THIRD EDITION

POLICE SUPERVISION AND MANAGEMENT

IN AN ERA OF COMMUNITY POLICING

Kenneth J. Peak

University of Nevada, Reno

Larry K. Gaines

California State University, San Bernardino

Ronald W. Glensor

Reno, Nevada, Police Department

Prentice Hall

Upper Saddle River, New Jersey

Columbus, Ohio

Library of Congress Cataloging-in-Publication Data
Peak, Kenneth J.,
Police supervision and management : in an era of community policing / Kenneth J. Peak, Larry K. Gaines, Ronald W. Gensor. — 3rd ed.
p. cm.
ISBN-13: 978-0-13-515466-3
ISBN-10: 0-13-515466-9
1. Police--Supervision of. I. Gaines, Larry K. II. Glensor, Ronald W. III. Title.
HV7936.S8P39 2010
363.2'2—dc22
2008041041

Editor in Chief: Vernon Anthony
Acquisition Editor: Tim Peyton
Editorial Assistant: Alicia Kelly
Media Project Manager: Karen Bretz
Director of Marketing: David Gesell
Marketing Manager: Adam Kloza
Marketing Assistant: Alicia Dysert
Production Manager: Wanda Rockwell
Creative Director: Jayne Conte
Cover Design: Bruce Kenselaar
Manager, Rights and Permissions: Zina Arabia
Manager, Visual Research: Beth Brenzel
Manager, Cover Visual Research & Permissions: Karen Sanatar
Image Permission Coordinator: Vickie Menanteaux
Full-Service Project Management/Composition: Nitin Agarwal, Aptara® Inc.
Printer/Binder: Hamilton Printing Co.

Pearson Education LTD.
Pearson Education Singapore, Pte. Ltd
Pearson Education, Canada, Ltd
Pearson Education–Japan
Pearson Education Australia PTY, Limited
Pearson Education North Asia Ltd
Pearson Educación de Mexico, S.A. de C.V.
Pearson Education Malaysia, Pte. Ltd

Prentice Hall
is an imprint of

www.pearsonhighered.com

10 9 8 7 6 5 4 3 2
ISBN-13: 978-0-13-515466-3
ISBN-10: 0-13-515466-9

DEDICATIONS

To Jen Peak, the newest member of our clan, who epitomizes what every elementary school teacher should be, and is now entering graduate work; and to her new stepdaughter and sidekick, Emma, who will one day be as luminous in her chosen field.

— K. J. P.

To my wife Jean; my children Ashley, Courtney, and Cody; and to my grandchildren Braedon, Luke, Dekan, Chloe, and Scooter. Because I allow projects such as this to steal valuable time from them.

— L. K. G.

To my wife Kristy, daughter Breanne, son-in-law Derek (Reno PD), grandaughter Addison, and son Ronnie.

—R. W. G.

CONTENTS IN BRIEF

EXPANDED TABLE OF CONTENTS

PREFACE

A comparatively large number of textbooks on police management and administration have been written over the past several decades, addressing the roles and responsibilities of chiefs of police or sheriffs. This text, however, focuses on first-line supervisors and middle managers and is grounded on the assumption that the reader is an undergraduate, possibly even a graduate, student or a neophyte practitioner, possessing but a fundamental knowledge of police organizations and operations. It is intended to help those persons learn more about the field of policing, as well as help those practitioners who are preparing for promotion, and new and experienced supervisors who are seeking to improve their skills. It will help to lay the foundation for the reader's future study and experience.

This text also assumes that a *practical* police supervision perspective is often lost in many administrative texts; therefore, while necessarily delving into some theory, this text is intended to focus on the practical aspects of a supervisor's or manager's job.

Those of us who have held a job or position, unless self-employed, have had a supervisor to whom we reported. That individual probably had a hand in showing us how to do our work and certainly was responsible for making sure that we did it properly. Even persons who have not yet entered the working world have experienced supervision in school, in sports, in the Boy Scouts or Girl Scouts, or in other nonwork settings. Supervision is a crucial element of any organized activity and is present in all organizations.

Our supervisors often reported to *their* supervisors, or managers. The managers coordinated and supervised the efforts of the lower-level supervisors as well as ensuring that the unit functioned as higher-level administrators envisioned. Supervisors and managers are the keys to quality work in any organization.

This book specifically concerns *police* supervision and management. In order to address these topics thoroughly and to provide as much useful information as possible, we must maintain a dual approach by looking at supervision and management broadly, while also focusing narrowly on these areas in police organizations. All supervisors and managers, whether in police departments, construction, or business firms, share similar concerns and duties. They manage people and activities.

It is also true that each and every organization is unique. Police departments in particular are different from most other organizations, for the simple reason that police work is different from most other vocations and occupations. Police officers have the unique authority to arrest people and investigate their activities. Also, police departments are not all made from the same mold. The New York City Police Department and the Chicago Police Department, the two largest departments in the United States, are different from the Las Vegas Police Department or the Nashville Police Department. Although all of these departments have the same or similar responsibilities, substantial variation within the police profession itself and the culture of the organization will make the jobs of police supervisors and managers unique and challenging. In addition, the police supervisors' and managers' jobs have recently been made even more specialized as a result of the implementation of community policing. Community policing has placed many new responsibilities on the police sergeant and manager.

During the course of a workday, police supervisors and managers directly oversee several employees in the performance of their activities and may even supervise a life-threatening situation or a critical incident or disaster. While a supervisor may not have ultimate command and control over critical incidents or disasters, he or she is often the first responder at the scene; his or her actions and directions to subordinates will be vital in determining the eventual success of the police in dealing with the problem. Managers are called to the scenes of major critical incidents to supervise groups of officers and to coordinate actions with other police units or agencies, such as the fire department or emergency medical services. Supervisors and managers essentially ensure that police operations unfold as planned.

TERMS USED THROUGHOUT THE BOOK

Although the terms *administration, management,* and *supervision* are often used synonymously, it should be noted that each is a unique concept that occasionally overlaps with the others. **Administration** encompasses both management and supervision. Administration is a process whereby a group of people are organized and directed toward achievement of the group's objective. The exact nature of the organization will vary among the different types and sizes of agencies, but the general principles used and the form of administration are often similar. Administration focuses on the overall organization and its mission and its relationship with other organizations and groups external to it. Administrators are often concerned with the department's direction and its policies and with ensuring that the department has the resources to fulfill its community's expectations. Police administrators generally include the chief, assistant chiefs, and high-ranking staff who support the chief in administering the department.

Management, which is also a part of administration, is most closely associated with the day-to-day operations of the various elements within the organization. For example, most police departments have a variety of operational units such as patrol, criminal investigation, traffic, gang enforcement, domestic violence, or community relations. The Los Angeles Police Department, the third largest police department in the country, has more than 200 specialized units. Each of these units is run by someone who is most aptly described as a manager. In most cases, these managers are captains or lieutenants. These managers ensure that their units fulfill their departmental mission and work closely with other units to ensure that conflict or problems do not develop. They also attend to planning, budgeting, and human resource or personnel needs to ensure that the unit is adequately prepared to carry out its responsibilities.

Supervision involves the direction of officers and civilians in their day-to-day activities, often on a one-to-one basis. Supervisors ensure that subordinate officers adhere to departmental policies, complete tasks correctly and on a timely basis, and interact with the public in a professional manner. Supervisors often observe their subordinates completing assignments and sometimes take charge of situations, especially when a deployment of a large number of officers is needed. They also work closely with managers to ensure that officers' activities are consistent with the unit's mission and objectives.

In the police organization, the first-line supervisor is usually a sergeant. We say *first-line* because sergeants are responsible for supervising those officers who are engaged in providing basic police services. Captains and lieutenants (called middle managers) also supervise, but they supervise persons who are also supervisors, and are more concerned with a unit's activities rather than with an individual officer's activities. In actuality, all ranking personnel from the chief to the sergeant supervise, but this text is concerned with supervision by sergeants and mid-level managers.

Finally, the terms *police officer, law enforcement officer,* and *peace officer* are also generally interchangeable. The primary difference is that peace officer refers to anyone who has arrest authority and usually includes correctional officers, probation officers, parole officers, and persons with special police powers. Correctional officers have specific police powers in their correctional facility workplace, and investigators of welfare or Medicaid fraud have limited peace officer powers. In this text, we are primarily concerned with police officers, who include municipal or rural officers; deputy sheriffs;

highway patrol; troopers; state police; and others holding local, state, or federal law enforcement officer status. For the purpose of this text, the term *police officer* will generally be used to refer to all the positions noted.

ORGANIZATION OF THE BOOK

This third edition's 16 chapters have been revised and reorganized to better provide the reader with an understanding of the key elements of police supervision and management, from both the theoretical and applied perspectives.

First, to fundamentally understand the challenges of police supervision and management, we consider the "big picture" of a police organization. Therefore, Part One, "The Supervisor in a Police Organization," introduces the broad concepts of supervision and management (including how and why police agencies are formally organized), the roles and responsibilities of supervisors and middle managers, how supervisors and managers lead and motive their subordinates, the purpose and functions of community oriented policing and problem solving (COPPS) and its related concepts, and effective communication and negotiation within an organization. COPPS is now policing's primary paradigm and, as seen in Chapter 4, has a profound impact on how police departments operate; this impact has filtered down to the supervisor and middle managers, and their challenge is to *make COPPS a part of daily practice.*

Part Two, "Supervising Human Resources," more narrowly examines the supervision of human resources. This section addresses training and professional development, personnel performance evaluation, stress and wellness, ethics and liability, and personnel rights and discipline in police organizations. This part essentially provides information on the "people" in the police organization. Somewhere between 75 and 90 percent of a police department's budget is for personnel. It is therefore important for the supervisor and manager to learn how to manage this important resource and ensure that the department's mission is achieved.

Part Three, "Supervising the Work of Police," contains information that is more applied in nature and looks at supervisors and managers at work, both on and off the street. It addresses what they need to know concerning the following key issues: officer deployment and scheduling, patrol and special operations (in patrol, investigations, traffic, and vehicle pursuits), responding to specific crime problems (domestic violence, drugs, gangs, school violence, and crimes in progress), and confronting disasters and critical incidents.

Part Four, "Major Challenges," focuses on what police supervisors and managers—indeed, policing in general—must do in order to face the threat of terrorism, and today's inherent focus on homeland security. Included in this part is an appendix that includes related wisdom of the ages—advice from Lao-Tzu, Confucius, and Machiavelli.

Also, note the following for each chapter:

- At the beginning of each chapter are "Key Terms and Concepts" and "Learning Objectives" sections, which give the reader an idea of the chapter's content as well as the major concepts and points to be drawn from it.
- Each chapter (except Chapter 1) concludes with two or more *case studies*—34 in total, disseminated throughout the book—that allow the reader to contemplate the kinds of problems that are routinely confronted by police supervisors and managers, and apply the chapter's materials.
- Discussion questions are also provided at the end of each chapter, to assist the reader in understanding the information contained therein. With a fundamental knowledge of the criminal justice system and a reading of the chapters, the reader should be in a position to engage in some critical

analyses—and even, it is hoped, some spirited discussions—of the issues involved and arrive at several feasible solutions to the problems presented.

ACKNOWLEDGMENTS

This third edition, and our collaborative effort in bringing it to fruition, was made possible with the input, counsel, guidance, and moral support of several people. The authors wish to acknowledge Tim Peyton, Acquistion Editor; Alicia Kelly, Editorial Assistant; and Wanda Rockwell, Production Liaison at Prentice Hall. In addition, we would like to acknowledge Nitin Agarwal, Project Manager; and Mona Newbatcher, copyeditor.

We are also grateful to the book's reviewers, who provided their insights and guidance and contributed a great deal toward making this a better effort (of course, we bear sole responsibility for any shortcomings in the final product).

Ken Peak
Larry K. Gaines
Ronald W. Glensor

ABOUT THE AUTHORS

Ken Peak is professor and former chairman of the Department of Criminal Justice, University of Nevada, Reno, where he was named "Teacher of the Year" by the university's Honor Society. He entered municipal policing in Kansas in 1970 and subsequently held positions as a nine-county criminal justice planner in Kansas; director of a four-state Technical Assistance Institute for the Law Enforcement Assistance Administration; director of university police at Pittsburg State University (Kansas); acting director of public safety, University of Nevada, Reno; and assistant professor of criminal justice at Wichita State University. He has published 21 textbooks (on general police, community policing, criminal justice administration, police supervision and management, and women in law enforcement), two historical books (on temperance and bootlegging), and more than 60 additional journal articles and invited book chapters. He served as chairman of the Police Section of the Academy of Criminal Justice Sciences and president of the Western and Pacific Association of Criminal Justice Educators. He received two gubernatorial appointments to statewide criminal justice committees while residing in Kansas and holds a doctorate from the University of Kansas.

Larry K. Gaines currently is a professor and chair of the Criminal Justice Department at California State University at San Bernardino. He received his doctorate in criminal justice from Sam Houston State University. He has police experience with the Kentucky State Police and the Lexington, Kentucky, Police Department. Additionally, he served as the executive director of the Kentucky Association of Chiefs of Police for 14 years. Dr. Gaines is also a past president of the Academy of Criminal Justice Sciences. His research centers on policing and drugs. In addition to numerous articles, he has co-authored a number of books in the field: *Police Operations; Police Administration; Managing the Police Organization; Community Policing: A Contemporary Perspective; Policing Perspectives: An Anthology; Policing in America; Drugs, Crime, and Justice; Criminal Justice in Action;* and *Readings in White Collar Crime.* His current research agenda involves the evaluation of police tactics in terms of their effectiveness in reducing problems and fitting within the community policing paradigm. He is also researching the issue of racial profiling in a number of California cities.

Ronald W. Glensor is a deputy chief of the Reno, Nevada, Police Department (RPD). He has more than 30 years of police experience and has commanded the department's patrol, administration, and detective divisions. He has been active in the development of, and training for, the RPD's community oriented policing and problem solving (COPPS) initiative since 1987 and has also provided COPPS training for more than 250 police agencies throughout the United States and in Canada, Australia, and the United Kingdom. He was the 1997 recipient of the prestigious Gary P. Hayes Award conferred by the Police Executive Research Forum for contributions in the policing field, served a six-month fellowship as problem-oriented policing coordinator with the Police Executive Research Forum in Washington, DC, and received an Atlantic Fellowship in public policy, studying repeat victimization at the Home Office in London. He is co-author of nine textbooks and anthologies and has also published in several journals and trade magazines. He is an adjunct professor at the University of Nevada, Reno, and instructs at area police academies and criminal justice programs. He holds a doctorate in political science from the University of Nevada, Reno.

PART ONE

The Supervisor in a Police Organization

CHAPTER 1

The Dynamics of Police Organizations

Key Terms and Concepts

- Administrative theory
- Bureaucracy
- Bureaucratic management
- Chain of command
- Classical organizational theory
- Community oriented policing and problem solving (COPPS)
- Employee-centered management
- Functional supervision
- Human relations theory
- Humanism
- Informal organization
- McGregor's Theory X/Theory Y
- Organization
- Organizational theory
- Police culture
- Police unions
- Policies and procedures
- POSDCORB
- Relatively identifiable boundary
- Rules and regulations
- Scientific management
- Span of control
- Social entity
- Specialization
- Systems theory
- Unity of command

Learning Objectives

After reading this chapter, the student will:

- understand the concept of organizations
- be able to explain how organizational theory evolved, including scientific management and bureaucracies
- describe several major elements of administrative theory, including POSDCORB, unity of command, span of control, policies and procedures, and rules and regulations
- understand rationales and purposes of police organizational design
- know how informal organizations, inertia, and unionization affect police organizations
- understand the basic philosophy underlying community policing and problem solving, and how organizations must be modified in order to accommodate this strategy

We are born in organizations, educated by organizations, and most of us spend much of our lives working for organizations. We spend much of our leisure time paying, playing, and praying in organizations. Most of us will die in an organization, and when the time comes for burial, the largest organization of all—the state—must grant official permission.

—AMITAI ETZIONI

No organization, regardless of its character, can rise higher than the quality and competency of its supervisory officials.

—AUGUST VOLLMER

INTRODUCTION

Supervision and management are extremely important factors in determining whether or not an organization achieves its mission and goals.

This chapter looks closely at organizations, first in general terms, and then examines the evolution of organizational theory, including scientific management and **bureaucratic management**. Next, we examine administrative theory, which includes universal methods of administration and a number of important concepts that have been used to help in the smooth operation of organizations. Rationales and purposes of police organizational design are then reviewed, followed by some influencial factors to consider: informal organizations, inertia, and employee unions. The chapter concludes with a view of how organizational change must accompany community policing and problem solving.

THE CONCEPT OF ORGANIZATIONS

Organizations are entities consisting of two or more people who cooperate to accomplish an objective or objectives. In that sense, certainly the *concept* of organization is not new. Undoubtedly, the first organizations were primitive hunting parties. Organization and a high degree of coordination were required to bring down huge animals, as revealed in fossils from as early as 40,000 B.C. Organizations today are much more complex, often involving thousands of people. The New York City Police Department has more than 39,000 officers who must be supervised and managed. Most organizations are much smaller. The majority of police departments in the United States have 10 or fewer officers. Regardless of size, all organizations are organized and managed.

An **organization** may be formally defined as "a consciously coordinated social entity, with a relative identifiable boundary, that functions on a relatively continuous basis to achieve a common goal or set of goals" (Robbins, 1990:4). The term *consciously coordinated* implies supervision. **Social entity** refers to the fact that organizations are composed of people who interact with one another and with people in other organizations. **Relatively identifiable boundary** alludes to the organization's goals and the public served (Gaines, Southerland, and Angell, 1991:43). Following is an analogy to assist in understanding organizations:

> Organization corresponds to the bones which structure or give form to the body. Imagine that the fingers were a single mass of bone rather than four separate fingers and a thumb made up of bones joined by cartilage so that they are flexible. The mass of bones could not, because of its structure, play musical instruments, hold a pencil, or grip a baseball bat. A police department's organization is analogous. It must be structured properly if it is to be effective in fulfilling its many diverse goals. (Gaines et al., 1991:9)

An organization, especially a police department, can be just as complex as the human body. All sorts of managerial processes occur in the police department: decision making, planning, leadership, motivation, and control of subordinates' behavior. Moreover, the many parts or units in a police department may include patrol, criminal investigation, traffic, juvenile services, gang unit, drug interdiction, or domestic violence. These processes and parts must operate in harmony if the department is to achieve its goals and objectives.

It is the supervisors and managers who are most often responsible for ensuring harmonious coordination in the police department. Supervisors are concerned with *tasks* and *human resources*. With the former, supervisors are responsible for ensuring that subordinate officers attend to their duties in a manner that is consistent with departmental expectations. They see that officers do their jobs the best way possible. Human resources refers to the fact that supervisors are responsible for people. People, especially in the workplace, often have problems and difficulties. Supervisors attempt to solve these problems and difficulties through training, supervision, and the provision of direction. Managers essentially have the same responsibilities, only at a higher level. In addition to being concerned with tasks and human resources, managers must ensure that the efforts of supervisors and officers collectively fulfill the unit's departmental responsibilities.

THE EVOLUTION OF ORGANIZATIONAL THEORY

The following section examines the development of **organizational theory**, which explains how an organization operates and provides the background for understanding productivity and leadership.

Scientific Management

Frederick Winslow Taylor, whom many consider to be the "father of **scientific management**," sought to refine management techniques by studying how workers might become more complete extensions of machines. Taylor (1911) was primarily interested in discovering the best means for getting the most out of employees—mostly the blue-collar workers at Bethlehem Steel in Pennsylvania where Taylor worked as chief engineer in 1898. Taylor maintained that management knew little about the limits of worker production and was the first to introduce time and motion studies to test his argument.

Taylor believed that by observing workers in action, wasted motions could be eliminated and production increased. He began by measuring the amount of time it took workers to shovel and carry pig iron. Taylor then standardized the work into specific tasks, improved worker selection and training, established workplace rules, and advocated close supervision of workers by a foreman.

The results were incredible; worker productivity soared. The total number of shovelers needed dropped from about 600 to 140, and worker earnings increased from $1.15 to $1.88 per day. The average cost of handling a long ton (2,240 pounds) dropped from $0.072 to $0.033.

Although criticized by unions for his management-oriented views, Taylor nonetheless proved that administrators must know their employees. His views caught on and soon emphasis was placed entirely on the formal administrative structure; later, such terms as *authority, chain of command, span of control,* and *division of labor* (discussed later) became part of the workplace vocabulary.

Taylor's work also spawned the idea of functional supervision, which is applicable to policing. In Taylor's time, supervisors were assigned to jobs but did not always have the technical expertise to adequately supervise their subordinates. **Functional supervision** entailed having several different supervisors on a job so that each one oversaw a particular aspect or part of the job—a part he or she had expertise in and could provide adequate supervision over. Functional supervision is important in policing. For example, a sergeant supervising criminal investigations must have expertise in investigations, while a sergeant in traffic must have expertise in accident investigation and selective enforcement techniques.

Bureaucratic Management

Police agencies certainly fit the description of an organization. First, they are managed by being organized into a number of specialized units. Administrators, managers, and supervisors exist to ensure that these units work together toward a common goal; each unit working independently would lead to fragmentation, conflict, and competition and would subvert the entire organization's goals and purposes. Second, police agencies consist of people who interact within the organization and with external organizations, and they exist to serve the public.

The development of an organization requires careful consideration, or the agency may be unable to respond efficiently to community needs. For example, the creation of too many specialized units in a police department (e.g., street crimes, bicycle patrol, media relations, or domestic violence) may obligate too many officers to these functions and result in too few patrol officers. As a rule of thumb, at least 55 percent of all sworn personnel should be assigned to patrol (Guyot, 1979: 253–284). Indeed, a recent survey by the U.S. Department of Justice, Bureau of Justice Statistics (1999) found that an

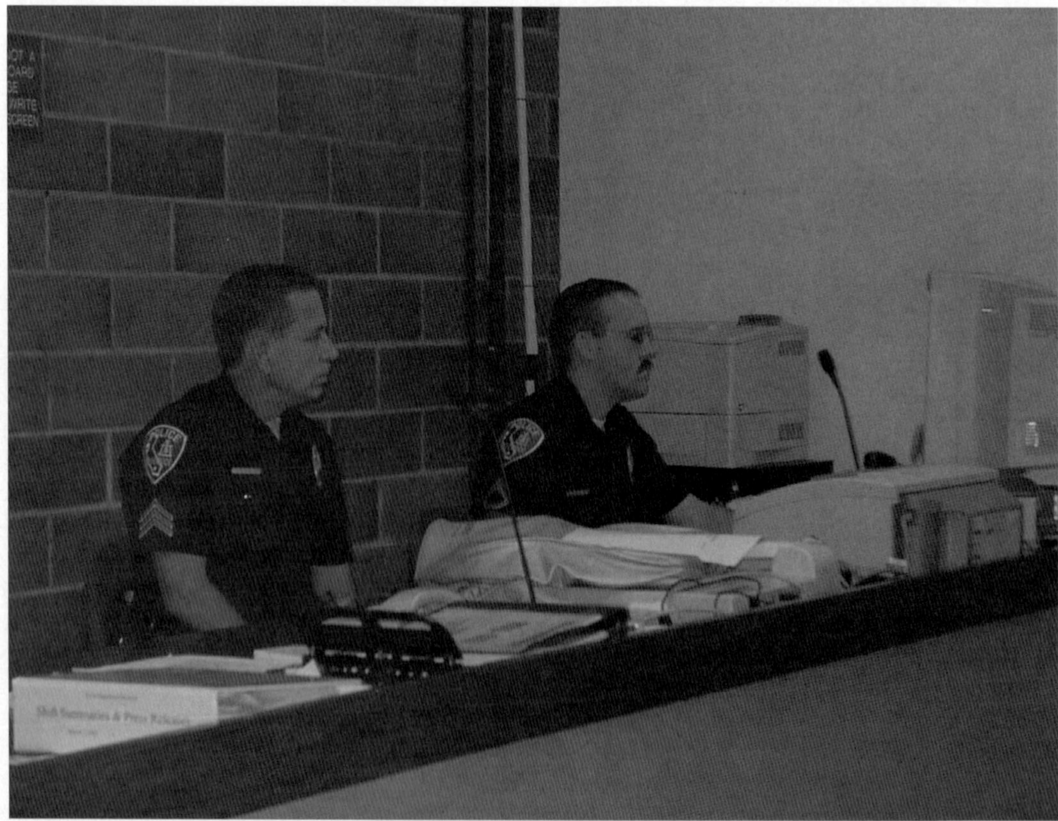

A patrol supervisor's day begins by giving officers vital information in briefing.
(Courtesy: Riverside, California, P.D.)

average of 63 percent of sworn officers in local police agencies were uniformed, with regular duties that included responding to calls for service.

Police administrators, through a mission statement, **policies and procedures**, a proper management style, and direction, attempt to ensure that the organization maintains its overall goals of crime suppression, order maintenance, and investigation, and that it works amicably with other organizations and people. As the organization becomes larger, the need becomes greater for people to cooperate to achieve organizational goals. (Formal organizational structures, which assist in this endeavor by spelling out areas of responsibility, lines of communication, and the chain of command, are discussed later.)

Police organizations in the United States are also *bureaucracies,* as are virtually all large organizations in modern society, such as the military, universities, and corporations (Gaines and Swanson, 1999). In popular terms, a **bureaucracy** has often come to be viewed in a negative light, as slow, ponderous, routine, complicated, and composed of "red tape," which frustrates its members and clients (Crozier, 1964). This image is far from the ideal or pure bureaucracy developed by Max Weber, the German sociologist, who claimed in 1947 that a bureaucratic organization,

> from a purely technical point of view, [is] capable of attaining the highest degree of efficiency and is the most rational known means of carrying out imperative control over human beings. It is superior to any other form in precision, in stability, in the stringency of its discipline, and in its reliability, and is formally capable of application to all kinds of administrative tasks. (Weber, 1947:337)

The administration of most police organizations is based on the traditional, pyramidal, quasi-military organizational structure containing the elements of a bureaucracy: specialized functions, adherence to fixed rules, and a hierarchy of authority. This pyramidal organizational environment is undergoing increasing challenges, especially as a result of the implementation of community policing by departments.

A simple structure indicating the hierarchy of authority or **chain of command** is shown in Figure 1-1.

To a large extent, police agencies are similar in their structure and management process. The major differences between agencies exist between the large and the very small agencies; the former will be more complex, with much more specialization, a hierarchical structure, and a greater degree of authoritarian style of command.

In the 1970s, experts on police organization, such as Egon Bittner (1970:51), were contending that the military-bureaucratic organization of the police was a serious handicap that created obstacles to the development of a truly professional police system. The reasons for this disillusionment include the quasi-military rank and disciplinary structures within police organizations; the lack of opportunity of management to match talent and positions; the organizational restrictions on personal freedom of expression, association, and dress; communication blockage in the tall structure; the organizational clinging to outmoded methods of operation; the lack of management flexibility; and the narrowness of job descriptions in the lower ranks of police organizations (Johnson, Misner, and Brown, 1981:53). This criticism continues today as proponents of community policing advocate that bureaucratic police departments should be decentralized so that decisions are made at lower levels of the department, allowing operational units to better meet citizen demands (Gray, Bodner, and Lovrich, 1997; Sparrow, Moore, and Kennedy, 1990).

Notwithstanding this growing disenchantment with the traditional bureaucratic structure of police organizations, this structure continues to prevail; for many administrators, it is still the best structure when rapid leadership and division of labor are required in times of crises (Gaines and Swanson, 1999). The traditional school of thought that each police supervisor can effectively supervise only seven employees is part of the reason for this "tall" organizational structure. A number of agencies

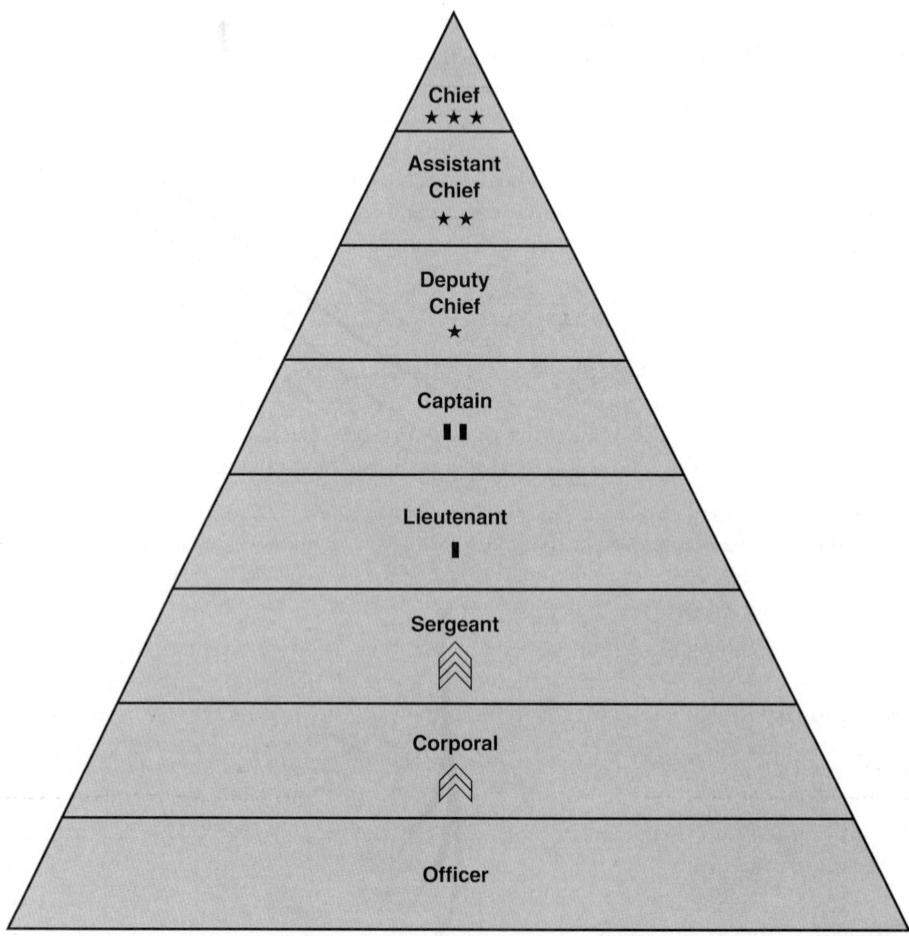

FIGURE 1-1 Traditional Pyramidal Chain of Command

have experimented with other approaches, and the results have been mixed. Most departments have elected to retain the classical police structure (Maguire, 1997).

Indeed, when police agencies have attempted to flatten the organizational structure, they have most often returned to the traditional organizational configuration. Perhaps an alternative is to keep a few features of the military model (such as police officers taking orders from superiors during critical incidents) and a few features of the bureaucratic model and then go beyond these to create a reasonably professional organization.

ADMINISTRATIVE THEORY

Administrative or management theory seeks to identify generic or universal methods of administration. Further, **administrative theory** is more compatible with the bureaucratic model than with scientific management, because it concentrates on broader principles. Key contributors to this school are Henri Fayol, Luther Gulick, and Lyndall Urwick.

The greatest contributions of Fayol, a French engineer, came from his experiences as a manager. His fame rests largely on his *General and Industrial Management* (1949), which includes the following principles:

1. Division of work: specialization
2. Authority: the right to give orders and to extract obedience
3. Discipline: the obedience, energy, behavior, and outward signs of respect as agreed upon by the organization and its employees
4. Unity of command: an employee receiving orders from only one supervisor
5. Unity of direction: with one leader and one plan for a group of activities having the same objective
6. Subordination of individual interest to the general interest
7. Remuneration of personnel
8. Centralization: a natural order of things
9. Scalar chain: the chain of superiors ranging from the ultimate authority to the lowest ranks, or chain of command
10. Order: a place for everyone and everyone in his or her place
11. Equity: the combination of kindness and justice
12. Stability of tenure of personnel: allowing employees to become familiar with their jobs and to be productive
13. Initiative at all levels of the organization
14. Esprit de corps and harmony: providing great strength

POSDCORB

Gulick and Urwick (1937) examined the role of administration in organizations and identified several key management functions. They articulated these functions using the acronym **POSDCORB** (for *p*lanning, *o*rganizing, *s*taffing, *d*irecting, *co*ordinating, *r*eporting, and *b*udgeting) as noted in Figure 1-2. Gulick and Urwick were most interested in how organizations might be structured and the role of managers within them. POSDCORB identified the key administrative activities that occupy the majority of a manager's time.

Gulick and Urwick also emphasized the need for coordinating the work by dividing labor within organizations. In police departments, this is known as specialization. **Specialization** means that similar tasks are grouped together so that they can be performed more efficiently. For example, many police

Planning—working out in broad outline the things that need to be done and the methods for doing them to accomplish the purpose set for the enterprise.
Organizing—establishment of the formal structure of authority through which work subdivisions are arranged, defined, and coordinated for the defined objective.
Staffing—the whole personnel function of bringing in and training the staff and maintaining favorable conditions at work.
Directing—the continuous task of making decisions, embodying them in specific and general orders and instructions, and serving as a leader of the enterprise.
Coordinating—the all-important duty of interrelating the various parts of the work.
Reporting—keeping those to whom the execution is responsible informed about what is going on, which includes keeping himself and his subordinates informed through records, research, and inspection.
Budgeting—all that goes with budgeting in the form of fiscal planning, accounting, and control.

FIGURE 1-2 POSDCORB

departments have traffic units that handle all police activities related to the enforcement of traffic laws. The division of labor in police agencies is evident when examining an organizational chart. (See Figure 1-4, an organizational chart for the Portland, Oregon, Police Bureau, on p. 17.)

Gulick and Urwick also saw the need in organizations for a hierarchy, whereby supervisors used a chain of command to coordinate orders and information from the top to the bottom of the organization. Sparrow, Moore, and Kennedy (1990) found that large American police departments averaged from nine to thirteen levels of rank or hierarchy.

Gulick and Urwick also believed that work should be coordinated in groups with one supervisor in charge. This concept, referred to as **span of control**, identified the number of persons reporting to a supervisor. Six to ten officers reporting to one supervisor is a commonly accepted span of control in policing, especially considering that patrol officers are assigned to a wide geographical area and that detectives often are investigating complicated criminal cases. Span of control is discussed more fully below.

Taylor's scientific management theory and Gulick and Urwick's principles of administration, with their emphasis on the technical and engineering side of management, became known as **classical organizational theory**. Classical organizational theory was quickly adopted by police in the first training schools in New York City and Berkeley, California, and influenced some of the early writers on police administration, including O. W. Wilson, V. A. Leonard, and August Vollmer. These theories remain the foundation for police management and supervision today.

Unity of Command

A related, important principle of hierarchy of authority is **unity of command**, an organizational principle that dictates that every officer should report to one and only one superior (following the chain of command). The unity of command principle applies to administrators and managers as well. That is, they do not skip over a sergeant or supervisor and give commands directly to an officer.

Ambiguity over authority occurs frequently in police organizations. Detectives and patrol officers often dispute who has authority over a criminal case; officers in two different patrol beats may disagree over who has responsibility for a call for service that is located on a beat boundary line. Numerous situations result in conflict because the lines of authority are unclear; as departments become larger and more complex, the amount of conflict naturally increases. The nature of conflict in the police setting is addressed in Chapter 5.

The unity of command principle also ensures that multiple and/or conflicting orders are not issued to the same police officers by several supervisors. For example, a patrol sergeant might arrive at a hostage situation and deploy personnel and give all the appropriate orders, only to have a shift lieutenant or captain come to the scene and countermand the sergeant's orders. This type of situation would obviously be counterproductive for all persons concerned. It is also important that all officers know and follow the chain of command at such incidents. In this example, the shift lieutenant or captain normally should consult with the sergeant before taking charge of the situation or giving any orders.

Span of Control

As mentioned above, span of control refers to the number of persons a superior officer can effectively supervise. At the top of the organizations the limit is small, normally three to five, and often larger at the lower levels depending on factors such as the capacity of the supervisor and those persons supervised, the type of work performed, the complexity of the work, the area covered by it, distances between elements, the time needed to perform the tasks, and the type of persons served. Normally, a patrol sergeant will supervise six to ten officers, while a patrol lieutenant may have four or five

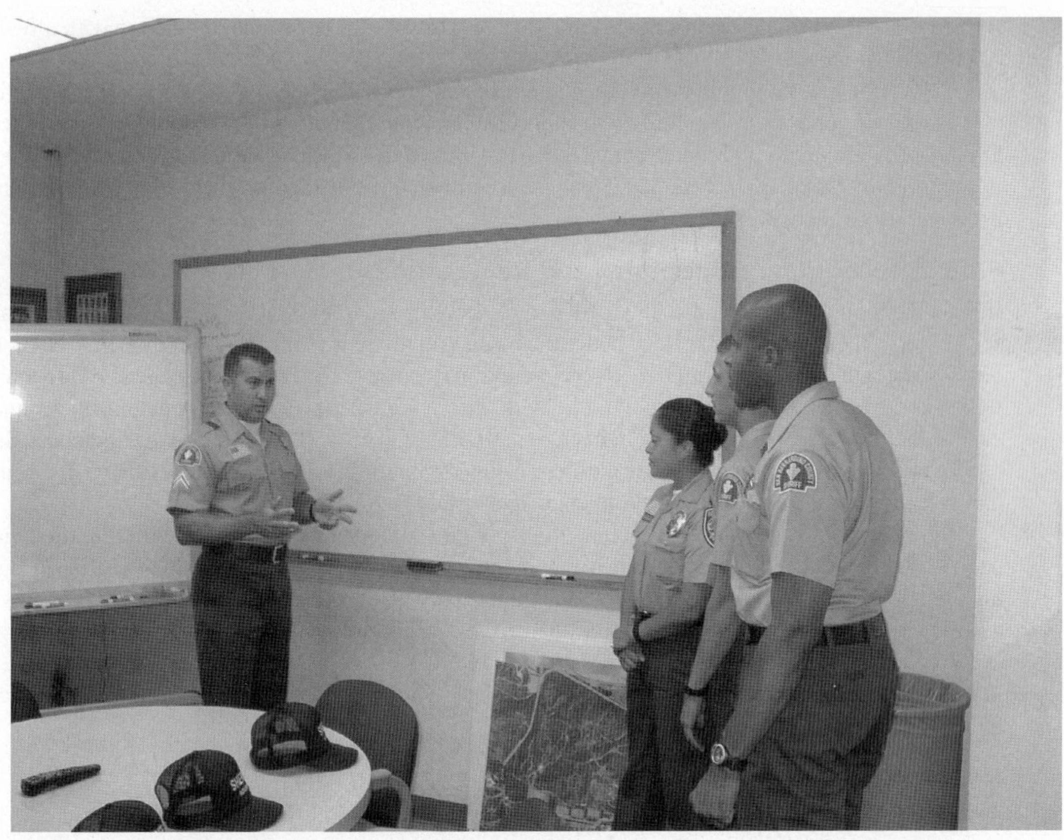

Interpersonal skills are essential for a supervisor's success.
(Courtesy San Bernardino County, California, S.O.)

sergeants reporting to him or her. This distribution of supervisors and managers applies to most of the units in a police department.

Several authors now advocate for higher spans of control, and argue that this is now the trend. It is believed that higher spans of control reduces such problems as: the distortion of information as it flows through the organization; slow, ineffective decision making and action; increased functional roadblocks and "turf protection;" emphasis on controlling the bureaucracy rather than on customer service; higher costs due to the lower number of managers and management support staff; and less responsibility assumed by subordinates for the quality of their work (Lane, 2006a). Some also argue that rank-and-file employees favor high spans of control because they receive less detailed and micromanaged supervision, greater responsibility, and a higher level of trust by their supervisors (Lane, 2006a).

Certainly span of control is also related to organizational communications, which is discussed in Chapter 5. Robert Bailey argued that "it is better to have a span of control that is too wide than to have too many layers of management. Every management layer adds another communication hurdle" (quoted in Lane, 2006a:29).

There is also a potentially major disadvantage to having a high span of control: a high span of control means there is much less time for any one supervisor to spend with any one subordinate. This limited time is reduced even more if a supervisor has to spend a large amount of time with a few new or problem employees.

Nevertheless, contemporary management theory holds that the classical (pre-1950s) belief in small spans of control for wielding close supervision over employees is, and should be, giving way to higher spans of control and flatter organizations. Although a consensus on the ideal rationale for span of control has not been reached, some experts recommend ratios ranging from 15 to 25 subordinates per supervisor (Lane, 2006b).

Policies, Procedures, and Rules and Regulations

In policing, policies, procedures, and rules and regulations are important for defining role expectations for officers. In essence, they specify how officers should do their jobs. The department relies on these directives to guide or control officers' behavior and performance. Because police agencies are intended to be service oriented in nature, they must work within well-defined, specific guidelines designed to ensure that all officers conform to behavior that will enhance public protection (Alpert and Smith, 1999). Police supervisors must control officer behavior, but, it is hoped that officers have the initiative and dedication to perform up to departmental standards.

Police agencies normally distribute their policies, procedures, and rules and regulations in the form of General Orders. Larger agencies may have as many as a hundred General Orders, covering topics such as code of conduct, use of force, and pursuit driving. The General Order normally begins with a policy statement about the subject and then follows with detailed procedures concerning how the order will work in practice. Figure 1-3 is an example of a police agency's General Order. Notice how the General Order provides fairly specific guidelines. Such orders provide officers specific guidance about various tasks and responsibilities.

Police officers have a great deal of discretion when answering calls for service or performing investigations (Walker, 1993). The task for the supervisor is to find the middle ground between wide discretionary authority possessed by the police and total standardization. The police role is much too ambiguous to become totally standardized, but it is also much too serious and important to be left completely to the total discretion of the officer. Officers will often seek a supervisor's opinion and guidance in discretionary matters. This requires that a supervisor is well informed about all policies, procedures, and rules and regulations. In some cases, the supervisor must seek clarification from his or her manager, especially in abnormal situations.

Policies are quite general and serve as guides to thinking, rather than action. Policies reflect the purpose and philosophy of the organization and help interpret those elements to the officers. An example of a policy might be that when answering calls at locations with a history of multiple calls, officers should attempt to identify the cause of the problems and take remedial action. A number of departments today are expanding on the idea of policies or guides and developing mission statements and value statements for officers. These mission and value statements are overarching guides that attempt to provide direction to officers as they perform their various job duties.

Procedures are more detailed than policies and provide the preferred methods for handling matters pertaining to investigation, patrol, booking, radio procedures, filing reports, roll call, use of force, arrest, sick leave, evidence handling, promotion, and many more job elements. Procedures describe how officers are to complete a specific task.

Rules and regulations are specific guidelines that leave little or no latitude for individual discretion. Some examples are requirements that police officers not smoke in public, check the operation of their vehicle and equipment before going on patrol, not consume alcoholic beverages within a specified number of hours of going on duty, arrive in court or at roll call early, or specify the type of weapons that officers carry on or off duty. Rules and regulations are not always popular, especially if

ANYWHERE USA POLICE DEPARTMENT GENERAL ORDER

Legal Advisor:	**Approving Deputy Chief:**	**Chief of Police:**

General Order No: 3/254.000

DOMESTIC VIOLENCE

Date Issued: November 4, 2007 **Last Review: NOV/08**

I. POLICY

The Anywhere USA Police Department recognizes that domestic violence has serious consequences to the family involved and necessitates prompt and thorough investigation. The Anywhere USA Police Department will investigate all calls for service involving domestic violence, recognizing that an aggressive policy of arresting domestic violence assailants leads to the reduction of domestic violence crimes and domestic homicides.

II. PROCEDURES

Officers will adhere to the arrest requirements as set forth under State Law PC 170.137:

170.137 Domestic violence: When arrest required; report required; compilation of statistics.

1. Except as otherwise provided in subsection 2, whether or not a warrant has been issued, a peace officer shall, unless mitigating circumstances exist, arrest a person when he has probable cause to believe that the person to be arrested has, within the preceding 24 hours, committed a battery upon his spouse, former spouse, any other person to whom he is related by blood or marriage, a person with whom he is or was actually residing, a person with whom he has had or is having a dating relationship, a person with whom he has a child in common, the minor child of any of those persons or his minor child.

2. If the peace officer has probable cause to believe that a battery described in subsection 1 was a mutual battery, he shall attempt to determine which person was the primary physical aggressor. If the peace officer determines that one of the persons who allegedly committed a battery was the primary physical aggressor involved in the incident, the peace officer is not required to arrest any other person believed to have committed a battery during the incident. In determining whether a person is a primary physical aggressor for the purposes of this subsection, the peace officer shall consider:

(a) Prior domestic violence involving either person;
(b) The relative severity of the injuries inflicted upon the persons involved;
(c) The potential for future injury;
(d) Whether one of the alleged batteries was committed in self-defense;

FIGURE 1-3 Example of a Police Agency's General Order

perceived as unfair or unrelated to the job. Nonetheless, it is the supervisor's responsibility to ensure that officers perform these tasks with the same degree of professional demeanor as other job duties. As Thomas Reddin, former Los Angeles police chief, stated:

> Certainly we must have rules, regulations and procedures, and they should be followed. But they are no substitutes for initiative and intelligence. The more a [person] is given an opportunity to make decisions and, in the process, to learn, the more rules and regulations will be followed (1966:17).

The Emergence of Humanism

Dissatisfaction with classical organizational theory began to develop in the 1930s. The emergence of labor unions had begun to put pressure on management to develop more humane and effective ways of managing and supervising workers. The human relations school of management evolved as a result of this dissatisfaction as well as from the Hawthorne experiments in the early 1930s.

The Hawthorne experiments provided the first glimpse of **human relations theory**. The Western Electric Company conducted a number of scientific management studies at its Hawthorne facilities in Chicago from 1927 through 1932. The experiments were an attempt to determine the level of illumination (light) and pattern of employee breaks that produced the highest levels of worker productivity. The researchers segregated a group of workers in an area and made numerous and varied changes in the levels of illumination and the length and number of work breaks. It was believed that if the optimal level of illumination and number and duration of work breaks could be discovered, employees would be more productive. Productivity increased as these two variables were manipulated. Ultimately, however, no consistent pattern in the changes in production relative to the changes in lighting and work breaks emerged. Productivity increased when work breaks were increased, and it increased when work breaks were reduced. The same pattern occurred when illumination was increased and reduced. Given the inconsistencies, the researchers could not discern why productivity was changing. Finally, the increases in productivity were attributed to worker job satisfaction from increased involvement and concern on the part of management. In essence, management's displayed concern for the workers, as evidenced in the experiment itself, resulted in higher morale and productivity.

Prior to the Hawthorne experiments, employers were not concerned with employees or their feelings. It was assumed that employees followed management's dictates. The Hawthorne experiments spurred a significant change in the relationship between management and employees. Management realized that individual workers and the work group itself could have just as much impact on productivity as management. The experiments signaled a need for management to harness worker energy and ideas so that management and workers could mutually benefit.

During the 1940s and 1950s, this research led to both private and public organizations recognizing the strong effect of the working environment and informal structures on the organization. In policing, attention was being paid to job enlargement and enrichment techniques to generate interest in the profession as a career. **Employee-centered management** approaches such as participatory management began to appear in policing. By the 1970s, there was also a move away from the traditional pyramid-shaped organizational structure to a more flattened structure with fewer mid-levels of management (Tenzel, Storms, and Sweetwood, 1976). This has resulted in an increase in responsibilities for managers and first-line supervisors as more responsibilities were delegated downward in the department.

McGregor's Theory X/Theory Y

Douglas McGregor (1966) was a proponent of a more humanistic and democratic approach to management. His work was based on two basic assumptions about people: **Theory X**, which views employees negatively and sees the need for structured organizations with strict hierarchal lines and close supervision; and **Theory Y**, which takes a more humanistic view toward employees, believing that they are capable of being motivated and productive. A further explanation of the assumptions about human nature and behavior that emerge from these divergent theories follows:

THEORY X

- The average employee dislikes work and will avoid it whenever possible.
- People are lazy, avoid responsibility, and must be controlled, directed, and coerced to perform their work.

- People are inherently self-centered and do not care about organizational needs.
- People will naturally resist change.

THEORY Y

- The average employee does not inherently dislike work.
- People will exercise self-control and are self-directed when motivated to achieve organizational goals.
- People are capable of learning and will not only accept, but will seek, responsibility.
- People's capacity for imagination, ingenuity, and creativity are only partially utilized.

Theory X portrays a dismal view of employees and their motivation to work and supports the traditional model of direction and control. In contrast, Theory Y is more optimistic and leads one to believe that motivated employees will perform productively. Also, Theory Y assumes some responsibility on the part of managers to create a climate that is conducive to learning and achieving organizational goals.

Although it may appear that Theory X managers are bad and Theory Y managers are good, McGregor did not support one style over the other. Administrators may need the flexibility of employing one or both theories, depending on the personnel involved and the situation. For example, a supervisor dealing with an officer resisting attempts to remediate unacceptable behavior may need to rely on a Theory X approach until the officer is corrected. On the other hand, a self-motivated and skilled officer given the task of developing a briefing training lesson plan may require limited supervision and therefore can be guided through the task by employing Theory Y.

The human relations approach, however, is not without its critics. There is concern that shifting the emphasis away from administration and structure to social rewards for employees would distract from the accomplishment of organizational goals. Critics also argue that it can lead employees to expect more rewards for less effort (Lynch, 1986). Gaines (1978) noted that classical theory was organization without people, while human relations theory was people without organization.

As a general rule, the police field found bureaucratic management to be more acceptable. In the first half of the last century, police managers were strongly influenced by the reform movement that swept the nation. Corruption was rampant and the key words for resolving the problems were "efficiency" and "control." The goals of progressive chiefs were to gain control of their departments and to reduce political influence. Human relations was viewed as vague, and the military model with its rank and structure was viewed as almost a perfect panacea for resolving the problems of police managers (More and Wegener, 1992). Moreover, police departments and police chiefs were accountable to the public. One method for the chief to ensure that people and units were operating as envisioned was to enact controls, which were best facilitated by the principles of classical management.

The Systems Approach

By the mid-1950s, it was apparent that classical organizational theory and the human relations approach were inadequate to ensure a productive organization. Consequently, a new theory, systems theory, began to evolve. **Systems theory** has its roots in biology. An organization is similar to a living organism. It absorbs energy, processes the energy into some kind of output such as services, and attempts to maintain an equilibrium with its environment.

The systems approach emphasizes the interdependence and interrelationship of each and every part to the whole. According to Luthans (1985:94), "A system is composed of elements or subsystems that are related and dependent upon one another. When these subsystems are in interaction with one another, they form a unitary whole."

The main premise of the theory is that to fully understand the operation of an entity, the entity must be viewed as a system or as a whole. The system can be modified only through changes in its parts. A thorough knowledge of how each part functions and the interrelationships among the parts must be present before modifications can be made (Certo, 1989).

This view opposes the way law enforcement agencies traditionally have been organized and have functioned. For example, detective units often work separate and apart from the remainder of the police department. It is not uncommon for other specialty units such as gangs, traffic, and street crimes to work in isolation as well. Functionally, what often occurs is that there are isolated subsystems with a limited interrelationship. The systems approach to management attempts to deal with this problem, trying to unify the various parts of the organization into a functioning whole.

A systems-oriented supervisor and other leaders must look at the big picture and continually analyze and evaluate how the entire organization is performing with respect to its missions, goals, and objectives. For example, in the case of a new policy regarding police pursuits, a systems-oriented supervisor would be conscious of how the new policy would affect all the organizational divisions, including patrol, investigations, administration, and training. A systems approach also takes into account the potential impact of decisions on external factors, such as the general public, political environment, and other criminal justice agencies. The goal is that all agencies and their units work together to resolve problems.

This section provided a brief introduction to organizational theory. Over time, three different schools of organizational thought have evolved: classical, human relations, and systems. Although various parts of human relations and systems theory can be applied to police organizations, most departments today still use classical theory as the basis for organizing (Maguire, 1997). Wycoff (1994) found that 61 percent of police administrators in her study reported that there was no need to change the organizational structure of their departments to implement community policing. Thus, it appears that many police administrators are content with current arrangements.

RATIONALES AND PURPOSES OF POLICE ORGANIZATIONAL DESIGN

All organizations have an organizational structure, be it written or unwritten, basic or highly complex. Administrators, managers, and supervisors use this organizational chart as a blueprint for action. The size of the organization depends on the demand placed on it and the resources available to it. Growth precipitates the need for more people, greater division of labor, specialization, written rules, and other such elements. Police administrators modify or design the structure of their organization to fulfill its mission.

An organizational chart reflects the formal structure of task and authority relationships determined to be most suited to accomplishing the police mission. The major concerns in organizing are

1. Identifying what jobs need to be done, such as conducting the initial investigation, performing the latent or follow-up investigation, and providing for the custody of evidence seized at crime scenes
2. Determining how to group the jobs, such as those responsible for patrol, investigation, and the operation of the property room
3. Forming grades of authority, such as officer, detective, corporal, sergeant, lieutenant, and captain
4. Equalizing responsibility—if a sergeant has the responsibility to supervise seven detectives, that sergeant must have sufficient authority to discharge that responsibility properly or he or she cannot be held accountable for any results (Robbins, 1976)

Perhaps the best way to understand police supervision and management is to examine a police organization. Figure 1-4 shows the organizational chart for the Portland Police Bureau, including the

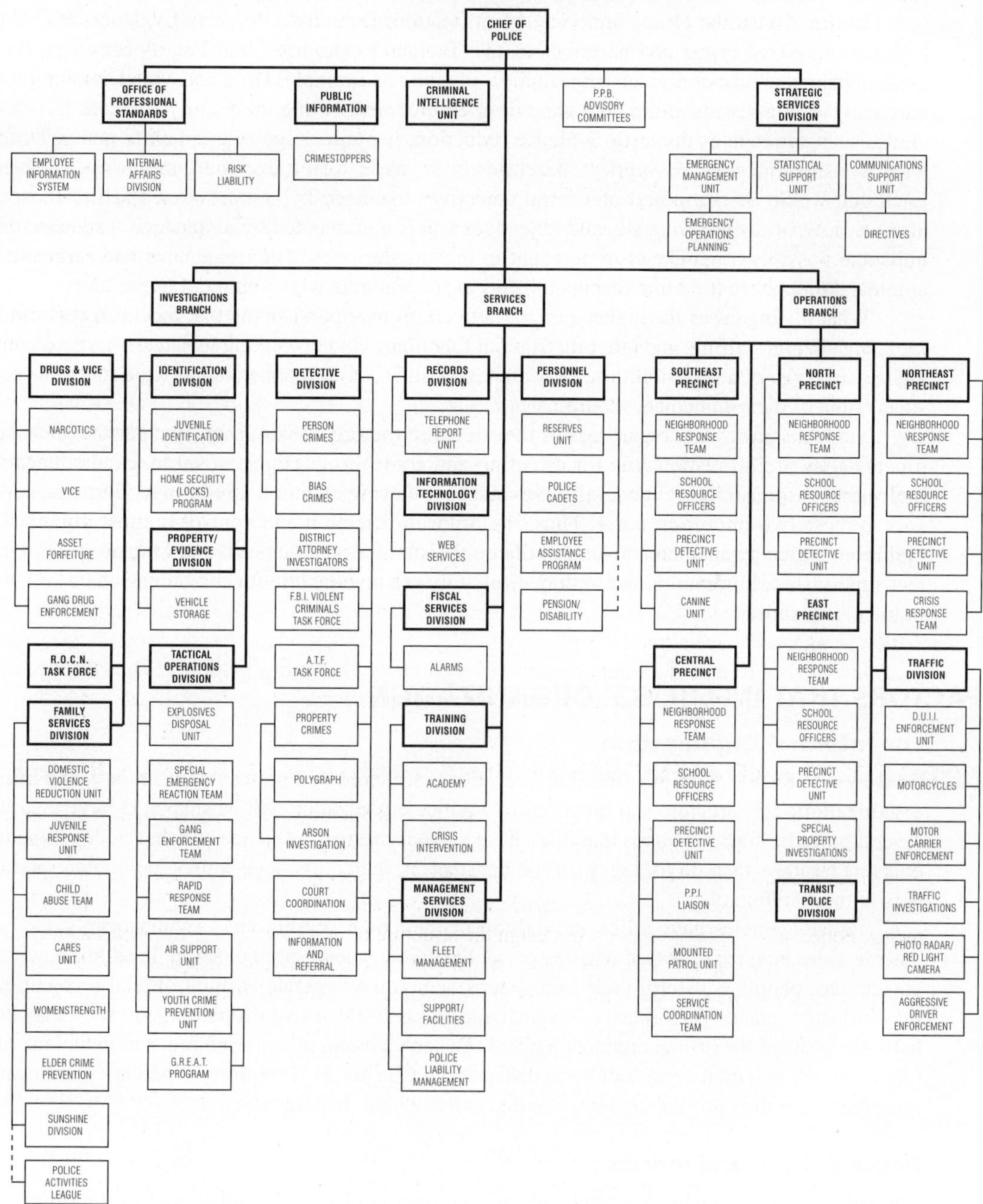

FIGURE 1-4 Portland Police Bureau 2008 organizational chart.
Used with permission; available at: http://www.portlandonline.com/shared/efm/image. cfm?id=35413

division of labor and responsibilities common to a fairly large department. Notice that each of the four major branches in the department contains a number of units. The Investigations Branch has seven **major divisions:** Drugs and vice, Identification, Detective, Property/Evidence, R.O.C.N. (a regional organized crime and narcotics team), Tactical Operations, and Family Services. Each of these divisions is further divided into smaller subunits; as example, Drug and Vice Division includes narcotics, vice, asset forfeiture, and gang drug enforcement, while the Family Services Division includes such subunits as domestic violence reduction, juvenile response, and child abuse. Drug and Vice Division includes air support, narcotics, vice, asset forfeiture, and gang drug enforcement. Each unit would be composed of several detectives managed by a supervisor. Each of those units also has a set of distinctive goals and objectives and is commanded by a manager, a captain in large units and possibly a lieutenant or sergeant in the smaller ones. The lieutenants and sergeants who command units have the same responsibilities as the captains who command larger units.

What distinguishes the higher-ranking officers from supervisors is that they also perform planning, organizing, staffing, and other managerial functions. Higher-ranking managers have executive as well as supervisory responsibilities. They are responsible for both organization-wide functions and the supervision of their immediate subordinates.

Since all managers, regardless of their level in the organization, must supervise their subordinates, they are all responsible for directing and controlling. Higher-level managers, because of their other responsibilities, generally are unable to devote as much attention as first-line supervisors to these two important tasks. Thus, the brunt of direction and control in most organizations, including police departments, usually falls on the shoulders of supervisors. Managers cannot neglect supervision, however, because they ultimately are responsible for the operation of larger units in the organization.

FACTORS THAT INFLUENCE ORGANIZATION

The Informal Organization

Existing side by side with the formal organizational structure of a police organization is the **informal organization**. The structure and functions of a police organization will be shaped in large measure by several powerful forces—forces that often have a much stronger influence over how a department conducts its business than do managers of the department, the courts, legislatures, politicians, and members of the community.

Police agencies have a life and culture of their own. Within any organization, some people emerge as leaders, regardless of whether or not they are in a leadership position. In addition, within organizations, people will form their own groups, which may operate without official recognition and may influence agency performance (Bennett and Hess, 2001). This informal organization may help or harm the goals of the formal organization and can carry gossip, misinformation, and malicious rumors (communication within organizations is discussed in Chapter 5). Therefore, supervisors and managers must recognize the informal organization that exists within their agency.

Police Culture and Inertia

The willingness to change is a fundamental requirement of today's police leaders, especially under **community oriented policing and problem solving (COPPS,** discussed thoroughly in Chapter 4). Police agencies must modify their culture from top to bottom. Change is never easy, however, because there is so much uncertainty accompanying it. It is much easier to proceed with the status quo, because "we've always done it this way."

Indeed, probably the most common characteristic of change is people's resistance to it. Adapting to a new environment or methods often results in feelings of stress or other forms of psychological discomfort. Resistance to change is likely when employees do not clearly understand the purpose, mechanics, or consequences of a planned change because of inadequate or misperceived communication.

Those who resist change are sometimes coerced into accepting it. Change in police agencies, particularly a major change, is frequently characterized by the use of centralized decision making and coercive tactics. Through the use of task forces, ad hoc committees, group seminars, and other participatory techniques, employees can become more directly involved in planning for change. By thoroughly discussing and debating the issues, a more accurate understanding and unbiased analysis of the situation is likely to result.

Any police executive contemplating change should do so in a manner that offers the greatest possibility of success. As Swanson, Territo, and Taylor (2001:642) noted:

> Conventional wisdom about change states that the way to change an organization is to bring in a new top executive, give the individual his or her head (and maybe a hatchet), and let the individual make the changes that he or she deems necessary. What the conventional wisdom overlooks are the long-term consequences of unilateral, top-down change.

The problem, then, with radical and unilateral change is the possibility of a severe backlash in the organization; a complementary problem for changes that are made gradually is that after many months or a few years of meetings, discussion, and planning sessions, nothing much has actually happened in the organization. Finding an appropriate pace for change to occur—neither too quickly and radically nor too slowly and gradually—is one of the most critical problems of planned organizational change.

Therefore, police managers and supervisors must be *viable change agents*. In any hierarchy, a person who oversees others is responsible for setting both the policy and the tone of the organization. Many police organizations boast talented and creative chief executives who, when participating in the change process, will assist in effecting change that is beneficial and lasting. As James Q. Wilson (1997:3) put it:

> The police profession today is the intellectual leadership of the criminal justice profession in the United States. The police are in the lead. They're showing the world how things might better be done.

Employee Organizations and Unions

Another factor that will affect police organization and practices is unionization. Although police unionization as a viable force has existed in this country less than 40 years, its impact has been considerable. Unions do in fact result in fewer administrative and management prerogatives; at the bargaining table, they have shaped the way policy decisions have been made in many ways. They have thwarted the creation of civilian review boards, advocated the election of "law and order" candidates, resisted the replacement of two-officer patrol cars with one-officer cars, litigated against personnel layoffs, lobbied for increased budgets, and caused the removal of chiefs and other high-ranking administrators. When the objectives of the union and the police leaders are the same, the union can be a powerful ally, however. Nonetheless, unions often compete with the administration for control of the department; many chiefs have left their posts in order to move to an agency that has a less powerful union. This raises the issue of accountability: To what extent can chief executives and managers be held responsible for the operation of the department (Swanson et al., 2001)? (Unions are discussed further in Chapter 11.)

CONTEMPORARY APPROACHES: COMMUNITY POLICING AND PROBLEM SOLVING

New Philosophy and Practices

Policing has now entered the era of community oriented policing and problem solving; this policing strategy has expanded across the United States and indeed around the world. There are, however, some important organizational considerations that arise if COPPS is to be accommodated within the police agency.

As we discussed earlier in this chapter, the traditional, bureaucratic form of policing, with its tight control and clear-cut rules, enforced by rigorous disciplinary systems, has some positive contributions for today's policing organization; however, many of these same features are counterproductive under COPPS. The professional era of policing of the early and mid-1900s inculcated a militaristic style of management and established rigid hierarchical lines of control. As a result, chief executives often placed great emphasis on their officers "going by the book" (the operations manual) and trying to avoid any chance of something going awry that would make their department look bad. Discipline was the watchword, managers were not to "rock the boat," and sergeants were expected to maintain strict control over patrol officers.

Under COPPS, police leaders must also be pioneers. This means

1. Shifting from telling and controlling employees to helping them develop their skills and abilities;
2. Listening to the customers in new and more open ways;
3. Solving problems, not just reacting to incidents;
4. Trying new things and experimenting, realizing that risk taking and honest mistakes must be tolerated to encourage creativity and achieve innovation; and
5. Avoiding, whenever possible, the use of coercive power to effect change (California Department of Justice, 1992).

An organizational transformation is a complex endeavor, and adopting COPPS requires a cultural and philosophical transformation within the entire police agency—including a decentralized, more flattened organizational structure (to encourage officer initiative) and changes in recruiting, training, awards systems, evaluation, promotions, and so forth.

It is essential that chief executives communicate the idea that COPPS is department-wide in scope. To get the whole agency involved, the chief executive must adopt four practices as part of the implementation plan:

1. Communicate to all department members the vital role of COPPS in serving the public. Executives must describe why handling problems is more effective than simply handling incidents.
2. Provide incentives to all department members to engage in COPPS. This includes a new and different personnel evaluation and reward system, as well as positive encouragement.
3. Reduce the barriers to COPPS that can occur. Procedures, time allocation, and policies all need to be closely examined.
4. Show officers how to address problems. Training is a key element of COPPS implementation. The executive must also set guidelines for innovation. Officers must know they have the latitude to innovate (Eck and Spelman, 1987:100-101).

Figure 1-5 demonstrates the principle components of COPPS implementation, tying together four key areas: leadership and administration, human resources, field operations, and external relations.

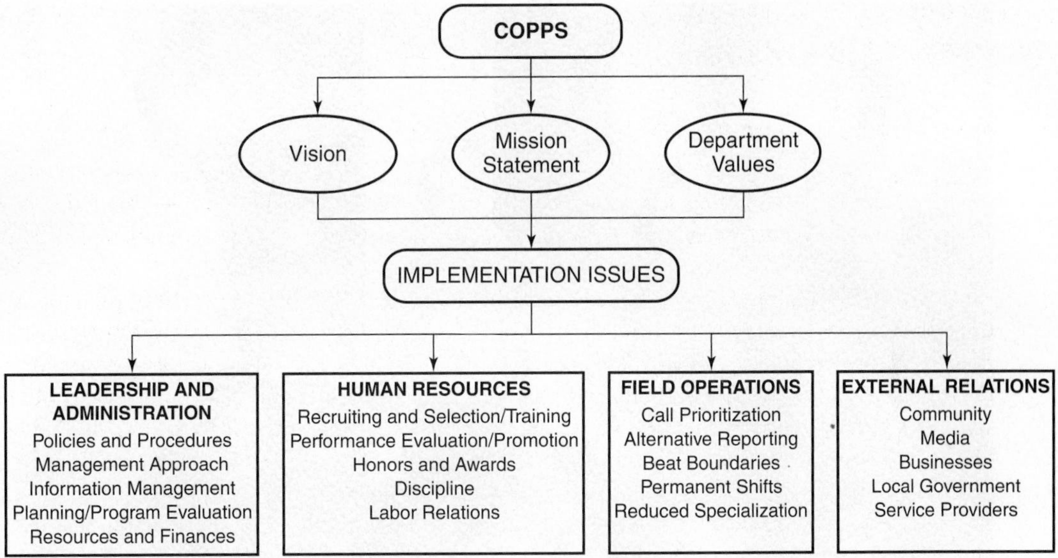

FIGURE 1-5 Principle Components of COPPS Implementation

Next is a brief example of how change to COPPS can be effected.

A Case Study in Change: Hayward, California

A good example of a police organization that modified its structure to adapt to COPPS is Hayward, California (Kocher, 1998). First, after determining that the city had a diverse ethnic composition, changes were made in the department's recruiting, hiring, training, and evaluation processes. The city's personnel and police departments began exploring the following questions:

1. Overall, what type of candidate, possessing what type of skills, is being recruited?
2. What specific knowledge, skills, and abilities reflect the COPPS philosophy—particularly problem-solving abilities and sensitivity to the needs of the community?
3. How can these attributes best be identified through the initial screening process?

Next, all personnel, both sworn and civilian, received training in the history, philosophy, and transition to COPPS. The department's initial training was directed to management and supervisory personnel to ensure they understood the agency's values, modifying the existing **police culture**, moving the organization from traditional policing to the new philosophy, and focusing on customer relations.

Performance and reward practices for personnel were also modified. Emphasizing quality over quantity (e.g., arrest statistics, number of calls for service, response times), new criteria included an assessment of how well a call for service was handled and what type of problem-solving approach was used to reach a solution for the problem. The department's promotional process was retooled, and a new phase was added to the department's promotional test (the "promotability" phase) to evaluate the candidate's decision-making abilities, analytical skills, communication skills, interpersonal skills, and professional contributions.

Collaborating with residents to resolve neighborhood problems is the foundation of community policing.
(Courtesy Charlotte, North Carolina, P.D.)

Obviously, the importance of having enlightened police executives, managers, and supervisors cannot be overemphasized under a COPPS philosophy.

Summary

This chapter has set the stage for the study of police supervision and management, defining organizations generally, then placing police agencies within the context of organizational and bureaucratic structures. Included were several important facets of supervision and management, including the evolution of organizational theory, several major administrative theories, and selected factors that influence organizations, such as employee unions. We also provided a glimpse into the current era of community oriented policing and problems solving–COPPS–which will be revisited several times in chapters to come (particularly in Chapter 4).

The reader will now have a better frame of reference for understanding the always challenging, and at times very difficult, positions of police supervisors and managers. The important part people in these positions play in human resource management is undisputed; they communicate, negotiate, train, evaluate, discipline, and deploy and must be sensitive to subordinates' needs and administrative goals and objectives. It will be seen in later chapters that, as first responders, supervisors must have a fundamental knowledge of a variety of major incidents and operations.

Items for Review

1. Explain what is meant by an organization.
2. Describe scientific management and bureaucratic management.
3. List the key management functions under POSDCORB.
4. Define *unity of command* and *span of control*.
5. Define and explain the differences between policies, procedures, and rules and regulations.
6. Explain McGregor's Theory X/Theory Y.
7. Review how the informal organization, resistance to change, and unionization can impact police organizations.
8. Discuss how organizational structures and functions might be modified in order to accommodate community policing and problem solving.

References

Alpert, G. P., and Smith, W. C. (1999). Developing police policy: An evaluation of the control principle. In L. Gaines and G. Cordner, eds., *Policing perspectives: An anthology*. Los Angeles: Roxbury Press, pp. 353–362.

Bennett, W. W., and Hess, K. (2001). *Management and supervision in law enforcement,* 3d ed. Belmont, CA: Wadsworth.

Bittner, E. (1970). *The functions of the police in a modern society*. Public Health Service Publication 2059. Washington, DC: U.S. Government Printing Office.

California Department of Justice, Attorney General's Office, Crime Prevention Center. (1992). *COPPS: Community oriented policing and problem solving*. Sacramento, CA: Author, pp. 67–68.

Certo, S. C. (1989). *Principles of modern management: Functions and systems,* 4th ed. Boston: Allyn & Bacon.

Crozier, M. (1964). *The bureaucratic phenomenon*. Chicago: University of Chicago Press.

Eck, J. E., and Spelman, W. (1987). *Problem-solving: Problem-oriented policing in Newport News*. Washington, D.C.: Police Executive Research Forum.

Fayol, H. (1949). *General and industrial management,* trans. Constance Storrs. London: Sir Isaac Pitman.

Gaines, L. K. (1978). Overview of organizational theory and its relation to police administration. In L. Gaines and T. Ricks, eds., *Managing the police organization*. St. Paul: West, pp. 151–178.

Gaines, L. K., Southerland, M. D., and Angell, J. E. (1991). *Police administration*. New York: McGraw-Hill.

Gaines, L. K., and Swanson, C. R. (1999). Empowering police officers: A tarnished silver bullet? In L. Gaines and G. Cordner, eds., *Policing perspectives: An anthology*. Los Angeles: Roxbury Press, pp. 363–371.

Gerth, H. H., and Mills, C. W. (1946). *From Max Weber: Essays in sociology.* New York: Oxford University Press.

Gray, K., Bodner, J., and Lovrich, N. P. (1997). Community policing and organizational change dynamics. In Q. Thurman and E. F. McGarrell, eds., *Community policing in a rural setting*. Cincinnati: Anderson Publishing, pp. 41–48.

Gulick, L., and Urwick, L. (1937). *Papers on the science of administration*. New York: Institute of Public Administration.

Guyot, D. (1979). Bending granite: Attempts to change the rank structure of American police departments. *Journal of Police Science and Administration* 7:253–284.

Johnson, T. A., Misner, G. E., and Brown, L. P. (1981). *The police and society: An environment for collaboration and confrontation.* Englewood Cliffs, NJ: Prentice Hall.

Kocher, C. J. (1998). A blueprint for developing responsible change. *Community Policing Exchange* (November/December): 1–6.

Lane, T. (2006a). Span of control for law enforcement agencies. *The Associate* (March-April):19-31.

Lane, T. (2006b). Span of control for law enforcement agencies. *The Police Chief* (October):74-83.

Luthans, F. (1985). *Organizational behavior*. New York: McGraw-Hill.

Lynch, R. G. (1986). *The police manager: Professional leadership skills*. Englewood Cliffs, NJ: Prentice Hall.

Maguire, E. R. (1997). Structural change in large municipal police organizations during the community policing era. *Justice Quarterly* 14(3):547–576.

McGregor, D. (1966). The human side of enterprise. In W. Bennis and E. Schein, eds., *Leadership and motivation.* Cambridge: MIT Press, pp. 5–16.

More, H. W., and Wegener, W. F. (1992). *Behavioral police management*. New York: Macmillan.

Reddin, T. (1966). Are you oriented to hold them? A searching look at police management. *The Police Chief* 3:17.

Robbins, S. P. (1976). *The administration process*. Englewood Cliffs, NJ: Prentice Hall.

Robbins, S. P. (1990). *Organizational theory: Structure, design and applications*. Englewood Cliffs, NJ: Prentice Hall.

Sparrow, M. K., Moore, M. H., and Kennedy, D. M. (1990). *Beyond 911: A new era for policing*. New York: Basic Books.

Swanson, C. R., Territo, L., and Taylor, R. W. (2001). *Police administration: Structures, processes, and behavior,* 5th ed. Upper Saddle River, NJ: Prentice Hall.

Taylor, F. W. (1911). *The principles of scientific management*. New York: Harper & Bros.

Tenzel, J., Storms, L., and Sweetwood, H. (1976). Symbols and behavior: An experiment in altering the police role. *Journal of Police Science and Administration* 4(1):21–27.

U.S. Department of Justice, Bureau of Justice Statistics (1999). *Law enforcement management and administrative statistics, 1997.* Washington, DC: Author.

Walker, S. (1993). *Taming the system*. New York: Oxford Press.

Weber, M. (1947). *The theory of social and economic organization*, trans. A. M. Henderson and Talcott Parsons. New York: Free Press.

Wilson, J. Q. (1997, September/October). Six things police leaders can do about juvenile crime. In *Subject to Debate* (newsletter of the Police Executive Research Forum).

Wycoff, M. (1994). *Community policing strategies*. Unpublished report, Police Foundation.

CHAPTER 2

Roles and Responsibilities

KEY TERMS AND CONCEPTS

- Active supervisor
- Assessment center
- Innovative supervisor
- Linking pin system
- Management by exception
- Middle manager
- Media relations
- PIO
- Police culture
- Supervisory tasks
- Promotion
- Supportive supervisor
- Traditional supervisor

LEARNING OBJECTIVES

After reading this chapter, the student will:

- know the various kinds of tests that are utilized with assessment centers and the advantages of using this approach in policing for hiring and promoting personnel
- understand the nature of supervisors' and managers' roles, and how both operate within the organizational structure
- be able to provide reasons why the first-line supervisor's role is felt to be the most difficult in the police hierarchy
- be able to explain how one prepares for and obtains promotion
- describe how the police culture and agency size affect supervision and management
- understand the police role in maintaining good media relations

Surround yourself with the best people you can find, delegate authority, and don't interfere.

—RONALD REAGAN

A man is known by the company he organizes.

—AMBROSE BIERCE

INTRODUCTION

Now that we have obtained a fundamental understanding of supervision, management, and organizations from Chapter 1, we realize that one of the most important members of an organization is the supervisor, who is directly and regularly in touch with those employees who actually do the work of the organization and interact with its customers and clients (Brown, 1992). If the supervisor fails to ensure that employees perform correctly, the unit will not be successful, causing difficulties for the manager—the lieutenant or captain. A police department is really nothing more than the sum total of all the units, and one problem unit can adversely affect other units and detract from the department's total effectiveness. This is particularly true for police organizations, because substantial interdependence exists among the various units in a police department. For example, if patrol officers do a poor job of writing reports when they respond to crimes, then the workload of detectives who later complete the cases' follow-up investigations will increase.

This chapter continues that general theme by identifying some important characteristics of policing and police organizations that make police supervision and management complex and distinctive. First, we examine the assessment center concept, and the advantages it provides in both the hiring and promoting of personnel. Then we discuss the supervisor's and manager's roles in terms of actual tasks performed. Next, we describe in broad terms how one goes about assuming the supervisory and managerial roles; this chapter section examines the various systems used by police departments to promote officers, the influence of agency size, some considerations for supervising and managing various units in the police organization, and the influence of the police culture. After discussing the important concept of media relations, the chapter concludes with two case studies.

FIRST THINGS FIRST: SELECTING THE BEST THROUGH THE ASSESSMENT CENTER

To obtain the most capable people for police middle-management and even supervisory positions (as well as chief executive positions), the assessment center method has surfaced as an efficacious means of hiring and promoting personnel. (*Note:* Sheriffs are normally elected, not hired or promoted into their position; thus, the assessment center is of little use for that position.) The assessment center method is now increasingly utilized for selecting people for all management or supervisory ranks. The assessment center process may include interviews; psychological tests; in-basket exercises; management tasks; group discussions; role-playing exercises such as simulations of interviews with subordinates, the public, and news media; fact-finding exercises; oral presentation exercises; and written communications exercises.

To better understand the advantages of the assessment center over traditional selection methods, a brief overview of the latter is in order. First, traditional methods typically consist of a written examination, credit for seniority, and a score or overall rating based on the candidate's past performance on the job. Typically the written examination is generic and is a basic, necessary starting point for the candidate, but alone it does not sufficiently ensure success in police administration and leadership. Nor does the recognition of long-term service alone guarantee that the candidate has the knowledge, skills, and abilities needed for higher-level positions. Finally, the use of past performance appraisal information is also not an accurate reflection of actual work effectiveness; supervisors have different standards and, for various reasons, may give inaccurate ratings. For these reasons, the assessment center method is used by many police agencies and is considered the most valid and reliable method to rank-order candidates (Hughes, 2006).

The first step is to identify behaviors important to the successful performance of the position. Job descriptions listing responsibilities and skills should exist for all executive, mid-management, and supervisory positions (such as chief, captain, lieutenant, sergeant, and so on). Then each candidate's abilities and skill levels should be evaluated using several of the techniques mentioned.

Individual and group role playing provides a hands-on exercise during the selection process. Candidates may be required to perform in simulated police–community problems (they conduct a "meeting" to hear concerns of local minority groups), to react to a major incident (explaining what they would do and in what order in a simulated shooting or riot situation), to hold a news briefing, or to participate in other such exercises. They may be given an in-basket situation in which they receive an abundance of paperwork, policies, and problems to be prioritized and dealt with in a prescribed amount of time. Writing abilities may also be evaluated: Candidates may be given 30 minutes to develop a use-of-force policy for a hypothetical or real police agency. This type of exercise not only illustrates candidates' written communications skills and understanding of the technical side of police work, but also shows how they think cognitively and build a case.

During each exercise, several assessors or raters analyze each candidate's performance and record some type of evaluation; when the assessment center process ends, each rater submits his or her individual rating information to the person making the hiring or promotional decision. Typically selected because they have held the position for which candidates are now vying, assessors must not only know the types of problems and duties incumbent in the position, but also should be keen observers of human behavior.

Assessment centers are logistically more difficult to conduct as well as more labor-intensive and costly than traditional interviewing procedures, but they are well worth the extra investment. Monies invested at the early stages of a hiring or promotional process can help avoid selecting the wrong person and can prevent untold problems for years to come. Good executives, middle managers, and supervisors make fewer mistakes and are probably sued less often.

THE SUPERVISORY ROLE

A Complex Position

From an organizational standpoint, the supervisor is often on the front line and caught in the middle. The supervisor deals with working employees on the one hand, and middle and upper management on the other. The concerns, expectations, and interests of labor and management are inevitably different and to some extent in conflict (Reuss-Ianni, 1983). Labor and management are, respectively, at the bottom and the top of the organization. It is management's responsibility to ensure that officers follow the dictates of policies and procedures and complete their assignments within the scope and mission of the department. Management has definite ideas about what officers should be doing and how they should do it. To some extent, management has developed a blueprint of the organization, and that blueprint outlines everyone's place and responsibilities. When officers do not follow the dictates outlined in the blueprint, the department is not effective.

Subordinate officers, on the other hand, have their own ideas about what is important and how they should perform their jobs. Officers often emphasize law enforcement tasks and deemphasize service tasks. Officers sometimes view the public negatively and act accordingly. This perception of the job often comes into conflict with management's, especially when management is implementing community policing. To help clarify this situation, Table 2-1 provides a listing of managers' and officers' expectations for supervisors.

Perhaps the best example of this today is the controversy over bias-based policing. Officers sometimes are overly aggressive and stop minority drivers to investigate them. Management expects officers in these situations to be courteous and to follow the letter and spirit of the law. Management in

TABLE 2-1 Management's and Officers' Expectations of Supervisors

Management's Expectations

- Interpret departmental policies, procedures, and rules and regulations and ensure that officers follow them.
- Initiate disciplinary action when officers fail to follow policies.
- Ensure that officers' paperwork and reports are accurate and filed on a timely basis.
- Train officers when they are deficient or unskilled.
- Complete performance evaluations.
- Ensure that officers treat citizens with respect, act professionally, and show equality.
- Ensure that officers' equipment and appearance are in order.
- Back up officers and review their performance when they answer calls for service.
- Take charge of high-risk or potential critical-incident situations.
- Make assignments to ensure that the objectives of the unit are met.

Officers' Expectations

- Interpret departmental policies, procedures, and rules and regulations to meet the needs of the officers.
- Handle disciplinary actions informally rather than taking direct action, especially regarding minor infractions.
- Advocate for officers when they request vacation or time off.
- Support officers when there is a conflict with citizens.
- Provide officers support and back-up at high-risk calls.
- Assist officers in getting better assignments and shifts.
- Emphasize law enforcement activities over providing services, community policing activities, or mundane assignments such as traffic control.
- Understand that officers need to take breaks and sometimes attend to personal needs while on duty.

many departments has voluntarily begun programs in which officers collect racial profiling data and information. Management expects supervisors to investigate or counsel officers whose statistics indicate biases or other problems. Their subordinates expect them to be understanding, to protect them from management's unreasonable expectations and arbitrary decisions, and to represent their interests. Management, though, expects supervisors to keep employees in line and to represent management and the overall department's interests.

There are several ways to place the supervisor's role in perspective. First, Likert (1961) visualized a **linking pin system** whereby each supervisor in the chain of command was a coordinator and conduit of information between the higher level of management and the lower level of workers. In this fashion, the supervisor is able to maintain a balance between upper-level expectations and subordinate expectations. When a directive flows downward in the department, the supervisor can explain it, put it in perspective relative to officers' needs and expectations, and sell the directive to subordinates. Such a process helps ensure that the directive is followed.

Others might view the position as a cushion where higher-level directives are mediated once they are issued. This softening of administrative intent sometimes results in less than desirable results. For example, a departmental policy may require officers to remain at the scene of an alarm until the owner arrives. Supervisors may allow officers to leave once the premise has been checked. A balance between departmental direction and subordinate needs must be maintained. Even when maintaining this balance, the manager or supervisor must ensure that the integrity of the directive is maintained. This is critical to the police organization.

Adding to the complexity of the supervisor's role is that the supervisor is the lowest managerial position in the department. A new supervisor, and especially one who is younger than some members

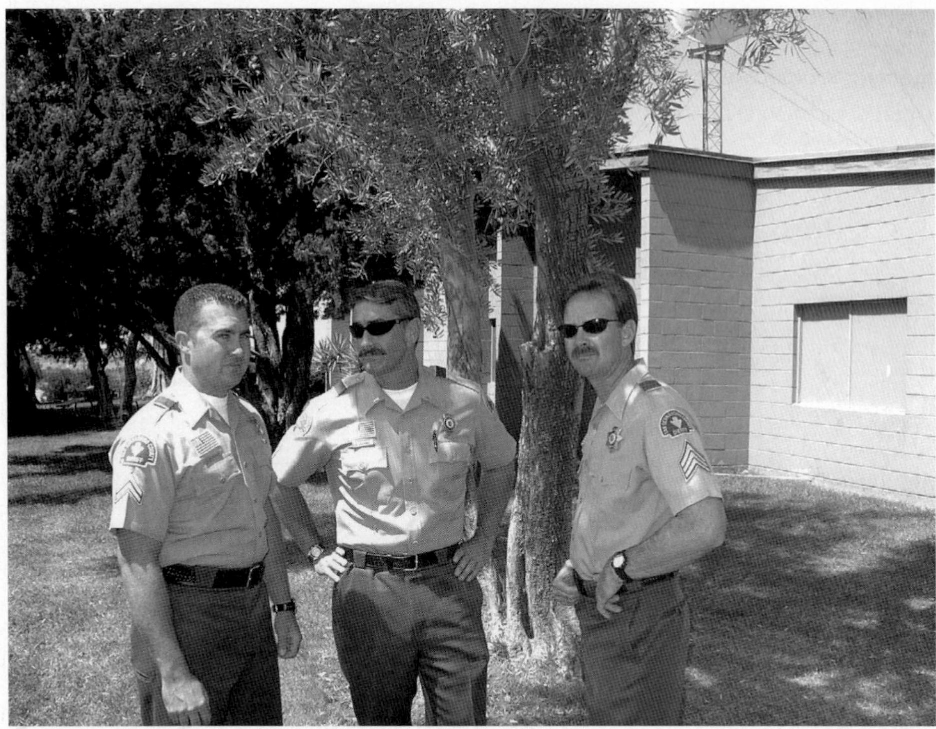

Promotion can put relationships under stress, as it brings official authority over former equals. *(Courtesy San Bernardino County S.O.)*

of the department, has to go through a transitional phase to learn how to exercise command and get cooperation from subordinates. The new supervisor is no longer responsible solely for her or his own personal behavior, but instead is responsible for the behavior of several other employees. The step from officer to supervisor is a big one that calls for a new set of skills and knowledge largely separate from that learned at lower levels in the organization.

Since supervisors are promoted from within the ranks, they are often placed in charge of their friends and peers. Long-standing relationships are put under stress when a new sergeant suddenly has official authority over former equals. Leniency or preferential treatment oftentimes is expected of new sergeants by their former peers. When new supervisors attempt to correct deficient behavior, their own previous performance may be recalled as a means of challenging the reasonableness or legitimacy of their supervisory action. Supervisors with any skeletons in their closets can expect to hear those skeletons rattling as they begin to use their new-found authority. This places a great deal of pressure on the supervisor.

The supervisor's role, put simply, is to get his or her subordinates to do their very best. This task involves a host of actions, including communicating, motivating, leading, team building, training, developing, appraising, counseling, and disciplining. Getting subordinates to do their best includes figuring out each one's strengths and weaknesses, defining good and bad performance, measuring performance, providing feedback, and making sure that subordinates' efforts coincide with the organization's mission, values, goals, and objectives.

Supervising a group of subordinates is made more difficult because of the so-called "human element." People are complex and sometimes unpredictable. Rules and principles for communicating,

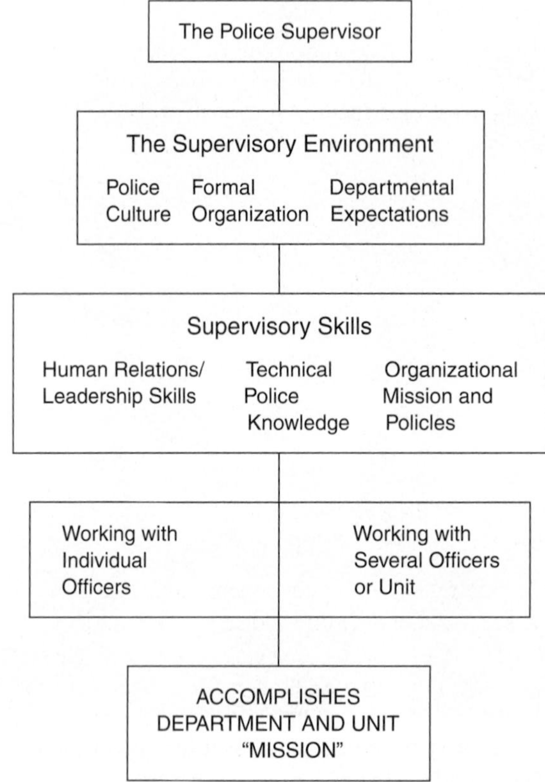

FIGURE 2-1 The Supervisory Process

leading, and similar supervisory tasks are rarely hard and fast because people react differently. What works for a supervisor in one situation may not work for that supervisor in another situation, much less for some other supervisor. Thus, supervisors have to learn to "read" subordinates and diagnose situations before choosing how to respond. Supervisors have to become students of human behavior and of behavioral science disciplines such as psychology and sociology.

Effective supervision is also difficult because the job is dynamic, not static. Even without any turnover of personnel, subordinates change over time as they age, grow, mature, and experience satisfaction and dissatisfaction in their personal and work lives. In addition, turnover is common as a result of retirements, promotions, and transfers to other units within the department. When new subordinates come under the supervisor's wing, the supervisor must learn the best way to handle these new subordinates and also be attuned to the new officers' effects on other subordinates and on the work group as a whole.

It is not only one's subordinates who change; the organization and its environment change over time. The organization's rules and expectations may change. The public may make new demands. Societal values evolve and change. Effective supervision over the long haul requires continuous monitoring and adaptation. The department expects the supervisor to keep up with such changes in order to better supervise subordinates. Subordinates, on the other hand, expect the supervisor to help them interpret and adapt successfully to this changing environment. The nature of the supervisor's role is reflected in Figure 2-1.

Police Supervisory Tasks

Police supervision shares with general supervision an emphasis on the direction and control functions. One illustration of this is the results of a job analysis of the sergeant position in the 500-officer Lexington, Kentucky, Police Department. A job analysis is used by human resource experts to document what incumbents in a position do. In Lexington, the following 10 tasks were rated most important according to incumbent *sergeants* (a job analysis of *patrol officers*, for determining training needs, is discussed in Chapter 6). They are listed with the most important first:

1. Supervises subordinate officers in the performance of their duties
2. Disseminates information to subordinates
3. Ensures that general and special orders are followed
4. Observes subordinates in handling calls and other duties
5. Reviews and approves various departmental reports
6. Listens to problems voiced by officers
7. Answers backup calls
8. Keeps superiors apprised of ongoing situations
9. Provides direct supervision on potential high-risk calls or situations
10. Interprets policies and informs subordinates

Tasks 1 and 9 on this list are global supervisory tasks that incorporate both direction and control. Tasks 2 and 10 are aspects of the directing function, while tasks 3, 4, and 5 are elements of control. Thus, 7 of these top 10 sergeant's tasks involve directing and controlling. The remaining three tasks provide interesting glimpses into some of the other duties and responsibilities performed by police supervisors: listening to subordinates' problems, notifying superiors of problems, and directly assisting subordinates in performing their work. Police supervisors provide an important communications link in the hierarchy between workers and management, as well as acting as a sounding board for problems and grievances. They also get involved in performing street police work from time to time.

Supervisory tasks can range from the mundane (such as preparing briefing logs and approving police reports) to the challenging (assigning priorities to investigations, training personnel in forced-entry procedures and handling a barricaded suspect call). Tasks may be administrative (preparing monthly activity reports, scheduling vacation leave), operational (securing major crime scenes, supervising street crime operations), general (maintaining inventory of equipment, coaching subordinates), or specialized (conducting stakeouts, training officers in how to use less than lethal munitions).

Types of Supervisors

Engel (2001) studied police supervisors and found four distinct types: traditional, innovative, supportive, and active. Each of these types of supervisors can be found in any police department. A particular supervisor's type is largely dependent on his or her experiences on the job and training and the department's organizational climate.

The **traditional supervisor** is law enforcement oriented. Traditional supervisors expect their subordinates to produce high levels of measurable activities such as traffic citations and arrests. They expect officers to efficiently respond to calls for service. They place a great deal of emphasis on reports and other paperwork. They provide officers with a substantial amount of instruction and oversight. To a great extent, traditional supervisors are task oriented. They tend to place greater emphasis on punishment than rewards and often believe that they do not have a great deal of power in the department. These supervisors see their primary role as controlling subordinates. Traditional supervisors often have morale and motivation problems with their subordinates.

The second type is the **innovative supervisor**, who is most closely associated with community policing. To some extent, innovative supervisors are the opposite of traditional supervisors. Innovative supervisors generally do not place a great deal of emphasis on citations or arrests. They also depend more on developing relationships with subordinates as opposed to using power to control or motivate. Innovative supervisors usually are good mentors, and they tend to coach rather than order. They are open to new ideas and innovations. Their ultimate goal is to develop officers so that they can solve problems and have good relations with citizens. Innovative supervisors sometimes have problems with officers who are task oriented or who emphasize enforcement and neglect community relations.

The **supportive supervisor**, like the innovative supervisor, is concerned with developing good relations with subordinates. The primary difference is that the supportive supervisor is concerned with protecting officers from what are viewed as unfair management practices. They see themselves as a buffer between management and officers. They attempt to develop strong work teams and motivate officers by inspiring them. Their shortcoming is that they tend to see themselves as "one of the boys," and they sometimes neglect to emphasize departmental goals and responsibilities.

The final category of supervisors according to Engel is the **active supervisor**, who tends to involve herself or himself in the field. Active supervisors sometimes are police officers with stripes or rank. They often take charge of field situations rather than supervising them. They are able to develop good relations with subordinates, because they are perceived as being hardworking and competent. Their shortcoming is that by being overly involved in some field situations, they do not give their subordinates the opportunity to develop.

In another study, Engel (2002) examined police supervision in Indianapolis, Indiana, and St. Petersburg, Florida. She found that the four types of supervision were fairly evenly distributed in the departments. The most effective form of supervision, however, was the active supervisor. Active supervisors are those who patrol, write tickets, and back calls. Subordinates working for active supervisors performed better in a number of areas, including problem solving and community policing. This led Engel to conclude that active or working supervisors were able to develop a more productive work unit because of their ability to lead by example. It seems that working supervisors inspire subordinates to be productive.

Engel did identify one issue with active police supervisors: they reported a higher incidence of use of force relative to other supervisors. The Christopher Commission (1991) examined use-of-force problems in the Los Angeles Police Department and cautioned police administrators that aggressive use of force is transmitted to subordinates through sergeants. Since active supervisors participate in the provision of police services, efforts should be made to ensure that they follow policies as well as that subordinates adhere to policies and procedures. Supervisors must not only be well trained and selected carefully, but they also must receive a measure of supervision from their superior.

THE MANAGER'S ROLE

Thus far, we have given substantial consideration to the supervisor. This section examines the role of the manager, especially the **middle manager**, in the police organization. Although every ranking officer in the police department exercises some managerial skills and duties, here we are concerned with the managers to whom first-line supervisors report, for they generally are unit commanders. In a mid-sized or large police agency, a patrol shift or watch may be commanded by a captain, who will have several lieutenants reporting to him or her. The lieutenants may assist the captain in running the shift, but when there is a shortage of sergeants as the result of vacations or retirements, the lieutenant may assume the duties of a first-line supervisor. The lieutenant's position in some departments may be a training ground for future mid-level managers or unit commanders.

Perhaps the best way to understand what these shift commanders do is to examine the tasks they perform, using as an example the medium-sized police department in Lexington, Kentucky. The 15 most important responsibilities for *lieutenants* include the following (this list is based on the frequency with which they are performed and their level of importance):

1. Assisting in supervising or directing the activities of the unit
2. Performing the duties of a police officer
3. Ensuring that departmental and governmental policies are followed
4. Preparing duty roster
5. Reviewing the work of individuals or groups in the section
6. Responding to field calls requiring an on-scene commander
7. Holding roll call
8. Preparing various reports
9. Reviewing various reports
10. Coordinating the activities of subordinates on major investigations
11. Meeting with superiors concerning unit operations
12. Maintaining time sheets
13. Notifying captain/bureau commander of significant calls
14. Answering inquiries from other sections/units, divisions, and outside agencies
15. Serving as captain/bureau commander in absence of same

Notice that some of the tasks (i.e., 4, 7, 8, and 12) performed by the lieutenants are purely administrative in nature. These administrative activities occur in every operational unit in the police department. The lieutenants in Lexington also perform supervisory functions in tasks 1, 3, 5, 6, 9, and 10. These functions include lieutenants overseeing officers and sergeants to ensure that different tasks are completed. This direct supervision generally focuses on the most critical tasks or those tasks that when performed incorrectly can result in dire consequences. Tasks 11, 13, 14, and 15 are managerial in nature. These are responsibilities that are generally vested with a unit commander, but many lieutenants perform them, especially in the absence of the captain. Finally, lieutenants perform the duties of a police officer (task 2). With their supervisory and managerial responsibilities, they engage in a limited amount of police work. It is seen from this list that lieutenants are involved in a wide scope of supervisory, managerial, and police duties.

Next, we examine the tasks generally performed by the captain, again using the Lexington Police Department as an example. The 15 most critical or important tasks performed by *captains* are as follows:

1. Issuing assignments to individuals and units within the section
2. Receiving assignments for section/unit
3. Reviewing incoming written complaints and reports
4. Preparing routine reports
5. Reviewing final disposition of assignments
6. Ensuring that subordinates comply with general and special orders
7. Monitoring crime and other activity statistics
8. Evaluating the work of individuals and units within the section
9. Maintaining sector facilities
10. Discussing concerns and problems with people
11. Attending various staff meetings
12. Maintaining working contacts and responding to inquiries from other sections of the division

13. Reviewing and approving overtime in section/unit
14. Monitoring section/unit operations to evaluate performance
15. Fielding and responding to complaints against subordinates

A review of these tasks shows that captains have more administrative responsibilities than lieutenants or sergeants. Tasks 2, 4, 7, 9, 10, 11, 12, 13, and 14 are administrative in nature. These tasks indicate that captains spend a substantial amount of time coordinating their units' activities with the activities of other units and overseeing the operation of their units. As an officer progresses up the chain of command, his or her responsibilities become more administrative. At the same time, captains also have supervisory responsibilities. Tasks 1, 3, 5, 6, 8, and 15 are basically supervisory in nature. Whereas a sergeant or lieutenant may be supervising individual officers, a captain is more concerned with tasks, unit activities, and the overall performance of the officers under his or her command.

Every commander and administrator in the department, including the police chief, possesses administrative and supervisory responsibilities to some extent. As can be seen from the previous lists, the unit commander functions like a police chief. The unit commander has many of the same responsibilities as the chief, but on a smaller scale. The chief performs these functions for the total department, while the unit commander is concerned only with one unit.

GETTING THAT FIRST PROMOTION: ASSUMING THE SUPERVISORY ROLE

This section first describes the means by which officers are promoted to supervisory positions. Then, we examine some of the more important aspects of policing and police organizations that distinguish police supervision from supervision in general. These include the wide variety of tasks found in and among police organizations, characteristics of police officers, the strength of the police culture, and the nature of police work itself.

Seeking Promotion

For most officers, the opportunity to attain the rank of supervisor or sergeant is an attractive one. Generally, lateral entry from one department to another in a supervisory or managerial rank does not occur. Lateral transfers happen, for the most part, at the officer level, and many police departments will select chiefs from outside the department, which perhaps is a form of lateral transfer. Officers' promotional opportunities, to a great extent, are limited to their present agency, and the waiting period for sergeant's vacancies to arise through retirement or promotion—especially in smaller agencies—can seem an interminable one.

Another administrative consideration that can filter into the promotional process is the knowledge that good officers do not automatically become good supervisors. Many good officers who are promoted to the rank of sergeant cannot divorce themselves from being "one of the troops" and are unable to flex their supervisory muscles when necessary. In short, a good sergeant must wear two hats, one of being a people-oriented, democratic leader with concern for subordinates, and another of a task-oriented leader who has the ability to command officers in field situations. Von der Embse (1987) notes that a good supervisor should spend at least 50 percent of his or her time managing. If less than 50 percent of a supervisor's time is spent on managing the unit, then the supervisor is not doing his or her job. The supervisor is spending too much time being a line officer.

At the same time, a good sergeant does not always make a good lieutenant or captain. A supervisor's job essentially entails the supervision of tasks and people. Positions above sergeant require more conceptual skills, such as planning, organizing, staffing, and budgeting. The police manager deals with groups of people and problems that encompass large geographical areas, while the supervisor generally interacts with individual officers and performs specific tasks. Substantial differences exist between the supervisor and the manager.

Obtaining Promotion

It is probably not uncommon for 60 to 65 percent or more of eligible officers to take the supervisor's test. Competition for promotion in most police agencies is normally quite keen. This is especially true because there are more people at the rank of officer than at any other rank in any given police department.

It should also be noted that, for several reasons, many excellent street cops do not wish to be promoted. Perhaps they want to remain one of the troops and do not believe that they could maintain the personal distance, perspective, or disciplinary authority needed at a higher rank. In addition, they might lose a lot of overtime pay if promoted or might be transferred to what they deem to be an undesirable shift. Others work in a particular unit, such as domestic violence, enjoy the work, and do not want to take the chance of being promoted away from their work. Some police officers find themselves a niche in the department and strive to stay there.

Others test for the wrong reasons. Many officers test simply for the experience, because of pressure from peers, through curiosity, or just to get off the streets for a short while (Van Maanen, 1989). Some have a need for power, but these individuals generally do not make good supervisors. Some officers see promotion as a means to obtaining a raise in salary, better working conditions, or an easier life. These officers, if promoted, do not make good superior officers. Promotions should be only for those who have a genuine interest in serving and improving the department.

A newly promoted sergeant. The rank of sergeant is one of the most difficult and challenging positions in a police organization.
(Courtesy Washoe County, Nevada, Sheriff's Office)

Promotions in most agencies are governed by departmental and civil service procedures, intended to guarantee legitimacy and impartiality for the process. In some jurisdictions, this is a fairly complicated process in which each step is strictly governed by law or regulation. Larger departments generally use a multifaceted procedure in which officers must compete in a series of tests or exercises. In smaller departments, the promotion examination may be nothing more than an interview with the chief of police, city manager, mayor, or city council. Supervisors are generally chosen from a final, rank-ordered list of names, often based on scores from written and oral tests. Some agencies include factors such as seniority, performance evaluations, and experience in the process. The most common promotion process in policing consists of a written test involving departmental policies, state statutes, and a reading list consisting of supervision, management, and criminal investigation books; an oral interview board; and the most recent performance evaluation.

After being promoted, several dynamics work to make the transition difficult. The new supervisor or manager confronts a solitary process. Many departments provide newly promoted officers with training prior to or after promotion and require that they complete a structured field-training program similar to the one new officers receive before being assigned to their new responsibilities. In some states, training for various supervisory and managerial ranks is mandated by statute. For example, in California, all lieutenants must complete the Commission on Police Standards and Training (POST) management training program. This multi-week course is designed to prepare lieutenants for their new jobs and includes topics such as leadership, motivation, scheduling, and complaint investigations. In many agencies, however, training is simply not available, and the newly promoted officer must rely on advice and counsel from peers and superiors.

Differences by Agency Size

A great deal of variety exists among the 16,000 or so police departments in the United States (Hickman and Reaves, 2006). Included in this group are general purpose police agencies, state police, sheriff's offices, highway patrols, state investigative agencies, and campus police departments. The agencies service small and large municipalities, merged metropolitan areas, counties, and entire states. Included also are federal law enforcement agencies and the police and security branches of the military.

Perhaps the greatest source of police organizational variation is size. A large number of American police agencies have fewer than 10 full-time sworn personnel. In many of these departments, especially those with five or fewer officers, the chief of police may be the only supervisor. In this situation, the chief must fulfill all the supervisory and managerial functions for the organization, a tall order that is made even more difficult by the 24-hour-a-day, 7-day-a-week nature of the police business. If the chief is the only supervisor, and if he or she works a normal 40-hour week, then for 128 hours each week, no supervisor is on duty. In other words, these chiefs are responsible for supervising their officers even though they are not usually on-duty with the officers. Often, these chiefs also perform police activities while they are on duty and serve as follow-up criminal investigators.

In slightly larger police organizations, particularly those with six to ten officers, the one or two sergeants in the agencies are, for all intents and purposes, assistant chiefs. They typically share both supervisory and managerial duties with the chief of police and are in operational command of the department much of the time. Out of necessity, they usually perform patrol, investigative, and other direct service activities as well. Figure 2-2 shows the varying ranks and managerial and supervisory duties that may exist in departments of varying size.

The larger the police agency, the more likely that the duties of supervisors (usually sergeants, but sometimes corporals as well) will be focused on overseeing their subordinates rather than on either doing police work or helping the chief manage the agency. In larger agencies, supervisors will ordinarily have a sufficient number of subordinates so that the supervisor is not expected to do much of the ac-

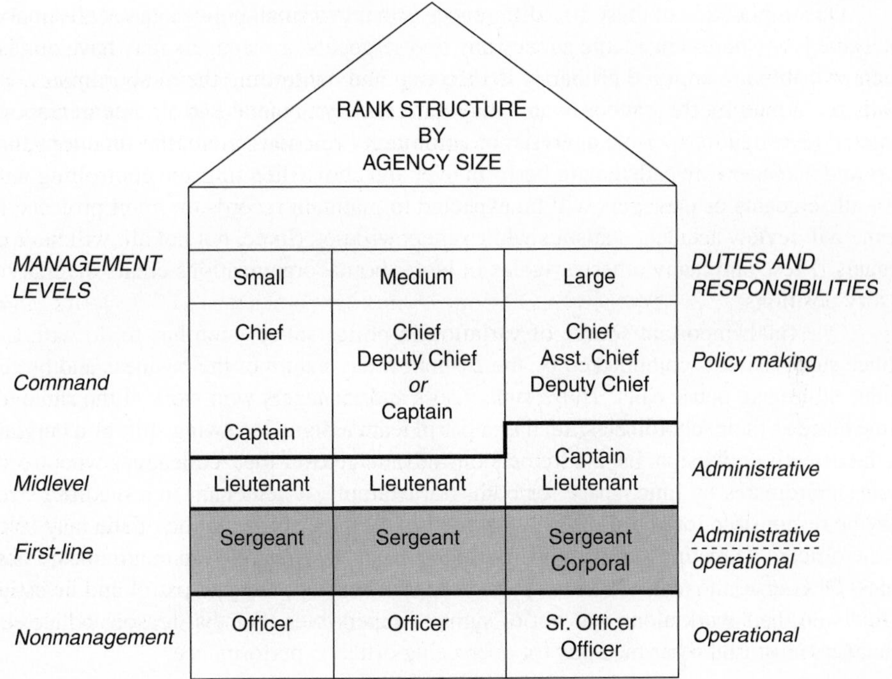

FIGURE 2-2 Rank Structure by Agency Size

tual police work (handling calls, investigating crimes, and so forth), and overseeing the subordinates is, in and of itself, a full-time job. The same goes for managers. In larger departments, they spend the majority of their time overseeing the operations of specific units.

Another important difference between small and large police agencies is the degree of specialization that affects supervisors. In small agencies with one or two supervisors, the subordinates under their direction and control do everything—engage in patrol, respond to calls for service, investigate crimes, organize crime prevention groups, present school-based programs, and so forth. Supervisors in small departments, like their officers, have to be experts in all facets of police work. In a larger agency, by contrast, a supervisor may be responsible only for a squad of detectives, or a squad of burglary detectives, or even a squad of residential burglary detectives. The range of activity under the supervisor's authority is generally narrower in larger agencies. On the other hand, the volume of work under the supervisor's control may be greater, as may be the number, expertise, and sophistication of subordinates.

Differences also exist between *large* and *medium-sized* departments at the middle-management levels. In a medium-sized department (with less specialization), the entire detective division might be commanded by a captain or lieutenant, with sergeants assigned to supervise detectives in units such as robbery/homicide, burglary, fraud, vice/narcotics, and juvenile crimes. A larger agency, however, might have a deputy chief of police in charge of the detectives, with one lieutenant managing crimes against property (such as burglary, fraud, cyber crimes, and auto theft units) and another responsible for crimes against persons (robbery/homicide, sexual assaults, juvenile crimes); furthermore, each of these specialized units would have a sergeant supervising its detectives. Finally, larger agencies might also have lieutenants and/or sergeants supervising regional task forces that address gang, narcotics, cyber, and juvenile crimes.

One implication of these size differences is that in a small police agency all supervisors perform the same job, whereas in a large agency any two sergeants or managers may have quite different jobs. Both probably are engaged primarily in directing and controlling their subordinates. But the kind of work performed by their subordinates may vary widely: general patrol, emergency operations, specialized investigations, crime analysis, or community relations. Also, the functions that the supervisors and managers are called on to perform over and above directing and controlling will likely differ. Not all sergeants or managers will be expected to maintain records on grant projects, but some will. Some will review accident statistics while others will not. Some, but not all, will have civilian subordinates. These and many other variables in larger police organizations create diversity among supervisory positions.

One final important source of variation in police supervision has to do with time and place. Police supervision is complicated by the 24-hour-a-day nature of the business and by the fact that the police still make house calls. Those supervisors and managers who work at the same time and in the same place as their subordinates, such as a patrol team assigned to swing shift or a burglary unit located in the detectives division, have a tremendous advantage over their colleagues who are separated from their subordinates by time, space, or both. For example, a lieutenant in a medium-sized department may be responsible for patrol officers assigned to all three shifts, but he or she may seldom see many of the officers. Directing and controlling are much easier when one can continuously observe subordinates. Of course, the reality of most police supervision, especially in patrol and investigations, is that officers do their work alone and out of sight of supervisors. For that reason, police supervisors and managers must find other methods for overseeing officers' performance.

Supervision of Patrol Officers

One of the most influential leadership theories holds that the nature of subordinates is the key determinant of which management style will be most successful (Hersey and Blanchard, 1988). Every indication is that this situational or contingency theory is quite applicable to police supervision (Southerland and Reuss-Ianni, 1992), and we will examine it in detail in Chapter 3. Here, we consider if any general characteristics of police officers have a pervasive impact on police supervision and management.

Some early studies suggested that policing attracts certain kinds of people with distinct personalities and philosophies. It was believed that conservative, authoritarian individuals with a preference for uniforms, weapons, and discipline were drawn to police work. Later studies, however, found that new police recruits scored surprisingly "normal" on psychological and intelligence tests. The most compelling characteristics that these recruits have in common are a desire to help others, an interest in job security, and perhaps some inclination toward risk taking and adventure. Otherwise, a police recruit class generally provides a good cross section of the population at large (Burbeck and Furnham, 1985).

Veteran police officers, however, clearly are different from the general population. As recruits, they may have started out much like their friends and neighbors, but police officers frequently become more rigid, more conservative, more cynical, and more suspicious as a result of adopting the police role and doing police work (Gaines and Kappeler, 2003). This is understandable, because they experience more anger, fear, and frustration than workers in most other fields. They see some of the worst things that people do to each other in the form of neglect, abuse, crime, and violence. And they have a good deal of lying, deception, suspicion, hatred, and violence directed at them. Given the rather dramatic and intense nature of policing and the police role, it would be odd if police officers' personalities and viewpoints were not affected. One manifestation of these effects on police officers is stress, a topic that is addressed fully in Chapter 8.

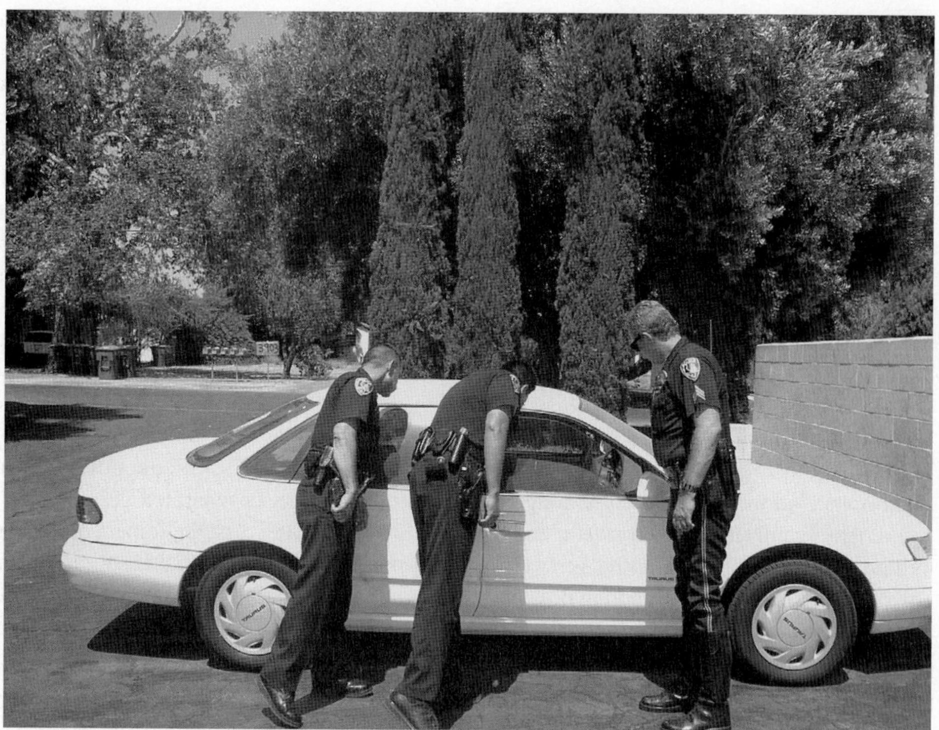

Assisting and guiding officers in the field is one of the primary functions of supervisors. *(Courtesy Riverside, California, P.D.)*

Also, and of equal importance, police superiors must attend to the emotional and psychological development of their subordinates and, in so doing, counter the occupational tendencies toward cynicism and stress-related mental and physical ill health just described. Perhaps the greatest responsibility given to police supervisors is that of guiding the moral and intellectual development of their subordinates (Muir, 1977). We discuss ethics, values, and liability issues in Chapter 9.

The superior's challenge is to restore balance in officers' lives, which are often thrown out of balance by the experience of policing. Today's superior cannot function like a military commander; he or she needs more than just unquestioned strength and toughness. Successful management and supervision utilize personal attributes such as empathy, caring, and nurturing, as well as street-wise attributes such as decisiveness, boldness, and toughness.

The Police Culture

As we discussed in Chapter 1, the role of the supervisor and manager is affected by the strength of the **police culture**, which is a determining factor in work behavior. For example, the number of traffic citations issued or number of arrests by officers is frequently determined by norms established by the work group—a condition we termed the *informal organization* in Chapter 1. And, on rare occasions, police cultures support flagrant forms of deviance: drinking on duty, brutalizing prisoners, selling drugs, and corruption (see Kappeler, Sluder, and Alpert, 1994; Kleinig, 1996).

These behaviors do occur and are a major concern to managers and supervisors. Major scandals such as those occurring in Los Angeles (planting evidence), New York (officers involved in drug corruption), and New Orleans (officers committing robbery-homicides) in recent years cause substantial damage to the police department.

Most police officers do not engage in flagrant deviance, of course, and not all police organizational cultures encourage or even allow such behavior. The police supervisory or managerial responsibility is to be especially familiar with the norms and values of the organization's culture. If these norms and values are consistent with official expectations, the superior officer can use the culture in directing and controlling subordinates' behavior. When the organizational culture supports unhealthy attitudes and deviant behavior, the job of managing or supervising is made much more difficult. Either subordinates must be convinced to reject the culture's deviant norms and values, or the culture itself must be changed. In some departments, speeding in marked patrol cars is routinely accepted by officers and the police culture. Yet, when officers speed while on duty but not while responding to an emergency call, it is not only dangerous, but it also undermines citizen satisfaction with the police. Citizens expect their police to abide by the same laws under which they are held accountable. In this case, supervisors must make an extraordinary effort to bring police behavior into compliance with laws and larger societal expectations.

Other characteristics of the police business provide supervisors with opportunities to resist a deviant organizational culture. For example, if a group of officers is separated geographically from the rest of the organization, or works at a different time from other officers, the impact of the organizational culture may be reduced, and the supervisor's opportunity to develop an alternative culture is heightened. Indeed, it is quite common in police departments to find distinct behavioral styles among different squads, shifts, and units; these styles are frequently the result of supervisors' own varying philosophies, styles, and values. This applies not only to deviant behavior, but also to day-to-day activities. Supervisors can have an impact on individuals' priorities. If a sergeant thinks the issuance of traffic citations is most important, then subordinates will likely make an effort to write more tickets. The police manager can reinforce this as well as provide some direct supervision of the sergeants.

The Ideal Versus the Real

Because supervision is such an important ingredient in police administration, it is necessary to examine how effective supervision is. Recall that supervision is not only conducted by first-line supervisors, but it also is an integral part of management. Police chiefs, their subordinate commanders, and unit commanders are engaged in the supervision of subordinates and police activities. Officers located at each higher level in the chain of command are responsible for supervising their immediate subordinates and ensuring that they, in turn, supervise officers under their command.

Research indicates that supervision is extremely weak in most police departments. For example, Engel (2000) examined supervision in Indianapolis, Indiana, and St. Petersburg, Florida. She found that supervisors who were active influenced officers' decisions in making arrests and in using force but did not exert a substantial amount of influence in other areas. Moreover, active supervisors constituted only about one-quarter of the supervisors in the department. Other supervisors had even less influence on officers.

There are several explanations for this occurrence. First, Van Maanen (1989) and Jermier and Berkes (1979) suggested that only when subordinates encounter a task that is unpredictable or has a high level of uncertainty associated with it do they rely on their supervisors to make decisions for them. Otherwise, subordinates tend to rely on their discretion and complete the task without conferring with a superior officer. Thus, it is unusual for officers to seek supervisory advice or intervention. Historically, police supervisors have been comfortable with this arrangement.

Along these same lines, many supervisors use the rule of **management by exception**, which states that a superior does not have the time to supervise all the activities under his or her control and, therefore, should devote energy and time only to those exceptional tasks or activities. When adhering to this rule, many supervisors and managers may neglect the daily activities that are part and parcel of the unit's overall responsibilities. This allows some critical activities to occur without supervision, and officers may deviate from departmental expectations.

Some may suggest that this lack of supervision is partially a consequence of the strong emphasis within police administration over the past decade or two on the human relations approach to management, which has accompanied the implementation of community policing. This is not the case, however. First, Gaines and Swanson (1999) suggest that in the past, police organizations have not been authoritarian but have been more lackadaisical. They have had the appearance of authoritarianism as a result of the uniforms and military rank, but for the most part police officers of the past had as much, if not more, discretion than today's officers. Police departments now likely have less discretion, as they have instituted more comprehensive policies and procedures and provided officers with better training.

Second, research indicates that community policing has not had much effect on the police organization. Zhao, Lovrich, and Robinson (2001) found that community policing has not changed the core mission of the police. Law enforcement remains committed to crime fighting as opposed to a greater orientation toward the maintenance of order. The implementation of community policing should result in a mission shift to order maintenance. In his survey of police departments, Maguire (1997) also found that police organizational structure has not changed appreciably as a result of community policing. Thus, community policing does not result in lax supervision. It also appears that some departments have not fully adopted community policing.

Police supervisors must enhance officer safety and help officers deal with the psychological effects of danger. Supervisors must also be wary of another reaction: Some officers see so much danger in every situation that their approach to citizens becomes uniformly heavy-handed and oppressive. Ultimately, police supervisors need to develop their officers into consistent and reliable decision makers.

Supervisors also need to ensure that their officers recognize and respect the varied functions of policing and overcome the view that work relating to order maintenance and social services is "not real police work." Supervisors should use performance appraisals, assignments, commendations, and other rewards and punishments under their control to drive home the message that all the varied functions of policing are legitimate aspects of police work.

In these situations, managers have the responsibility of reviewing the work of their supervisors. If a patrol sergeant becomes lax and does not ensure that officers follow the dictates of departmental policies, it is up to the manager to catch and correct such omissions. This is usually accomplished by reviewing complaints against officers and use-of-force and other routine reports and by frequently meeting with supervisors and discussing priorities and problems. Managers must hold their supervisors accountable and remain abreast of what is occurring in their units.

MEDIA RELATIONS

News dissemination is a delicate undertaking for the police; news organizations, especially the television and print media, are highly competitive businesses that seek to obtain the most complete news in the shortest amount of time, which often translates to wider viewership and therefore greater advertising revenues for them. From one perspective, the media must appreciate that a criminal investigation can be seriously compromised by premature or excessive coverage. From another legitimate viewpoint, the public has a right to know what is occurring in the community, especially as it concerns crime. Therefore, it is only prudent to have an open and professional relationship with the media in which each side knows and understands its responsibilities. It is therefore also important that someone in the agency—either the chief executive, his/her designee, or a trained Public Information Officer (**PIO**)—knows how to perform public speaking, and what kind and how much information they should divulge to media outlets.

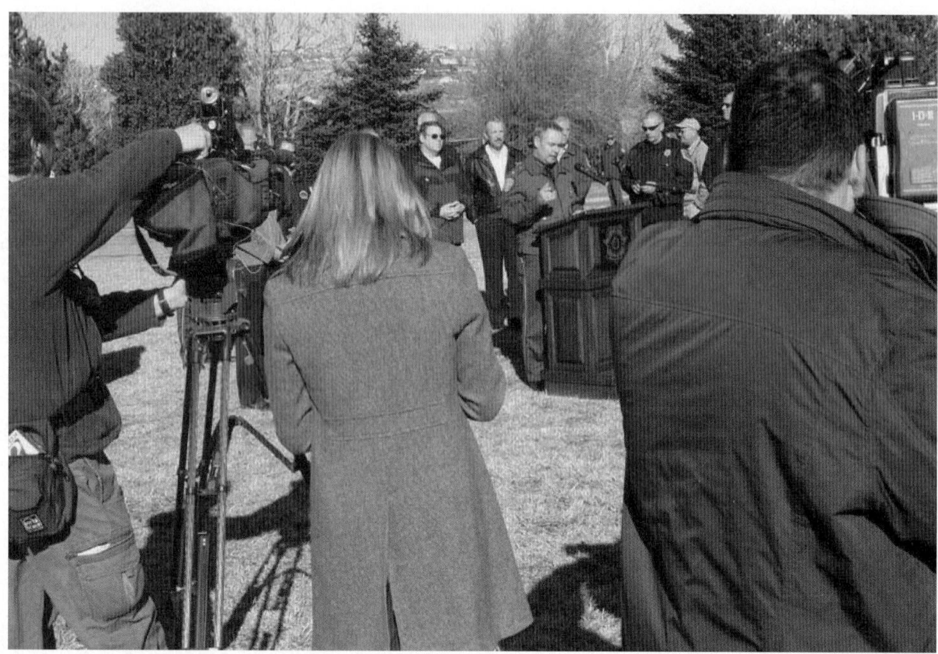

News dissemination is a delicate yet important undertaking for agency leaders and public information officers. *(Courtesy Washoe County, Nevada, Sheriff's Office)*

Unfortunately, many police executives (a good number of whom involuntarily left office) can speak of the results of failing to develop an appropriate relationship with the media. One example is a former police chief in a medium-sized western city who sported a bumper sticker on his vehicle stating "I don't trust the liberal media." This action obviously did not endear him to the local newspaper, nor did it help him in editorials and articles when an issue concerning his involvement in a sexual harassment allegation became public, and he ultimately resigned. This chief obviously did not recognize the power of the pen, and that you "Don't argue with someone who buys his ink by the barrel!"

Certainly every police agency, large or small, should have a written media policy that is grounded on certain basic precepts:

- Never lie or embellish a story; do not refuse to talk with media representatives.
- Never slowly release details of a story in tiny scraps, because the media may assume that the police are hiding something.
- Do not lash out at the press; it only makes matters worse.
- Do not try to shift the blame unnecessarily; if the agency was responsible for something going wrong, assume accountability for it.
- Look at the big picture; avoid making bad news bigger by dwelling on scandals, faults, mistakes, and other embarrassments.
- Honor your promises. For example, if you tell a reporter "I'll get back to you," be sure to do so.
- Remember that the best news is that bad news really will pass, and soon there are sunny days. (Garner, 2004:22-24)

A media policy should stress to the individual officers that their interaction with an individual reporter, either positive or negative, will affect how the entire agency is viewed–by both the reporter, and possibly the public. A good relationship will help the agency to control what information the public receives and can also help to alleviate the problem of the media hounding detectives and others for updates and information.

Because it is important to "speak with one voice," the agency should also explain to all personnel the proper steps for referring reporters up the chain of command, what the chain is, and where they are on the chain. There are five basic approaches: (1) only the agency head speaks; (2) anyone can speak; (3) the senior ranking officer at the scene can speak; (4) only designated personnel can speak; (5) and only the PIO can speak. Note, too, that the normal chain of command may not be the chain of command when dealing with the media; a rank-and-file officer may be designated as the PIO and can be the next step in the chain as opposed to a detective or higher ranking officer (Donlon-Cotton, 2005).

Nowhere is it written on the officer's badge or pocket Miranda card that dealing with the press will always be easy or that the news they have to share will always be positive. However, in adhering to the above guidelines, the specter of agency "bad press" will hopefully but held at bay.

CASE STUDIES

Following are two case studies that enable the reader to consider some of the substantive issues described in the chapter and to consider some options as solutions to problems.

Case Study #1

Adapting to the Role: The Laissez-Faire Supervisor

Sgt. Tom Gresham is newly promoted and assigned to patrol on the graveyard shift; he knows each officer on his shift, and several are close friends. Sgt. Gresham was an excellent patrol officer and prided himself on his reputation and ability to get along with his peers. He also believed this trait would benefit him as a supervisor. From the beginning, Sgt. Gresham believed that he could get more productivity from his officers by relating to them at their level. He made an effort to socialize after work and took pride in giving his team the liberty of referring to him by his first name. Sgt. Gresham also believed that it was a supervisor's job to not get in the way of "good" police work. In his view, his team responded tremendously, generating the highest number of arrest and citation statistics in the entire department. Unfortunately, his shift was also generating the highest number of citizen complaints—yet, few complaints were sustained by internal affairs. It was Gresham's opinion that complaints are the product of good, aggressive police work. He had quickly developed the reputation among subordinates as being "a cop's cop." One Monday morning, Sgt. Gresham is surprised when he is called in to his patrol captain's office; the internal affairs lieutenant is also present. They show Gresham a number of use-of-force complaints against his team over the past week while Sgt. Gresham was on vacation. Despite his captain's efforts to describe the gravity of the situation, Gresham failed to grasp the seriousness of the complaints, and how his supervisory style may have contributed to them.

Questions for Discussion:

1. What do you think are some of Sgt. Gresham's problems as a new supervisor?
2. As his captain, what kind of advice would you give to Gresham?
3. What corrective action must Sgt. Gresham take immediately with his team of officers?

Case Study #2

No One Said It Would Be Easy....

Officer John Knox is 25 years old, married, and has two young children. He is a graduate of the local university, and was one of the top academy graduates. He is bilingual, serves as an interpreter as needed, and enjoys the respect of neighborhood leaders. Officer Knox received outstanding performance ratings during his first three years of service, but his last rating was only satisfactory. This is his second year of graduate school at the university, and his total energies have been devoted to the completion of his master's degree. Since beginning his master's work a year ago, his work performance has deteriorated to the point of becoming marginal: his responses to calls for service have been less than stellar, as have his enforcement of traffic laws, community problem solving efforts, and other endeavors. Furthermore, you, as his newly promoted supervisor, are aware that Knox has been parking his vehicle and studying, rather than solving problems on his beat. Two weeks ago, his wife phoned you saying that she and Knox are having serious domestic issues; she added that she is certain he has met another woman at the university, and that his conduct is rapidly becoming a subject of neighborhood gossip. Today a news reporter phones your receptionist and states that a report was received about an hour ago on the police radio scanner that Officer Knox had been discovered in his car at the bottom of a ravine in a secluded part of the county, and upon arriving there the reporter witnessed Knox in the car with a well-known woman who is a dean at the university. The reporter wants to interview you and is on hold. You know that the agency's PIO is on vacation.

Questions for Discussion:

1. What do you have the receptionist tell the reporter? Do you talk to him or not? If so, what do you say?
2. What steps do you take after dealing with the reporter?
3. What are the key issues presented in this situation?
4. How do you deal with these key issues?

Case Study #3

Seeing the Big Picture

Sgt. Henry Garcia, a college-educated 18-year veteran, scored near the top in his promotional exam. His career has essentially involved time spent in the planning/research and the training divisions. He also teaches report writing at the area academy. Garcia believes very strongly that officers are only as good as the reports they write. He believes his officers should write exceptional reports, and he devotes most of his time to reviewing officers' reports, counseling them on report content, and recommending changes and revisions. His demands require officers to spend inordinate amounts of time with their report-related duties (accruing much overtime in the process). Garcia often uses his team's reports at the recruit academy as examples of "good" police work. Arrests in his division are the lowest in the agency, but the division has the highest number of reported offenses. Sgt. Garcia often asks his officers why the arrest and crime statistics are so poor, but they fail to respond to him. Frustrated, he schedules an appointment to see his superior, a lieutenant, to discuss the problems.

Questions for Discussion:

1. As the lieutenant, what would you tell Sgt. Garcia are the reasons for the crime problem in his district and his relations with his team?
2. What might you suggest to rectify this situation?

Summary

This chapter focused on the complex demands and considerations of police management and supervision, including a very good means of determining who should wear the bars and stripes (of captains, lieutenants, sergeants, and so on)–the assessment center.

A number of important characteristics of policing and police organizations were identified that indicate that police management and supervision are complex and problematic. To a great extent, supervision and management at all levels of a police department are the fuel that makes the department operate. When there are supervisory and management problems at any level in the police department, they will negatively affect officers and units.

We learned how managers and supervisors assigned to different units, particularly patrol and investigations, are affected by their unit's mission and activities. We described how one goes about assuming a supervisory or managerial position, using a variety of promotional processes, as well as the supervisor's and manager's roles in terms of actual tasks performed. The influence of agency size and the police culture were also shown to be important considerations. Also of considerable importance was the discussion of the need for the police to maintain positive relations with the media, to know the chain of command for talking with the media, the kinds of information they can and should be given, and other facets of police-media relations. The chapter's three case studies provided some substantive issues for the reader to use for applying chapter information.

Items For Review

1. Explain how the supervisor's and manager's roles are uniquely difficult and complex.
2. Describe the possible component parts of an assessment center, and the advantages of using this approach to hiring and promoting personnel.
3. Delineate the means by which one is promoted to a supervisory level, some of the factors that

influence whether or not one is promoted, and some of the problems that one faces on assuming the role.

4. What are the supervisor's and manager's tasks?
5. What are some of the major aspects of patrol work that supervisors and managers must oversee?
6. What kinds of supervisors exist in the police organization and how effective are they?
7. Explain some of the means of achieving positive media relations, and the kinds of behaviors that should be avoided in dealing with media representatives.

References

Barker, T., and Carter, D. (1990). Fluffing up the evidence and covering your ass: Some conceptual notes on police lying. *Deviant Behavior* 11:61–73.

Brown, M. F. (1992). The sergeant's role in a modern law enforcement agency. *The Police Chief* (May):18–22.

Burbeck, E., and Furnham, A. (1985). Police officer selection: A critical review of the literature. *Journal of Police Science and Administration* 13:58–69.

Christopher Commission. (1991). *Report of the independent commission on the Los Angeles Police Department.* Los Angeles: City of Los Angeles.

Donlon-Cotton, C. (2005). Model media policy. *Law and Order* (October):18-19.

Engel, R. S. (2002). Patrol officer supervision in the community policing era. *Journal of Criminal Justice* 30:51–64.

Engel, R. S. (2001). Supervisory styles of patrol sergeants and lieutenants. *Journal of Criminal Justice* 29:341–355.

Engel, R. S. (2000). The effects of supervisory styles on patrol officer behavior. *Police Quarterly* 3(3):262–293.

Gaines, L., and Kappeler, V. (2003). *Policing in America.* Cincinnati: Anderson.

Gaines, L. K., and Swanson, C. (1999). Empowering police officers: A tarnished silver bullet? In L. Gaines and G. Cordner, eds. *Policing perspectives: An anthology.* Los Angeles: Roxbury Press, pp. 363–371.

Garner, G. W. (2004). Handling bad press. *Law and Order* (September):22-24.

Hersey, P., and Blanchard, K. H. (1988). *Management of organizational behavior: Utilizing human resources,* 5th ed. Englewood Cliffs, NJ: Prentice Hall.

Hickman, M. J., and Reaves, B. A. (2006). *Local police departments, 2003.* Washington, DC: Bureau of Justice Statistics.

Hughes, F. (2006). Does the benefit outweigh the cost? Using assessment centers in selecting middle managers. *The Police Chief* (August):106-111; see also Hales, C. (2005). Pros and cons of assessment centers. *Law and Order* (April):18-22.

Jermier, J. M., and Berkes, L. J. (1979). Leader behavior in a police command bureaucracy: A closer look at the quasi-military model. *Administrative Science Quarterly* 24:1–23.

Kappeler, V., Sluder, R., and Alpert, G. (1994). *Forces of deviance: Understanding the dark side of policing.* Prospect Heights, IL: Waveland.

Kleinig, J. (1996). *The ethics of policing.* Cambridge, England: Cambridge University Press.

Likert, R. (1961). *New patterns of management.* New York: McGraw-Hill.

Maguire, E. R. (1997). Structural change in large municipal police organizations during the community policing era. *Justice Quarterly* 14(3):547–576.

Muir, W. K., Jr. (1977). *Police: Streetcorner politicians.* Chicago: University of Chicago Press.

The Museum of Broadcast Communications, "Police programs," http://www.museum.tv/archives/etv/P/htmlP/policeprogra/policeprogra.htm (Accessed January 4, 2007)

Reuss-Ianni, E. (1983). *Two cultures of policing: Street cops and management cops.* New Brunswick, NJ: Transaction Books.

Southerland, M. D., and Reuss-Ianni, E. (1992). Leadership and management. In G. W. Cordner and D. C. Hale, eds., *What works in policing? Operations and administration examined.* Cincinnati, OH: Anderson, pp. 157–177.

Van Maanen, J. (1989). Making rank: Becoming an American police sergeant. In R. G. Dunham and G. P. Alpert, eds., *Critical issues in policing: Contemporary readings.* Prospect Heights, IL: Waveland, pp. 146–151.

Von der Embse, T. (1987). *Supervision: Managerial skills for a new era.* New York: Macmillan.

Zhao, J., Lovrich, N., and Robinson, T. H. (2001). Community policing: Is it changing the basic functions of policing? Findings from a longitudinal study of 200+ municipal police agencies. *Journal of Criminal Justice* 29:365–377.

CHAPTER 3

Leadership and Motivation within the Police Organization

Key Terms and Concepts

- Achievement, power, and affiliation motives
- Authority
- Benevolent-authoritarian leadership
- Conceptual skills
- Consultative leadership
- Contingency theory
- Culture of discipline
- Developing leadership skills
- Empowerment
- Expectancy theory
- Exploitive-authoritarian leadership
- "Great" police organizations
- Katz's technical, human, conceptual skills
- Leadership styles
- Leading v. managing
- Likert's leadership systems
- Managerial grid
- Maslow's hierarchy of needs
- Maturity-immaturity theory
- McClelland's achievement, power, and affiliation motives
- Mintzberg model for CEOs
- Motivation-hygiene theory
- Participative leadership
- Planning cycle
- Power
- Situational leadership
- Station house sergeants and street sergeants
- Strategic planning
- Supervisors and managers as leaders
- Trait theory
- Zone of indifference

Learning Objectives

After reading this chapter, the student will:

- comprehend what is involved in transforming a "good" police organization into one that is "great"
- know the basic leadership theories, and how leadership skills are developed
- have a working knowledge of motivating personnel in the workplace, and how motivational strategies may be applied in the police agency
- understand the difference between leading and managing

- understand empowerment—its importance for today's policing and its levels and stages
- be aware of the major roles of police executives, using the Mintzberg model of chief executive officers
- be able to explain the basic precepts of strategic thinking and planning for strategic management
- explain what is meant by adaptive change, and how it applies to police leaders
- be able to discuss how leadership can fail in a police department
- know which leadership styles are best for the police agency

Of the best leader, when he is gone, they will say: We did it ourselves.

—CHINESE PROVERB

It is time for a new generation of leadership, to cope with new problems and new opportunities. For there is a new world to be won.

—JOHN F. KENNEDY

INTRODUCTION

Previous chapters identified the first-line supervisor and the middle manager as two of the most important and influential members of a police organization, whose primary functions involved directing and controlling the work of subordinates. That discussion was limited to the functional duties and tasks, or the mechanics of these positions. Here we delve deeper, exploring the motivational side of supervision and management, or the "art of leadership." We explore why some supervisors and managers are capable of capturing the hearts and minds of their subordinates and arouse their passion to perform extraordinary tasks, while others struggle to gain officers' compliance to simple directions.

We open the chapter with a discussion of how some experts say today's leaders must fundamentally approach personnel administration in order to move an organization from one that is "good" to one that is "great." We then consider relevant definitions and the kinds of traits that make good leaders, and look at the difference between *power* and *authority.* Next, we examine empowerment; a model of what chief executive officers actually do; and how police supervisors, managers, and executives must be able to think and plan strategically. Then some early theories of motivation (both content and process theories) are discussed that have stood the test of time, and then we look at several prominent theories concerning leadership, as well as leadership styles that do and do not work in the policing setting. We then discuss why leading in the new millennium is so difficult, and why police leaders must shift their expectations, attitudes, or habits of behavior to address today's problems. Next is a brief analysis of why leaders fail, and the chapter concludes with three case studies that provide the reader with an opportunity to view relevant issues and to integrate the information and possible solutions presented in the chapter.

It is important to remember that behind every good practice lies a good theory. Theory and practice are inextricably intertwined. Thus, we look at the primary theories behind employee satisfaction, motivation, and leadership. We might also point out that many books examine leadership theories in length; thus, in this chapter we limit our coverage to comparatively brief overviews of related theories for policing.

MOVING FROM A "GOOD" TO A "GREAT" POLICE ORGANIZATION

Jim Collins (2001) wrote a best-selling book entitled *Good to Great: Why Some Companies Make the Leap and Others Don't,* which sought to answer the compelling question: can a good company become a great company and, if so, how? Collins and his team of assistants searched for companies that made a "leap to greatness" defined by stock market performance and long-term success; they found 11 companies that met their criteria, and spent more than 10 years studying what made them great. Acknowledging the growing interest in his book by non-business entities, later Collins (2005) published a monograph entitled *Good to Great and the Social Sectors*, delineating how his lessons could be modified to fit government agencies. Certainly much of the success of **"great" police organizations** has to do with the leadership.

Collins coined the term "Level 5 leader" to describe the highest level of executive capabilities (Levels 1 through 4 are highly capable individual, contributing team member, competent manager, and effective leader). Level 5 executives are ambitious, but their ambition is directed first and foremost to the organization and its success, not to personal renown. Level 5 leaders, Collins stressed, are "fanatically driven, infected with an incurable need to produce results" (quoted in Wexler et al., 2007:5).

Such leaders, Collins found, do not exhibit enormous egos; instead, they are self-effacing, quiet, reserved, even shy. Perhaps this has to do with the nature of their organizations. Unlike a business executive, police leadership has to answer to the public; unions and civil service systems further inhibit their power. Therefore, Level 5 leadership in a police organization may involve a greater degree of "legislative" types of skills–relying heavily on persuasion, political currency, and shared interests to create the conditions for the right decisions to happen (Wexler et al., 2007).

Collins also likes to use a bus metaphor when talking about igniting the transformation from good to great:

> The executives who ignited the transformations . . . did not first figure out where to drive the bus and then get people to take it there. No, they *first* got the right people on the bus (and the wrong people off the bus) and *then* figured out where to drive it (emphasis his) (Wexler et al., 2007:6).

In fact, Collins wrote, "The main point is not about assembling the right team—that's nothing new" (Wexler et al., 2007:6). Rather, the main point is that great leaders assemble their teams *before* they decide where to go. The executive who hires the right people does not need to waste time looking for ways to manage and motivate them; the right people will be self-motivated. Good-to-great organizations, Collins found, also have a **culture of discipline** in which employees show extreme diligence and intensity in their thoughts and actions, always focusing on implementing the organization's mission, purpose, and goals (Wexler et al., 2007).

People are not an organization's most important asset; rather, the *right* people are. When police executives are appointed or promoted, they inherit nearly all of their personnel, including poor performers who are unenthusiastic about the organization's vision and philosophy. Some of these people may be near retirement (about ready to "get off the bus"). Collins states that picking the right people and getting the wrong people off the bus are critical. *By whatever means possible, personnel problems have to be confronted in an organization that aspires to greatness* (Wexler et al., 2007:22).

This is why performance evaluations are so critical. Unfortunately, however, many police departments still have not created evaluation tools that adequately reflect the work police do. The tendency is to measure what is easy to measure: "orderliness" (neatness, attendance, punctuality) and conformity to organizational rules and regulations. A consultant to a Texas police agency asked how employees could be expected to act like supervisors, managers, and leaders when everyone in the organization was evaluated through an instrument that was "designed to control a 20-year old, high-testosterone male who was armed with a gun and given a fast car to drive" (Wexler et al., 2007:24). Until police agencies invest in valid and reliable instruments for measuring the real work of policing, it will remain very difficult to move the non-performers out of the organization.

As an illustration, when William Bratton became police commissioner in New York City, he decided he had to reach down at least two generations to get leaders who were motivated to improve the organization. Overnight he wiped out several generations of command staff, which was unheard of in New York. He promoted Jack Maple, then a lieutenant in the Transit Police, to deputy commissioner for crime control; Maple designed CompStat, the revolutionary crime-fighting strategy now used in countless agencies around the world (see Chapter 4). The message from a Level 5 leader is clear: it is no longer business as usual.

Perhaps the most difficult part of achieving greatness is in *sustaining* that greatness. Police chiefs have notoriously short tenure in office. Therefore, in their world, some of Collins's principles may be particularly important—for example, finding Level 5 leaders who pay close attention to preparing for the next generation of leaders, giving managers authority to make key decisions, sending them to leadership academies and conferences, encouraging them to think on their own, and ask questions. We term this "succession planning," and discuss this major aspect of police leadership and motivation more in Chapter 6.

SUPERVISORS AND MANAGERS AS LEADERS

A Problem of Definition

Leadership is the heart and soul of any organization. The idea of leadership has been with us for quite a long time, yet widespread debate and disagreement as to its characteristics and meaning continue. As Bennis and Nanus (1985:5) observe, there has been long-standing difficulty in defining leadership: "Like love, leadership . . . is something everyone knew existed but nobody could define." It is clear that leadership is elusive, and everyone in a supervisory or managerial position must make every attempt to possess it.

Early ideas about leadership assumed that it was a matter of birth: the so-called "Great Man" theory of leadership. Leaders were born into leadership positions (e.g., monarchs). History has shown, however, that many of these born leaders were actually ineffective ones. When this view failed to explain leadership, it was replaced by the notion that great events made leaders of people who excelled in extraordinary situations. Moses, Julius Caesar, Martin Luther, Abraham Lincoln, Winston Churchill, Harry Truman, Gandhi, Martin Luther King, Jr., and many others sought to assert their influence when time and social events intersected to make them great leaders. This definition is also inadequate, because there have been many instances requiring a leader, but one has failed to materialize. For example, one might conjecture that Los Angeles police executives failed to exert proper leadership in the Rodney King incident of 1991, and during the riots in its aftermath.

Many other leadership theories have gained interest. Some looked at the leader; others looked at the situation. None, Bennis and Nanus (1985) argue, has stood the test of time. Now, they believe, we have an opportunity to appraise our leaders and ponder the essence of power. They maintain that today's leadership environment must be examined in three major contexts: commitment (maintaining a strong work ethic, with employees working at full potential); complexity (keeping abreast of legal, financial, and technological changes that have profound effects on organizations); and credibility (being recognized by other members of the department as a leader).

The word *leadership* is widely used and has resulted in as many definitions as there have been studies of the subject. Some commonly used definitions include the following:

- "Leadership is the process of directing the behavior of others toward the accomplishment of some objective." (Certo, 1989:351)
- "The process of influencing the activities of an individual or a group in efforts toward goal achievement in a given situation." (Hersey and Blanchard, 1988:86)
- "The process of directing and influencing the task-related activities of group members." (Stoner and Freeman, 1992:472)

Another leadership perspective that must be considered is subordinate acceptance of leadership. Bernard (1938) notes that followers must respect and accept a leader's orders and directives if they are to be followed. This entails that the leader develop relationships with followers, and directives must be within the boundaries of organizational norms and established policies. It means that leaders must sometimes sell their instructions to subordinates to gain compliance. Too often there is a **zone of indifference** in which subordinates do not respect their leader or they question his or her directives. When this occurs, compliance is, at best, minimal. This means, as Bernard notes, that a leader's authority is delegated upward, not downward.

It is clear that supervisors use various methods for motivating officers. There is no one best way to manage and lead people in every situation. Leader style is largely dependent on the situation and the capabilities of those being led. In fact, supervisors may need to rely on a combination of strategies to be effective leaders. A number of leadership and motivation theories are addressed in this chapter, and an effective leader will need to rely on several of them, depending on the situation at hand.

Developing Leadership Skills

Katz (1974) identified three essential skills that leaders should possess: technical skills, human skills, and **conceptual skills**. Figure 3-1 illustrates these skills and how they apply to managers and supervisors. Notice that technical skills are most important at the lower supervisory ranks while conceptual skills preoccupy the higher ranks in an organization. Katz defined a *skill* as the capacity to translate knowledge into action in such a way that a task is accomplished successfully. Each of these skills, when performed effectively, results in the achievement of objectives and goals, which is the primary thrust of management and supervision.

Technical skills are those a manager needs to ensure that specific tasks are performed correctly. They are based on proven knowledge, procedures, or techniques. A supervisor's technical skills may involve knowledge in areas such as high-risk tactics, law, and criminal procedures. The police sergeant usually depends on training and departmental policies for technical knowledge. The areas in which

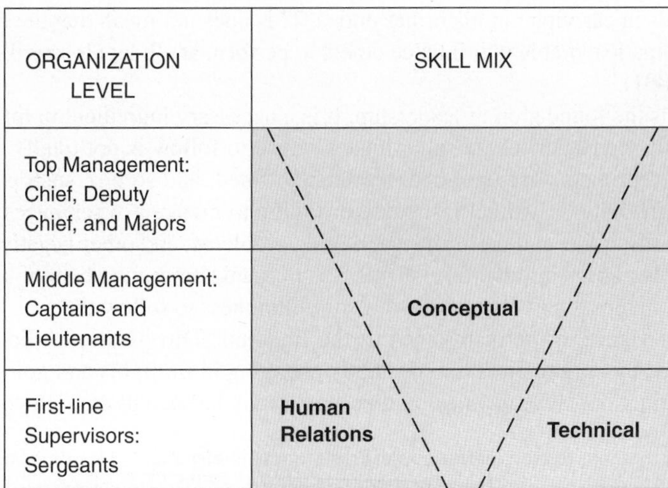

FIGURE 3-1 The Leadership Skill Mix in a Police Department
Source: Charles R. Swanson, Leonard Territo, and Robert W. Taylor, *Police Administration: Structures, Processes, and Behavior,* 3rd ed. (New York: Macmillan, 1993), p. 169.

managers need technical skills include computer applications, budgeting, strategic planning, labor relations, public relations, and human resources management. The manager must also have a knowledge of the technical skills required for the successful completion of tasks that are within his or her command.

Human skills involve working with people and include being thoroughly familiar with what motivates employees and how to utilize group processes. Katz visualized human skills as including "the executive's ability to work effectively as a group member and to build cooperative effort within the team he leads" (p. 63). Katz added that the human relations skill involves tolerance of ambiguity and empathy. Tolerance of ambiguity means that the manager is able to handle problems when insufficient information precludes making a totally informed decision. Empathy is the ability to put oneself in another's place or to understand another's plight. The practice of human skills allows a manager to provide the necessary leadership and direction, ensuring that tasks are accomplished in a timely fashion and with the least expenditure of resources.

Conceptual skills, according to Katz, involve "coordinating and integrating all the activities and interests of the organization toward a common objective" (p. 65). Katz considered such skills to include "an ability to translate knowledge into action" and emphasized that these skills can be taught to actual and prospective managers and supervisors. Thus, good managers and supervisors are not simply born but can be trained to assume their responsibilities.

All three of these skills are present in varying degrees for each management level. As one moves up the hierarchy, conceptual skills become more important and technical skills less important. The common denominator for all levels of management is *human* skills. In today's unionized and litigious environment, it is inconceivable that a manager or supervisor could neglect the human skills.

Power, Authority, and Leadership

While considering the nature of leadership, it is important to remember that organizations exist to accomplish missions and goals that citizens cannot or will not achieve alone. Within organizations, and certainly within those of the police, employees are granted the authority and power to morally and legally accomplish their tasks. Authority and power are related but separate concepts, however. **Authority** is a grant made by the formal organization to a position, which the person occupying that position wields in carrying out his or her duties. This does not mean that the person receiving that authority is automatically able to influence others to perform at all, let alone willingly (Swanson, Territo, and Taylor, 2001).

Power is the foundation of leadership. It is a necessary ingredient in influencing others to act or perform. While the leader whose subordinates refuse to follow is not totally without power (subordinates may be reprimanded, suspended, terminated, fined, and so on), such power must be used judiciously; both invoking it without just cause or failing to invoke it when necessary may contribute to a breakdown in discipline and performance, morale problems, and other negative side effects.

Power also arises in the informal side of an organization; members of a work group give one or more of their members power by virtue of their willingness to follow them on the basis of that person's charisma, experience, or heroism (such as the fictional "Dirty Harry," who was respected by peers while criticized by his superiors for constantly engaging in firefights and going "against the book").

The distinction between *power* and *authority* may be seen in the following example:

> A 10-year veteran, female, uniformed officer (Jones) is dispatched to a domestic violence scene and finds that a woman has clearly been assaulting her husband. The officer's sergeant, Blair, who has only recently been promoted from an office position, hears the call on the radio and shows up at the scene just as the female officer is preparing to leave without effecting an arrest. Sgt. Blair wants to know why Jones is not taking the woman to jail; it is clear that she is the assailant and the municipal ordinance

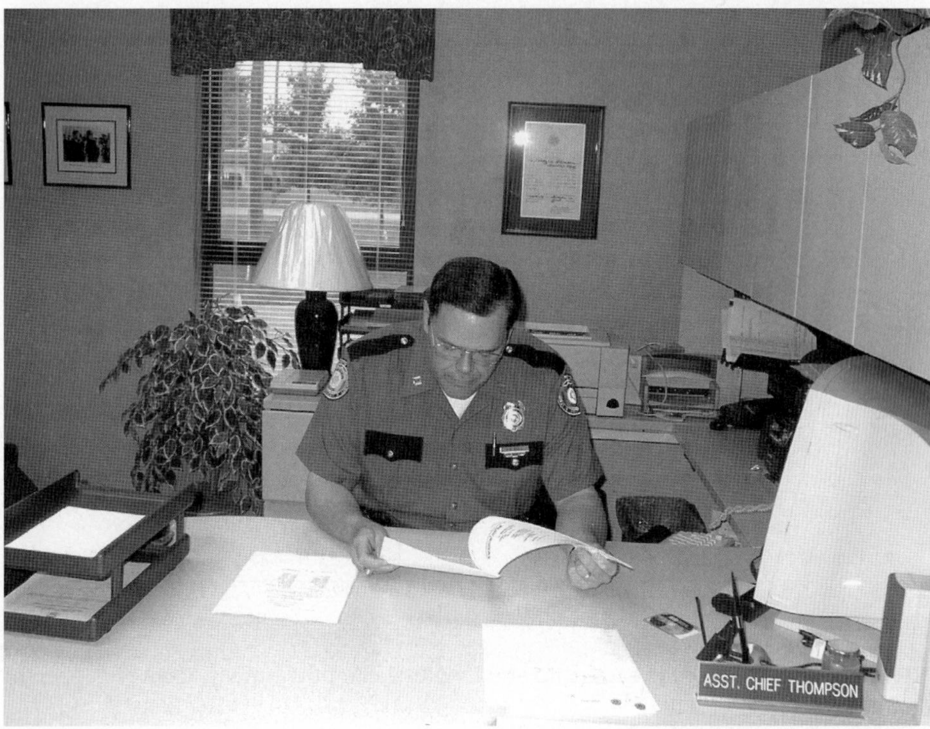

The higher one's rank in a police hierarchy, the more important it becomes to be able to conceptualize and develop necessary policies and procedures.
(Courtesy Lexington, Kentucky, Police Department)

requires an arrest. Jones tells her sergeant that she has personal knowledge from previous calls to the residence that the husband has until now been beating the wife with frequency, and therefore she will not take the woman into custody. The sergeant then directs Jones to make the arrest anyway, and she refuses, gets in her patrol car, and leaves. Later, Sgt. Blair files charges for refusal to obey the direct order of a superior, and Jones is suspended without pay for four days. Although wearing the "stripes" and possessing the *authority* they carry, Sgt. Blair's lack of experience contributed to his inability to influence Officer Jones to handle the situation according to the city ordinance. This led to Blair's relying on and invoking his *power* to discipline Jones. Jones, in this example, refused to recognize Blair's authority as a sergeant. Blair then resorted to power to force Jones to recognize or understand his authority and to solve the problem.

Empowerment

Today much is being written about the importance of **empowerment**, which is also known as participative management, dispersed leadership, open-book management, or industrial democracy. Today's officers are more highly trained and educated in a variety of subjects and have learned to think independently. Therefore today's policing—particularly in this community-oriented policing and problem solving era (COPPS; see Chapters 1 and 4) demands the self-initiated thinking, innovation, and freedom that result from employee empowerment (Gove, 2007). Certainly the greater acceptance of COPPS by the rank and file may directly hinge on officers having greater latitude and authority

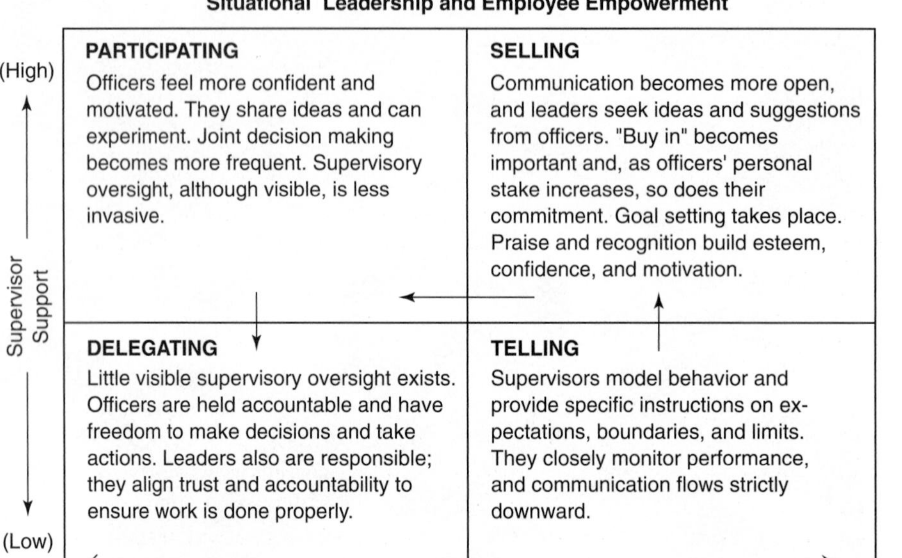

FIGURE 3-2 Situational Leadership and Employee Empowerment, from *FBI Law Enforcement. Bulletin,* Sept. 2007, p. 10

(Wuestewald, 2006). Furthermore, continuing an important theme we mentioned above (and discuss in Chapter 6)—succession planning—empowerment also follows the theory and practice of developing future leaders, as those on the front lines learn valuable leadership skills.

Supervisors at all levels should also recognize that empowering employees offers the benefits of decreased work-related stress, increased job satisfaction, higher employee involvement and contributions, and positive outcomes. This empowerment may range from the delegation of power (such as allowing officers flexibility to change work hours, meeting with citizen groups, selecting equipment for a particular function, or serving on a temporary crime task force) to simply having more communication, goal setting, and feedback. But with greater empowerment comes greater accountability; skilled supervisors must carefully balance both and not vest too much attention to one, thus "tipping the scale" and causing problems; excessive freedom may cause workers to feel alienated or confused, while too much oversight can lead to micromanagement low morale (Gove, 2007).

According to Gove (2007), those police leaders striving to empower their employees will find guidance from the **situational leadership** model (discussed below). In its most basic framework, the model details a continuum of leader and follower actions that progresses through four cycles, shown in Figure 3-2. The figure shows the process beginning with the "telling" supervisor, who provide specific instructions and closely monitor the performance of their subordinates; the supervisor then moves into a "selling" phase, where communication becomes more open, leaders seek ideas from subordinates, employees are granted more "buy-in" with decision making, and praise and recognition are used. The third phase, "participating," involves officers becoming more confident and sharing ideas; joint decision making becomes more frequent, and supervision is not invasive. Finally, the delegating phase involves very little supervisory oversight (while employees are held accountable for their actions and decisions); trust and accountability are balanced properly. The end result involves much more than merely delegating tasks; it culminates in a more confident, self-directed, and motivated officer (Gove, 2007).

Applying Mintzberg's View of Chief Executives

Police leadership actually encompasses many roles. Police chief executive officers (CEOs)—and many middle managers and supervisors—practice behaviors and tasks as set forth by Henry Mintzberg. Following is an overview of the roles assumed and tasks performed by the leaders of the police agency using the Mintzberg model's *interpersonal*, *informational*, and *decision-maker* roles as an analytic framework (Mintzberg, 1975).

THE INTERPERSONAL ROLE The CEO's interpersonal role includes figurehead, leadership, and liaison duties. As a *figurehead*, the CEO performs various ceremonial functions. Examples include riding in parades and attending other civic events; speaking before school and university classes and civic organizations; meeting with visiting officials and dignitaries; attending academy graduation and swearing-in ceremonies and some weddings and funerals; and visiting injured officers in the hospital. Like the mayor who cuts ribbons and kisses babies, the CEO performs these duties simply because of his or her position within the organization; the duties come with being a figurehead.

The *leadership* function requires the CEO to motivate and coordinate workers while resolving different goals and needs within the department and the community. For example, a chief or sheriff may have to urge the governing board to enact a code or ordinance that, whether popular or not, is in the best interest of the jurisdiction. CEOs also provide leadership in such matters as bond issues (e.g., to raise money for more officers or to build new stationhouse facilities) and advise the governing body on the effects of proposed ordinances.

The role as *liaison* is performed when the CEO of a police organization interacts with other organizations and coordinates work flows. It is not uncommon for police executives from one geographic area—the police chief, the sheriff, the ranking officer of the local highway patrol office, the district attorney, the campus police chief, and so forth—to meet informally each month to discuss common problems and strategies. Also, the chief executives serve as liaisons between their agencies and others in forming regional police councils, narcotics units, crime labs, dispatching centers, and so forth. They also meet with representatives of the courts, the juvenile system, and other criminal justice agencies.

THE INFORMATIONAL ROLE The second major role of CEOs under the Mintzberg model is the informational role. This role involves the CEO in monitoring/inspecting and disseminating information and acting as spokesperson. In the *monitoring/inspecting* function, the CEO constantly looks at the workings of the department to ensure that things are operating smoothly (or as smoothly as a police agency can be expected to run). This function is often referred to as "roaming the ship," and many CEOs who have isolated themselves from their personnel and from the daily operations of the agency can speak from sad experience of the need to be alert and to create a presence. Many police executives use daily staff meetings to discuss any information about the past twenty-four hours that might affect the department.

The *dissemination* tasks involve getting information to members of the department. This may include memorandums, special orders, general orders, and policies. The *spokesperson* function is related, but it is more focused on getting information to the news media. This is another very difficult task for the chief executive; news organizations are in a competitive field in which scoops and deadlines and the public's right to know are all-important. Still, the media must understand those occasions when a criminal investigation can be seriously affected by premature or overblown coverage. We discuss police-media relations in more detail in Chapter 2.

THE DECISION-MAKER ROLE Finally, as a decision maker, the CEO of a police organization serves as an entrepreneur, a disturbance handler, a resource allocator, and a negotiator. As *entrepreneur*, the CEO must sell ideas to the governing board or the department. Ideas might include new computers or a new communications system, a policing strategy (such as community-oriented policing and problem solving), or different work methods, all of which are intended to improve the organization. Sometimes there is a blending of roles, as when several police executives band together (functioning as liaisons) and go to the state attorney general and the legislature to lobby (in an entrepreneurial capacity) for new crime-fighting laws.

As a *resource allocator*, the CEO must be able to say no to subordinates. However, subordinates should not be faulted for trying to obtain more resources or for trying to improve their unit as best they can. The CEO must have a clear idea of the budget and what the priorities are and must listen to citizen complaints and act accordingly. For example, ongoing complaints of motorists speeding in a specific area will result in a shifting of patrol resources to that area or neighborhood.

As a *negotiator*, the police manager resolves employee grievances and sits as a member of the negotiating team for labor relations. As a member of management, the CEO is often compelled to argue against demands made by police bargaining units that would benefit the rank and file. These situations can become uncomfortable and even disastrous—as in some cities, where the police have engaged in work stoppages, work speedups, work slowdowns, or other such tactics.

Strategic Thinking and Planning for Strategic Management

DIFFERENT WAYS OF THINKING AND PLANNING Today it is not enough for police leaders to think in terms of the "here-and-now." The world is changing too rapidly, and one who is thinking in contemporary terms will quickly find himself or herself out of date and sync with society. They must think, plan, and manage in what are called *strategic* terms.

In order for a chief executive to engage in strategic management, he or she must first be a strategic *thinker* and *planner*. This means seeing both the big picture and its operational implications. As Heracleous observed, the purpose of strategic thinking is to discover novel, imaginative strategies that can rewrite the rules of the competitive game and to envision potential futures, significantly different from the present. Strategic thinking refers to a creative, divergent thought process. It is a mode of strategy making that is associated with reinventing the future (Herocleous, 1998:481).

Strategic thinking is therefore compatible with strategic planning. Both are required in any thoughtful strategy-making process and strategy formulation. The creative, groundbreaking strategies emerging from strategic thinking still have to be operationalized through convergent and analytical thought (strategic planning). Thus, both strategic thinking and strategic planning are necessary, and neither is adequate without the other for effective strategic management (Lawrence, 1999). As Herocleous (1998:482) stated,

> It all comes down to the ability to go up and down the ladder of abstraction, and being able to see both the big picture and the operational implications, which are signs of outstanding leaders and strategists.

Figure 3-3 shows how strategic thinking and planning relate to strategic management.

Strategic planning involves more people than the chief executive; major transformation within an organization should be guided by teams under the direction of strategic managers—command and support staff members who have the expertise, credibility, and competence to get the job done (Charrier, 2004).

Strategic planning is both a leadership tool and a process. It is primarily used for one purpose: to help an organization do a better job—to focus its energy, ensure that members of the organization are working toward the same goals, and assess and adjust an organization's direction in response to a

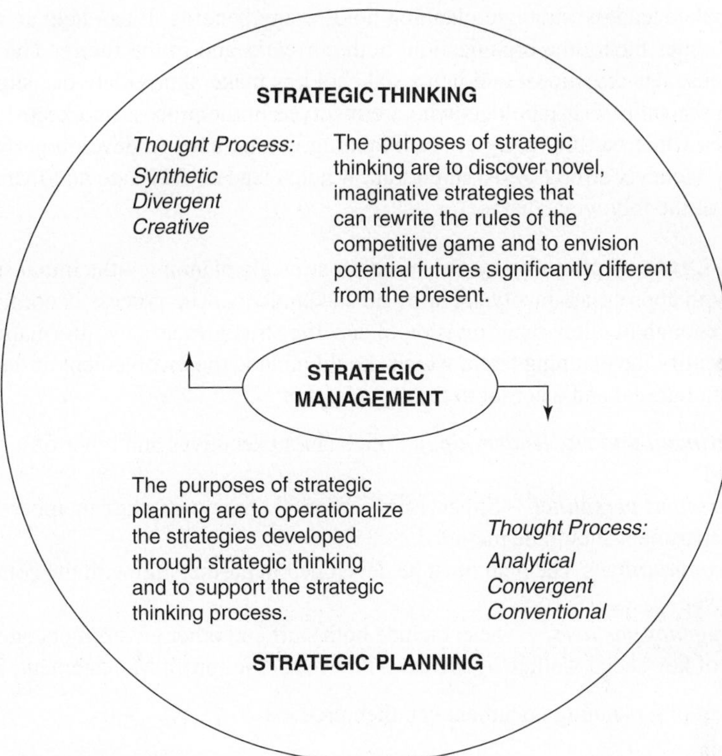

FIGURE 3-3 Strategic Thinking and Strategic Planning
Source: Loizos Heracleous, "Strategic Thinking or Strategic Planning?" *Long Range Planning* 31 (June 1998):485. Used with permission.

changing environment. Strategic planning is therefore a disciplined effort to produce fundamental decisions and actions that shape and guide what an organization is, what it does, and why it does it, with a focus on the future. Its aim is to achieve competitive advantage.

Strategic planning also includes the following elements:

- It is oriented toward the future and looks at how the world could be different five to ten years in the future. It is aimed at creating the organization's future.
- It is based on thorough analysis of foreseen or predicted trends and scenarios of possible alternative futures.
- It thoroughly analyzes the organization, both its internal and external environment and its potential.
- It is a qualitative, idea-driven process.
- It is a continuous learning process.
- When it is successful, it influences all areas of operations, becoming a part of the organization's philosophy and culture (Peak and Glensor, 2008:169).

Excellent examples of strategic plans may be found for the Federal Bureau of Investigation at: http://www.fbi.gov/publications/strategicplan/strategicplanfull.pdf; the information technology plan of the U.S. Department of Justice for 2006-2011, is available at: http://www.justice.gov/archive/jmd/2006itplan/index.html#direction.

For police leaders, strategic planning holds many benefits. It can help an agency anticipate key trends and issues facing the organization, both currently and in the future. The planning process explores options, sets directions, and helps stakeholders make appropriate decisions. It facilitates communication among key stakeholders who are involved in the process and keeps organizations focused on outcomes while battling daily crises. Planning can be used to develop performance standards to measure an agency's efforts. Most important, it helps leaders facilitate and manage change (which is the subject of the following chapter).

PLANNING CYCLE A **planning cycle** is used for strategic planning—the initial steps to be taken in the process—with appropriate involvement by all stakeholders. The process is not fixed, however; it must be flexible enough to allow rapid revision of specific strategies as new information develops. The first step is to identify the planning team, which should include the involvement of the following key stakeholders, both internal and external to the organization:

a. ***Department and city leadership.*** Police chief executives and other officeholders should be involved.
b. ***Department personnel.*** Supervisors, officers, non-sworn staff members, and all members of the department should be included.
c. ***The community.*** The plan must be developed in partnership with the community it is designed to serve.
d. ***Interagency partners.*** These include both staff and other government agencies and representatives of key social welfare agencies (Alliance for Nonprofit Management, 2007).

Development of a planning document can then proceed.

STRATEGIC MANAGEMENT Strategic management is therefore a systems management approach that uses the proper thinking and planning approaches that are discussed above. Community policing, external and internal environments, political influences, homeland security, and new technologies are molding the profession into a highly complex structure. To be successful in this environment, executives need to set their course.

Leaders in the organization move change across organizational boundaries. A small team of personnel is assembled to analyze operational functions, identify inefficiencies, review systems integration, and detect gaps in management communications that hinder performance. Major transformation within an organization cannot rest with one person, but should be guided by teams under the direction of strategic managers—command and support staff members who have the expertise, credibility, and competence to get the job done.

MOTIVATION THEORY

Toward Attaining Goals

Motivation generally refers to "the set of processes that arouse, direct, and maintain human behavior toward attaining some goal" (Greenberg and Barron, 1995:126). This definition implies that motivation consists of several areas. First, "arousal" refers to getting subordinates interested in performing some action. Some people are self-motivated and do not require a stimulus from a supervisor. Others, however, require direction or prodding. Second, this definition implies that people make choices about their behavior, such as about the amount and quality of their work. Management, through policies, direction, and consultation, can assist employees in making the correct choices. Finally, motivation is about maintaining productive behavior. Leaders must strive to have their subordinates working

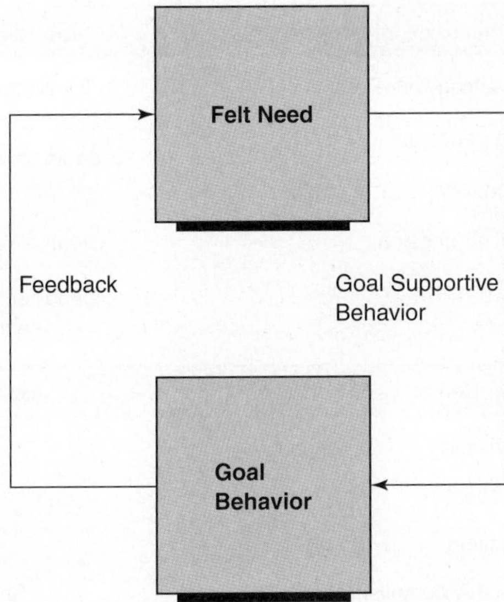

FIGURE 3-4 The Needs–Goal Model of Motivation
Source: Samuel Certo, *Principles of Modern Management: Functions and Systems,* ed. (Needham Heights, MA: Simon and Schuster, 1989), p. 377.

constantly to achieve goals. At its most fundamental level, motivation involves a *needs-goal model,* in which an individual seeks to fulfill a need (see Figure 3-4). The need is then transformed into some behavior that is directed toward satisfying that need. For example, when someone becomes hungry, behavior becomes directed toward buying, preparing, and eating food. If a person is unable to satisfy a need, he or she becomes frustrated. This frustration may lead to greater effort by the employee or withdrawal and mediocre productivity. When a subordinate cannot achieve his or her goals, problems may arise.

Motivating employees on the job is not so simplistic. Therefore, motivation theory helps us understand the "why" of people's behavior. It is often misunderstood as something that supervisors do to employees. In reality, it is more internal and relates to an individual's needs, wants, and desires. But what exactly sparks an employee's desire to achieve a higher level of performance is not easily identified. What is clear, however, is that what motivates one employee to perform may not motivate another employee at all.

Motivation theories may be divided into two general categories: content theories and process theories. Content theories focus on the individuals' needs, wants, and desires and attempt to explain internal needs that motivate people's behavior. Process theories attempt to explain how people are motivated and focus on the interplay of the individual with forces in the workplace.

Content Theories: Maslow, Argyris, Herzberg, and McClelland

MASLOW'S HIERARCHY OF NEEDS Abraham Maslow founded the humanistic school of psychology during the 1940s. Maslow's (1954) work focused on human needs and wants. He viewed people as perpetually "wanting" in nature and described their needs as insatiable. According to Maslow, people's needs are not random but progress in a "hierarchy of needs" from survival to security, social, ego-esteem, and self-actualization needs, as shown in Figure 3-5.

Self-actualization Needs	Job-related Satisfiers
Reaching Your Potential	Involvement in Planning Your Work
Independence	Freedom to Make Decisions Affecting Work
Creativity	Creative Work to Perform
Self-expression	Opportunities for Growth and Development

Esteem Needs	Job-related Satisfiers
Responsibility	Status Symbols
Self-respect	Merit Awards
Recognition	Challenging Work
Sense of Accomplishment	Sharing in Decisions
Sense of Competence	Opportunity for Advancement

Social Needs	Job-related Satisfiers
Companionship	Opportunities for Interaction with Others
Acceptance	Team Spirit
Love and Affection	Friendly Coworkers
Group Membership	

Safety Needs	Job-related Satisfiers
Security for Self and Possessions	Safe Working Conditions
Avoidance of Risks	Seniority
Avoidance of Harm	Fringe Benefits
Avoidance of Pain	Proper Supervision
	Sound Company Policies, Programs, and Practices

Physical Needs	Job-related Satisfiers
Food	Pleasant Working Conditions
Clothing	Adequate Wage or Salary
Shelter	Rest Periods
Comfort	Labor-saving Devices
Self-preservation	Efficient Work Methods

FIGURE 3-5 Maslow's Hierarchy of Needs
Source: A.H. Maslow, *Motivation and Personality,* 2d ed. (New York: Harper & Row, 1970).

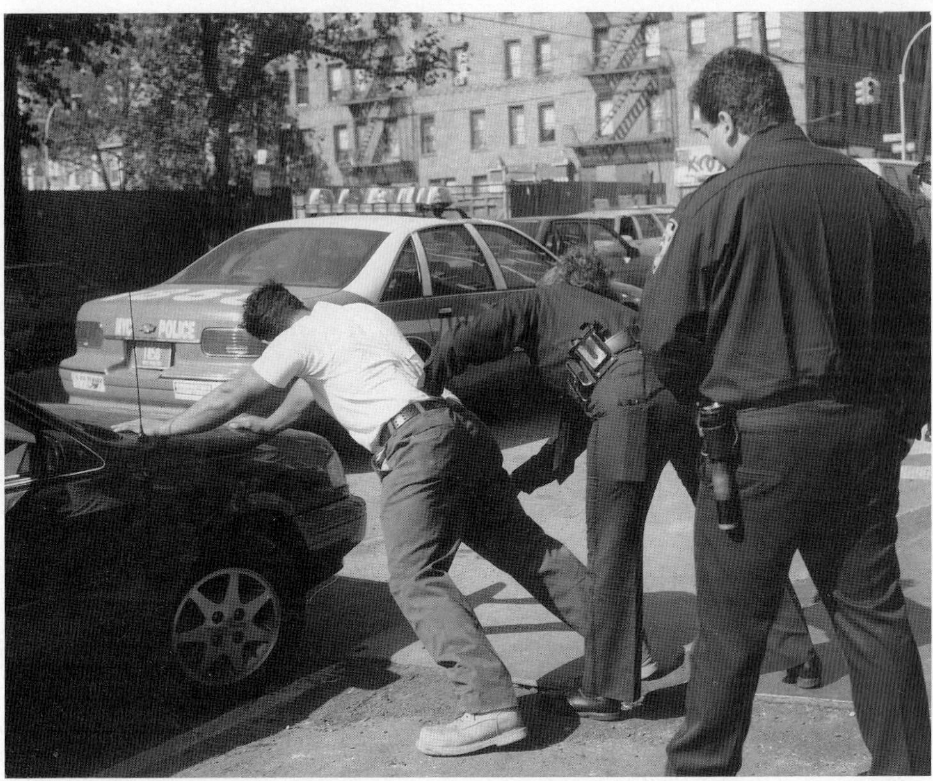

Many of the tasks performed by field officers are self-directed.
(Courtesy NYPD Photo Unit)

Maslow asserted that people are motivated by their lowest level of unsatisfied need. Once a lower need is satisfied, higher needs are sought. An important implication to motivation theory is understanding that a satisfied need is no longer a motivator of behavior. Simply stated, people who have their security needs met can be motivated only by higher needs.

What are the implications of this theory for the police organization? According to Maslow's hierarchy, a supervisor will better understand officers' performance and what motivates them by identifying their unfulfilled needs. There must also be a recognition that different officers may be at various levels in the hierarchy of needs and, therefore, are not necessarily motivated by the same wants. For example, a rookie officer may be most concerned with successfully completing the probationary period; therefore, security is that officer's primary concern and motivator. For the more veteran officer interested in promotion, motivation may derive from the esteem and status level. The supervisor may be successful in motivating this officer by delegating team leader duties and assisting the officer in preparing for the sergeant's exam.

ARGYRIS'S MATURITY-IMMATURITY THEORY Argyris's (1957) maturity-immaturity continuum also furnishes insight on human needs. According to Argyris, people naturally progress from immaturity to maturity. They develop needs for more activity and relative independence and often behave in many different ways. They also have deeper interests, consider a relatively long-term perspective, and show more awareness of themselves and more control of their own destiny. Argyris viewed an effective

Dissatisfaction: Hygiene or Maintenance Factors	Satisfaction: Motivating Factors
1. Company policy and administration	1. Opportunity for achievement
2. Supervision	2. Opportunity for recognition
3. Relationship with supervisor	3. Work itself
4. Relationship with peers	4. Responsibility
5. Working conditions	5. Advancement
6. Salary	6. Personal growth
7. Relationship with subordinates	

FIGURE 3-6 Herzberg's Hygiene Factors and Motivators

organization as one requiring employees to be self-responsible, self-directed, and self-motivated. He argued that motivation can be maximized when each employee pursues goals and experiences psychological growth and independence. He noted that the organization has a responsibility to structure the work environment so that employees can grow and mature.

HERZBERG'S MOTIVATION-HYGIENE THEORY In 1968, Frederick Herzberg developed a motivation theory based on a study of 200 engineers who were queried about when they were satisfied and dissatisfied with their jobs. The findings led Herzberg to identify two vital factors that are found in all jobs: (1) items that influence the degree of job dissatisfaction, called maintenance or *hygiene* factors, which relate mostly to the work environment; and (2) factors that influence the degree of job satisfaction, called *motivators,* which relate to the work itself. The items that comprise Herzberg's hygiene and motivator factors are shown in Figure 3-6.

Herzberg distinguished between job satisfaction and motivation. Indeed, using his scheme, an officer can be dissatisfied and motivated at the same time. If negative hygiene factors are present in a job, workers will become dissatisfied. Addressing these factors, such as by increasing salary, generally will not motivate people to do a better job, but it will keep them from becoming dissatisfied. In contrast, if motivating factors are high in a particular job, workers generally are motivated to do a better job. People tend to be more motivated and productive as more motivators are built into their job situation (Certo, 1989).

The process of incorporating motivators into a job situation is called *job enrichment.* Subordinates are given more responsibilities, allowed to be involved in more complex cases, and have the opportunity to provide input into those decisions that directly affect them. The most productive employees are involved in work situations with desirable hygiene factors and motivating factors. This relates to **Maslow's hierarchy of needs** as well; for example, hygiene factors (such as a pay raise) can help to satisfy physical, security, and social needs, while motivating factors (for example, an award for outstanding performance) can satisfy employees' esteem and self-actualization needs.

According to Herzberg, hygiene factors may attract people to join an organization, but they do not provide the intrinsic satisfaction in the work itself that motivates people to perform at higher levels. Intrinsic motivation can come only from what the individual does through job responsibilities and subsequent satisfaction gained from job accomplishment. It appears that people are influenced more by intrinsic motivators than by hygiene factors. Put more simply, job satisfaction appears to be more important to most people than pay and benefits. A supervisor who conducts frequent team meetings to keep officers informed about departmental matters and to dispel rumors, who delegates additional duties to those officers ready to accept new challenges and compliments their work, and who solicits officers' participation in decision making whenever possible is appealing to their intrinsic motivators.

MCCLELLAND'S ACHIEVEMENT, POWER, AND AFFILIATION MOTIVES McClelland (1964), another humanistic theorist, believed that individual needs were acquired over time and as a result of experience. From his studies, he identified three motives or needs that are important to an individual within an organizational environment:

1. ***Need for achievement***—the need to succeed or excel. Some individuals must have standards or benchmarks to separate success from failure, and they have an internal force (motivation) that drives them toward accomplishment.
2. ***Need for power***—the need to exert control over one's environment. Some individuals have an internal desire to make decisions and ensure that others abide by those decisions.
3. ***Need for affiliation***—the need to establish and maintain friendly and close interpersonal relationships (social need).

Individuals who have a compelling drive to succeed are more interested in personal achievement than the rewards for their success. Such people have a desire to do things better; they seek situations in which they can attain greater personal responsibility; and they quickly volunteer for complex, challenging assignments. As they work through an assignment, they must have immediate and continuing feedback on their performance. If not carefully monitored and controlled, such individuals may develop a workaholic personality.

McClelland notes that power and affiliation needs are closely related to success. Successful managers and supervisors have a greater need for power and a lower need for affiliation. This type of individual is willing to take charge of a situation and act without undue regard for the social implications of decisions. If the need for power overshadows the affiliation need, however, managers and supervisors may become Machiavellian types who concentrate on their own success rather than on that of the organization or its personnel.

McClelland's theory has broad implications. The administrator should identify the high achievers and place them in positions where their attributes would best meet the department's needs. Some positions call for affiliation-oriented people, while others require achievers. When there is a crisis situation, a problem area within the department, or a new program is being developed and implemented, planning and operations are best handled by a high achiever. This internally motivated individual will take charge and exert all his or her energy toward ensuring that the assignment is completed successfully.

Process Theory: Vroom's Expectancy Theory

In reality, the motivation process is much more complex than is depicted by the needs-goal model shown in Figure 3-4 on p. 59, and advocated by the content theorists. Content theories focus solely on the individual and, to a great extent, neglect the effects of the work environment on the individual. Vroom's (1964) **expectancy theory** was developed in the 1960s and addresses some of the complexities. This theory holds that people are motivated primarily by a felt need that affects behavior; however, Vroom's theory adds the issue of motivation *strength*—an individual's degree of desire to perform a behavior.

Vroom's expectancy model is shown in equation form in Figure 3-7. According to this model, motivation strength is determined by the perceived value of performing a task or job and the perceived probability that the work performed will result in an appropriate reward. That is, an individual is motivated if he or she perceives that the effort will be rewarded and if the value of the reward is equal to or greater than the amount of effort or work. Generally, individuals tend to perform the behaviors that maximize rewards over the long term.

Expectancy theory suggests that officers who experience success will feel more competent and therefore will be more willing to take risks in improving performance levels. When officers know that certain behaviors will produce anticipated departmental rewards, they are motivated. For example, an

Motivation strength	=	Perceived value of result of performing behavior	×	Perceived probability that result will materialize

FIGURE 3-7 Vroom's Expectancy Model of Motivation in Equation Form

officer may be motivated to participate in a community policing project knowing that it could result in a higher performance rating, departmental letter of commendation, and improved promotional prospects. If such rewards are not forthcoming, the officer will be less enthusiastic when participating in similar projects in the future.

LEADING VERSUS MANAGING

Leading is related to managing. In this chapter, however, we maintain that effective leadership goes well beyond the basic management functions described at the beginning of the chapter. Bennis and Nanus (1985:21) help us understand the broader role of supervision in their discussion of management and leadership: "To be a manager is to bring about, to accomplish, to have charge of, responsibility for, to conduct. Leading, on the other hand, is influencing, guiding in direction, course, action, opinion." They go on to say that managers are people who "do things right," and leaders are people who "do the right things." Managers are more efficiency driven and focus on mastering routine activities, while leaders are driven by vision and judgment. Managers tend to be bean counters, while leaders focus on achieving desired results.

In this regard, the following statement was developed by United Technological Corporation and provides much food for thought:

> People don't want to be managed. They want to be led. Whoever heard of a world manager? World leader[s], yes. They don't manage. The carrot always wins over the stick. Ask your horse. You can *lead* your horse to water, but you can't *manage* him to drink. If you want to manage somebody, manage yourself. Do that well and you'll be ready to stop managing. And start leading. (Quoted in Bennis and Nanus, 1985:22)

Another clear distinction between the leader and the manager is organizational consensus on overall goals—having a vision. According to Bennis and Nanus (1985:92), by focusing attention on a vision, the leader operates on the *emotional* and *spiritual resources* of the organization, on its values, commitment, and aspirations. The manager, by contrast, operates on the *physical resources* of the organization, its capital, human skills, raw materials, and technology. As they put it,

> Any competent manager can make it possible for people to earn a living [and] see to it that work is done productively and efficiently, on schedule, and with a high level of quality. It remains for the effective leader, however, to help people in the organization know pride and satisfaction in their work. (Bennis and Nanus, 1985:92)

They added: "The essential thing in organization leadership is that the leader's style *pulls* rather than *pushes* people on. Leading is a responsibility, and the effectiveness of this responsibility is reflected in the attitudes of the led" (Bennis and Nanus, 1985:80–81).

We concur that a successful police supervisor must be a good manager as well as a good leader. As Whisenand and Ferguson explained (1996:13), "If you're a competent manager, you are getting the most out of your resources. If you're a competent leader, you are pointing their energy in the right direction." It is therefore important that the supervisor manage departmental resources in as efficient a manner as possible, while also motivating and inspiring employees to perform to the best of their ability. Therein lies the influential art of leadership that instills the sense of esprit de corps or common purpose that imbues successful cohesive teams.

LEADERSHIP THEORIES

We now discuss trait, behavioral, and situational theories that attempt to explain leadership behavior. Whereas trait theories are based on the intrinsic qualities a leader possesses, behavioral theories explain leadership by examining what the leader does. Situational theories maintain that effective leadership is a product of the fit between the leader's traits or skills and the situation in which he or she is to exercise leadership. Finally, contingency theories, to a degree, merge and extend trait and behavioral theories by examining how the environment or workplace affects leadership and the leader.

Trait Theory

Early leadership studies of the 1930s and 1940s focused on the individual and assumed that some people were born leaders, and that good leaders could be studied to determine the special traits that leaders possess. From an organizational standpoint, this **trait theory** had great appeal. For example, in the police field it was assumed that all that was needed was for leaders with these special traits to be identified and promoted to managerial positions within the department.

Researchers have attempted to identify those special traits that separate successful leaders from poor leaders for more than 50 years. For example, Davis (1940) found 56 different characteristics or traits that he considered important. While admitting it was unlikely that any manager would possess all 56 traits, he said the following 10 traits were required for executive success: intelligence, experience, originality, receptiveness, teaching ability, knowledge of human behavior, courage, tenacity, and a sense of justice and fair play.

The age-old assumption that leaders are born and develop their technical, human, and conceptual skills was completely discredited, because researchers have been unable to agree or present empirical evidence to support its claims (Tannenbaum and Weschler, 1961). There are too many traits that a good leader must possess, and some good leaders possess some of the traits, while other good leaders do not. Additionally, there are traits that good leaders possess that bad leaders also possess. Consequently, it is now believed that certain traits and skills increase the *likelihood* that a given person will be an effective manager. There are no guarantees, however.

Behavioral Theories

The *behavioral* approach focuses on a leader's behavior in relation to the environment. Studies at the University of Michigan and Ohio State University and Blake and Mouton's "managerial grid" led the early research of behavioral theories leadership. These studies were important because they studied leadership in real-life situations.

UNIVERSITY OF MICHIGAN AND OHIO STATE UNIVERSITY STUDIES The University of Michigan conducted a series of studies of leadership behavior in relation to job satisfaction and productivity in business and industrial work groups. The researchers determined that leaders must have a sense of the task to be accomplished as well as the environment in which the followers worked. They found the following to be the beliefs of a successful leader:

1. The leader assumes the leadership role is more effective relative to managers who fail to exhibit leadership.

2. The closeness of supervision will have a direct bearing on the production of employees. High-producing units had less direct supervision; highly supervised units had lower production. Conclusion: Employees need some area of freedom to make choices. Given this, they produce at a higher rate.
3. Employee-orientation is a concept that includes the manager's taking an active interest in subordinates. It is the leader's responsibility to facilitate employees' accomplishment of goals (Bennett and Hess, 2001).

Ohio State University began its study of leadership in 1945 and identified leadership behavior in two dimensions: initiating structure and consideration. *Initiating structure* referred to supervisory behavior that focused on the achievement of organizational goals and included characteristics such as assigning subordinates to particular tasks, holding subordinates accountable for following rules and procedures, and informing subordinates of what is expected of them. *Consideration* was directed toward a supervisor's openness concerning subordinates' ideas and respect for their feelings as persons and included characteristics such as listening to subordinates, being willing to make changes, and being friendly and approachable. It was assumed that high consideration and moderate initiating structure yielded higher job satisfaction and productivity than did high initiating structure and low consideration (Sales, 1969).

THE MANAGERIAL GRID The managerial grid, developed by Robert Blake and Jane Mouton (1962), has received a lot of attention since its appearance and is based on and expands the research conducted at the universities of Ohio State and Michigan.

The **managerial grid** (Figure 3-8) has two dimensions: concern for production and concern for people. Each axis or dimension is numbered from 1, meaning low concern, to 9, indicating a high concern. The horizontal axis represents the concern for production and performance goals, and the vertical axis represents the concern for human relations or empathy. The way in which a person combines these two dimensions establishes a leadership style in terms of one of the five principal styles identified on the grid.

The points of orientation are related to styles of management. The lower left-hand corner of the grid shows the 1,1 style (representing a minimal concern for task or service and a minimal concern for people). The lower right-hand corner of the grid identifies the 9,1 style. This type of leader would have a primary concern for the task or output and a minimal concern for people. People are seen as tools of production. The upper left-hand corner represents the 1,9 style, often referred to as "country club management," with minimum effort given to output or task. The upper right, 9,9, indicates high concern for both people and production—a team management approach of mutual respect and trust. In the center, a 5,5, "middle-of-the-road" style, the leader has a "give a little, be fair but firm" philosophy, providing a balance between output and people concerns (Favreau and Gillespie, 1978).

These five **leadership styles** can be summarized as follows:

1. Authority-compliance management (9,1)
2. Country club management (1,9)
3. Middle-of-the-road management (5,5)
4. Impoverished management (1,1)
5. Team management (9,9)

Swanson and Territo (1982) attempted to investigate the extent to which Blake and Mouton's various styles are utilized by police managers. They surveyed managers from 166 different departments and found that almost 40 percent of the participants reported that they primarily used the team

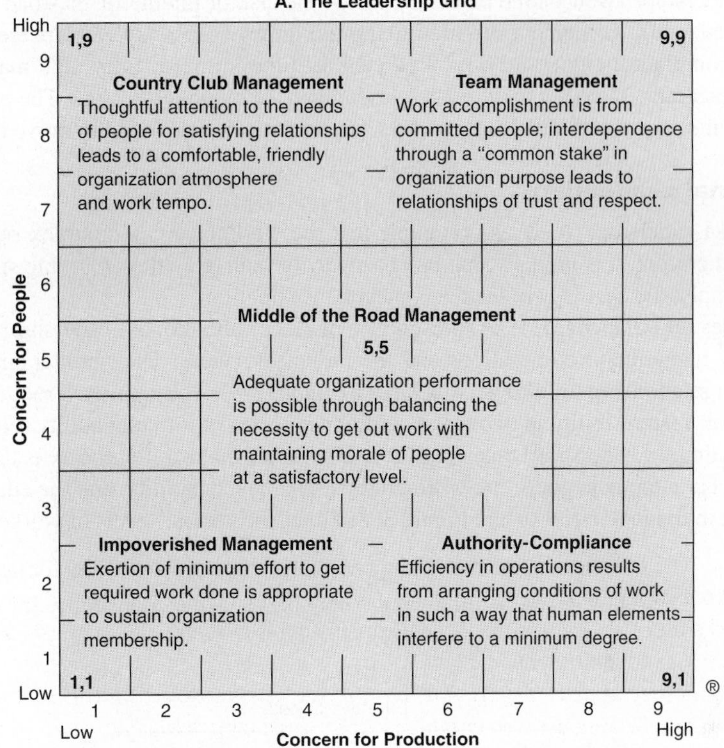

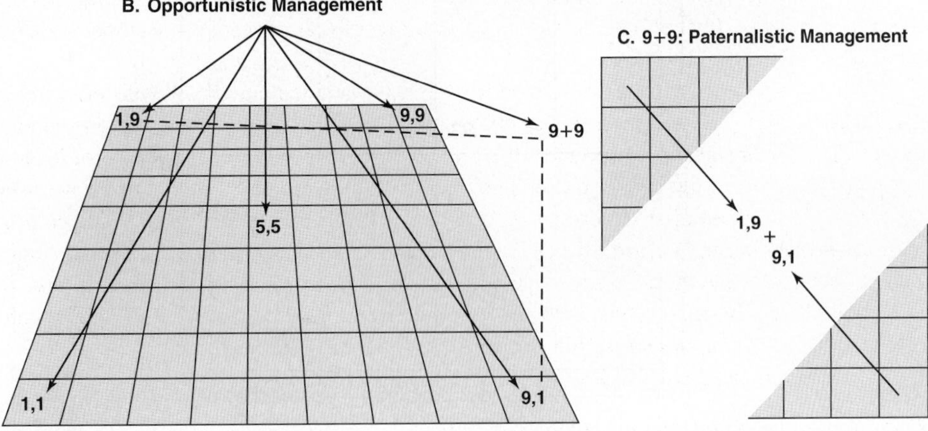

FIGURE 3-8 The Leadership Grid

Source: The Leadership Grid® figure, Paternalism Figure and Opportunism from *Leadership Dilemmas—Grid Solutions,* by Robert R. Blake and Anne Adams McCanse (Formerly the Managerial Grid by Robert R. Blake and Jane S. Mouton). Houston: Gulf Publishing Company, (Grid Figure: p. 29, Paternalism Figure: p. 30, Opportunism Figure: p. 31). Copyright 1991 by Scientific Methods, Inc. Reproduced by permission of the owners.

style of leadership. Twenty-nine percent reported the task or middle-of-the-road style as their primary form of leadership, 15 percent reported using the impoverished style, 11 percent reported using the authority-compliance form, and only 9 percent said they were country club managers. Swanson and Territo's research indicates a variety of styles being used by police leaders. The predominant style they found was the team style. The leaders who were not team leaders need to move in that direction.

Situational Leadership®

Situational Leadership® theories recognize that the workplace is a complex setting subject to rapid changes. Therefore, it is unlikely that one best way of managing these varying situations would be adequate. Simply, the best way to lead depends on the situation.

Hersey and Blanchard (1988) presented a model of Situational Leadership® that has been used in training by many major corporations and the military services. Their model emphasizes the leader's behavior in relationship to followers' behavior (Figure 3-9). This approach requires the leader to evaluate follower responsibility in two ways: willingness (motivation) and ability (competence).

Situational Leadership® takes into account worker maturity; *maturity* is defined as the capacity to set high but attainable goals, the willingness to take responsibility, and the education and/or experience of the individual or the group. Figure 3-9 defines the various levels of worker maturity as follows:

M1: The followers are neither willing nor able to take responsibility for task accomplishment.

M2: The followers are willing but are not able to take responsibility for task accomplishment.

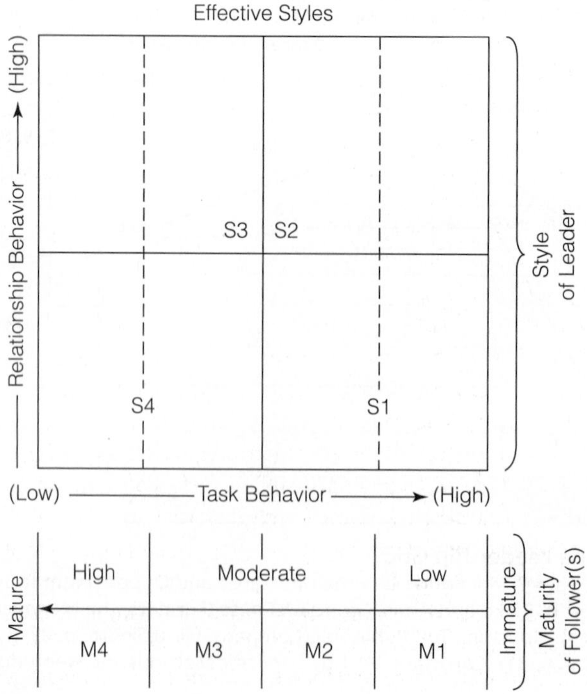

FIGURE 3-9 Situational Leadership® Model
(Copyrighted material. Reprinted with permission of Center for Leadership Studies, Escondido, CA 92025. All rights reserved.)

M3: The followers are not willing but are able to take responsibility for task accomplishment.

M4: The followers are willing and able to take responsibility for task accomplishment (Hersey and Blanchard, 1988).

Task behavior, shown in Figure 3-9, is essentially the extent to which a leader engages in one-way communication with subordinates; relationship behavior is the extent to which the leader engages in two-way communication (by providing positive reinforcement, emotional support, and so on). Four basic styles of leadership are associated with task accomplishment. They operate similarly to those on the managerial grid. They are characterized as follows:

S1: *Telling.* High task–low relationship style characterized by one-way communication in which the leader defines the roles of followers and tells them what, how, when, and where to do various tasks.

S2: *Selling.* High task–high relationship behavior is provided by two-way communication and socioemotional support to get followers to voluntarily buy into decisions that have been made.

S3: *Participating.* High relationship–low task behavior indicates both leader and follower have the ability and knowledge to complete the task.

S4: *Delegating.* Low relationship–low task behavior gives followers the opportunity to "run their own show" with little supervision (Swanson, Territo, and Taylor, 2001).

As the maturity level of followers develops from immaturity to maturity, the appropriate style of leadership moves in a corresponding way (Hersey and Blanchard, 1988). For example, a police supervisor who has a subordinate whose maturity is in the M3 range would be most effective employing an S3 style of leadership.

Hersey and Blanchard asserted that leaders could reduce their close supervision and direction of individuals and increase delegation as followers' readiness to complete tasks increased. The difficulty of this style of leadership is its dependence on leaders to diagnose follower ability and then adjust their leadership style to the given situation. This is often easier said than done.

Contingency Theory

Several researchers (Burns and Stalker, 1961; Woodward, 1965) attempted during the late 1950s and early 1960s to show that no one leadership style was appropriate for all job situations. Some jobs require one type of leadership, while another may require a different one. For example, a leader's style in a barricaded-person situation would be different from that of the same leader working with officers confronting a burglary problem. Therefore, situational theories of leadership are based on the concept of leader flexibility: Successful leaders must change their leadership style as they confront different situations. But can leaders be so flexible as to employ all major styles? Obviously, not all leaders are capable of such flexibility. It may be that leaders are locked into a particular style as a result of their personalities and job experiences.

Fred Fiedler (1965) developed one strategy for overcoming these obstacles, which is to change the organizational situation to fit the leader's style, and not vice versa. According to Fiedler, leader–member relations (the degree to which the leader feels accepted by the followers), task structure (the degree to which the work to be done is outlined clearly), and power of the leader (discussed later) should be considered when assigning leaders. Police departments commonly move sergeants with investigative experience into detective units to capitalize on their knowledge. According to Fiedler, it may be just as important to evaluate the sergeant's leadership style and ability to ensure that it matches the leadership situation.

The basic components of **contingency theory** then are that (1) among people's needs is a central need to achieve a sense of competence, (2) the ways that people fulfill this need vary from person to person, (3) competent motivation is most likely to occur when there is a fit between task and organization, and (4) a sense of competence continues to motivate people even after competence is achieved (Plunkett, 1983). It seems that not only are subordinates unhappy when they have a leader whose style does not match the job, but the leader may also be just as unhappy and unmotivated. Contingency theory argues that authoritarian leaders are more effective in performing structured and organized tasks. Human relations–type leaders are best suited for performing unstructured and uncertain tasks. Understanding this distinction requires that managers and supervisors tailor jobs to fit people or give people the skills, knowledge, and attitudes they will need to become competent (Burns and Stalker, 1961; Plunkett, 1983).

Position Power and Personal Power

Perhaps the two most often confused terms in management and supervision are *power* and *authority*. Authority is the right to command or give orders and is based on one's rank or position in the department. The extent to which an individual is able to influence others so they respond to orders is power. The greater this ability, the more power an individual is said to have. Further, a person can have rank but little or no power, and conversely, a person can have power but no rank within the department.

The total power a manager possesses is made up of position power and personal power. *Position power* is power derived from the organizational position a manager holds. In general, moves from lower-level management to upper-level management accrue more position power for a manager. *Personal power* is power derived from a manager's relationships with others (Certo, 1989).

Managers and supervisors can increase their total power by increasing their position power or their personal power. Position power can generally be increased by a move to a higher organizational position, but managers and supervisors usually have little personal control over moving upward in the department. They do, however, have substantial control over the amount of personal power they hold over other organizational members. To increase personal power, a manager can attempt to develop:

1. ***A sense of obligation in other organizational members that is directed toward the manager.*** If a manager is successful in developing this sense of obligation, other workers think they should rightly allow the manager to influence them, within certain limits. Doing personal favors for others is a basic strategy.
2. ***A belief in other organizational members that the manager possesses a high level of expertise within the organization.*** To increase the perceived level of expertise, the manager must quietly make significant achievement visible to others and rely heavily on a successful track record and respected professional reputation.
3. ***A sense of identification that other organizational members have with the manager.*** The manager can strive to develop this identification by behaving in ways that other organizational members respect and by espousing goals, values, and ideals commonly held by them.
4. ***The perception in other organizational members that they are dependent on the manager.*** The main strategy the manager should adopt is a clear demonstration of the amount of authority that he or she possesses over organizational resources. This is aptly reflected in the managerial version of the Golden Rule: "He who has the gold makes the rules." (Kotter, 1977)

LEADERSHIP STYLES

We now examine the styles of leadership that are sometimes displayed in police organizations. When researchers could not agree on universally accepted leadership traits, they began to study leadership styles. An early focus of the style theory of leadership resulted in the adoption of a single style based on a manager's rank or position in the department. Here, we examine two different typologies of leadership styles, one by Likert and another by Van Maanen (1984), who examines police leadership in terms of station house sergeants and street sergeants.

Likert's Leadership Systems

Likert's (1961) management systems are a good way to conceptualize the differences across organizational theories. Likert examined a number of industrial plants in an attempt to discover the style of leadership used by various managers. He was primarily interested in determining those leaders who were successful and why. Likert identified four distinct leadership types: exploitive-authoritarian, benevolent-authoritarian, consultative, and participative. Figure 3-10 shows these types in a continuum from low employee involvement to high involvement and interaction.

- ***Exploitive-Authoritarian Leadership:*** The exploitive-authoritarian leader has no confidence or trust in subordinates, and subordinates are not allowed to provide input into decisions. Policies and decisions are formulated by top management and filter down the chain of command. There is little superior-subordinate interaction, and when there is, it is usually negative or directive in nature. Superiors generally attempt to motivate subordinates through fear, threats, and punishment. Employees become frustrated and join together in informal groups to protect themselves from top management and to oppose unpopular policies. The exploitive-authoritarian style of leadership thwarts motivation and causes officers to concentrate only on attaining minimum productivity levels. This style of leadership is obviously inappropriate in policing, because police officers' activities cannot be highly or easily controlled as a result of the types of activities performed and the high degree of discretion officers must have when dealing with crime and calls for service. Moreover, first-line supervisors seldom provide close supervision of officers, which is a key component of the exploitive-authoritarian style. If this style of leadership exists in law enforcement, it exists only in a few isolated cases.
- ***Benevolent-Authoritarian Leadership:*** The benevolent-authoritarian style is somewhat more positive than the exploitive-authoritarian style. With this style, most policies and decisions are made by top management and are distributed through the chain of command, but sometimes managers and supervisors listen to subordinates' problems. More interaction takes place between first-line supervisors and line employees than in the exploitive-authoritarian style. Superiors frequently are willing to listen, but they continue to make all the decisions. Subordinates still view superiors with caution and distrust, but not to the point that they oppose organizational goals. They feel somewhat frustrated because they have little input into daily activities, especially those that directly affect them. This style of leadership permeates many traditionally organized police departments and is responsible for many of the motivational problems in these departments. (A possible reason for the existence of authoritarian leaders in police work is that the enforcement aspect of policing is, to a great extent, authoritarian, thereby attracting this type of individual.) Many officers working under this leadership style concentrate on accomplishing their assigned tasks, but they seldom go beyond them because of the lack of encouragement and the possibility of getting into trouble with their superiors. Hence, there is no real motivation to succeed, which is a necessary part of a successful organization. No statistics are available on the extent to which particular leadership styles exist in police organizations, but many police leaders likely are benevolent-authoritarian or consultative.

Operating Characteristic	Exploitive Authoritarian System	Benevolent Authoritarian System	Consultative	Participative
Motivation	Economic security marked with fear & threats	Economic and occasionally status rewards coupled with some punishment	Economic, ego, and desire for new experiences. Occasional punishment	Economic, ego, and full involvement in the organization and shared power
Communication Processes	Very little and downward	Little and mostly downward	Quite a bit, up and down the organization	Substantial throughout the organization
Character of interaction-influence	Little interaction, usually distrustful	Some interaction with caution on the part of subordinates	Moderate interaction and a moderate level of trust and confidence	Extensive collegial interaction with a high degree of trust and confidence
Decision making	Centralized with top administrators	Policy dictated by top administrators with some decisions resting with mid-level managers	Broad policies made at top with lower level echelons having input into programs	Decisions made throughout the organization with lower level subordinates having input in all decisions
Goal setting	Goals set by top administrators and orders issued by administrators. Directives resisted by subordinates	Goals set by top administrators and orders issued by administrators with some discussion by subordinates	Goals and orders issued after discussion with subordinates. Goals and orders have some level of acceptance by subordinates	Goals established through group participation with high levels of acceptance by work group
Control Processes	Formalized controls established by top management which are resisted by subordinates	Control rests primarily at the top with resistence from subordinates	Moderate delegation of authority and responsibility with subordinates having some input in performance expectations	Concern for performance throughout the organization coupled with collegiality
Productivity	Mediocre productivity	Fair to good productivity	Good productivity	Excellent productivity

FIGURE 3-10 Likert's System Organizational Characteristics
Adapted from: Likert, R. (1967). *The Human Organization: Its Management and Value.* New York: McGraw-Hill Book Co., pp14-24.

- ***Consultative Leadership:*** **Consultative leadership** involves management's establishment of goals and objectives for the department with subordinates making some of the decisions on methods of goal achievement (i.e., strategic and tactical decisions). A more positive relationship exists between superiors and line personnel as problems and possible solutions are discussed openly and freely. Employees are encouraged to become involved by providing input into some decisions and unit goals. Positive rewards are emphasized and punishment is used to motivate only in extreme cases. Whole or parts of police departments formally or informally adhere to this leadership style. This is especially true in larger police departments in which operational units have a great deal of autonomy (Toch, 1997). For example, the leadership style in drug units often is consultative. Officers in these units likely have substantial discretion in how they attack an area's drug problem. This style of leadership tends to emphasize involvement and esteem rewards and leads to a more positive motivational climate.

- ***Participative Leadership:*** The **participative leadership** style involves subordinates having input not only into tactical decisions, but also into policy formulation. It is a team approach whereby everyone has input in the organization's goals and objectives and operational strategies and tactics. The participative style implies that police officers provide direct input into what the department should be doing. Witte, Travis, and Langworthy (1990) found that officers at all levels within police departments favored the use of participatory management, but that only those officers in administrative positions believed that they were allowed an adequate level of participation. All other officers believed that they were not allowed adequate participation in decision making and strategic planning. Managers sometimes are given objectives that are counter to the expectations of officers. Such disagreements on policy usually center on law enforcement versus service roles. If there is a high degree of trust within the police organization, however, this may be only a minor problem. In the vast majority of cases, subordinates should be allowed to have some level of input into decisions. An open discussion of such matters generally brings about compliance and cooperation.

Police organizations must move toward the latter two styles of leadership. Approximately 80 percent of any police department's budget is devoted to salaries for personnel, and personnel represent an important resource in police agencies. These resources must be used to their maximum advantage. The consultative and participatory styles of leadership create a positive motivational atmosphere in which officers are more likely to be concerned about doing an excellent job in accomplishing objectives.

Station House Sergeants and Street Sergeants

To learn the differences in leadership style as a function of workplace, we consider an interesting study of a 1,000-officer police department by John Van Maanen (1984), who identified two contrasting types of police sergeants: "station house" and "street." Station house sergeants have been out of the "bag" (uniform) since before their promotion to sergeant and prefer to work inside in an office environment once they win their stripes. This preference is clearly indicated by the nickname of "Edwards, the Olympic torch who never goes out" given to one sergeant. Station house sergeants immerse themselves in the management culture of the police department, keeping busy with paperwork, planning, record keeping, press relations, and fine points of law. Their strong orientation to conformity also gave rise to nickname "by the book Brubaker."

In contrast, Van Maanen (1984) found that street sergeants were serving in the field when promoted; consequently, they had a distaste for office procedures and a strong action orientation as suggested by nicknames such as "Shooter McGee" and "Walker the Stalker." Moreover, their concern was not with conformity, but with "not letting the assholes take over the city."

Station house sergeants and street sergeants are thought of differently by those whom they supervise: Station house sergeants "stood behind their officers," whereas street sergeants "stood beside their officers." Station house sergeants might not be readily available to officers working in the field but can always be located when a signature is needed and are able to secure more favors for their subordinates. Street sergeants occasionally interfere with the autonomy of their subordinates by responding to and handling a call assigned to a subordinate.

Station house sergeants spend considerable time learning routines, procedures, and skills that will improve future promotional opportunities. Furthermore, they are making contacts with senior police commanders who can give them important assignments and possibly influence future promotions. In contrast, street sergeants may gain some favorable publicity and awards for their exploits, but they are also more likely to have citizen complaints against them, be investigated by internal affairs, or be sued. Consequently, street sergeants are regarded by their superiors as "good cops" but difficult people to supervise. In short, the action-oriented street sergeant may not go beyond a middle-manager's position in a line unit such as patrol or investigation.

LEADING IN THE NEW MILLENIUM: NO EASY ANSWERS

One person whose voice has been increasingly heard in the leadership arena is Ronald Heifetz. As author of *Leadership Without Easy Answers* (1994), director of the Leadership Education Project, and instructor of what is reported to be the single most popular course at Harvard's Kennedy School of Government, Heifetz has focused on the practical problems of leadership.

Much of Heifetz's work centers on what he terms "adaptive change," which he calls for when a problem cannot be solved with one's existing knowledge and skills and requires people to make a shift in their expectations, attitudes, or habits of behavior. To clarify his intended meaning, let us consider how Heifetz describes differences in adaptive problems and technical problems. There are problems, he says, that are *technical* only—a mechanic repairs a car, a surgeon repairs a broken bone, and so on. Such problems are fixable by experts. On the other hand, there are problems that an expert alone cannot fix, and that require people in the community to change their values, behavior, and attitudes.

Heifetz cites as an example the drug abuse problem—an adaptive problem treated as if it were technical. When President George H. W. Bush came into office it was one of the most devastating problems in the nation; he and his experts devised a $9 billion plan, appointed a "drug czar," named it a "war." People were delighted to hear all of this, and did not want to be told that the problem of drug abuse is much deeper, emanating from a lack of community spirit, poverty, disorder in neighborhoods, and so on (Flower, 2007).

Heifetz argues that mere technical fixes will not work with drug and other social problems. Rather, our leaders must call for adaptive change, which is engaged through the conferred authority of those being led (a very important point, by the way, that we will not delve into here). Heifetz proposes four principles for bringing about adaptive change:

1. Be able to recognize when the challenge requires adaptive work for resolution; understand the values and issues at stake in the situation.
2. Remember that adaptive change will cause distress in the people being led. The leader should keep the distress in the tolerable range (too much stress can be defeating, and too little stress does not motivate people).
3. Keep the focus on the real issue—do not get sidetracked by denial, scapegoating, and so on, as these are "work avoidance mechanisms."
4. Ensure that the people who need to make the change take the responsibility for doing the work of change themselves (Heifetz, 1994).

When problematical situations arise that cannot be resolved through old "tried and true" methods, this approach will help to provide the leader with a perspective to help people resolve it.

WHY LEADERS FAIL

The previous discussion of theories and methods of leadership—some of which were developed several decades ago—is intended to help managers and supervisors avoid failure. In today's stop-and-go, ever dangerous, litigation-vulnerable world of policing, the price paid for incompetent supervision is too high; there is little room for error. Moreover, it means that we must not depend on on-the-job-training but must develop our leaders before they are placed in leadership positions.

Some supervisors are too preachy, rigid, cold, uncaring, and vindictive, while others are too friendly, accommodating, or self-centered. Thus far, we have addressed how a supervisor, manager, or administrator should lead. However, it is also helpful to examine how a leader should *not* conduct business. The following are some types of "problem bosses":

1. ***Ticket Punchers:*** They maneuver daily to advance in status, power, and rank. Promotion is paramount, and they will do whatever is necessary to get ahead.
2. ***Spotlighters:*** They require attention and center stage, demanding recognition for all the positive results. When things go awry, they are quick to disappear. They rarely share the successes with others.
3. ***Mega-delegators:*** These people seldom do real work and view themselves as "participatory managers." They accomplish nothing, while everyone else is working hard.

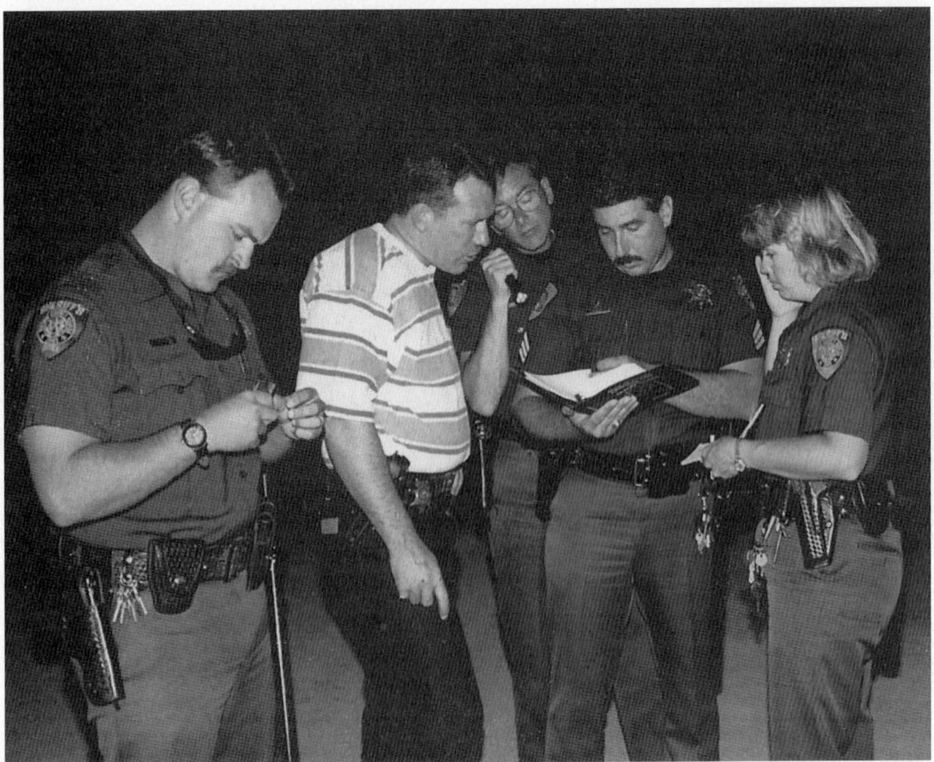

Supervisors are often responsible for coordinating the responses of patrol and specialized units, such as detectives and crime scene technicians at crime scenes.
(Courtesy Washoe County, Nevada, Sheriff's Office Photo Unit)

4. ***Micromanagers:*** These bosses are either insecure or perfectionists or need to control every aspect of work; they seek feedback incessantly and require frequent reporting. They expend too much energy on details rather than getting the job done.
5. ***One Best Style:*** These managers believe that only one style of managing guarantees success. In other words, if you mimic this person's style, you're a winner. They are too inflexible in too many situations.
6. ***Control Takers:*** These people crave power; force is foremost, control is critical, and being correct is imperative. They too often cannot delegate and do not allow their subordinates to grow with the job.
7. ***The Phantoms:*** These bosses are uncomfortable with social interaction, preferring to remain invisible or secreted away in their offices. They are uneasy empowering others. They are usually excellent test takers and thus are able to attain positions of command (Whisenand and Ferguson, 1996).

Finally, Steven Brown (1989) provided a list of 13 fatal errors that can erode a leader's effectiveness:

1. Refuse to accept personal accountability
2. Fail to develop people; operations should function successfully in your absence
3. Try to control results instead of activities
4. Join the wrong crowd
5. Manage everyone in the same way
6. Forget the importance of service
7. Concentrate on problems rather than objectives
8. Be a buddy, not a boss
9. Fail to set standards
10. Fail to train your people
11. Condone incompetence
12. Recognize only top performers
13. Try to manipulate people

A number of pitfalls are waiting for the police supervisor or manager. Being a good leader entails a great deal of hard work. The best leaders are those who are actively involved with their subordinates and the department. They have a vision of where they are going, and they adhere to a set of values to guide their actions.

CASE STUDIES

The following three case studies provide some substantive information and issues for the reader to use for applying chapter information. The first one is a "warm-up," where you must first consider, identify, and stake out your own personal management style. The others demand more in terms of using chapter material.

Case Study #1

The New Kid on the (Lieutenant's) Block

You are a newly promoted lieutenant and have decided that a priority is to schedule an open meeting with your sergeants to discuss your priorities and any problems, and then for you to respond to any questions. At the meeting's conclusion, a sergeant raises her hand and says the sergeants are quite concerned about what they might expect in terms of your management style, particularly as it concerns personnel discipline, rewards, and motivation. She further asks you to explain why you believe this style to be the best for you.

Question for Discussion

1. Based on the readings in this chapter, which management style would you say is probably your own? Explain why you feel this one is best and suits your personality.

Case Study #2

The "Rising Star" Who Falls Too Far

Detective Thurmond Thomas is a "rising star" in the Bentley County Sheriff's Department, and at age 25 is the youngest officer there ever to be promoted to rank of detective. Recently married, Thomas is excited about his new assignment and is looking forward to the day-shift hours and weekends off. Thomas begins his new assignment with great desire, often volunteering for the less popular cases and working a lot of overtime. He is doing everything possible to make a good impression on his more experienced peers. Sgt. Wise takes a particular liking to Thomas and is making every effort to recognize his good work among the other detectives. He even suggests that Thomas consider being promoted at the soonest possible time and offers to coach him for the promotional exam. Everything appears to be going well for young Thomas. After a couple of months, however, Sgt. Wise begins to notice that Thomas is using a lot of sick time and has lost much of his enthusiasm for the job. Wise meets with Thomas to discuss the matter. Thomas explains that he is now uncomfortable in the detective division and does not fit in with the rest of the detectives. He adds that the others simply ignore him, never inviting him to lunch or coffee. Sgt. Wise decides that Thomas is simply lacking self-confidence due to his young age. He then discusses Thomas's concerns and his potential with the other detectives, in hopes of improving relations. Instead, matters only worsen, and now the lieutenant is directing Wise to investigate Thomas's sick days to determine if he is abusing his leave time.

Questions for Discussion

1. What is your assessment of this situation?
2. Does Sgt. Wise correctly understand the nature of the problem?
3. How would you describe Thomas's problem, using the motivation theories discussed in the chapter?
4. What could Sgt. Wise have done differently?

Case Study #3

Where to Begin When a Veteran Comes In

Officer Maria Sanchez has 17 years of experience, mostly as a detective in undercover narcotics and vice. She is a capable officer with numerous departmental commendations and awards for her work. As a result, Sanchez was selected to be a member of an elite multi-agency vice and narcotics task force. On the first day of her new assignment, Sanchez met with her new supervisor, Sgt. Webster. He is from a neighboring agency and does not know Sanchez outside the selection interview process and review of her personnel file. Sgt. Webster was also recently assigned to the unit from patrol division where he gained the reputation of being somewhat of a perfectionist and detail person. Webster assumed responsibility for breaking in all new team members to ensure they knew exactly what, when, where, and how they should perform their tasks. Webster had developed a four-week orientation for all new members. After two weeks of basic orientation, including an elementary review of drug law, raid procedures, vice laws, and so on, Sanchez becomes extremely frustrated with Sgt. Webster and asks why she is not being allowed to participate in drug and vice raids with the rest of her team. She argues that she has worked with the task force on many occasions, is very familiar with operational procedures, and could demonstrate her abilities if Webster would only allow her to work with the rest of the team. Webster denies her request, saying she has to finish the orientation just the same as everyone else does. The next day, Sanchez submits a memo to the lieutenant in charge of the task force, requesting to be reassigned back to her agency. In the memo, Sanchez states that she believes Sgt. Webster is treating her differently from other people in the unit and does not have any respect for her past experience and work. She does not believe she can work under these conditions, in which she is "being treated like a child."

Questions for Discussion

1. Could this problem have been avoided? If so, how?
2. What situational style of leadership was Sgt. Webster employing?
3. How would you assess the maturity level of Officer Sanchez?
4. What style of situational leadership would be more appropriate for this situation?

Summary

This chapter has examined several management theories that are of interest to supervisors and managers, including what motivates employees, how managers are distinguished from leaders, theories of leadership, and quality leadership and team building. In addition to covering these theories, we discussed the importance of empowering employees, how to think and act strategically, and pointed out several theories and approaches that have not succeeded. One can learn much from a failed approach.

It should be remembered that all of these elements and issues of management and supervision revolve around one very important feature of the workplace: people. Perhaps that is what Heifetz meant when he wrote that there are no "easy answers." The major point being emphasized in this chapter may well be that managers and supervisors must know their people, and how to motivate them. To be effective in the labor-intensive field of policing, superior officers should first learn all they can about this most valuable asset, just as much as they must learn about agency policies and procedures and new technology. Effective leaders are made, not born; thus, they must also receive the requisite training and education for performing well. An educated approach is far better than simply marching the new leader off the plank, to either sink or swim.

Items For Review

1. What is involved in taking a "good" organization and making it "great?"
2. Contrast what is meant by "leader" versus "manager."
3. Describe situational leadership and how it applies to the police leader.
4. Review some of the ways in which a manager can increase his or her personal power.
5. Explain how and why a police leader would empower his or her subordinates.
6. How would Mintzberg's model for chief executives apply to chiefs of police, sheriffs, and their middle managers?
7. Review how one must first think strategically in order to manage the organization in a strategic manner.
8. There are a number of theories of motivation. How might these theories be applied in the police setting?
9. Explain what Heifetz meant by "adaptive change," including its four principles, and how it applies to police supervision and management.
10. Delineate several ways in which a leader can fail, and how failure can be avoided.

References

Alliance for Nonprofit Management, Strategic planning, http://www.allianceonline.org/FAQ/strategic_planning/what_is_strategic_planning.faq (Accessed October 5, 2007).

Argyris, C. (1957). *Personality and organization.* New York: Harper & Bros.

Bennett, W. W., and Hess, K. (2001). *Management and supervision in law enforcement.* Belmont, CA: Wadsworth.

Bennis, W., and Nanus, B. (1985). *Leaders.* New York: Harper & Row.

Bernard, C. (1938). *The functions of the executive.* Cambridge, MA: Harvard University Press.

Blake, R. R., and Mouton, J. S. (1962). The developing revolution in management practices. *Journal of the American Society of Training Directors* 16:29–52.

Brown, S. B. (1989). *Fatal errors managers make: And how you can avoid them.* Police Leadership Report, The National Law Enforcement Leadership Institute, Safety Harbor, Florida, 1(3):6–7.

Burns, T., and Stalker, G. M. (1961). *The management of innovation.* London: Tavistock.

Certo, S. C. (1989). *Principles of modern management: Functions and systems,* 4th ed. Boston: Allyn & Bacon.

Charrier, K. (2004). The role of the strategic manager. *The Police Chief* (June):60.

Collins, J. (2001). *Good to great: Why some companies make the leap . . . and other don't.* New York: HarperCollins.

Collins, J. (2005). *Good to great and the social sectors.* New York: HarperCollins.

Davis, R. C. (1940). *Industrial organization and management.* New York: Harper & Bros.

Favreau, D. F., and Gillespie, J. E. (1978). *Modern police administration.* Upper Saddle River, NJ: Prentice Hall.

Fieldler, F. (1965). Engineer the job to fit the manager. *Harvard Business Review* 43 (September/October): 115–122.

Flower, J. (2007). A conversation with Ronald Heifetz: Leadership without easy answers. http://www.well.com/bbear/heifetz.html (Accessed October 18, 2007).

Gove, T. G. (2007). Empowerment and accountability: Tools for law enforcement leaders. *FBI Law Enforcement Bulletin* (September):8–13.

Greenberg, J., and Baron, R. (1995). *Behavior in organizations.* Upper Saddle River, NJ: Prentice Hall.

Heifetz, R. A. (1994). *Leadership without easy answers.* Cambridge, Mass.: The Belknap Press of Harvard Press.

Herocleous, L. (1998). Strategic thinking or strategic planning? *Long Range Planning* 31:481–487.

Hersey, P., and Blanchard, K. H. (1988). *Management of organizational behavior.* Upper Saddle River, NJ: Prentice Hall.

Herzberg, F. (1968). One more time: How do you motivate employees? *Harvard Business Review* (January/February):53–62.

Katz, R. L. (1974). Skills of an effective administrator. *Harvard Business Review* 52 (September–October): 90–101.

Kotter, J. (1977). Power, dependence, and effective management. *Harvard Business Review* (July/August):128–135.

Lawrence, E. (1999). *Strategic thinking: A discussion paper*. Ottawa, Ontario, Can.: Public Service Commission of Canada, Research Directorate, Policy, Research, and Communications Branch, April 27th.

Likert, R. (1961). *New patterns of management.* New York: McGraw-Hill.

Maslow, A. H. (1954). *Motivation and personality.* New York: Harper & Row.

McClelland, D. (1964). *The achieving society.* Princeton, NJ: Van Nostrand Reinhold.

Mintzberg, H. (1975). The Manager's job: Folklore and fact, *Harvard Business Review* 53 (July–August):49–61.

Peak, K. J., and Glensor, R. W. (2008). *Community policing and problem solving: Strategies and practices*, 5th ed. Upper Saddle River, NJ: Prentice Hall.

Plunkett, W. R. (1983). *Supervision: The direction of people at work.* Dubuque, IA: Wm. C. Brown.

Sales, S. M. (1969). Supervisory style and productivity: Review and theory. In Larry Cummings and William E. Scott, eds., *Readings in organizational behavior and human performance.* Homewood, IL: Richard D. Irwin.

Stoner, J. A., and Freeman, R. E. (1992). *Management,* 5th ed. Upper Saddle River, NJ: Prentice Hall.

Swanson, C. R., and Territo, L. (1982). Police leadership and interpersonal communications styles. In J. Greene, ed., *Police and police work.* Beverly Hills: Sage.

Swanson, C. R., Territo, L., and Taylor, R. W. (2001). *Police administration,* 5th ed. Upper Saddle River, NJ: Prentice Hall.

Tannenbaum, R., and Weschler, I. R. (1961). *Leadership and organization: A behavioral science approach.* New York: McGraw-Hill.

Toch, H. (1997). The democratization of policing in the United States: 1895–1973. *Police Forum* 7(2):1–8.

U.S. Department of Justice (2007), Information technology strategic plan, http://www.usdoj.gov/jmd/ocio/2006strategic_plan.htm (Accessed October 6, 2007).

Van Maanen, J. (1984). Making rank: Becoming an American police sergeant. *Urban Life* 13:155–176.

Vroom, V. H. (1964). *Work and motivation.* New York: Wiley.

Wexler, C., Wycoff, M. A., and Fischer, C. (2007). *Good to great: Application of business management principles in the public sector.* Washington, D.C.: Office of Community Oriented Policing Services and Police Executive Research Forum.

Whisenand, P. M., and Ferguson, F. (1996). *The managing of police organizations.* Upper Saddle River, NJ: Prentice Hall.

Witte, J. H., Travis, L. F., and Langworthy, R. H. (1990). Participatory management in law enforcement: Police officer, supervisor, and administrator perceptions. *American Journal of Police* 9(4):1–24.

Woodward, J. (1965). *Industrial organization: Theory and practice.* London: Oxford University Press.

Wuestewald, T. (2006). Can empowerment work in police organizations? *The Police Chief* (January): 48–55.

CHAPTER 4

Community Policing and Problem Solving

KEY TERMS AND CONCEPTS

- Analysis
- Assessment
- Community oriented policing and problem solving (COPPS)
- CompStat
- Crime prevention through environmental design (CPTED)
- Geographic information system (GIS)
- Mapping
- Problem analysis triangle
- Response
- S.A.R.A.
- Scanning
- Situational crime prevention (SCP)

LEARNING OBJECTIVES

After reading this chapter, the student will:

- know how community oriented policing and problem solving differs from traditional policing, and the four-step process used by police to address crime and neighborhood disorder
- comprehend several approaches to crime prevention, including situational crime prevention and crime prevention through environmental design
- understand the key roles of first-line supervisors and middle managers in implementing and maintaining community policing and problem solving, and list the characteristics of a good problem-solving supervisor
- be able to explain how the street officer must be viewed by supervisors and managers under the community policing philosophy and be granted considerably more freedom and trust for problem-solving activities
- be able to delineate how police officers may obtain the time necessary for engaging in problem-solving activities
- understand the function of the CompStat crime control model

The difficulty lies, not in the new ideas, but in escaping from old ones.

—JOHN MAYNARD KEYNES

We are continually faced with a series of opportunities, brilliantly disguised as insoluble problems.

—JOHN GARDNER

INTRODUCTION

As stated by one source, community oriented policing has "become a mantra for police chiefs and mayors in cities big and small across the country" (Witkin and McGraw, 1993:28), and has rapidly become entrenched. As will be seen, what we term community oriented policing and problem solving (COPPS) has spread rapidly across the nation; indeed, this philosophy and strategy is now the current era of policing, and is in its third generation. This chapter provides a closer look at COPPS and examines the important roles of supervisors and managers within this strategy.

First we provide definitions and an illustration of this strategy, including the four-step problem-solving process. Next we look at two related approaches for viewing and addressing crime: crime prevention through environmental design (CPTED) and situational crime prevention. Following that is a discussion of several implementation and leadership issues as they relate to the COPPS philosophy, focusing on the key roles of first-line supervisors, middle managers, and executives. It will be seen that the importance of these individuals—particularly the sergeants, lieutenants, and captains—in the successful launching and maintenance of COPPS cannot be overstated. Next is a discussion of the importance of giving freedom and prominence to the street officer, and then we look at several means by which adequate time may be obtained for officers to engage in problem solving. Other important implementation considerations are also presented.

Our last—but major—topic of discussion in this chapter concerns a management tool for analyzing and addressing crime: CompStat. Included is its function, how it modifies roles of police leaders, and some examples of its application (some leadership opportunities and caveats are presented in Chapter 6). The chapter concludes with two case studies.

THE NATURE OF COMMUNITY POLICING AND PROBLEM SOLVING PRACTICES: AN OVERVIEW

By the Numbers: Emphasis and Extent

A recent report by the U.S. Bureau of Justice Statistics stated that 58 percent of all police agencies, employing 82 percent of all officers in the nation, now have full-time personnel performing COPPS functions (see Table 4-1). Furthermore, nearly four in ten such agencies, employing 72 percent of all officers, train their recruits in COPPS-related skills such as problem solving, S.A.R.A. (discussed below), and developing community partnerships (see Table 4-2).

Clearly, today's police supervisors and managers must understand this strategy from its foundational precepts and methods of looking at crime (assuming the role of "street-level criminologists"), to practical, fundamental aspects such as freeing time for their patrol officers to develop long-term solutions to neighborhood disorder.

A Change in Philosophy and Methods: An Illustration

COPPS represents a dramatic shift from the traditional methods of policing. What exactly is COPPS? Following is a definition that captures the essence of this concept:

> Community oriented policing and problem solving (COPPS) is a proactive philosophy that promotes solving problems that are criminal, affect our quality of life, or increase our fear of crime, as well as other community issues. COPPS involves identifying, analyzing, and addressing community problems at their source (Peak and Glensor, 2008:85).

One of the strongest advocates of this approach to policing is the California Department of Justice, which has published several monographs on the subject and has taken the position that

TABLE 4-1 Full-Time Community Policing Officers in Local Police Departments, By Size of Population Served, 2003

	Community policing officers		
Population served	Percent of agencies using	Total number of officers	Average number of full-time sworn*
All sizes	58%	54,849	7
1,000,000 or more	100%	4,756	287
500,000–999,999	89	4,135	120
250,000–499,999	85	3,388	94
100,000–249,999	89	5,152	33
50,000–99,999	88	5,329	14
25,000–49,999	80	6,071	10
10,000–24,999	62	7,582	7
2,500–9,999	55	11,377	5
Under 2,500	52	7,060	3

*Excludes agencies that did not employ any full-time community policing officers.

TABLE 4-2 Community Policing Training in Local Police Departments, by Size of Population Served

	Percent of agencies that trained personnel for 8 or more hours in community policing		
Population served	Total	All	Some
New officer recruits			
All sizes	39%	31%	8%
1,000,000 or more	81%	81%	0%
500,000–999,999	79	76	3
250,000–499,999	88	85	3
100,000–249,999	84	76	8
50,000–99,999	72	63	9
25,000–49,999	67	58	9
10,000–24,999	59	51	8
2,500–9,999	40	29	11
Under 2,500	23	17	6
Inservice sworn personnel			
All sizes	48%	17%	31%
1,000,000 or more	75%	31%	44%
500,000–999,999	49	17	32
250,000–499,999	64	20	44
100,000–249,999	72	19	53
50,000–99,999	71	17	54
25,000–49,999	66	17	49
10,000–24,999	60	18	42
2,500–9,999	50	16	34
Under 2,500	37	18	19

TABLE 4-2 *(Continued)*

Civilian personnel			
All sizes	12%	4%	8%
1,000,000 or more	25%	6%	19%
500,000–999,999	25	6	19
250,000–499,999	32	3	29
100,000–249,999	42	5	37
50,000–99,999	29	4	25
25,000–49,999	30	4	26
10,000–24,999	18	6	12
2,500–9,999	12	5	7
Under 2,500	4	2	2

*During 1-year period ending June 30, 2003.

Source: U.S. Department of Justice, Bureau of Justice Statistics, Local Police Departments, 2003 (Washington, D.C.: Author, May 2006), pp.19–20.

> Community Oriented Policing and Problem Solving is a concept whose time has come. This movement holds tremendous promise for creating effective police-community partnerships to reclaim our communities and keep our streets safe. COPPS is not "soft" on crime; in fact, it is tougher on crime because it is smarter and more creative. Community input focuses police activities; and, with better information, officers are able to respond more effectively with arrests or other appropriate actions. COPPS can unite our communities and promote pride in our police forces (California Department of Justice, 1993:iii).

Two principal and interrelated components emerge from these two definitions: community engagement (partnerships) and problem solving. Although separate and distinct, they are not mutually exclusive. Engaging the community without problem solving provides no meaningful service to the

The professional era of policing emphasized crime fighting. Shown are officers of NYPD's Emergency Services unit, formed in 1926 to drive criminals from the street.
(Courtesy NYPD Photo Unit)

public. Problem solving without partnerships risks overlooking the most pressing community concerns. Thus, the partnership between police departments and the communities they serve is essential for implementing a successful program in community policing.

COPPS, with its focus on collaborative problem solving, seeks to improve the quality of policing. This is no simple task, however, and several steps must be taken to accomplish it: (1) Police must be equipped to define more clearly and to understand more fully the problems they are expected to handle, (2) the police must develop a commitment to analyzing problems, and (3) police must be encouraged to conduct an uninhibited search for the most effective response to each problem (Goldstein, 1987:5–6). The S.A.R.A. process (discussed later) provides the police with the tools necessary to accomplish these steps.

To assist in understanding this definition, we present two scenarios; the first is an example of how a neighborhood problem is treated under the traditional, reactive style of policing:

> Police noted a series of disturbances in a relatively quiet and previously stable residential neighborhood. Although the neighborhood's zoning had for years provided for late-night cabaret-style businesses, none had existed until the "Nite Life," a live-music dance club, opened. Within a few weeks, the police dispatcher received an increased number of complaints about loud music and voices, fighting, and screeching tires late into the night. Within a month's time, at least 50 calls for service had been dispatched to the club to restore order. Evening shift officers responded to calls and restored order prior to midnight, but graveyard shift officers would have to again restore order when called back to the scene by complaining neighbors after midnight.

This second scenario illustrates how this same matter might be handled using the COPPS approach:

> The evening-shift area patrol sergeant identified the disturbances as a problem. The initial information-gathering phase revealed the following: large increases in numbers of calls for service (CFS) in the area on both the evening and graveyard shifts; several realtors had contacted council members to complain about declining market interest in the area and to say that they were considering suing both the owner of the new business and the city for the degradation of the neighborhood; a local newspaper was about to run a story on the increase in vehicle burglaries and damage done to parked vehicles in and around the cabaret's parking lot. The team also determined that the consolidated narcotics unit was investigating both employees and some of the late-night clientele of the business as a result of several tips that narcotics were being used and sold in the parking lot and inside the business.
>
> The officers and their sergeant gathered information from crime reports, a news reporter about to publish the story, neighboring business owners, and the department's crime analysis unit. Information was also gathered concerning possible zoning and health department violations. Officers then met with the business owner to work out an agreement for reestablishing the quality of life in the neighborhood to its previous levels and to decrease the department's CFS. First, the business licensing division and the owner were brought together to both reestablish the ground rules and provide for a proper licensing of all the players. This resulted in the instant removal of an unsavory partner and in turn his "following" of drug users and other characters at the business. The landlord agreed to hasten landscaping and lighting of the parking lots and provided a "sound wall" around the business to buffer the area residents. Agreements were reached to limit the hours of operation of the live music of the business. The cabaret's owner and all of his employees were trained by the area patrol teams in pertinent aspects of the city code (such as disturbing the peace, minors in liquor establishments, and trespassing laws). The police experienced a reduction in CFS in the area. Area residents, although not entirely happy with the continuing existence of the business, acknowledged satisfaction of their complaints; no further newspaper stories appeared regarding the noise and disorder in the neighborhood.

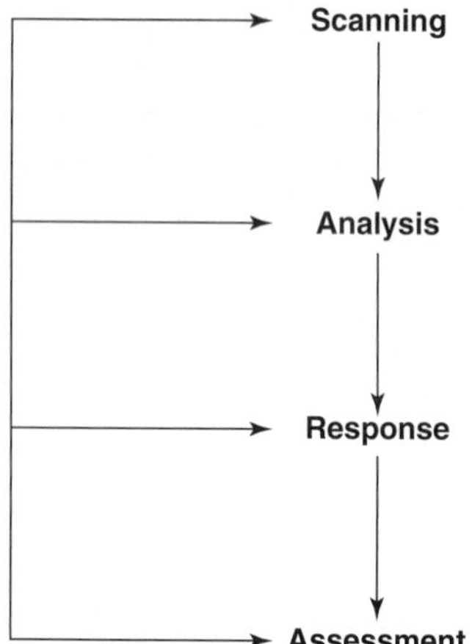

FIGURE 4-1 S.A.R.A. Problem Solving Process
Source: John E. Eck and William Spelman, *Problem Solving: Problem-Oriented Policing in Newport News* (Washington, DC: U.S. Department of Justice, National Institute of Justice, 1987), p. 43.

In this example, the police not only responded to the concerns of the neighborhood residents, they also developed a better understanding of both the area's businesses and residents and established a working relationship with all involved. By co-opting the services of the other municipal entities, police also learned of new and valuable resources with which to share some of the burden of future demands for governmental service.

The S.A.R.A. Process

This illustration of COPPS at work employed four steps toward solving the problems created by the Nite Life club. These four steps comprise the problem-solving process called **S.A.R.A.**:

Scanning: the initial information-gathering stage by the supervisor
Analysis: the more in-depth information-gathering stage, involving crime reports, the crime analysis unit, a news reporter, and zoning and health departments
Response: involved a number of meetings, improved the lighting and landscaping, agreements
Assessment: a follow-up look at CFS in the area

Figure 4-1 shows the S.A.R.A. process. This process provides officers with a logical step-by-step framework to identify, analyze, respond to, and evaluate crime, the fear of crime, and neighborhood disorder. This approach, with its emphasis on in-depth analysis and collaboration, replaces officers' short-term, reactive responses with a process vested in longer-term outcomes.

Next, we briefly discuss each component of the S.A.R.A. process in more detail (for a more complete discussion of this process, see Peak and Glensor, 2008, Chapter 3).

SCANNING: PROBLEM IDENTIFICATION Scanning means problem identification. It initiates the problem-solving process by conducting a preliminary inquiry to determine if a problem really exists and whether further analysis is needed. A problem is different from an isolated incident, which is something police are called to or happen on that is unrelated to any other incidents in the community. A problem can be defined as a cluster of two or more similar or related incidents that are of substantive concern to the community and to the police.

The problems derived from repeated incidents may vary and include:

- A series of burglaries at an apartment complex
- Drug activity at a city park
- Thefts of a particular type of car from several lots
- Graffiti at a particular location or jurisdiction
- Parking and traffic problems
- A series of gang-related drive-by shootings
- Robberies of convenience stores
- Juvenile loitering related crime at a mall
- Aggressive panhandling at a downtown center
- Repeat alarms to commercial businesses

Numerous resources are available to the police for identifying problems, including calls for service data (especially repeat calls), crime analysis information, police reports, and officers' own experiences. Other sources of information include other governmental agencies, public and private agencies, businesses, media reports, and information obtained from the public. Scanning helps the officer determine whether a problem really exists before moving on to more in-depth analysis.

ANALYSIS: DETERMINING THE EXTENT OF THE PROBLEM **Analysis** is the heart of the problem-solving process. It is the *most difficult* and *most important* step in the S.A.R.A. process. A common criticism of incident-driven policing is that officers often skip analysis in their haste to find solutions. Without analysis, long-term solutions are limited and the problem is likely to persist.

In this step, officers gather as much information as possible from a variety of sources. A complete and thorough analysis consists of officers identifying the seriousness of the problem, all persons affected, and the underlying causes. Officers should also assess the effectiveness of current responses.

Many tools are available to assist with analysis. Crime analysis may be useful in collecting, collating, analyzing, and disseminating data relating to crime, incidents not requiring a report, criminal offenders, victims, and locations. **Mapping** and **geographic information systems (GIS)** can identify patterns of crime and hot spots. Police offense reports can also be analyzed for suspect characteristics, MOs, victim characteristics, and information about high-crime areas and addresses. Computer-aided dispatch is also a reliable source of information, because it collects data on all incidents and specific locations from which an unusual number of events require a police response.

One explanation of crime may be found in routine activity theory (Cohen and Felson, 1979), which postulates that a crime will occur when three elements are present: (1) a suitable victim, (2) a motivated offender, and (3) a location. If one of these three elements is addressed or removed, the crime will not occur. The **problem analysis triangle** (Figure 4-2) helps officers to visualize the complexities of crime and the relationship among its three elements.

RESPONSE: FORMULATING TAILOR-MADE STRATEGIES Once a problem has been clearly defined, officers may seek the most effective responses. Responses should be developed in consideration of each side of the problem analysis triangle. Focusing solely on the offender leaves room for new offenders because the location or victims have not been changed.

We have stressed the importance of long-term solutions; however, officers cannot ignore the fact that more serious situations may require immediate action. For example, in the case of an open-air drug market involving rival gang violence, police may initially increase the number of patrols in the area to arrest offenders, gain control of public space, and secure the safety of residents and officers. Once this

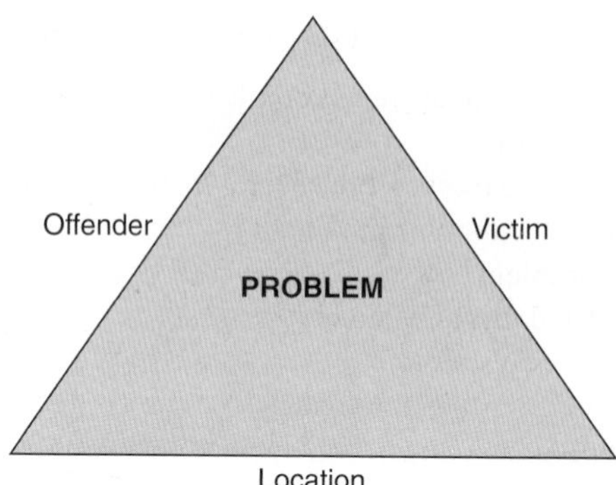

FIGURE 4-2 Problem Analysis Triangle
Source: Bureau of Justice Assistance, U.S. Department of Justice, *Comprehensive Gang Initiative: Operations Manual for Implementing Local Gang Prevention and Control Programs*, draft (October 1993), pp. 3–10.

is accomplished, longer-term responses that include the collaborative efforts of officers, residents, and other agencies may be considered.

Responses to substantive problems rarely involve a single agency or tactic or quick fix. For example, arrest is often viewed as the only response to a problem even though it is rarely sufficient to provide more permanent resolutions. More appropriate responses often involve the police and public and other appropriate entities, including businesses, private and social service organizations, and other governmental agencies.

Officers have many options to respond to problems; however, they should not expect to eliminate every problem they take on. With some social problems, such as gangs and homelessness, elimination is impractical and improbable.

Other important prevention tools for COPPS are crime prevention through environmental design (CPTED) and situational crime prevention, discussed below.

ASSESSMENT: EVALUATING OVERALL EFFECTIVENESS The final stage is **assessment**. Officers evaluate the effectiveness of their responses and use the results to revise their responses, collect more data, or even redefine the problem. For some problems, assessment is simple: observing a location to see if a problem resurfaces. For example, in one East Coast city, when asked how he determined that his COPPS efforts in a local park were successful, an officer simply mentioned that more families were using the park.

In most cases, however, assessments should be comprehensive and include measures such as before/after comparisons of crime and calls for service data, environmental crime prevention surveys, and neighborhood fear reduction surveys. The nature of the problem often dictates the method of assessment.

NEW APPROACHES FOR VIEWING AND ADDRESSING CRIME: CPTED AND SITUATIONAL CRIME PREVENTION

Crime prevention began in policing as a "lock it or lose it" concept, with police giving citizens advice about how to target-harden and protect their residences and businesses from potential offenders. But we now have a much better understanding of crime theories–and more sophisticated approaches to crime control—and make crime prevention the responsibility of all officers and community members. Two very important crime prevention concepts that are part and parcel to the problem-solving process are crime prevention through environmental design (CPTED) and situational crime prevention (SCP). We briefly define them both:

CPTED is defined as the "proper design and effective use of the environment that can lead to a reduction in the fear and incidence of crime, and an improvement in the quality of life" (Jeffrey, 1971:117). At its core are three principles that support problem-solving approaches to crime:

1. ***Natural access control.*** Natural access control includes the existence of doors, shrubs, fences, and gates to deny admission to a crime target and to create a perception among offenders that there is a risk in selecting the target.
2. ***Natural surveillance.*** Natural surveillance includes the proper placement of windows, lighting, and landscaping to increase the ability of those who care to observe intruders as well as regular users, allowing them to challenge inappropriate behavior or report it to the police or the property owner.
3. ***Territorial reinforcement.*** Using such elements as sidewalks, landscaping, and porches helps distinguish between public and private areas and helps users exhibit signs of "ownership" that send "hands off" messages to would-be offenders.

Situational crime prevention (SCP) is a targeted means of reducing crime, providing a framework for strategies to prevent crime by making settings less conducive to unwanted or illegal activities; it focuses on the environment rather than on the offender, while making criminal activity less attractive to offenders. SCP is a problem oriented approach that examines the roots of a problem and identifies a unique solution to the problem. SCP relies on the rational choice theory of crime, which asserts that criminals choose to commit crimes based on the costs and benefits involved with the crime. For example, a potential offender will commit a high-risk crime only if the rewards of the crime outweigh the risks (Clarke, 1997).

Crime prevention goals can be divided into five primary objectives, each of which is designed to dissuade the criminal by making the crime too hard to commit, too risky, or too small in terms of rewards to be worth the criminal's time and effort (Clarke, 1997):

1. ***Increasing the effort needed to commit the crime.*** Crimes typically happen because they are easy to commit. Casual criminals are eliminated by increasing the effort needed to commit a crime, by doing the following:
   Target hardening: installing physical barriers (such as locks, bolts, protective screens, and mechanical containment and antifraud devices to impede an offender's ability to penetrate a potential target).
   Controlling access: installing barriers and designing walkways, paths, and roads so that unwanted users are prevented from entering vulnerable areas.
   Deflecting offenders: discouraging crime by giving people alternate, legal venues for their activities (such as separating fans of rival teams after athletic events).
   Controlling facilitators: facilitators are accessories who aid in the commission of crimes. Controlling them is achieved by universal measures (such as firearm permit regulations) and specific measures (metal detectors in community centers).
2. ***Increasing the risks associated with the crime.*** Following are examples for increasing the risks associated with a crime, to convince potential offenders they will be caught:
   Entry and exit screening: screening methods might include guest sign-ins or a required display of identification.
   Formal surveillance: using security personnel and hardware (such as CCTV and burglar alarms) is a deterrent to unwanted activities.
   Informal surveillance: the presence of building attendants, concierges, maintenance workers, and attendants increases site surveillance and crime reporting.
   Natural surveillance: the surveillance provided by people as they go about their daily activities makes potential offenders feel exposed and vulnerable.

3. ***Reducing the rewards.*** Reducing the rewards from crime makes offending not worthwhile to offenders, by such means as:
   Target removal: eliminating crime purposes from public areas. Examples include a no-cash policy and keeping valuable property in a secure area overnight.
   Identifying property: using indelible marks, establishing ownership, and preventing individuals from reselling the property.
   Removing inducements: removing temptations in advance, such as razing dilapidated houses or fixing broken windows and light fixtures.
4. ***Reducing the provocations.*** The environment may provoke crime and violence; studies show that certain lighting improves people's mood and morale in the workplace.
5. ***Removing the excuses.*** Many offenders say, "I didn't know any better," so this strategy involves informing them of the law, such as posting an enforceable "no trespassing" sign.

IMPLEMENTATION AND LEADERSHIP ISSUES

To make COPPS a part of an organization's philosophy and practice requires an entire organizational transformation that cannot be accomplished overnight. Gaining the support of the agency's supervisors and managers represents a major step in implementing COPPS. Next, we discuss some of the needs and problems of accomplishing this task.

The Key to Success: First-Line Supervisors

The successful implementation of COPPS requires the support of the first-line supervisor. This can be a daunting task, however, and the sergeant is arguably the most important ranking individual within the police organization in terms of whether or not COPPS will succeed or fail. The link between street officers and the organization is the sergeant; however, there is some cause for supervisors' reluctance to change. As Goldstein (1990:29) noted:

> Changing the operating philosophy of rank-and-file officers is easier than altering a first-line supervisor's perspective of his or her job, because the work of a sergeant is greatly simplified by the traditional form of policing. The more routinized the work, the easier it is for the sergeant to check. The more emphasis placed on rank and the symbols of position, the easier it is for the sergeant to rely on authority—rather than intellect and personal skills—to carry out their duties. [S]ergeants are usually appalled by descriptions of the freedom and independence suggested in problem oriented policing for rank-and-file officers. The concept can be very threatening to them. This . . . can create an enormous block to implementation.

Supervisors often cannot overcome the idea that giving officers the opportunity to be creative and take risks does not diminish their own role or authority.

Supervising in a COPPS environment means a change from being a "controller," primarily concerned with rules, to being a "facilitator" and "coach" for officers involved in problem solving. Supervisors must learn to encourage innovation and risk taking among their officers and be well skilled in problem solving, especially in the analysis of problems and evaluation of efforts. Conducting a workload analysis (discussed briefly in Chapter 12) and finding the time for officers to problem solve and engage with the community (discussed later) are important aspects of supervision.

The St. Petersburg, Florida, police department identified the characteristics of the "ideal" sergeant under the COPPS philosophy (Quire, 1998:8):

Availability	Leadership
Flexibility	Champion
Innovative	Trustworthy

Widely experienced
Facilitator
Open-minded
Sense of humor
Supportive
Buffer
Good speaker
Respected
Risk taker
Coach
Dependable

The Police Executive Research Forum (1990:4) also provided a list of characteristics for a good COPPS supervisor:

1. Allows officers the freedom to experiment with new approaches.
2. Insists on good, accurate analyses of problems.
3. Grants flexibility in work schedules when requests are appropriate.
4. Allows officers to make most contacts directly and paves the way when they are having trouble getting cooperation.
5. Protects officers from pressures within the department to revert to traditional methods.
6. Runs interference for officers to secure resources and protects them from criticism.
7. Knows what problems officers are working on and whether the problems are real.
8. Knows officers' beats and important citizens in them, and expects subordinates to know them even better.
9. Coaches officers through the S.A.R.A. process, giving advice and helping to manage their time.
10. Monitors officers' progress and, as necessary, prods them along or slows them down.
11. Supports officers, even if their strategies fail, as long as something useful is learned in the process—and the process was well thought through.
12. Manages problem-solving efforts over a long period of time; does not allow efforts to end just because they get sidetracked by competing demands for time and attention.
13. Gives credit to officers and lets others know about their good work.
14. Allows officers to talk with visitors or at conferences about their work.
15. Identifies new resources and shares them with officers.
16. Stresses cooperation, coordination, and communication within and outside the unit.
17. Coordinates efforts across shifts and beats and with outside units and agencies.
18. Realizes that this style of policing cannot simply be ordered; officers and detectives must come to believe in it.

COPPS supervisors should also understand that not all patrol officers or detectives will like this kind of work or be good at it. Supervisors must also realize that they need to avoid isolating the problem-solving function from the rest of the department. This could create the illusion that the problem-solving unit is composed of "privileged prima donnas" who receive benefits that other officers do not. Also, supervisors should not allow the COPPS initiative to become a mere public-relations campaign; the emphasis is always on results (Police Executive Research Forum, 1990).

Executives and Managers

COPPS requires changing the philosophy of leadership and management throughout the entire organization. First, the agency's executive leadership, with input from managers and supervisors, should develop a new *vision/values/mission statement.* All *policies and procedures* should be reviewed to ensure they conform to the department's COPPS objectives. The organization should also invest in

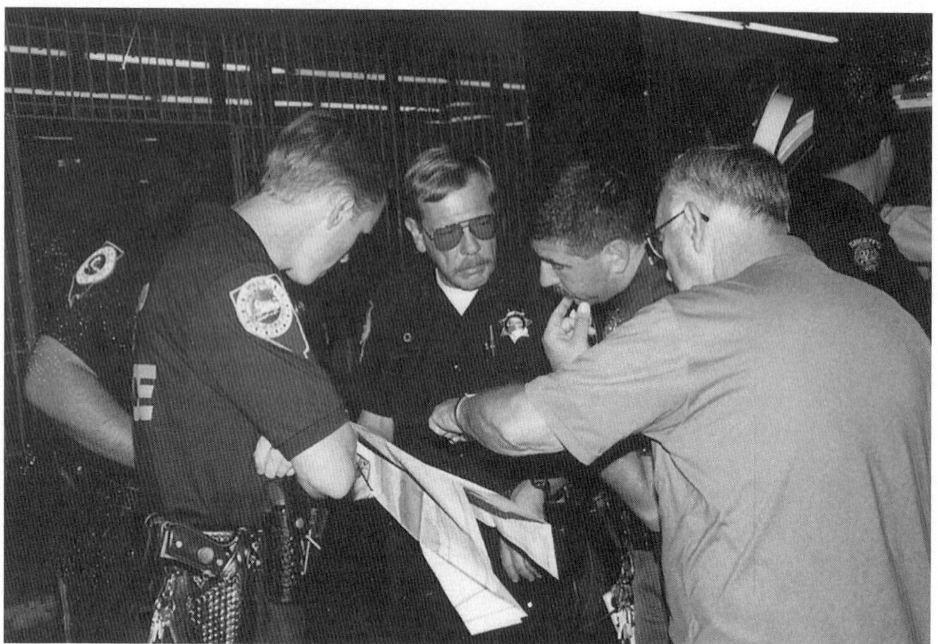

Interagency cooperation is essential for solving community problems.
Courtesy Washoe County, Nevada, Sheriff's Office Photo Unit.

information systems that will assist officers in identifying patterns of crime and support the problem-solving process. Progressive leaders will need to prepare for this millennium by engaging in *long-term strategic planning* and continuous *evaluation processes.*

Regarding managers, Robinette (1993) asserted that the traditional police middle manager (as well as the first-line supervisor) is largely unprepared by training and experience for the requirements of the COPPS strategy. Indeed, few street officers see their managers as sources of guidance and direction, but rather as authority figures to be satisfied by numbers of arrests and citations, the manner in which reports are completed, and so on. Normandeau and Leighton (1990:49) explained what must be done:

> Like most large, public service agencies, the requirements for innovation in policing include: changing the formal corporate values as well as the subculture of "front-line" policing; having an inspired chief executive who is committed to the new approach; having a motivated and experienced level of middle management which can implement the new approach in operational terms; recognizing innovations that come from the street level of policing; and obtaining support for the new approach and the risks that it runs from the police governing authorities and from the local community.

In many instances, the ultimate challenge to a police organization is to change its hierarchical, paramilitary structure. Managers and executives working within a flattened, COPPS-oriented organization often require new skills to ensure the successful adaptation and functioning of the police organization (Province of British Columbia, 1993:56). Exhibit 4-1 is an example of an attempt by one agency—the Seattle, Washington, Police Department—to support leadership in its transition to COPPS.

Valuing the Line Officer

The shift to COPPS centers on those singular individuals who comprise the "backbone" of policing—the patrol officers. The most powerful resources an organization possesses are thinking, creative, and

EXHIBIT 4-1 Ambitious in Seattle: Leadership Conferencing and Tool Kits

The Seattle, Washington, Police Department (SPD), in collaboration with the Police Executive Research Forum, has offered a three-day conference entitled "Leadership Sessions to Support Problem Oriented Policing." The purpose of the conference is to "provide a forum for inspiration, motivation, guidance, and practical tools to leaders who are committed to supporting problem solving in their agencies." Invitees include police supervisors, managers, and researchers. Topics include ethical challenges for leaders, politics inside and outside the organization, examining the organization from top to bottom to see how every system and structure supported problem oriented policing, and leadership.

Included is a three-day course entitled "Leadership Skills" for field training officers, supervisors, and managers; it includes coaching, feedback, facilitation, leadership, and cultural competency. Also, a "Training of Trainers" for police and community academies was developed to assist community and police instructors to incorporate the mission and values of the organization into every phase of academy training. The course also includes adult learning theory, gender inclusiveness, and facilitation skills.

Source: Norm Stamper, "A Training Menu to Support Problem Oriented Policing" (Seattle, WA: Seattle Police Department, 1997).

innovative police officers who, when supported by information, the community, training (in problem identification, analysis, and response), and internal support systems that reward and motivate them, are capable of providing long-term solutions to problems.

A major departure of COPPS from the conventional style of policing lies with the view that the line officer is given much more discretion and decision-making ability and is trusted with a much broader array of responsibilities. The necessary shift to a COPPS perspective centers on supervisors, who should encourage officers to take the initiative in identifying and responding to beat problems. This recognizes the potential of college-educated officers "who have been smothered in the atmosphere of traditional policing" (Goldstein, 1987:17). It also gives officers a new sense of identity and self-respect; they are more challenged and have opportunities to follow through on individual cases and analyze and solve problems, which will give them greater job satisfaction. Using patrol officers in this manner also allows the agency to provide sufficient challenges not only for the better educated officers, but also for those officers who remain unpromoted throughout their careers. We ought to be recruiting as police officers people who can "serve as mediators, as dispensers of information, and as community organizers" (Goldstein, 1987:21).

COPPS appeals to the reasons why most officers chose policing as a profession. When asked why they originally wanted to join police forces, police officers consistently say they joined in order to help people (Sparrow, 1988). By emphasizing work that addresses people's concerns, and giving officers the discretion to develop solutions, COPPS helps make police work more rewarding.

Another Management and Supervisory Dilemma: Gaining Time for Officers to Solve Problems

One of the debates often heard with respect to COPPS is whether officers have enough time to engage in problem-solving activities. On the one hand, officers complain that they are going from call to call and have little time for anything else. On the other hand, police managers and supervisors might contend that there is plenty of time for problem solving because calls account for only 50 to 60 percent of an officer's time. The supervisor would seem to be caught in the middle of this debate and is certainly in a key position to determine whether or not adequate time is indeed available to the patrol officers and, if not, that it be made so.

Obviously, citizens' calls for service are important and cannot be ignored. But the aim should be to handle these calls in an efficient and expedient manner. There are four methods for overcoming the problem of finding time for problem solving while still handling calls effectively:

1. ***Allow units to perform problem-solving assignments as self-initiated activities.*** Under this approach, a unit would contact the dispatcher and go out of service for a problem-solving assignment. The unit would be interrupted only for an emergency call in its area of responsibility. Otherwise, the dispatcher would hold nonemergency calls until the unit becomes available, or send a unit from an adjacent area after holding the call for a predetermined amount of time.
2. ***Schedule one or two units to devote a predetermined part of their shift to problem solving.*** As an example, a supervisor could designate one or two units each day to devote the first half of their shift or even just one hour to problem solving. Their calls would be handled by other units so that they have an uninterrupted block of time for problems. Of course, this approach means that the other units will be busier. The tradeoff is that problem solving gets done and the supervisor can rotate the units designated for these activities.
3. ***Take more reports over the telephone.*** The information in nonemergency incidents is recorded on a department report form and entered in the department's information system as an incident or crime. The average telephone report taker can process four times as many report calls per hour compared to a field unit.
4. ***Review the department policy on "assist" units.*** In some departments, several units show up at the scene of a call even though they are not needed. This problem is particularly acute with alarm calls. A department should undergo a detailed study on the types of calls for which assist units are actually appearing, with the aim of reducing the number of assists. In addition, officers should be discouraged from assisting other units unless it is necessary.

As a more general approach, a department should review its patrol plan to determine whether units are fielded in proportion to workload. Time between calls is a function not just of the number of incoming calls, but also of the number of units in the field. More units result in more time between calls.

As noted in Chapter 12, delaying response time to calls for service can also provide more time for officers. Response time research has determined that rapid responses are not needed for most calls. Slower police responses to nonemergency calls have been found satisfactory to citizens if dispatchers tell citizens an officer might not arrive at their home right away, and nonsworn employees can handle noncrime incidents (Eck and Spelman, 1989). Figure 4-3 provides a 15-step exercise that may help supervisors capture more time for officers to engage in problem solving (Vaughn, n.d.).

Other Important Considerations

In addition to leadership, organizational culture, field operations, and external relations are also important for the successful implementation of COPPS (Glensor and Peak, 1996). We briefly examine those three elements next.

1. Assemble a group of patrol officers and emergency communications center personnel representing each shift.
2. Have each of them write down three to five locations where the police respond repeatedly to deal with the same general problem and people.
3. Determine that average number of responses to those locations per month and approximately how long the problem has existed.
4. Determine the average number of officers who respond each time to those incidents.
5. Determine the average length of time involved in handling the incidents.
6. Using the information from points 3, 4, and 5, determine the total number of staff hours devoted to each of these problem locations. Do this for the week, month, and year.
7. Identify all the key players who either participate in or are affected by the problem—all direct and indirect participants and groups such as the complaining parties, victims, witnesses, property owners and managers, bystanders, and so forth.
8. Through roundtable discussion, decide what it is about the particular location that allows, or encourages, the problem to exist and continue.
9. Develop a list of things that have been done in the past to deal with the problem, and a candid assessment of why each has not worked.
10. In a free-flowing brainstorming session, develop as many traditional and nontraditional solutions to the problem as possible. Include alternative sources such as other government and private agencies that could be involved in the solution. Encourage creative thinking and risk taking.
11. After you have completed the brainstorming session, consider which of those solutions are (a) illegal, (b) immoral, (c) impractial, (d) unrealistic, or (e) unaffordable.
12. Eliminate all those that fall in categories (a) and (b).
13. For those that fall in categories (c), (d), and (e,) figure out if those reason derive from thinking in conventional terms like "We've never done it this way," "It won't work," "It can't be done." If you are satisfied that those solutions truly are impractical, unrealistic, or unaffordable, then eliminate them, too. If there is a glimmer of hope that some may have merit with just a little different thinking or approach, then leave them.
14. For each remaining possible solution, list what would have to be done and who would have to be involved to make it happen. Which of those solutions and actions could be implemented relatively soon and with a minimum of difficulty?
15. If the solution were successful, consider the productive things officers could do with the time that would be recaptured from not having to deal with the problem anymore.

FIGURE 4-3 15-Step Exercise to Recapture Officers' Time
Source: Jerald R. Vaughn, *Community-Oriented Policing: You Can Make it Happen* (Clearwater, FL: National Law Enforcement Leadership Institute, n.d.), pp. 6–7. Used with permission.

ORGANIZATIONAL CULTURE Human resources is the "heart and soul" of organizational culture. For employees, it answers the question, "What's in it for me?" Any major change in an organization requires that a review of all human resources is conducted. Community engagement and problem solving require new skills, knowledge, and abilities for everyone in the organization. Therefore, areas such as *recruiting, selection, training, performance evaluations, promotions, honors and awards,* and *discipline* should be reviewed to ensure they promote and support the organization's transition to COPPS. Agencies must also work closely with the various *labor organizations,* which will be concerned with any proposed changes in shifts, beats, criteria for selection, promotion, and discipline. It is wise to include labor representatives in the planning and implementation process from the beginning.

FIELD OPERATION The primary concern with field operations is to structure the delivery of patrol services so as to assist officers in dealing with the root causes of persistent community problems.

The first issue raised is whether a *specialist vs. generalist* approach will be used. It is not uncommon, especially in larger police agencies, to begin COPPS implementation with an experimental district composed of a team of specially trained officers. The experience of many agencies, however, suggests that department-wide implementation should occur as quickly as possible. This will eliminate the common criticism that COPPS officers do not do "real police work" and receive special privileges. If allowed to fester, this attitude can quickly impair any implementation efforts. The need for available time presents a supervisory challenge that begins with *managing calls for service,* which requires comprehensive workload analysis, call prioritization, alternative call handling, and differential response methods discussed in Chapter 12. A *decentralized approach* to field operations involves assigning officers for a minimum of one year to a beat and shift to learn more about a neighborhood's problems.

EXTERNAL RELATIONS Collaborative responses to neighborhood crime and disorder are essential to the success of COPPS. This requires new relationships and the sharing of information and resources among the police and community, local governmental agencies, service providers, and businesses. It requires that agencies educate and inform their external partners about police resources and neighborhood problems using surveys, newsletters, community meetings, and public service announcements. The *media* also provide an excellent resource for police to educate the community. Press releases about collaborative problem-solving efforts should be sent to the media and news conferences held to discuss major crime reduction efforts.

An officer works with citizens to improve the overall safety of a shopping mall.
Courtesy Community Policing Consortium.

COMPSTAT

Utilizing Information Technology to Manage Crime

A relatively new crime management tool used in the problem-solving process is known as **CompStat**, which is a "strategic control system" designed for the collection and feedback of information on crime and related quality of life issues. This "emerging police managerial paradigm" is said to be "revolutionizing law enforcement management and practice" (DeLorenzi, Shane, and Amendola, 2006), and some have called it "perhaps the single most important organizational/administrative innovation in policing during the latter half of the 20th century." Furthermore, CompStat has been summarized as follows: "Collect, analyze, and map crime data and other essential police performance measures on a regular basis, and hold police managers accountable for their performance as measured by these data" (DeLorenzi, Shane, and Amendola, 2006).

Since the CompStat process was introduced by the New York City Police Department in 1994, it has been widely adopted: a national survey found that 58 percent of large agencies (those with 100 or more sworn officers) had either adopted or were planning to implement a CompStat-like program. CompStat is partly responsible for contributing to significant improvements in the way many organizations control crime and conduct daily business. The core management theories of CompStat, "directing and controlling," have been demonstrated to be effective means for controlling crime. But the CompStat process also has an inherent opportunity for developing leaders, instilling in people a sense of willingness to accomplish the goals of the organization using initiative and innovation (DeLorenzi, Shane, and Amendola, 2006). (This aspect of CompStat is discussed in Chapter 6, in the leadership development section.)

It is obviously imperative that police supervisors and managers understand the basics of this approach–especially given that, unfortunately, today it seems that CompStat is often oversimplified. Many believe that CompStat refers to aggressive or data-driven policing, where police commanders are frequently grilled about crimes in their areas of responsibility—and they are even castigated, transferred, or demoted after a lifetime of service if they failed to do something about it. According to police scholar Phyllis McDonald, this perception of CompStat "does a disservice to its management principles and its potential for other jurisdictions" (McDonald, 2002).

The key elements of CompStat are as follows:

- Specific objectives
- Accurate and timely intelligence
- Effective tactics
- Rapid deployment of personnel and resources
- Relentless follow-up and assessment (Grant and Terry, 2005)

CompStat pushes all precincts to generate weekly crime activity reports so that they can be held accountable for the achievement of several objectives. Crime data are readily available, offering up-to-date information that is then compared at citywide, patrol, and precinct levels. The role of commanders has changed under CompStat: they stop simply responding to crime, and begin proactively thinking about ways to deal with it in terms of suppression, intervention, and prevention. Commanders must explain what tactics they have employed to address crime patterns, what resources they have and need, and with whom they have collaborated. Brainstorming problem-solving sessions ensue about proactively responding to the crime problems, and suggestions for strategies are made at subsequent meetings, with relentless follow-up by top brass to further ensure accountability (Grant and Terry, 2005).

Over time, CompStat has evolved to include other data: census demographics, arrest and summons activity, average response time, domestic violence incidents, unfounded radio runs, personnel absences, and even citizen complaints and charges of officer misconduct. Many scholars and practitioners believe that CompStat has played a prominent role in the significant crime reductions seen across the nation.

Certainly the impact CompStat has had on police management practices cannot be denied, while another benefit has been the significant increase in job satisfaction by those who feel empowered by the problem-solving process (discussed above) (Grant and Terry, 2005).

Figure 4-4 summarizes CompStat's crime-reduction principles and how each successive principle flows from the preceding one.

Using CompStat Data: An Example

Next we provide some fundamentals about how to *present, compare, and map* data. Although some of this information may well be beyond the training of some readers—e.g., the section that discusses descriptive statistics—we feel it is important to at least present the *process,* as well as an overview of what is available with CompStat analyses. Here are the three steps:

1. The first step involves descriptive statistics, or presenting the data so that everyone, from commanders down to patrol officers, can readily understand the relevant information. Data may be presented and described in a number of ways: aggregate increase or decrease; simple percentages (including increase or decrease over previous time frames); ratio and rates; incidents compared to population; mean, median, and mode; pie charts, line charts, bar charts, histograms; and so on. Figure 4-5 shows these means by which data may be presented.
2. The second step in presenting data, comparing, is designed to reveal the relationship between two or more crimes. These statistics are called *measures of association*, and they enable crime analysts to quantify the strength and direction of a relationship—to uncover the connections between crimes, and to make predictions. For example, suppose a crime analyst was interested in seeing if a relationship existed between CFS pertaining to drug sales and shootings. After gathering the appropriate data, by calculating the measure of association (such as a Pearson's r), the analyst can determine the strength of the relationship and its direction. Suppose a strong, positive relationship was found between these two variables (i.e., the two crimes of drug sales and shootings); one might infer that the two crimes were closely related and, as one of the crimes increased, so would the other. A prediction could then be made that the more CFS for drug sales, the higher the number of shootings. The analyst would do well to remember, however, that this strong positive relationship does not automatically prove such a connection exists, but this association would serve as an important clue about causation. *Comparing* the data allows analysts and commanders to consider adjusting or compensating for shifts in trends or patterns. Appropriate charts should display the information for each beat, zone, or precinct, as well as city- or county-wide area, including the aggregate difference and percentage change in reported incidents (see Figure 4-6). The data should also be depicted in temporal (time) distribution, so that commanders can see when crimes occur.
3. The final step, *mapping data* (called *spatial analysis*), can detect where criminals travel. Analysts can create overlays of CFS versus arrests effected, unsolved burglaries with known burglars' residences, or CFS with abandoned buildings. Analysis can create specialty maps, such as locating sex offenders' residences, recovered guns, recovered stolen autos, and thefts of auto parts. Most important, they can display data to show hot spots, or areas of concentrated crime (discussed more fully next); then the police can develop appropriate intervention strategies (Shane, 2004:17–18).

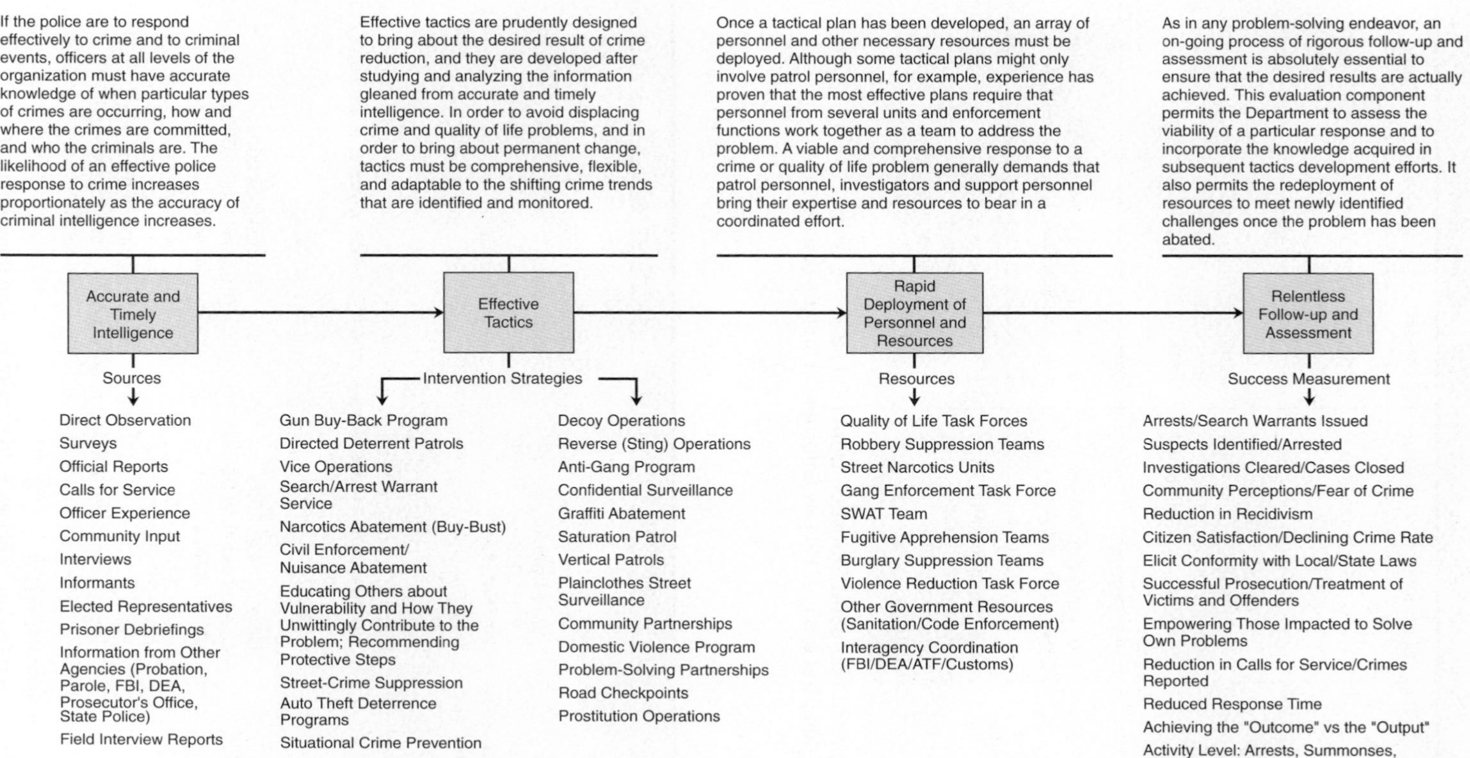

COMPSTAT Process: Crime Control Strategy (Courtesy of the FBI LEB, April 2004)
Crime Reduction Principles
If the police are to respond effectively to crime and to criminal events, officers at all levels of the organization must have accurate knowledge of when particular types of crimes are occurring, how and where the crimes are committed, and who the criminals are. The likelihood of an effective police response to crime increases proportionately as the accuracy of criminal intelligence increases.
Effective tactics are prudently designed to bring about the desired result of crime reduction, and they are developed after studying and analyzing the information gleaned from accurate and timely intelligence. In order to avoid displacing crime and quality of life problems, and in order to bring about permanent change, tactics must be comprehensive, flexible, and adaptable to the shifting crime trends that are identified and monitored.
Once a tactical plan has been developed, an array of personnel and other necessary resources must be deployed. Although some tactical plans might only involve patrol personnel, for example, experience has proven that the most effective plans require that personnel from several units and enforcement functions work together as a team to address the problem. A viable and comprehensive response to a crime or quality of life problem generally demands that patrol personnel, investigators and support personnel bring their expertise and resources to bear in a coordinated effort.
As in any problem-solving endeavor, an on-going process of rigorous follow-up and assessment is absolutely essential to ensure that the desired results are actually achieved. This evaluation component permits the Department to assess the viability of a particular response and to incorporate the knowledge acquired in subsequent tactics development efforts. It also permits the redeployment of resources to meet newly identified challenges once the problem has been abated.
Accurate and Timely Intelligence
Effective Tactics
Rapid Deployment of Personnel and Resources
Relentless Follow-up and Assessment
Sources
Direct Observation
Surveys
Official Reports
Calls for Service
Officer Experience
Community Input
Interviews
Informants
Elected Representatives
Prisoner Debriefings
Information from Other Agencies (Probation, Parole, FBI, DEA, Prosecutor's Office, State Police)
Field Interview Reports
Intervention Strategies
Gun Buy-Back Program
Directed Deterrent Patrols
Vice Operations
Search/Arrest Warrant Service
Narcotics Abatement (Buy-Bust)
Civil Enforcement/ Nuisance Abatement
Educating Others about Vulnerability and How They Unwittingly Contribute to the Problem; Recommending Protective Steps
Street-Crime Suppression
Auto Theft Deterrence Programs
Situational Crime Prevention
Decoy Operations
Reverse (Sting) Operations
Anti-Gang Program
Confidential Surveillance
Graffiti Abatement
Saturation Patrol
Vertical Patrols
Plainclothes Street Surveillance
Community Partnerships
Domestic Violence Program
Problem-Solving Partnerships
Road Checkpoints
Prostitution Operations
Resources
Quality of Life Task Forces
Robbery Suppression Teams
Street Narcotics Units
Gang Enforcement Task Force
SWAT Team
Fugitive Apprehension Teams
Burglary Suppression Teams
Violence Reduction Task Force
Other Government Resources (Sanitation/Code Enforcement)
Interagency Coordination (FBI/DEA/ATF/Customs)
Success Measurement
Arrests/Search Warrants Issued
Suspects Identified/Arrested
Investigations Cleared/Cases Closed
Community Perceptions/Fear of Crime
Reduction in Recidivism
Citizen Satisfaction/Declining Crime Rate
Elicit Conformity with Local/State Laws
Successful Prosecution/Treatment of Victims and Offenders
Empowering Those Impacted to Solve Own Problems
Reduction in Calls for Service/Crimes Reported
Reduced Response Time
Achieving the "Outcome" vs the "Output"
Activity Level: Arrests, Summonses, Field Interviews

FIGURE 4-4 CompStat Process: Crime Control Strategy
Source: Jon M. Shane, "CompStat Design, "FBI Law Enforcement Bulletin (May 2004): 12–21.

Appropriate Statistics (Courtesy of FBI LEB, May 2004)					
Descriptive analysis	Maximum	Minimum	Mean	Median	Mode
	Violent and nonviolent crime summary		Aggregate increase or decrease		Standard deviation
Frequency distribution	Percentage increase or decrease	Proportion across categories	Ratio and rates Incidents to population Performance to police officers		
Organization and presentation of data	Pie charts (for percentage of total)		Bar charts (for aggregate data or rate; e.g., incidents per 100,000 people)		
	Line charts (frequency polygon); add trend lines to establish direction		Histograms with a normal curve (e.g., response time analysis)		Crosstab charts

FIGURE 4-5 Appropriate CompStat Statistics, from FBI LEB
Source: Jon M. Shane, "CompStat Design, "FBI Law Enforcement Bulletin (May 2004): 14.

Data Comparison (Courtesy of FBI LEB, May 2004)					
				Diff.	% +/-
Day to day	One chart for each week of the Compstat period				
Week to week	Current week	vs.	Previous week	+5	+3%
Month to month	March 2003	vs.	April 2003	-18	-27%
Quarter to quarter	Jan, Feb, Mar	vs.	Apr, May, Jun	+32	+44%
Half year to half year	1st 6 months	vs.	2nd 6 months	-63	-40%
Year to year	2002	vs.	2003	-27	-2%
Year to date	January 1, 2003 to present date			Aggregate	
Last 12 months	March 15, 2002 to March 14, 2003			Aggregate	
Custom date	Any time period (days, weeks, months, quarters, years, decades)				

Comparisons for each period against the prior period

Week	Current week 2003	vs.	Same week 2002
Month	Current month 2003	vs.	Same month 2002
Quarter	Jan, Feb, Mar 2003	vs.	Jan, Feb, Mar 2002
Half year	1st 6 months 2003	vs.	1st 6 months 2002
Year	Jan 1, 2003 to present	vs.	Jan 1, 2002 to present
12 months	Jan 18, 2002 to Jan 17, 2003	vs.	Jan 18, 2001 to Jan 17, 2002
Custom	Any custom date period compared with the prior date period		

FIGURE 4-6 Data Comparison Chart
Source: Jon M. Shane, "CompStat Design, "FBI Law Enforcement Bulletin (May 2004): 16.

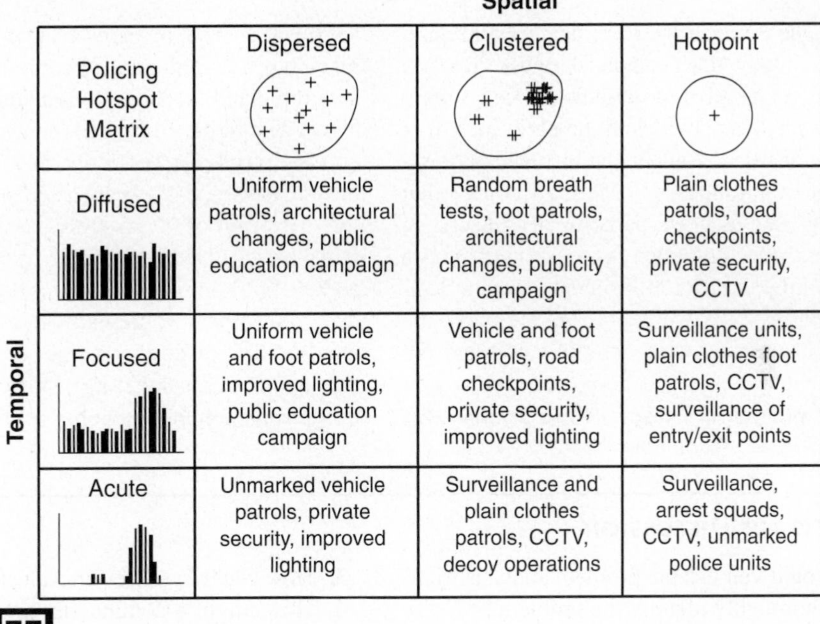

Spatial

Policing Hotspot Matrix	Dispersed	Clustered	Hotpoint
Diffused	Uniform vehicle patrols, architectural changes, public education campaign	Random breath tests, foot patrols, architectural changes, publicity campaign	Plain clothes patrols, road checkpoints, private security, CCTV
Focused	Uniform vehicle and foot patrols, improved lighting, public education campaign	Vehicle and foot patrols, road checkpoints, private security, improved lighting	Surveillance units, plain clothes foot patrols, CCTV, surveillance of entry/exit points
Acute	Unmarked vehicle patrols, private security, improved lighting	Surveillance and plain clothes patrols, CCTV, decoy operations	Surveillance, arrest squads, CCTV, unmarked police units

Temporal

FIGURE 4-7 Temporal/Spatial Intervention Matrix
Source: Jon M. Shane, "CompStat Design, "FBI Law Enforcement Bulletin (May 2004): 18.

Figure 4-7 is a matrix showing the kinds of intervention strategies that might be used to address crime that is experiencing different temporal (time) and spatial (space) occurrences. For example, in the lower-left of the matrix, it is shown that, where crimes that are being committed and are heavily concentrated in terms of time of day/week and at a particular hot spot, the police would want to use surveillance, arrest squads, CCTV, and unmarked police cars.

As noted earlier, Chapter 6 includes some CompStat opportunities—and caveats—as it applies to leadership development.

CASE STUDIES

Following are two case studies that will provide the reader with opportunities to apply S.A.R.A. and to see how COPPS differs from the traditional reactive policing approach.

Case Study #1

Problems Plague the Park

Paxton Park holds tremendous significance for the predominately older African American and Hispanic residents of the city's Hillsborough District. Referred to as "instant park," it was literally constructed within a day by residents during the late 1960s. Since then, it has deteriorated and become a haven for drug dealers and gang members. Today, few residents dare use the park. Residents frequently report to the police all manner of suspicious activities in the park, including sightings of persons under the influence harassing children and houses bordering the park that are being used as crash pads for drug users. In most instances, the police response is to send a police unit by the park to disperse the drug dealers. Few arrests are ever made. On occasion, the countywide consolidated narcotics unit and the department's special weapons and tactics unit initiate a program to make massive arrests. This approach usually involves a large number of arrests, but it also generates complaints of excessive force and racism by offenders and residents alike. The department has also initiated a narcotics tip line for residents, but few calls have been made since it was installed six months ago. Sgt. Brewer was recently assigned to the Hillsborough District. She has recently attended a COPPS training seminar and believes that the drug and other problems at the park could be handled in a different manner than in the past. She calls a team meeting to discuss how they might approach the problem.

Questions for Discussion

1. How would you use the problem analysis triangle to thoroughly identify the problem?
2. What responses might be considered by the team (be sure to include all organizations that could help)?
3. How could Sgt. Brewer evaluate their successes?
4. How might a commander under the CompStat model approach this problem with the precinct's managers and supervisors? What kinds of information would be requested?

Case Study #2

The Horrendous Highway Hangout

The Burger Barn is the most popular fast-food restaurant in town and it is open 24 hours a day. It is located in the middle sector of town where two highways intersect; this is a busy four-lane commercial area that is adjacent to a low-income residential area consisting of mobile homes, apartment complexes, and small single-family homes. Sgt. Maas has noticed a tremendous increase in calls for service at the location and on checking computer-aided dispatch records, discovers that CFS to the Burger Barn had indeed increased to nearly 90 per month. Further analysis reveals that the majority of CFS occur during the late night/early morning hours, peaking between 1:00 A.M. and 3:00 A.M. The CFS mostly involve large crowds of juveniles, fights, noise disturbances, shots fired, and traffic congestion and accidents. A few police officers have even been injured while attempting to break up fights. The restaurant's manager has attempted to limit access to the building during the peak hours, allowing only five juveniles inside at any one time. This approach has resulted in long lines forming outside and has increased the number of disturbances and fights. Employees are frequently harassed by angry customers waiting for service in the building. Many of the juveniles are cruising and driving carelessly, paying little attention to the traffic signals and contributing significantly to congestion, which is creating a backup on the adjoining highway, generating a letter of complaint from the state highway patrol to the police chief.

Questions for Discussion

1. How would you thoroughly *analyze* the problem using the problem analysis triangle?
2. What *responses* may be considered (be sure to include all organizations that could help)?
3. How could Sgt. Maas *evaluate* their successes?

Summary

This chapter has examined community policing and problem solving from several perspectives: its philosophy and methods (including a problem solving model); crime prevention (including the environment and ways of making crime less attractive); the implementation of COPPS and support needed from police supervisors and managers; and CompStat, the new management tool for managing crime.

It has become clear to this nation's nearly 17,000 police agencies that they cannot single-handedly contain the crime and neighborhood disorder problems that afflict society, create fear, and drain our federal, state, and local resources. These officers have discovered that COPPS—with its emphasis on community engagement and problem solving—carries the best potential for success in resolving substantive and recurring community problems.

It was also made clear in this chapter that police supervisors and managers are key to making this strategy work. It was shown that if these leaders are not viewed as a major part of the implementation and maintenance of the COPPS strategy, and do not provide officers with the kind of prominent role and freedom they require to be able to analyze and respond to community problems, then this approach to crime and disorder will inevitably fail.

Items for Review

1. Describe COPPS in general, focusing on how it differs in philosophy and practice from the traditional, reactive policing model.
2. Explain the four-step S.A.R.A. problem-solving process.
3. Review the major tenets and approaches of the CPTED and situational crime prevention concepts.
4. Describe the important role of the first-line supervisors and managers in the implementation and ongoing maintenance of COPPS; include a list of at least 10 characteristics of a good problem-solving supervisor.
5. Explain how the street officer must be viewed by supervisors and managers in terms of being granted freedom and trust for problem-solving activities.
6. Delineate how police officers may obtain the time necessary for engaging in problem-solving activities.
7. Explain how CompStat functions, and provide an illustration of its workings.

References

California Department of Justice, Attorney General's Office. (1993). *Community oriented policing and problem solving: Definitions and principles*. Sacramento, CA: Author.

Clarke, R. V. (1997). *Situational crime prevention: Successful case studies* (2d ed.). Monsey, N.Y.: Criminal Justice Press.

Cohen, L. E., and Felson, M. (1979). Social change and crime rate trends: A routine activity approach. *American Sociological Review* 44 (August):588–608.

DeLorenzi, D., Shane, J. M., and Amendola, K. L. (2006). The CompStat process: Managing performance on the pathway to leadership. *The Police Chief*, http://www.Theiacp.org/foundation/Foundation.htm (Accessed October 22, 2007).

Eck, J., and Spelman, W. (1989). A problem-oriented approach to police service delivery. In Dennis Jay Kenney, ed., *Police and policing: Contemporary issues*. New York: Praeger, pp. 87–119.

Glensor, R. W., and Peak, K. J. (1996). Implementing change: Community oriented policing and problem solving. *FBI Law Enforcement Bulletin* 7:14–20.

Goldstein, H. (1990). *Problem-oriented policing*. New York: McGraw-Hill.

Goldstein, H. (1987, 12 June). Problem-oriented policing. Paper presented at the Conference on Policing: State of the Art III, National Institute of Justice, Phoenix, AZ.

Grant, H. J., and Terry, K. J. (2005). *Law enforcement in the 21st century.* Boston: Allyn & Bacon, pp. 329–330.

Jeffrey, C. R. (1971). *Crime prevention through environmental design*. Beverly Hills, CA: Sage.

McDonald, P. (2002). *Managing police operations: Implementing the New York crime control model—CompStat.* Belmont, CA: Wadsworth, p. 1. Also see Buerger, M. E. (2005). COMPSTAT: A strategic vision. *The Associate* (January-February):18–23.

Normandeau, A., and Leighton, B. (1990). *A vision of the future of policing in Canada: Police-challenge 2000, background document*. Ottawa: Solicitor General Canada, Police and Security Branch (October):49.

Peak, K. J., and Glensor, R. W. (2008). *Community policing and problem solving: Strategies and practices,* 5th ed. Upper Saddle River, NJ: Prentice Hall.

Police Executive Research Forum (1990). Supervising problem-solving. Washington, DC: Author, training outline.

Province of British Columbia, Ministry of Attorney General, Police Services Branch. (1993). *Community policing advisory committee report*. Victoria, British Columbia, Canada: Author, p. 56.

Quire, D. S. (1998). Officers select "ideal" supervisors. Washington, DC: Community Policing Consortium, *Community Policing Exchange* (March/April):8.

Robinette, H. M. (1993). Supervising tomorrow. *Virginia Police Chief* (Spring):10.

Shane, J. M. (2004). CompStat design. *FBI Law Enforcement Bulletin* (May):17–18.

Sparrow, M. K. (1988). Implementing community policing. National Institute of Justice. *Perspectives on Policing,* No. 9 (November):6.

Vaughn, J. R. (n.d.). *Community oriented policing: You can make it happen*. Clearwater, FL: National Law Enforcement Leadership Institute.

Witkin, G., and McGraw, D. (1993). Beyond "Just the facts, ma'am." *U.S. News and World Report* (2 August):28.

CHAPTER 5

Communication and Negotiation

Key Terms and Concepts

- Communication: process, barriers, types
- Conflict resolution
- Jargon
- Negotiation
- Organizational conflict
- Prenegotiation stage
- Radio codes
- Stereotyping

Learning Objectives

After reading this chapter, the student will:

- understand the communications process, including types of formal and informal communication
- know the major barriers to effective communication, including problems with electronic methods of communicating
- better understand the unique nature of police communications, specifically their jargon and codes
- know how police use negotiations to effectively communicate ideas and information in order to gain greater compliance to orders and directives
- understand the nature of organizational and group conflict
- be able to effectively mediate conflict when it occurs

The difference between the right word and the almost right word is the difference between lightning and lightning bug.

—Mark Twain

The right of every person "to be let alone" must be placed in the scales with the right of others to communicate.

—Chief Justice Warren Burger

INTRODUCTION

Communication is obviously very important in every segment of our society. As Mark Twain stated earlier, there can be a vast difference between using the "right word" and the "almost right word;" to that quote we might add another, by noted Italian-American linguist Mario Pei (1961:4-5), who wrote:

> Rightly or wrongly, most people consider language as an index of culture, breeding, upbringing, personality, sometimes even of intelligence, decency, and integrity. Under the circumstances, it is unwise, not to say harmful, to pay no heed to your language. Ignorance or improper use of language can easily interfere with your success and advancement. It can take money out of your pocket.

All of police work is coordinated and conducted through communication. Members of policing, regardless of rank, spend a significant portion of a workday communicating with citizens, other officers, or superiors. Essentially, police departments run on information and communications. It is also critical that officers learn communications skills in light of our discussion in Chapter 4 concerning the contemporary application of the community oriented policing and problem-solving (COPPS) concept; solving problems will place officers in environments where they are the linchpin for mobilizing communities, other organizations, and resources towards crime reduction and prevention efforts.

A companion process to communication is **negotiation**. A good supervisor must be skilled in negotiations. When we think of negotiations, we think of people attempting to work out a problem when there is appreciable disagreement. However, negotiation actually occurs in most communications (including collective bargaining in policing, which is discussed in detail in Chapter 11). A police chief can issue an order, but it will not necessarily be followed unless it is accepted and understood. Negotiation skills legitimize the order, while communications skills transmit it clearly to subordinates. Therefore, to some extent, negotiation is the art of gaining compliance or selling people on an idea. How to successfully negotiate conflicts is addressed in this chapter.

The chapter opens with a general look at the communication process, including barriers to effective communication. We then look at police communications specifically, with emphasis on their jargon and codes. Next, we examine the art of negotiating, including various approaches and tactics, and then turn to conflict—its nature, levels, and sources, and how to cope with it. The chapter concludes with two case studies.

THE ACT OF COMMUNICATING

A Large Part of the Workday

Communication is a complex process. Indeed, communications, formal or informal, written or verbal, serve to link people and activities. We use a variety of technologies to communicate, including telephones, fax machines, the Internet, and police computers and radios. Yet, people seldom give much thought to how they communicate and the content of their communications. When there are errors in communication, or when information is not communicated effectively, a greater probability exists that those receiving the information will not fully grasp the meaning of the communication, and mistakes can result. Proper communication essentially serves to make a group of workers into a team and provides a means to coordinate people and work.

Several studies have examined the amount of communications in the police department. Mayo (1983) found that police executives spent about 70 percent of their time communicating, with the overwhelming majority of their communication occurring in meetings. A substantial amount of communication occurs at all levels of the organization. Supervisors communicate with a variety of people at all levels of the department. More and Wegener (1996) reported that about 55 percent of supervisors' communications is with subordinates. Approximately 26 percent of their communications is with superiors in the department, while only 4 percent is with other supervisors. Only 15 percent of a supervisor's communications is with the public. They also examined the tasks performed by sergeants and found that 51 percent of the tasks involved some form of communication. Their statistics indicate that sergeants spend most of their time working with and supervising subordinates.

Another study of supervisors found that they spent about 80 percent of their time communicating. The various types of communication in which they engaged are as follows: 45 percent listening, 30 percent talking, 16 percent reading, and 9 percent writing (Von der Embse, 1987). It appears that about 39 percent of the time supervisors are communicating to others, and 61 percent of the time someone is communicating to the supervisor. Supervisors spend more time receiving information than providing it. This study indicates that police supervisors are extensively involved in the communications process, and that they communicate with an array of people.

The Communication Process

Communication has been defined as "the process by which the sender—a person, group, or organization—transmits some type of information (the message) to another person, group, or organization (the receiver)" (Greenberg and Baron, 1995, p: 330). Lussier (1999) expands this definition by noting that communications occur with the intent to (1) influence, (2) inform, or (3) express feelings or opinions. Thus, the act of communicating is a complicated transaction between two or more parties that occurs with the intention of having an impact. In reality, communicating is a complicated process wrought with pitfalls that can lead to mistakes or ineffective communications. Figure 5-1 provides a detailed schematic for communicating and shows how complicated communications really are.

The process begins with the communicator or sender wishing to communicate an idea or information to another person(s) or organization. The first step in the communication process is that the sender must *encode* the idea or information—translate it into a form such as writing, language, or nonverbal communication. The encoding process can be difficult, especially if the sender is attempting to communicate a set of complex ideas. Although people may have little difficulty conceptualizing complex ideas, they sometimes have trouble putting them into the proper words or language so that others can understand the full meaning of their ideas. In other instances, the communicator may have difficulty in communicating. That is, some people are restricted by a limited vocabulary or their understanding of language.

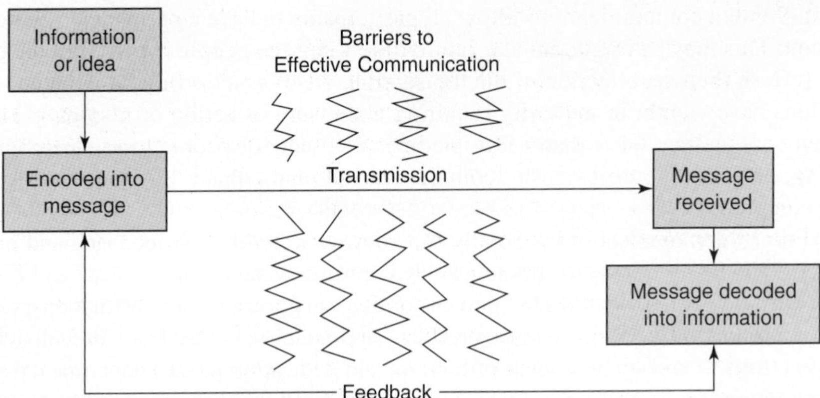

FIGURE 5-1 The Communications Process

Once a message has been encoded, the sender must select a communications *channel* through which a message is transmitted or sent to the recipients. The primary communications channels are formal and informal. Within these two channels, communications can be written, verbal, and nonverbal. *Formal communications* are the official transmission of information in the organization, and they generally follow the police department's chain of command or organizational chart. Formal communications generally are written in the form of letters, memoranda, or orders. *Informal communications* are usually oral and are used to convey a variety of official and unofficial information throughout the department. Formal and informal communication are discussed below.

When deciding on the channel to use, the communicator also selects a medium. *Medium* refers to the manner in which the message is sent. It may be written and sent in the form of a memorandum or policy, or it may be verbal at a meeting, on the telephone, or through a one-on-one conversation. It is important to select the proper medium when communicating. For example, if a lieutenant wants to discuss staffing problems with his or her sergeants, a face-to-face meeting would be more effective than a memorandum or a telephone call.

Once information is transmitted to a recipient, the recipient must *decode* the message, or conceptually translate the information into meaningful knowledge. When people receive new information, they typically give it meaning by comparing it with past experiences and knowledge, which can be either a help or a hindrance. The receiver may have difficulty internalizing its full implication or, in the worst case, may reject it entirely.

It is important that the receiver have the same conceptual impression of the information as that envisioned by the individual transmitting the message. If inconsistencies occur, then the desired information has not been fully internalized. One way of ensuring full internalization is *feedback:* the process whereby the sender initiates additional two-way communications to test the receiver's comprehension and understanding of the information communicated. Feedback serves to ensure that everyone received the correct information. The level of feedback should increase (1) as the content of messages becomes more complex, (2) when it is critical that receivers have the information, (3) when the information is drastically different from past information or operating procedures, and (4) when there are disruptions in the communications process itself. The supervisor has the responsibility for ensuring that information is properly exchanged.

Formal and Informal Communication

Formal and informal communications, discussed briefly earlier, can be written or verbal. Generally, however, formal communications are written, while informal communications are verbal. Written communications allow all participants to have a permanent record of the communication. This may be important at a future time when the people involved in the communications must refresh their recollection of the transaction. Also, as an official document, written communications have weight or authority requiring a measure of action or response. The problem with written communication is that it is sometimes difficult for people to reduce complex issues into writing, and there is no two-way communication or feedback to ensure that the message was fully comprehended.

Formal communications generally flow downward, although feedback and information about problems and issues are sometimes transmitted upward by subordinates. Katz and Kahn (1966) found that downward communications fall into one of five categories: (1) job instructions; (2) rationale or explanations about jobs; (3) procedures, practices, and policies; (4) feedback on individual performance; and (5) efforts to encourage a sense of mission and dedication toward departmental goals. Thus, official communications serve a variety of purposes for managers and supervisors. An example would be a patrol division captain who observes problems with offense reports being submitted late by officers;

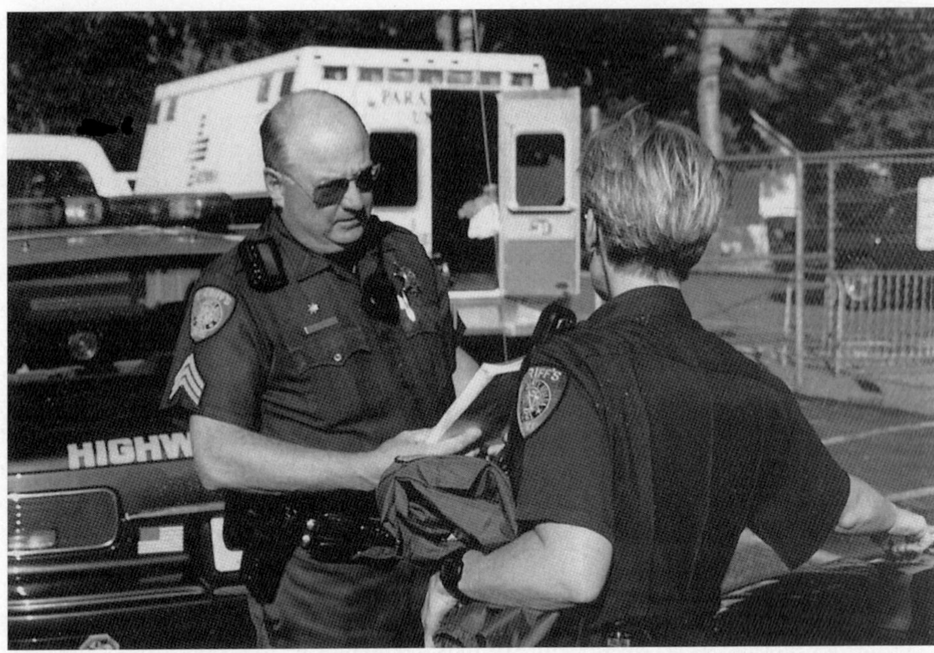

Establishing two-way communication with officers is essential for the supervisor.
(Courtesy Washoe County, Nevada, Sheriff's Office Photo Unit.)

the captain then writes a memorandum to his lieutenants and sergeants, informing them that all such reports must be turned in to and reviewed by a supervisor by the end of the shift.

Informal communications are generally accomplished via conversations and informal notes. For example, a supervisor on a shift may leave a note for a supervisor on the following shift to have the officers check a residence because of reports of prowlers or suspicious persons. In this example, although the note is a form of informal communications, it is being used in an official capacity. By leaving a note, the supervisor is able to communicate rapidly and effectively without going through the chain of command. Instead of leaving a note, the supervisor could have waited for the next shift supervisor to tell him or her directly about the problem. This face-to-face conversation would have allowed the sergeant to fully explain what had happened and what actions the sergeant took. In essence, informal communications can be used for formal or informal purposes. They allow officers to communicate rapidly without going through the chain of command.

Informal communications typically consist of "interpersonal networking" (Schermerhorn, Hunt, and Osborn, 1994) and quasi-formal exchanges of information between co-workers. Such exchanges typically use verbal and nonverbal communications. Oftentimes, members of an organization find that formal communications are inadequate for accomplishing communications activities. When this occurs, people tend to use informal networks through which they contact others to obtain official information, or they work unofficially with others to solve problems. For example, officers will use informal communications to get information about a new commander and his or her priorities.

Informal communications essentially allow information to flow more freely and rapidly. In their review of excellent organizations, Peters and Waterman (1983) found that increased levels of informal communications were associated with organizational success. Indeed, managers and supervisors who can rapidly gain information or discuss problems with subordinates and managers throughout the police department have an important advantage.

Another type of informal communications are rumors, or the *grapevine,* so termed because it zigzags back and forth across organizations like a grapevine. There is probably *no* type of organization in our society that has more grapevine information than that found in police agencies. Departments even establish "rumor control" centers during major riots. Policing is a 24-hour per day, 7-day per week occupation, so rumors are easily carried from one shift to the next as officers discuss issues such as pay raises, assignments, new policies or procedures, and other matters that affect them at work or at home.

Although it may carry many falsehoods, cynicism, and employee malice, the grapevine has several potential benefits, including that it is fast; it operates mostly at the place of work; and it supplements regular, formal communication. It can be a tool for management to get a feel for employees' attitudes, to spread useful information, and to help employees vent their frustrations. Without a doubt, the grapevine is a force for supervisors to reckon with on a daily basis. Some officers initiate false information in the grapevine to cause dissension or disruptions in the formal organization. Efforts should be made to monitor the information being communicated informally in the work group and take measures to ensure that false information does not result in problems in work group performance.

BARRIERS TO EFFECTIVE COMMUNICATION

The act of communicating occurs under a variety of circumstances. For example, a lieutenant may be coordinating a crime scene where he or she must communicate to subordinates while maintaining the integrity of the scene, keeping witnesses separated, and providing assistance to injured persons. It is extremely difficult for the lieutenant to effectively communicate to all the sergeants, officers, and civilians in this situation. The lieutenant must ensure that everyone receives the appropriate orders or directions.

Many distractions can occur in any type of situation. Such distractions are commonly referred to as *noise,* which is anything that disrupts the communications process (Van Fleet and Peterson, 1994). The different types of noise that the supervisor should be aware of when communicating are discussed in the following sections.

Perceptual Problems

Perceptual problems occur when either the sender's or the receiver's perception of the other affects how the message is sent or received. One such perceptual problem is *status*. To a great extent, people judge the significance and accuracy of information by the status and ability of the sender. Information from an assistant chief will be received differently from information that is given by a lieutenant, even though both officers provide their receivers with accurate information. All information should be evaluated on its own merits. Another perceptual problem is **stereotyping***:* Judgments are made about communications because of the sender's traits or qualities. For example, it is assumed that a police union leader and a police captain would likely interpret the same information differently, because of their relative orientations about the department. The information should be given due consideration, regardless of where it emanated from.

A third perceptual problem is the *value judgments* people make about information. If the information is consistent with old information or values, it generally is given more credibility. If it is not, receivers sometimes have difficulty accepting or internalizing it. Supervisors should take extra precautions when attempting to communicate new or radically different information.

A fourth perceptual problem involves semantics. *Semantic problems* refer to instances when the receiver improperly decodes a message because symbols or verbiage used by the sender is interpreted differently by the receiver. Certain words have different meanings to different people. Semantic problems can be overcome through the feedback process or by restating the same information several times. Semantic problems perhaps are the most difficult problems to detect in the communication process, especially when there is no feedback.

Physical Barriers

Physical barriers to communication are those attributes and activities in the immediate environment that interfere with or detract from the communications process. If police officers are spread over a wide area, it is more difficult to communicate effectively with them. It is distracting when a supervisor tries to counsel subordinates in an office while answering the telephone. Every effort should be made to ensure that communications are free of such barriers. When barriers do exist, the sender should delay communicating or take special precautions to ensure that receivers obtain information correctly.

This discussion illustrates that communicating is a complicated process and that the person communicating a message should give careful consideration to how to convey the message. The following elements should be considered prior to communicating:

1. The sender's purpose
2. The sender's and receiver's positions in the department, perceptions, and listening skills
3. The content of the message
4. Available methods for sending the message
5. Possible interpretations of the message and its content
6. The sender's desired results

Communicating Electronically

Certainly the ubiquitous electronic mail, or e-mail, system of communication can and does present a barrier to effective communications (a problem that is greatly exacerbated by persons trying to operate a motor vehicle while sending a text message!).

Prior to e-mail people wrote business letters or memorandums, generally carefully thought out and subjected to several drafts before the final product was delivered. Now e-mails are sent rapidly and on the fly, often not carefully thought out. We also talked more—in person and on the phone. If upset with someone, we might normally take the time to calm ourselves before confronting him or her in person; yet how many of us have quickly dispatched an e-mail we later regretted?

We would do well to remember that only 7 percent of the message we intend to communicate is in our words—and that this is why e-mail messages get easily misinterpreted. Certainly issues can quickly escalate out of control when e-mails are not understood or sent properly in context.

These shortcomings become even more potentially critical in police work, where people's lives—both inside and outside the department—stand to be seriously affected by poor communications. People in policing must remember, therefore, to express themselves very carefully in e-mail. They should first write the e-mail and save it as a draft, review it, and, make any necessary changes. Once an e-mail is sent off, it is too late to change it (Chrysalis Performance Strategies, Inc., 2007).

POLICE COMMUNICATIONS: "CODE TALKERS"

Import, Methods, and a Unique Dialect

As indicated earlier, the ability of the police to communicate effectively with individuals (many of whom are highly educated and very articulate) and groups is paramount. Imagine the damage that can be done to people's lives if, for example, an offense report is not properly prepared and therefore fails to accurately convey to supervisors, or to the district attorney, what actually happened in a criminal matter. Or imagine the potential harm that might be if an officer is unable to convey orally in court, on the witness stand, the actual facts of a criminal matter. Police also must communicate clearly in developing policies and procedures, and rules and regulations that control daily organizational operations.

Like physicians, lawyers, construction workers, and all other occupations and professions, the police also have their own jargon and slang that they use on a daily basis. To the police, an offender might be a "perp," for perpetrator; a "subject" is simply someone of interest that they are talking with, while a "suspect" is someone suspected of committing a crime. An "interview" is the officer's attempt to obtain basic information about a person (name, address, date of birth, and so forth), while an "interrogation" is questioning that same person about his knowledge of, or involvement in, a crime. Such **jargon** and slang helps officers to communicate among themselves.

The police also communicate with one another by talking on and listening to their squad car radios, using **radio codes**, and have done so since the 1920s. The codes that are actually used may vary somewhat from agency to agency, but a fairly common listing of codes is provided in Table 5-1.

Police agencies generally have detailed instructions and do's and don'ts in their policies and procedures regarding the use of radios. The task falls to supervisors to ensure that officers' radio transmissions are as concise, complete, and accurate as possible; officers are also instructed, again normally in their policies and procedures manuals, that they are to refrain from making unprofessional, rude, sarcastic, or unnecessary remarks while on their radio; those who fail to abide by these rules will quickly be admonished or even disciplined by their supervisors.

The police also communicate with the use of the phonetic alphabet, which was designed to avoid confusion between letters that sound alike, when, for example, radioing in the name of a person or a license plate number to the dispatcher. For example, a "d" might easily be confused with a "b," and an "m" with an "n". So, if radioing in a license plate number that is "DOM-123," the officer would say "David Ocean Mary 1- 2-3". This allays any possible confusion on the receiver's part. Table 5-2 shows the standard police and military phonetic alphabets.

The police are fully aware that many citizens and the media are able to listen to their communications by using inexpensive police scanners; citizens will often "chase" officers to calls, and arrive at a crime or accident scene before the officer can. Certainly the media are in a "need to know" position in terms of letting the public know of emergencies and crime occurrences. Many citizens, however, will use their scanners to know where the police are—and possibly for the purpose of knowing when and where it is most advantageous to commit a crime. For instance, a burglar who knows that an officer is out of service at an accident scene or in a restaurant may well use that information to know when and where to gain entry; and a drug trafficker will not pass up an opportunity to keep tabs on the police's whereabouts. Many agencies have therefore tried to prevent citizens from listening to their police scanners by encrypting all their radio communications. However, those persons who are willing to pay for expensive decoders can obtain them.

Most police agencies have three or more radio frequencies. The most common frequencies are the primary or main channel, which carries the bulk of the traffic, including dispatch; an administrative channel to handle administrative manners; and a car-to-car channel to allow uninterrupted communications between individual patrol units. Larger agencies, such as the Chicago Police Department, may use more than 100 frequencies, with many of their police divisions, bureaus, and specialized units having their own channels (Birzer and Roberson, 2008).

Improving Communications

The act of communicating can be troublesome because of the many inherent problems that can arise, as seen above. The most effective way to communicate is to be aware of potential pitfalls and take action

TABLE 5-1 Partial List of Standard Radio Codes Used by Many Agencies

Code	Meaning	Code	Meaning
10-1	Signal weak	10-50	Traffic accident
10-2	Signal good	10-51	Request tow truck
10-3	Stop transmitting	10-52	Request ambulance
10-4	Message received	10-54	Livestock on roadway
10-5	Relay	10-55	Intoxicated driver
10-6	Busy	10-56	Intoxicated pedestrian
10-7	Out of service	10-57	Hit-and-run accident
10-8	In service	10-58	Direct traffic
10-9	Repeat	10-59	Escort
10-10	Fight in progress	10-60	Squad in vicinity
10-11	Animal problem	10-61	Personnel in vicinity
10-12	Stand by	10-62	Reply to message
10-13	Report conditions	10-63	Prepare to copy
10-14	Prowler report	10-64	Local message
10-15	Civil disturbance	10-65	Network message
10-16	Domestic problem	10-66	Cancel message
10-17	Meet complainant	10-67	Clear for network message
10-18	Urgent	10-68	Dispatch information
10-19	Go to station	10-69	Message received
10-20	Location	10-70	Fire alarm
10-21	Phone____	10-71	Advise of nature of fire
10-22	Disregard	10-72	Report progress of fire
10-23	Arrived at scene	10-73	Smoke report
10-24	Assignment complete	10-74	Negative
10-25	Report to____	10-75	In contact with____
10-26	Detaining suspect	10-76	En route to____
10-27	Driver's license information	10-77	E.T.A.
10-28	Vehicle registration information	10-78	Request assistance
10-29	Check for wants/warrants	10-79	Notify coroner
10-30	Unauthorized use of radio	10-80	Pursuit in progress
10-31	Crime in progress	10-81	Breathalyzer report
10-32	Person with gun	10-82	Reserve lodgings
10-33	Emergency, stand by	10-83	School crossing detail
10-34	Riot	10-84	E.T.A.
10-35	Major crime alert	10-85	Arrival delayed
10-36	Correct time	10-86	Operator on duty
10-37	Investigate suspicious vehicle	10-87	Pick up
10-38	Stop suspicious vehicle	10-88	Advise of telephone number
10-39	Use lights and siren	10-89	Bomb threat
10-40	Respond quickly	10-90	Bank alarm
10-41	Beginning shift	10-91	Pick up subject
10-42	Ending shift	10-92	Illegally parked vehicle
10-43	Information	10-93	Blockage
10-44	Permission to leave	10-94	Drag racing
10-45	Dead animal	10-95	Subject in custody
10-46	Assist motorist	10-96	Detain subject
10-47	Emergency road repair	10-97	Test signal
10-48	Traffic control	10-98	Escaped prisoner
10-49	Traffic signal out	10-99	Wanted

Source: Michael Birzer and Cliff Roberson, *Police Field Operations: Theory Meets Practice* (Boston: Pearson, 2008), p. 405.

TABLE 5-2 Phonetic Alphabet

There are two general phonetic alphabets used in the United States. Law enforcement agencies generally use the one on the left, while fire agencies primarily use the one on the right.

	Law Enforcement		
A	Adam	N	Nora
B	Boy	O	Ocean
C	Charles	P	Paul
D	David	Q	Queen
E	Edward	R	Robert
F	Frank	S	Sam
G	George	T	Tom
H	Henry	U	Union
I	Ida	V	Victor
J	John	W	William
K	King	X	X-ray
L	Lincoln	Y	Young
M	Mary	Z	Zebra
	Fire and Military		
A	Alpha	N	November
B	Bravo	O	Oscar
C	Charlie	P	Papa
D	Delta	Q	Quebec
E	Echo	R	Romeo
F	Foxtrot	S	Sierra
G	Golf	T	Tango
H	Hotel	U	Uniform
I	India	V	Victor
J	Juliet	W	Whiskey
K	Kilo	X	X-ray
L	Lima	Y	Yankee
M	Mike	Z	Zulu

Source: Michael Birzer and Cliff Roberson, *Police Field Operations: Theory Meets Practice* (Boston: Pearson, 2008), p. 406.

to counteract them when they occur. This section provides information that can be used to overcome communication problems.

Face-to-face communication is the most effective way of communicating because it can maximize the feedback between the sender and receiver. Supervisors should not only be open to feedback, but they must also solicit it to ensure that communications are received and understood.

Furthermore, many police departments have invested in computer network systems and in-car computers or terminals that facilitate the communications process. These systems also allow officers to communicate through electronic mail (e-mail), which can substantially enhance formal and informal communications throughout a police department. It allows officers to communicate at any time and encourages feedback through its messaging system.

Another method of enhancing communications is empathy. *Empathy* is the act of putting oneself in another's position. The communicator should be receiver oriented and consider how the message will affect the receiver. If a supervisor understands how information will affect the listener, then he or she can better organize and present the message so that it has a greater chance of being accepted by the listener. At the same time, the sender should participate in *active listening*—coaxing or assisting the other's communication. This is accomplished by asking questions, providing comments, and being especially attentive when information is being provided. When supervisors actively listen to subordinates, especially when they have just given them information about policies or directives, they actively engage the subordinates in feedback to ensure that they comprehend the information.

THE ART OF NEGOTIATING

Definition and Function

Negotiation is a form of communicating. The ability to effectively negotiate with others is an important characteristic, and it essentially consists of effectively communicating with other people. Negotiations play a key role when management and employees attempt to agree on a new contract or working conditions. In this instance, the two sides communicate until an agreement is reached. When the two sides communicate effectively, they are more likely to arrive at an agreement. Donnelly, Gibson, and Ivancevich (1995:433) defined negotiations as "the collaborative pursuit of joint gains and a collaborative effort to create value where none previously existed."

When a group of people discuss an issue, there likely will be conflict or disagreement. For example, officers often disagree with departmental policies regarding pursuit driving, arrest procedures, or dealing with citizens. Racial profiling is a primary example. Police agencies often examine officers' actions in terms of their effects on public relations and community support, while officers tend to emphasize their law enforcement role. Officers resent that their patrol stops and citations are being reviewed for racial profiling patterns. Communication and negotiations are sometimes necessary to ensure that policies and actions are properly balanced. Situational leadership, as discussed in Chapter 3, plays a key role in getting things done, and supervisors must learn to apply various leadership styles to different situations. This is a key part of negotiating.

One can easily see the need for negotiation skills when dealing with the public. For example, when a police officer encounters a domestic violence situation or a barroom fight, the situation is best handled when the officer can talk or negotiate the combatants into submission. Negotiation is an important tool that is used in a variety of situations.

Approaches to Negotiating

Effective negotiations occur when issues of substance are resolved and the working relationships among the negotiating parties are improved or at least not harmed (Schermerhorn, 1996). Because negotiations sometimes occur over a long period of time, it is critical that the parties attempt to maintain good working relationships. It is not in the interest of a particular side to decimate the other side, because they likely will meet again in a similar situation.

Three criteria are used to judge the effectiveness of negotiations: quality, cost, and harmony (Schermerhorn, 1996). First, *quality* refers to attempts by both sides to come to a win-win solution. In some cases, one side may be more interested in using the negotiations as a form of disruption. For example, when officers lodge complaints about minor issues and reject honest efforts to resolve them, they are probably attempting to be disruptive as opposed to pursuing legitimate concerns. Such actions are counterproductive and have substantial long-term costs to everyone involved.

Cost does not refer to the amount of money involved with negotiations, but rather to the time and energy spent negotiating. When two sides have a disagreement, it is in everyone's best interest to resolve it as soon as possible. When supervisors allow a problem to drag on and worsen, they can cause the unit to suffer in terms of lost effectiveness and reduced morale.

Finally, *harmony* refers to the feelings of personnel about the department and its members after the conflict or problem is resolved. If a supervisor orders subordinates to conform to a departmental policy or order without explaining its importance to the police, then work group harmony is damaged or lost. Furthermore, it may take a considerable amount of time for the supervisor to recapture the collegiality that was destroyed. To a great extent, negotiation involves selling ideas to gain acceptance and compliance.

The Prenegotiation Stage

Negotiation is a process that occurs in steps; the first is the **prenegotiation stage**. Negotiators must prepare themselves in advance. Three important elements comprise the prenegotiation stage. First, the negotiator must fully understand what is at issue. In some cases, this is rather simple, such as whether or not space is available in the training schedule for personnel to receive training. But when the issues are complex, as is often the case in collective bargaining, it may be a fairly difficult task to come to some understanding about what is at stake. The successful negotiator is able to ferret out the real issues when conflict occurs.

Second, it is important for the negotiator to be empathetic and understand the other side's position. In some cases, officers may be making demands that are totally out of the question, or they may not be feasible because of budget constraints or personnel limitations. In other cases, however, officers may be making demands as a result of a problem that adversely affects their ability to perform their assigned duties. For example, officers may complain about how beats are configured. Some officers may be overworked as a result of beat boundaries, while others have too little to do. Thus, it is important for the supervisor to become thoroughly familiar with officers' concerns before attempting to address them.

Third, the successful negotiator understands all the options before sitting down to negotiate. For example, if a sergeant is aware that officers are upset about a particular policy, then the sergeant should research it prior to discussing it. A new departmental policy may prohibit officers from eating meals outside their beats. For officers working early morning hours, this policy might pose a major problem, especially if there are no restaurants on their beat and their home is outside the beat area. The graveyard shift supervisor might need to independently study the situation and recommend a policy change to the chief executive.

Personal Factors Affecting Negotiations

Cohen (1980) examined successful negotiations and identified three important factors that identify a successful negotiator: power, time, and information. *Power* refers to the negotiator's ability to influence or have an impact on the other side. Power can be used in a positive or negative way. Rewards often are greater motivators than the threat of punishment. Further, power in negotiations does not necessarily refer to the power derived from one's position. Other sources of power include technical expertise or association with other powerful individuals in the department.

Time is also an important factor. The previous section discussed the importance of eliminating conflicts, because if they are drawn out, they can have a greater negative impact on the work unit. Sometimes it is best to extend negotiations, however. This allows tempers to cool. For example, if some officers are upset over a new policy, it is perhaps best to discuss it with them after they have had time to think about it. In some cases, the issue becomes less important over time. The good negotiator understands time and uses it to his or her advantage.

Finally, *information* is the most important tool when negotiating. When a person is knowledgeable about an issue, he or she is in a much better position to negotiate. Often knowledge disarms adversaries since a great deal of conflict often is the result of misunderstandings or misinformation.

Negotiation Tactics

A number of tactics are available to the negotiator. If all the information about the other side as well as possible options have been collected, the negotiator is better able to select a set of tactics that will result in a desired outcome. Donnelly et al. (1995) identified a number of tactics from which the negotiator can select:

1. ***Good-guy/bad-guy team.*** The good-guy and bad-guy ploy has long been used by the police when interrogating suspects. The bad guy tends to be a hard liner who refuses to give an inch. The good guy comes in later after the opponent has had time to reflect on the extreme position and makes several accommodations. This ploy helps negotiations move the other side toward the middle, especially when the other side is intransigent.
2. ***The nibble.*** The nibble occurs when a small concession is made in order to facilitate movement on the other side. A nibble often gives the negotiator the leverage to obtain a greater concession. The nibble usually is the first step in a series of concessions on both sides to come to an agreement.
3. ***Joint problem solving.*** Joint problem solving occurs when both sides recognize the need to identify an acceptable solution. If at all possible, this is the method that should be used; but in most circumstances, other tactics are required to get the parties to the point that they will engage in joint problem solving.
4. ***Power of competition.*** Competition with other units or agencies can be used to gain cooperation or compliance. Every unit commander in the police department constantly battles for additional personnel. The police executive can sometimes get these unit commanders to agree to perform additional tasks by providing new officers. The competition for additional officers often can lead to agreements about workload.
5. ***Splitting the difference.*** Splitting the difference occurs when both sides simultaneously move to a mutually acceptable position. Splitting differences can be effective only after each side has become thoroughly familiar with the other side's negotiating position.
6. ***Lowballing.*** Lowballing occurs when one side makes a ridiculously low offer in an effort to scare the other side into a negotiating position. Lowballing also disguises the real distance between the two sides. Lowballing is also used to try to get the other side to move substantially as a result of negotiating. The best reaction to lowballing is to hold one's position until the offering side reshapes its negotiating position. This method of negotiation frequently is not effective in police organizations.

Guidelines for Conducting Negotiations

Although every negotiation will proceed differently, some general guidelines may be helpful (Stoner and Freeman, 1992):

1. Have and understand your objectives. This includes the rationale for the objectives and their relative importance.
2. Do not hurry when negotiating. Information is far more important than time, and information is lost when negotiating is hastily done.
3. When there is doubt, consult others for the facts. It often is extremely difficult to break agreements that are the result of negotiations.
4. Ensure that you have access to supporting documentation and data as the negotiations become more formal.
5. Maintain some measure of flexibility in your position.
6. Attempt to discover the driving force behind the other side's request.

7. Do not become deadlocked over minutiae or some singular point.
8. Ensure that you allow room for your opponent to save face. Total defeat of an opponent leads to long-term resentment and future problems.
9. Focus on listening throughout the negotiating, and pay close attention to the other side.
10. Make sure that your emotions are controlled, regardless of how the negotiations proceed.
11. During the negotiations process, ensure that you listen and consider every word. Nail down statements into precise, understood language.
12. Try to understand your opponents.

These guidelines can assist the supervisor when negotiating with subordinates, peers, or superiors.

Negotiation by Police Managers and Supervisors

Police managers and supervisors must constantly negotiate with their subordinates and be able to ensure their maximum compliance with orders, directives, and assignments. In some cases, orders are clearly within the bounds of reason and the purview of the superior's authority. In these cases, the orders generally are unquestioned. In some cases, however, the superior may issue an order that is not understood or is outside the range of past practices, and the subordinate may come to question it. For example, while a sergeant can order an officer to perform certain tasks, it is generally more effective if a consensus is reached, and a consensus can normally be reached only through discussion and negotiation. A supervisor is better able to induce voluntary compliance when he or she is able to negotiate effectively. The exception would be emergencies or critical incidents, when the officer is expected to follow orders without delay.

Police supervisors also must often negotiate with their superiors and peers. They must argue their case when there are personnel shortages, when members of the unit are given too many responsibilities, or when the unit needs new equipment. Negotiations skills allow the manager or supervisor to better present his or her case and ultimately be more successful.

Conflict between units over assignments sometimes occurs, resulting in managers and supervisors having to negotiate with peers about working conditions. For example, officers engaged in community policing projects may work contrary to patrol or investigative operations. Detectives and patrol officers sometimes have disputes over cases and arrests. When such conflicts occur, they must be negotiated.

It becomes even more evident that negotiation is important when we consider the nature of police work. Police officers are often called on to engage in activities that are perceived as being less important or not as prestigious as other tasks. For example, most police officers would rather investigate a homicide or robbery than direct traffic after a high school football game. Directing traffic is not as interesting, nor will it reap the same amount of prestige or publicity that a successful homicide investigation might bring to the officer. Nonetheless, directing traffic is a vital function to be performed by the police department. Indeed, there are many more mundane tasks for officers than there are exciting ones. Yet, all of these tasks must be performed and be performed well. Without a doubt, the efforts of a supervisor with negotiations skills will increase the probability that officers will perform these tasks more effectively.

COPING WITH CONFLICT

Thus far, we have discussed communications and negotiations. This section examines conflict and conflict resolution. Communication and negotiations skills are necessary to avoid conflict. Regardless of the efforts put forth by managers and supervisors, however, conflict erupts. This section describes how best to deal with it.

The Nature of Organizational Conflict

Conflict is a natural phenomenon, occurring in all organizations. **Organizational conflict** is a situation in which two or more people disagree over issues of organizational substance and experience some emotional antagonism with one another (Schermerhorn et al., 1994). Conflict has four key elements: (1) individuals or groups with opposing interests, (2) acknowledgment that the opposing viewpoints or interests exist, (3) the belief by parties that the other will attempt to deny them their goal or objective, and (4) one or both sides of the conflict have overtly attempted to thwart the other's goals and objectives (Greenberg and Baron, 1995). These elements require that overt action has occurred, but conflict may exist prior to that action. If the level of antagonism between the parties is substantial, then conflict will exist without any action by either of the parties.

Conflict should be viewed as a continuous process, occurring against a backdrop of relationships and events. Conflict is inevitable when there are people, relationships, and activities. Thus, conflict is not an isolated, short-term event, but rather it is something that managers and supervisors will encounter on a continuing basis. Conflict as a process also affects and involves a variety of people and activities within the organization. It tends to spread and cut across other activities. Finally, it can result from a variety of causes, ranging from personal to professional; personal conflict affects professional relationships just as professional conflict affects personal relationships (Thomas, 1992).

The nature of police work often leads to conflict. Few citizens are pleased when they encounter a police officer, regardless of the nature of the encounter. Such encounters often require intervention and negotiation by a supervisor. In other instances, the police supervisor is seen as the person in the middle who must mediate the impact of departmental policies on subordinate officers. Officers tend to expect supervisors to make policies realistic in their application, while managers expect supervisors to

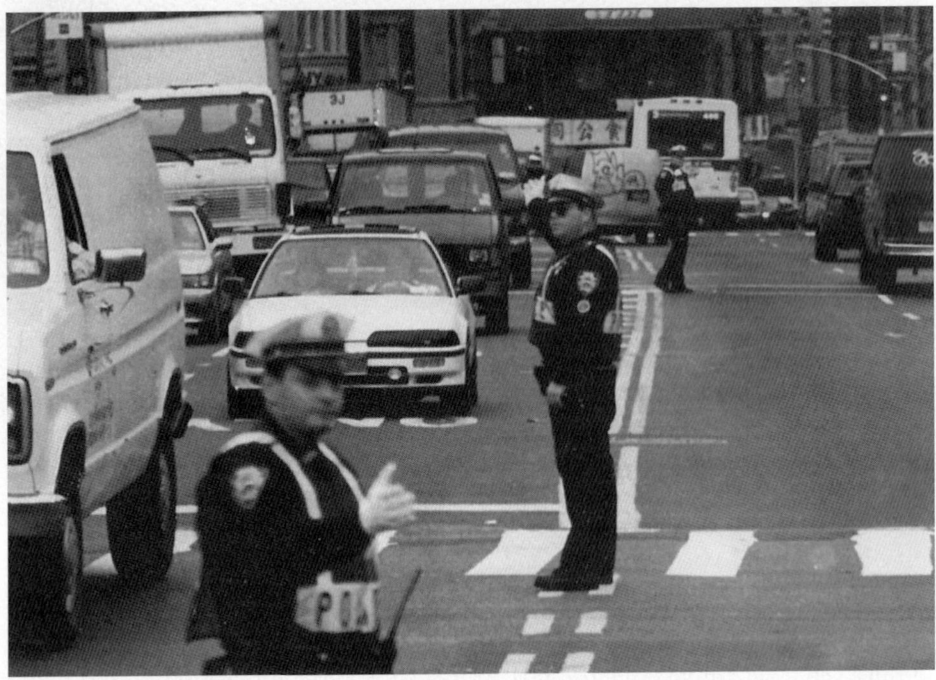

It is often a challenge for supervisors to motivate officers who are assigned to less prestigious functions, such as traffic control.
(Courtesy NYPD Photo Unit.)

follow the letter of the law with regard to policies and procedures. Such differences of opinion often lead to conflict.

Levels of Conflict

Conflict can occur throughout an organization. For example, two precinct commanders may develop a conflict over resources. Both may need additional officers in order to properly staff their patrol beats. Specialized services such as the jail, community relations, or crime prevention often compete with patrol and criminal investigation for officers. At another level, conflict may develop between detectives and patrol officers when both are attempting to solve the same case. Two officers may engage in conflict when they request to work the same beat or shift. Managers and supervisors should be aware of the conflict swirling around them, since this conflict will likely have some impact on them or their units. With this in mind, conflict can occur at four levels within the agency:

1. ***Intrapersonal:*** An individual has a conflict within him- or herself.
2. ***Interpersonal:*** Individuals have a conflict with others in the unit or department.
3. ***Intergroup:*** Work groups within the organization develop a conflict.
4. ***Interorganizational:*** Different organizations are at odds as the result of some issue or event.

Intrapersonal conflict occurs when the individual is not content or satisfied with what is occurring in his or her life. The conflict may be work related, such as dissatisfaction with an assignment or

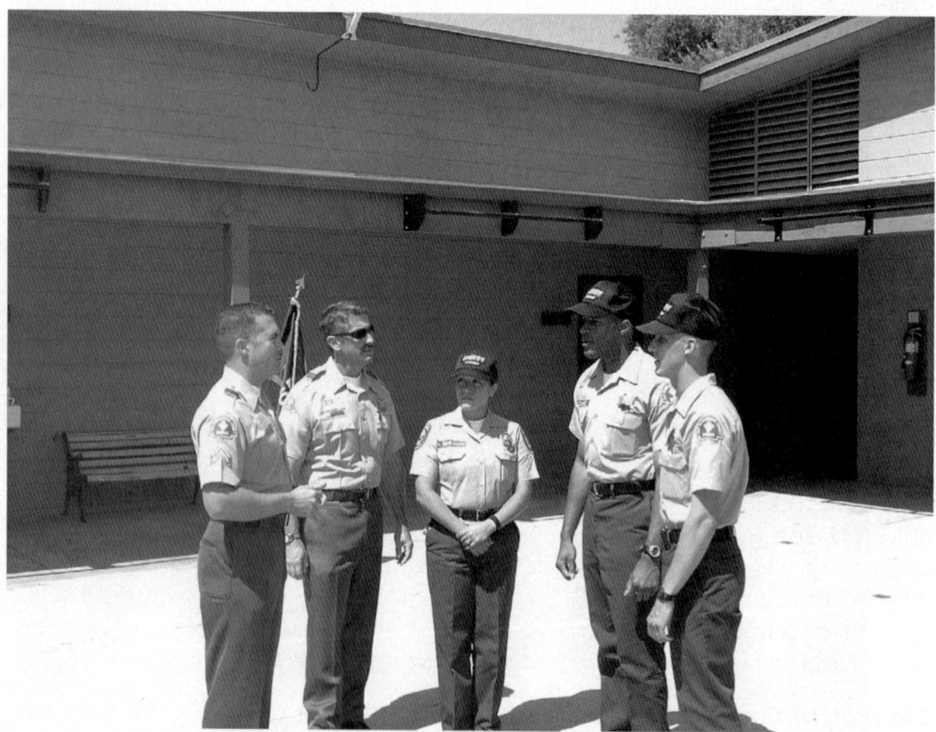

Conflict can occur within organizations, such as when different divisions of the agency compete for personnel and other resources.
(Courtesy San Bernardino, California, Sheriff's Office.)

potential for promotion. It may also be related to the individual's personal life. An officer may be experiencing problems at home or in some other part of his or her life (police officer stress and wellness is discussed in Chapter 8). Such conflict generally manifests itself in withdrawal or aggression. When a supervisor observes changes in a subordinate's demeanor or personality, the change should be investigated and support provided to the officer. Attempts should be made to prevent the problem from affecting work or resulting in overly aggressive behavior when dealing with the public.

Interpersonal conflict occurs when members of the work group have personal disagreements and conflicts with one another. Whenever several people work together, conflict is inevitable. Again, the conflict can be the result of the job or can be personal in nature. For example, some officers may become agitated because they perceive that their work schedule or assignments are not equitable relative to others. They may become jealous or threatened by other officers' productivity. Personality conflicts may develop and must be addressed. Often such conflict will not be dealt with by supervisors, who hope that it will dissipate. In most cases, however, if not addressed, interpersonal conflict will only worsen and, ultimately, affect the productivity and collegiality of the work group.

Intergroup conflict occurs when officers in one unit have conflict with the officers in another unit. A good example of intergroup conflict occurred on the popular television show *NYPD Blue.* A homicide occurred on the street that separated two precincts. Detectives from one precinct moved the body to the other side of the street, forcing detectives from the other precinct to investigate the case. Needless to say, when the detectives who were investigating the case learned what the other detectives had done, a significant confrontation ensued. Work activities must be carefully monitored and any possible conflicts among work groups must be mediated. Sergeants must be prepared to intervene and mediate such disputes, and in some cases, it may require raising the issue with managers. Regardless, the conflict should not be allowed to manifest itself in aggressive, unprofessional acts. Decisive action is required.

Finally, *interorganizational* conflict occurs when there are problems between the police department and other organizations. Unfortunately, law enforcement is not always the united, amicable, cooperative "family" that outsiders perceive it to be. It is not at all uncommon for a county sheriff's office and a municipal police department in the county to have problems or conflict because of professional jealousy or for reasons relating to "turf protection." For example, the city police department may resent deputies performing undercover operations in the city without coordinating their efforts. Indeed, turf battles and refusal to communicate and cooperate between certain federal law enforcement agencies have been long-standing issues and are well known in police circles. These interdepartmental problems often are due to a rift between the respective agency administrators and do not directly involve lower-ranking supervisors or their respective responsibilities. Nevertheless, such disagreements ultimately can affect managers and supervisors, because when the actual conflict occurs, it occurs between line officers.

Conflict sometimes occurs between the judiciary and the police. A judge may require that officers not wear their weapons in court. Most police officers would be highly offended at such a requirement. Nonetheless, it is a requirement that must be followed. In this case, the supervisors must counsel officers about the possible impact of their not following the directive, which is being held in contempt of court or having cases dismissed, and emphasize that the object of going to court is to present evidence in the best possible manner. In other words, the officers must get beyond the order and attend to the business at hand. At another level, a supervisor must communicate officers' concerns up the chain of command to the chief of police, to intercede in the problem and possibly have the order rescinded.

Sources of Conflict in Police Organizations

Conflict can occur for a variety of reasons. Most often, it can be categorized as organizational or interpersonal. Greenberg and Baron (1995) have identified a number of causes of conflict, which are addressed in Figure 5-2.

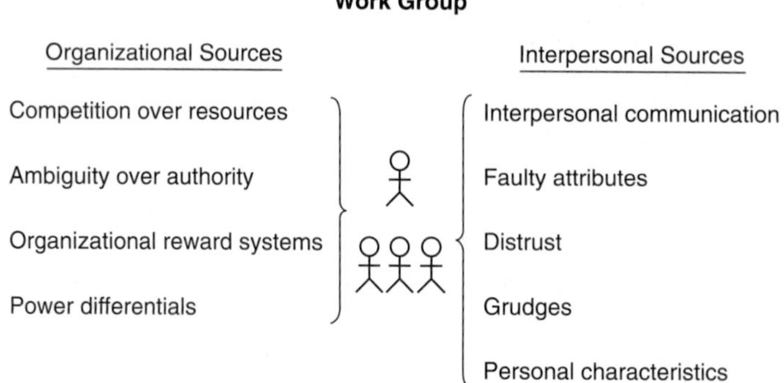

FIGURE 5-2 Causes of Conflict in Organizations

ORGANIZATIONAL CAUSES One source of conflict is *competition over resources,* which occurs when units or sections within a police department compete for personnel, responsibilities, equipment, and other tangibles related to the job. Indeed, if supervisors are doing their job, they will constantly strive to obtain greater amounts of personnel or equipment. When resources become available, everyone generally attempts to garner as many of them as possible. Competition for resources inevitably leads to conflict, especially when the parties resort to political measures to obtain their objectives. For example, a commander may go to a member of the city council to lobby for a particular program, bypassing the normal staff decision-making process concerning resource allocation in the department. While not acceptable, this often occurs.

A second source of conflict is *ambiguity over authority,* which refers to instances when two units or supervisors believe they have authority over a situation or personnel. It is similar to a breach in the span of control, discussed in Chapter 1. As an example, detectives will allow patrol officers to do as much work as possible on low-profile cases but immediately take control of high-visibility cases such as sex crimes, homicides, or large drug arrests.

Third, *organizational reward systems* cause conflict. Organizational reward systems consist of tangible and intangible benefits. Tangible benefits include extra pay in the form of overtime or specialists' pay, new equipment, and new vehicles. Intangible benefits include prestige and media exposure. Detectives frequently receive vast amounts of publicity when they solve a major case, while other units, even though they may have been central to the investigation, receive little if any recognition. Because of the nature of their work, some units have more equipment; and some units, such as traffic, may be afforded substantial amounts of overtime. As perceptions of inequality increase as a result of a department's reward system, so will job dissatisfaction and conflict. It is almost impossible to have all rewards distributed evenly within a police agency, because of the nature of the work. Efforts should be made, however, to ensure equity in a department's reward system.

Fourth, conflict results when there is a *power differential* within the police department. A power differential refers to some members having more power than others and usually occurs as a result of "nonlegitimate" power. For example, the chief may have spent most of his or her career in the traffic unit and now favors that unit over others. Individuals in the organization, because of their assignment, past work record, or personal relationships, may have closer ties with the chief or other high-ranking commanders, affording them higher levels of power and access. Each of these instances can cause animosity and conflict within the police organization.

Problems of power differential occur at lower levels of an organization as well as across units. When those at the lower levels, such as officers or sergeants, believe that they have little input in decisions and that they are not appreciated by the department, they will feel frustration and be more likely to engage in conflict. For example, the planning unit may develop a new policy and not adequately consider its consequences on the officers it affects. Line officers may come to see the policy as a bureaucratic hindrance. Line personnel should be allowed input into the policy decision, and the policy's use and rationale should be fully explained to officers.

INTERPERSONAL CAUSES The *failure to properly communicate* is a common interpersonal cause of conflict. The information or message may not be complete, contain faulty information, or be communicated in such a way as to antagonize the receiver. Supervisors sometimes do not take the time to ensure that their message is complete or to obtain suitable feedback to ensure that their subordinates clearly understand the message. Managers sometimes fail to consider how a decision will affect officers and sergeants. In other cases, managers and supervisors may be curt or discourteous when communicating to subordinates. These examples show the importance of proper communications, and when effective communications are not used, subordinates may become frustrated, which ultimately leads to conflict.

A second interpersonal cause of organizational conflict is *faulty attributes*—the intentions or rationale for an action is misunderstood by someone who is directed to complete some task. In such cases, the assignment is seen as an act of malevolence rather than a legitimate request. For example, when a detective supervisor requests that a detective recontact some witnesses in a case, the detective may see the request as harassment, while the supervisor may believe that the detective's report contained insufficient information. Faulty communications often lead to faulty attributions in the workplace.

Third, *distrust* creates a great deal of conflict. For example, a substantial amount of distrust exists between some citizens and the police (Gaines, Kappeler, and Vaughn, 1999). At the organizational level, officers may distrust other officers or units within the department. Most officers, if not all, distrust officers assigned to the Internal Affairs Unit. Some officers may come to distrust officers working in the Domestic Violence Unit, because at some point a domestic violence unit may have complained because an officer did not make an arrest in a mandatory arrest situation. Officers may come to distrust superiors. An officer may come to distrust a sergeant because the sergeant fails to communicate adequately, to back the officer when there is a problem, to keep a promise about an assignment, or imposes disciplinary action when the officer believes that he or she made an honest mistake. Innumerable situations may result in officers coming to distrust one another. Unfortunately, these situations are seldom addressed and resolved, which leads to festering conflict.

Fourth, people develop and tend to hold *grudges* against others in the department. Grudges may be personal in nature—two officers attempt to date the same person or an officer sells another officer an automobile that turns out to require unforeseen repairs. Or, grudges can be professional in nature—an officer withholds information in a case so he or she can make the arrest, or one officer reports another officer's deviant or improper behavior to superiors. Grudges may occur for a variety of reasons. It is important to understand that they may last a number of years, and in some cases, officers never forgive the person toward whom they hold a grudge.

Finally, an officer's *personal characteristics* may lead to conflict. Personal characteristics refer to attributes such as curtness, inability to communicate clearly, a need to pry into others' business or affairs, or being unorganized and often failing to perform adequately. All sorts of people can be labeled as difficult or uncooperative. Generally, it is the nature of their personality that causes them to have difficulties with others. These people are frequently difficult to work with, and the reactions of others to them often antagonizes, rather than appeases, them.

SUPERVISORS' AND MANAGERS' ROLES IN CONFLICT RESOLUTION Supervisors and managers can choose to deal with conflict using a variety of strategies. Good senior police managers will constantly monitor the supervisors and managers within their command. This entails meeting with and talking with all of them periodically. The effective manager will maintain good communications so that he or she will know what is transpiring within the unit. At the same time, the manager should openly discuss problems with supervisors. In essence, managers should hold supervisors accountable and direct them to resolve problems. As discussed in Chapter 2, supervisors sometimes avoid intervening in difficult situations. Good managers push supervisors into working with difficult situations.

There is no one way to deal with conflict because it manifests itself in many ways, and a different set of factors is always contributing to it. It is important, however, for the supervisor to be able to recognize conflict when it occurs and quickly take action. As noted earlier, negotiations skills play a key role in conflict resolution. Such skills are necessary to mediate between the combatants when conflict occurs. The goal of conflict resolution is to eliminate the causes of conflict and reduce the potential for additional conflict in the future.

Intervention in conflict essentially involves two supervisory skills: cooperativeness and assertiveness (Schermerhorn, 1996). *Cooperativeness* refers to a superior officer's attempts to cooperate with the conflicting parties and work toward a solution. *Assertiveness* is shown when the superior orders or directs combatants to behave in a certain manner, usually in accordance with departmental policies and procedures. Assertiveness does not attempt to alleviate the conflict, rather to remove its manifestations from the workplace.

Figure 5-3 shows the conflict management grid, which contains five means of addressing conflict, along with corresponding levels of cooperativeness and assertiveness. Perhaps the most common

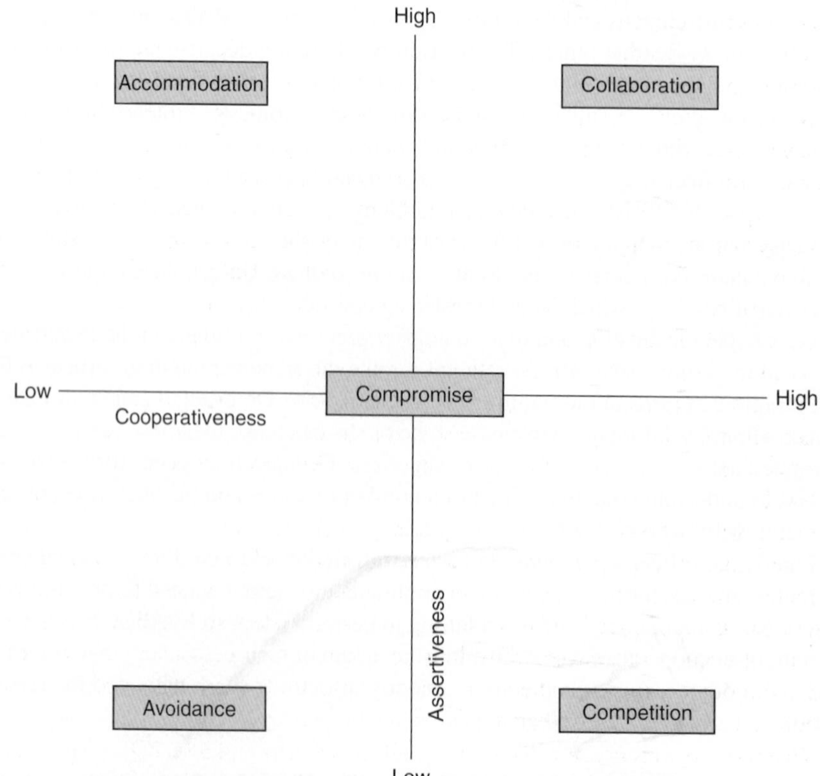

FIGURE 5-3 Conflict Management Grid

reaction to conflict is *avoidance;* the superior refuses to recognize its existence and hopes that it simply will go away. Conflict is seldom resolved without intervention on a timely basis, however, and when it is left to its own designs, it will have a negative impact on the conflicting parties and their associates in the work group. Intervention in conflicts is generally difficult, personal, and uncomfortable and can be a highly emotional ordeal that can result in additional conflict between the negotiator and the parties involved. Thus, there is a natural tendency to avoid dealing with conflicts. This, of course, is a mistake since the problem likely will only worsen.

A second strategy for handling conflict is *accommodation,* or smoothing. Accommodation involves minimum intrusion on the part of the superior, who attempts to smooth over differences between those engaged in the conflict. Accommodation requires a high level of cooperativeness and a low level of assertiveness on the part of the superior. The superior does not attempt to assert his or her authority but tries to induce a higher level of cooperativeness. Actual differences are avoided so that harmony may be achieved. A sergeant involved in accommodation would attempt to work more closely with the officers engaged in the conflict. The sergeant would attempt to become more personable, engaging the officers in conversation about departmental and extradepartmental issues. Here, the sergeant would attempt to make the issues at the center of conflict a low priority.

A third conflict resolution strategy is *competition.* The superior intervenes and meets with the combatants, forcing them to present all the facts about the situation and then making a decision. The conflict becomes a competitive situation with a clear winner and loser. It involves a maximum degree of assertiveness with little or no cooperation on the part of the supervisor. Obviously, this strategy does not resolve the underlying cause of the conflict and may result in its reoccurring at a later time. It should be used only as a last resort.

An example of competition occurs when patrol officers and detectives dispute cases or arrests. On completing a preliminary investigation, patrol officers will generally turn the case over to detectives. When patrol officers make an arrest or are close to making an arrest in a high-profile case, however, they resent giving the case, and its inherent credit, to detectives. Thus, case assignment becomes a "winner take all" proposition unless other accommodations are made. Some departments have resolved this type of situation by allowing patrol officers to work with detectives throughout the follow-up investigation so that credit is shared. This arrangement also provides invaluable experience and training to patrol officers, which ultimately results in improved investigative skills.

A fourth strategy to resolve conflict is *compromise,* which involves a mix of cooperation and assertiveness. The intervening superior officer searches for a solution that satisfies all parties involved in the conflict. It is a process whereby everyone generally gains something, but at the same time it accommodates others. It is essentially a search for a middle ground. Sergeants frequently use compromise when they make the work schedule. They attempt to divide days off and hours worked so that everyone is accommodated to some extent. At the same time, few officers are totally happy with the arrangement.

Finally, conflict resolution can involve *collaboration.* Superior officers attempt to work through problems to fully address everyone's concerns. Sergeants should consult with or involve managers when attempting to solve problems. Managers often have to give their consent to solutions; therefore, it can be fruitful to have them involved in the beginning. Collaboration involves having all parties discuss the issues and look for solutions. Debate helps to clear any impediments and allows participants to understand the other side's issues. Once this occurs, people are more willing to work with one another toward a solution. Collaboration is akin to problem solving when the problem or cause of conflict is identified and removed or solved.

Whenever there is conflict, there likely will be winners and losers. Avoidance and accommodation generally result in lose-lose conflict resolution outcomes because the conflict is never really addressed, and no one really attains his or her objectives. If the conflict is allowed to continue, it will ultimately result in ill feelings that affect work relations for some time. Competition and compromise strategies generally result in win-lose outcomes, where one side wins and the other side loses. Again, this ending will have negative effects on at least one side of the conflict. Competition and compromise fail to address the root causes of conflict and even though a temporary solution can be found, the conflict will probably reoccur. Only collaboration attempts to seek solutions whereby all sides win. Collaboration attempts to impress on all the parties that it is mutually beneficial for a solution that is acceptable to everyone to be identified. Collaboration attempts to engage people in problem solving, and it encourages them to work out differences.

A supervisor may use all of these strategies when dealing with conflict. Obviously, collaboration results in the best outcome, but in some cases the situation and the people involved in the conflict may prohibit the use of a collaborative strategy. Jealousies and dislikes among the parties involved in the conflict may be too deeply ingrained. In that case, other resolution strategies must be used.

CASE STUDIES

Following are two case studies that will provide some insight into how communications can pose dilemmas for supervisors and managers.

Case Study #1

The Lieutenants' Latency

In recent months it has become increasingly apparent to your deputy chief of operations that the watch commanders (lieutenants) and, by extension, sergeants, are not communicating, coordinating, or cooperating well toward meeting the organization's mission and goals. Specifically, three central issues are at the core of the matter:

1. Several patrol lieutenants have recently been attempting to improve the quality of officers' reports by rejecting those that are deemed unacceptable. Other lieutenants have taken the view that, with all of the other pressures on officers to perform, this concern about reports is far too "nitpicky."
2. Six months ago all patrol vehicles in the department were equipped with mobile data computers (MDCs) to improve officer efficiency in the field and to relieve the burden on the Communications section. Now, however, it is clear that differences of opinion exist about when it is practical and appropriate to use the MDCs; the deputy chief has learned that officers are in fact using them infrequently in the field, and practically never during traffic stops. This has naturally resulted in a heavy burden being placed again on Communications. Some lieutenants have differences of opinion about when/how MDCs should be used.
3. Due to the above two issues, both sergeants and patrol officers, perceiving the differences in how lieutenants view the matters, have been "shopping" for lieutenants who are more "sensitive" to their side, and have them approve their reports.

These are just three examples of several where watch commanders are not communicating or working well together. This is the *overarching* problem, resulting in increased animosity between lieutenants and decreasing consistency between shifts. Clearly, the need exists for greater strength and consensus among mid-level managers. In sum, each lieutenant is either part of the problem, or a part of the solution.

Questions for Discussion

1. Using the information provided, follow the steps below to evaluate the problem and make suggestions for ways to resolve the problem. You are encouraged to think outside the box and include *all* levels of command in your assessment and suggestions.
   - **A.** Evaluate the overall problem. Be specific and concise as to what are the causal factors.
   - **B.** Write an impact statement. Tell how these specific problems if left unchecked can have wide-ranging negative consequences throughout the agency.
   - **C.** Recommend change. Be explicit as to what you feel must be done to rectify the problems, especially as they relate to interaction between management, supervisory, and rank-and-file personnel.

Case Study #2

The Case of "Superman" on Patrol

Officer "Spike" Jones recently transferred back to patrol division after three years in a street crimes unit, where he was involved with numerous high-risk arrests of dangerous offenders. He has built a reputation within the department as being a highly skilled tactical officer, he is team leader of the agency's special operations (SWAT) team, and he is also a trainer in special operations and tactics at the regional police academy. For these reasons, Jones's supervisor was pleased to have him assigned to the team, to impart his knowledge and experiences to the other officers. Indeed, when Jones first comes to the team, the supervisor praises his accomplishments in front of the other officers. Within a month, however, the supervisor begins to notice a wide rift developing between Jones and the rest of the team. Jones is overheard on several occasions discussing the menial work of patrol, saying it's not "real" police work. He is always trying to impress other officers with his experiences; he also says he cannot wait to get out of patrol and into another specialized, high-risk assignment. The team members complain to the supervisor that Jones does not fit in. After two months, this rift has grown much wider, and the supervisor is noticing that the other officers have begun to be slow in backing up Jones at calls. Upon questioning some of the team members, they tell the supervisor that "Superman Jones doesn't need our help anyway."

Questions for Discussion

1. As the supervisor concerned, how would you mediate the conflict that is developing within your team?
2. What kinds of strategies can the supervisor employ to reduce or eliminate the rift that has developed within the team?
3. What does the supervisor need to do with the other team members? What kinds of compromises or adjustments do the team members need to make in order to include Jones as part of their team?
4. What does the supervisor need to do with Jones? What kinds of compromises or adjustments does Jones need to make in order to become a team member?

Summary

This chapter has addressed the interpersonal dynamics surrounding organizational communication, the unique forms of police communication, negotiation, and conflict resolution. These activities must be mastered if supervisors and managers are to effectively oversee and direct subordinates and activities. Indeed, the chapter revealed that there are a number of barriers to, and problems with, communication that must be accounted for and dealt with. Leadership, to a great extent, involves superiors interacting with people, and the activities discussed in this chapter form a foundation for effective interaction. They allow the superior officer to translate departmental goals and objectives into action.

Communication is the effective transmittal of information, ideas, and directives to others. In order to interact and ensure that departmental goals are fulfilled, a leader must possess good communications skills. Communications, formal or informal, written or verbal, serve to link people and activities. In reality, tasks are accomplished in police organizations through communications.

Likewise, negotiations play an important role in a supervisor's success. To a great extent, successful policing involves reaching a consensus about police goals and objectives. Not everyone agrees with what should be done or how it should be done, however. Negotiation skills are often used to make officers accept or see the importance of following departmental procedures.

Finally, conflict is a natural phenomenon and occurs in all organizations. A substantial amount of conflict is the result of poor communications skills; oftentimes, effective negotiation skills are called on to resolve conflict. The supervisor must understand that conflict is almost always present; it is the nature of organizations and work groups. Steps must be taken to resolve conflict when it exists. This chapter identified a number to ways to accomplish this.

Items For Review

1. Describe the extent and methods by which people communicate.
2. Explain barriers to effective communications, including problems with communicating electronically.
3. Review how the police uniquely communicate in general, with codes and jargon.
4. Describe how police supervisors communicate.
5. How do managers and supervisors negotiate? Review the tactics they use, the phases that are involved, and the guidelines that apply to successful negotiation.
6. Define organizational conflict, its levels and sources.
7. Explain how managers and supervisors can engage in conflict resolution.

References

Birzer, M. L., and Roberson, C. (2008). *Police field operations: Theory meets practice*. Boston: Pearson.

Christopher, W. (1991). *Summary: Report of the independent commission on the Los Angeles Police Department*. Los Angeles: City of Los Angeles.

Chrysalis Performance Strategies, Inc. (2007). Approaching change. http://www.teamchrysalis.com/AC/V2/AC212_e-mail_communication.htm (Accessed October 8, 2007).

Cohen, H. (1980). *You can negotiate anything*. Toronto: Bantam Books.

Donnelly, J. H., Gibson, J. L., and Ivancevich, J. M. (1995). *Fundamentals of management,* 9th ed. Chicago: Irwin.

Gaines, L., Kappeler, V., and Vaughn, J. (1999). *Policing in America*. Cincinnati: Anderson.

Greenberg, J., and Baron, R. A. (1995). *Behavior in organizations,* 5th ed. Upper Saddle River, NJ: Prentice Hall.

Katz, D., and Kahn, R. (1966). *The social psychology of organizations*. New York: Wiley.

Lussier, R. (1999). *Human relations in organizations: Applications and skill building*. New York: McGraw-Hill.

Mayo, L. (1983). *Analysis of the role of the police chief executive*. Ann Arbor: University Microfilms.

More, H. W., and Wegener, W. F. (1996). *Effective police supervision,* 2d ed. Cincinnati: Anderson.

Pei, M. (1961). *Language for everybody: What it is and how to master it.* Greenwich, CT.: Devin-Adair Company.

Peters, T. J., and Waterman, R. H. (1983). *In search of lessons from America's best-run companies*. New York: Warner Books.

Schermerhorn, J. R. (1996). *Management,* 5th ed. New York: Wiley.

Schermerhorn, J. R., Hunt, J. G., and Osborn, R. N. (1994). *Managing organizational behavior,* 5th ed. New York: Wiley.

Stoner, J. A., and Freeman, R. E. (1992). *Management,* 5th ed. Upper Saddle River, NJ: Prentice Hall.

Thomas, K. W. (1992). Conflict and negotiation processes in organizations. In M. Dunnette and L. Hough, eds., *Handbook of industrial and organizational psychology,* 2d ed., Vol. 3. Palo Alto: Consulting Psychologists Press, pp. 651–718.

Van Fleet, D. D., and Peterson, T. O. (1994). *Contemporary management,* 3rd ed. Boston: Houghton Mifflin.

Von der Embse, T. J. (1987). *Supervision: Managerial skills for a new era*. New York: Macmillan.

PART TWO

Supervising Human Resources

CHAPTER 6

Training, Education, and Professional Development

Key Terms and Concepts

- Academy training
- Assessing training needs
- Bloom's taxonomy
- CompStat for professional development
- Field training officer (FTO)
- Higher education
- In-service training
- Liability issues
- On-line distance education programs
- Paramilitary training
- Police training officer (PTO)
- Problem-based learning
- Professional development
- Professional organizations
- Roll call training
- Stress academies
- Supervisor training academy

Learning Objectives

After reading this chapter, the student will:

- understand how to determine whether or not individual types of training are good investments for patrol officers
- know the major types of training that exist in policing, as well as some methods for developing and delivering that training
- understand similarities and differences in the functions between the FTO and PTO post-academy training approaches
- understand why policing is in a "crisis stage" with respect to its future leadership
- know what is meant by professional development, and some means available for developing future police leaders
- be aware of the advantages—and potential pitfalls—that can exist in an online distance education program
- be able to explain how CompStat can be a very useful tool for leadership development—but with some inherent limitations
- understand some of the major liability issues with training

A man can seldom—very, very seldom—fight a winning fight against his training: the odds are too heavy.

—Mark Twain

If you think education is expensive, try ignorance.

—Derek Bok

INTRODUCTION

Training is one of the most critical functions performed by today's police organizations. It can also be one of the most critical, because of liability and public trust and treatment issues. It is a primary responsibility of supervisors and managers. Our society's growing crime, economic, and legal problems challenge the police to acquire and maintain the knowledge, skills, and abilities necessary to cope with the ever-changing and challenging world. Proper training provides a vital link to employee performance appraisal, discussed in Chapter 7.

This chapter begins with a discussion of how a supervisor or manager can determine whether or not particular types of training are "right" for their officers and a good return on investment. Next is a brief examination of the two fundamental types of training—technical and discretionary. Following that is an overview of the various methods available for instructing police officers, both during and after the recruit academy phase; included are the various types of academies, the field training and police training programs, and roll call and in-service methods. Means of assessing training needs are then reviewed, as well as materials that are useful in the endeavor. Then, we examine the important subject of professional development for supervisors and managers, and how policing is now confronted with a "crisis stage" as many baby boomers who are now in supervision and management are preparing to retire. We look at the requisite skills, training, and higher education that are needed, including the professional online programs and organizations that are available for leadership development. Then we examine how CompStat, discussed in Chapter 4, presents some opportunities—and inherent limitations—for professional development of police managers and supervisors. A review of **liability issues** is presented next, and the chapter concludes with three case studies.

WHAT IS THE "RIGHT" TRAINING FOR A RETURN ON MY INVESTMENT?

Police leadership has a vested interest in insuring proper training for their officers; given that there are hundreds of training opportunities available each month, knowing which programs are worth the expense and officers' absence for attendance is often difficult. Consider the following three questions when trying to determine whether or not the training has value as a return on investment:

1. What does the training attempt to teach? Quality training depends on solid learning objectives, which should at least indicate what the students will be able to do when the training is completed, and what level of mastery and under what conditions the students will be able to complete the task.
2. Is the skill being taught needed? Any training will be worthless if the officer will not use it. The first step is to require a detailed explanation as to how the agency will benefit from the officer's gaining the skills trained. Second, if needed, the supervisor or manager should specify that after attending the training, the returning officer should pass on the training's benefits to other officers.

3. Will the officer be able to use the new skills soon after training? Adults will quickly lose any new skills that they do not use soon after learning. Therefore, the training event should allow for plenty of practice time—and continue those sessions after the training ends (Brown, 2006).

TECHNICAL AND DISCRETIONARY TRAINING

Training enables police departments to ensure that officers have the knowledge, skills, and abilities to perform the varied tasks that are part of law enforcement. Policing is a complicated job because citizens expect the police to respond to many requests for service as well as to combat crime and disorder. Training is a process whereby officers receive information about how to respond. Lussier (1999) distinguishes training from development by noting that training focuses on the current job and development is future oriented, preparing officers for other jobs in the organization.

For example, a department may provide patrol officers with training so that they can be more effective patrol officers. At the same time, some training should be devoted to preparing them to work in investigations, traffic, juvenile, domestic violence, and so on. They should also receive some preparatory work on being promoted to sergeant. Developmental activities ensure that a department has adequate human resources to staff all the positions in the department. Here, we use the term *training* to refer to both processes.

With that rationale in mind, training has two important aspects: technical and discretionary. *Technical* aspects refer to providing officers with information about the procedures and laws for doing the job. Many of these procedures are outlined in departmental policies, and the laws refer to statutes as well as case law. *Discretionary* aspects refer to the training officers receive about how to apply procedures and law and the ramifications should the procedures and law be applied inappropriately.

An example that illustrates both aspects of training is weaponless defense training. Police departments provide officers with technical training to ensure that they are capable of using various defensive tactics, such as search and handcuffing techniques commonly used in the line of duty. They also provide discretionary training whereby officers may be taught data about officer-involved deaths during the year, upcoming changes to weaponless defense techniques, or new legislation regarding use of certain techniques such as the carotid hold. In essence, police officers are not effective unless they possess both the technical and discretionary skills associated with the job.

METHODS OF POLICE INSTRUCTION

Training is a critical function of police agencies in general, and supervisors specifically have a responsibility to ensure that their officers are well trained. Unit effectiveness is directly tied to training. This section addresses the training methods used in the police organization. They include basic or academy training, problem-based learning, field training officer (FTO) programs, roll call training, and in-service training.

Basic or Academy Training

NATURE AND EXTENT New recruits begin their career with **academy training**, which is one of the strongest investments in their training by police departments (Figure 6-1 shows the minimum academy hours mandated by state). Today there are about 625 state and local police academies operating in the United States. The median number of hours offered in basic recruit training is 720 hours across all academies; among academies also conducting field training (discussed below), the median number of hours is 180. The greatest amount of required training time is in firearms skills (a median of 60 hours), followed by physical fitness (50 hours), investigations (45 hours), self-defense (44 hours), patrol

Training requirements for new officer recruits in local police departments, by size of population served

Population served	Average number of hours required					
	Academy			Field		
	Total	State-mandated	Other required	Total	State-mandated	Other required
All sizes	628	588	40	326	147	179
1,000,000 or more	1,016	689	327	513	153	360
500,000–999,999	920	588	332	561	104	456
250,000–499,999	950	620	330	652	200	452
100,000–249,999	815	642	173	624	253	371
50,000–99,999	721	657	64	598	268	330
25,000–49,999	702	657	46	527	210	317
10,000–24,999	672	642	30	442	164	279
2,500–9,999	630	597	32	314	151	162
Under 2,500	577	542	35	199	106	93

Note: Average number of training hours excludes departments not requiring training.

FIGURE 6-1 Average academy and field training requirements by population served
Source: U.S. Department of Justice, Bureau of Justice Statistics, *Local Police Departments*, 2003. Washington, D.C.: Author, May 2006, p 9.

procedures (40 hours), emergency vehicle operations (36 hours), and basic first aid/CPR (24 hours). Eighty-three percent of academies train on identifying community problems, and nearly 60 percent provide training on the S.A.R.A. problem solving process (discussed in Chapter 4). About 80 percent provide some type of terrorism training; the most common types of terrorism training are weapons of mass destruction (57 percent), the nature of terrorism (48 percent), and relevant governmental agencies (44 percent) (U.S. Department of Justice, 2005).

Table 6-1 provides a more complete breakdown of the various topics instructed at the basic academies, including percent of academies offering the topic area and median number of hours of instruction required.

TYPES AND METHODS Academy training usually lasts three to six months and includes classroom instruction on a variety of topics. In the past, most larger agencies administered their own academies and utilized their own staff as instructors; however, this is not generally the case today. The high cost of administering and staffing an academy has led agencies to seek less expensive alternatives, such as regional training centers. These training centers have changed the environment of police academy training.

In many states, community colleges are the sites for a regional police academy. In Ohio, Minnesota, and California, a student can go to a community college and earn state law enforcement certification while earning an associate's degree. In other states, the community college provides the training and bestows some college credit on the officers while in the academy. The officers later can use the credit toward a degree. A number of positions in each class are reserved for people who are interested in becoming police officers but have not yet been hired. These students pay their own expenses and fees and receive a certificate of completion, but they are not guaranteed employment.

Other states have developed a system of regional academies that are not associated with colleges and that service all the departments in the region. These academies are self-sufficient and provide complete basic training, as well as specialized courses and in-service training. In some cases, people who are interested in

TABLE 6-1 Academies providing basic instruction on various topics, and number of hours of instruction required

Training topic	Percent of academies providing training in topic area	Median number of hours of instruction required
Firearms skills	99 %	60 hrs.
Basic first-aid/CPR	99	24
Emergency vehicle operations	99	36
Self-defense	99	44
Criminal law	98	40
Domestic violence	98 %	12 hrs.
Ethics and integrity	98	8
Investigations	98	45
Patrol procedures/techniques	98	40
Juvenile law and procedures	98	8
Constitutional law	96 %	11 hrs.
Cultural diversity	95	8
Health and fitness	95	50
Officer civil/criminal liability	93	6
Human relations	92	11
Use of non-lethal weapons	91 %	12 hrs.
Community policing	90	8
Stress prevention/management	86	6
Hate crimes/bias crimes	85	4
Mediation skills/conflict management	83	8
Domestic preparedness	78 %	8 hrs.
Problem solving (for example, SARA, CAPRA)	64	6
Computers/information systems	59	8
Basic foreign language (such as, survival Spanish)	35	16

Note: SARA stands for Scanning, Analysis, Response, Assessment. CAPRA stands for Clients, Acquiring and analyzing information, Partnerships, Response, Assessment.

Source: U.S. Department of Justice, Bureau of Justice Statistics, *State and Local Law Enforcement Academies, 2002.* Washington, D.C.: Author, May 2006, p 9.

becoming police officers but have not yet been hired are allowed to pay their way through the academy and receive certification. However, they are not guaranteed employment. The certification does make them attractive as prospective police officers since the department does not have the expense of training them.

Basic training academies provide instruction on a wide range of topics, from skills training in the areas of firearms and first aid to discretionary areas such as police ethics, use of force, handling domestic violence calls, and relations with citizens. Figure 6-2 provides a breakdown of the topics and hours that are included in California's academy training. The hours associated with each block are minimum standards, and some departments provide additional training in some of the areas.

The topic included in Figure 6-2 are meant to provide recruits with the knowledge, skills, and ability to perform as police officers. When departments fail to train their officers adequately, the

California Basic Academy Curriculum

Domain Number	Domain Description	Minimum Hours
1.	Ethics and Professionalism	8
2.	Criminal Justice System	4
3.	Community Relations	12
4.	Victimology/Crisis Intervention	6
5.	Introduction to Law	6
6.	Crimes Against Property	10
7.	Crimes Against Persons	10
8	General Criminal Statutes	4
9.	Crimes Against Children	6
10.	Sex Crimes	6
11.	Juvenile Laws	6
12.	Controlled Substances	12
13.	ABC Law	4
14.	Laws of Arrest	12
15.	Search and Seizure	12
16.	Concepts of Evidence	8
17.	Report Writing	40
18.	Vehicle Operations	24
19.	Use of Force	12
20.	Patrol Techniques	12
21.	Vehicle Pullovers	14
22.	Crimes in Progress	16
23.	Handling Disputes	12
24.	Domestic Violence	8
25.	Unusual Occurrences	4
26.	Missing Persons	4
27.	Traffic Enforcement	22
28.	Traffic Investigation	12
29.	Preliminary Investigations	42
30.	Custody	4
31.	Physical Fitness	40
32.	Weaponless Defense	60
33.	First Aid/CPR	21
34.	Firearms/Chemical Agents	72
35.	Information Systems	4
36.	Persons with Disabilities	6
37.	Gangs	8
38.	Crimes Against the Justice Process	4
39.	Weapon Violations	4
40	Hazardous Materials	4
41.	Cultural Awareness	24
	[a]**Additional hours added** TOTALS	599

FIGURE 6-2 California POST Curriculum
Source: Adapted from California P.O.S.T.

departments can be liable. In *City of Canton v. Harris* (1989), the U.S. Supreme Court ruled that departments were liable under Title 42 U.S. Code section 1983 when officers violated citizens' rights as a result of a failure to train. Ross (2000) examined about 1,500 of these lawsuits and found the following areas in which the police have been challenged as the result of inadequate training: use of force, false arrest or detention, search and seizure, failure to protect, detainee suicide, use of emergency vehicles, and the provision of medical assistance. A number of studies found that the basic academy was inadequate in preparing officers for the job. Ness (1993) found this to be the case in Illinois, and Marion (1998) found similar issues in Ohio.

In addition to providing officers with the necessary tools to be a police officer and to protect against liability, the basic academy serves to instill a commitment to law enforcement in officers. The academy is part of a socialization process whereby officers not only learn official information, but also learn unofficial boundaries and rules (Bayley and Bittner, 1997; Little, 1990). As Niederhoffer noted, "The cord binding the rookie to the civilian world is clipped at the police academy, where the beginner is taught fundamentals of the job" (1967:45).

Some issues must be examined when considering the basic academy. First, a number of police training academies across the country still use the paramilitary format for entry-level training (these are also known as **stress academies**). Their proponents argue that this style of training is a time-proven and highly effective method of training, that produces highly disciplined, fully functional, and physically fit police officers. These recruits are residential (unable to leave training during the week), and, according to proponents of stress academies, recruits are given the benefit of physical training, time management instruction, military drill or work assignments, and awarding or taking away of privileges (Gundy, 2007).

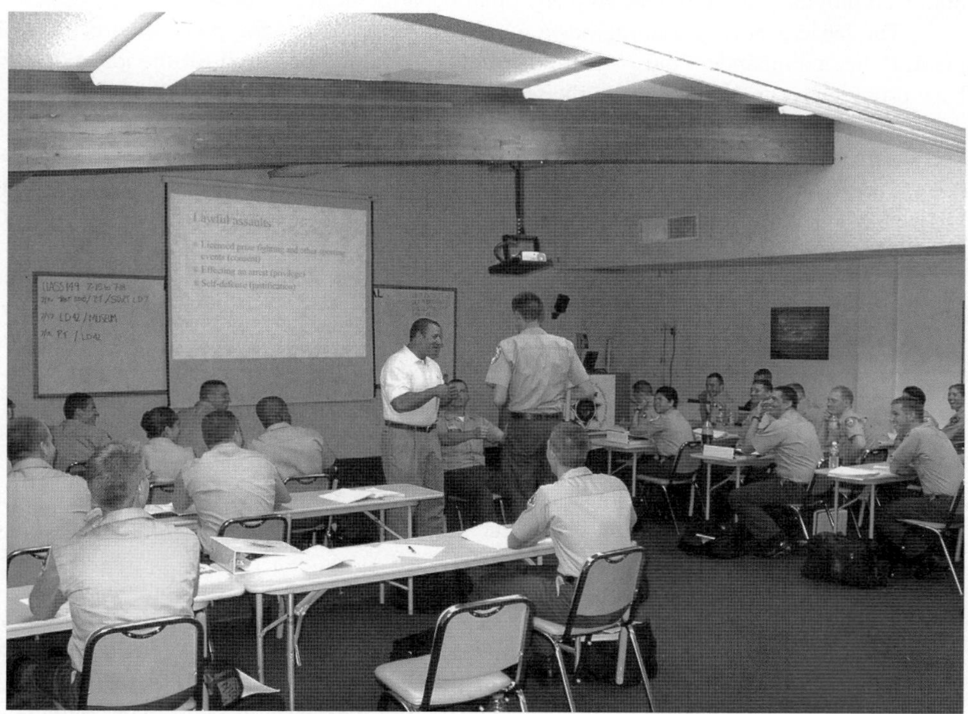

Training academies provide new officers with necessary skills.

Other observers, however, believe that you cannot teach discipline in the academy; a recruit already possesses it or not as a result of past socialization and education. A recruit's discipline level can best be measured through the background investigation and psychological screening. Violanti (1993) examined high-stress training and found that recruits tend to use a variety of maladaptive responses to this training, such as having difficulty making some decisions or needing close supervision. These responses inhibit the learning process and may also result in problems once the recruit is on the job. Post (1992) found that recruits actually learned better in nonstress academies.

STATE CERTIFICATION Once a recruit graduates from the academy, the state's commission or board of Peace Officers Standards and Training (POST) awards a basic certificate of completion. Over the years, POSTs have also developed intermediate, advanced, managerial, and executive certificates for police officers; these certificates, above the basic level, are generally categorized as "advanced" certificates. Each certificate requires a specified number of hours of training and/or higher education in various areas such as investigation, management, and operations.

The purpose of advanced certification programs is to enhance lifelong learning and career development for the officer. Over the years, advanced POST certification and higher education have become popular bargaining issues for police unions and associations. Some agencies offer as much as a 5 percent pay increase for an advanced certificate or a combination of advanced certificates and a four-year college degree. This system provides strong motivation for some officers to continue their education and training.

In some states, basic certification is tied to police discipline; that is, officers are required to have the certification in order to be a police officer. In some cases, if an officer's disciplinary infraction is substantial, the POST will revoke his or her certification. This means that the officer then is unable to obtain employment as an officer with any other department in the state.

The basic academy training has a number of implications for every level of the police department. Police commanders must ensure that new officers are prepared for the job. When new officers have problems, it generally falls on the sergeants to remedy any identified problems.

FIELD TRAINING OFFICER (FTO) AND POLICE TRAINING OFFICER (PTO) PROGRAMS Following the completion of a basic academy, most departments assign their new officers to either a **Field Training Officer (FTO)** or a **Police Training Officer (PTO)** program. We discuss the similarities and differences between the two programs.

The FTO program serves two primary functions. First, it has a training function. Some aspects of the job can be learned only through experience. These are demonstrated and taught by the FTOs. Second, the FTO program is an evaluation phase that determines if new officers have the ability to be police officers–whether or not the new officer can adequately apply the information he or she learned while in the academy. If not, the officer is terminated. Thus, the FTO program is actually a training and a selection device.

FTO programs are based on the San Jose, California, Police Department model of 1968. A typical FTO program, as shown in Figure 6-3, is divided into three phases and ideally takes 52 weeks, although many departments have shortened the program to about 14 weeks. Each phase is designed to help the recruit learn a particular set of tasks.

The first three phases in the 14-week program are about four weeks' duration each, and the last phase consists of a final two-week evaluation. The trainee is normally assigned to different FTOs and different shifts during each of the first three phases. This provides the officer with maximum exposure and experience before returning to the original FTO for the final phase. If an officer does not do well during any of the three phases, he or she may be required to repeat the phase. The content of each phase of training is as follows:

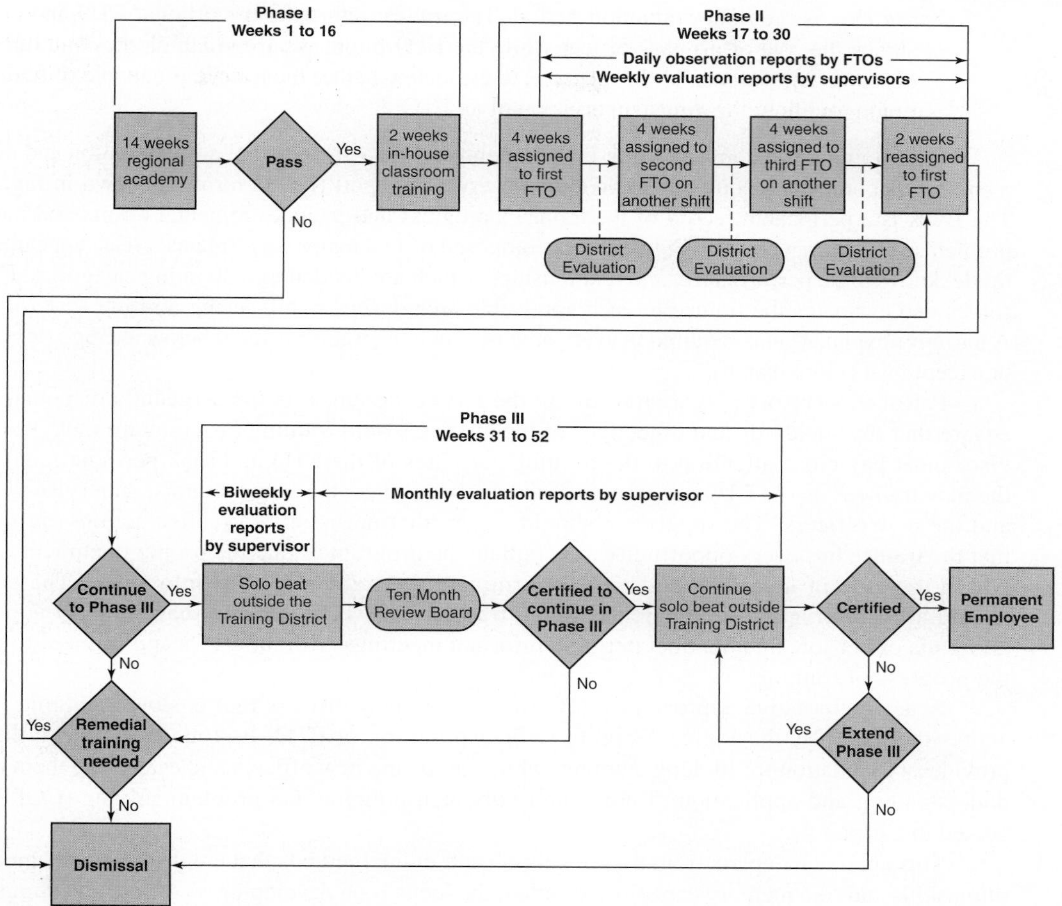

FIGURE 6-3 Schematic for FTO Program
Source: M. S. McCampbell, *Field Training for Police Agencies: State of the Art*. Washington, DC: U.S. Department of Justice, National Institute of Justice, 1997, pp. 4–6.

Phase I is the introductory phase. The trainee is taught certain basic skills, including officer safety and other areas of potential liability to the organization and officer. This phase serves as an orientation for the new officers; their demonstration of a willingness to learn from experienced officers is an important part of this phase.

Phase II is a continuation of Phase I; however, the training becomes more intense. The trainee begins to apply his or her mastery of basic skills. The routine activities of report writing, traffic enforcement, and crime scene investigations become routine for the trainee during this phase. Whereas Phase I consisted primarily of training, Phase II includes a larger measure of evaluation.

Phase III is the last phase of directly supervised formal training. It is characterized by advanced skills training and polishing those skills already learned. This is also an opportunity for the FTO to review those tasks previously accomplished and to ensure that the trainee is prepared for the final phase.

Phase IV is the final evaluation period. The trainee returns to the original FTO and assumes the role of primary officer while the FTO might wear civilian clothes and only observe. The purpose of this phase is to evaluate whether the trainee is capable of functioning without the direct supervision of an FTO.

Field training programs are labor intensive and require a great deal of administration and management. FTOs complete a comprehensive daily observation report (DOR) form, as shown in Figure 6-4. The DOR is a permanent record of the trainee's progress and includes remedial efforts and identified problems. The form, shown in Figure 6-4 is composed of five major performance areas: appearance, attitude, knowledge, performance, and relationships, which are divided into 30 rating categories. FTO observes and evaluates the trainee in each applicable area during a shift, using a rating scale of 1 to 7. A narrative explanation is required in every area in which the trainee is rated below average (less than 2) or exceptional (more than 6).

Patrol supervisors play a vital role in the FTO program. It is the sergeant's responsibility to ensure that the standards and objectives of the agency's field training program are met. The supervisor must pay close attention to the training activities of the FTO and seek periodic feedback on the new trainees as the FTO program progresses. In essence, the sergeant must supervise the FTOs and the new officers. The supervisor should ensure that necessary corrective actions are taken so that the trainee has every opportunity to complete the program or that the proper documentation exists in the case of a recommendation to terminate the trainee from employment. The sergeant should also observe the interaction between trainee and FTO to ensure that the FTO is properly doing his or her job, and conduct periodic informal meetings with the FTOs and trainees to discuss the progress of training.

A new, alternative approach to FTO for training new officers that is slowly gaining traction across the nation is the Police Training Officer program, or PTO. Its founders believe that PTO provides a foundation for lifelong learning, while embracing new officers and evaluating them on their understanding and application of community oriented policing and problem solving (COPPS, discussed in Chapter 4).

This approach departs from traditional police training methods that emphasize mechanical repetition skills and rote memory capabilities; rather, the focus is on developing an officer's learning capacity, leadership, and problem-solving skills. Its theoretical underpinnings include adult–and problem-based learning. Regarding one's learning capacity, Malcolm Knowles (1981) believed in self-directed learning, and that adults should acquire the skills necessary to achieve the potentials of their personalities, understand their society, and be skilled in directing social change. Furthermore, adults should learn to react to the causes, not the symptoms, of behavior.

Problem-based learning (PBL) is a learning process that stimulates problem solving, critical thinking, and team participation, and attempts to make learning relevant to real-world situations (Barrows, 1980). In PBL, the trainee engages in self-teaching; trainees *begin* with a problem, rather than following the traditional approach whereby a class is given a problem to solve at the end of the class. The aim of PBL is not solely to solve the problem, but also to help the students fill gaps in their knowledge and involve them in self-directed learning techniques. The police trainee decides what information is needed and develops a course of action to solve the problem. This approach to learning teaches the trainees to look at problems from a broader perspective, and encourages them to explore, analyze, and think systemically.

Additionally, Benjamin **Bloom's taxonomy** (1956) was felt to be highly relevant to PTO. Bloom's cognitive domain for learning was utilized, which emphasizes intellectual outcomes. Bloom's taxonomy of six learning activities, in ascending order, is as follows:

Date ____________ Daily Observation Report No.________________________

Trainee's Last Name First (MI) No. FTO's Last Name First (MI) No.

RATING INSTRUCTIONS: RATE OBSERVED BEHAVIOR WITH REFERENCE TO THE SCALE BELOW. COMMENT ON THE MOST AND LEAST STATISFACTORY PERFORMANCE OF THE DAY. A SPECIFIC COMMENT IS REQUIRED ON ALL RATINGS OF "2" OR LESS AND "6" AND ABOVE. CHECK "N. O." IF NOT OBSERVED. IF TRAINEE FAILS TO RESPOND TO TRAINING, CHECK "N. R. T." BOX AND COMMENT.

WATCH WORKED ______________
FTO PHASE ______________
ASSIGNMENT ______________

R.T.	No.	NOT ACCEPTABLE BY FTO STANDARDS 1	2	3	ACCEPTABLE LEVEL <4>	SUPERIOR BY FTO STANDARDS 5	6	7	N.O.	N.R.T	
											APPEARANCE
[ ] [ ]	1.	1	2	3	4	5	6	7	[]	[]	GENERAL APPEARANCE
											ATTITUDE
[ ] [ ]	2.	1	2	3	4	5	6	7	[]	[]	ACCEPTANCE OF FEEDBACK-FTO
[ ] [ ]	3.	1	2	3	4	5	6	7	[]	[]	ATTITUDE TOWARDS POLICE WORK
											KNOWLEDGE
											DEPARTMENT POLICIES AND PROCEDURES REFLECTED IN:
[ ] [ ]	4.	1	2	3	4	5	6	7	[]	[]	VERBAL/WRITTEN TESTING
[ ] [ ]		1	2	3	4	5	6	7	[]	[]	FIELD PERFORMANCE
											CRIMINAL STATUTES REFLECTED IN:
[ ] [ ]	5.	1	2	3	4	5	6	7	[]	[]	VERBAL/WRITTEN TESTING
[ ] [ ]		1	2	3	4	5	6	7	[]	[]	FIELD PERFORMANCE
											MUNICIPAL ORDINANCES REFLECTED IN:
[ ] [ ]	6.	1	2	3	4	5	6	7	[]	[]	VERBAL/WRITTEN TESTING
[ ] [ ]		1	2	3	4	5	6	7	[]	[]	FIELD PERFORMANCE
											TRAFFIC ORDINANCES REFLECTED IN:
[ ] [ ]	7.	1	2	3	4	5	6	7	[]	[]	VERBAL/WRITTEN TESTING
[ ] [ ]		1	2	3	4	5	6	7	[]	[]	FIELD PERFORMANCE
											PERFORMANCE
[ ] [ ]	8.	1	2	3	4	5	6	7	[]	[]	DRIVING SKILL: NORMAL CINDITIONS
[ ] [ ]	9.	1	2	3	4	5	6	7	[]	[]	DRIVING SKILL: STRESS CONDITIONS
[ ] [ ]	10.	1	2	3	4	5	6	7	[]	[]	ORIENTATION/RESPONSE TIME
[ ] [ ]	11.	1	2	3	4	5	6	7	[]	[]	ROUTINE FORMS: COMPLETE/ACCURATE
											REPORT WRITING
[ ] [ ]	12.	1	2	3	4	5	6	7	[]	[]	ORGANIZATION/DETAILS
[ ] [ ]	13.	1	2	3	4	5	6	7	[]	[]	GRAMMER/SPELLING/NEATNESS
[ ] [ ]	14.	1	2	3	4	5	6	7	[]	[]	APPROPRIATE TIME USED
[ ] [ ]	15.	1	2	3	4	5	6	7	[]	[]	FIELD PERFORMANCE: NON-STRESS
[ ] [ ]	16.	1	2	3	4	5	6	7	[]	[]	FIELD PERFORMANCE: STRESS
[ ] [ ]	17.	1	2	3	4	5	6	7	[]	[]	INVESTIGATIVE SKILL
[ ] [ ]	18.	1	2	3	4	5	6	7	[]	[]	INERVIEW/INTERROGATION
[ ] [ ]	19.	1	2	3	4	5	6	7	[]	[]	SELF-INITIATED FIELD ACTIVITY
[ ] [ ]	20.	1	2	3	4	5	6	7	[]	[]	OFFICER SAFETY: GENERAL
[ ] [ ]	21.	1	2	3	4	5	6	7	[]	[]	OFFICER SAFETY: SUSPECTS/PRISONERS
[ ] [ ]	22.	1	2	3	4	5	6	7	[]	[]	VOICE COMMAND
[ ] [ ]	23.	1	2	3	4	5	6	7	[]	[]	PHYSICAL SKILL
[ ] [ ]	24.	1	2	3	4	5	6	7	[]	[]	PROBLEM SOLVING/DECISION MAKING RADIO
[ ] [ ]	25.	1	2	3	4	5	6	7	[]	[]	USE OF CODES/PROCEDURES
[ ] [ ]	26.	1	2	3	4	5	6	7	[]	[]	LISTEN AND COMPREHEND
[ ] [ ]	27.	1	2	3	4	5	6	7	[]	[]	ARTICULATION/TRANSMISSION
											RELATIONSHIPS
[ ] [ ]	28.	1	2	3	4	5	6	7	[]	[]	CITIZENS IN GENERAL
[ ] [ ]	29.	1	2	3	4	5	6	7	[]	[]	ETHNIC GROUPS OTHER THAN OWN
[ ] [ ]	30.	1	2	3	4	5	6	7	[]	[]	OTHER DEPARTMENT MEMBERS
											MINUTES OF REMEDIAL TIME

FIGURE 6-4 Daily Observation Report

1. Knowledge: remembering or recalling previously learned material
2. Comprehension: understanding meaning, and explaining and restating ideas
3. Application: applying learned material in new and different situations
4. Analysis: categorizing material into segments and demonstrating their relationships
5. Synthesis: grouping or combining the separate ideas to form a new whole and to establish new relationships
6. Evaluating the material for appropriate outcomes based on established criteria

PTO covers two primary training areas: substantive topics (the most common activities in policing) and core competencies (the required, common skills which officers engage in, and are required to utilize in daily performance of their duties). New officers must successfully pass 15 core competencies, which are specific skills, knowledge, and abilities that have been identified as essential for good policing. A learning matrix (see Figure 6-5) serves as a guide for trainees and trainers during the training period, and demonstrates the interrelationships between the core competencies and daily policing activities during the eight phases of the PTO program (Peak et al., 2007).

Reno PTO Learning Matrix

	Phase A Nonemergency Incident Response	Phase B Emergency Incident Response	Phase C Patrol Activities	Phase D Criminal Investigation
Core Competencies				
Police Vehicle Operations	A1	B1	C1	D1
Conflict Resolution	A2	B2	C2	D2
Use of Force	A3	B3	C3	D3
Local Procedures, Policies, Laws, Philosophies	A4	B4	C4	D4
Report Writing	A5	B5	C5	D5
Leadership	A6	B6	C6	D6
Problem-Solving Skills	A7	B7	C7	D7
Community-Specific Problems	A8	B8	C8	D8
Cultural Diversity & Special Needs Groups	A9	B9	C9	D9
Legal Authority	A10	B10	C10	D10
Individual Rights	A11	B11	C11	D11
Officer Safety	A12	B12	C12	D12
Communication Skills	A13	B13	C13	D13
Ethics	A14	B14	C14	D14
Lifestyle Stressors/ Self-Awareness/Self-Regulation	A15	B15	C15	D15
Learning Activities	Introduction of Neighborhood Portfolio Exercise	Continuation of Neighborhood Portfolio Exercise	Continuation of Neighborhood Portfolio Exercise	Final Neighborhood Portfolio Presentation
	Problem-Based Learning Exercise	Problem-Based Learning Exercise	Problem-Based Learning Exercise	Problem-Based Learning Exercise
Evaluation Activities	Weekly Coaching	Weekly Choaching	Weekly	Weekly

FIGURE 6-5 The PTO Learning Matrix, from the federal Office of Community Oriented Policing Services.
Source: U.S. Department of Justice, Office of Community Oriented Policing Services, http://www.cops.usdoj.gov/files/RIC/Publications/pto_manual.pdf (accessed October 23, 2008).

Roll Call Training

Roll call occurs during the 15 to 30 minutes prior to the beginning of a tour of duty. This time is used by unit commanders to prepare officers for patrol. Roll call sessions usually begin with a sergeant assigning officers to their respective beats. Information about wanted and dangerous persons and major incidents on previous shifts is usually disseminated. Other matters may also be addressed, such as issuing officers court subpoenas, explaining new departmental policies and procedures, and discussing shift- and beat-related matters.

Roll call meetings also afford an excellent opportunity for the department to update officers' knowledge and to present new ideas and techniques. For example, when the department changes a policy or adopts a new one, it is presented in roll call. Officers can then ask questions and clarify its meaning. Such two-way communication leads to a better understanding of the policy. It also allows the department to address issues, such as officer safety. **Roll call training** provides an opportunity to clarify a department's policy regarding, say, traffic stops and, it is hoped, enhance officer safety.

In-Service Training

Changes in departmental policies and procedures, court decisions, and operational strategies and techniques demand that training be an ongoing process throughout a police officer's career. It is simply unreasonable to expect that the knowledge gained during academy training or specialized training can serve an officer for an entire career. **In-service training** is the most commonly utilized method for maintaining and improving officer performance and competency and may also reduce the likelihood of citizen complaints and future litigation. In-service training is also used to recertify, refresh, or provide new information to officers in the most critical areas of their job, including weapons qualification, driving, defensive tactics, first aid, and changes in the law (Moore and Stephens, 1991).

Creating an effective in-service training program presents many challenges for the department. First, few departments have adequate funds to provide training beyond what is mandatory by law or for those issues that create the greatest public concern or liability. Scheduling training can also be a nightmare. In-service and specialized training often result in staffing shortages in areas where officers attending the training are assigned. For example, the legislature in California recently mandated that every police officer receive four hours of training on racial profiling within a two-year period. The San Bernardino Sheriff's Department has more than 1,400 deputies. It took a considerable amount of resources and planning to meet this legislative mandate within the two-year time frame. This training will also result in units having personnel shortages, which will be extremely problematic for sergeants and unit commanders. In other words, the work does not stop when officers go to training.

Labor agreements can also hinder training. Some police officer contracts may prohibit agencies from moving officers off an evening shift to train on day shift without compensation at an overtime rate. Agencies may also be required by contract to maintain certain established staffing levels, further complicating the task of ensuring that officers are properly trained.

Sergeants and unit commanders play a key role in in-service training. They try to ensure that their subordinates are assigned to in-service courses that will provide them with additional skills for their current assignment. Detective sergeants want to ensure that newly appointed detectives receive the proper training in criminal investigation. Also, when sergeants observe officers who have deficiencies or problems with some aspect of the job, it may be more effective to remedy the deficiency through training as opposed to disciplinary action.

ASSESSING TRAINING NEEDS

Training evolves from a logical and cyclical process. The training cycle contains five interrelated components: training needs assessment, establishing objectives, program development, delivering training, and conducting an assessment.

Training must be based on organizational goals and employee needs. The latter are determined by conducting surveys and interviews with officers, supervisors, citizens, and elected officials; reviewing lawsuits and citizen complaints; and looking at what other agencies are doing (Rossett, 1987). A training needs assessment is the foundation for developing a training curriculum. It ensures that the training will meet the needs of the organization and employees. The failure to conduct such a needs assessment may result in the training having no practical application in the minds and functions of the officers.

The most common method of validating training or determining training content is the *job analysis,* which consists of surveying all or a sample of officers to determine what they do on the job. The job analysis generates a list of tasks and the knowledge, skills, and abilities associated with each of the tasks. This information then is used to develop training objectives, the building blocks of a good training program. Figure 6-6 shows the top 30 tasks performed by Lexington, Kentucky, police officers in order of importance as determined by a departmental job analysis.

Training objectives identify what the trainer hopes to accomplish during the course of a session. They should clearly define the nature of the training and its intended outcomes. In essence, objectives should address what the trainee is expected to learn. They relate directly to expected performance and generally serve as benchmarks for testing purposes.

After needs and objectives have been established, the training can be developed. This is when the trainer decides the "who, what, when, where, why, and how" of the course. The information is assembled and developed into a structured lesson plan that serves as a guide for the instructor to present the information. Time, available resources, costs, and type of audience are all factors requiring consideration in the development of training. At the same time, student learning materials should be developed. Too often training consists of the lecture method whereby information is provided to officers by an instructor. Officers should be provided source material that should be read prior to the lecture to maximize training. Too many training programs neglect providing this necessary source material.

After the training has been presented, an evaluation of its effectiveness should follow. Training that is currently successful and applicable may soon become outdated. The two most common methods of assessing training are examinations and student evaluations. The Federal Bureau of Investigation's Instructor Development Course recommends four steps to complete a total course assessment:

1. Evaluation reaction: How well did the trainee like the training?
2. Learning evaluation: What principal facts and techniques were learned?
3. Behavior evaluation: What job behavior resulted from the training program?
4. Results: What were the tangible results of the program (reduced costs, improved performance, reduced liability)?

At first glance, we may think that the new officer's reaction to the training is not important. If he or she did not like or understand the training, however, there is a high probability that learning did not take place. It is important that officers enjoy and be involved in the training process. The question of evaluation reaction can be answered in a well-constructed evaluation form. A sample training evaluation form is shown in Figure 6-7.

POLICE OFFICER TASK LIST

PATROL DUTIES

1. Patrols to establish a presence, reduce opportunities for crime, detect crimes, and render service to citizens.
2. Searches for or observes for wanted persons, suspect vehicles, or evidence.
3. Responds to crimes in progress.

EQUIPMENT OPERATION

4. Maintains firearms proficiency.
5. Operates various police vehicles as assigned.

PUBLIC CONTACT

6. Responds to citizen requests for police service or assistance such as directions, stranded motorists, etc.
7. Deals with distressed individuals to calm them, explain police procedures, and obtain their cooperation.

HANDLING DISTURBANCES

8. Responds to special situations such as barricaded persons, hostages, riots, etc.
9. Responds to disorders in order to prevent physical injuries and damage and restore peace.
10. Intervenes in fights, separates participants and attempts to restore order.

TRAFFIC ENFORCEMENT

11. Handles traffic control at construction sites, other special events and projects, and accident scenes.
12. Observes motorists to detect violations, safely pulls over violators, and takes appropriate police action.

CRIME AND ACCIDENT INVESTIGATION

13. Interviews complainants, victims, suspects, and/or witnesses to gather information relating to the investigation or locating individuals.
14. As first responder at a crime/accident scene, radios for assistance, protects scene, detains witnesses, performs rescue operations as needed.
15. Searches for and collects evidence at a crime scene or accidents.
16. Speaks to informants to gather information and possible leads about recent crimes.
17. Searches premises or property with a search or arrest warrant or with consent of the owner.

APPREHENSION AND ARREST

18. Serves domestic violence papers, restraining orders, protective orders, etc.
19. Arrests suspected law violators, with or without a warrant, observing legal requirements.
20. Takes necessary precautions against blood-borne pathogens.
21. Uses force necessary to affect an arrest using physical force, OC spray, or baton.
22. Searches persons for stolen property, concealed weapons or illegal substances, observing legal requirements.
23. Fires weapon at suspect in line of duty.

COURT PREPARATION AND TESTIMONY

24. Meets with attorney to provide case facts, discuss evidence, prepare for testimony, etc.
25. Gathers and organizes all records, reports and information needed for grand jury or court presentation.
26. Testifies in court regarding the facts of the case as known first-hand, evidence collected, notes, actions taken, etc.

REPORTS, RECORDS, AND PAPERWORK

27. Writes reports in narrative form, describing activities, events, investigations, enforcement actions taken, etc.
28. Completes various departmental forms and paperwork.

TRAINING

29. Attends in-service training classes, workshops, and conferences.
30. Reads and remains abreast of department general orders, bulletins, policies, etc.

FIGURE 6-6 Top 30 Police Officers' Tasks, Lexington, Kentucky, Police Department

Instructor:______________ Course:______________

In an effort to improve this course, we would appreciate your candid comments concerning the following items. Thank you for your cooperation.

1. How would you rate the content of this course in terms of its value to you?

Poor		Average		Excellent
1	2	3	4	5

2. Do you believe the course objectives were met by the instructor?

   Yes No Partially

   Comments:
3. What topical area covered was of most benefit to you?
4. Identify the weak areas of the course that either need to be strengthened or eliminated.
5. How would you rate the overall performance of the instructor?

Poor		Average		Excellent
1	2	3	4	5

6. Was the instructor prepared, with adequate material, and was a lesson plan used?
7. Can you offer any suggestions to help the instructor improve?
8. Please offer any other comments or suggestions you think will improve the quality of this course.

FIGURE 6-7 Sample Training Evaluation Form

Student examinations are used to measure learning. Most training programs have an examination at the end of the training. When training programs span several weeks, as they do at the basic academy, tests are administered weekly or at the end of each major block of instruction. Instructors too often rely on multiple-choice tests to measure learning. Such tests show only how well facts are memorized, and not whether material was actually learned. Multiple-choice tests should be supplemented with role-play exercises, simulations, and other testing in which the trainees actually use the material learned. For example, if veteran officers are being trained on the use of a new report, they should be given a case study and should complete a copy of the form at the end of the training.

Behavior is measured by sergeants and unit commanders and generally is documented by the administration of performance appraisals, which are addressed in the following chapter. That is, once the training was completed, did the trainee's behavior change to incorporate the training program's content? Commanders must then ensure that sergeants reinforce the training as a result of the supervision process.

Finally, we must ensure that the results are what was intended. The officer may apply the principles learned in the training, but the outcomes do not match expectations. In this case, the training itself is deficient. It does not prepare officers for the situations they meet. As part of their evaluation of officers and activities, sergeants should look for such problems. When they are observed, they should be communicated to the training staff so that the training curriculum can be altered.

PROFESSIONAL DEVELOPMENT

A "Crisis Stage": Preparing Future Leaders with Succession Planning

Soon the administration, management, and supervision of police agencies could be in a crisis stage, at least unless measures are taken in the near future to prepare for what is coming: the current aging, turnover, and retirement of "baby boomers" and other generational employees. Today an essential part of every chief's job is to prepare colleagues in the organization for the next advance in their careers; indeed, today the mark of a good leader is ensuring a ready supply of capable leaders for the future.

Thorough preparation of successors can help a chief establish an important legacy—one that will sustain the improvements and progress that have been made, offer opportunities for mentoring, and instill the importance of the organization's history. An approach is to use a strategic planning process (discussed in Chapter 3) to determine the key competencies needed at every level of the organization over the next five years. Then, key personnel are given assignments to develop these competencies in those areas, showing them they can perform outside of what may now be for them a comfort zone. The chief can then equip the organization to close the gap between strategic intent and current performance—or, as one chief put it, "keep the talent pipeline flowing" (Davis and Hanson, 2006:5).

Chiefs need to take a long view and look at succession planning and leadership development as a continuous process that changes organizational culture. To provide for the ongoing supply of talent needed to meet organizational needs, chiefs should use recruitment, development tools (such as job coaching, mentoring, understudy, job rotation, lateral moves, higher-level exposure, acting assignments, and instructing) and career planning (Davis and Hanson, 2006:5).

Organizations may already have a sufficient pipeline of strong leaders—people who are competent with the ground-level, tactical operations but who are not trained in how to look at the big picture. While not everyone can excel at both levels of execution, it is certain that an effort must be made to help prospective leaders to develop a broader vision—as one author put it, prepare employees to take on broader roles and "escape the silos" (Ready, 2004:97). To build police leaders who do not see the world in zero-sum terms but instead can appreciate the bigger picture requires people to leave their comfort zones and by offering them challenging assignments in different roles (Ready, 2004).

A number of excellent police promotional academies and management institutes exist for developing chief executives as well as middle managers and supervisors in the kinds of skills described above as well as later in this chapter. Two of these training programs are described in Exhibit 6-1 and Exhibit 6-2.

EXHIBIT 6-1 The Madison, Wisconsin Leadership Promotional Academy

Developing the Right People

In the 1980s, then-Chief David Couper instituted the Leadership Promotional Academy in the Madison, Wisconsin, Police Department (MPD). The academy is a two-week course open to anyone who wishes to compete for promotion, with the approval of the individual's supervisor, Work performance during the previous year must be judged satisfactory. The academy consists of 10 days of classes, covering several topics each day. The chief opens with a history and overview of "quality" in the MPD and discussed the organizational mission and core values. Ethical leadership is another topic. A class on current issues in policing is held, and other classes covering organizational roles, policies, and procedures are taught by as many as 30 MPD members representing every rank. On the second day, students are introduced to the promotional project, which s a key component of the course. Each student is expected to identify and analyze some work process or system in the MPD that may need improvement and to suggest an idea for improving it. They write papers and make an oral presentation to the members of the management team who are responsible for the area under scrutiny. The advantages of the academy are multiple: students learn about the organization and about leadership theories and practices; they meet organizational leaders; course coordinators and class teachers get hands-on leadership training; and the entire organization benefits from the generation of new ideas. Most important, the process helps to ensure that all aspiring leaders have basic preparation, and it helps to identify those persons who are best qualified to become leaders.

Source: Wexler, C., Wycoff, M. A., and Fischer, C. (2007). *Good to Great Policing: Application of Business Management Principles in the Public* Sector (U.S. Dept. of Justice, Office of Community Oriented Policing Services; Police Executive Research Forum), p.27.

EXHIBIT 6-2 SMIP Builds Leaders

One of the experiences that helped shape my career was my attendance at PERF's Senior management Institute for Police (SMIP), which provided the best executive leadership program for me personally. This program excels because superb instructors provide an excellent forum during the three-week period. they use an applied, case-based curriculum and rigorously demand thinking in ways one might not be accustomed to. The combination of the intensive curriculum and spending three weeks working with, and learning from, a group of peers presented an excellent learning environment. As a course graduate and chief, I have witnessed others return form that program better able to accomplish tasks with higher levels of responsibility.

Source: Robert W. McNeilly, Jr., former chief of police, Pittsburgh, Pennsylvania, quoted in Wexler, C., Wycoff, M. A., and Fischer, C. (2007). *Good to Great Policing: Application of Business Management Principles in the Public* Sector (U.S. Dept. of Justice, Office of Community Oriented Policing Services; Police Executive Research Forum), p.28.

In addition, *agencies* can provide skill development opportunities by having those persons with leadership potential do such things as: plan an event, write a training bulletin, update policies or procedures, conduct training and research, write a proposal or grant, counsel peers, become a mentor, write contingency plans, and so forth. Meanwhile, the *individual* can be laying plans for the future through such activities as: undertaking academic coursework, participating and leading in civic events, attending voluntary conferences and training sessions, reading the relevant literature, studying national and local reports, guest lecturing in college or academy classes, engaging in research, and so on (Michelson, 2006).

Developing Supervisors and Managers: Requisite Skills

Once officers are promoted to a higher-level position, an entirely different world of policing emerges for them. Supervisors are the backbone of an organization. Promotion forces them into situations they may never have experienced. The dual demands of operations and administration are overwhelming at times and require an entirely new set of knowledge and skills to be successful. At the same time, when a sergeant is promoted to lieutenant, he or she assumes more responsibility in the administration of a unit. This also entails making many more decisions that ultimately affect the unit's operations.

The International Association of Chiefs of Police (IACP, 1985:81) noted that being promoted "represents probably the most critical and challenging adjustment for the employee who must, for the first time, supervise the performance of others in the agency." In other words, a promotion entails that the newly promoted officer perform an almost entirely new job. Unfortunately, most police departments do not provide newly promoted officers with the training that they need. Once promoted, they may receive some guidance from a superior officer, but it generally is assumed that they are ready to accept their new responsibilities as a result of having been on the job for a number of years.

Many of today's police recruits engage in computer-assisted training.

Sandwith (1993) examined supervisory and management training needs. He noted that these needs went well beyond the technical aspects of the job. He identified five domains or areas in which promoted officers need competence. First, they need conceptual skills. They need to be able to grasp and understand the inner workings of their units (i.e., they need to see the larger picture). It also means that they must be able to translate goals and objectives into action. Second, they need leadership skills. Officers do not necessarily need to possess leadership skills. Once promoted, however, leadership is a necessity. Third, they must possess interpersonal skills. They must be able to effectively communicate to subordinates and others. Fourth, they must possess administrative skills. They must be able to plan, complete reports, and otherwise ensure that the unit and officers are functioning according to expectations. Finally, they need technical skills. Even though they are not functioning as officers, they must completely understand how the job is to be performed. Otherwise, they are not able to provide adequate supervision.

Although a specialized course on supervision will provide the new sergeant with professional management skills and knowledge, the application of new knowledge is often provided via a field training program similar to that discussed earlier for patrol officers. For example, some agencies require that new sergeants complete a structured field training program lasting up to six or more weeks before being assigned to supervise a team of officers. A shift lieutenant assumes the role of FTO and utilizes a critical task manual to evaluate the newly promoted supervisor's field performance. A number of supervisory dimensions are evaluated, including role identification, leadership, employee performance appraisal, discipline, employee relations, training, report review, and critical incident management. Then, on completion of the field training program, the sergeant is assigned to manage a team of officers in a uniformed patrol division.

	Instructed by Trainer Trainer's Initials/Date	Satisfactorily Understood Trainee Initials
Training: The supervisor will understand the responsibilities of being a trainer		
1. Understands the instructional role of the supervisor.		
2. Understands the elements of the agency's FTO program and supervisory responsibilities.		
3. Understands the need to plan, schedule, and conduct roll call training.		
4. Understands the need to evaluate the training subordinates received:		
a. To ensure it meets their needs.		
b. To ensure they are applying what they learned.		
5. Is aware of the training resources that are available within the agency.		
6. Understands the career development process and provides subordinates proper guidance.		
7. Understands the concepts of *vicarious liability* and *failure to train.*		
8. Critical Incident Management: The supervisor will demonstrate an understanding of the agency's procedures in managing critical incidents utilizing the Critical Incident Checklist:		
a. Bomb threats		
b. Barricaded suspect		
c. Command post operations		
d. Hazardous materials spills		
e. Use of SWAT/Hostage negotiations		
f. Multiagency operations		
g. Officer-involved shootings		
h. Other disasters		

UPON COMPLETION PLACE IN MASTER TRAINING FILE

FIGURE 6-8 Supervisor's Critical Task Guide

Figure 6-8 is an example of the training and critical incident sections of a critical task manual for supervisors.

Few departments have a program of this nature for anyone promoted above the rank of sergeant. Training at these higher levels consists of on-the-job training in which a superior officer makes assignments to the newly promoted lieutenant or captain and then monitors his or her progress. In fact, few national training programs are aimed at officers above the rank of sergeant.

Next, we discuss other related aspects of a supervisor's professional development in supervision and management: training, education, literature, and professional and civic organizations.

A Supervisors' Training Academy?

As discussed above, the typical entry-level recruit is required to study for a median of 720 hours—18 weeks—prior to becoming a full-fledged officer. But what about training for new supervisors? Should there not be a basic supervisory academy as well, especially given that this is widely viewed as the most difficult promotional move in policing (from patrol officer to sergeant)? Classes for new supervisors are an excellent way for them to learn about ethics, motivation, evaluation, discipline, organizational communication, liability, and other essential topics. In a perfect world, participating in a supervisory "FTO" program, such as that described above for new recruits, would be mandatory for new supervisors. However, budget constraints dictate otherwise. Still, a mentoring program for new supervisors should be plausible. Pairing up a new supervisor with a more experienced one would benefit both parties, allowing the new supervisor to learn the above topics from the veteran (this assumes, of course, that the veteran supervisor was instructed in those areas) and the experienced supervisor to gain new and fresh ideas. If it is true, as is commonly stated, that supervision and management are a science that can be taught, then these "newbies" can surely be groomed and educated to become outstanding leaders (Nowicki, 2007).

Regarding supervisory training for PTO, discussed above, the Reno, Nevada, Police Department (RPD) has adapted its patrol officers' PTO problem for that purpose. This program, called Police Training Sergeants (PTS), places newly promoted supervisors in a supervised training period that utilizes similar adult and problem-based principles developed for PTO. Moreover, a "PTL" program is currently under development by the RPD for the rank of lieutenant.

Of course, the type of leadership promotional academy that is shown in Exhibit 6.1, in Madison, Wisconsin, is an excellent method for achieving the goal of educating new supervisors.

Higher Education

ARGUMENTS PRO AND CON Today a relatively small proportion of police officers have, or are required to have, a college degree. Indeed, of all local police agencies, only 8 percent require officers to have some college; 9 percent require a two-year college degree, and only 1 percent require a four-year degree. These low percentages are certainly surprising in light of the reports of numerous studies, courts, and national commissions—as early as the 1960s—that have concluded that higher education is essential for police officers.

Abundant empirical evidence indicates that college-educated police officers are better officers. Compared to less-educated officers, research findings have shown that college-educated police officers: have significantly fewer founded citizen complaints, have better peer relationships, are likelier to take a leadership role in the organization, tend to be more flexible, are less dogmatic and less authoritarian, take fewer leave days, receive fewer injuries, have less injury time, have lower rates of absenteeism, use fewer sick days, and are involved in fewer traffic accidents In addition, they have greater ability to analyze situations and make judicious decisions, and have a more desirable system of personal values. Furthermore, college graduates are significantly less likely to violate their department's internal regulations regarding insubordination, negligent use of a firearm, and absenteeism than officers who lack a college degree (Mayo, 2006).

A major argument by police administrators against requiring a college degree for entry-level officers is that the recruitment of minorities will greatly suffer—which is particularly problematic in a time when agencies seek to diversify their ranks. However, a number of jurisdictions argue just as strongly that this is not a problem, and offer evidence—albeit anecdotal—that the reverse is actually true and that maintaining the college requirement has a number of benefits:

- The Arlington, Texas, Police Department has required police officers to have bachelor's degrees since about 1983, and has successfully recruited officers, even protected-class officers. In fact, people from these protected classes have made up about two-thirds of each of its recruit classes since 1986.

- Dover Township, New Jersey, has required a two-year associate's degree since 1978, and a four-year degree since 1994; it also recruits heavily on college campuses, and advertises widely in the mainstream media, including cable television.
- Lakewood, Colorado, had required bachelor's degrees for its officers (known as agents) since 1970, and today many agents have graduate degrees, including law degrees. LPD street officers are generalists; among the highest paid officers in the states, 60 of their agents have become chiefs of police and sheriffs in other agencies across the nation.
- Tulsa, Oklahoma, police instituted a bachelor's degree requirement in 1996. Educational incentives are offered today, and the requirement has not made recruiting more difficult. TPD has also found that its educated officers maintain a much higher degree of community involvement and have a lifelong-learning mentality (Mayo, 2006).

Some studies, however, have found negative effects of higher education. Critics believe that educated officers are more likely to become frustrated with their work and that their limited opportunities for advancement will cause them to leave the force early. Furthermore, they argue that police tasks that require mostly common sense or street sense are not performed better by officers with higher education (Worden, 1990). These studies found that it had no positive effect on officers' public service orientation (those with a degree displayed less orientation toward public service than those without a degree) (Miller and Fry, 1976), and that college-educated officers attach less value on obedience to supervisors than officers without a college education (Hudzik, 1978).

Online Programs

Online distance learning can be an effective and efficient way for modern police agencies and managers to improve their education. The Internet has revolutionized higher education, and it offers police personnel a means to obtain college degrees or certification in a wide variety of fields. This form of education is increasing by about 15 percent per year; roughly 1.5 million Americans are enrolled in online higher education programs (Jarrell and Woodall, 2006).

Not all programs are the same, however. A typical program may involve a mix of off-campus/on-campus work, with some residency requirement that may require weekly class meetings or one to two weeks of on-campus attendance during a semester (and often require that students take examinations on campus, in a monitored atmosphere). Other programs require students to be online at the same time as other class members, while still others allow students to do coursework whenever their schedule allows it, relying on accessing audio or video presentations, e-mail and message boards, and so forth (Jarrell and Woodall, 2006).

Quality is a natural concern, so prospective students should do thorough research before choosing a school. The first thing to look for is accreditation. Distance learning institutions should meet the same standards traditional schools are held to; and, normally, regional accreditation is more rigorous to obtain than national accreditation, so look for the former. The quality of faculty is also important; look for a combination of academic and practical credentials in instructors. Other students, likewise, should be high quality as well; other online students should be mature, professionally involved, self-disciplined, and highly motivated. Another concern is cost. The tuition at distance learning institutions often compares favorably with traditional schools (they do not charge all the ancillary costs one typically finds at a traditional institution, such as health-care fees, parking, and, obviously, housing, commuting, food, and other costs associated with living away from home) (Jarrell and Woodall, 2006).

Although online students don't physically go to a classroom to learn, it must be emphasized that online learning is hard work—perhaps even more so than attending classes at a traditional institution. Online programs are typically self-paced, so it takes a great degree of self-discipline to stay on track

EXHIBIT 6-3 A Police Chief's Distance Learning Experiences

Even experienced chiefs realize that their personal, professional, and organizational success depends on their ability and willingness to learn. It had been 20 years since I had finished my bachelor's degree in administration of justice and I had some doubts about going back to college. I turned to e-learning and distance education. I knew that if I were to decide on this method, it had to meet certain criteria: a highly recognized university with accreditation; professors who were a mix of Ph.D.'s and practitioners; professionally diverse classes with both returning and traditional students; cohort (learning team) structure; non-law enforcement curriculum; focus on building leaders more than producing scholars; and treatment of students as scholars. Search engines produced a large number of institutions offering online master's degrees, but the real work came with the careful examination of entrance requirements, cost, residency requirements, testing methods, method of course delivery, the application process, and course and program content. I found three that met my criteria. For almost two years, I found time to go online, read my assignments, produce projects, and learn about communications and leadership. [At work] there was the energy and thrill of doing things better and with more purpose. My classmates were brilliant young people, with a great mix of ideas. I graduated (valedictorian), and consider this to be the best thing I have done for my community and myself since joining the police department. I strongly urge all chiefs to reach out, take a chance, and grow.

Source: Adapted from Charles E. Samarra, Chief of Police, Alexandria, Virginia, in "Distance Learning is Practical—Even for Chiefs," *The Police Chief*, August 2006, pp. 49-51.

and not fall behind. One who tends to procrastinate may find it a difficult experience—and nearly impossible to graduate!

Exhibit 6-3 describes the experience of a current police chief with distance learning.

Professional Organizations

Another mark of professionals is that they organize in order to share information and further their interests. No organizations focus exclusively on police supervision, as far as we know, but there are several prominent national organizations for police specialists and police managers. Regular or associate membership in these organizations would generally be open to police supervisors. Seven general-purpose **professional organizations** are briefly described next.

International Association of Chiefs of Police: the primary membership organization of police chief executives. Provides publications, training, consulting, and other membership services and holds a major annual conference. See http://www.iacp.org/about/.

International Association of Law Enforcement Planners: a membership organization catering to police planners, analysts, and middle managers. Provides a newsletter, credentials police planners, maintains a database of police programs, and holds an annual conference. See http://www.ialep.org/.

National Organization of Black Law Enforcement Executives: a membership organization that represents and gives a voice to African Americans in policing. Develops new programs and provides various membership services. See http://www.noblenatl.org/.

National Sheriffs Association: the primary membership organization for sheriffs, an often overlooked group of law enforcement executives. Provides publications, training, consulting, and other membership services and holds an annual conference. See http://www.sheriffs.org/.

Police Executive Research Forum: a membership organization for police chief executives of larger jurisdictions. Requires a college degree for membership. Conducts studies; develops new programs; provides publications, training, and consulting; and holds an annual meeting. See http://www.policeforum.org/.

National Association of Field Training Officers: a membership organization composed of field training officers. Promotes the dissemination of information on FTO programs. See http://www.nafto.org/.

Police Section, Academy of Criminal Justice Sciences: the primary membership organization for faculty teaching criminal justice in colleges and universities. Provides a newsletter for its members and helps organize the police portion of the annual conference. Members include police and criminal justice practitioners and students in addition to teachers and researchers. See: http://www.acjs.org/.

USING COMPSTAT FOR LEADERSHIP DEVELOPMENT: OPPORTUNITIES AND CAVEATS

Useful Attributes

In Chapter 4 we discussed CompStat, the crime analysis and police management process introduced by the New York City Police Department in 1994 that has been widely adopted as a crime analysis management process nationwide. Where this strategy is employed, CompStat reflects the paradigm of modern policing: adding accountability to all levels of a police agency (Shane, 2004). But the CompStat process also provides major opportunities for the development of leaders. Next we discuss those opportunities—as well as some inherent caveats.

In its earlier stages of development—and still today in some agencies—the CompStat process is viewed as a quasi-military, intimidating approach. More specifically, at CompStat meetings, police leaders often employ demeaning, deprecating, or other offensive language, raising their voices with subordinates who are not abreast of crime issues in their sectors, or not doing enough to address them. Such an approach may well be counterproductive for developing competent leaders who will take greater initiative and more effectively solve problems. Rather, public CompStat meetings should be a time to exercise command presence and establish accountability—not a time for criticizing personnel in front of an audience of colleagues, subordinates, and members of other government agencies.

Today, leadership theory holds that law enforcement executives should adopt a participative management style, also known as democratic leadership, for daily business, except when emergencies arise (Schroeder, Lombardo, and Strollo, 1995). Therefore, an autocratic management style that includes public criticism can cause resentment among subordinates, rather than a sense of teamwork or a spirit of cooperation. This style may also inhibit the development of future leaders and undermine the cooperative leadership process. Leadership is learned behavior, and new leaders can be developed through properly designed leadership experiences. Activities like coaching, mentoring, action-learning, and 360-degree feedback are key elements of leadership development (Hernez-Broome and Hughes, 2004).

Prior to the public CompStat meeting, a pre-CompStat meeting should first be held, in private and between the chief executive and the individual commander. Thus both will understand the data and the underlying conditions in the beat sector, and then the commander can work with staff to devise effective strategies and tactics, giving officers the latitude to be creative with their problem solving efforts (International Association of Chiefs of Police, 1999). Then, at the actual CompStat meeting, public praise and accolades should be given where justified; commanders should publicly recognize outstanding performance, explaining the analyses and tactics that resulted in successful crime reduction and problem solving. The CompStat process, when used effectively for accountability and problem solving, can be a means for developing potential leaders and promoting cooperative and creative leadership. The CompStat podium can also be a place where new and hopeful supervisors and officers aspire to stand someday (DeLorenzi, Shane, and Amendola, 2006).

Inherent Limitations

The proper application of CompStat—particularly as it concerns leadership development—can have significant limitations, however, as noted by Willis, Mastrofski, and Weisburd (2007) in their examination of CompStat use in three cities (Lowell, Massachusetts; Minneapolis, Minnesota; and Newark, New Jersey). First, middle managers were not recruited based on their analytical skills, nor were they likely given much training in crime analysis or provided with support staff trained in criminology, research methods, statistics, or crime mapping. Furthermore, they noted (as was pointed out above) that although more police are becoming college-educated, most are not, and they were simply expected to learn a complex, new technical task on the job. Therefore, they observed no commanders conducting in-depth crime analyses to determine the underlying causes of problems, or how to mobilize responses to crime. Significant time and resources would have to be invested in developing managers' analytic skills for any chance at realizing the vision of CompStat–training that would take the commanders away from their other numerous and necessary tasks. Such training would not only place a burden on the organization, but would also disrupt traditional career advancement avenues that place a high value on learning the craft on the street before advancing to higher rank (Willis, Mastrofski, and Weisburd, 2007).

LIABILITY ISSUES

Chapter 9 discusses the broad issue of liability; thus, it is given only brief attention here. Federal and state laws hold agencies and their supervisors liable for acts of negligence. The importance of training from a liability perspective cannot be overemphasized. The failure to train officers and supervisors in this regard has resulted in costly litigation against departments; furthermore, the negligence of police supervisors is currently one of the most frequently litigated areas of liability. The public's inclination to sue individual officers, supervisory personnel, and chiefs of police is quite strong. The courts have sent a clear message: Supervisors may be held accountable for the negligence and wrongful acts of their subordinates.

Supervisors are expected to keep their personnel properly informed and trained and to take necessary action to correct problems and prevent future harm. The failure to do so may result in a lawsuit for failing to act or properly train personnel. Thibault, Lynch, and McBride (1995) provide the following checklist to help agencies and supervisors guard against liability:

1. Do not allow untrained officers to perform any field police duties.
2. Official departmental policies should be reflected in training. Critical issues such as deadly force, pursuit driving, arrest procedures, and weaponless defense should be carefully outlined in the context of academy and updated in-service training courses.
3. All lesson plans, policies, training bulletins, and instructional techniques should be reviewed periodically and updated.

The supervisor must be a trainer, coach, and mentor. Here, a supervisor trains S.W.A.T. officers in team movement.
(Courtesy Reno, Nevada, Police Department)

CASE STUDIES

The following three case studies provide some substantive issues for the reader to use for applying information from this chapter on training.

Case Study #1

In the Hot Seat: Developing a New Training Model

You are the shift commander, a lieutenant, on the evening shift of a medium-sized city police department. Your captain has become increasingly disheartened with the old field training officer (FTO) training program, as she does not believe that it best suits the needs for today's community policing era. You are initially charged with developing an outline for a new program that incorporates problem solving, using what you know about community policing and problem solving as well as existing training methods.

Questions for Discussion

1. What would be some of the topics you would want to cover in this program?
2. How would you measure whether or not officers were learning how to solve problems?
3. How would you build in some hands-on learning experiences for the class members? What kinds of community problems would you include?

Case Study #2

An FTO "Drives" Her Points Home

Six months have passed since the Arturo Hills Police Department lost its first officer to a traffic accident. A probationary officer was killed when his vehicle collided at an intersection with a passenger vehicle, also killing the female driver and her two young children. An investigation of the accident determined that the officer was responding to a business alarm and ran through a stop sign at 50 miles per hour. It was determined that the circumstances did *not* warrant the speed involved and concluded that the accident was avoidable. A lawsuit quickly ensues, and lawyers representing the family of the woman and her two children begin by reviewing the department's training files. They learn that 54 percent of the agency's accidents involved probationary officers, and that 90 percent of those employees were trained by the same field training officer (FTO): Nancy Banks. Banks is a veteran officer with 12 years of patrol experience; she is the department's pursuit driving instructor. She tells probationary officers assigned to her shift that she loves working nights because of its freedom from the administrative "brass hats" and the boring school and shoplifting calls that are so common on day shift. For Banks and her officers, stop signs and stop lights do not exist on the graveyard shift, because "only 'cops and crooks' are out." Banks is hard on the recruits, uses FTO information to terminate a greater proportion of new officers than her peers, and pushes their driving skills to the limit during in-progress calls. A few recruits have complained to the shift commander about the dangers involved with the driving style that she teaches and requires, but their concerns are ignored.

Questions for Discussion

1. What lessons can be learned from this case?
2. Could the department have done anything differently in the administration of its FTO program to keep this situation from developing?
3. Should a supervisor have known about the potential problems and intervened? How?

Case Study #3

The "Too Cool for School" Supervisor, or How to Conduct Training in Absentia

Sergeant Arnold Kazinsky has been with the state police for nearly 30 years. His reputation for being a no-nonsense, hard-nosed veteran is legendary, as are stories about the record number of citations he has written over the years. Kazinsky often yearns for a return to the days when troopers were hired and given a map, a citation book, and the keys to a cruiser and assigned to work by their sergeant. Kazinsky does not agree with the new, contemporary emphasis on trooper training and believes that the troopers' time can be better spent on the road instead of in the classroom. When state headquarters issues a series of officer safety videos to be shown at briefings, in typical fashion Kazinsky does not take the training seriously. He plays the videotapes during briefings as told but turns down the volume so low that it is almost impossible to hear them; furthermore, he does not distribute the accompanying handout materials for discussion and even leaves the room while the training video is playing, allowing the troopers freedom to banter among themselves at will. Meanwhile, Trooper Benjamin Scott, who has just completed the nine-month basic training academy, is assigned to work for Sgt. Kazinsky. Scott idolizes the legendary Kazinsky and wants to do his best to please his first supervisor. At briefing, even with the training video sound turned low, Scott strains to watch and hear the video intently, in hopes of picking up some new methods for doing his job better. That evening, Scott is dispatched to a suspicious person call at a highway truck stop. Scott uses a frisk technique he saw earlier that day on the briefing video, patting the suspect down with one hand while holding his shotgun in the other. The shotgun accidentally discharges, killing the suspect. Internal Affairs later discovers that the video was actually a demonstration on how *not* to frisk a suspect; the discussion during the video and handout materials made that fact clear, and a training staff member was supposed to be present to emphasize the point. Without any training or supervisory personnel making this clear to all who saw the video, the viewers did not get this major point.

Questions for Discussion

1. Did Kazinsky err? If so, how? Is he civilly liable?
2. Do you feel Trooper Scott is blameworthy?
3. This chapter discussed different types of training. How can training create liability for supervisors?
4. How can training that is national in scope be in conflict with local ordinances or policies? What should an agency do to ensure that the wrong training information is not distributed to officers?

Summary

This chapter has examined police training and education from a number of perspectives: how to judge training in terms of its cost and usefulness; methods of instruction (i.e., unique challenges of teaching adults, recruit academy, post-academy field training, roll call, in-service); assessing training needs;

professional development (including online distance education programs, CompStat, and other means of preparing future leaders for higher promotion); and liability issues that attend the training function. The underlying theme—and a major one—is that today's police agencies more than ever need to ensure that their officers are well trained; the effectiveness of the agency and the specter of liability depend on it.

The changing nature of our society and its laws, coupled with increasing technology and diversity, places incredible demands on officers, supervisors, and managers to maintain the skills, knowledge, and abilities to perform their duties proficiently. Supervisors and managers are in a unique position in an organization's structure to assess officers' training needs and to provide employees with the necessary instruction and guidance. We also noted that training is important for supervisors themselves; among the avenues of professional growth for police supervisors are training, education, literature, and professional and civic organizations that contribute to career development.

This chapter noted that training begins in the academy and continues throughout one's career, in a variety of methods, settings, and circumstances. These means allow a department substantial flexibility while ensuring that personnel are well trained. The failure to properly train or recognize the need for training can create tremendous liability for an organization. Liability alone requires that agencies take training seriously and obligate the necessary people and resources to organize, plan, and document all courses taught.

Items For Review

1. Explain how one can determine whether or not a particular offering of police training would be a good investment.
2. Review the major methods for a patrol officer's receiving training, including those that occur in the academy, immediately upon going to patrol, and later (in-service) methods.
3. Describe the similarities and differences between field training officer (FTO) and police training officer (PTO) programs.
4. Explain why it is said that police leadership is now confronting a "crisis stage."
5. Describe what may be done in the form of professional development in order to address the problem in item #4 above.
6. Delineate some of the advantages—and potential pitfalls—that one should consider in an online distance education program.
7. Review how CompStat may be highly beneficial in professional development of police; include some of the limitations that might adhere to the full realization of CompStat's function and promise.
8. Explain how supervisors may be liable for inadequate training of their subordinates.

References

Barrows, H., and Tamblyn, R.M. (1980). *Problem based learning*. New York: Springer.

Bayley, D., and Bittner, E. (1997). Learning the skills of policing. In R. Dunham and G. Alpert, eds., *Critical issues in policing*. Prospect Heights, IL: Waveland, pp. 114–138.

Bloom, B. S. (1956). *Taxonomy of educational objectives, handbook I: The cognitive domain.* New York: David McKay.

Brown, S. (2006). Choosing the right training: Four questions for return on investment. *The PoliceChief* (September):26-28.

City of Canton v. Harris, 57 U.S.L.W. 4263 (1989).

Davis, E., and *Hanson, E.* (2006). Succession planning: Mentoring future leaders. Washington, D.C.: Police Executive Research Forum, *Subject to Debate* (June):5.

DeLorenzi, D., Shane, J. M., and Amendola, K. L. (2006). The CompStat process: Managing performance on the pathway to leadership. *The Police Chief*, http://www.Theiacp.org/foundation/Foundation.htm (Accessed October 22, 2007).

Gundy, J. (2007). Paramilitary training in police academies. *Law and Order* (June):22-30.

Hernez-Broome, G., and Hughes, R. L. (2004). Leadership development: Past, present, and future. *Human Resource Planning* 27(1):25.

Hoover, J., Glensor, R. W., and Peak, K. J. (2002, March 9). The next generation field training officer (FTO) program: A problem-based learning model. Paper presented at the annual conference of the Academy of Criminal Justice Sciences. Anaheim, CA.

Hudzik, J. K. (1978). College education for police: Problems in measuring component and extraneous variables," *Journal of Criminal Justice* 6 (1978):69–81.

International Association of Chiefs of Police. (1985). *Police supervision*. Arlington, VA: Author, p. 130.

International Association of Chiefs of Police. (1999). Police leadership in the 21st century: Achieving and sustaining executive success. http:www.theiacp.org/documents/pdfs/Publications/policeleadership%2Epdf (Accessed July 26, 2006).

Jarrell, C., and Woodall, B. (2006). Online higher education is law enforcement-friendly. *The Associate* (November-December):28-36. For an excellent review of the program offerings and locations of a number of online education programs, see also Gavigan, J. (2007). Accredited law enforcement programs. *Law and Order* (June):88-98.

Knowles, M. (1981). Andragogy in action. San Francisco: Jossey-Bass.

Little, R. (1990). The police academy: Toward a typology of modes of anticipatory occupational socialization among a sample of police recruits. *Police Journal* (April):159–167.

Lussier, R. N. (1999). *Human relations in organizations: Applications and skill building*. New York: McGraw-Hill.

Marion, N. (1998). Police academy training: Are we teaching recruits what they need to know? *Policing: An International Journal of Police Strategies & Management* 21(1):54-79.

Mayo, L. (2006). College education and policing. *The Police Chief* (August):20-40.

Michelson, R. (2006). Succession planning for police leadership. *The Police Chief* (June):16-22.

Miller, J., and Fry, L. (1976). Reexamining assumptions about education and professionalism in law enforcement. *Journal of Police Science and Administration* 4 (1976):187–98.

Moore, M. H., and Stephens, D. W. (1991). *Beyond command and control: The strategic management of police departments*. Washington, DC: Police Executive Research Forum.

Ness, J. J. (1993). The relevance of basic law enforcement training—Does the curriculum prepare recruits for police work: A survey study. *Journal of Criminal Justice* 19: 181-193.

Niederhoffer, A (1967). *Behind the shield: The police in urban society*. New York: Doubleday.

Nowicki, E. (2007). Training for supervisors. *Law and Order* (June):18-20.

Peak, K. J., Pitts, S., and Glensor, R. W. (2007). From 'FTO' to 'PTO': A contemporary approach to post-academy recruit training. Paper presented at the annual conference, Academy of Criminal Justice Sciences, Seattle, Washington, March 22.

Post, G. M. (1992). Police recruits: Training tomorrow's workforce. *FBI Law Enforcement Bulletin* 61(3):19–24.

Ready, D. A. (2004). How to grow leaders. *Harvard Business Review* (December):93-100.

Ross, D. L. (2000). Emerging trends in police failure to train properly. *Journal of Police Strategies and Management* 23(2):169–193.

Rossett, A. (1987). *Training needs assessment.* Upper Saddle River, NJ: Educational Tech. Publications.

Sandwith, P. (1993). A hierarchy of management training requirements: The competency domain model. *Public Personnel Management* 22(1):43–62.

Schroeder, D. J., Lombardo, F., and Strollo, J. (1995). *Management and supervision of police personnel* Binghamton, NY: Gould, p. 9.

Shane, J. M. (2004). CompStat design. *FBI Law Enforcement Bulletin* (May 2004):17-18.

Thibault, E. T., Lynch, L. M., and McBride, R. B. (1995). *Proactive police management,* 3d ed. Upper Saddle River, NJ: Prentice Hall.

U.S. Department of Justice., (2005). *State and local law enforcement training academies, 2002*. Washington, D.C.: Author.

U.S. Department of Justice., Bureau of Justice. Statistic (2006). *Local police departments, 2003.* Washington, D.C.: Author.

Violanti, J. M. (1993). What does high stress police training teach recruits? An analysis of coping. *Journal of Criminal Justice* 21:411–417.

Willis, J. J., Mastrofski, S. D., and Weisburd, D. (2007). Making sense of CompStat: A theory-based analysis of organizational change. *Law and Society Review* 41(1) (March):147-188.

Worden, R. E. (1990). A badge and a baccalaureate: Policies, hypotheses, and further evidence, *Justice Quarterly* 7 (September):565–92.

CHAPTER 7

Evaluation Methods and Performance Appraisal

KEY TERMS AND CONCEPTS

- Accountability
- Behaviorally Anchored Rating Scale (BARS)
- Citizen surveys
- CompStat
- Effectiveness
- Efficiency
- Equity
- Mixed format scale
- Performance appraisal
- Performance targeting
- Productivity
- Strategic planning
- Total quality management

LEARNING OBJECTIVES

After reading this chapter, the student will:

- understand both productivity measurement and performance appraisal, and how they can be used in a police department
- understand how community policing has affected the measurement of police productivity
- understand the different forms or scales that are used to collect performance appraisal information
- comprehend how performance targeting can increase a police officer's performance
- know how commanding officers and supervisors are evaluated under New York City's CompStat program

Excellence is to do a common thing in an uncommon way.

—BOOKER T. WASHINGTON

Excellent firms don't believe in excellence, only in constant improvement and constant change.

—TOM PETERS

INTRODUCTION

Police departments provide a host of services to the communities they serve. There is an array of goals including law enforcement, traffic and accident control, miscellaneous services, and maintaining order. As such, police departments are goal seeking. They have been established to render these services to the community, and therefore, they should be accountable for how well these services are delivered. Accountability infers that we should attempt to measure and evaluate performance.

Police and other governmental agencies are different from the public sector. In the private sector, performance—and its success or failure—is measured by profits. If a business fails to make a profit, it likely will close or its stockholders will sell their stock, devaluing the company. Conversely, public governmental agencies do not have a profit margin—they provide services to citizens and communities. This makes it inherently more difficult to measure productivity and performance. Police departments, nonetheless, are created to provide a host of services, and police managers must attempt to determine how well these services are delivered and whether they are delivered at an adequate level. Performance must be appraised.

In exploring several issues surrounding police performance evaluation and appraisal, this chapter is divided into two primary sections: productivity measurement and performance appraisal. First examining productivity measurement, we focus on police department productivity and measurement. Included here are definitions of productivity, planning, and problem solving, and how police managers and supervisors collect information about departmental and unit productivity and subordinates' activities. CompStat, a system designed to increase productivity and accountability at the manager's level, is also discussed.

Next, in examining performance appraisal, we look at the formal process police departments establish to measure officers' performance and provide them with feedback on their performance. This section includes an overview of performance appraisal, rating forms, improving rater performance, providing feedback, how subordinates can accomplish appraisals of supervisors, and performance targeting. The chapter concludes with two cases studies.

PRODUCTIVITY MEASUREMENT

What Is Productivity?

Productivity measurement is important because managers and supervisors must make judgments about the relative success of their subordinates and operational units. This generally entails comparing their productivity to some standard. In some cases, officers are compared to one another using averages; in other instances, they are compared to some universal departmental or unit standard. The latter method is inherently superior to the former for two reasons. First, if averages are used, half of the officers, regardless of productivity, will always be below the average. Second, the use of averages means that the work group, rather than supervisors or administrators, is setting productivity levels. This often occurs with traffic enforcement officers who tend to have work-group–established quotas that are lower than the number of citations that can be easily written in a given shift. Regardless of the method used, supervisors are faced with the prospect of developing productivity measures to accomplish this function.

A host of potential measures exist. Nearly every activity a police officer performs can be measured (with the exception of crime prevention, as it is not possible to know whether or not directed patrol in an area or some other activity has reduced crime); this infers that every police unit can be evaluated in terms of performance. It is critical to focus on the *correct* measure, however, because officers pattern their behavior and activities using prescribed performance standards and expectations. For example, if a patrol sergeant emphasizes traffic citations or field interviews, officers will tend to write more tickets and possibly neglect other activities. If the same sergeant fails to comment about or investigate officers' performance at domestic violence calls, officers may develop the attitude that such calls are unimportant and feel free to deal with them less judiciously. Thus, productivity measurement is important in molding police officer behavior and contributes heavily to overall departmental effectiveness.

Productivity theoretically refers to how well the police provide services to citizens. It is the relationship between the resources used by a police department and the amount or level of services provided (Kuper, 1975). Schermerhorn (1996:6) notes that productivity is a "summary measure of the quantity of work performance, with resource utilization considered." These definitions point to four general concerns when attempting to measure productivity: efficiency, effectiveness, equity, and accountability. We briefly discuss each concern.

Efficiency refers to the accomplishment of a given task with a minimum expenditure of resources. Constituents want to minimize costs while maximizing outputs (desired outcomes such as services, arrests, or stolen property recovered by the police). The various strategies to accomplish a given task must be considered and the ones that not only achieve desired objectives but also do so at the lowest cost should be implemented. For example, should detectives or patrol officers be assigned to teams? How many patrol units should be dispatched to calls? Can the department take some citizen reports by telephone?

The calculation of efficiency measures is no easy task; costs of activities are generally computed by examining the number of personnel, amount of equipment and staff support, and the amount of noncapital supplies (such as gasoline, paper, and electricity consumed by the program). The cost of outputs, on the other hand, is either difficult or impossible to compute. For example, how can we determine how many accidents or deaths were prevented by setting up a drunk-driving check lane? Nonetheless, the police should strive to increase organizational efficiency.

Gaines, Famega, and Bichler (2007) provide an example of efficiency. They conducted a study of police responses to burglar alarms and found that in Fontana, California, the department received 8,529 alarms in one year. Of this total, only 22 were actually burglaries or some other crime, and only one arrest was made as a result of responding to all the alarm calls. It was estimated that average response consumed 16.77 minutes of time per officer, with two officers being dispatched to each call. The average hourly wage of officers was $53.75. Thus, the alarm calls cost the department $256,603 for the year; however, this cost included only patrol officer salaries, and the actual costs are considerably higher if overhead costs such as dispatching, administration, and so forth, are considered. Obviously, if the department could reduce its burglar alarm calls, it would result in substantial savings in fiscal and personnel resources.

Managers maximize efficiency through program planning, while supervisors can increase efficiency through proper assignment and supervision. The commander of the criminal investigation unit must examine the volume of reported crimes and then decide how to allocate detectives. These decisions require the commander to ensure that functions or units within the detective division are staffed at the proper level. Too many detectives in an area will result in wasted personnel. On the other hand, too few detectives results in a lowered clearance rate. Once allocation decisions are made, supervisors must ensure that detectives handle cases properly and expediently.

Effectiveness refers to how well the task is performed, regardless of cost, as a result of program activities: Were program goals met? The calculation of measures of effectiveness requires the identification of goals and goal achievement strategies. If objectives were not completely met, how close did the program come to doing so? For example, a police supervisor might decide to implement a problem-solving initiative in an area with low-income housing that has had high numbers of calls for service (CFS) during the past six months. A goal might be set to reduce the number of CFS by 25 percent in the next two months. Strategies to achieve this objective might include increased patrol, increased citizen contacts, crime prevention activities, neighborhood cleanups, and problem solving. If officers are given an assignment or dispatched to a call, did they satisfactorily resolve the situation? If officers must repeatedly return to family disturbance calls, it may indicate that they are taking inappropriate measures on the first occasion. Supervisors must use follow-up calls and activities to ensure that officers make every effort possible to adequately manage situations.

Equity refers to the quality of police services delivered to various groups in the community (Hepburn, 1981). All citizens' problems should receive the same level of concern. This is accomplished through operational planning. Equity in police services frequently becomes a political focal point. Citizens are concerned with the number of patrol units in their area, the probability of being victimized, and the response time of the police. If police services in their area are perceived to be consistent with those of other areas, citizens are more likely to have a positive image of the police. To a large extent, equity is at the root of the recent bias-based policing controversy. For years, the police did little in many minority neighborhoods. Minorities often received fewer or inferior services and viewed this as an inequitable situation (Gaines and Kappeler, 2008). As a result of community policing and problem solving, the police today are attacking crime, drug, and disorder problems in many minority communities. The end result is that more minorities are being stopped and questioned by the police more frequently. This can result in a perception of inequity since minorities are stopped at higher rates than nonminority citizens. On the other hand, if the police continue to allow greater levels of lawlessness in some areas relative to others, equity becomes an issue.

Finally, **accountability** refers to whether or not resources are used for proper purposes and infers that the police are public servants and, consequently, should provide services that meet public concerns and needs (Gaines and Kappeler, 2008). Moore (2003) notes that citizens have a right to demand that their police departments be accountable. Police officers too often see their role as that of "crime fighters" and want to subjugate other responsibilities. Research indicates, however, that the public consistently requests the police to be more involved in peacekeeping and service activities than in law enforcement activities (Gaines and Kappeler, 2008). Managers and supervisors must ensure that officers understand their role in society and meet these citizen expectations.

EXHIBIT 7–1 Measuring Accountability Citywide: Colorado Springs

The Colorado Springs, Colorado, Police Department recently implemented a new organizational performance evaluation system called the Police Accountability and Service Standards (PASS), which is a measurement system to evaluate police services and determine whether or not the agency is working effectively and efficiently. The four main goals of PASS are to (1) provide a method of accountability to the city for providing a high level of service and maintaining a secure community, (2) establish priorities of the community's needs, (3) assess the agency's ability to provide services for those needs, and (4) identify resources spent and needed to accomplish agency goals. PASS analyzes six categories of service standards: response times, clearance rates, neighborhood policing, citizen satisfaction with police services, vice and narcotics activity, and officer deployment. PASS attempts to identify the best practices in the agency, while addressing those practices that are not performing up to standard. Outcome measures were developed for each category of service standard, to explain why the department was or was not able to meet the individual standards.

Source: Information provided by the Colorado Springs Police Department; see also "Beyond the Numbers: How Law Enforcement Agencies Can Create Learning Environments and Measurement Systems," *The Police Chief,* April 2002, pp. 164–173.

Numbers of reports, citations, and arrests by officers are traditional performance measures still in use by many police agencies.
(Courtesy Reno, Nevada, Police Department.)

Traditional Views Relative to Police Productivity

The police historically have been more concerned with efficiency than effectiveness, equity, or accountability. Police managers and supervisors have been primarily concerned with the number of activities generated by officers or units. Such measures include number of citations issued, number of arrests, percentage of cases cleared by arrest, number of citizen complaints about police services and conduct, conviction rates, and amount of stolen property recovered. These conventional measures, some of which are collected by most agencies for the FBI's Uniform Crime Reports (UCR), have been used as the primary source of officer performance criteria; however, they do not indicate that the department, unit, or officers are striving to achieve specified goals and objectives or that they are achieving them. Police officers may write large numbers of traffic citations, but if they are written at locations where there are few accidents or for violations other than those that contribute to accidents at specific locations, the officers' efforts will not contribute to the objective of reducing the number of traffic accidents.

This does not mean that managers and supervisors should not monitor traditional measures of productivity. Research indicates that officers vary in their outputs. For example, Walsh (1985) examined the arrests for one precinct in New York City and found varying rates of felony arrests across patrol officers. He found that 63 officers did not make a felony arrest during the year; 59 officers had 1 to 8 arrests; 19 officers had 9 to 20 felony arrests; and 15 officers had 25 to 69 felony arrests. These data indicate that some officers were exerting more effort, especially in the area of felony investigations, than other officers. Walsh's data demonstrates the importance of productivity monitoring. Every critical area of police work can be examined similarly. However, activity monitoring does not equate to evaluating the department's response to community problems.

Spelman (1988) compared traditional police productivity measures to bean counting. Police managers or supervisors too often focus on the number of activities, rather than what the activities are supposed to accomplish. For example, if the number of arrests increases from one year to the next, does this mean that the department is doing better? Police activities should be directed toward some problem or goal. The police are productive when they solve some problem or accomplish a desired goal. (Note how commanders are now being evaluated in New York City Police Department, as an outgrowth of the city's CompStat strategy, discussed later.)

What is a Productive Police Department Today?

A productive police department is engaged in a number of processes that provide a variety of services to its constituents. Obviously, effectiveness, efficiency, equity, and accountability are guiding principles when delivering these services. However, how should a department focus on and interact with a community? The National Institute of Justice (1997) identified six attributes of a healthy police department, with *healthy* being operationalized as maximally serving the community.

First, a department knows what it wants to accomplish. It has articulated goals and objectives. This means that the department has scanned the community and identified specific problems and has taken action to deal with them. Police departments must be proactive, especially at the operational level. This equates to the implementation of a variety of strategies and tactics.

Second, a healthy or productive department knows its citizens. What do citizens, citizen groups, and neighborhoods desire from their police? Police departments should serve the interests of the citizens they serve. This entails understanding citizens' needs and perceptions at the lowest level. Each neighborhood may have its own unique problems, and citizens expect the police to address them. This means that policing is tailored to meet these demands and expectations.

Third, a police department should know its business. That is, it constantly monitors activities to determine if services are increasing, and if so, which services are increasing and where they are allocated. This means examining calls for service, arrests, traffic accidents, crimes, and other activities or services provided by the police. When these indices are monitored by time and geography, a department can better understand current levels of service and future trends.

Fourth, a department must understand the demands of the business. Police departments have limited resources, personnel, and budgets. These resources also include others in the community that provide a support function for police services, such as other agencies and partnerships. A department must understand where and the activities for which these resources are expended. The department must ensure that it maintains the budget so that goals and objectives can be met. It also allows managers to anticipate budgetary needs as service levels increase.

Fifth, a good department knows its people. Police managers and supervisors must know what motivates their subordinates, and develop reward structures that maintain high levels of motivation. Managers and supervisors must ensure that officers are prepared for their job assignments. They must determine whether officers have the correct training and the personality or ability to work in a particular assignment. For example, a highly productive patrol officer may not necessarily be a good investigator. Interests and personality often determine the assignments for which an officer is best suited.

Finally, a productive police department provides its constituents with feedback on police activities and what is occurring in the jurisdiction. If police officials expect citizens to cooperate and provide information and support to the department, they must meet with these groups and explain what the department is doing about their problems. Managers and supervisors should meet with officials from those agencies that work with the department on police related activities. Most importantly, police managers and supervisors should provide feedback to their subordinates regarding the job that is being done and those goals and objectives that are important. When police managers and supervisors interact with other groups, these groups are more likely to help and support police activities.

The above sections described some of the principles that identify a productive police department. The following section examines how productivity has been measured. Traditional methods largely have been inaccurate and represent a more bureaucratic perspective about productivity. Later sections will examine more current methods that attempt to incorporate contemporary principles regarding productivity.

IMPROVING POLICE PRODUCTIVITY: PLANNING AND PROBLEM SOLVING

Police departments must constantly strive to improve productivity by looking for better ways of providing services to citizens and monitoring expenses. At the same time, departments must be able to better identify problems. Four important innovations have contributed to improved productivity: planning, problem solving, citizen surveys, and CompStat. These innovations are addressed in this section.

If a police agency is to be effective in its productivity, a large percentage of its officers' activities must relate to solving some community problem or helping citizens. Police departments have attempted to accomplish this objective through **strategic planning,** which is an administrative process that drives agency vision, mission, and goals; it may also be defined as "a systematic, and continuous process of analyzing internal and external conditions in order to make more accurate decisions that effectively deal with problems and issues" (Law Enforcement Assistance Administration, 1975:2). Planning, roughly stated, is deciding what the police agency should be doing; it is the linking of current activities to future conditions. It is decision making regarding operational activities based on anticipated contingencies (Gaines et al., 1991). Planning results in goals and objectives for the department and individual units within the department. Once goals and objectives are identified, activities must be implemented to accomplish them. Activities can be in the form of programs, strategies, and tactics.

As shown in Figure 7-1, top-level administrators monitor and evaluate the environment or community and identify the department's mission and police department goals. This process results in tone and direction for the department. Here, strategies and responsibilities are assigned to individual units in the department. Mid-level managers then break these goals down into unit-level objectives and develop

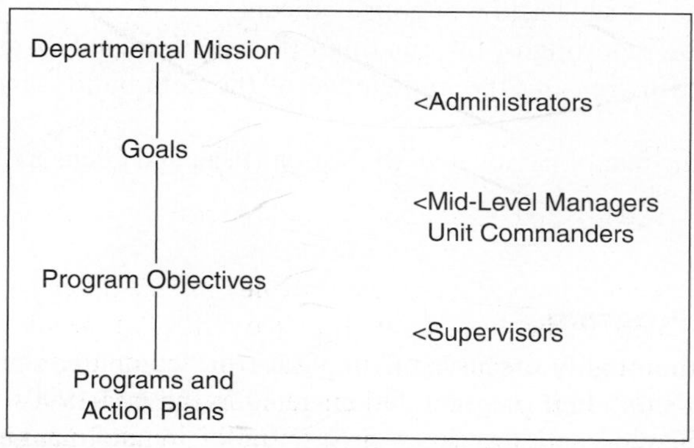

FIGURE 7-1 The Planning Process

programs to accomplish the objectives. Finally, supervisors are charged with ensuring that officers perform according to operational plans and achieve the desired objectives. They ensure that work is conducted as envisioned. The planning process becomes the link between internal measures or productivity and external needs.

This planning model has a number of problems. First, police departments have difficulty identifying overall goals for the department and as such often resort to general statements that provide little direction for lower-level managers and supervisors (Hoover, 1993). Second, when goals are identified, it becomes difficult to make adjustments when the environment changes. This inflexibility results in discrepancies between services being provided by the department and actual community need. Third, lower-level managers and supervisors often have little input into the system. They are not involved in designing work activities or performance measures; furthermore, they are provided little opportunity to criticize or make adjustments in organizational activities that are not working properly.

Another similar organizational form that enhances police productivity is community oriented policing and problem solving (COPPS), which is discussed in detail in Chapter 4. Essentially, COPPS focuses on concerns in the community. Problem solving is the primary tactic used in this strategy, with the police department attempting to identify a problem and then developing a plan to solve it. Each problem is handled differently, depending on the nature of the problem, and the police department works with other units of government or private agencies in deploying solutions.

The evaluative criteria employed in the traditional policing model, such as crime rates, clearance rates, and response times, have been problematic when applied to the professional model itself and are even less appropriate for the COPPS model. Geller and Swanger (1995) argue for a marriage between the quality and quantity of performance criteria, noting "who cares how many coffee beans we have if the java tastes nasty!" (p.152). These measures also fail to gauge the effect of crime prevention efforts. Under a COPPS philosophy, the department must change its criteria for determining the quality of officer performance. Following are some of the criteria that might be used in this appraisal:

- Identifying and solving local crime and disorder problems through a police-community consultation process
- Increasing reporting rates for both traditional crime categories and nontraditional crime and disorder problems
- Reducing the number of repeat calls for service from the same addresses
- Improving the satisfaction with police services by public users of those services, particularly with victims of crime
- Increasing the job satisfaction of police officers
- Increasing the reporting of information of local crime and disorder problems by community residents and increasing the knowledge of the community and its problems by local beat officers
- Decreasing the fear of personal victimization (Peak and Glensor, 2008:194)

COMPSTAT

The New York Program

In Chapter 4 we thoroughly discussed CompStat (for "computer statistics")—the New York City Police Department's (NYPD) program that emerged in the mid-1990s. **CompStat** is a computerized tool for tracking the most serious crimes in New York City and mapping them to determine patterns

EXHIBIT 7–2 Assessing NYPD Commander Performance

NYPD's CompStat program has become an agency-wide philosophy that guides much of what the organization does, and it has been expanded to include accountability over and appraisal of many non–crime-fighting facets of the department. Another unique feature of the rapidly spreading reach of CompStat is the manner in which the organization's commanders are evaluated. Statistics are gathered for generating a profile of commanding officers and assessing their performance. Commander Profile Reports scrutinize the commander's performance on a variety of management variables, including the commander's appointment date, years in rank, and the amount of education and specialized training he or she received. In addition, each profile contains non-crime statistics such as the amount of overtime generated by members of his or her command, the number of department vehicle accidents, absence rates, and the number of civilian complaints.

Adapted from Jim McKay (2002). CompStat for the 21st century. *Government Technology* (July):30, 32

and trends through crime analysis, and to hold commanders accountable for reducing crime in their areas.

CompStat has become a business management tool, being adopted by departments throughout the country. In addition to analyzing crimes, officials can keep track of officer overtime, citizen complaints, and even building maintenance and how quickly a police vehicle is returned to the streets after being serviced (McKay, 2002).

Four principles govern CompStat: timely and accurate intelligence, rapid deployment, effective tactics, and relentless follow-up and assessment. The assessments contain information gathered and mapped electronically; several maps can be overlapped to form layers of statistical information that can be projected onto video screens. A dense pattern of dots, or hot spots, on a map suggests a spree of criminal activity and means someone is going to be held accountable for the causes and solutions (McKay, 2002).

In essence, CompStat brings accountability to policing (Willis, Mastrofski, and Weisburd, 2004). By examining crime maps, managers can identify problems with some level of specificity. Once problems are identified, managers can devise strategies and tactics to counteract them. Because CompStat is a continuous process, it allows managers and supervisors to have a "real time" view of crime problems. It allows for continuous and instantaneous planning.

CompStat also includes a statistical profile of NYPD's commanding officers, as explained in Exhibit 7-2.

The map contained in Figure 7-2 shows the burglaries for a portion of Fontana, California. Some areas have larger numbers of burglaries than other areas. Patrol commanders can use the map to assign officers and deploy different police strategies. A variety of maps can be generated. For example, burglaries for one week, one month, or six months or more can be mapped. Maps showing a variety of crimes can be mapped. For example, a unit commander may be interested in FBI Part I crimes or all violent crimes in an area. The maps serve to: (1) assist in devising strategies, (2) focus attention and police resources, and (3) hold commanders and supervisors accountable for their operations. CompStat has been a significant innovation in law enforcement.

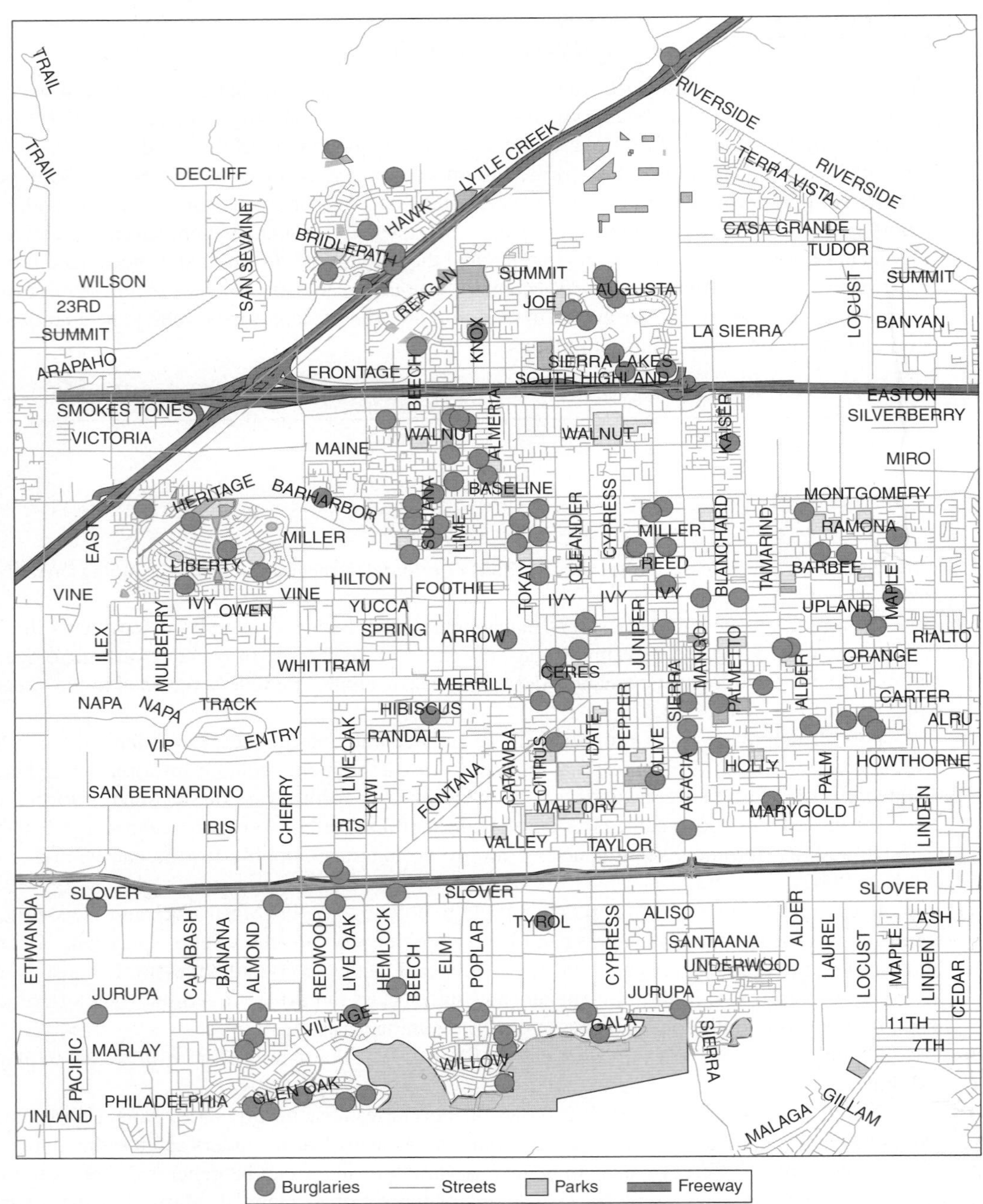

FIGURE 7-2 Crime map of Fontana, California
(Provided by the Fontana, California Police Department)

CITIZEN SURVEYS

Another important method of identifying problems and focusing police efforts is **citizen surveys**, which add a measure of accountability to police services (Moore and Braga, 2003). As discussed above, police departments should be responsive to citizen needs and expectations. One method of identifying these needs is citizen surveys. Citizen surveys can provide a great deal of information:

1. Perceptions of crime problems
2. Perceptions of disorder in the area
3. Fear of crime
4. Citizen satisfaction with police services and performance
5. Citizen satisfaction with other related governmental services

Surveys can be stratified to meet the department's informational needs. For example, the department can perform business or residential surveys. People residing in apartment complexes, especially high-crime complexes, can be surveyed. Finally, information can be collected by neighborhood or area allowing the police to identify and concentrate on neighborhood problems. Citizen surveys are an important part of COPPS and policing in general. Table 7-1 shows the extent of citizen surveying that is being done by local police departments; essentially, 22 percent of all agencies, employing 43 percent of all officers, survey citizens in their jurisdictions; furthermore, as shown in Figure 7-3, a majority of the departments use surveys to evaluate agency performance (76 percent) or to provide information to officers (61 percent); other common uses are shown in the figure.

Wells, Horney, and Maguire (2005) investigated the utility of citizen feedback on police officers. Unfortunately, they found that feedback has had little effect on officers' performance, attitudes, or activities. The research demonstrates that police managers and supervisors must make a more concerted effort to ensure that survey results and other citizen feedback are incorporated in officers' activities. Managers can accomplish this through enhanced supervision and the incorporation of citizen feedback into policies and directives.

Although surveys are very useful in identifying problems in the community, they also serve as an accountability tool. Surveys can be used to evaluate the department as a whole and individual units. When survey results are examined across time, e.g., six month or yearly intervals, administrators and

TABLE 7-1 Surveying of citizens by local police departments, by size of population served, 2003

	Percent of agencies that surveyed citizens during 12-month period ending June 30, 2003 regarding—				
Population served	Any topic	Satisfaction with services	Perceptions of crime problems	Reporting of crimes to law enforcement	Personal crime experiences
All sizes	22%	17%	12%	10%	7%
1,000,000 or more	31%	25%	13%	6%	19%
500,000–999,999	43	43	30	30	24
250,000–499,999	58	58	50	33	28
100,000–249,999	53	48	38	26	30
50,000–99,999	45	40	34	27	25
25,000–49,999	38	33	25	12	16
10,000–49,999	28	26	19	12	13
2,500–9,999	19	15	8	8	6
Under 2,500	17	10	8	9	2

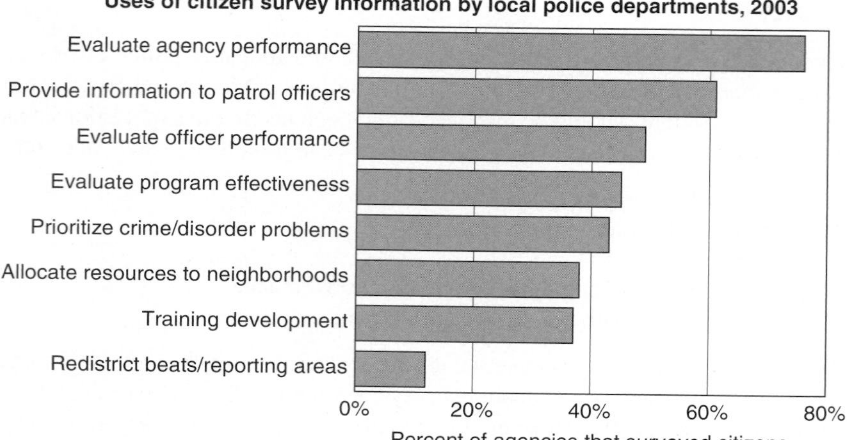

FIGURE 7-3 "Uses of Citizen Survey Information by Local PDs," from p. 22 of *Local Police Departments, 2003*; available at: http://www.ojp.usdoj.gov/bjs/pub/pdf/1d03.pdfno

managers can determine if improvements have been made. If not, corrective actions, whether it is new programming, better supervision, or the reallocation of officers, can be taken.

Productivity is an important issue in policing. Productivity can be measured using a variety of tools. Departments should provide as much productivity information to managers and supervisors as possible. Too often, managers and supervisors fail to measure and take steps to improve productivity. When this occurs, the department is usually stagnant and not effective in meeting the needs of the community. Every manager and supervisor in the police organization should constantly evaluate productivity so that they know where they need to be and what changes must be made to get there.

PERFORMANCE APPRAISAL

Rationale and Purposes

When performance appraisal is discussed, many people focus solely on individual officers. Officers are an important part of the performance evaluation process, but they only represent one part of the picture. Performance and productivity measurement must consider all levels of the police department.

Figure 7-4 shows the police hierarchical structure. As noted in the figure, administrators are concerned with the department's overall productivity–types and level of services provided to the community. Middle managers are responsible for individual units in the department, e.g., patrol shifts, criminal investigation, traffic, etc. The individual units are responsible for providing specific services and have a number of duties. These middle managers must be concerned with the performance of subordinates and the unit's overall productivity; they must determine whether goals and objectives are being met. Finally, sergeants are assigned to these units, and their primary responsibility is to ensure that their subordinate officers carry out assignments as expected. To a great extent, a police department is the sum of its many parts, and attention must be given to each part as well as the total or complete police department.

The monitoring and maintenance of productivity and performance standards are not easy tasks; many managers and supervisors, both new and old, find the obligation to evaluate and appraise subordinates' performance to be quite daunting. But for most managers and supervisors, this is a "make or

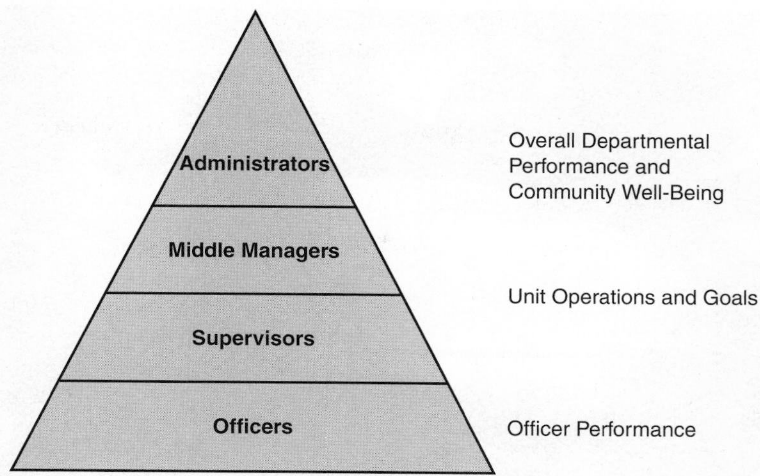

FIGURE 7-4 Police Department Productivity and Performance by Organizational Level

break" component of management. One can hardly be called a leader if he or she does not fairly and accurately rate subordinates and unit activities. Moreover, if this is not accomplished, the department and community may suffer as a result of poor performance.

According to Mathis and Jackson (1997:343), **performance appraisal** is "the process of evaluating how well employees do their jobs compared with a set of standards and communicating that information to those employees." Thus, in order for a department to have an effective performance evaluation system, it must have (1) performance standards, (2) a method of measuring performance, and (3) a way to provide officers with feedback relative to their performance. Departments have used a variety of names to refer to the performance appraisal process: performance evaluation, activity audit, employee rating, or performance review. Generally, performance appraisal is a formal process whereby supervisors examine subordinates' performance, rate their performance, and provide them with feedback about their behavior. It is a formal process because departments generally evaluate all officers at the same time using the same rating form and system. Once supervisors rate their subordinates, most departments require unit commanders to review and approve the ratings.

A department's formal performance appraisal process should co-exist with and be parallel to the constant and informal evaluation of subordinates' behavior and performance by managers and supervisors. The informal process allows supervisors to collect information for the performance appraisal, and it allows them to take action and change subordinates' behavior that does not comply with the department's expectations. A captain should monitor the activities of his or her lieutenants and sergeants just as sergeants should constantly oversee the activities of their officers. Neither the formal process nor the informal process should supplant the other.

Police departments generally identify three reasons for a formalized performance appraisal:

1. To standardize the nature of the personnel decision-making process so that the rights of the job incumbent are fully represented
2. To assure the public that the agency representatives are fully qualified to carry out their assigned duties
3. To give the job incumbent necessary behavior modification information to maintain behaviors that are appropriate (Landy and Goodin, 1974:167)

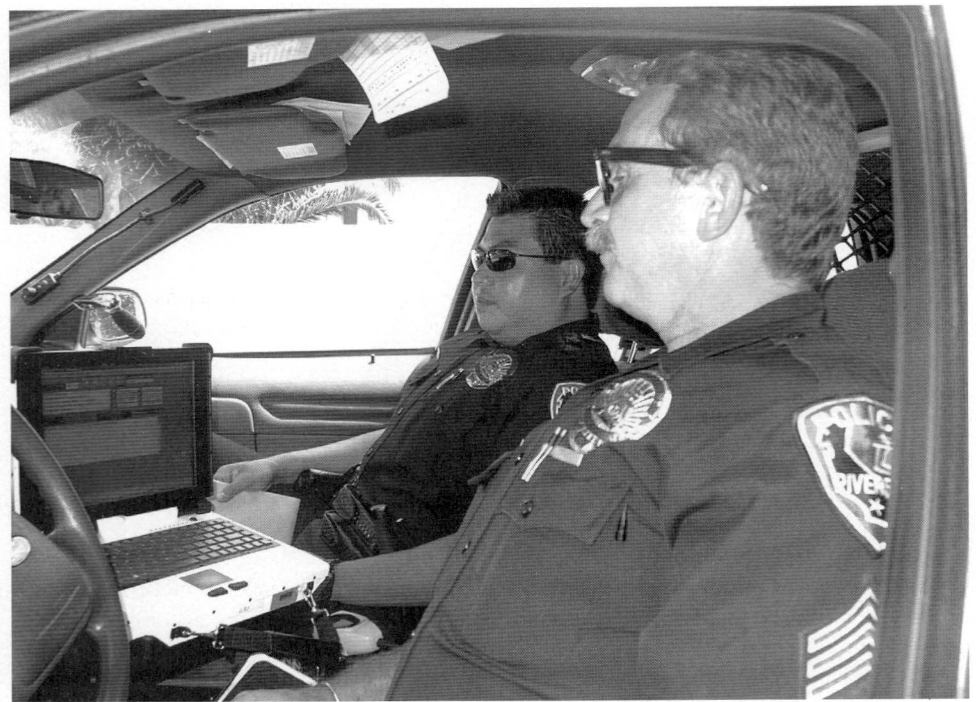

Superior officers, regardless of rank, should constantly provide officers with feedback. *(Courtesy Riverside, California, Police Department.)*

Performance appraisal, in essence, is an accountability and control process. It is a system for ensuring accountability because the results can be used to evaluate individual officers and units within the police department, or the department as a whole. Administrators are able to make a number of comparisons by examining the results of performance appraisals. It is a control process because the results can be used by managers to direct and change subordinates' behavior. Supervisors can counsel individual officers who do not perform at expected levels and managers can discuss results with supervisors and unit commanders when unit productivity does not reach expected levels.

More specifically, the performance appraisal serves a number of organizational purposes: formalized feedback to employees, recruitment and selection, training, field training officer evaluation, horizontal job changes, promotions, compensation management, and discipline.

Formalized Feedback to Employees. Superior officers, regardless of rank, should constantly provide subordinates with feedback about their performance. This activity is the very essence of supervision. The quality and quantity of this feedback varies tremendously even within a given police department. Some supervisors will closely supervise their subordinates and constantly counsel them about their performance, while other supervisors may only discuss performance occasionally with their subordinates. Other supervisors may abdicate this responsibility altogether. The department should provide the structure—a minimum agenda—to guide the evaluation and the resulting feedback session. Also, the department should establish a policy that dictates the time and frequency of appraisals. A formal feedback session for subordinates is the most important purpose for performance appraisals, although formal feedback sessions should be supplemented with informal counseling on a continuous basis.

Recruitment and Selection. As a formal process, performance appraisal provides a structure whereby supervisors can collectively have input into recruitment and selection criteria. Personnel specialists should examine performance appraisals to identify personnel weaknesses or deficiencies. As problems are identified, they should be used to target pools of people for recruitment and to refine selection tests and criteria.

Training. The performance appraisal process should identify deficiencies or problems with officers' performance, especially those officers who recently graduated from the basic training academy. In some instances, these deficiencies are the result of improper training or the lack of training. The training staff should review the results of annual performance evaluations to identify training deficiencies. Adjustments can then be made in the recruit or basic training program or provide veteran officers with in-service training programs.

Field Training Officer (FTO) Evaluation. As discussed in Chapter 6 (along with the newly developed PTO program), most police departments have an FTO program for their new officers, which represents a special type of performance appraisal. The program is designed to allow the department to determine whether officers should be retained. These field training evaluations are extremely important, because if the officer is retained after the probationary period, he or she can be dismissed only by showing cause. This creates a situation in which departments are forced to retain officers who are mediocre or who constantly cause minor problems. Below average or problem-causing officers should be dismissed during the probationary period. These evaluations can also serve to provide feedback to the training process.

Horizontal Job Changes. An accurate performance appraisal system will document officers' strengths and weaknesses. Many police departments have specialized units, such as traffic, criminal investigation, or planning, that require officers to have a variety of skills and different levels of job knowledge. Commanders of these units can review performance appraisal information to identify those officers who possess the best skills and productivity levels for these units. The performance appraisal can provide invaluable information when making decisions about transfers across units.

Promotions. The performance appraisal is one of the most common measures used in the promotion process. A survey by the International Association of Chiefs of Police (IACP) and the Police Foundation (PF) showed that 32 percent of the departments surveyed used performance evaluations in their promotion system (IACP and PF, 1973). Only written tests and oral boards were used more frequently. The performance appraisal allows the department to consider officers' past behavior when making promotional decisions. Generally, past behavior is the best predictor of future behavior. When performance is used for promotions, police departments should use promotability ratings (Cederblom, 1991). The difference between promotability ratings and performance appraisals is that promotability ratings concentrate on job dimensions or criteria that are important for the next level supervisory position while performance appraisals focus on important job behaviors for the officer's current position. Officers should be evaluated on their performance relative to the new position rather than on how well they perform in the old position.

Compensation Management. A number of departments base annual salary increments on the performance appraisal. Officers in the Lexington, Kentucky, Police Department must have a minimum of 70 percent on their annual performance appraisal in order to receive their annual salary increment. Other departments provide merit raises for officers who receive high rankings. For example, the 10 officers who receive the highest performance appraisal scores for the department might receive an extra 5 percent merit raise. Performance appraisals are used extensively in determining raises for police officers.

Discipline. In some instances, the performance appraisal can be used as a basis to discipline officers. This is especially applicable when an officer fails to meet departmental expectations but does not do anything that violates policies or lies outside the bounds of acceptable behavior. Performance that is consistently below average or otherwise deficient can be documented on the performance appraisal form. If an officer fails to correct the behavior and receives several such deficient evaluations, the department might take disciplinary action. The performance appraisal formally documents unacceptable behavior and provides a record of the feedback to the officer.

Potential Problems

One of the problems with performance appraisals is that police managers attempt to use them for multiple purposes. The purpose of the ratings generally affects how supervisors rate their subordinates. For example, supervisors tend to be more lenient when ratings are used for promotions as compared to when they are used strictly for counseling. Consequently, when a department attempts to use a single set of ratings for multiple purposes, it tends to distort the ratings and create a variety of problems. Given that performance appraisal is such a critical part of supervision, police departments should consider developing a variety of rating schemes.

It should also be understood that performance appraisal is not an event but functions as a process. Even though the performance appraisal may be administered only once or twice a year within a given department, a great deal of activity precedes it and occurs after its administration. Adequate attention must be given to these details if the performance appraisal process is to effectively accomplish its objectives.

Defining Rating Criteria

Defining rating criteria is a three-step process. First, the job is studied in an attempt to identify what should be measured by the performance appraisal system. This includes reviewing job descriptions, job-task analysis information, and other job-related information, such as departmental policies and procedures, to identify the critical and most important activities associated with the position. This process ultimately should provide a listing of job activities and measures of their relative importance. Hence, the most important job components can be identified for measurement.

Second, once this is accomplished, performance standards must be established. That is, at what level must subordinates perform these tasks or activities for their behavior to be deemed unacceptable, acceptable, or above average? When rating subordinates' work behavior, raters must have fairly specific standards to guide their decision making. Furthermore, subordinates must be made aware of standards so that they can evaluate their own work. These performance standards must then be captured on the performance appraisal rating form, the third step in the process.

Job criteria and performance standards must be articulated within the performance appraisal system. That is, the department must develop rating forms and guidelines that are provided to everyone prior to their usage. Every officer must be trained on the system prior to implementing it. Police administrators cannot expect subordinates to perform at acceptable levels unless the subordinates have been informed of the standards.

When Bradley and Pursley (1987) developed a performance appraisal system for the North Little Rock, Arkansas, Police Department, they identified 202 unique tasks that were critical or frequently performed by the officers. They also identified 23 skills, knowledge, and abilities (SKAs) that were necessary to perform the tasks. The 23 SKAs were then grouped into eight general categories: job knowledge, decision making, dependability, initiative, equipment use, communication, demeanor, and relations with others. The performance appraisal system was then developed around these eight dimensions.

Unfortunately, many performance ratings focus on mundane or bureaucratic activities or officer traits. Lilley and Hinduja (2006) examined over 1,400 rating dimensions used in police performance appraisals and found that the overwhelming majority of rating factors focused on internal procedures such as radio protocols, completing departmental forms, and dress code. These types of rating dimensions actually related to supervision and discipline rather than performance. Performance appraisals should focus on activities that are important in terms of accomplishing unit objectives.

Finally, it should be noted that performance appraisal ratings represent unique measures of officer performance. Falkenberg, Gaines, and Cordner (1991) investigated the constructs or dimensions used in performance appraisals. They found that the measurements were distinctive from other psychological dimensions or scores on management tests. They concluded that performance appraisals provided productivity information that could not be obtained through other means.

Choosing Among Rating Forms

Managers have a variety of rating forms from which to choose when developing a performance appraisal system. Each form has its strengths and weaknesses. The purposes of the performance appraisal should dictate the type of form used by a department. The following sections examine the various forms.

GRAPHIC RATING FORM Perhaps the simplest rating form, the graphic rating form, is that shown in Figure 7-5. The graphic rating form lists the job dimensions to be rated and provides a space for the rater to select a numerical rating. When using the rating form in Figure 7-5, the supervisor would merely place an "X" or a check mark in the box that best describes the officer's performance. For example, if the officer's performance in public relations skills was "good," it would be so noted. The supervisor would make this determination by considering the officer's behavior as well as citizen input (both complaints and commendations).

DIMENSION	UNSATISFACTORY	FAIR	GOOD	SUPERIOR	EXCEPTIONAL
Relationship with Others					
Quantity and Quality of Work					
Communications Skills					
Attendance and Punctuality					
Public Relations Skills					

FIGURE 7-5 Graphic Rating Form for Rating Police Officers

A variation on the graphic rating form is the numerical rating form. The only difference between these two forms is that the descriptive adjectives at the top of the form in Figure 7-5 are replaced by numbers, generally ranging from 0 to 10 or 50 to 100. When a numerical rating form is used, the rater is allowed to provide a numerical score, which allows the rater a wider range of possible scores. For example, the rating "fair" may be replaced by a range of 61 to 70. The rater can then give the officer a score within this range. Hughes (1990) notes that the majority (approximately 70 percent) of police departments use a numerical rating form.

The foremost difficulty with graphic rating forms is that they lack reliability. Police departments generally have several people involved in rating. Sergeants from each shift or unit are responsible for rating their officers. The difficulty arises in interpreting the descriptive adjectives or numbers used in the scale. For example, one supervisor may rate a subordinate good on a dimension, while another supervisor will rate the same employee superior. As the number of supervisors involved in the rating process increases, so does the number of errors or inconsistencies. The problem is that each supervisor has associated different meanings with the adjectives or numbers. The form does not provide the raters with information to assist in giving the ratings a meaning.

BEHAVIORALLY ANCHORED RATING SCALE Another variation of the graphic rating scale is the **Behaviorally Anchored Rating Scale (BARS)** (Bradley and Pursley, 1987). The BARS attempts to provide the rater with more information about performance standards and, therefore, lead to more accurate and reliable ratings. Figure 7-6 provides an example of a BARS for rating officers' handling of domestic violence situations. Notice that in addition to a numerical rating scale and an adjective rating scale, the form includes weighted descriptions of police officer behavior or performance when handling these situations. The form contains "fixed standard" information. When rating a subordinate, the

DIMENSION: HANDLING DOMESTIC VIOLENCE SITUATIONS

Extremely good	+ 7	Uses good judgment in determining proper action. Always considers what performance is best for the victim. Will also attempt to discover a workable solution for the aggressor. Will consider actions for the short term as well as the long term.
Good performance	+ 6	Generally uses good judgment in determining proper action. Always considers what is best for the victim but does not necessarily take action that considers the aggressor or a long-term solution.
Slightly good performance	+ 5	Responds to calls. Generally collects information that is helpful in deciding what action to take. Sometimes considers both the victim and the perpetrator. Usually makes the correct decision.
Adequate performance	+ 4	Responds to calls. Attempts to collect information that is helpful in deciding what action to take. Attempts to help the victim but usually does not consider the perpetrator. Sometimes makes the correct decision.
Slightly poor	+ 3	Responds to the calls and takes information from the complainant and other witnesses. Usually will only do the minimum necessary action. Not interested in problem solving at all.
Poor performance	+ 2	Only interested in answering the call and takes the action that is the most expedient for the officer. Always does the absolute minimum. Sometimes takes action that escalates the situation.
Unacceptable	+ 1	Responds to calls because he or she has to. Sometimes becomes embroiled in the conflicts and too frequently leaves the situation worse than before police intervention.

FIGURE 7-6 Behaviorally Anchored Rating Scale

Duties, Responsibilities And Projects	Measures of Results/ Performance Standards	Results
Ability to make decisions.	Officer consistently makes sound decisions. Demonstates self-confidence that decisions will be proper. Demonstrates proper application of police discretion. Uses proper application of the Kentucky Revised Statutes and the Revised Code of Ordinances. Functions well with limited amount of supervision and direction.	Employee consistently uses good judgment and makes sound decisions. Employee is highly confident in all situations and demonstrates proper discretion on all types of calls for service. Employee properly applies statutes when placing charges or taking reports. Employee requires a limited amount of supervision and direction.

FIGURE 7-7 Patrol Duties, Measurement, and Performance Standards, Lexington, Kentucky, PD

supervisor attempts to select the description that best fits how the officer typically handles family disturbances. The primary advantage of BARS is that the descriptions assist the supervisor in making better ratings and to be more consistent when rating several subordinates.

MIXED FORMAT

A performance appraisal format that is being adopted by departments is the mixed format. The **mixed format scale** uses multiple rating formats. For example, in Lexington, Kentucky, the performance appraisal consists of three sections using different rating formats. In the first section, setting forth the position duties and responsibilities, each unit in the police department identifies key or important duties and responsibilities that are to be rated. The second step is to develop measures or performance standards much like the behavioral rating scales, which are included in the Measure of Results/Performance Standards column. Supervisors then rate subordinates in narrative form using the measures of performance in the Results column. Figure 7-7 provides an example of one of the duty areas for patrol in the position responsibilities section of the Lexington, Kentucky, performance rating form.

The advantage to this format is that it allows different units to identify critical or important position responsibilities. Detective units can tailor their position responsibilities to their jobs rather than having everyone in the department use the same rating dimensions. Moreover, the Position Responsibilities can be changed every rating cycle to place more emphasis on new or more important Position Responsibilities. Figure 7-8 provides examples of position responsibilities that can be used by various operational units in the police organization.

The second section on the mixed format form includes a set of items that are rated using a graphic or numerical rating scale. These items are much like the items contained in Figures 7-7 and 7-8, above. The items contained in this section are standardized, allowing comparisons across the department. It provides a measure of consistency providing managers with information about how well all officers are performing.

The third and final section in the mixed format performance appraisal is the Develop Plans Section. This section has two primary areas: (1) Performance Strengths and (2) Development Needs. The supervisor describes the ratees' strengths in the Performance Strengths Area. This serves as positive feedback. It reinforces positive or good work habits. In the Development Needs Area, the supervisor lists areas of needed improvement. All supervisors must identify Development Needs. This ensures that the performance appraisal process works to improve officers' performance. Moreover, these Development Needs are discussed with the officer and reinforced. Managers can review the suggested

PATROL	INVESTIGATIONS	TRAFFIC	DOMESTIC VIOLENCE
Able to Make Decisions	Able to Effectively Conduct Investigations	Maintains Adequate Levels of Activity	Follows Procedures and Laws Relative to Domestic Violence Cases
Interacts with Citizens Well	Effectively Presents Cases in Court	Targets Areas with Large Numbers of Traffic Crashes When Engaged in Selective Enforcement	Works with Patrol Officers to Ensure that Procedures are Followed
Able to Complete Special Assignments Such as Problem Solving	Effectively Follows Laws of Arrest, Search, and Seizure	Able to Investigate Traffic Crashes and Document Circumstances	Works with Victims to Ensure Prosecution
Adheres to Departmental Regulations When Performing Patrol Duties	Able to Present Evidence in Court	Able to Interact with Public Effectively	Ensures That Victims Have Access to Assistance Such as Shelters

FIGURE 7-8 Examples of Position Responsibilities

Development Needs Areas for officers under their command to ensure that subordinates are moving in the right direction.

The mixed format performance rating system is comprehensive in that it provides feedback to officers and uses a targeted approach. Units within the department are able to develop performance standards, which help to get officers to concentrate on important parts of the job. The graphic rating section allows the department to collect performance information across the department. Finally, the Develop Plans Section allows supervisors to target individual officer performance and behavior. Subordinates are provided with specific information about how to improve.

COMMUNITY POLICING AND PERFORMANCE APPRAISALS

Although a majority of the police agencies in the United States have adopted community policing, a remaining problem has been to get officers and units at the lower levels of the police department to adopt the strategy (Kappeler, and Gaines, 2005). One way to facilitate acceptance is to adopt community policing activities into the performance appraisal system. This helps to identify the important aspects or activities associated with the strategy, and it provides a mechanism for rewarding officers who excel in community policing activities. Oettmeier and Wycoff (1997) noted that the Houston, Texas, Police Department used the performance appraisal to solidify that department's community policing efforts. Figure 7-9 shows some of the criteria Houston used. Note that the performance objectives provide substantial guidance to officers in performing community policing.

Even though community policing has been the primary strategy in many American police departments, community policing has not been integrated into police performance appraisals on a wide scale. Lilley and Hinduja (2006) report that community policing attributes have not been used in most community policing departments when measuring performance. Departments still emphasize bean counting and adherence to police policies. Many performance appraisal systems remain mechanistic and fail to encourage or reinforce community policing activities. Departments must endeavor to include community policing and other important dimensions in departmental performance appraisals.

Community Policing Performance Dimensions for the Houston Police Department

Tasks/Activities

Activities are listed beneath the tasks they are intended to accomplish.
Several activities could be used to accomplish a number of different tasks.

1. **Learn characteristics of area, residents, businesses**
   a. Study beat books
   b. Analyze crime and calls-for-service data
   c. Drive, walk area and make notes
   d. Talk with community representatives
   e. Conduct area surveys
   f. Maintain area/suspect logs
   g. Read area papers (e.g., "shopper" papers)
   h. Discuss area with citizens when answering calls
   i. Talk with private security personnel in area
   j. Talk with area business owners/managers
2. **Become acquainted with leaders in area**
   a. Attend community meetings, including service club meetings
   b. Ask questions in survey about who formal and informal area leaders are
   c. Ask area leaders for names of other leaders
3. **Make residents aware of who officer is and what s/he is trying to accomplish in area**
   a. Initiate citizen contacts
   b. Distribute business cards
   c. Discuss purpose at community meeting
   d. Discuss purpose when answering calls
   e. Write article for local paper
   f. Contact home-bound elderly
   g. Encourage citizens to contact officer directly
4. **Identify area problems**
   a. Attend community meetings
   b. Analyze crime and calls-for-service data
   c. Contact citizens and businesses
   d. Conduct business and residential surveys
   e. Ask about other problems when answering calls
5. **Communicate with supervisors, other officers and citizens about the nature of the area and its problems**
   a. Maintain beat bulletin board in station
   b. Leave notes in boxes of other officers
   c. Discuss area with supervisor
6. **Investigate/do research to determine sources of problems**
   a. Talk to people involved
   b. Analyze crime data
   c. Observe situation if possible (stakeout)
7. **Plan ways of dealing with problem**
   a. Analyze resources
   b. Discuss with supervisor, other officers
   c. Write Patrol Management Plan, review with supervisor
8. **Provide citizens information about ways they can handle problems (educate/empower)**
   a. Distribute crime prevention information
   b. Provide names and number of other responsible agencies; tell citizens how to approach these agencies
9. **Help citizens develop appropriate expectations about what police can do and teach them how to interact effectively with police**
   a. Attend community meetings/make presentations
   b. Present school programs
   c. Write article for area paper
   d. Hold discussions with community leaders
10. **Develop resources for responding to problem**
    a. Talk with other officers, detectives, supervisors
    b. Talk with other agencies or individuals who could help
11. **Implement problem solution**
    a. Take whatever actions are called for
12. **Assess effectiveness of solution**
    a. Use data, feedback from persons who experienced the problem, and/or personal observation to determine whether problem has been solved
13. **Keep citizens informed**
    a. Officers tell citizens what steps have been taken to address a problem and with what results
    b. Detectives tell citizens what is happening with their cases

FIGURE 7-9 Performance Dimensions for the Houston Police Department
Source: Oettmeier, T., and Wycoff, M. *Personnel Performance Evaluations in the Community Policing Context.* Washington, DC: Community Policing Consortium, 1997.

IMPROVING RATER PERFORMANCE

Perhaps the most notable problem associated with performance appraisals is raters' ability to accurately evaluate subordinates. DeNisi, Cafferty, and Meglino (1984) described the rating process as a complicated operation whereby supervisors need to constantly collect, encode, store, and retrieve information for rating purposes. Many personnel experts, however, believe that this process results in more problems than the form or system utilized. The following sections expound on rating problems and possible solutions.

Rater Errors

Rater errors refer to problems that potentially occur anytime superiors rate subordinates. Errors occur for a variety of reasons, and they must be controlled if the department is to have an effective performance appraisal system. The following is a discussion of some of the most common rater errors.

Halo Effect. The halo effect occurs when a rater evaluates a subordinate high or low on all rating dimensions because of one dimension. For example, a sergeant may believe that patrol officers should write a generous number of traffic citations. Officers who tend to write more citations receive higher ratings in all categories, while those who do not write above average numbers of tickets receive only average or below average ratings. In this example, the sergeant allows the number of citations written by officers to cloud his or her judgment about other rating dimensions.

Recency Problem. Recency problem refers to when a recent negative or positive event unduly affects an officer's ratings. An officer may make a traffic stop that results in the seizure of several pounds of cocaine and the arrest of several mid-level drug dealers immediately prior to the end of the rating period. The sergeant doing the ratings may give this arrest undue weight and rate the officer high. It may not matter that the arrest was the only felony arrest made by the officer during the rating period, and that the officer's performance overall was less than average. Ratings should represent the average performance during the total rating period.

Rater Bias. Rater bias refers to raters' values or prejudices distorting their ratings. People have all sorts of biases that can affect ratings: religious, racial, gender, appearance, existence of a disability, prior employment history, or membership in civic clubs and organizations. Biases can help or detract from an officer's ratings. Biases are one of the most difficult rater errors to overcome.

Constant Error Problem. Some raters are too strict, others may be too lenient, while still others tend to rate everyone in the middle. For example, a new sergeant may rate all his subordinates lower in order to show improvement in the next rating period. These rating patterns affect the outcome of combining the ratings for several different raters. When ratings are combined, some officers have a distinct advantage or disadvantage over others.

Unclear Standards. Unclear standards is a problem when there is little agreement about the rating dimensions or associated standards. For example, sergeants may be asked to rate their subordinates on productivity. One sergeant may define productivity one way, while another may define it differently. Varying interpretations of rating dimensions substantially affect ratings. If sergeants' ratings are to be consistent, they must have a clear, corresponding understanding of the standards being used.

These five errors represent the most common rating errors. Raters can make a number of other mistakes. For example, raters tend to value officers who are more like themselves or dislike those who are different. This can apply to a person's appearance, background, education, hobbies, and so on. First impressions by new officers may also have an undue impact on subsequent ratings. Finally, officers who previously had high-profile assignments may have an advantage over other officers because of their being perceived as better. Innumerable factors that have nothing to do with officers' performance can affect their performance appraisal ratings.

Rater Training

One of the most important methods for controlling rater error is rater training. Too often, supervisors are given performance appraisal forms and expected to accurately complete them. Research indicates that the rating process is extremely complicated (DeNisi et al., 1984) and that rater training is one of the better administrative mechanisms for improving ratings. In a survey of police officers, Coutts and Schneider (2004) found that many felt that raters were poorly trained, and this lack of training resulted in inadequate performance appraisals and lowered morale within the department. Bernardin and Buckley (1981) identified three key performance appraisal areas that require training: enhanced observational skills, a common frame of reference for raters, and the ability to be critical.

Enhanced Observational Skills. As noted earlier, the rating process involves several steps: collecting information, encoding the information into a meaningful form, storing the information, and finally, retrieving the information for rating purposes. Raters must be taught to gather and store pertinent information in a fashion that enhances the rating process.

When faced with the prospect of having to complete performance appraisal forms for their subordinates, supervisors often hurriedly ponder past activities, make judgments about those activities, and prepare to complete the required forms. This haste generally results in consideration of only partial data and leads to errors such as the halo effect or recency.

Raters can be trained to collect and store information for the rating process. Supervisors should be taught to observe and critically analyze subordinates' performance. The key here is to focus on critical job events. They should also be trained to keep diaries of subordinates' behavior and activities throughout the rating period. In an effort to ensure that all pertinent information is considered, raters should retain both positive and negative information, regardless of its magnitude. A few exceptional examples of work behavior should not counterbalance an otherwise below average performance period. Likewise, one or two mistakes should not overly blemish a productive work period.

Common Frame of Reference. In an effort to reduce the error of unclear standards, training should be provided to all raters to ensure that they clearly understand, accept, and adhere to the rating standards. Raters must use a common frame of reference when completing performance appraisals. For example, if sergeants are rating subordinates on interpersonal relationships, each sergeant involved should have the same understanding of what interpersonal relationships mean. If variation occurs among the sergeants, some officers will be treated unfairly, departmental morale will be affected, and the intended purposes of the performance appraisals will not be fulfilled. Behavioral anchors such as those found on a BARS are helpful in eliminating this problem, but a training program that exposes all raters to a thorough and complete discussion of the rating dimensions, their meanings, and expected behavior will substantially reduce rater error. A training program can provide raters with video-recorded examples or vignettes of critical incidents of the job. Supervisors' ratings can be analyzed and discussed in a classroom atmosphere to foster more accurate ratings.

Critical Appraisal of Subordinates. As mentioned earlier, one of the major problems associated with performance appraisals is that raters oftentimes are too lenient and rate all or most of their subordinates too high. They fail to critically appraise subordinates' activity and behavior and reflect that appraisal in their ratings. This occurs for a number of reasons. It is a natural behavioral reaction since almost everyone attempts to avoid confrontations. Supervisors may fail to properly supervise subordinates and believe that they could not adequately explain or defend lower ratings. Raters may evaluate everyone high because low ratings may cast a doubt on the rater's ability to supervise. Another reason is that supervisors may not properly understand departmental expectations and therefore cannot accurately distinguish a poor performance from a good one.

A training program can emphasize the standards used to evaluate officers, and it can be used to underscore the importance of making accurate ratings that distinguish good, average, and below average performers. Training can indoctrinate raters on how ratings are used and the importance of making distinctions in ratings. In the end, training is one of the most important mechanisms that a department can use to enhance the accuracy of ratings.

It is important that officers are evaluated on their individual assignments. A footbeat officer would not necessarily be evaluated on the exact same criteria as one who is assigned to detectives, traffic, or training.
(Courtesy NYPD Photo Unit.)

DIFFERENT APPROACHES TO APPRAISAL

Using Peer and Self-Evaluations

For the most part, performance appraisals have been viewed as a management prerogative in policing. That is, performance appraisals have been used almost exclusively by management to evaluate subordinates. Few departments have experimented with or used peer evaluations (Gaines and Falkenberg, 1992; Love, 1981a, 1981b) or subordinate evaluations of superiors (McEvoy, 1987).

Peer evaluations refer to officers completing performance appraisal forms for the other officers within their work group. One supposed benefit of peer evaluations is that as the result of closer working relationships, officers possess more information about their colleagues than do supervisors and can consequently make better appraisals. It is questionable as to whether or not officers have more knowledge about their peers than do their supervisors, but they unquestionably have different information. The circumstances in which police work is conducted among peers is probably quite different from the interactions among police officers and their supervisors. The inclusion of this information in the performance appraisal process could be beneficial.

Love (1981a, 1981b) noted that the primary concerns with peer evaluations are reliability, validity, friendship bias, and negative user reactions. Love's research indicated that peer evaluations were just as reliable and valid as performance appraisals. Furthermore, he did not find that friendship bias affected ratings. When placed in a position of rating peers, officers would attempt to consider only those aspects of a peer's performance that related to the rating dimensions. Finally, they, like many supervisors, found performance rating to be a negative experience.

Gaines and Falkenberg (1992) investigated peer evaluations in an attempt to determine what they measured. They examined the relationships among peer ratings and a number of psychological dimensions, management qualities, and departmental performance appraisals. No consistent relationships were identified. They concluded that peer evaluations represent unique measures of performance, which provide information that otherwise is not included in performance appraisals.

Finally, self-evaluations must also be considered (Kakar, 1998). It may be beneficial to a department to have officers complete self-evaluations to identify their own strengths and deficiencies. Supervisors could compare the department's performance appraisal with the individual's self-evaluation to identify areas of agreement, blind spots, and areas of over evaluation. The self-evaluation could also serve as an excellent catalyst when discussing performance with subordinates.

The extent to which agencies are using peer, subordinate, or self-evaluations is not known. Police managers should be open-minded and use the type of rating system that best meets the needs of the department.

Subordinate Appraisal of Supervisors

McEvoy (1987) investigated subordinate appraisals of managers, with the following findings:

1. Subordinate appraisals frequently have been used for management development rather than evaluation purposes, but anecdotal reports of their use for both purposes are generally positive.
2. Managers report that subordinate feedback is helpful in improving their performance.

3. A substantial amount of "halo" exists in subordinate appraisals of their managers as they tend to rate superiors on only one dimension rather than differentiating the multiple dimensions that are commonly used on the rating forms.
4. A modest positive correlation exists between ratings by subordinates and ratings of the same individuals by superior officers, indicating some level of validity or agreement.

McEvoy's research revealed that subordinate ratings were effective in predicting manager success. He compared the results of subordinate appraisals to the results of an assessment center and found that subordinate appraisals more effectively predicted future performance appraisal scores. He also found that regardless of the number of dimensions used in such ratings, subordinates tended to rate superiors on one universal dimension.

PROVIDING APPRAISAL FEEDBACK

A critical component of the performance appraisal process is subordinate feedback. Substantial efforts should be exerted to ensure that this purpose is effectively achieved. The previous sections addressed a number of mechanical aspects of performance appraisal, including how to prepare raters for rating. It is just as important for supervisors to prepare for feedback sessions. There are a number of steps in this process:

1. Prior to a feedback session, supervisors should refresh their memories regarding the ratee's productivity record. Departmental printouts and other productivity records should be reviewed. This information should be discussed as a supplement to the performance appraisal itself.
2. Supervisors should know what they are going to say or the major points they will cover before the interview. Furthermore, the supervisor should ensure that the feedback session does not become sidetracked; the officer's performance should remain the focal point at all times. These interviews should be planned or mapped out prior to the interview. Supervisors should even rehearse interviews when possible.
3. Both positives and negatives should be discussed. Positive reinforcement of good work habits is just as important as eliminating negative ones.
4. Force the ratee to discuss his or her performance. This can be accomplished by asking questions or requesting the ratee to comment about his or her performance. This helps the subordinate to realistically evaluate his or her behavior.
5. Force the ratee to develop a performance plan. If an officer is substantially below expectations, require the officer to present a plan explaining how he or she will improve his or her performance. The plan can be verbal or written, but it is critical that a plan be presented. The plan can be used in subsequent counseling sessions should they be necessary.
6. Leave the subordinate with a clear understanding of what is expected. This can be accomplished by providing the officer with goals and objectives, discussing other officers' performance, and reinforcing overall departmental goals. Regardless of the method used, subordinates must have clear ideas of what is expected of them if they are to be good employees.

No matter what methods a department uses to evaluate police officer performance, the system will be only as good as the feedback sessions that supervisors provide subordinates. Unfortunately, many supervisors take this responsibility too lightly and do only a mediocre job during the performance appraisal feedback session. They often are uncomfortable with this responsibility and avoid it, and even worse, there is evidence that some supervisors inflate ratings to avoid what they perceive as a confrontation with their subordinates (Roberts, 2003; Smith, Harrington, and Houghton, 2000). Police managers must ensure that effective feedback sessions are conducted by supervisors.

EFFECTIVENESS OF PERFORMANCE APPRAISALS

What Works? Reasons for Ineffectiveness

The performance appraisal is an important supervisory tool. Theoretically, it should assist in increasing productivity and contribute to a police department's overall performance. Sometimes it is not effectively used, and the police department fails to reap its benefits. Walsh (1990) surveyed 122 police sergeants from several small and medium-size police departments and found that 87 percent reported that the performance evaluation was of little utility to them. That is, it was not helpful in their job as supervisors. The most common reasons given as to why performance appraisals were ineffective were

1. The performance criteria are subjective.
2. The systems lack managerial control. This creates rater inconsistency and favoritism.
3. Supervisors have little input into the process but are its major users.
4. The forms are filed and mean nothing.
5. Management is not concerned about performance—just making sure that things run smoothly is the main concern.
6. Supervisors' performance assessments are changed by administrators who have not observed the officer perform on a daily basis. (p. 101)

Walsh's findings clearly indicate that police departments must pay more attention to how their performance appraisal systems function. The problems voiced by the supervisors in Walsh's study are the result of deficiencies or problems that were addressed earlier. Such problems also indicate that departments are failing to use the information produced through performance appraisals. Police managers must put forth the effort to ensure that performance appraisals are functioning as envisioned by the department.

Performance Targeting

Halachmi (1993) recognized these same deficiencies and believes that police departments should abandon traditional performance appraisals and adopt performance targeting. **Performance targeting** occurs when the subordinate and the supervisor jointly identify performance goals for the subordinate and how they are to be achieved. Such an arrangement provides the subordinate with superior direction, and it creates an obligation on the part of the supervisor to work with the subordinate to ensure that the subordinate has the resources to accomplish assigned goals.

Performance targeting can be used at all levels within the chain of command. It is a modified form of management by objectives (MBO), in which a superior officer identifies objectives for the next subordinate level. This ensures that activities throughout the department are ultimately tied to the department's primary goals. Thus, a patrol captain could use a modified form of CompStat and identify priorities for each of his or her patrol squads. The patrol supervisors would then work with their officers to ensure that the objectives were met. The officers would then be evaluated on how well they contributed to accomplishing these objectives, rather than on global standards that usually are used on performance appraisals.

The Bainbridge, Ohio, Police Department implemented a modified performance targeting system (Kramer, 1998). The department identified a number of performance dimensions for which officers are evaluated. Unit commanders could select from the list for an individual officer or for an entire unit. Only important dimensions for a specific job were selected. The system gave the department a measure of flexibility allowing managers to have a focused evaluation. This allowed supervisors to select performance areas and provide officers with better direction. The mixed format performance appraisal format discussed earlier in this chapter is best suited for performance targeting.

CASE STUDIES

Following are two case studies that enable the reader to consider some of the substantive issues involved with appraising officer performance and to consider some possible solutions.

Case Study #1

Knowing Your People, or Searching for Hidden Meanings

You are a supervisor in Bay City, recently transferred from the robbery/homicide section of detectives to day shift patrol. You begin your new assignment by reviewing crime reports and calls for service data for the area and meeting with each of your officers to discuss their view of the area's problems and their work productivity. The south area of the district is divided geographically into five beats, consisting of single-family homes, small commercial businesses, and several large apartment complexes. Approximately 50,000 citizens live in the area; most are middle-class white and Hispanic people who reside and work in the area. Crime analysis data reveals that the most prevalent crime problems are daytime burglaries and thefts of property from the apartment complexes, juvenile drinking, and vandalism. The vandalism is not gang related and is mostly spray paint tagging of schools and businesses. There are three main thoroughfares through the area, but traffic accidents are low in comparison with the rest of the city. After reviewing three of your officers' past performance evaluations, you determine that Officer Stengel leads the patrol division in felony arrests. Her follow-up investigations have led to the identification of two groups of daytime burglars who were truants from the local school. A review of other performance areas shows similar good effort. Officer Robbins has just completed his probationary period. Troubled by the vandalism, he began working with the city attorney and local business owners on an ordinance that would ban the sale of spray paint to juveniles. Robbins makes every effort to work on this project between calls for service, but some of his fellow officers have complained about having to handle some of his calls. Officer Franklin has 10 years' experience and would like to work a motorcycle traffic assignment. Selections will be made in six months. In an effort to demonstrate his interest in that assignment, Franklin currently leads the department in the number of citations written. He also leads the department in citizen complaints of rude behavior, but only 2 of 10 complaints in the past three months were sustained. Assume that you are about to engage in an annual performance appraisal for each officer.

Questions for Discussion

1. What are your observations of each officer's performance?
2. Do you have any concerns about any of the behaviors demonstrated by any of the officers?
3. Do the officers satisfactorily address the district's problems?
4. Are there any other issues that may require your attention? If so, how would you handle those issues?
5. Which performance appraisal system (among those described in this chapter) would you opt to use?

Case Study #2

Seeing the World (and Subordinates) Through Rose-Colored Glasses

Sgt. Wilcox is a 10-year veteran, having worked mostly in the fraud section of detectives. She is recently assigned to day shift patrol division and assumes responsibilities for a team of mostly experienced and capable officers. Wilcox believes in a participative management style and therefore thinks that her officers should be involved in setting their work goals and objectives and should participate in the performance evaluation process. Wilcox meets with her team and outlines her approach to performance evaluations. Believing that this should be a positive experience for all, she instructs her officers to keep an individual log of their more notable achievements during the performance period. At the end of the rating period, Wilcox uses their top five accomplishments as a basis for their annual evaluation. When the first rating period is completed, Wilcox is pleased to find that her officers received some of the highest performance ratings in the department. However, she recently learns from her lieutenant that other supervisors are voicing criticisms of her evaluation methods. She is now confused about her evaluation method.

Questions for Discussion

1. What, if any, do you perceive to be the good aspects of Wilcox's personal method of evaluation?
2. What problems might arise from Sgt. Wilcox's rating system?
3. What rater errors are being committed, if any? What might be the basis for the peer supervisors' criticisms?

Summary

This chapter has addressed two important issues in police management: productivity measurement and performance appraisals. First-line supervisors are primarily responsible for a department's productivity. They supervise line personnel and must ensure that officers are not only productive, but also that their activities have a demonstrable effect on community problems. Managers and commanders, on the other hand, must assist in the development of programs and strategies that result in officers being able to accomplish goals and objectives. Thus, productivity is best accomplished through a team effort with management, supervisors, and officers working to provide services to the community.

One way departments manage productivity is through performance evaluations. Performance evaluations are formalized feedback sessions at which supervisors advise their subordinates about the quantity and quality of their activity. One of the purposes of the performance appraisal is to use it as a supervisory tool to direct officers' behavior. Moreover, performance appraisals should be used throughout the chain of command or anywhere there is a superior-subordinate relationship.

Performance appraisals also serve a variety of other departmental functions. When they are used for more than one function, the process becomes complicated and stated objectives may not easily be accomplished. The critical aspect about performance appraisals is that they represent a system, and as such, every aspect of the system, from developing rating forms to training supervisors to rate and provide feedback to officers, must be managed properly. If any one link in the system is defective, the total system will be damaged.

Items for Review

1. Describe what is meant by productivity measurement, and what are the primary tools used to enhance and measure productivity.
2. Explain how efficiency, effectiveness, equity, and accountability are of concern when attempting to measure productivity.
3. Review the characteristics of today's productive police department.
4. Describe how evaluation criteria employed in the traditional policing model, such as crime rates, clearance rates, and response times, have been problematic when applied to the community oriented policing and problem solving strategy.
5. Define and explain CompStat, how it originated, and how commanders are evaluated under this strategy.
6. Define performance appraisal and describe its purposes and uses.
7. Describe the various rating forms that supervisors may employ in a performance appraisal system, as well as some of the strengths and weaknesses of each.
8. Explain how citizen surveys can enhance police measurement and appraisal.
9. Delineate some of the problems and errors that exist when raters attempt to evaluate subordinates.
10. Explain some of the advantages, disadvantages, and problems of having subordinates rate their supervisors.

References

Bernardin, H. J., and Buckley, M. R. (1981). Strategies in rater training. *Academy of Management Review* 6(2):205–212.

Bradley, D. E., and Pursley, R. D. (1987). Behaviorally anchored rating scales for patrol officer performance appraisal: Development and evaluation. *Journal of Police Science and Administration* 15(2):37–44.

Cederblom, D. (1991). Promotability ratings: An underused promotion method for public safety organizations. *Public Personnel Management Journal* 20(1):27–34.

Coutts, L., and Schneider, F. (2004). Police officer performance appraisal systems: How good are they? *Policing: An International Journal of Police Strategies & Management* 27(1): 67-81.

DeNisi, A., Cafferty, T. P., and Meglino, B. M. (1984). A cognitive view of the performance appraisal process: A model and research propositions. *Organizational Behavior and Human Performance* 33:360–396.

Falkenberg, S., Gaines, L. K., and Cordner, G. W. (1991). An examination of the constructs underlying police performance appraisals. *Journal of Criminal Justice* 19:351–359.

Gaines, L., and Falkenberg, S. (1992). Anatomy of peer evaluations: What do they measure? *Justice Professional* 6(1):39–46.

Gaines, L., Famega, C., and Bichler, G. (2007). *Police Response to Burglar Alarms Study: San Bernardino County*. Report to the San Bernardino County Police Chiefs and Sheriff's Association.

Gaines, L. and Kappeler, V. (2008). *Policing in America*. Cincinnati: Anderson Publishing.

Gaines, L., Southerland, M. D., and Angell, J. E. (1991). *Police administration*. New York: McGraw-Hill.

Geller, W. A., and Swanger, G. (1995). *Managing innovation in policing: The untapped potential of the middle manager*. Washington, DC: Police Executive Research Forum.

Halachmi, A. (1993). From performance appraisal to performance targeting. *Public Personnel Management* 22(2):323–344.

Hepburn, J. R. (1981). Crime control, due process, and measurement of police performance. *Journal of Police Science and Administration* 9(1):88–98.

Hoover, L. T. (1993). Police mission: An era of debate. In L. Hoover, ed., *Police management: Issues and perspectives*. Washington, DC: Police Executive Research Forum, pp. 1–30.

Hughes, F. (1990). *Performance appraisal systems in law enforcement*. Unpublished doctoral dissertation, Michigan State University, East Lansing.

International Association of Chiefs of Police and the Police Foundation. (1973). *Police personnel practices in state and local governments*. Washington, DC: Police Foundation.

Kakar, S. (1998). Self-evaluations of police performance: An analysis of the relationship between police officers' education level and job performance. *Policing: International Journal of Police Strategies and Management* 21(4):632–646.

Kappeler, V., and Gaines, L. (2005). *Community policing*. Cincinnati: Lexis-Nexis.

Kramer, M. (1998). Designing an individual performance evaluation system. *FBI Law Enforcement Bulletin* 67(3):20–27.

Kuper, G. H. (1975). Productivity: A national concern. In J. Wolfle and J. Heaphy, eds., *Readings on productivity in policing*. Washington, DC: Police Foundation, pp. 1–10.

Landy, F., and Goodin, C. (1974). Performance appraisal. In O. Stahl and R. Staufenberger, eds., *Police personnel administration*. North Scituate, MA: Duxbury, pp. 180–181.

Law Enforcement Assistance Administration. (1975). *Criminal justice planning workbook.* Washington, DC: Author.

Lilley, D., and Hinduja, S. (2006). Officer evaluation in the community policing context. *Policing: An International Journal of Police Strategies & Management* 29(1):19-37.

Love, K. G. (1981a). Accurate evaluation of police officer performance through the judgment of fellow officers: Fact or fiction? *Journal of Police Science and Administration* 9(2):143–149.

Love, K. G. (1981b). Comparison of peer assessment methods: Reliability, validity, friendship bias, and user reaction. *Journal of Applied Psychology* 66(4):451–457.

Mathis, R., and Jackson, J. (1997). *Human resource management*. St. Paul: West.

McEvoy, G. M. (1987). Using subordinate appraisals of managers to predict performance and promotions: One agency's experience. *Journal of Police Science and Administration* 15(2):118–124.

McKay, J. (2002). CompStat for the 21st century. *Government Technology* (July):30, 32.

Moore, M. (2003). *The Bottom Line in Policing: What Citizens Should Value (and Measure!) in Police Performance*. Washington, DC: Police Executive Research Forum.

Moore, M., and Braga, A. (2003). Measuring and improving police performance: The lessons of CompStat and its progeny. *Policing: An International Journal of Police Strategies & Management* 26(3):439–453.

National Institute of Justice. (1997). *Measuring what matters (Part Two): Developing measures of what the police do.* Washington, DC: Author.

Oettmeier, T., and Wycoff, M. (1997). *Personnel performance evaluations in the community policing context*. Washington, DC: Community Policing Consortium.

Peak, K. J., and Glensor, R. W. (2008). *Community policing and problem solving: Strategies and practices,* 5th ed. Upper Saddle River, NJ: Prentice Hall.

Roberts, G. (2003). Employee performance appraisal system participation: A technique that works. *Public Personnel Management* 32(1):89-98.

Schermerhorn, J. (1996). *Management*. New York: John Wiley & Sons.

Spelman, W. (1988). *Beyond bean counting: New approaches for managing crime data*. Washington, DC: Police Executive Research Forum.

Smith, W., Harrington, K., and Houghton, J. (2000). Predictors of performance appraisal discomfort: A preliminary examination. *Public Personnel Management* 29(1):21-32.

Walsh, W. F. (1990). Performance evaluation in small and medium police departments: A supervisory perspective. *American Journal of Police* 9(4):93–109.

Walsh, W. F. (1985). Patrol officer arrest rates: A study of the social organization of police work. *Justice Quarterly* 2(3):271–290.

Wells, W., Horney, J. and Maguire, E. (2005). Patrol officer responses to citizen feedback: An experimental analysis. *Police Quarterly* 8(2):171–205.

Willis, J., Mastrofski, S., and Weisburd, D. (2004). CompStat and bureaucracy: A case study of challenges and opportunities for change. *Justice Quarterly* 21(3):463–496.

CHAPTER 8

Stress, Wellness, and Employee Assistance Programs

Key Terms and Concepts

- Chronic stress
- Employee assistance program (EAP)
- Distress
- Eustress
- General adaptive syndrome (GAS)
- Social support
- Stress
- Team building
- Traumatic stress
- Wellness

Learning Objectives

After reading this chapter, the student will:

- understand the nature and causes of stress in policing
- know the primary intrinsic stressors for police officers, supervisors, and managers, and their impact over the course of a career
- be able to list ways in which police officers may reduce stress levels, and the responsibility of supervisors and managers in this endeavor
- know the meaning of health and wellness
- know how employee assistance programs function, their five key elements, and how they help officers to cope with substance abuse and other personal problems

There are two ways of meeting difficulties: you alter the difficulties or you alter yourself meeting them.

—Phyllis Bottome

Health is a state of complete physical, mental and social well being, and not merely absence of disease or infirmity.

—Heave

INTRODUCTION

There is a side of policing, and its supervision and management, that we would prefer to ignore: the stress that is induced by the job. Indeed, Sir W. S. Gilbert observed that "When constabulary duty's to be done, the policeman's lot is not a happy one" (quoted in Bartlett, 1992:529). Furthermore, William A. Westley (1970:3) observed that "The policeman's world is spawned of degradation, corruption and insecurity. He walks alone, a pedestrian in Hell."

Many people with whom the police interact are heavily armed and arrogant. Indeed, being a police officer today has been described as a "stop-and-go nightmare" (Witkin, Gest, and Friedman, 1990:32). The job of policing has never been easy, but the danger, frustration, and family disruption of the past have been made worse by the drug war and violent criminals who have more contempt for the police than ever before. Furthermore, as will be seen later, compounding this situation is that the officer's own organizational policies and practices often generate more stress than the streets.

Therefore, police supervisors, managers, and administrators have become increasingly concerned about the health and welfare of their employees and must ensure that employees are mentally and physically prepared for the challenges of the workplace. Police officers' health, both mental and physical, affects their jobs. In some cases, negative attributes associated with health may result in lost productivity or an inability to make good decisions, and in other cases, it may result in early retirements. Healthy police officers are more likely to efficiently serve the public needs. This chapter focuses on the supervisor's role in recognizing and dealing with stress.

The chapter begins with a definition of stress and the patterns of its effects over a career. Following that is a discussion of the major stressors that are specific to police work, from both inside and outside the organization. The effects of stress on the individual officer as well as the agency are then examined, including ways of coping with it. Employee wellness programs are reviewed, including a discussion of employee assistance programs. After an overview of how police supervisors and managers can assist in stress recognition and treatment, the chapter concludes with two case studies.

UNDERSTANDING POLICE STRESS

Nature and Types

Police work is different from any other occupation in our society. Our police system is society's primary mechanism for controlling aberrant and illegal behavior. As such, society vests police officers with a substantial amount of authority—a level of authority possessed by no other occupation—including the right to employ deadly force or to deny someone his or her freedom.

This work environment can and does have adverse effects on police officers. It creates **stress**, which may be defined as a force that is external in nature that causes both physical and emotional strain upon the body. The late Hans Selye, who is known as "the father of stress research," defined stress as a nonspecific response of a body to demands placed on it. Succinctly, stressors are situations or occurrences outside of ourselves that we allow to turn inward and cause problems.

Stress can be positive or negative. Positive stress is referred to as **eustress**, while negative stress is called **distress**. When people think about stress, they usually focus on negative stress and negative situations; however, positive events in our lives can create stress. For example, an officer's promotion to sergeant is a positive experience, but at the same time, it creates stress. The officer has to react and adjust to the new position. The promotion, although positive for the officer's career, is somewhat psychologically disruptive.

Traumatic stress is the result of an extremely stressful event, such as a line-of-duty shooting or a hostage situation. This stress is immediate and has a significant and profound impact on the officer.

On the other hand is **chronic stress**, which generally represents the accumulation of the effects of numerous stressful events over time. Each can adversely affect a police officer and result in physical, emotional, and psychological problems. Traumatic stress may subside over time, but chronic stress for many police officers is ever-present. If an officer cannot cope with a traumatic stressful event or manage the long term effects of chronic stress, he or she may suffer from its consequences.

Selye (1981) formulated the **general adaptive syndrome (GAS)** to describe the stress process. GAS consists of three stages: (1) alarm, (2) resistance, and (3) exhaustion. The *alarm stage* occurs when the stressful event happens and the individual becomes aware of the event. Psychological and physiological reactions follow. A variety of psychological reactions can surface, including fear, anxiety, depression, apprehension, or aggressiveness. Physiological reactions include an increase in heart rate and a release of adrenaline into the bloodstream. If the threat subsides, the individual ultimately returns to a normal state.

Resistance is the process whereby the individual attempts to cope or co-exist with the stress. The threat remains, but the individual continues to muster the strength to endure and contend with the situation. Resistance is characterized by continued psychological and physiological changes or adaptations in the individual. *Exhaustion* is the point at which the individual is no longer able to effectively cope with the stressful situation. If the stress continues, the individual experiences physical, emotional, or psychological problems. Physiological responses can be as severe as a heart attack. Emotional responses include withdrawal, lack of motivation, and anxiety. Psychologically, an individual may reach the point where he or she cannot properly function at work or home. For example, an officer may be unable to nurture his or her children or withdraw from all social responsibilities such as church, children's education, or interaction with family members.

No human being can exist in a continuous state of stress. The body strives to maintain its normal state, homeostasis, and to adapt to the alarm, but it can actually develop a disease in the process. Thus, it is extremely important for police agencies to recognize stress and its impact on officers and their productivity.

There are two competing views of the causes of stress for police officers (Gaines and Kappeler, 2008). First, police stress is viewed as a *personal pathology*. Here, police officers are seen as being deficient in some way, unable to handle the rigors of the job. It is postulated that some officers do not have the "right stuff" to be police officers. The problem lies totally within the psyche of the stressed police officer. This perspective essentially postulates that police departments are created and police agencies must recruit officers who can withstand the strain associated with the job. It means that police departments must develop selection procedures that "screen in" those officers who are mentally and physically fit for police work—officers who are resistant to stress.

The second view is that stress is the result of structural problems or the pathology of the environment, especially the police organization itself. This perspective recognizes that police managers and supervisors must accept that certain aspects of the job and the operation of the police department result in stress. It recognizes that over time, almost, if not everyone in the department, will experience stress. Obviously, police managers must recognize the level of stress induced as a result of the job and organization, and take actions to reduce stress through organizational change and employee development.

Patterns of Stress During a Police Career

A limited amount of research has examined stress patterns in police departments. Dietrich (1989) and Violanti (1983) attempted to articulate police officer stress patterns based on years of service. They identified several stages of stress, which are based on Niederhoffer's (1967) four stages of police career development as shown in Figure 8-1. The first five years of a police officer's career can be described as a period of *alienation and alarm*. Officers essentially experience a reality shock; they discover that

Author	Stages				
Niederhoffer (1967) and Violanti (1983)	Alarm stage (0–5 yrs.)	Disenchantment stage (6–13 yrs.)		Personalization stage (14–20 yrs.)	Introspection stage (20+ yrs.)
Dietrich (1989)	Alienation from nonpolice world (0–5 yrs.)	Emotional shutdown (5–10 yrs.)	Emotional unsureness (10–15 yrs.)	Namelessness (15–20 yrs.)	Maintaining the status quo (20–35 yrs.)

FIGURE 8-1 Stress Patterns by Years of Service

the job is substantially different from what they first imagined. As a result of the many negative situations in which they intervene, officers come to view citizens as the enemy. Police officers generally have a negative outlook on life during this phase of their career.

The second phase may be characterized as the *disenchantment phase*. Violanti postulated that this phase generally lasts from years 6 through 13. Officers become extremely disappointed, emotionally detached, and bitter about the job during this period. To a great extent, they withdraw during these years as a result of not being able to reconcile the realities of police work with their perception of "how the world ought to be." These feelings often spill over into family life, causing additional stress. This is the peak period for police officer stress.

It appears that police officers get back on track during years 14 through 20 in the *personalization phase*. During this period, they become more interested in their families and outside activities. They may engage in hobbies and second jobs to satisfy their interests. It is a period when police work begins to become secondary. That is, during this phase officers come to realize that their jobs are not their lives and there are other, more important aspects to life. Their negativism tends to subside during this phase, and they are less bitter and cynical about the job and citizens they serve. They often become more helpful and engaging when they respond to calls or become involved in other job-related activities. They come to realize that police work is nothing more than a job.

Finally, as their career approaches 20 years, police officers become *introspective* about their jobs. That is, they typically do their jobs and avoid worrying about job-related problems such as failing to get promoted, not being able to meet citizen expectations, or the demands of their superiors. They tend to take life in stride, realizing that the job is only a small part of life. They tend to focus even more on their families and their own personal needs.

These stress phases have two implications for supervisors. First, it should be noted that supervisors themselves are not immune from this stress paradigm. They frequently develop stress symptoms that affect their own performance. Supervisors must remain focused and exert every effort possible to ensure that they and their subordinates work toward departmental goals and objectives. Second, supervisors must be able to recognize the symptoms and stages of stress and help officers deal with them. Supervisors must provide social support, training, counseling, and, when necessary, outside intervention to reduce the debilitating effects of stress on officers.

SOURCES OF POLICE STRESS

A number of researchers have examined the general categories of stress (Barker and Carter, 1994; Zhao, Hi, and Lovrich, 2002). Police officers can experience job stress as the result of a wide range of problems and situations. Derogatis and Savitz (1999) advise that stress is multi-dimensional, necessitating

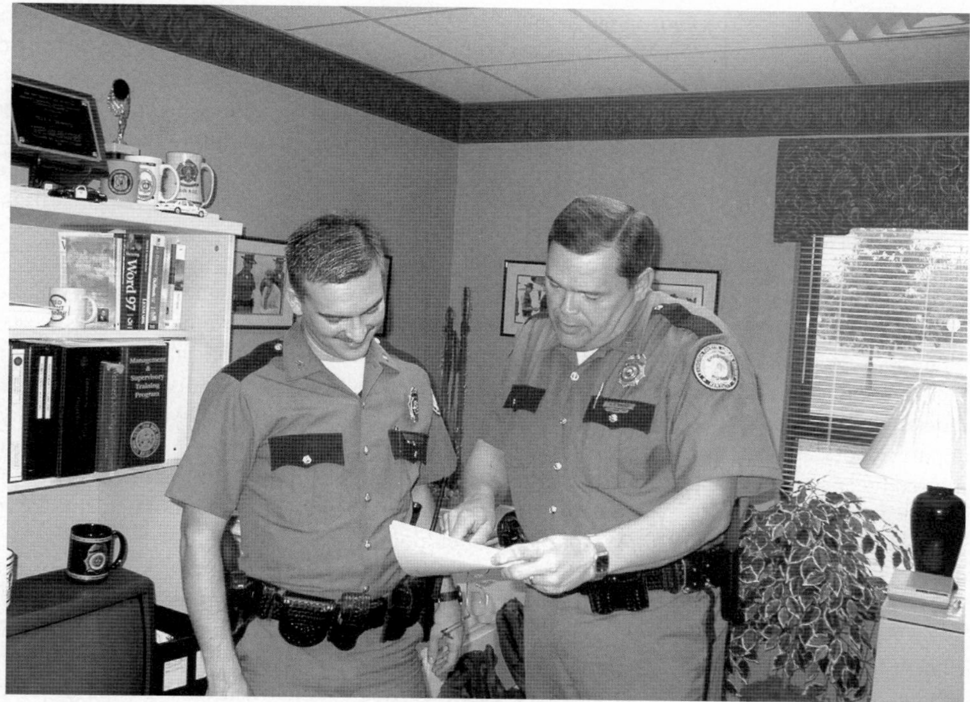

The authoritarian nature of police organizations creates stress for supervisors as well as for officers. Here, a sergeant receives directions from a captain.
(Courtesy Lexington, Kentucky, Police Department.)

officers to react to a number of environmental and personal cues. Stress can come from a number of directions. Basically, police stressful events fall within one of four general categories: (1) organizational and administrative practices, (2) the criminal justice system, (3) the public, and (4) stress intrinsic to police work itself.

Organizational Sources

A primary source of stress is the police organization itself. One survey of police officers in eight medium-sized departments found that organizationally based problems were the most stressful problems for police officers (Crank and Caldero, 1991). Police departments typically are bureaucratic, authoritarian organizations (Franz and Jones, 1987; Harrison and Pelletier, 1987; Langworthy, 1992). As Zhao and his colleagues (2002) note, the "dark side of bureaucracy" creates a substantial amount of stress for officers. Police agencies are unique in their operation and consequently place a number of restrictions on how police officers conduct their activities.

A police department's authoritarian nature creates stress for individual officers in several ways. First, police departments follow strict rules and regulations that are dictated by top management. Line officers and first-line supervisors seldom have direct input into their formulation, resulting in officers feeling powerless and alienated about the decisions that directly affect their jobs. Second, these rules dictate how officers specifically perform many of their duties and responsibilities. They are created to provide officers with guidance and direction. Police officers, however, sometimes view them as mechanisms used by management to restrict their freedom and discretion or to punish them. Officers also view rules as protection for the department when officers make incorrect decisions or errors. In these instances, departments sometimes use rules to avoid liability when officers' actions are challenged in civil actions.

Kirschman (1997) and Lord, Gray, and Pond (1991) identified a number of other organizational stressors, which include inadequate training, volume of paperwork required of officers, limited opportunities for advancement, shift work, understaffing, and the amount of work or calls assigned to officers. Indeed, a number of problems confront the modern police department. Unfortunately, many departments do not have the resources to resolve them.

It is also necessary to discuss some of the problems faced by female police officers. Policing is a male-dominated occupation, and female officers do not have the same standing in a number of police agencies. Studies tend to indicate that the primary source of stress for female officers is sexual harassment and treatment different from that which males receive in the workplace. Women officers report that they are given different assignments, are the object of jokes (especially those with a sexual orientation), are propositioned by male officers, and generally are victimized by gender stereotyping in the department (Haarr and Morash, 1999; Morash, Kwak and Haarr, 2006). Many such behaviors are prohibited by sexual harassment statutes, and any other behaviors of this nature are totally unprofessional. Supervisors must ensure that female officers are treated equally in the workplace and are not sexually harassed—from both humanitarian and legal standpoints. Even though female officers are exposed to different stressors, research indicates that females are not more stressed than male officers (McCarty, Zhao, and Garland, 2007).

One of the key factors relating to organizational stress is the size of the department. Morash and Haarr (1991) found that officers in larger departments tended to experience more stress than officers in smaller departments. Some researchers suggest that the personal relationships that develop in smaller departments help mediate organizational stress (Brooks and Piquero, 1998). Police managers must understand that as a department grows and becomes more complex, officers are often subjected to greater levels of stress. This means that managers and supervisors, especially in larger departments, should labor to establish better work teams and camaraderie.

The Criminal Justice System

The criminal justice system itself can be a source of stress when officers have difficulty interacting with other components of the system or complying with the decisions made and actions taken by other criminal justice agencies. Each component of the criminal justice system affects the other components. For example, judges have openly displayed hostile attitudes toward the police, or prosecutors have not displayed proper respect to officers, arbitrarily dismissing cases, having them appear in court during regularly scheduled days off, and advocating rulings restricting police procedures (Brooks and Piquero, 1998). Another example occurs when parole officers and probation officers do an inadequate job of supervising parolees, which results in their being involved in an inordinate amount of crime. The courts have the most direct impact on police officers and probably are the greatest source of stress from the criminal justice system.

Police managers and supervisors have an obligation to ensure that police officers understand and appreciate their role within the criminal justice system, and, for their mental health, they need to let go of the case following their arrest of the subject and not be fazed by the plea bargaining (or acquittals) that might ensue.

At the same time, police managers must continually monitor the activities of other criminal justice agencies and, when problems are identified, take action to reduce or eliminate the problem. In 2001, the San Bernardino, California, Police Department noticed that the California Department of Corrections and Rehabilitation was "dumping" parolees in the city. Many of the parolees had been arrested and convicted in other counties, but were paroled in San Bernardino. Consequently, the city had a disproportionately high number of parolees, which resulted in an increase in crime. The police department worked with the city attorney to force the Department of Corrections and Rehabilitation to limit the number of parolees released in the city. This eventually resulted in less crime problems for the police.

The Public

Most citizens recognize that the police perform an important function in our society, but there are numerous individuals and groups that view the police less positively or negatively (Brown and Benedict, 2002). In addition to combating criminal activities, the police provide many important services that otherwise would not be available. When police officers perform these services, however, they become involved in conflicts or negative situations. They arrest citizens; they write tickets; and they give citizens orders when intervening in domestic violence or disorder situations. Often, to resolve problems, they make half of the participants happy, but the other half are unhappy.

The problem is that police officers develop unrealistic or inaccurate ideas about citizens as a result of their negative encounters (Albrecht and Green, 1977). For example, Crank and Caldero quoted one officer as saying, "Anytime you deal with the public they have certain images, stereotypes, and expectations of you.... Most people aren't happy to see the police, as it is usually some sort of negative contact" (1991:345). Skolnick (1994) noted that police officers often view all citizens as "symbolic assailants" who are not only unfriendly, but are also potentially dangerous. These images result in stress for police officers, especially when they are dealing with citizens.

In order to reduce police stress in this area, managers and supervisors must ensure that officers keep their relationship with citizens in proper perspective. This is achieved by open, straightforward discussions of public attitudes and encounters with citizens. It also means that managers must emphasize the importance of good police public relations as well as the fact that the majority of citizens support and respect the police.

Stressors Intrinsic to Police Work

Police work is fraught with situations that pose physical danger to officers. Anytime officers confront a felon, especially if drugs are involved, there is the potential for physical violence. Domestic violence, felonies in progress, and fight calls often require officers to physically confront suspects. It would seem that police work itself, since it includes dealing with dangerous police activities and dangerous people, would be the most stressful part of police work. Certainly traumatic incidents such as the bombings of the World Trade Center in New York and the Federal Building in Oklahoma City, plane crashes, and natural disasters can require long-term follow-up support for law enforcement personnel. The Federal Bureau of Investigation has created a Critical Incident Stress Management Program to provide immediate interventions and long-term treatment of trauma, which is a model for other law enforcement agencies to follow (McNally and Solomon, 1999). Police departments must establish similar services and make them readily available not only for officers who experience traumatic stress, but also for officers who are exposed to chronic stress.

Another major job-related stressor involves undercover work. The glamorous depiction of undercover officers in books, movies, and other media does not adequately portray the stress that is caused by the overall nature of the work—the isolation, danger, relationships with suspects, loss of personal identity, protracted periods of removal from family and friends, and fear of discovery (Band and Sheehan, 1999).

Research, however, tends to indicate that police work may not be excessively stressful for officers. A number of researchers have found that organizationally induced stress was a far greater problem

Painful sights on the ocean floor overcome police divers.
(Courtesy NYPD Photo Unit)

(Stinchcomb, 2004). Police officers understand that the job has some dangers, but they do not see them as overwhelming problems.

Regardless, the supervisor's role is to ensure that police officers view their jobs and responsibilities realistically. Police officers cannot be complacent when confronting potentially hazardous situations, for example, by using poor defensive posture when talking with a subject who is standing near the officer or sitting in his or her vehicle, which substantially increases the probability of physical injury. First-line supervisors must ensure that officers follow established policies and procedures. These orders are developed to provide as much protection to officers as possible. Commanders have a responsibility to ensure that the department's policies ensure maximum safety for officers. Also, as a result of performing command inspections and direct observations of subordinates performing field duties, they should ensure that policies are followed and that they accomplish the desired results.

Incidents that Provoke Stress

As noted above, stress is multi-dimensional and there are numerous events or situations that can lead to stress. In addition each situation has a magnitude dimension. That is, some events or conditions are more stressful for officers than others. There have been several studies that have attempted to identify those events that are stressful for police officers (Garcia, Nesbary, and Gu, 2004; Sewell, 1983; Violanti and Aron, 1994).

TABLE 8-1 Twenty-five Most Stressful Law Enforcement Critical Life Events

1. Violent death of a partner in the line of duty
2. Dismissal from the force
3. Taking a life in the line of duty
4. Shooting someone in the line of duty
5. Suicide of an officer who is a close friend
6. Violent death of another officer in the line of duty
7. Murder committed by a police officer
8. Duty-related violent injury (shooting)
9. Violent job-related injury to another officer
10. Suspension
11. Passed over for promotion
12. Pursuit of an armed suspect
13. Answering a call to a scene involving violent nonaccidental death of a child
14. Assignment away from family for a long period of time
15. Personal involvement in a shooting incident
16. Reduction in pay
17. Observing an act of police corruption
18. Accepting a bribe
19. Participating in an act of police corruption
20. Hostage situation resulting from aborted criminal action
21. Response to a scene involving the accidental death of a child
22. Promotion of inexperienced/incompetent officer over you
23. Internal affairs investigation against you
24. Barricaded suspect
25. Hostage situation resulting from a domestic disturbance

Source: J. Sewell, *FBI Law Enforcement Bulletin,* 50(4), 1981

Table 8-1 provides a listing of 25 stressful situations based on previous surveys categorized using the above sources of police stress.

An examination of Table 8-1 reveals that the majority of stressors are organizational or those intrinsic to police work. It should be noted that the most stressful events in the intrinsic category occur very infrequently, and indeed, the average officer will experience very few of these events in his or her career. On the other hand, many of the organizational stressors occur very frequently. This may be why research shows that organizational stressors result in the most concern for officers.

EFFECTS OF STRESS

The preceding sections defined stress, its sources, and some of its resultant problems. Given that stress is a significant problem in policing, departments must endeavor to reduce and, where possible, eliminate stress. As such, a number of actions may be taken to accomplish this objective. Prior to discussing these actions, however, the effects of stress on the officer and the agency must be examined.

Potential Officer Afflictions

It has been estimated that at any point in time, 15 percent of a department's officers will be in a burnout phase. These officers account for 70 to 80 percent of all the complaints against their department, including physical abuse, verbal abuse, and misuse of firearms. If officers do not relieve the pressure, they eventually may suffer heart attacks, nervous breakdowns, back problems, headaches, psychosomatic illnesses, and alcoholism (Daviss, 1982). They may also manifest excessive weight gain or loss; combativeness or irritability; excessive perspiration; excessive use of sick leave; excessive use of alcohol, tobacco, or drugs; marital or family disorders; inability to complete an assignment; loss of interest in work, hobbies, and people in general; more than the usual number of "accidents," including vehicular and other types; and shooting incidents (Fishkin, 1988). An extreme reaction to stress is suicide. Police are at a higher risk for committing suicide because of their access to firearms, continuous exposure to human misery, shift work, social strain and marital difficulties, physical illness, and alcohol addiction. Police are eight times more likely to commit suicide than to be killed in a homicide and three times more likely to kill themselves than to die in job-related accidents ("What's killing America's cops?" 1996; see also Vila, 2000).

Another stress-induced problem is *negative public image*. Stressed police officers have a tendency to view everyone negatively. For example, an officer may respond to an assault call and do little to solve the case. The officer's actions are the result of his or her feeling that the victim likely got what he or she deserved. When officers have a pronounced negative image of the public, they tend to exert little effort to do the job correctly.

As noted earlier, no human being can exist in a continuous state of alarm. Often, however, the problem of stress is exacerbated by the reluctance of police officers to admit they have problems. They often avoid seeking professional psychological help, fearing that they will be placed on limited duty or be labeled "psychos" by their peers. As they start to acknowledge the problem, many police departments are attempting to improve their recruit screening and provide better counseling programs.

It is imperative that officers learn to manage their stress before it causes deep physical and/or emotional harm. One means is to view the mind as a "mental bucket" and strive to keep it full through hobbies or activities that provide relaxation. Exercise, proper nutrition, and positive lifestyle choices (such as not smoking, and moderation with alcohol) are also essential for good health.

Stress can have a number of effects on police officers. First, officers can experience *emotional exhaustion*. When officers are stressed in the workplace, they can become emotionally exhausted, and this usually takes its toll in the home. Officers who are emotionally exhausted often withdraw or do not have the energy to cope with problems at home. They tend to isolate themselves from their families. This further compounds the stress problem because problems in the home contribute to the level of chronic stress in the workplace.

Officers under a great deal of stress tend to experience a *hardening of their emotions*. Officers tend to detach and isolate themselves emotionally from the job and their families. It becomes more difficult for the officer to express basic emotions such as love, joy, excitement with accomplishments of their children, or basic involvement in many family functions. The officer appears to be uncaring and impersonal. In some cases, this hardening of emotions leads to sexual problems such as an inability to be intimate or infidelity. These emotional responses to stress further contribute to the officer's chronic stress.

Effects on the Officer's Family

Police officers who are experiencing enhanced levels of stress tend to *be overprotective of their families*. They become overly concerned with the actions and whereabouts of family members. They tend to view all other citizens as "symbolic assailants" who have the potential to harm family members. This overprotectiveness leads to increased levels of conflict within the family as the officers tend to restrict the activities of other members of the family to an unacceptable degree. Moreover, work stress often leads to conflict within the home. As officers become stressed, they begin to carry emotional baggage. They become depressed, aggressive, withdrawn, and so forth, which affects relationships with significant others. This results in police officers having a high divorce rate.

Police officer stress also results in stress among family members. As family members are exposed to the negativism on the part of the officer, they too become stressed. They tend to worry more about the officer and the environment. Researchers have identified a number of stressors that family members develop:

- Shift work
- Concern over the spouse's cynicism, need to feel in control in the home, or inability or unwillingness to express feelings
- Fear that the spouse will be hurt or killed in the line of duty
- Officers and others' excessively high expectations of their children
- Avoidance, teasing, or harassment of the officer's children by other children because of the parent's job
- Presence of a gun in the home
- The officer's 24-hour role as a law enforcer
- Perception that the officer prefers to spend time with co-workers rather than with family members
- Too much or too little discussion of the job
- Family members' perception of the officer as paranoid or excessively vigilant and overprotective of them
- Problems in helping the officer cope with work-related problems
- Critical incidents or the officer's injury or death on the job (NIJ, 2000)

This listing demonstrates that police officers' family members are exposed to a number of stressors that other people are not. These situations result is an escalation of emotional conflict within the household. Without intervention, the family is doomed to divorce or constant strife. Not only must police departments attempt to deal with police officer stress, but they must also develop programming that assists in relieving stress in the home.

Effects on the Agency

A study by the National Institute of Justice interviewed nearly 100 stress-management program directors, police administrators, mental health providers, union and association officials, officers and their families, and civilians. The respondents agreed that the negative effects of stress on individuals typically harm agencies as well as officers, leading to:

- Reduced morale
- Public relations problems
- Labor-management friction
- Civil suits stemming from stress-related shortcomings in personnel performance
- Tardiness and absenteeism
- Increased turnover due to leaves of absence and early retirements
- Added expenses of training and hiring new recruits, as well as paying overtime, when the agency is short-staffed due to turnover (Finn, 1997)

REDUCING STRESS IN THE POLICE ORGANIZATION

As illustrated in the above discussion, it is obvious that police managers and supervisors have a vested interest in reducing police officer stress. Any reduction will result in a more effective and productive police organization and the avoidance of a number of human resource problems. In this section, we explore some of the methods used to reduce stress. Three primary methods are discussed: (1) social support and team building, (2) organizational restructuring, and (3) wellness programs.

Social Support and Team Building

Social support refers to communications and actions that lead individuals to believe that they are cared for, important, and an integral part of a network of mutual obligations. Social support can be emotional in nature—people let others know that they care for them—and instrumental—the providing of assistance, such as money or doing another's work. Social support buffers or moderates the conditions of work, thus making it less stressful (Kaufmann and Beehr, 1989). Social support can be an important factor in mediating stress in policing.

Supervisors and managers must increase their ability to provide support services to officers—not only in traumatic situations, but also on a daily basis. Officers constantly need support and encouragement. Graf (1986) has identified several strategies to increase organizational support for officers. Departments should attempt to reduce officer cynicism, which is most pronounced during the first 10 years of an officer's career (see Figure 8-1 earlier in this chapter). This is done through direct intervention by supervisors to correct behavior and change officer attitudes. It also involves supervisors becoming involved in a wider range of officer problems. Supervisors should be supportive but also ensure that officers' behavior is within acceptable boundaries.

Social support is an important part of team building, but **team building** goes further. Teams have a collective sense of accountability and cooperatively strive to achieve objectives. Teams function when there is continuous communication and shared expectations. When teamwork replaces individualism, officers feel better about their jobs, are less cynical, are more productive, and feel less stress. Managers and supervisors should endeavor to build positive intra-group relations.

Organizational Restructuring

As noted above, the primary causes of stress in the police organization is the organization itself. Thus, one way to reduce the amount of stress in policing is to reduce organizational stress. This is best accomplished by implementing more decentralization and allowing officers and work groups to have more control over decision making, the identification of objectives, and the implementation of police tactics and strategies. Too often, police departments adhere to standard operating procedures when a problem can best be solved innovatively. Officers should have more discretion to innovate when problem solving. Second, communication within work groups as well as across work groups should be encouraged and facilitated. Patrol officers should be given more latitude to work with detectives, traffic officers, domestic violence specialists, and persons from outside agencies when attempting to tackle a problem. Officers should be given the freedom to make decisions. Commanders and supervisors should take on more of a coordinative role as opposed to purely being supervisors and work schedulers. All of these activities result in officers having more investment in the department and the work they perform, which reduces stress and increases productivity.

EMPLOYEE WELLNESS PROGRAMS

When we contemplate health, we not only consider disease, but we also assess diet, mental outlook, and social integration and skills. This approach has come to be known as **wellness**, which means that individuals will adopt a lifestyle that will help them achieve their highest level of well-being. This does not mean that everyone must achieve perfect wellness, but everyone should constantly be aware of the implications of his or her actions and strive for a more healthy lifestyle that includes physical exercise, a good diet, moderate or no consumption of alcohol or drugs, avoidance of tobacco products, and the use of a seatbelt when in a vehicle.

Five important dimensions are subsumed within wellness (Anspaugh, Hamrick, and Rosato, 1991). In order to move toward optimal health or wellness, individuals must improve their lifestyle in each of the following areas:

1. ***Spiritual.*** Spirituality refers to the belief in some force or belief system, such as religion, science, nature, or a higher power. It includes the individual's ethics, values, and morals. It provides direction and enables people to discover and act out their basic purposes in life.
2. ***Social.*** Social skills are extremely important in life. People must have the ability to interact with others in their environment, and they must have the ability to form intimate relationships with significant others. Individuals must be socially mature to the point that they are tolerant of ideas and opinions that are different from their own.
3. ***Emotional.*** An individual is emotionally healthy when he or she is able to express feelings and to understand the feelings and emotions of others. One must be able to control stress and deal with people and situations under adverse conditions.
4. ***Intellectual.*** People must be able to continuously learn and use newly acquired information. This is a necessary component for coping with the job, environment, and life in general. People who fail to absorb new information have difficulty keeping up with our ever-changing society.
5. ***Physical.*** The physical dimension implies that individuals not only maintain an adequate level of physical ability to perform the job, but that they also strive to achieve physical well-being. This ability is measured in terms of cardiovascular capacity, body fat, and nutrition. It also means that individuals will avoid tobacco products and drugs and other substances and activities that adversely affect their health.

Each of these dimensions is important to a healthy life. An overcommitment to one area and the neglect of other areas will not result in any appreciable improvement in a person's life or wellness. Individuals must examine their lives with respect to each of these dimensions.

A study conducted in 1998 examined the health of police officers. The study focused on risky behaviors: alcohol consumption, nicotine usage, inadequate exercise, being overweight, and stress symptoms. The researchers found that 83 percent of officers had problems in at least one area with the consumption of alcohol being the most frequent problem. The researchers found that female officers had almost as many problems as male officers (Richmond, Wodak, Kehoe, and Heather, 1998). The study revealed that unhealthy lifestyles remain a significant health issue for policing. Tanigoshi, Kontos, and Remley (2008) found that when officers are provided with health counseling, their health and lifestyles improve. Thus, police departments need to invest in such programming, which, in the end, will pay for themselves through productivity increases and reduced injuries and sick time.

EMPLOYEE ASSISTANCE PROGRAMS

Historically, police departments hired or sought the volunteer services of ministers and priests to serve as department chaplains. The use of chaplains was seen as the primary tool with which to deal with human problems. Later, formal programs were developed to deal with alcohol problems among police officers. For example, the Chicago Police Officers' Fellowship began in 1955 to work with officer alcoholism, the New York City Alcohol Program was started in 1966, and Boston assigned a full-time officer to a departmental alcohol program in 1959.

It was not until the 1970s and 1980s, when increasing numbers of departments began to implement **employee assistance programs (EAPs)**, that employee assistance was recognized as an important human resource tool. In addition to alcohol rehabilitation programs, some departments hired psychologists or counselors. The psychologists not only worked with the alcohol dependent officers, but they also worked with officers who were suffering from stress or had been involved in critical events such as shootings. Finally, the drug epidemic of the 1990s created a need for drug counseling. A number of departments started drug testing and counseling programs that were housed within EAPs.

Five Key Elements

Although police agencies have implemented wellness programs, for the most part, they are piecemeal or incomplete. A comprehensive wellness program should include five elements: (1) physical fitness, (2) stress management, (3) psychological and mental health, (4) nutrition and dietary-related problems, and (5) alcohol/chemical dependency. Church and Robertson (1999) surveyed state police agencies and found that 29 had wellness programming, but none had programs addressing all five elements. The 20 agencies that did not offer wellness programs to its officers did, however, offer at least one program or element. Church and Robertson also found that when wellness programs were offered, they were administered in such a fashion as to discourage their use. Often there was a lack of confidentiality, facilities were often restricted to headquarters and not geographically convenient for field officers, and officers were fearful of using programs such as alcohol or drug counseling for fear of being stigmatized.

Police officers experience a number of problems that can necessitate their use of an EAP, including drug and alcohol abuse and marital problems. Police agencies need a comprehensive wellness program to assist officers in coping with stress, but if that fails or is absent, an EAP should be available to assist officers who experience significant amounts of stress or whose health is jeopardized by stress. This is especially true when job stress results in drinking problems, substance abuse, psychological problems such as depression, or family management problems.

Alcohol Abuse and Counseling

Excessive drinking and alcoholism remain a problem in policing. For example, Kroes (1976) estimated that 25 percent of police officers have a serious drinking problem. Another study found that 20 percent of officers in one department abused drugs while on duty (Kraska and Kappeler, 1988). Van Raalte (1979) found that 67 percent of officers in one department admitted to drinking on duty. This research is somewhat outdated, but it does demonstrate that officers have substance abuse problems. Seldom will officers admit to such problems, making it difficult to gather more current, accurate statistics. Nonetheless, it remains a problem.

Police officers are a close-knit group who work and relax together, often in isolation from other people. When they unwind, they generally use alcohol. When officers' drinking becomes excessive, other officers and frequently supervisors and the department cover up for them. In the end, however, covering up drinking problems postpones officers' seeking or being required to obtain assistance. When drinking behavior remains untreated, it quite often leads to legal and departmental problems.

Officers with drinking problems usually have identifiable symptoms that can serve to alert the supervisor. They tend to deny that they have a drinking problem; they often drink alone; they cannot control the amount of alcohol they consume; they crave alcohol; they have an increased tolerance to its effects; they have memory blackouts; and they develop a physical dependence on alcohol. Officers with drinking problems also tend to use more sick time and have other personal problems as a result of their drinking. Obviously, supervisors who encounter such problems among their subordinates must see that they obtain professional assistance.

The death of a fellow officer is one of the most traumatic experiences that officers will face during their career.
(Courtesy Washoe County, Nevada, Sheriff's Office)

Drug Abuse and Counseling

Drug abuse can also be present among officers, although it is not known if it is a significant problem. What is known, however, is that drug testing reduces the incidence of drug usage among police officers. If officers know they are going to be tested, they are less likely to use drugs. A number of departments require officers in selected assignments such as narcotics or special response teams to submit to drug testing, and some departments require officers being transferred to such units to be tested.

If an officer is found to be using illegal drugs, the police department is faced with a difficult decision: What should be done with the employee? There are a number of arguments for immediate termination. First, the police officer has committed a crime. Second, the officer has associated with known criminals when obtaining the illegal drugs. And third, the officer's drug use poses a liability problem for the police department.

Immediate termination is counter to a humane view of police personnel administration, however. It should be realized that job stress may be the primary contributing factor to the drug usage. Second, the department has a significant investment in each of its officers, and a termination decision should not be taken lightly. Finally, problem officers can be salvaged and returned to work as productive officers. Thus, termination, although an acceptable choice for officers with chronic drug problems, may not be the best solution for officers who had not previously caused the department any problems or had not otherwise been in trouble. Factors considered in making this decision include the severity of the offense (type and amount of drug used and whether or not the officer went beyond mere usage), prior drug and disciplinary problems, and the probability of the officer being rehabilitated.

CASE STUDIES

The following two case studies provide the reader with some insights concerning how quickly stress can be generated and its effect on police officers; also included are some of the difficult decisions that supervisors, managers, and administrators have to make regarding stressful situations involving their subordinates.

Case Study #1

Near Shootout at K-9 Corral

The headlines read "Near Shootout at K-9 Corral." The department is stunned by the events of Sunday evening. During a weekly training session, K-9 Officer Tom Watson pointed his duty weapon at Officer Jack Connolly and threatened to shoot him during an argument. Fortunately, no one was injured, but Watson is under investigation for assault. Officer Watson's friends are not surprised. Since joining the K-9 Unit three months ago, he has been the subject of intense teasing, especially by Connolly, who liked to imitate Watson's stuttered speech. Watson is very sensitive about his speech and attended three years of therapy at the local university before gaining enough confidence to take the police officer test. Lately, Connolly's teasing has become more personal—he has imitated Watson's stutter over the police radio. When other officers and dispatchers began to join in, Watson asked Sgt. Aldous to speak with Connolly. Aldous explained that all new guys got teased and warned him not to make the situation worse by complaining. For the next two weeks, Watson called in sick on the six days that he and Connolly would have worked together. Just prior to the incident, Watson's fiancé had broken up with him (telling Watson she had a new love interest), he had learned that he owed a significant amount of money in back taxes to the government, and he was bitten on the hand by another K-9 handler's dog during practice exercises. When Connolly initiated his teasing on the day in question, Watson burst into a rage of vulgarities and threats, drew his service revolver, and pointed it at Connolly; other officers tackled and disarmed Watson.

Questions for Discussion

1. What were some of the issues and precipitating factors leading to this incident?
2. Were there any warning signs? If so, what were they?
3. Could this incident have been avoided? If so, how?
4. What were Sgt. Aldous's responsibilities in this matter? Did he meet those responsibilities?

Case Study #2

An Agency at the End of Its ROP

Hill City is a relatively small community of about 80,000 people, whose police department has developed an aggressive Repeat Offender Program (ROP). Its eight hand-picked and specially trained officers engage in forced entries into apartments and houses, serving search warrants on the "worst of the worst" wanted felons. Their work is dangerous and physical, thus all of ROP's officers are in top physical condition. The supervisor overseeing the ROP team, Sgt. Lyle, was a drill instructor in the military prior to joining the force. He has developed an impressive training regimen for the ROP officers. They usually work out on their own time at least once a week, have high esprit de corps, and pride themselves on never losing a suspect or a physical confrontation. They often go out partying together to "blow off steam." They generally consider themselves to be elite and "head and shoulders above the rest." One day, while the team was attempting to serve a robbery warrant at a local motel, the suspect escaped through a rear window and led three ROP officers on a foot pursuit. After running extremely hard for about six blocks, the officers became exhausted and were unable to maintain their chase.

The following week, the same suspect robbed a fast-food establishment, and during his escape he killed a clerk and seriously wounded a police officer. Irate because the ROP team failed to catch the suspect earlier, many Hill City patrol officers begin to criticize the ROP team—whose members they consider to be overly exalted prima donnas—with one officer stating to a newspaper reporter that the entire team should be disciplined and that ROP should be disbanded. In one instance, a fight nearly ensued between two officers. The situation has now reached a boiling point, causing nearly all officers to take one side or another, fomenting a lot of stress and turmoil within the small agency, and causing officer requests for sick leave and vacation time to spike as never before. Sensing the urgency of the situation, and that his agency is being torn apart both from within and without, the chief asks all administrators (two deputy chiefs) and middle managers (four lieutenants) for input to deal with the public and the press, reduce the internal strife, and determine if any procedural or training issues require the department's attention. He further asks his six supervisors to provide input concerning means of reducing or ending the high level of hostility among patrol officers.

Questions for Discussion

1. Should Sgt. Lyle shoulder any responsibility for the suspect situation and its aftermath (dissension within the department)? What kinds of inquiries might you make to determine whether or not this is the case?
2. Given that this seems to have become an agency-wide stress problem, what might the deputy chiefs, lieutenants, and sergeants recommend to the chief?
3. Should the ROP team be disbanded or continued under different supervision, training, and methods of operation

Summary

This chapter has addressed police officer stress, wellness, and employee assistance programs. These three areas represent critical issues in police supervision and management. Police departments must plan for meeting the needs of their human resources just as they plan for the purchase of capital equipment or for operations. When human resources are neglected, it results in lost productivity and public confidence. Too often, police departments neglect or take their personnel for granted. People are a department's most important asset.

This chapter demonstrated that the supervisor and manager play a key role in employee stress reduction and wellness. Supervisors must constantly evaluate their subordinates, make judgments about their stress and wellness, and, when necessary, encourage officers to seek help. This is a key function of supervision.

Managers, on the other hand, must provide support to the supervisors. They must also ensure that departmental resources are available to combat the stress problem and to provide assistance to officers who have become debilitated as a result of stress. First-line supervisors can work with officers to reduce stress, but managers are the ones who must supply the resources and tools to accomplish the mission.

Items for Review

1. Explain the dimensions and processes of stress.
2. Describe the typical stress pattern by years of police service.
3. Examine the four general areas of police work that contribute to stress.
4. Explain how police personnel may attempt to manage their stress levels.
5. Describe the kinds of measures supervisors can undertake to assist officers in dealing with their stress.
6. Explain the function of an employee assistance program.

References

Albrecht, S., and Green, M. (1977). Attitudes toward the police and larger attitude complex and implications for police-community relationships. *Criminology* 15:67–86.

Anspaugh, D. J., Hamrick, M. H., and Rosato, R. D. (1991). *Wellness: Concepts and applications.* St. Louis: Mosby.

Band, S. R., and Sheehan, D. C. (1999). Managing undercover stress: The supervisor's role. *FBI Law Enforcement Bulletin* (February):1–6.

Barker, T., and Carter, D. (1994). *Police deviance.* Cincinnati: Anderson.

Bartlett, J., ed. (1992). *Familiar quotations,* 16th ed. Boston, MA: Little, Brown.

Brooks, L., and Piquero, N. (1998). Police stress: Does department size matter? *Policing: An International Journal of Police Strategies and Management* 21(1):600–617.

Brown, B., and Benedict, W. (2002). Perceptions of the police. *Policing: An International Journal of Police Strategies & Management* 25:543-580.

Church, R., and Robertson, N. (1999). How state police agencies are addressing the issue of wellness. *Policing: An International Journal of Police Strategies & Management* 22:304-312.

Crank, J. P., and Caldero, M. (1991). The production of occupational stress in medium-sized police agencies: A survey of line officers in eight municipal departments. *Journal of Criminal Justice* 19:339–349.

Daviss, B. (1982). Burnout. *Police Magazine* (May):24–27.

Derogatis, L., and Savitz, K. (1999). The SCL-90-R, Brief Symptom Inventory (BSI): An introductory report. In M. Maruish (ed.). *The use of psychological testing for treatment, planning and outcomes assessment.* Mahwah, NJ: Lawrence Erlbaum.

Dietrich, J. F. (1989). Helping subordinates face stress. *Police Chief* 56(11):44–47.

Finn, P. (1997). Reducing stress: An organization-centered approach. *FBI Law Enforcement Bulletin* (August):22–28.

Fishkin, G. L. (1988). *Police burnout: Signs, symptoms and solutions*. Gardena, CA: Harcourt Brace Jovanovich.

Franz, V., and Jones, D. (1987). Perceptions of organizational performance in suburban police departments: A critique of the military model. *Journal of Police Science and Administration* 15(2):153–161.

Gaines, L., and Kappeler, V. (2008). *Policing in America*, 6th ed. Cincinnati: Lexis-Nexis.

Garcia, L., Nesbary, D., and Gu, J. (2004). Perceptual variations of stressors among police officers during an era of decreasing crime. *Journal of Contemporary Criminal Justice*, 20:38-45.

Graf, F. A. (1986). The relationship between social support and occupational stress among police officers. *Journal of Police Science and Administration* 14(3):178–186.

Haarr, R., and Morash, M. (1999). Gender, race and strategies of coping with occupational stress in policing. *Justice Quarterly* 16(2):303–306.

Harrison, E. F., and Pelletier, M. A. (1987). Perceptions of bureaucratization, role performance, and organizational effectiveness in a metropolitan police department. *Journal of Police Science and Administration* 15(4):262–270.

Kaufmann, G. M., and Beehr, T. A. (1989). Occupational stressors, individual strains, and social supports among police officers. *Human Relations* 42(2):185–197.

Kirschman, E. (1997). *I love a cop: What police families need to know*. New York: Guilford Press.

Kraska, P., and Kappeler, V. (1988). A theoretical and descriptive study of police on-duty drug use. *American Journal of Police* 8(1):1-36.

Kroes, W. (1976). *Society's victim, the policeman: An analysis of job stress in policing.* Springfield, IL: C.C. Thomas.

Langworthy, R. H. (1992). Organizational structure. In G. W. Cordner and D. C. Hale, eds., *What works in policing?* Cincinnati: Anderson, pp. 87–105.

Lord, V., Gray, D., and Pond, S. (1991). The police stress inventory: Does it measure stress? *Journal of Criminal Justice* 19:139–149.

McCarty, W., Zhao, J., and Garland, B. (2007). Occupational stress and burnout between male and female police officers. *Policing: An International Journal of Police Strategies & Management*, 30:672-691.

McNally, V. J., and Solomon, R. M. (1999). The FBI's critical incident stress management program. *FBI Law Enforcement Bulletin* (February):20–25.

Morash, M., and Haarr, R. (1991). Gender, workplace problems, and stress in policing. Paper presented at the annual meeting of the Academy of Criminal Justice Sciences, Nashville, TN.

Morash, M., Kwak, D., and Haarr, R. (2006). Gender differences in the predictors of police stress. *Policing: An International Journal of Police Strategies & Management* 29:541–563.

National Institute of Justice. (2000). *On-the-job stress in policing*. Washington, DC: NIJ.

Niederhoffer, A. (1967). *Behind the shield: The police urban society.* Garden City, NY: Doubleday.

Richmond, R., Wodak, A., Kehoe, L., and Heather, N. (1998). How healthy are the police? A survey of lifestyle factors. *Addiction*, 93:1729-1738.

Selye, H. (1981). *Stress without distress*. Philadelphia: Lippincott.

Sewell, J. D. (1983). The development of a critical life events scale for law enforcement. *Journal of Police Science and Administration* 11(1):109–116.

Skolnick, J. (1994). *Justice without trial: Law enforcement in a democratic society.* New York: Wiley.

Stinchcomb, J. (2004). Searching for stress in all the wrong places: Combating chronic organizational stressors in policing. *Police Practice and Research* 5:259-277.

Tanigoshi, H., Kontos, A. and Remley, T. (2008). The effectiveness of individual wellness counseling on the wellness of law enforcement officers. *Journal of Counseling & Development* 86: 64-74.

Van Raalte, R. (1979). Alcohol as a problem among police officers. *Police Chief*, 44:38-40.

Vila, B. (2000). *Tired cops: The importance of managing police fatigue*. Washington, DC: Police Executive Research Forum.

Violanti, J. M. (1983). Stress patterns in police work: A longitudinal study. *Journal of Police Science and Administration* 11(2):211–216.

Violanti, J. M., and Aron, F. (1994). Ranking police stressors. *Psychological Reports* 75:825-826.

Westley, W. A. (1970). *Violence and the police.* Cambridge, MA: The MIT Press.

What's killing America's cops? (1996). *Law Enforcement News* (November 15):1.

Witkin, G., Gest, T., and Friedman, D. (1990). Cops under fire. *U.S. News and World Report* (December 3):32–44.

Zhao, S., Hi, N., and Lovrich, N. (2002). Predicting five dimensions of police officer stress: Looking more deeply into organizational settings for sources of police stress. *Police Quarterly*, 5: 43-62.

CHAPTER 9

Ethics, Inappropriate Behaviors, and Liability

Key Terms and Concepts

- Absolute ethics
- Accepted lying
- Bias-based policing
- Civil liability
- Code of Conduct
- Code of Ethics
- Contagious shooting
- Deontological ethics
- Deviant lying
- Duty of care
- Dynamic Resistance Response Model (DRRM)
- Entrapment
- Ethics
- Excessive force
- Failure to protect
- Gratuities
- Knapp Commission
- Model of circumstantial corruptibility
- Negligence
- Noble cause corruption
- Proximate cause
- Relative ethics
- Slippery slope
- Use of force
- Workplace harassment

Learning Objectives

After reading this chapter, the student will:

- have a basic understanding of absolute and relative ethics, and their relationship to policing, and what supervisors and managers can and must do to maintain a culture of integrity
- be able to explain what is meant by *noble cause corruption*, and what supervisors and managers must do to recognize and deal with it
- know the kinds of improper or illegal officer behaviors that supervisors and managers must address
- understand what is meant by *contagious shooting*, and why it is so inflammatory
- define and provide distinctions between acceptable and deviant lying by police
- know the definitions of *bias-based policing* and *workplace harassment*, and be able to explain why they can be so problematic in policing
- be able to define *proximate cause* and *failure to protect*

- know the meaning of *gratuities*, and reasons for and against their receipt by officers, and the DSSR model for examining the roles of both givers and receivers of gifts
- be knowledgeable about how supervisors can be liable if they are negligent in their supervision of officers
- describe the nature and use of 42 U.S. Code Section 1983
- be able to explain what protections against liability police have in vehicle pursuits, and the kinds of actions that can result in their being liable for damages.

Watch your thoughts, for they become words.
Watch your words, for they become actions.
Watch your actions, for they become habits.
Watch your habits, for they become character.
Watch your character, for it becomes your destiny.

- UNKNOWN

INTRODUCTION

Few chapters in this book are as important in their content as this one. It concerns serious police transgressions, violations of public trust, and areas of liability. Police supervision and management, being very concerned with people and their behaviors, are heavily implicated in these areas. The responsibility for ensuring that subordinates act correctly relative to their position, in an acceptable and effective manner, lies squarely at their door.

First, we frame the question of ethics with two opening scenarios—the first is an extreme illustration, perhaps, but one that demonstrates an ethical issue in which the police can become involved. Next, we discuss ethics generally, including its philosophical underpinnings and types, and then move to the matter of ethical problems specific to police supervision and management, including the police codes of ethics and conduct. Following that is a review of inappropriate police behaviors as they relate to ethical conduct; included here are sections on lying and deception, gratuities and corruption, **use of force**, sexual relations, workplace harassment, and **bias-based policing**. Finally, the liability of police supervisors is addressed in terms of holding them and their subordinates accountable for their actions. The chapter concludes with three case studies.

LAYING THE FOUNDATIONS OF ETHICS: TWO SCENARIOS

1. Does the End Justify the Means?

Assume that the police have multiple leads that implicate Smith as a pedophile, but they have failed in every attempt to obtain a warrant to search Smith's car and home where evidence might be present. Officer Jones feels frustrated and, early one morning, takes his baton and breaks a rear taillight on Smith's car. The next day he stops Smith for operating his vehicle with a broken taillight; he impounds and inventories the vehicle and finds evidence leading to Smith's conviction on 25 counts of child molestation and possession of pornography. Jones receives accolades for the apprehension.

2. You and the Oral Interview

During oral interviews for police positions, applicants are often placed in hypothetical situations to test their ethical beliefs and character. For example, assume that you are a police officer who is clearing a retail office supplies store in the early morning hours that was found to have an unlocked door and window. On leaving the building, you observe another officer, Brown, remove a $250 gold writing pen from a display case and place it in his uniform pocket. What would you do?

This kind of question commonly befuddles applicants for police positions. "How am I *supposed* to answer? Do they want to hire someone who will rat on their fellow officer? Should I protect the officer? Overlook the matter? Or merely tell Brown never to do it again?" Unfortunately, applicants are often more preoccupied with a self-debate concerning how they "should" respond than with a true introspective assessment of where they stand on the question.

What Does the Oral Board Want to Hear?

How does a values-laden police agency *want* and *expect* its applicants to respond to these two scenarios? First, bear in mind that criminal justice agencies do not wish to hire someone who has ethical shortcomings. It is simply too potentially dangerous and expensive—from both litigation and morality standpoints—to take the chance of bringing someone who is corrupt into an agency (possibly for many years).

Was Officer Jones's act regarding the taillight legal? Should his actions, even if improper or illegal, be condoned for "serving the greater public good"? Did Jones use the law properly? How close is he to "planting evidence" on an innocent citizen just because he doesn't like him? Assume that a supervisor observed Jones breaking the taillight; what action(s), if any, should follow?

Before responding to a scenario concerning Officer Brown's theft of the pen, the applicant should also consider the following issues: Is this likely to be the first time that Brown has stolen something? Don't the police arrest and jail people for this same kind of behavior? If the police were to overlook this act, how much *should* the officer be allowed to steal before determining that it's wrong (this is a tongue-in-check, rhetorical query!)?

In short, police administrators should *never* expect or hope that an applicant will say that it is proper for an officer to steal. Furthermore, it would be incorrect for an applicant to believe that police do not want to hear someone "rat out" another officer. People should never acknowledge that stealing or other such activities are to be overlooked.

We invite the reader to keep these scenarios and questions in mind as we discuss ethics and ethical dilemmas.

ETHICS, GENERALLY

Philosophical Foundations

The term *ethics* is rooted in the ancient Greek idea of character. **Ethics** involves doing what is right or correct and is generally used to refer to how people should behave in a professional capacity. Many people would argue, however, that there should be no difference between one's professional and personal lives. Ethical rules of conduct essentially should transcend everything a person does.

A central problem with understanding ethics is that there is always the question as to "whose ethics?" or "which right?" This becomes evident with controversies such as the death penalty, abortion, use of deadly force, or gun control. How individuals view a particular controversy largely depends on their values, character, or ethics. Both sides on controversies such as these believe they are morally right.

Another area for examination is **deontological ethics**, which does not consider consequences but instead examines one's duty to act. The word *deontology* comes from two Greek roots, *deos* meaning duty, and *logos* meaning study. Thus, deontology means "the study of duty." When police officers observe a violation of law, they have a duty to act. Officers frequently use this as an excuse when they issue traffic citations that, on their face, have little utility and do not produce a beneficial result for society as a whole. When an officer writes a traffic citation for a prohibited left turn at two o'clock in the morning when no traffic is around, the officer is fulfilling a departmental duty to enforce the law. From a utilitarian standpoint (which judges an action by its consequences), however, little if any good was served. Here, duty trumped good consequences.

Immanuel Kant, an eighteenth-century philosopher, expanded the ethics of duty by including the idea of "good will." People's actions must be guided by good intent. In the previous example, the officer who wrote the traffic citation for an improper left turn would be acting unethically if the ticket was a response to a quota or to some irrelevant cause. On the other hand, if the citation was issued because the officer truly believed that it would result in some good, he or she would have been performing an ethical action.

Some people have expanded this argument even further. Kania (1988) argued that police officers should be allowed to freely accept gratuities because such actions would constitute the building blocks of positive social relationships between the police and the public. In this case, duty is used to justify what under normal circumstances would be considered to be unethical. Conversely, if the officers take the gratuity for self-gratification rather than to form positive community relationships, then the action would be considered unethical by many.

Absolute and Relative Ethics

Broadly speaking, ethical issues in policing have been affected by three critical factors (O'Malley, 1997): (1) the growing level of temptation stemming from the illicit drug trade; (2) the potentially compromising nature of the police organizational culture—a culture that exalts loyalty over integrity, with a "code of silence" that protects unethical, corrupt officers; and (3) the challenges posed by decentralization (flattening the organization and pushing decision making downward) through the advent of community oriented policing and problem solving (COPPS). The latter concept is characterized by more frequent and closer contacts with the public, resulting in the minds of many observers in less accountability and, by extension, more opportunities for corruption.

POINT OF AGREEMENT: ABSOLUTE ETHICS Ethics usually involves standards of fair and honest conduct, and what we call the conscience, the ability to recognize right from wrong, and actions that are good and proper. There are absolute ethics and relative ethics. **Absolute ethics** issues have only two sides; something is either good or bad, black or white. The original interest in police ethics focused on unethical behaviors such as bribery, extortion, excessive force, and perjury, which were always considered wrong. Other contemporary examples would be that police officers, it is universally agreed, should not be selling drugs or pocketing protection money.

AREAS OF DISAGREEMENT AND CONTROVERSY: RELATIVE ETHICS AND NOBLE CAUSE CORRUPTION Issues of **relative ethics** are more complicated and can have a multitude of sides with varying shades of gray. Here, the problem lies with the fact that allegations of corruption can mean different things to different people. If a community appears to accept relative ethics, especially in police dealings with, say, gang members or drug traffickers, it may send the wrong message to the police: that there are few boundaries placed on police behavior, and that, at times, "anything goes" in their fight against crime. As Kleinig (1996:55) pointed out, giving false testimony to ensure that a public menace is "put away" or the illegal wiretapping of an organized crime figure's telephone might sometimes be viewed as "necessary" and "justified," though wrong.

When relative ethics are given life and practiced in overt fashion by the police, it is known as **noble cause corruption**—what Thomas Martinelli (2006:150) defined as "corruption committed in the name of good ends, corruption that happens when police officers care too much about their work."

Imprisoned Officer Michael Dowd is highlighted during an NYPD internal affairs workshop. *(Courtesy NYPD Photo Unit)*

This viewpoint is also known as the "principle of double effect." It holds that when an act is committed to achieve a good end (such as an illegal search) and an inevitable but intended effect is negative (the person who is searched eventually goes to prison), then the act might still be justified.

Officers might "bend the rules," such as not reading a drunk person his rights or performing a field sobriety test; planting evidence; issuing "sewer" tickets (i.e., writing a person a ticket but not giving it to him, resulting in a warrant issued for failure to appear in court); "testilying" (e.g., lying in court about the defendant's actions); or "using the magic pencil," where police officers write up an incident in a way that criminalizes a suspect. A powerful tool for punishment, noble cause corruption carries with it a different way of thinking about the police relationship with the law; officers operate on a standard that places personal morality above the law. They become legislators *of* the law, and act as if they *are* the law (Crank and Caldero, 2000:75).

Such activities can be rationalized by some officers, however. As a Philadelphia police officer put it, "When you're shoveling society's garbage, you gotta be indulged a little bit" (U.S. Department of Justice 1997:62). Nonetheless, when officers participate in such activities and believe the ends justify the means, they corrupt their own system.

CHALLENGES FOR POLICE LEADERS

Recognizing and Addressing Noble Cause Corruption

Obviously the kinds of ends-justifies-means, noble cause behaviors that are mentioned above often involve arrogance on the part of the police and ignore the basic constitutional guidelines their occupation demands. Middle managers must be careful not to take a hard-line view that their subordinates always tell the truth and follow the law. For their part, when red flags surface, supervisors must look deep for reasons behind this sudden turn of events, and make reasonable inquiries into the cause (Martinelli,

2006). They must not fail to act, lest noble cause corruption be reinforced and entrenched; their inability to make the tough decisions that relate to subordinate misconduct can be catastrophic.

A supervisory philosophy of discipline based on due process, fairness, and equity, combined with intelligent, informed, and comprehensive decision making is best for the department, its employees, and the community. This supervisory philosophy demonstrates the moral commitment employees look for in their leaders and the type that is expected in police service (Martinelli, 2006).

Some experts in the field of police ethics blame supervisors for problems involving officers' lapses in ethic. For example, Edward Tully (1998:7) stated the following:

> Show me a law enforcement agency with a serious problem of officer misconduct and I will show you a department staffed with too many sergeants not doing their job. [Leaders must] recognize the vital and influential role sergeants play within a police organization. They should be selected with care, given as much supervisory training as possible, and included in the decision making process. Sergeants are the custodians of the police culture, the leaders and informal disciplinarians of the department, and the individual most officers look to for advice.

Perhaps a more tempered view of the daunting task confronting supervisors in reducing or preventing ethical lapses by officers is offered by Vicchio (1997:8–9); he believes that it is nearly impossible to prevent unethical officers from misbehaving if they are so inclined:

> No supervision of police officers can keep bad cops from doing bad things. There are simply too many police officers and too few supervisors. There will never be enough supervision to catch everyone.

Tully (1998:3), however, did underscore the vast amount of temptation that confronts today's officers and what must be done toward combating it:

> Socrates, Mother Teresa, or other revered individuals in our society never had to face the constant stream of ethical problems of a busy cop on the beat. One of the roles of [police leaders] is to create an environment that will help the officer resist the temptations that may lead to misconduct, corruption, or abuse of power. The executive cannot construct a work environment that will completely insulate the officers from the forces which lead to misconduct. Help is needed from the labor associations, and support is needed from the executive, legislative, and judicial branches of government. The ultimate responsibility for an officer's ethical and moral welfare rests squarely with the officer.

We further discuss the supervisor's and manager's roles later in the chapter.

Codes of Ethics and Conduct

Fair and Pilcher (1991) argued that one of the primary purposes of ethics is to guide police decision making. Codes of ethics provide more comprehensive guidelines than law and police operational procedures and answer questions that may otherwise go unanswered. When in doubt, police officers should be able to consider the ethical consequences of their actions or potential actions to evaluate how they should act or proceed. It is impossible for a police department to formulate procedures that address every possible situation an officer may encounter. Therefore, other behavioral guidelines must be in place to assist officers when making operational decisions.

Some police officers, however, take the attitude that if a particular behavior is not prohibited by law or policy, then it is permissible. Conversely, if actions are not mandated, they merely represent an option. Such an attitude points to a general failure of police ethics. Their actions should be guided by what is "right" for the situation and individuals involved, not what is required or prohibited.

Toward this end, law enforcement has adopted a **Code of Ethics**, which is shown in Figure 9-1. In 1989, the International Association of Chiefs of Police replaced the Code of Ethics with a Police **Code of Conduct**, shown in Figure 9-2. This code is broader and incorporates value statements that

LAW ENFORCEMENT CODE OF ETHICS

All law enforcement officers must be fully aware of the ethical responsibilities of their position and must strive constantly to live up to the highest possible standards of professional policing.

The International Association of Chiefs of Police believes it is important that police officers have clear advice and counsel available to assist them in performing their duties consistent with these standards, and has adopted the following ethical mandates as guidelines to meet these ends.

PRIMARY RESPONSIBILITIES OF A POLICE OFFICER

A police officer acts as an official representative of government, and is required and trusted to work within the law. The officer's powers and duties are conferred by statute. The fundamental duties of a police officer include serving the community, safeguarding lives and property, protecting the innocent, keeping the peace, and ensuring the rights of all to liberty, equality and justice.

PERFORMANCE OF THE DUTIES OF A POLICE OFFICER

A police officer shall perform all duties impartially, without favor or affection or ill will and without regard to status, sex, race, religion, political belief or aspiration. All citizens will be treated equally with courtesy, consideration and dignity.

Officers will never allow personal feelings, animosities, or friendships to influence official conduct. Laws will be enforced appropriately and courteously and, in carrying out their responsibilities, officers will strive to obtain maximum cooperation from the public. They will conduct themselves in appearance and deportment in such a manner as to inspire confidence and respect for the position of public trust they hold.

DISCRETION

A police officer will use responsibly the discretion vested in the position and exercise it within the law. The principle of reasonableness will guide the officer's determinations and the officer will consider all surrounding circumstances in determining whether any legal action shall be taken.

Consistent and wise use of discretion, based on professional policing competence, will do much to preserve good relationships and retain the confidence of the public. There can be difficulty in choosing between conflicting courses of action. It is important to remember that a timely word of advice rather than arrest—which may be correct in appropriate circumstances—can be a more effective means of achieving a desired end.

USE OF FORCE

A police officer will never employ unnecessary force or violence and will use only such force in the discharge of duty as is reasonable in all circumstances.

Force should be used only with the greatest restraint and only after discussion, negotiation, and persuasion have been found to be inappropriate or ineffective. While the use of force is occasionally unavoidable, every police officer will refrain from applying the unnecessary infliction of pain or suffering and will never engage in cruel, degrading, or inhuman treatment of any person.

CONFIDENTIALITY

Whatever a police officer sees, hears, or learns of, which is of a confidential nature, will be kept secret unless the performance of duty or legal provision requires otherwise.

Members of the public have a right to security and privacy, and information obtained about them must not be improperly divulged.

INTEGRITY

A police officer will not engage in acts of corruption or bribery, nor will an officer condone such acts by other police officers.

The public demands that the integrity of police officers be above reproach. Police officers must, therefore, avoid any conduct that might compromise integrity and thus undercut the public confidence in a law enforcement agency. Officers will refuse to accept any gifts, presents, subscriptions, favors, gratuities, or promises that could be interpreted as seeking to cause the officer to refrain from performing official responsibilities honestly and within the law. Police officers must not receive private or special advantage from their official status. Respect from the public cannot be bought; it can only be earned and cultivated.

(Continued)

COOPERATION WITH OTHER OFFICERS AND AGENCIES

Police officers will cooperate with all legally authorized agencies and their representatives in the pursuit of justice.

An officer or agency may be one among many organizations that may provide law enforcement services to a jurisdiction. It is imperative that a police officer assist colleagues fully and completely with respect and consideration at all times.

PERSONAL/PROFESSIONAL CAPABILITIES

Police officers will be responsible for their own standard of professional performance and will take every reasonable opportunity to enhance and improve their level of knowledge and competence.

Through study and experience, a police officer can acquire the high level of knowledge and competence that is essential for the efficient and effective performance of duty. The acquisition of knowledge is a never-ending process of personal and professional development that should be pursued constantly.

PRIVATE LIFE

Police officers will behave in a manner that does not bring discredit to their agencies or themselves.

A police officer's character and conduct while off duty must always be exemplary, thus maintaining a position of respect in the community in which he or she lives and serves. The officer's personal behavior must be beyond reproach.

FIGURE 9-1 Code of Ethics (IACP)
Source: The International Association of Chiefs of Police. Used with permission.

Police Code of Conduct

All law enforcement officers must be fully aware of the ethical responsibilities of their position and must strive constantly to live up to the highest possible standards of professional policing.

The International Association of Chiefs of Police believes it important that police officers have clear advice and counsel available to assist them in performing their duties consistent with these standards, and has adopted the following ethical mandates as guidelines to meet these ends.

Primary Responsibilities of a Police Officer

A police officer acts as an official representative of government who is required and trusted to work within the law. The officer's powers and duties are conferred by statute. The fundamental duties of a police officer include serving the community, safeguarding lives and property, protecting the innocent, keeping the peace and ensuring the rights of all to liberty, equality and justice.

Performance of the Duties of a Police Officer

A police officer shall perform all duties impartially, without favor or affection or ill will and without regard to status, sex, race, religion, political belief or aspiration. All citizens will be treated equally with courtesy, consideration and dignity.

Officers will never allow personal feelings, animosities or friendships to influence official conduct. Laws will be enforced appropriately and courteously and, in carrying out their responsibilities, officers will strive to obtain maximum cooperation from the public. They will conduct themselves in appearance and deportment in such a manner as to inspire confidence and respect for the position of public trust they hold.

Discretion

A police officer will use responsibly the discretion vested in his position and exercise it within the law. The principle of reasonableness will guide the officer's determinations, and the officer will consider all surrounding circumstances in determining whether any legal action shall be taken.

Consistent and wise use of discretion, based on professional policing competence, will do much to preserve good relationships and retain the confidence of the public. There can be difficulty in choosing between conflicting courses of action. It is important to remember that a timely word of advice rather than arrest—which may be correct in appropriate circumstances—can be a more effective means of achieving a desired end.

Use of Force

A police officer will never employ unnecessary force or violence and will use only such force in the discharge of duty as is reasonable in all circumstances.

The use of force should be used only with the greatest restraint and only after discussion, negotiation and persuasion have been found to be inappropriate or ineffective. While the use of force is occasionally unavoidable, every police office will refrain from unnecessary infliction of pain or suffering and will never engage in cruel, degrading or inhuman treatment of any person.

Confidentiality

Whatever a police officer sees, hears or learns that is of a confidential nature will be kept secret unless the performance of duty or legal provision requires otherwise.

Members of the public have a right to security and privacy, and information obtained about them must not be improperly divulged.

Integrity

A police officer will not engage in acts of corruption or bribery, nor will an officer condone such acts by other police officers.

The public demands that the integrity of police officers be above reproach. Police officers must, therefore, avoid any conduct that might compromise integrity and thus undercut the public confidence in a law enforcement agency. Officers will refuse to accept any gifts, presents, subscriptions, favors, gratuities or promises that could be interpreted as seeking to cause the officer to refrain from performing official responsibilities honestly and within the law. Police officers must not receive private or special advantage from their official status. Respect from the public cannot be bought; it can only be earned and cultivated.

Cooperation with Other Police Officers and Agencies

Police officers will cooperate with all legally authorized agencies and their representatives in the pursuit of justice.

An officer or agency may be one among many organizations that may provide law enforcement services to a jurisdiction. It is imperative that a police officer assist colleagues fully and completely with respect and consideration at all times.

Personal-Professional Capabilities

Police officers will be responsible for their own standard of professional performance and will take every reasonable opportunity to enhance and improve their level of knowledge and competence.

Through study and experience, a police officer can acquire the high level of knowledge and competence that is essential for the efficient and effective performance of duty. The acquisition of knowledge is a never-ending process of personal and professional development that should be pursued constantly.

Private Life

Police officers will behave in a manner that does not bring discredit to their agencies or themselves.

A police officer's character and conduct while off duty must always be exemplary, thus maintaining a position of respect in the community in which he or she lives and serves. The officer's personal behavior must be beyond reproach.

FIGURE 9-2 Police Code of Conduct
Source: The International Association of Chiefs of Police. Used with permission.

express more contemporary police administrative concerns. The Code of Ethics and the Police Code of Conduct are taught in most training academies and made available to officers in many departments. They provide the trappings of professionalism but may actually exert little control over police officer behavior. Generally, state statutes and departmental policy, which are more specific and less theoretical, govern police behavior.

INAPPROPRIATE POLICE BEHAVIORS

Most of the efforts to control police behavior are rooted in statutes and departmental orders and policies. These written directives stipulate inappropriate behavior and, in some cases, the behavior or actions that are expected in specific situations. However, written directives cannot address every contingency and officers must often use their discretion. These discretionary decisions should be guided by ethics and values.

Some observers have referred to illegal police behavior as a "**slippery slope**": Officers tread on solid or legal grounds but at some point slip beyond the acceptable into illegal or unacceptable behavior. These slippery slopes serve as a point of analysis for the behaviors addressed in this section, which discusses areas in which officers can get into trouble: (1) lying and deception, (2) acceptance of gratuities and corruption, (3) improper use of force, (4) verbal and psychological abuse, (5) violations of civil rights, and (6) improper sexual relationships.

Officer Lying and Deception

Police officers lie or deceive for different purposes and under varying circumstances. In some cases, their misrepresentations are accepted and considered to be an integral part of a criminal investigation, while in other cases they are not accepted and are viewed as violations of law. Barker and Carter (1994, 1990) examined police lying and perjury and developed a taxonomy that centered on **accepted lying** and deviant lying. *Accepted lying* includes police activities to apprehend or entrap suspects. This type of lying is generally considered to be trickery. **Deviant lying**, on the other hand, refers to occasions when officers commit perjury to convict suspects or are deceptive about some activity that is illegal or unacceptable to the department or public in general.

Accepted Lying. Deception has long been used by the police to ensnare violators and suspects. For many years, it was the principal method used by detectives (particularly undercover agents) and police officers to secure confessions and convictions (Kuykendall, 1986). It is allowed by the law, and to a great extent, it is expected by the public. Gary T. Marx (1982:170) identified three methods of, or situations where the police may attempt to use trickery with a suspect:

1. Offering the illegal action as a part of a larger socially acceptable and legal goal. Here, the target may be convinced that the criminal activity is legal and desirable; for example, a person suspected of involvement in white collar crimes might be told that their involvement will bring a major industry to their city, and, conversely, that the opportunity will be lost if they do not, say, accept bribe money.
2. Disguising the illegal action so that the suspect does not know the action is illegal. Ignorance of the law, of course, is not an excuse for its violation. However, the situation seems different (at least, ethically) when one is led into illegal activities by a government agent who claims that no wrongdoing is occurring, and creates a subterfuge in order to make it appear to the suspect that nothing illegal is happening.
3. Morally weakening the suspect so that the suspect voluntarily becomes involved. This involves an agent attempting to create or aggravate conditions in the target. For example, suspects have been convinced to eventually take bribes after government agents, learning the target was a drug addict or alcoholic, provide them drugs or liquor. Such persons may be more susceptible to persuasion and less able than most citizens to distinguish right from wrong.

The courts have long accepted deception as an investigative tool. In *Illinois v. Perkins* (1990), the U.S. Supreme Court ruled that police undercover agents who are posing as inmates are not required to administer the *Miranda* warning to incarcerated inmates when investigating crimes. The Court essentially separated trickery from coercion. Coercion is strictly prohibited, but trickery by police officers is unquestionably acceptable. Lying, although acceptable by the courts and the public in certain circumstances, does result in an ethical dilemma. It is a dirty means to accomplish a good end; the police use untruths to gain the truth relative to some event.

Another problem with deception is entrapment. ***Entrapment*** occurs when the idea of a crime begins with the police rather than the suspect, and the police facilitate the commission of a criminal act. The courts examine the offender's predisposition to commit the crime. If no predisposition exists, then the police have engaged in entrapment. Should police undercover officers be allowed to give drugs to suspects so that the suspects can be apprehended for possession? Should suspects be encouraged by undercover police officers to burglarize a business so that the suspects can be arrested?

Deviant Lying. In their taxonomy of police lying, Barker and Carter (1994) identified two types of deviant lying: lying that serves legitimate purposes and lying that conceals or promotes crimes or illegitimate ends.

Lying that serves legitimate goals occurs when officers lie to secure a conviction, obtain a search warrant, or conceal police omissions during an investigation. Lying becomes an effective, routine way to sidestep legal impediments. When left unabated by police supervisors, managers, and administrators, lying can become organizationally accepted as an effective means to nullify legal entanglements and other obstacles that stand in the way of convictions. Examples include officers misrepresenting the fact that they used the services of confidential informants to secure search warrants, concealing that an interrogator went too far and coerced a confession, or perjuring themselves to gain a conviction.

Lying to conceal or promote police criminality is, without a doubt, a very egregious form of police deception. Examples of this form of lying range from officers' lying to conceal their using excessive force when arresting a suspect to obscuring the commission of a criminal act. Barker and Carter (1990) and Skolnick (1982) reported that the practice is commonplace in some departments. They reasoned that the police culture approves and, in some cases, promotes it.

Deception and lying must be dealt with. First, supervisors must fully understand what is acceptable and what is not acceptable behavior; a line must be drawn. Second, this information must be communicated to officers on a regular basis. Third, supervisors must inquire into and actively supervise officers' cases. If supervisors inquire into and investigate the extent of deception and lying by individual officers, officers are less likely to engage in unacceptable deception. Finally, when problems are identified, supervisors must take immediate disciplinary action. If supervisors promote deception by failing to respond to it, they are only worsening the problem.

Accepting Gratuities

Gratuities are commonly accepted by police officers as a part of their job. Restaurants and convenience stores frequently give officers free or half-price food and drinks, while a number of other businesses routinely give officers discounts for services or merchandise. Many police officers and departments accept these gratuities as a part of the job, while other departments "draw the short line," having policies prohibiting such gifts and discounts and arguing that "the only clean item of value is your paycheck."

There are two basic arguments against police acceptance of gratuities. First is the slippery slope argument, discussed earlier, which proposes that gratuities are the first step in police corruption. Once gratuities are received, police officers' ethics are subverted and officers are open to additional breaches of their integrity. Also, officers who accept minor gifts or gratuities are then obligated to provide the donors with some special service or accommodation. Second, some propose that receiving a gratuity is wrong since officers are receiving rewards for services that, as a result of their employment, they are obligated to provide.

Kania (1988) attempted to categorically justify police officers' acceptance of gratuities. He argued that shopkeepers and restaurant owners often feel an indebtedness toward the police, and gratuities provide an avenue of repayment. He also maintained that the acceptance of gratuities does not necessarily lead to the solicitation of additional gratuities and gifts or corruption. Officers are able to differentiate what is appropriate and develop their own ethical standards and adhere to them.

Withrow and Dailey (2004) have recently offered a uniquely different viewpoint toward gratuities. They propose a "**model of circumstantial corruptibility**," stating that the exchange of a gift is influenced by two elements: the role of the giver and the role of the receiver. In this model, the role of the giver determines the level of corruptibility; the giver is either taking a position as a:

- *presenter,* who offers a gift voluntarily without any expectation of a return from the receiver;
- *contributor*, who furnishes something toward a result and expects something in return; or a
- *capitulator*, who involuntarily responds to the demands of the receiver.

The role of the receiver of the gift is obviously very important as well. In the model, the receiver can act as an:

- *acceptor,* who receives the gift humbly and without any residual feelings of reciprocity;
- *expector,* who looks forward to the gift and regards it as likely to happen, and will be annoyed by the absence of the gift; or
- *conqueror,* who assumes total control over the exchange and influence over the giver.

The function of the model, Withrow and Dailey (2004) argue, is centered on the intersection of the giver and the receiver. For example, when the giver assumes the role of the presenter and the receiver is the acceptor, the result is a giving exchange, and corruption does not occur. However, if giver and receiver occupy other roles, corruptibility can progress to higher levels of social harm, which they term a "hierarchy of wickedness." Bribery results when something of value is given and the giver expects something in return, while the receiver agrees to conform his behavior to the desires of the giver. This model is not clear-cut, however, because the confusion of roles between givers and receivers is inevitable.

Withrow and Dailey's model is distinguishable from Kania's view that the police should be encouraged to accept minor gratuities to foster good relations; rather, Withrow and Dailey encourage the police to consider the role of the giver as well as their own intentions when deciding whether or not to accept a gratuity. In certain circumstances, the exchange of *any* gratuity is ethical or unethical regardless of its value.

Notwithstanding Kania's arguments, above, history and studies have shown the dysfunctional and corrupting influence gratuities can have on law enforcement. Perhaps the most notorious and disgraceful example can be found in the ***Knapp Commission*** *Report on Police Corruption* in New York City (1972). The commission found that a large number of officers were not only accepting gratuities, but that the active solicitation of gratuities and gifts was institutionalized within the department. If the gifts and gratuities were not forthcoming, the police often issued summonses or otherwise harassed the shopkeeper or business owner. The commission characterized a majority of the officers as "grass-eaters," who freely accepted gratuities and sometimes solicited minor payments and gifts; others were described as "meat-eaters," who spent a significant portion of the workday aggressively seeking out situations that could be exploited for financial gain. These officers were corrupt and were involved in thefts, drugs, gambling, prostitution, and other criminal activities.

Once a police department decides on a policy, it should ensure that all officers are familiar with the policy; and certainly supervisors and managers must fully enforce it and ensure that the following measures are taken. First, supervisors should inquire about activities and continually stress the department's policies. Second, supervisors should aggressively investigate any evidence or indication that officers may be violating the department's policies. These actions are necessary to ensure that officers' actions regarding gratuities do not get out of hand.

Improper Use of Authority and Force

As noted earlier, citizens bestow a substantial amount of authority on police officers. A central problem in police supervision occurs when officers improperly use this authority. Improper use of authority can range from being disrespectful to the inappropriate use of deadly force. To this end, Carter (1994) has attempted to provide a typology of abuse of authority by police officers. His categories include (1) physical abuse and excessive force, (2) verbal and psychological abuse, and (3) legal abuse and violations of civil rights.

PHYSICAL ABUSE AND EXCESSIVE FORCE Physical abuse and **excessive force** can occur when the police use either deadly or non-deadly force. The use of excessive physical force often results in substantial public scrutiny. Indeed, such instances of improper use of police authority and excessive force have received national attention. Perhaps the most well-known incident was the Rodney King case in 1991, involving the Los Angeles Police Department. This incident had profound effects at the national level on policing and how citizens view law enforcement. Local incidents may not receive national media coverage, but they oftentimes have the same dramatic, chilling effects in a community. All police officers are judged by the actions of one or a few officers.

Regardless of the type of force used, it must be used by police officers in a legally accepted manner. Police officers are allowed to use only that force necessary to effect an arrest. Thus, the amount of force that a police officer uses is dependent on the amount of resistance demonstrated by the person being arrested. This concept is taught to police officers in training academies. Figure 9-3 below shows a good means of visualizing what is the proper use of force in a given situation.

A MODERN APPROACH TO DETERMINING THE PROPER USE OF FORCE How much force is reasonable for a police officer to use against a suspect? An enormous amount of thought was invested in responding to that question over the past 30 years, leading to the development of various force continuums. Shaped like a staircase, ladder, wheel, or something else, these traditional use of force continuums attempted to determine which type of force (usual ranging from mere presence to verbal commands, empty-hand control holds, personal weapons, less-lethal weapons, carotid restraint, and deadly force) an officer could use in response to a suspect's behavior.

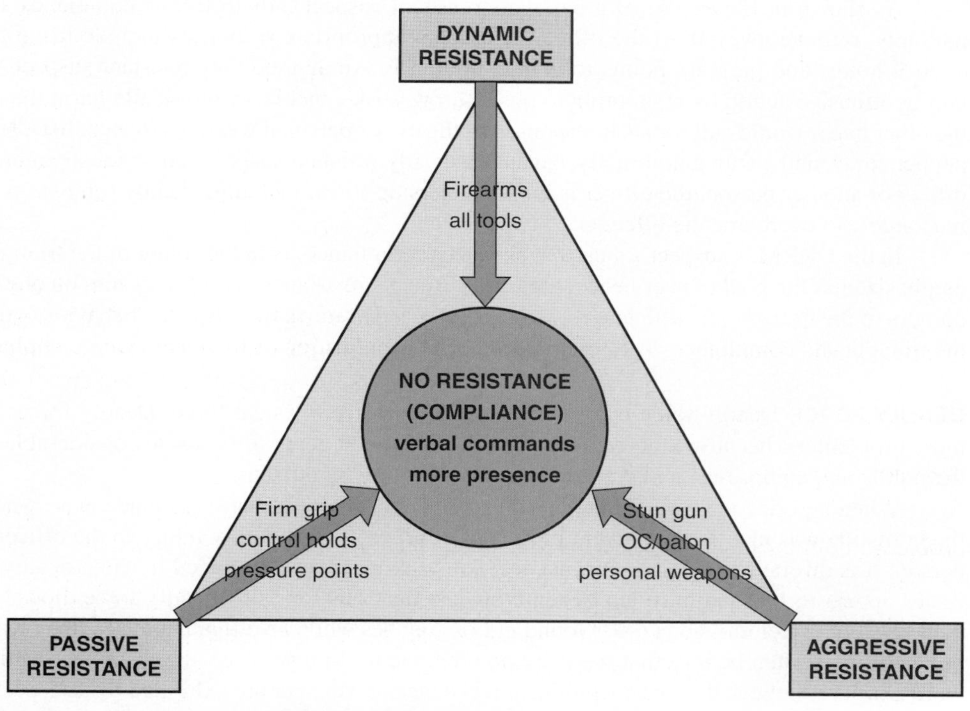

FIGURE 9–3 The Dynamic Resistance Response Model
Source: FBI *Law Enforcement Bulletin, Sept. 2007*

Even when agency policies accompanied the continuum (as they always should), such continuums have always been confusing to most police officers. "How far and when do I 'climb the next rung' of the ladder" sort of confusion could and did exist. Such continuums also fail to properly represent the dynamic encounter between the officer and a resistant suspect and to take into account the wide array of tools that are available to officers today; it is too difficult for a department to dictate by a continuum in what situations, say, a baton or pepper spray or Taser or other less-lethal weapons, should be used.

Instead, many agencies now have policies requiring their officers to be "objectively reasonable" in their use of force; an example of the language defining what is objectively reasonable is as follows:

> In determining the necessity for force and the appropriate level of force, officers shall evaluate each situation in light of the known circumstances, including, but not limited to, the seriousness of the crime, the level of threat or resistance presented by the subject, and the danger to the community.

A new approach to determining proper use of force has recently been developed by two special agents of the Federal Bureau of Investigation and asserts to "more accurately reflect the intent of the law and the changing expectations of society" and provides officers with "simple, clear, unambiguous, and consistent guidelines in the use of force" (Joyner and Basile, 2007:17).

Known as the **Dynamic Resistance Response Model (DRRM)**, this approach combines a use of force continuum with an application of four broad categories of suspects. *Dynamic* indicates that the model is fluid, and *resistance* demonstrates that the suspect controls the interaction. In this view, a major failing of past continuums has been that the emphasis is on the officer and the amount of force used. DRRM instead emphasizes that the suspect's level of resistance determines the officer's response. The model also delineates suspects into one of four categories (see Figure 9-3).

As shown in Figure 9-3, if a passively resistant suspect fails to follow commands and perhaps attempts to move away from the officer or escape, appropriate responses include using a firm grip, control holds, and pressure points to gain compliance. An aggressively resistant suspect–one who is taking offensive action by attempting to push, throw, strike, tackle, or physically harm the officer—on the other hand, would call for such responses as the use of personal weapons (hands, fists, feet), batons, pepper spray, and a stun gun. Finally, because a deadly resistant suspect can seriously injure or kill the officer or another person, the officer is justified in using force, including deadly force, as is *objectively reasonable* to overcome the offender.

In the DRRM, a suspect's lack of resistance (compliance) is in the center of the triangle, which is emphasized as the goal of every encounter. If a suspect's resistance level places him on one of the three corners of the triangle, the officer's response is intended to move the suspect's behavior to the center of the triangle and compliance. The sole purpose of the application of force is to gain compliance.

DEADLY FORCE Deadly force is an extension of excessive physical force. Deadly force, however, is more problematic because of its outcome and the fact that it generally leads to considerable scrutiny by the public and authorities; and it can also result in rioting by citizens.

When a police officer deliberately kills someone, a determination is made as to whether or not the homicide was justified to prevent imminent death or serious bodily injury to the officer or another person. It is difficult to detail the police decision-making process involved in using deadly force. Two issues appear to be used fairly consistently as justifications for using deadly force, however. First, as the Christopher Commission (1991) found in Los Angeles while investigating the Rodney King incident, police officers often believe that there are no effective mid-range force alternatives or tactics. In other words, officers believe that once significant resistance and danger are exhibited by a suspect, their only alternative is to use deadly force. This situation can be corrected by training and ensuring that officers adhere to the use-of-force model shown above.

Second, Fyfe (1986) opined that officers used the split-second syndrome to justify shootings, especially when bad shootings occur. The split-second syndrome essentially implies that officers must make deadly force decisions in a matter of a precious few seconds. Fyfe noted that the syndrome makes three assumptions. First, no two shootings are alike; therefore, it is virtually impossible to establish principles that can be used to diagnose potential shooting situations. Second, because of the stress and time limitations, it should be expected that police officers will make errors. The circumstances, stress, and time limitations should justify police actions, and any criticism of police officers is unwarranted, especially by nonpolice personnel who do not understand police procedures or do not have an appreciation of the problems encountered by officers. Third, any evaluation of police decision making should be based on the perceived exigencies. If a citizen has or is perceived to have committed an act justifying deadly force, any subsequent shooting by the police should be deemed necessary or permissible.

Fyfe further asserted that adherence to the split-second syndrome can lead to unnecessary violence. In many shooting instances, police officers have the time to analyze the situation and make reactive decisions. Police officers can avoid split-second decision situations by taking actions before the situation escalates. When there are fight calls or calls involving weapons, officers should deploy tactics or obtain assistance that reduces the need for deadly force.

Police supervisors have the primary responsibility for ensuring that officers respond to various calls correctly. Supervisors should counsel officers when they become lax and make sure they use proper procedures when approaching a suspect or answering a call. If officers follow procedures, the need to make split-second decisions about using deadly force will diminish.

CONTROVERSY WITH "CONTAGIOUS" SHOOTINGS Clearly, nothing can inflame a community and raise tensions like police shootings. And there has been no dearth of high-profile police shooting incidents during the early part of this millennium:

- In April 2007 three NYPD officers were indicted for manslaughter and reckless endangerment for a shooting incident where they fired 50 rounds at a car of unarmed men leaving a bachelor party at a strip club; the groom died on his wedding day (Milton, 2007). The incident heightened racial tensions and, for many people, brought to mind the 1999 New York police killing of an unarmed West African, Amadou Diallo, who officers shot as he was reaching for his wallet, firing 41 shots and striking him 19 times.
- In July 2005, more than 30 Los Angeles officers, including its SWAT team, responded to a hostage situation and were caught in a crossfire from the front and back of an auto sales lot; the 19-month old daughter of the suspect was killed. The Police Commission found poor communication and a breakdown in command and control during the incident, and that 17 officers needed additional training. The probe involved microscopic analysis of about 130 bullets and more than 100 casings involving 13 firearms (*Los Angeles Times*, 2007).

These are what is known in police parlance as **contagious shooting**—gunfire that spreads among officers who believe that they, or their colleagues, are facing a threat. It spreads like wildfire, and often leads to an outcry from community leaders or family members. The phenomenon appears to have happened again in 2005, when eight officers fired 43 shots at an armed man in Queens, New York, killing him. In July 2005, three officers fired 26 shots at a pit bull that had bitten a chunk out of an officer's leg in a Bronx apartment building. And there have been other episodes: in 1995, in the Bronx, officers fired 125 bullets during a bodega robbery, with one officer firing 45 rounds (Wilson, 2007).

Incidents that also involve minority group members will often heighten the tension and lead to charges of racism against the entire police agency; one columnist offered that "it is the police culture,

The homeless often claim to be victims of police abuse and harassment.

more than race, that is at the crux of the problem . . . a mentality of brutality" (*Washington Post*, 2000). In response to excessive use of force by police, one organization, Human Rights Watch, stated in a report entitled *Shielded from Justice: Police Brutality and Accountability in the United States*, that:

> Police abuse remains one of the most serious and divisive human rights violations in the United States. The excessive use of force by police officers, including unjustified shootings, severe beatings, fatal chokings, and rough treatment, persists because overwhelming barriers to accountability make it possible for officers who commit human rights violations to escape due punishment and often to repeat their offenses. (1998)

Human Rights Watch (1998) also noted in the report that officers who repeatedly commit human rights violations tend to be a small minority, but that they are protected, routinely, by the silence of their fellow officers and by flawed systems of reporting, oversight, and accountability; by the scarcity of meaningful information about trends in abuse; data lacking regarding the police departments' response to those incidents; and their plans or actions to prevent brutality.

Paradoxically, for all their severity and inflammatory nature, the extent of police shootings is largely unknown. As the *New York Times* (2001:A1) stated:

> We like to think we live in the information age. For all the careful accounting, however, there are two figures Americans don't have: the precise number of people killed by the police, and the number of times police use excessive force. Despite widespread public interest and a provision in the 1994 Crime Control Act requiring the Attorney General to collect the data, statistics on police shootings and use of non-deadly force continue to be piecemeal products of spotty collection, and are dependent on the cooperation of local police departments. No comprehensive accounting for the nation's 17,000 police department exists.

The *Times* suggests that this lack of accurate statistics makes it impossible to draw meaningful conclusions about deadly encounters between the police and the civilian population, and that the major reason for the vacuum is the failure of the police in many cities to keep and report accurate figures that distinguish between what the police see as "justifiable" shootings—those in which the suspect posed a serious threat—and incidents where an officer may have unlawfully fired at an unarmed civilian (*New York Times*, 2001).

VERBAL AND PSYCHOLOGICAL ABUSE Police officers sometimes abuse citizens by berating or belittling them. They antagonize citizens knowing that as police officers they are wrapped in the shroud of authority, and that citizens must take the abuse. One of the most common methods used by police officers to verbally abuse citizens is profanity. Research indicates that profanity is used for a variety of reasons: as a source of power to control others (Selnow, 1985), as a weapon to degrade or insult others (Paletz and Harris, 1975), as a method of alienating others (Selnow, 1985), as a method of labeling others (Warshay and Warshay, 1978), and as a way of defying authority (Paletz and Harris, 1975). Unfortunately, profanity has become a part of the police culture and many officers' everyday speech. When profanity is used liberally in the work setting, it increases the likelihood that it will be used inappropriately.

Profane language tends to polarize a situation. A citizen will either passively submit or respond aggressively, in either case causing the citizen to distrust and dislike the police. When police officers use profanity, especially in an aggressive manner, the focus shifts from the problem to the officer's language; and when it is used aggressively, profanity can easily create greater physical risks to the officer. Furthermore, even if the officer intended to resolve the situation, it may no longer be possible because of the harm caused by the language. And, because it can incite situations, profanity also increases the potential for liability and citizens' complaints; therefore, it also heightens the possibility of the officer's facing administrative action.

For all these reasons, the use of profanity by the police toward citizens is not justified, wise, or advised. Supervisors should discourage its use and review every instance in which an officer used profanity with a citizen.

LEGAL ABUSE AND VIOLATIONS OF CIVIL RIGHTS Legal abuse and civil rights violations consist of police actions that violate a citizen's constitutional or statutory rights. This abuse usually involves false arrest, false imprisonment, and harassment. For example, a police officer may knowingly make an unlawful search, charge the suspect with a crime, and then lie about the nature of the search. Another example occurs when police officers hassle a criminal to gain information or hassle a business owner to obtain some monetary gain.

Supervisors and managers play a key role in preventing legal abuse and violations of citizens' civil rights. Supervisors frequently back up officers when responding to calls and observe situations that lead to an arrest. They should ensure that officers' decisions to arrest are based on probable cause, not some lesser standard. They should also review arrest reports and question officers when arrests are not observed to ensure that the arrests meet the probable cause standard.

This is critical since research has long indicated that officers frequently base their decisions to arrest on factors such as a suspect's demeanor (Smith and Visher, 1981), socioeconomic status (Black and Reiss, 1967; Friedrich, 1977), race (Brooks, 1986; Smith and Visher, 1981), age (Brooks, 1986; Freidrich, 1977), relationship between the suspect and victim (Friedrich, 1977; Smith and Visher, 1981), and the preference of the complainant (Brooks, 1986; Smith and Visher, 1981). When police officers allow such factors to substitute for probable cause, they are abusing their authority. Officers should provide the same level of services to all citizens, and they should use consistent decision-making criteria when making an arrest that exclude race, gender, or social standing.

Improper Sexual Relations

Although no accurate data exists, it seems that a significant number of officers engage in improper sexual relationships. While studying deviance in a southern city, Barker (1994) found that the officers believed that about one-third of the department engaged in improper sexual relationships while on duty. This in itself is problematic, because officers who participate in this activity are not only showing poor judgment in doing so, they may also be compromising their ability to objectively enforce the law. Although many of the liaisons could be deemed romantic encounters, some of them may very well be associated with illicit activities.

Sapp (1994) noted that because of their authority, police officers have a number of opportunities to sexually harass citizens. They have the authority to stop and talk with citizens, and in many cases, they can limit their freedom. They also perform work activities while unsupervised and in relative isolation. Although the majority of police officers may never sexually harass other citizens, a significant number do.

Because sexually related improprieties can and do occur, police supervisors and managers must be vigilant of such inappropriate behaviors, seven types of which have been identified (Sapp, 1994):

1. ***Nonsexual Contacts That Are Sexually Motivated.*** An officer will stop another citizen without legal justification to obtain information or get a closer look at the citizen.
2. ***Voyeuristic Contacts.*** Police officers attempt to observe partially clad or nude citizens. They observe apartment buildings or college dormitories. In other cases, they roust citizens parked on lovers' lanes.
3. ***Contacts with Crime Victims.*** Crime victims generally are emotionally distraught or upset and particularly vulnerable to sexual overtures from officers. In these instances, officers may make several return visits and calls with the intention of seducing the victim.
4. ***Contacts with Offenders.*** In these cases, officers may conduct body searches, frisks, and patdown searches. In some cases, officers may demand sexual favors. Offenders' complaints of sexual harassment will not be investigated by a department without corroborating evidence, which seldom exists.
5. ***Contacts with Juvenile Offenders.*** In some cases, officers have exhibited some of the same behaviors with juveniles that they have with adults, such as patdowns, frisks, and sexual favors. There have also been cases in which officers assigned as juvenile or school liaison officers have taken advantage of their assignment to seduce juveniles.
6. ***Sexual Shakedowns.*** Police officers demand sexual services from prostitutes, homosexuals, and others engaged in criminal activity as a form of protection.
7. ***Citizen-Initiated Sexual Contacts.*** Some citizens are attracted to police officers and attempt to seduce them. They may be attracted to the uniform, authority, or the prospect of a "safe" sexual encounter. In other cases, the citizen may be lonely or may want a "break" when caught violating the law.

Improper sexual activities undermine the effectiveness of a police department in two ways. First, they create a public relations nightmare. When sexual deviance cases involving the police become known, citizens lose respect for their police, tend to be less cooperative, and are less likely to support them politically. Second, they undermine the operational effectiveness of a department. When these problems occur, officers tend to believe they are immune from disciplinary controls and can do their jobs as they please.

Supervisors and managers must closely scrutinize subordinates' activities to prevent or reduce the incidence of sexual misconduct. If they fail to investigate or pursue allegations of sexual misconduct, in essence they are condoning it. This only leads to additional and possibly more outrageous conduct on the part of some of the officers. Supervisors may not be able to completely eliminate such behavior, but through thoughtful supervision, they can minimize it.

Workplace Harassment

Although sexual harassment has been a major concern in the nation for several decades—and is even outlawed in the Code of Federal Regulations (see 29 C.F.R. 1604.11(a))—today the more contemporary approach is for agencies to have a broader policy that applies to all forms of **workplace harassment**. All such harassment is a form of discrimination that violates Title VII of the Civil Rights Act of 1964 and other federal laws.

Unwelcome verbal or physical conduct based on race, color, religion, sex (whether or not of a sexual nature), national origin, age (40 and over), disability (mental or physical), sexual orientation, or retaliation constitutes harassment when:

1. the conduct is sufficiently severe to create a hostile work environment; or
2. a supervisor's harassing conduct results in a change in employment status or benefits (such as demotion, termination, failure to promote, and so on) (Federal Communications Commission, 2007).

In a hostile work environment, unwelcome comments or conduct based on sex, race, or other legally protected characteristics unreasonably interferes with an employee's work performance or creates an offensive work environment. Examples of such actions include:

- Leering in a sexually suggestive manner
- Making offensive remarks about looks, clothing, body parts
- Touching in a way that makes an employee uncomfortable, such as patting, pinching, brushing against another's body
- Sending or telling suggestive letters or notes, or telling sexual or lewd jokes
- Using racially derogatory words, phrases, epithets

A claim of harassment generally requires that: the complaining party be a member of a statutorily protected class; was subjected to unwelcome verbal or physical conduct; the unwelcome conduct complained of was based on his or her membership in that protected class; and the unwelcome conduct affected a term or condition of employment and unreasonably interfered with his or her work performance.

Any employee wishing to initiate an Equal Employment Complaint (EEO) arising out of the prohibited conduct described above must contact an EEO official within 45 days of the incident (Federal Communications Commission, 2007).

A "Hot Button" Issue: Bias-Based Policing

A contemporary issue in which police find themselves open to criticism and even disciplinary action involves bias-based policing. This issue has driven a deep wedge between the police and minorities, many of whom claim to be victims of this practice. Indeed, a New Jersey state police superintendent was fired by that state's governor for statements concerning racial profiling that were perceived as racially insensitive.

Many people remain convinced that the justice system unfairly draws minorities into its web, and that police methods are at the forefront of this practice. Bias-based policing, also known as racial profiling or "driving while black or brown" (DWBB)—occurs when a police officer acts on a personal bias and stops a vehicle simply because the driver is of a certain race (Neubauer, 1999:62).

Anecdotal evidence of bias-based policing has been accumulating for years, and now many people and groups (such as the American Civil Liberties Union) believe that all "pretext" traffic stops are wrong, because the chance that racism and racial profiling will creep into such stops is high.

For their part, many police executives defend such tactics as an effective way to focus their limited resources on likely lawbreakers; they argue that profiling is based not on *prejudice* but on *probabilities*—the statistical reality that young minority men are disproportionately likely to commit crimes. As explained by Bernard Parks, an African American and former police chief of Los Angeles,

> We have an issue of violent crime against jewelry salespeople. The predominant suspects are Colombians. We don't find Mexican-Americans, or blacks, or other immigrants. It's a collection of several hundred Colombians who commit this crime. If you see six in a car in front of the Jewelry Mart, and they're waiting and watching people with briefcases, should we play the percentages and follow them? It's common sense (quoted in Kennedy, 1999:31).

Still, it is difficult for the police to combat the public's perception that traffic stops of minorities simply on the basis of race are widespread and prejudicial in nature.

The best defense for the police may be summarized in two words: *collect data* (see, for example, Aether Systems, 2001; Garrett, 2001; Oliver and Zatcoff, 2001). Collecting traffic stop data helps chiefs and commanders determine whether officers are stopping or searching a disproportionate number of minorities and enables them to act on this information in a timely fashion (Garrett, 2001:103). In 1999, Connecticut was the first state to require all its municipal police agencies and the state police to collect race data for every police-initiated traffic stop (Cox, 2001); by mid-2001, at least 34 states either had enacted laws that included data collection or were considering data-collection legislation. It is anticipated that eventually all states will require the tracking of race data for all contacts. Technology that is available to the police, including mobile data computers and wireless handheld devices, is being adapted for this purpose (Aether Systems, 2001).

Figure 9-4 shows a race data traffic stop form for the state of Connecticut.

The International Association of Chiefs of Police has issued a comprehensive policy statement on biased policing and data collection. The association "believes that any form of police action that is

State of Connecticut
Traffic Stops Statistics

Department — ORI:______________________ Town:______________________

Date:___/___/___ Time:_____:_____ Age:______

Gender: Male Female Unknown

Race: (Circle One)
W - White
B - Black
I - Indian Amer./Alaskan Native
A - Asian/Pacific Islander
U - Unknown

Ethnicity: (Circle One)
H - Hispanic
N - Not Hispanic
U - Unknown

Stop Nature: I - Investigation, Criminal

Statute:______________________

Vehicle Search: (Circle One)
Y - Yes
N - No
V - Violation, Motor Vehicle
E - Equipment, Motor Vehicle

Disposition: (Circle One)
U - Uniform Arrest Report
M - Misdemeanor Summons
I - Infraction Ticket
V - Verbal Warning
W - Written Warning
N - No Disposition

Event Number:__________
(as defined by your department)

FIGURE 9-4 Connecticut Traffic Stops Statistics Form, State of Connecticut, Interim Report of Traffic Stops Statistics, January 2001, http://web.wtnh.com/Report_Narrative.pdf (Accessed November 25, 2008)

based solely on the race, gender, ethnicity, age, or socioeconomic level of an individual is both unethical and illegal," but that data-collection programs "must ensure that data is being collected and analyzed in an impartial and methodologically sound fashion" (Voegtlin, 2001:8).

CIVIL LIABILITY

General Types of Liability

Supervision and management is about behavior, for it is the direct responsibility of supervisors and managers to monitor and regulate officers' behavior and when necessary, to take disciplinary action to ensure that negligent or illegal behavior does not recur in the future. This section explores some of the legal consequences when police supervisors fail to control officers' behavior.

In the years following the Civil War and in reaction to the states' inability to control the Ku Klux Klan's lawlessness, Congress enacted the Ku Klux Klan Act of 1871. This was later codified as Title 42, U.S. Code Section 1983. Its statutory language is as follows:

> Every person who, under color of any statute, ordinance, regulation, custom, or usage of any State or Territory, subjects, or causes to be subjected, any citizen of the United States or any other person within the jurisdiction thereof to the deprivation of any rights, privileges, or immunities secured by the Constitution and laws, shall be liable to the party injured in an action at law, suit in equity, or other proper proceeding for redress.

This legislation is intended to provide civil rights protection to all persons protected under the act, when a defendant acts "under color of law" (misuses power of office). It is also meant to provide an avenue to the federal courts for relief of alleged civil rights violations.

Several factors have contributed to a surge in Section 1983 actions. First, some lawyers believe that a better caliber of judges and juries can be found in the federal forum. Federal judges, who are appointed for life, can be less concerned about the political ramifications of their decisions than the locally elected judges. Furthermore, federal rules of pleading and evidence are uniform, and federal procedures of discovery are more liberal. Just as important, Section 1988 of the Civil Rights Act in 1976 allowed attorney's fees to the "prevailing party" over and above the award for compensatory and punitive damages. This provision in the law did as much to spur the use of Section 1983 as any other factor.

Supervisors must be mindful that a certain level of liability is attached to the job when they fail to supervise correctly. They should also remember that plaintiffs generally attempt to include as many officers, supervisors, and administrators in the lawsuit as possible to enhance the probability that the award will be greater and the defendants will have the ability to pay it. This is commonly referred to as the "deep pockets" approach.

Supervisors may incur liability for what their subordinates do. Supervisors have direct and vicarious liability. *Direct liability* is incurred for the actions of supervisors themselves, while *vicarious* or *indirect liability* refers to when supervisors are held liable for the actions of their subordinates. For direct liability to exist the supervisor must actively participate in the act. Supervisors may incur direct liability in the following ways (del Carmen, 1989):

1. They authorize the act. They give officers permission to do something that ultimately results in liability.
2. They are present when an act for which liability results occurs. They stand by and watch an act occur and fail to take corrective action.
3. They ratify the act. Once the act is completed, they fail to admonish or take corrective action when it comes to their attention.

One of the most commonly litigated areas of liability is **negligence**. *Simple negligence* occurs when a supervisor fails to provide the degree of care and vigilance required for a situation, while *gross negligence* is a deliberate indifference to life or property. Generally, the courts require gross negligence to hold a supervisor liable.

As a result of case law, there are currently five areas in which supervisors have been found liable as a result of negligence: (1) negligent assignment, (2) negligent failure to supervise, (3) negligent failure to direct, (4) negligent entrustment, and (5) negligent failure to investigate or discipline (del Carmen, 1991:227). These areas of liability fall squarely with the supervisor and are discussed next.

Negligent assignment occurs when the supervisor assigns a task to a subordinate without first determining that the subordinate is properly trained or capable of performing the required work. Negligent assignment also occurs when a supervisor determines that an employee is not qualified for a position but fails to relieve the employee of the assignment.

An example of negligent assignment would be a supervisor who allows a subordinate to assume the duties of a police officer without receiving firearms training. If the officer then inappropriately shoots a citizen, the supervisor as well as the officer would be liable. A second example would be an officer who has had several complaints of sexual harassment and supervisors fail to reassign the officer to a position within the department that eliminates the opportunity for sexual harassment. Even if disciplinary action was taken, supervisors must eliminate any opportunity for the act to recur. Supervisors must pay particular attention to their subordinates' behavior and make assignments to ensure that problems do not occur.

Negligent failure to supervise occurs when the supervisor fails to properly oversee subordinates' activities. The court in *Lenard v. Argento* (1983) held that at a minimum a plaintiff must demonstrate that the supervisory official authorized (implicitly or explicitly), approved, or knowingly acquiesced in the illegal conduct. For example, if a supervisor knows that an officer on a number of occasions has used more force than was necessary to effect an arrest and fails to take corrective action, the supervisor can be held liable for failure to supervise in a subsequent action. Thus, anytime a supervisor becomes aware of a problem, action must be taken to rectify the problem. The courts have also examined individual cases. In *Grandstaff v. City of Borger* (1985), police officials were held liable for failing to take supervisory action after officers mistakenly opened fire and shot an innocent bystander who was attempting to help the officers. The court reasoned that the department's failure to reprimand, discipline, or fire officers constituted a failure to supervise. Supervisors' failure to act is an abdication of authority, and the courts consider this to be negligent supervision.

Negligent failure to direct occurs when supervisors fail to advise subordinates of the specific requirements and limits of the job. For example, if a police department fails to provide officers with the limits of when they can use deadly force and officers subsequently use deadly force inappropriately, the responsible supervisors can be held liable. Negligent failure to direct has specific application relative to departmental policies and procedures. If a department does not have a policy dealing with a sensitive area and officers subsequently act inappropriately, the department will be found negligent for failure to direct. Supervisors must be knowledgeable about departmental policies and be able to properly advise officers about their content.

Negligent entrustment occurs when supervisors entrust officers with equipment and facilities and fail to properly supervise the officers' care and use of the equipment, and subsequently the officers commit an act using the equipment that leads to a violation of a citizen's federally protected rights. The government in these cases must show that the officer in question was incompetent and the supervisor knew of the incompetence. A supervisor's defense in negligent entrustment is that the employee was competent to use the equipment and was properly supervised.

Supervisors must investigate complaints and work activities and take proper disciplinary actions when required. Clearly, police departments must have adequate disciplinary procedures and they must function to protect the rights of citizens. If a supervisor or department covers up or is inattentive to complaints of police misconduct, the department and supervisor are liable. Too often supervisors attempt to stall, discourage, or disregard complainants when they attempt to protest police officer actions. Such actions can ultimately lead to *negligent failure to investigate or discipline charges*.

Obviously, a department's and supervisor's defense in such cases is to establish a record of strong disciplinary procedures within the agency. This is accomplished through strong actions and documentation. Plaintiffs, on the other hand, will attempt to show that either no action or inadequate action took place.

Next we discuss several other areas of liability that are important for police supervisors and managers to know.

Other Areas of Potential Liability

PROXIMATE CAUSE is established by asking "but for the officer's conduct, would the plaintiff have sustained the injury or damage?" If the answer to this question is no, then **proximate cause** is established, and the officer can be held liable for the damage or injury. This requirement of negligence limits liabilities, however, in situations where damage would have occurred regardless of the officer's behavior (Kappeler, 2005). An example is where an officer is involved in a high-speed chase and the offending driver strikes an innocent third party. Generally, if the officer was not acting in a negligent fashion and did not cause the injury, there would be no liability on the officer's part (*Fielder v. Jenkins*, 1993).

Proximate cause may be found in such cases as an officer leaving the scene of an accident aware of dangerous conditions (e.g., spilled oil, smoke, vehicle debris, stray animals) without proper warning to motorists.

PERSONS IN CUSTODY AND SAFE FACILITIES Courts generally recognize that police officers have a **duty of care** to persons in their custody. This means that police officers have a legal responsibility to take reasonable precautions to ensure the health and safety of persons in their custody—keeping detainees free from harm, rendering medical assistance when necessary, and treating detainees humanely (*Thomas v. Williams*, 1962).

This general duty of care to persons in police custody seldom results in liability for self-inflicted injury or suicide because these acts are normally considered to result from the detainee's own intentional conduct, rather than from some form of police negligence (*Guice v. Enfinger*, 1980). For example, if a prisoner's suicide is "reasonably foreseeable," the jailer owes the prisoner a duty of care to help prevent that suicide. If the suicidal tendencies of an inmate are known, the standard of care required of the custodian is elevated.

Another area of police liability, one that involves both persons in custody and proximate cause, is the need to provide safe facilities. Courts have even considered the design of detention facilities as a source of negligence, such as in a Detroit case where the construction of a jail's holding cell did not allow officers to observe detainee's movements; the construction of the cell doors hampered detainee supervision, there were no electronic monitoring devices for observing detainees, and there was an absence of detoxification cells required under state department of corrections rules. Therefore, following a suicide in this facility, the court concluded that these conditions constituted building defects and were the proximate cause of the decedent's death (*Davis v. City of Detroit*, 1986).

FAILURE TO PROTECT This form of negligence may occur if a police officer fails to protect a person from a known and foreseeable danger. These claims most often involve battered women. There are, however, other circumstances that can create a duty to protect people from crime. Informants, witnesses, and other people dependent on the police can be a source of police liability if police fail to take reasonable action to prevent victimization. The officer's conduct cannot place a person in peril or demonstrate deliberate indifference for their safety.

For example, one morning a California man named Penilla was on the porch of his home and became seriously ill. His neighbors called 911, and two police officers arrived first. They found him to be in grave need of medical care, cancelled the request for paramedics, broke the lock and door jam on the front door of Penilla's residence, moved him inside the house, locked the door, and left. The next day, family members found Penilla dead inside the house as a result of respiratory failure. His mother sued under Section 1983, and the court found that the officers' conduct clearly placed Penilla in a more dangerous position than the one in which they found him (*Penilla v. City of Huntington Park*, 1997).

VEHICULAR PURSUITS In Chapter 13 we will discuss the operational aspects of vehicular pursuits, including supervisors' roles and liabilities. Here we briefly cover the amount of force that may be used in such occurrences.

In 2007 the U.S. Supreme Court issued a major decision concerning the proper amount of force the police may use during high-speed vehicle pursuits. The fundamental question was whether or not the level of force used was proportionate to the threat of reckless and dangerous driving. The incident involved a 19-year old Georgia youth driving at speeds up to 90 miles per hour and covering nine miles in six minutes with a deputy sheriff in pursuit. The chase ended in a violent crash that left the youth a quadriplegic; his lawyers argued that the Fourth Amendment protects against the use of such excessive force and high-speed drivers having their cars rammed by police (by intentionally stopping a fleeing vehicle in such a manner, a "seizure" occurs for Fourth Amendment purposes). Conversely, the deputy's lawyers argued that such drivers pose an escalating danger to the public and must be stopped to defuse the danger. The Court held, 8-1, that "A police officer's attempt to terminate a dangerous high-speed car chase that threatens the lives of innocent bystanders does not violate the Fourth Amendment, even when it places the fleeing motorist at risk of serious injury or death" (*Scott v. Harris*, 2007:13).

Still, the police must act reasonably in such instances or they may be found civilly liable. Police officers are afforded no special privileges or immunities in the routine operation of their patrol; in non-emergency situations they have no immunity for their negligence or recklessness and are held to the same standard of conduct as private citizens. When responding to emergency situations, however, most jurisdictions afford the police limited immunity—some protections and privileges not given to private citizens—and are permitted to take greater risks that would amount to negligence if undertaken by citizens' vehicles (*Seide v. State of Rhode Island*, 2005).

CASE STUDIES

The following three case studies demonstrate some of the ethical dilemmas in which supervisors and managers may find themselves.

Case Study #1

Company's Comin'

You and your partner, a senior deputy, are dispatched on a "found property" call. When you contact the reporting persons, they tell you they have found what appears to be stolen property in the field behind their fence. You find the following: a high-powered microscope, an HD television set, and a DVD player; obviously the burglar got scared away and left the items in the field. You inventory the property and give a receipt to the reporting party, who states they wish to claim the property if, after 30 days, the rightful owner is not found. When you return to the patrol car, your partner tells you he is expecting a "hoard" of people at his home this weekend for the Super Bowl, and that he could really use the television set to "take the load off" their living room. He adds that he is going to "borrow" it for a few days, take it home for the Super Bowl, and then return it on Monday to the property room.

Questions for Discussion

1. How would you handle this situation? Would you discuss this matter with anyone? If so, with whom?
2. Is there any way(s) in which this situation can be made worse? How?

Case Study #2

Redneck Causes Escalation to Black and Blue

Officer Burns is known to have extreme difficulty in relating to persons of color and others who are socially different from himself. Burns admits to his sergeant that he grew up in a prejudiced home environment and that he has little sympathy or understanding for people "who cause all the damn trouble." The officer never received any sensitivity or diversity training at the academy or within the department. The supervisor fails to understand the weight of the problem and has very little patience with Burns. So, believing it will correct the matter, the supervisor decides to assign Burns to a minority section of town so he will improve his ability to relate to diverse groups. Within a week, Burns responds to a disturbance at a housing project where residents are partying noisily and a fight is in progress. Burns immediately becomes upset, yelling at the residents to quiet down; they fail to respond, so Burns draws his baton and begins poking residents and ordering them to comply with his directions. The crowd immediately turns against Burns, who then has to call for backup assistance. After the other officers arrive, a fight ensues between residents and officers, and several officers and residents are injured and numerous arrests are made. The following day the neighborhood council meets with the mayor, demanding that Burns be fired and threatening a lawsuit.

Questions for Discussion

1. Is there any liability or negligence present in this situation? If so, what kind?
2. Could the supervisor have dealt with Burns's lack of sensitivity in a better manner? If so, how?

Case Study #3

Getting the Job Done

Gothamville is a Midwestern city with a high crime rate and poor relations between the police and the public. The new reform mayor and police chief campaigned on a platform of cleaning up crime in the streets and ineffectiveness of government. They launched a commission to investigate what was termed a "litany of problems" within the police department. The investigation found that officers routinely lied about the probable cause for their arrests and searches, falsified search warrant applications, and basically violated rules of collecting and preserving evidence. They were also known to protect each other under a "shroud of secrecy" and to commit perjury in front of grand juries and at trials. These problems were found to be systemic throughout the agency; however, greed and corruption were not the motivating factors behind officers' giving perjured testimony. Officers believed that their false testimony and other such activities were the only means by which they could put persons they believed guilty behind bars. Worse yet, the study also found that prosecutors routinely tolerated or at least tacitly approved of such conduct. The study also found that many police officers did not consider giving false testimony to be a form of corruption, which they believed implies personal profit. Instead, they viewed testifying as just another way to "get the job done."

Questions for Discussion

1. Do you believe that the officers' means of lying about the basis for their arrests and searches justified the end result of making arrests?
2. What about the prosecutors' tolerance of the officers' unethical behavior? To what ethical standards should the prosecutor's office be held?
3. As a supervisor, when these kinds of behaviors come to light, what punishment, if any, do you think is warranted for the persons involved?
4. What actions, if any, could a supervisor take to oversee officers' activities to prevent and detect such behaviors?

Summary

This chapter has examined police behavior from ethical and legal standpoints. We first defined the philosophical underpinnings and types of ethics; discussed the vital role of police supervisors and managers in monitoring officers' activities and addressing any breaches of ethical behavior; and identified the kinds of specific activities that can be problematic for officers, supervisors, managers, and organizations (e.g., lying, accepting gratuities, improper use of authority and force, workplace harassment, and biased policing). We also considered how supervisors might be found liable for the inappropriate acts and deeds of their subordinates.

Ethics form the foundation for police officer behavior. It is important that officers understand ethics and the role ethics plays in their profession. Officers and departments must come to grips with the ethical boundaries of police work to ensure that the boundaries are not violated. Police supervisors, furthermore, must shoulder the responsibility for failure to properly supervise their subordinates. Supervisors and managers—more so the former—are the primary control mechanisms in any police department, and they must ensure that officers perform to acceptable standards in all areas involving ethics. Supervisors, in closer contact with officers, must understand the mission, values, goals, and moral positions of policing in general, as well as within their own organizations, and then apply them to their subordinates. Failure to do so, history has shown, will result in civil (tort) action against supervisors—a difficult means by which society can hold its police supervisors accountable for failing to properly oversee their subordinates. It is a bitter pill to swallow, but it is the price to be paid; surely it is preferable for supervisors and managers to do all that is possible to ensure that ethical matters are first and foremost addressed in-house, rather than in the courthouse.

Items for Review

1. Define ethics, and provide examples of what is meant by relative as well as absolute ethics (including noble cause corruption).
2. Describe the vital role of police leaders, especially first-line supervisors, in preventing and addressing problems of patrol officer ethics.
3. Define and provide distinctions between acceptable and deviant lying by police.
4. Explain what constitutes improper use of force by the police.
5. Describe police use of force as set forth in the Dynamic Resistance Response Model (DRRM), to include its application to four broad categories of suspects.
6. Define gratuities and give common reasons for and against their receipt by officers.
7. Explain the roles of givers and receivers in Withrow and Dailey's model of circumstantial corruptibility, and whether or not a gratuity—large or small—can ever be accepted under this model.
8. Provide a thorough explanation of both workplace harassment and bias-based policing.
9. Define what is meant by "contagious shootings."
10. Explain the two types of liability that police supervisors may incur, as well as the five areas of liability.
11. Define duty of care and failure to protect, and how they apply to police supervisors and officers.
12. Explain the potential for police liability vehicle pursuits, including any protections police enjoy against liability in such pursuits; provide examples of actions in vehicle pursuits that may result in police being liable for damages.
13. Describe the nature and use of 42 U.S. Code Section 1983.

References

Aether Systems, Mobile Government Division. (2001). Special report II: Overcoming the perception of racial profiling. *Law and Order* (April):94–101.

Barker, T. (1994). An empirical study of police deviance other than corruption. In T. Barker and D. Carter, eds., *Police deviance*. Cincinnati: Anderson, pp. 123–138.

Barker, T., and Carter, D. (1994). Typology of police deviance. In T. Barker and D. Carter, eds., *Police deviance*. Cincinnati: Anderson, pp. 3–12.

Barker, T., and Carter, D. (1990). "Fluffing up the evidence and covering your ass": Some conceptual notes on police lying. *Deviant Behavior* 11:61–73.

Black, D., and Reiss, A. (1970). Police control of juveniles. *American Sociological Review* 35:63–77.

Brooks, L. W. (1986). Determinants of police orientations and their impact on police discretionary behavior. Unpublished Ph.D. dissertation. Institute of Criminal Justice & Criminology, University of Maryland.

Carlan, P. E., and Byxbe, F. R. (2000). Managing sexual harassment liability: A guide for police administrators. *The Police Chief* (October):124–129.

Carter, D. (1994). Theoretical dimensions in the abuse of authority. In T. Barker and D. Carter, eds., *Police deviance*. Cincinnati: Anderson, pp. 269–290.

Christopher Commission. (1991). *Report of the independent commission on the Los Angeles police department*. Los Angeles: City of Los Angeles.

County of Sacramento v. Lewis, 118 S.Ct. 1708 (1998).

Cox, S. M. (2001). Racial profiling: Refuting concerns about collecting race data on traffic stops. *Law and Order* (October):61–65.

Crank, J. P., and Caldero, M. A. (2000). *Police ethics: The corruption of noble cause.* Cincinnati: Anderson.

Davis v. City of Detroit, 386 N.W.2d 169 (Mich. App. 1986).

del Carmen, R. V. (1991). *Civil liabilities in American policing*. Englewood Cliffs, NJ: Brady.

del Carmen, R. V. (1989). Civil liabilities of police supervisors. *American Journal of Police* 8(1):107–136.

Fair, F. K., and Pilcher, W. D. (1991). Morality on the line: The role of ethics in police decision-making. *American Journal of Police* 10(2):23–38.

Federal Communications Commission. (2007). Understanding workplace harassment. http://www.fcc.gov/owd/understandin-harassment.html (Accessed October 18).

Fielder v. Jenkins, 833 A.2d 906 (N.J. Super. A.D. 1993).

Friedrich, R. J. (1977). The impact of organizational, individual, and situational factors on police behavior. Ph.D. dissertation. Department of Political Science, University of Michigan.

Fyfe, J. (1986). *Police personnel practices*. Washington, DC: International City Management Association.

Garrett, R. L. (2001). Changing behavior begins with data. *Law Enforcement Technology* (April): 100–108.

Grandstaff v. City of Borger, 767 F.2d 161 (5th Cir. 1985).

Guice v. Enfinger, 389 So.2d 270 (Fla. App. 1980).

Higginbotham, J. (1988). Sexual harassment in the police station. *FBI Law Enforcement Bulletin* 9:22–29.

Human Rights Watch. (1998). *Shielded from justice: Police brutality and accountability in the United States*. New York: Author.

Illinois v. Perkins, 110 S.Ct. 2394 (1990).

Joyner, C., and Basile, C. (2007). The dynamic resistance response model. *FBI Law Enforcement Bulletin* (September):15-20.

Kania, R. (1988). Police acceptance of gratuities. *Criminal Justice Ethics* 7(2):37–49.

Kappeler, V.E. (2005). *Critical issues in police civil liability* (4th ed.). Long Grove, IL: Waveland.

Kennedy, R. (1999). Suspect policy. *The New Republic* (September 13):30–35.

Kleinig, J. 1996. *The ethics of policing*. New York: Cambridge University Press.

Knapp Commission Report on Police Corruption. (1972). New York: George Braziller.

Kuykendall, J. 1986. The municipal police detective: An historical analysis. *Criminology* 24(1): 175–201.

Lenard v. Argento, 699 F.2d 874 (7th Cir. 1983).

Los Angeles Times. (2007). LAPD shooting blamed on poor supervision. latimes.com, http://www.latimes.com/news/local/los_angeles_metro/la-me-pena6dec06,0,5058221,print.story?coll=la-commun-los_angeles_metro (Accessed January 12).

Martinelli, T. J. (2006). Unconstitutional policing: The ethical challenges in dealing with noble cause corruption. *The Police Chief* (October):148–155.

Marx, G. T. (1982). Who really gets stung? Some issues raised by the new police undercover work. *Crime & Delinquency* (28):165–193.

Milton, P. (2007). Grand jury indicts 3 in NYPD shooting. http://abcnews.go.com/US/wireStory?id=2957956 (Accessed April 19).

Neubauer, R. (1999). Quoted in Keith W. Strandberg, Racial profiling. *Law Enforcement Technology* (June):62.

New York Times. (2001). When the police shoot, who's counting? (April 29:A1).

Oliver, J. A., and Zatcoff, A. R. (2001). Lessons learned: Collecting data on officer traffic stops. *The Police Chief* (July):23–29.

O'Malley, T. J. (1997). Managing for ethics: A mandate for administrators. *FBI Law Enforcement Bulletin* (April):20–25.

Paletz, D. L., and Harris, W. F. (1975). Four-letter threats to authority. *Journal of Politics* 37:955–979.

Penilla v. City of Huntington Park, 115 F.3d 707 (9th Cir., 1997).

Sapp, A. D. (1994). Sexual misconduct by police officers. In T. Barker and D. Carter, eds., *Police deviance*. Cincinnati: Anderson, pp. 187–200.

Scott v. Harris, 550 U.S. _____ (2007) (Docket No. 05-1631).

Seide v. State of Rhode Island, 875 A.2d 1259 (2005).

Selnow, G. W. (1985). Sex differences in uses and perceptions of profanity. *Sex Roles* 12:303–312.

Skolnick, J. L. (1982). Deception by police. *Criminal Justice Ethics* 1(2):27–32.

Smith, D. A., and Visher, C. (1981). Street-level justice: Situational determinants of police arrest decisions. *Social Problems* 29:167–178.

Thomas v. Williams, 124 S.E.2d 409 (Ga. App. 1962).

Tully, E. (1998). Misconduct, corruption, abuse of power: What can the chief do? *Beretta USA Leadership Bulletin*. www.berettabulletin.com (14 January 1998).

U.S. Department of Justice, National Institute of Justice, Office of Community Oriented Policing Services. (1997). *Police integrity: Public service with honor*. Washington, DC: U.S. Government Printing Office.

Vicchio, S. J. (1997). Ethics and police integrity. *FBI Law Enforcement Bulletin* (July):8–12.

Voegtlin, G. (2001). Biased-based policing and data collection. *The Police Chief* (October):8.

Warshay, D. W., and Warshay, L. H. (1978). Obscenity and male hegemony. Paper presented at the annual meeting of the International Sociological Association, Detroit, Michigan.

Washington Post. (2000). L.A. police corruption case continues to grow (February 13, p. 1A).

Wilson, M. (2007). 50 shots fired, and the experts offer a theory. http://www.nytimes.com/2006/11/27/nyregion/27fire.html?ei=5088&en=357cf73362b1de61&ex=1322283600&partner=rs&pagewanted=print (Accessed January 10).

Withrow, B. L., and Dailey, J. D. (2004). When strings are attached. In eds. Thurman, Q. C., and Zhao, J., *Contemporary policing: Controversies, challenges, and solutions*. Los Angeles: Roxbury, pp. 319–326.

CHAPTER 10

Officers' Rights and Discipline

Key Terms and Concepts

- Alcohol and drug testing
- Citizen's complaint
- Disposition
- Early warning system
- Freedom of speech
- Grievance
- Misuse of firearms
- Moonlighting
- Peace Officers' Bill of Rights
- Religious practices
- Restrictions on constitutional rights
- Searches and seizures
- Sexual misconduct

Learning Objectives

After reading this chapter, the student will:

- understand police officers' rights and limitations in areas such as freedom of speech, searches and seizures, religious practices, moonlighting, alcohol and drug use, and residency, according to legislative enactments and court decisions
- know the various forms of disciplinary action that can be taken by police leaders against officers
- understand how complaints against the police can be investigated in a fair manner
- understand how early warning systems may be employed by police leadership toward identifying and treating problem officers

The price of greatness is responsibility.
—Winston Churchill

No man is fit to command another that cannot command himself.
—William Penn

INTRODUCTION

Chapter 9 discussed ethics and inappropriate police behaviors, some of which may result in individual police supervisors or managers being found liable. This chapter essentially extends that discussion, by examining officer rights and discipline. These aspects of policing are especially delicate and important aspects of supervision and management; if they are ignored or handled improperly, they can foster serious internal and external problems, increased liability, and a loss of public respect and trust.

The police, more than most segments of government, are under the close scrutiny of the public. The media and some citizens stand ready to criticize the police when an incident goes awry. Therefore, it is important that police agencies develop sound disciplinary policies and ensure that supervisors and managers are properly trained to intervene in problems early. These leaders must also have a good working knowledge of departmental rules and regulations, as well as the resources available for dealing with disciplinary issues.

This chapter begins with an overview of the **Peace Officers' Bill of Rights** and several areas in which their constitutional rights are limited under the U.S. Constitution and federal court decisions because of the nature of their work and their position in society. We then look at the nature of complaints against officers, how they are investigated, and the kinds of outcomes and punishments that may result. Next we examine the **early warning system** concept for identifying problem officers, and following that is a discussion of some legal consequences of failure to properly supervise officers. The chapter concludes with two case studies.

Note that a related area of police discipline—grievances and appeals—is discussed in Chapter 11, which concerns unions and labor relations.

PEACE OFFICER'S BILL OF RIGHTS

Although they may be compelled to give up certain rights in connection with an investigation of on-duty misbehavior or illegal acts, police officers generally are afforded the same rights, privileges, and immunities outlined in the U.S. Constitution for all citizens. These rights are the basis for legislation such as the Peace Officers Bill of Rights (discussed next), labor agreements, court decisions and civil service and departmental rules and regulations that guide an agency's disciplinary process. One mechanism to protect police officers from undue or coercive police investigations is the Peace Officers' Bills of Rights.

Beginning in the 1990s, police officers have insisted on greater procedural safeguards to protect them against what they perceive as arbitrary infringement on their rights. These demands have been reflected in statutes enacted in many states, generally known as the "Peace Officers Bill of Rights." These statutes confer on an employee a property interest (i.e., their job is to be viewed as their property) in his or her position and mandate due process rights for peace officers who are the subject of internal investigations that could lead to disciplinary action. These statutes identify the type of information that must be provided to the accused officer, the officer's responsibility to cooperate during the investigation, the officer's rights to representation during the process, and the rules and procedures concerning the collection of certain types of evidence, especially the interrogation of the officer.

For example, the California Peace Officer Bill of Rights states:

> When any public safety officer is under investigation and subjected to interrogation by his or her commanding officer, or any other member of the employing public safety department, that could lead to punitive action, the interrogation shall be conducted under the following conditions. For the purpose of this chapter, punitive action means any action that may lead to dismissal, demotion, suspension, reduction in salary, written reprimand, or transfer for purposes of punishment.

a. The interrogation shall be conducted at a reasonable hour, preferably at a time when the public safety officer is on duty, or during the normal waking hours for the public safety officer, unless the seriousness of the investigation requires otherwise. If the interrogation does occur during off-duty time of the public safety officer being interrogated, the public safety officer shall be compensated for any off-duty time in accordance with regular department procedures, and the public safety officer shall not be released from employment for any work missed.
b. The public safety officer under investigation shall be informed prior to the interrogation of the rank, name, and command of the officer in charge of the interrogation, the interrogating officers, and all other persons to be present during the interrogation. All questions directed to the public safety officer under interrogation shall be asked by and through no more than two interrogators at one time.
c. The public safety officer under investigation shall be informed of the nature of the investigation prior to any interrogation.
d. The interrogating session shall be for a reasonable period taking into consideration gravity and complexity of the issue being investigated. The person under interrogation shall be allowed to attend to his or her own personal physical necessities. (California Government Code Section 3303)

As noted in the statute, police officers who are under investigation are afforded certain rights. Peace Officer Bill of Rights statutes ensure that police officers are not subjected to coercive interrogations or questioning. Additionally, most Peace Officer Bill of Rights contain language that requires the department to provide a written notice of charges; they provide that officers have a right to representation, either an attorney or a union representative; they prohibit the use of a polygraph; and they often establish procedures specifying how the information obtained in an interrogation can be used.

It is imperative that supervisors and managers become thoroughly familiar with statutes, contract provisions, and existing rules between employer or employee, so that procedural due process requirements can be met, particularly in disciplinary cases when an employee's property interest might be affected. If procedural guidelines are not followed, it may result in the police department not being able to take action against an officer who has committed a crime or disciplinary infraction.

POLICE OFFICERS' CONSTITUTIONAL RIGHTS

Over the years, the courts and legislatures have bestowed or recognized a number of rights that police officers possess. Many of these rights are constitutionally guaranteed, but others have been adopted by legislative bodies or through union negotiations. The following provides an overview of some of these rights.

Free Speech

Although the right of **freedom of speech** is one of the most fundamental of all rights of Americans, the Supreme Court indicated in *Pickering v. Board of Education* (1968:568) that "the State has interests as an employer in regulating the speech of its employees that differ significantly from those it possesses in connection with regulation of the speech of the citizenry in general." Thus, the state may impose restrictions on its employees that it would not be able to impose on the citizenry at large. These restrictions must be reasonable, however.

A police regulation may be found to be an unreasonable infringement on the free speech interests of officers if overly broad. A Chicago Police Department rule prohibiting "any activity, conversation, deliberation, or discussion which is derogatory to the Department" is a good example of one that is unreasonable as such a rule obviously prohibits all criticism of the agency by its officers, even in private conversation (*Muller v. Conlisk,* 1970:901). Essentially, a department cannot arbitrarily regulate officers' speech. However, if officers make statements that adversely affect the department's operation, such as leaking information about an ongoing investigation, or make false statements, the courts generally will prohibit the speech.

A related area is political activity. As with free speech, governmental agencies may restrict the political behavior of their employees to prevent employees from being pressured by their superiors to support certain political candidates or engage in political activities, under threat of loss of employment or other adverse action. The federal government and many states have such statutes.

A police officer may also be protected because of his or her political affiliations. An example is a case involving the Sheriff's Department in Cook County, Illinois, where a newly elected sheriff, a Democrat, fired the chief deputy of the process division and a bailiff of the juvenile court because they were Republicans. The Supreme Court ruled that it was a violation of the employees' First Amendment rights to discharge them from non-policymaking positions solely on the basis of their political party affiliation (*Connick v. Myers,* 1983; *Jones v. Dodson,* 1984).

At the same time, police departments cannot restrict police officers' off-duty political activities. That is, they have the right to run for certain political offices as long as those offices do not create a conflict of interest or interfere with the officer's performance of duties, e.g., school board. Moreover, police departments cannot restrict an officer's off-duty political activities. That is, officers are allowed to support and campaign for political candidates.

The First Amendment's reach also includes appearance. For example, the Supreme Court upheld the constitutionality of a regulation of the Suffolk County, New York, Police Department that established several grooming standards regarding hair, sideburn, and moustache length for its male officers to make officers readily recognizable to the public and to maintain the esprit de corps within the department (*Kelley v. Johnston,* 1976).

Searches and Seizures

The Fourth Amendment to the U.S. Constitution protects the right of the people to be secure in their persons, houses, papers, and effects against unreasonable **searches and seizures**. In an important case in 1967, the Supreme Court held that the amendment also protected individuals' reasonable expectations of privacy, not just property interests (*Katz v. United States,* 1967).

The Fourth Amendment usually applies to police officers when they are at home or off duty in the same manner that it applies to all citizens. Because of the nature of their work, however, police officers can be compelled to cooperate with investigations of their behavior when ordinary citizens would not. Examples include searches of equipment and lockers provided by the department to the officers. The officers have no expectation of privacy that affords or merits protection (*People v. Tidwell,* 1971). Lower courts, however, have established limitations on searches of employees themselves. The rights of prison authorities to search their employees arose in a 1985 Iowa case, in which employees were forced to sign a consent form allowing such searches as a condition of hire; the court disagreed with such a broad policy, ruling that the consent form was too broad and intruded on the employee's normal reasonable expectation of privacy (*McDonell v. Hunter*, 1985).

Police officers may also be forced to appear in a lineup, a clear "seizure" of their person. Lineups normally require probable cause, but a federal appeals court upheld a police commissioner's ordering 62 officers to appear in a lineup during an investigation of police brutality, holding that "the governmental interest in the particular intrusion [should be weighed] against the offense to personal dignity and integrity." Again, the court cited the nature of the work, noting that police officers do "not have the full privacy and liberty from police officials that [they] would otherwise enjoy" (*Biehunik v. Felicetta,* 1971:230).

Self-Incrimination

The Supreme Court has also addressed questions concerning the Fifth Amendment as it applies to police officers who are under investigation. In *Garrity v. New Jersey* (1967), a police officer was ordered by the attorney general to answer questions or be discharged. The officer testified that information obtained as a result of his answers was later used to convict him of criminal charges. The U.S. Supreme Court held that the information obtained from the officer could not be used against him at his criminal trial, because the Fifth Amendment forbids the use of coerced confessions. Today, the *Garrity* rule essentially states that if an officer is compelled to provide self-incriminating information or statements, such statements cannot be used in a criminal proceeding. However, they may be used to discipline or discharge the officer as long as such interrogations are not prohibited by the state's Peace Officer Bill of Rights, other statutes, or union contract. *Garrity* requires that when police wrongdoing occurs, the department must make a decision as to pursue the matter criminally or civilly before interrogating the officer.

It is proper to fire a police officer who refuses to answer questions that are related directly to the performance of his or her duties, provided that the officer has been informed that any answers may not be used later in a criminal proceeding. Although there is some diversity of opinion among lower courts on the question of whether or not an officer may be compelled to submit to a polygraph examination, the majority of courts that have considered the question have held that an officer can be required to take the examination (*Gabrilowitz v. Newman,* 1978). However, there are a number of states that prohibit requiring officers to take a polygraph. For example, the California Peace Officer Bill of Rights states:

> No public safety officer shall be compelled to submit to a polygraph examination against his will. No disciplinary action or other recrimination shall be taken against a public safety officer refusing to submit to a polygraph examination, nor shall any comment be entered anywhere in the investigator's notes or anywhere else that the public safety officer refused to take a polygraph examination, nor shall any testimony or evidence be admissible at a subsequent hearing, trial, or proceeding, judicial or administrative, to the effect that the public safety officer refused to take a polygraph examination (California Government Code, Section 3307).

Religious Practices

Criminal justice work often requires that personnel are available and on duty 24 hours per day, 7 days a week. Although it is not always convenient or pleasant, such shift configurations require that many criminal justice employees work weekends, nights, and holidays. It is generally assumed that one who takes such a position agrees to work such hours and abide by other conditions of the job (i.e., carrying a weapon, as in a policing position). There are occasions, however, when one's religious beliefs are in direct conflict with the requirements of the job, such as conflicts between one's work assignment and attendance at religious services or periods of religious observance. In these situations, the employee may be forced to choose between the job and his or her religious beliefs. However, departments generally must make "reasonable accommodations," which may include allowing the officer to trade shifts or take vacation time. A department does not have to make accommodations that interfere with the operation of the department.

Title VII of the Civil Rights Act of 1964 prohibits religious discrimination in employment. Thus, Title VII requires reasonable accommodation of religious beliefs, but not to the extent that the employee has complete freedom of religious expression (*United States v. City of Albuquerque,* 1976; see also *Trans World Airlines v. Hardison,* 1977).

Sexual Misconduct

Although we discussed **sexual misconduct** in Chapter 9, it deserves further mention here. To be blunt, criminal justice employees have ample opportunity to become engaged in affairs, incidents, trysts, dalliances, or other behavior that is clearly sexual in nature. In addition, a number of police "groupies" do in fact chase police officers and others in uniform.

Instances of sexual impropriety in police work can range from casual flirting while on the job to becoming romantically involved with a foreign agent whose principal aim is to learn delicate matters of national security. And there have been all manner of incidents between those extremes, including the discipline of female police officers who posed nude in magazines. Sapp (1994) noted that police sexual misconduct generally falls within one of seven categories:

1. Nonsexual contacts that are sexually motivated
2. Voyeuristic contacts
3. Contacts with crime victims
4. Contacts with offenders
5. Contacts with underage females
6. Sexual shakedowns
7. Citizen-initiated contacts (p. 188).

There is little information describing how prevalent police sexual misconduct is. However, McGurrin and Kappeler (2002) examined 66 newspapers from across the United States and uncovered more than 700 cases of police sexual misconduct. In many instances, the police behavior was serious, involving rape and sexual assault, warranting felony charges against officers. These statistics indicate that the problem is pervasive and serious. It behooves supervisors and commanders to continually monitor activities and proactively investigate any charges or suspicious behavior on the part of officers.

Residency Requirements

Many governmental agencies specify that all or certain members in their employ must live within the geographical limits of their employing jurisdiction. In other words, employees must reside within the county or city of employment. Such residency requirements have been justified by employing agencies, particularly in criminal justice, on the grounds that employees should become familiar with and be visible in the jurisdiction of employment. Additionally, they should reside and pay taxes in their employing jurisdiction. Perhaps the strongest rationale given by employing agencies is that criminal justice employees must live within certain proximity of their work in order to respond quickly in the event of an emergency. The U.S. Supreme Court has ruled that such requirements are reasonable and do not violate constitutional safeguards (*McCarthy v. Philadelphia Civil Service Commission*, 1976).

Moonlighting

The courts have traditionally supported police agencies placing limitations on the amount and kinds of outside work their employees can perform (*Brenckle v. Township of Shaler,* 1972; *Cox v. McNamara,* 1972; *Flood v. Kennedy,* 1963; *Hopwood v. City of Paducah,* 1968). Police restrictions on **moonlighting** range from a complete ban on outside employment to permission to engage in certain forms of work-work that would not result in a conflict of interest for officers. When moonlighting is allowed and regulated, the regulations generally prohibit officers from working where they may be required to use their police powers. When officers use their police powers in other jobs, it substantially increases the likelihood of civil liability for the department.

Misuse of Firearms

Police agencies generally have policies regulating the use of handguns and other firearms by their officers, both on and off duty. The courts have held that such regulations need only be reasonable and that the burden rests with the disciplined police officer to show that the regulation was arbitrary and unreasonable (*Lally v. Department of Police,* 1974). Police firearms regulations tend to address three basic issues: (1) requirements for the safeguarding of the weapon, (2) guidelines for carrying the weapon while off duty, and (3) limitations on when the weapon may be fired.

Courts and juries are dealing more harshly with police officers who misuse their firearms. The current tendency is to "look behind" police shootings in order to determine if the officer acted negligently or the employing agency negligently trained and supervised the officer or employee. Courts have awarded damages against police officers and/or their employers for other acts involving **misuse of firearms**, such as when an officer shot a person while intoxicated and off duty in a bar (*Marusa v. District of Columbia,* 1973); an officer accidentally killed an arrestee with a shotgun while handcuffing him (*Sager v. City of Woodlawn Park,* 1982); an unstable officer shot his wife five times and then committed suicide with an off-duty weapon the department required him to carry (*Bonsignore v. City of New York,* 1981); and an officer accidentally shot and killed an innocent bystander while pursuing another man at nighttime (the officer had received no instruction on shooting at a moving target, night shooting, or shooting in residential areas) (*Popow v. City of Margate,* 1979). These cases illustrate the importance of training and ensuring that officers receive all required training. It also demonstrates that training curricula must be comprehensive and up-to-date.

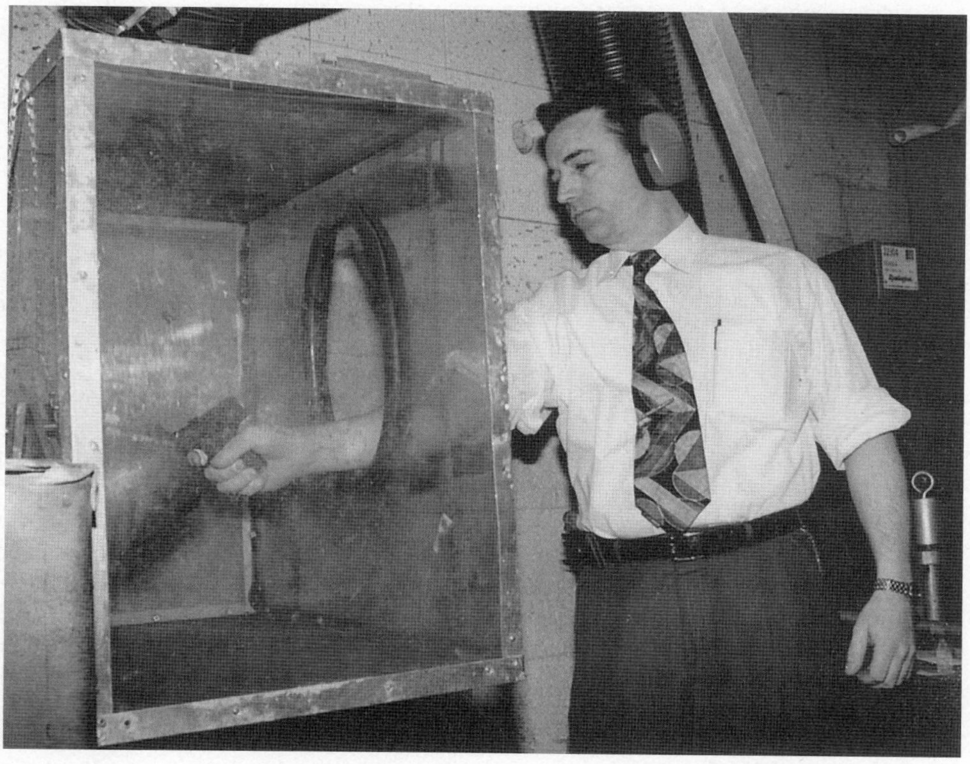

An officer's personal weapon will be tested thoroughly following any incident where it was discharged.
(*Courtesy NYPD Photo Unit*)

Alcohol and Drug Testing in the Workplace

It is obvious, given the extant law of most jurisdictions and the nature of their work, that criminal justice employees must not be "walking time bombs," but must be able to perform their work with a "clear head," unbefuddled by alcohol or drugs (*Hester v. Milledgeville,* 1984; *Krolick v. Lowery,* 1969). Police departments often specify in their manual of policy and procedures that no alcoholic beverages will be consumed within a specified period prior to reporting for duty. Such regulations have been upheld uniformly as rational because of the hazards of the work. Enforcing such regulations will occasionally result in criminal justice employees being ordered to submit to drug or alcohol tests.

In March 1989, the U.S. Supreme Court issued a major decision on drug testing of public employees in the workplace in *National Treasury Employees Union v. Von Raab,* which upheld drug testing when there was no indication of a drug problem in the workplace and held that although only a few employees test positive, drug use is such a serious problem that the program could continue. It stated that the Customs Service had a compelling interest in having a "physically fit" employee with "unimpeachable integrity and judgment" (*National Treasury Employees Union v. Von Raab,* 1989:38). Today, police departments have policies that require police officers—perhaps even the entire agency—to submit to random drug testing. There are basically two types of policies. First, some departments require drug testing when officers transfer in or out of special units such as narcotics or SWAT. The second policy is that all officers or officers assigned to certain units are subject to random drug testing. Drug and alcohol testing may also be required as a part of a disciplinary investigation.

This section has provided information on employee rights and protection. The following section examines police internal investigative processes and how police misconduct is regulated. Police disciplinary action is a complicated process that requires that departments protect accused officers' rights. However, the police must have discipline in order to provide the public with the best possible services and to avoid civil liability and public criticism.

THE NEED FOR POLICIES AND GUIDELINES

Throughout its history, policing has experienced allegations of misconduct and corruption. In the late 1800s, New York police sergeant Alexander "Clubber" Williams epitomized police brutality, as he spoke openly of using his nightstick to knock a man unconscious, batter him to pieces, or even kill him. Williams supposedly coined the term *tenderloin* when he commented, "I've had nothing but chuck steaks for a long time, and now I'm going to have me a little tenderloin" (Morris, 1951:112). Williams was referring to opportunities for graft in an area of downtown New York that was the heart of vice and nightlife, often referred to as Satan's Circus. This was Williams's beat, where his reputation for brutality and corruption became legendary (Inciardi, 1996).

Although police corruption and brutality are no longer openly tolerated, a number of events throughout history have demonstrated that the problem still exists and requires the attention of police officials. Incidents such as the beating of Rodney King by officers in the presence of supervisors, the controversy surrounding the testimony of former Los Angeles police detective Mark Fuhrrman during the O. J. Simpson trial, as well as major corruption scandals in the New York, Philadelphia, and New Orleans police departments, have led many people to believe that police misbehavior today is worse than during the riotous 1960s (MacNamara, 1995). This perception about corruption is supported by the Mollen Commission's 1994 report on the New York City Police Department, which suggested that a worsening pattern of corruption existed then and at higher levels in the organization than was the case 20 years earlier (Gaffigan and McDonald, 1997). It is apparent why the issue of police misconduct is at the forefront of the policing agenda.

TABLE 10-1 Written Policy Directives Pertaining to Officer Conduct and Appearance in Local Police Departments, by Size of Population Served, 2003

	Percent of agencies with a written policy on—	
Population served	**Conduct and appearance**	**Off-duty conduct**
All sizes	94%	86%
1,000,000 or more	100%	100%
500,000–999,999	100	94
250,000–499,999	100	100
100,000–249,999	100	99
50,000–99,999	100	97
25,000–49,999	100	96
10,000–24,999	99	93
2,500–9,999	97	91
Under 2,500	89	76

Source: Hickman, M., and Reaves, B. (2006). *Local Police Departments*, 2003, Washington, D.C.: Bureau of Justice Statistics.

TABLE 10-2 Conduct Regulated by Police Departments

Failure to conform with laws	Engaging in conduct unbecoming an officer
Seeking gifts, gratuities, or bribes	Engaging in vice activities
Citizen complaints	Failure to be courteous
Failure or late to report for duty	Dereliction of duty
Incompetence	Operation of departmental vehicles in an unsafe manner
Improper use of police equipment	Dissemination of confidential information
Dishonesty	Failure to complete reports
Improper treatment of prisoners	Improper use of force
Use of alcohol or drugs on duty	Loitering in bars in uniform
Failure to obey lawful orders	Appearance
Abuse of position or police power	Failure to report being arrested in another jurisdiction
Cowardice	Insubordination

Officer misconduct and violations of departmental policy are the two principal areas that involve discipline (McLaughlin and Bing, 1987). Officer misconduct includes acts that harm the public, such as corruption, harassment, brutality, and civil rights violations. Violations of policy may involve a broad range of issues, including substance abuse and insubordination or minor violations of dress and punctuality.

Police departments must have policies and procedures to guide police officer behavior. Police officers must be informed of behavioral expectations, and this is accomplished through policies. As noted in Table 10-1, the majority of departments have policies regulating officer conduct and appearance.

Police departments enact policies that address a range of police officer behavior. Table 10-2 provides a listing of areas of police conduct that normally are addressed in policies.

WHEN TROUBLE HAPPENS: THE NATURE AND INVESTIGATION OF COMPLAINTS

Forms of Complaint Investigations

There are a variety of mechanisms used by departments to investigate and process police complaints. Generally speaking, there are differences across departments, depending on the extent to which responsibility and authority for processing the complaints is vested with some form of citizen board or the police department. To this end, Liederbach, Boyd, Taylor, and Kawucha (2007) have identified four forms of complaint investigations based on the mix of police and civilian participation in the process. First is the internal police review, where total responsibility of the investigation and disposition of complaints is vested with the department. Second, in the auditor format, a civilian body reviews complaint investigations to ensure fairness and comprehensiveness. Third is the citizen inclusive board (sometimes referred to as a civilian review board), where a civilian body has exclusive jurisdiction on the investigation and disposition of complaints. Finally, the monitor form is where a citizen body oversees the police investigation and has authority to intervene by recommending additional investigative efforts or reviewing the merits of the findings of the police board.

Civilian review of the police is a highly charged topic: the police are adamantly opposed to it and civil liberties groups and citizens are in favor of it. Police officers are suspect of civilians who have no police training or experience examining their split-second decisions. On the other hand, many citizen groups feel that the police do an inadequate job of policing themselves, with departments often failing to take citizen complaints or failing to properly investigate them (see Walker, 2001). The police unions in New York and Philadelphia were responsible for abolishing citizen review boards in those cities. Nonetheless, Walker notes that 80 percent of the large departments in the United States have some form of citizen review. Citizen review of the police often becomes a political issue with police unions supporting candidates who are opposed to citizen oversight.

The following section traces the complaint processing and investigative process. Regardless of the agency involved, the process is very similar across departments.

Complaint Origin

A *personnel complaint* is an allegation of misconduct or illegal behavior against an employee by anyone inside or outside the organization. *Internal complaints* arise within the organization and may involve supervisors who observe officer misconduct, officers who complain about supervisors, supervisors who complain about other supervisors or middle managers, civilian personnel who complain about officers, and so on. For example, in a study of a Midwestern police department, Liederbach and his colleagues (2007) found that 12.2 percent of the total complaints were initiated internally. *External complaints* originate from sources outside the organization and usually involve the public and constitute the largest volume of complaints. The most common external complaints are citizens' complaints where individual citizens complain or charge police misconduct.

Supervisors may receive complaints from primary, secondary, and anonymous sources. A *primary* source is the victim or a witness. A *secondary* source is a party other than the victim, such as an attorney, school counselor, or parent of a juvenile. Generally, a secondary source is an individual who learns of the misconduct from a primary source. An anonymous source is unknown, and the complaint may be delivered to the police station via a telephone call or unsigned letter.

Every complaint, regardless of the source, must be accepted and investigated in accordance with established policies and procedures. Some complaints, however, may be disposed of without the formality of an investigation. In some cases, the accused employee's actions clearly may be within departmental policy, and a simple communication to that effect to the citizen by a supervisor would resolve the matter. Such may be the case of a citizen who is offended that officers would handcuff an elderly shoplifting suspect. Other complaints may be so trivial that further inquiry or investigation is not necessary. For example, a citizen's call to the watch commander with a general complaint that too many police officers are employed by the city is not an issue that would be handled within a disciplinary process.

Anonymous complaints are the most difficult to investigate because there is no opportunity to obtain further information or question the complainant about the allegation. Anonymous complaints are additionally troublesome for the supervisor because they negatively affect the employee's morale. Officers may view these types of complaints as unjust and frivolous and question why the department gives them any attention whatsoever. Supervisors and managers must help officers understand that complaints, regardless of their source, cannot be ignored or disregarded, and that disciplinary processes are designed to protect both the officer and organization, as well as preserve the public's trust.

Police leaders should also be aware that the most bizarre of accusations may prove true. In one western city, an anonymous complaint was received alleging that a marked city police vehicle was observed in another city 120 miles away and across state lines during the early morning hours. It was discovered that officers working in the rural outskirts of the city were making bets on how far they could travel and return during the course of a shift. Photos of officers in uniform standing next to their vehicle and the city limits sign of the city in question were discovered and used as evidence against the officers during their disciplinary hearing.

Types and Receipt

Supervisors and managers may handle complaints informally or formally. The seriousness of the allegation and preference of the complainant usually dictate whether a complaint will be investigated in a formal or informal manner. A formal complaint involves a written, signed, and/or tape-recorded statement of the allegation, and the complainant requests to be informed of the investigation's disposition.

An informal complaint is an allegation of minor misconduct made for informational purposes that can usually be resolved without the need for more formal processes. If a citizen calls the watch commander to complain about the rude behavior of a dispatcher but does not wish to make a formal complaint, the supervisor may simply discuss the incident with the dispatcher and resolve it through informal counseling as long as more serious problems are not discovered and the dispatcher does not have a history of similar complaints. However, some departments require that all complaints, no matter how minor or trivial, be handled via a formal complaint investigation process (see Figure 10-1, an example of a complaint form used to initiate a personnel investigation).

These examples are typical of the majority of complaints handled by supervisors. Few complaints involve serious acts of physical violence, excessive force, or corruption. Wagner and Decker (1997) found that the majority of complaints against officers fall under the general categories of verbal abuse, discourtesy, harassment, improper attitude, and ethnic slurs. These comprise the issues that supervisors contend with on a daily basis.

The process for receiving a complaint should be clearly delineated by departmental policy and procedures. Generally, a complaint will be made at a police facility and referred to a senior officer in charge to determine its seriousness and need for immediate intervention. Complaints will usually be accepted from any person who feels injured or aggrieved. Complaints may be made through a variety of means, including in person, by mail, or over the telephone. Some departments allow citizens to file complaints electronically by completing forms on the department's Internet Web page. Worrall (2002) found that as a department improves or makes reporting easier, there will be an increase in the number of complaints filed.

The manner in which an agency receives citizens' complaints can say much about the agency's philosophy and rigor in this regard. Diop Kanau, executive director of the Police Complaint Center, a nonprofit organization that assists victims of police misconduct, believes that the police often intend to investigate the complainant instead of the officer. In one-third of the agencies he studied, complainants had to take a polygraph test if they wanted to file a complaint, and in another agency of fewer than 30 officers, the police insist on getting the date of birth from any caller reporting a crime. "This is preposterous,"

****

Control Number___________

Date & Time Reported ________________

Location of Interview ________________

Interview ________Verbal ________Written ________Taped

Type of Complaint: _____Force _____Procedural _____Conduct
_____Other (Specify)

Source of Complaint: _____In Person _____Mail _____Telephone
_____Other (Specify)

Complaint originally Received by: _____Supervisor _____On Duty Watch Commander _____Chief
_____IAU _____Other (Specify)

Notifications made: Received by: _______Division Commander _______Chief of Police
_______On-Call Command Personnel
_______Watch Commander _______Other (Specify)

Copy of formal personnel complaint given to complainant? _____Yes _____No

****

Complainant's name: ____________________

Address: ____________________ Zip__________

Residence Phone: ____________________

Business Phone: ____________________

DOB: __________ Race: __________ Sex: __________ Occupation: __________

****

Location of Occurrence: ____________________

Date & Time of Occurrence: ____________________

Member(s) Involved:
(1) ____________________
(3) ____________________

Member(s) Involved:
(2)____________________
(4)____________________

Witness(es) Involved:
(1) ____________________
(3) ____________________

Witness(es) Involved:
(2)____________________
(4)____________________

****

(1) _____ Complainant wishes to make a formal statement and has requested an investigation into the matter with a report back to him/her on the findings and actions.

(2) _____ Complainant wishes to advise the Police Department of a problem, understand that some type of action will be taken, but does not request a report back to him/her on the findings and actions.

****

CITIZEN ADVISEMENTS

(1) If you have not yet provided the department with a signed written statement or a tape-recorded statement, one may be required in order to pursue the investigation of this matter.

(2) The complainant(s) and/or witness(es) may be required to take a polygraph examination in order to determine the credibility concerning the allegations made.

(3) Should the allegations prove to be false, the complainant(s) and/or witness(es) may be liable for criminal and/or civil prosecution.

____________________ ________________
Signature of Complainant Date & Time

____
Signature of Member Receiving Complaint

FIGURE 10-1 Police Department Formal Personnel Complaint Report

Kanau opined. "They're running a warrant check on the caller; they're assuming you must've had a run in with a cop, and they can use any information they get to undermine your credibility" (quoted in Pedersen, 2001:140).

Investigating Complaints

The investigation of complaints is a bifurcated process. Generally, all investigations and the management of complaint investigations is controlled and coordinated by an internal affairs unit (IAU). If the complaint or charge is significant, investigators from internal affairs will handle the complaint totally. If it is an informal complaint, it will be handled by a supervisor. In some cases, internal affairs will forward minor formal complaints to the unit commander for investigation. The commander will then assign the case to a supervisor who conducts the investigation. Once the investigation is completed, it is reviewed by the unit commander and internal affairs. Finally, in some cases, unit supervisors will be assigned to assist internal affairs in the investigation.

After being assigned an investigation, supervisors review all the available evidence: documents, statements, reports, and photographs. They likely will review dispatch tapes and videotapes if they exist. This initial review examines all departmental, victim, and witness information. This review provides details about the charges, circumstances around the incident, and points of contention between the officers and victims and witnesses.

Next, all the parties involved are interviewed. There is a specific order in which the interviews should be conducted: witnesses first, so that supervisors can develop questions for the complainant and the subject officer, who will be interviewed later. Witness interviews should be tape-recorded. Prior to every interview, supervisors should prepare a list of questions and then, prior to asking the questions, explain the purpose of the interview and give the witnesses an opportunity to provide a narrative statement. Then, the supervisors can follow up with specific questions and be confrontational (when the evidence or other witnesses have provided facts to the contrary) or challenging (if the witnesses' responses to confrontational questions are not believable) (Arnold, 1998). The goal is not to exonerate or convict the officer, but to collect factual information so that a decision can be made after all the evidence has been collected and analyzed.

After interviewing witnesses, supervisors should have a solid understanding of the case and prepare a list of questions to ask the complainant. This interview should also be tape-recorded, and the complainant should be allowed to enter a statement, give his or her side of the story, and provide independent recollection of dates, times, and descriptions. Following this, supervisors should ask specific questions regarding the incident and if the complainant has information unavailable when the complaint was filed, such as the names of witnesses.

With regard to subject officer interviews, supervisors must review their applicable state statutes or confer with their legal advisors regarding peace officers' rights while under investigation. It must then be determined if the officer wants to have an attorney or representative present. As with other interviews, supervisors should prepare a list of specific questions beforehand and tape-record the interview. The officer should be informed of the nature of the investigation and then be allowed to provide a narrative statement about the incident. After taking the statement, supervisors should ask the officer specific questions, such as "What did you do?" "What did you say?" "Did you say ______________ to the complainant?" Posing questions in this manner (instead of, say, "Do you recall . . . ?" or "Have you ever . . . ?") is a more effective way to obtain concrete details. If the officer's statements contradict the evidence, supervisors must ask confrontational questions in a professional manner; while this may be unpleasant, supervisors have a professional duty to determine the facts (Arnold, 1998).

An investigative report must then be written that contains all the relevant facts of the case. The format of this report should follow agency protocol. Generally, the investigator will summarize the charges and organize the evidence showing those pieces of evidence that support the charge and the evidence that is contradictive of the charges. Investigators may or may not provide an opinion as to the disposition of the charges. In most cases, such decisions are made at a higher level within the police organization. Investigative reports are reviewed by managers and executives and may resurface in a later grievance hearing or a possible civil suit. Therefore, the reports must be detailed, accurate, thorough, and unbiased.

There are questions about the thoroughness and accuracy of police investigations. For example, recently the Los Angeles Police Commission, a civilian oversight body, reviewed a sample of 60 complaints filed against police officers in that city. The commission found flaws in 29 of the investigations. They found that investigators inaccurately recorded statements, failed to interview witnesses, and in some cases did not identify the accused officers (Rubin, 2008). In another case, the New York State Police and the New York Office of the Attorney General conducted an investigation of officer wrongdoing and found 19 inadequately investigated cases. Some of the infractions could have resulted in criminal charges against troopers; drunken driving, assault, drug use, and bribery (Soper, 2006). Obviously, police agencies must promulgate and follow policies that ensure that all complaints are comprehensively investigated.

Determination and Disposition

Once an investigation is completed, a determination as to the culpability of the accused employee is made. Each allegation should receive a separate adjudication. Following are the categories of dispositions that are commonly used:

Unfounded. The alleged act(s) did not occur.
Exonerated. The act occurred, but it is lawful, proper, justified, and/or in accordance with departmental policies, procedures, and rules and regulations.

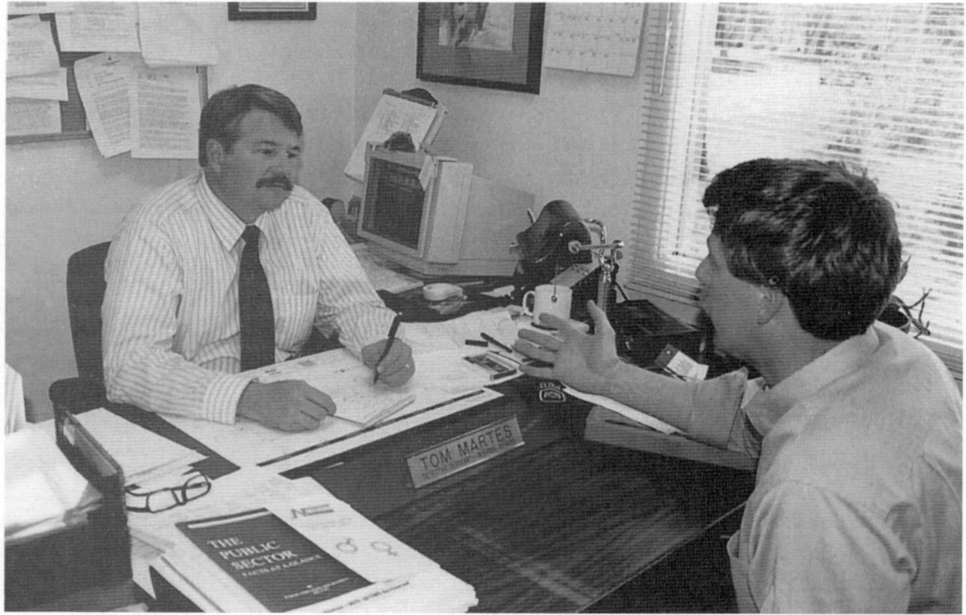

The internal affairs office is the locus of investigations for allegations of police misconduct. Here an internal affairs supervisor interviews an officer.

Not sustained. There is insufficient evidence to prove or disprove the allegations made.
Misconduct not based on the complaint. Sustainable misconduct was determined but is not part of the original complaint. For example, a supervisor investigating an allegation of excessive force against an officer may find the force used was within departmental policy, but that the officer made an unlawful arrest.
Closed. An investigation may be halted if the complainant fails to cooperate or it is determined that the action does not fall within the administrative jurisdiction of the police agency.
Sustained. The act did occur and it was a violation of departmental rules and procedures. Sustained allegations include misconduct that falls within the broad outlines of the original allegation(s).

Once a determination of culpability has been made, the complainant should be notified of the department's findings (see Figure 10-2). Details of the investigation or recommended punishment will not be included in the correspondence. As Figure 10-2 shows, the complainant will normally receive only information concerning the outcome of the complaint, including a short explanation of the finding along with an invitation to call the agency if further information is needed.

Police Department
3300 Main Street
Downtown Plaza
Anywhere, USA 99999
June 20, 2000

Mr. John Doe
2200 Main Avenue
Anywhere, U.S.A.

Re: Internal Affairs #000666-98
Case Closure

Dear Mr. Doe:

Our investigation into your allegations against Officer Smith has been completed. It has been determined that your complaint is SUSTAINED and the appropriate disciplinary action has been taken.

Our department appreciates your bringing this matter to our attention. It is our position that when a problem is identified, it should be corrected as soon as possible. It is our goal to be responsive to the concerns expressed by citizens so as to provide more efficient and effective services.

Your information regarding this incident was helpful and of value in our efforts to attain that goal. Should you have any further questions about this matter, please contact Sergeant Jane Alexander, Internal Affairs, at 555-9999.

Sincerely,

I.M. Boss,
Lieutenant
Internal Affairs Unit

FIGURE 10-2 Citizen's Notification of Discipline Letter

Level and Nature of Action

When an investigation against an employee is sustained, the sanctions and level of discipline must be decided. Management must be careful when recommending and imposing discipline because of its impact on the overall morale of the agency's employees. If the recommended discipline is viewed by employees as too lenient, it may send the wrong message that the misconduct was insignificant. On the other hand, discipline that is viewed as too harsh may have a demoralizing effect on the officer(s) involved and other agency employees and result in allegations that the leadership is unfair. This alone can have significant impact on the esprit de corps or morale of the agency.

We have discussed the importance of having a disciplinary process that is viewed by employees as fair and consistent, meaning that similar violations receive similar punishments. It is also important that discipline is progressive and more serious sanctions are invoked when repeated violations occur. For example, a third substantiated violation of rude behavior may result in a recommendation for a one-day suspension without pay, whereas a first offense may be resolved through documented oral counseling or a letter of reprimand. Listed next are disciplinary actions commonly used by agencies in order of their severity:

Counseling. This is usually a conversation between the supervisor and employee about a specific aspect of the employee's performance or conduct; it is warranted when an employee has committed a relatively minor infraction or the nature of the offense is such that oral counseling is all that is necessary. For example, an officer who is usually punctual but arrives at briefing 10 minutes late two days in a row may require nothing more than a reminder and warning to correct the problem.

Documented Oral Counseling. This is usually the first step in a progressive disciplinary process and is intended to address relatively minor infractions. It is provided when no previous reprimands or more severe disciplinary action of the same or similar nature have occurred.

Letter of Reprimand. This is a formal written notice regarding significant misconduct, more serious performance violations, or repeated offenses. It is usually the second step in the disciplinary process and is intended to provide the employee and agency with a written record of the violation of behavior. It identifies what specific corrective action must be taken to avoid subsequent more serious disciplinary steps.

Suspension. This is a severe disciplinary action that results in an employee's being relieved of duty, often without pay. It is usually administered when an employee commits a serious violation of established rules or after a written reprimand has been given and no change in behavior or performance has resulted.

Demotion. In this situation, an employee is placed in a position of lower responsibility and pay. It is normally used when an otherwise good employee is unable to meet the standards required for the higher position or the employee has committed a serious act requiring that he or she be removed from a position of management or supervision.

Transfer. Many agencies use the disciplinary transfer to deal with problem officers; officers can be transferred to a different location or assignment, and this action is often seen as an effective disciplinary tool.

Termination. This is the most severe disciplinary action that can be taken. It usually occurs when previous serious discipline has been imposed and inadequate or no improvement in behavior or performance has occurred. It may also be used when an employee commits an offense so serious that continued employment would be inappropriate.

The public release of disciplinary investigations generally is dependent upon state statutes. For example, in California all such records can be accessed only by a court order, and in Kentucky, all such records are available to the public as a result of the state's open records law. Another record retention factor is permanence. Some states allow the purging of disciplinary records after a period of time. The maintenance of IAU files is a matter of confidentiality, making any violation an unlawful act. Therefore, the maintenance and security of IAU files is often assigned to the IAU supervisor, and they are maintained in accordance with state laws.

DETERMINING THE FINAL OUTCOME

The final disposition of the internal affairs investigation is a two-pronged process. First, as noted above, there is a departmental disposition. In most jurisdictions, the chief of police is responsible for determining the final outcome. His or her decision may be based on the recommendation of the IAU or an internal hearing board. In some jurisdictions, the internal hearing board may decide on a final disposition, and the chief only reviews or ratifies it. Jurisdictions that have some form of civilian review are quite similar, although who makes the final decision varies. Some civilian review panels have the authority to make the final decision, while in other cases the civilian review panel only reviews the outcome and makes recommendations to the department.

Once a decision is made, officers often have a right to appeal their punishment to a higher authority. In essence, a police disciplinary action is a civil action, and officers often have the right to appeal their cases in court. When cases are appealed to courts, in some states the courts review the record only to determine if there was a violation of the officer's rights. Other states require that the case be heard *de novo,* whereby the court considers all the evidence and renders a decision relative to guilt and punishment. Once this process is completed, and the officer disagrees with the outcome, he or she can appeal the case to higher courts.

AVERTING PROBLEMS: THE EARLY WARNING SYSTEM

Purposes and Functions

It has become a truism among police leadership that 10 percent of their officers cause 90 percent of the problems. Indeed, some research has indicated that as little as 2 percent of all officers are responsible for 50 percent of all citizen complaints. The Independent Commission on the Los Angeles Police Department (Christopher Commission) (1991) found that a small number of officers were responsible for a disproportionate number of use-of-force incidents. Five percent of the LAPD officers accounted for more than 20 percent of the use-of-force reports. Problem officers are well known to their leaders, their peers, and to the residents of the areas in which they work (Walker, Alpert, and Kenney, 2001:1). Toch (1995) has characterized these officers as *chronic deviants*–officers who consistently create problems.

The early identification of and intervention with employee misconduct or performance problems are vital to preventing ongoing and repeated incidents. Today, a number of departments have implemented early warning systems. An early warning system (EWS) is a database police management tool designed to identify officers whose behavior is problematic and to provide a form of intervention to correct that performance. A department uses an EWS to intervene before such officers are in a situation that warrants formal disciplinary action. The system alerts the department to these individuals and warns the officers while providing counseling or training to help them change their problematic behavior. EWS should not be viewed as an alarm clock, however; it is not a mechanical device that automatically sounds an alarm. Rather, it is an extremely complex, high-maintenance administrative operation that requires close and ongoing human attention.

The first EWS was implemented by the Miami Police Department. In Miami, the system collected information on four types of incidents:

1. ***Complaints.*** An officer receiving five or more complaints or inconclusive complaints in a two-year period.
2. ***Use of Force.*** An officer involved as a principal in five or more use-of-force incidents in a two-year period.
3. ***Reprimands.*** An officer receiving five or more reprimands in a two-year period.
4. ***Discharge of Firearms.*** An officer who has three or more discharges in a five-year period (Walker, et al., 2000).

There are variations to the Miami model. For example, departments include other problem behaviors such as at-fault traffic crashes while in departmental vehicles. Some departments use a cumulative index where a number of total incidents result in some form of remediation for the officer. The EWS generally is housed in the IAU or in the human resource section of the department.

Nearly 4 of every 10 (39 percent) of all municipal and county law enforcement agencies that serve populations greater than 50,000 people either have an EWS in place or are planning to implement one. Most (67 percent) require three complaints in a given time frame (normally a 12-month period) to identify a problem officer. Furthermore, in most systems (62 percent), the initial intervention consists of a review by the officer's immediate supervisor. Almost half (45 percent) involve other command officers in counseling the officer. And nearly all agencies with an EWS monitor an officer's performance after the initial intervention (Walker et al., 2001).

Obviously, one of the primary components in an EWS is police officers' use of force, and it is important to accurately collect this information. Many police departments now require officers to complete use-of-force reporting forms to collect information. These forms are required anytime an officer uses any physical force, which often is broadly defined and may include defensive tactics (physical contact), batons, oleo capsicum (pepper) spray, Tasers, and firearms. By reviewing and approving use-of-force reports, the supervisor must make a judgment concerning whether the officer is acting within departmental policies and regulations. Figure 10-3 provides an example of a use-of-force form.

The use of an EWS appears to have a dramatic effect on reducing citizen complaints and other indicators of problematic police performance. Recently in Minneapolis, citizen complaints against officers dropped by 67 percent one year after the intervention; in New Orleans, that number dropped by 62 percent (Walker et al., 2001). These systems also have a significant effect on police supervisors, initiating their responsibility to monitor officers who have been identified by the program.

Benefits and Potential Drawbacks

No disciplinary system is perfect, but developing a system to identify potential problems early offers many benefits. An EWS has potential drawbacks, however. The overall success of any system depends on how employees perceive its benefits and drawbacks. Reiter (1993) identified the benefits of an EWS:

1. An employee's career may be salvaged before the problem gets too serious.
2. It forces supervisors, particularly in field operations, to become actively involved in employee development.
3. It may provide necessary progressive discipline steps to support termination of an employee who fails to respond to remediation and other supervisory techniques.
4. The agency can gain valuable information that can be used to develop positive changes in training, equipment, tactics, and policy.

Date:
Type of Incident:
Location of Occurrence:

Officer Involved: Badge Number:
Area/Div Assigned: State Compensation Claim Filed Y/N____
Injuries/Officer: ___None ___Treat/rel ___Hospitalized ___Fatal
Other Officers Involved: ___ Yes ___ No Number___

Subject #1
Name (Last, First, Middle)
Sex, Race, DOB:
Level of Resistance: ___ None ___ Physical ___ Firearm ___ Other Weapon
Injuries to Subject: ___Y/N
If Yes: ___Treated/Released ___Hospitalized ___Fatal
Type of Force Used: ___ Physical ___ Capstun ___ K-9 ___Firearm ___ Carotid
___ Other (specify):
Charges:

Subject #2
Name (Last, First, Middle):
Sex, Race, DOB:
Level of Resistance: ___ None ___ Physical ___ Firearm ___ Other Weapon
Injuries to Subject: ___ Y/N
If Yes: ___ Treated/Released ___ Hospitalized ___ Fatal
Type of Force Used: ___ Physical ___ Capstun ___ K-9 ___ Firearm ___ Carotid
___ Other (specify):
Charges:

Witnesses

#1 Name (Last, First, Middle):
Address & Phone:

#2 Name (Last, First, Middle):
Address & Phone:

#3 Name (Last, First, Middle):
Address & Phone:

Supervisor:
Further Investigation Required ___No Further Investigation Required
Date: Signature:

Shift Lieutenant:
Further Investigation Required ___No Further Investigation Required
Date: Signature:

Division Commander:
Further Investigation Required ___No Further Investigation Required
Date: Signature:

FIGURE 10-3 Supervisor's Use of Force Form

5. Properly documented action in this system may defend the agency against a "custom and practice" allegation in a civil suit (i.e., that certain inappropriate behaviors of officers were routine, customary, and practiced often).
6. A workable and articulated system may encourage greater community confidence in the agency's ability to control and manage itself.

There may be several potential drawbacks to the use of an EWS, however, such as the following (Reiter, 1993):

1. The use of an EWS could have an adverse impact on an individual employee's career, particularly if used inappropriately by supervisors or managers.
2. The system could restrict some employees' field performance if they developed an attitude that "no action is safe action."
3. Some supervisors may simply go through the motions of their role and not truly become involved and supportive of the system.
4. If the police agency does create and implement such a system and then fails to use it, the agency could be harmed by failure to identify a problem employee.
5. This system could be used by a plaintiff's attorney to accumulate resource information that might be helpful in a subsequent civil lawsuit.

On balance, it would seem that the benefits of an EWS outweigh the potential drawbacks. This system provides police leaders with vital information for early identification of and intervention with employee problems and may also protect the agency against litigation.

Developing a Preventive Policy

A carefully constructed policy on disciplinary matters can serve as a blueprint for the development of effective procedures. The Police Executive Research Forum (PERF) developed a model policy on how to handle officer misconduct. The purpose of establishing an internal affairs process is threefold: It engenders the trust and confidence of the public, helps supervisors and managers identify problems and areas that need increased direction or training, and helps protect the rights and due process of citizens and officers. Following are the essential components of PERF's (1981:2) model policy:

Prevention of Misconduct: Agencies should make every effort to eliminate any organizational conditions that may foster, permit, or encourage improper behavior by their employees. Preventing misconduct should be an agency's primary means of reducing and controlling it.
Recruitment and Selection: Testing that includes written psychological exams and interviews may ensure that the highest quality individuals are hired and protect against the selection of those who may be unsuited for the difficult tasks of police work.
Training: Ethics training should be included as a major component of recruit training and revisited periodically in in-service classes. Departments should develop systems to ensure that rules, procedures, and outcomes of disciplinary processes are communicated to officers.
Written Directives Manual: Every officer should receive a complete manual of departmental general orders, procedures, and training bulletins. Particular attention should be paid to sections dealing with misconduct and officers' responsibility and accountability to protect the civil rights of all citizens.

Supervisory Responsibility: Properly training supervisors is critical to ensuring that officers' performance conforms to departmental policies and procedures. Emphasis should be placed on methods of identifying problems early, counseling and intervention strategies, training needs, and providing professional referral for more serious problems.

Data Collection and Analysis: It is mandatory that records are kept of all internal affairs actions. General information should be communicated throughout the agency for training purposes. An EWS will assist agencies in early intervention and prevention of problems.

LEGAL CONSIDERATIONS

Negligent failure to discipline is an area that involves both policy and supervisory liability. What are the consequences of an agency's failure to develop an adequate policy and a system to investigate and prosecute violations by officers? Is an agency required to develop a system for receiving and handling citizen complaints against an officer? Generally, case law has held that liability exists if the plaintiff is able to prove that the disciplinary process was so lacking that officers believed no consequences would result from their actions. The bases of this belief include numbers of citizen complaints, how discipline is handled, and the department's failure to take action in matters that needed intervention.

In *Parish v. Luckie* (1992), the plaintiff claimed that she was victim of a false arrest and rape by a member of the police department. The court found that the department had a history of ignoring and covering up complaints of physical and sexual abuse by officers. The officer in question also had a history of violent conduct. The chief would investigate only complaints against officers that were in writing and improperly applied the standard of "beyond a reasonable doubt" to determine whether or not the case was sustained.

An example of a supervisor's failure to address problems is *Gutierrez-Rodriguez v. Cargegena* (1989). Puerto Rican drug agents came upon the plaintiff and his girlfriend in a parked car. The agents approached the vehicle in civilian clothes and with weapons drawn. The plaintiff, seeing them approaching, started his car and attempted to drive away. Without warning or notice that they were police officers, the officers began firing at the car, striking the plaintiff in the back and permanently paralyzing him. The plaintiff sued the squad, the supervisor, and the police chief in federal court under Section 1983. The court found evidence of numerous complaints against the supervisor (13 separate citizen complaints filed against him in three years). The court awarded a $4.5 million judgment.

Liability may also be established in the department's past practices. In *Bordanaro v. McLeod* (1989), the court found that the agency had a widespread practice of unconstitutional warrantless entries and that the chief had knowledge or should have known that the practice was occurring. The court observed that when a large number of officers are conducting themselves in a like manner, that alone is evidence of an established practice by the department.

In *Ramos v. City of Chicago* (1989), however, the plaintiff alleged that he was beaten by police without provocation and that his beating was the result of an institutionalized practice by the Chicago Police Department, but the court did not find the city liable. The court concluded that six unrelated incidents of police brutality over a 10-year period in a police department of more than 10,000 officers failed to prove that a policy or custom existed that condoned brutality. This case is important in that it considered the size of the department and its location in its decision.

CASE STUDIES

Following are two case studies, challenging the reader to look at disciplinary issues and determine what, if any, supervisory style changes or punitive measures are appropriate for the circumstances.

Case Study #1

Making Enemies Fast: The "Misunderstood" Disciplinarian

Sgt. Jerold Jones does not understand why his officers appeal all of his disciplinary recommendations. He takes matters of discipline seriously; it commonly takes him three to four weeks to investigate minor matters—three to four times longer than other supervisors. Jones believes that by doing so, he shows great concern for his officers and, in fact, does not even question the officers about their behavior until the investigation is nearly complete and he has interviewed everyone involved in the matter. Jones decides to speak to his officers about the matter. He is surprised when they tell him that they do not trust him. Indeed, they fail to understand why so much time is needed for him to investigate the minor incidents. They believe that he is being secretive and is always looking for ways to find fault with their performance. Jones argues that his recommendations are consistent with those of other sergeants and provides some examples of similar cases that were handled by various supervisors. Apparently unconvinced by Jones's argument, the next day an officer appeals one of Jones's disciplinary recommendations concerning a minor traffic accident.

Questions for Discussion

1. Are the officers' allegations of Sgt. Jones's unfairness valid?
2. What requisites of sound disciplinary policy may Jones not understand that may be leading to the officers' appeals?
3. Under the circumstances, should Jones simply ignore the officers' complaints? Are their perceptions that important?

Case Study #2

Downtown Sonny Brown

Officer Sonny Brown works the transport wagon downtown and has worked this assignment on day shift for several years. Because of his length of service in this assignment, he has earned the nickname "Downtown" Brown. He loves "hooking and booking" drunks and takes great pride in keeping the streets safe and clean. Local business owners appreciate his efforts, even once honoring him as the Chamber of Commerce "Officer of the Year." Sgt. Carol Jackson is recently promoted and receives her first patrol assignment to the downtown district. As it has been a while since she worked patrol, she decides to ride with Brown for a couple of days to learn about the district and its problems. She is pleased at the warm reception Brown receives from business merchants but quickly becomes concerned about some of his heavy-handed methods of dealing with drunks. When questioned about his tactics, Brown replies, "This ain't administration, Sarge, it's the streets, and our job is to sweep 'em clean." Jackson speaks with Brown's former supervisor, who said he had received several verbal complaints against Brown from citizens, but none could be substantiated. Apparently no one was interested in the word of a drunk against a popular officer. Two days later, Sgt. Jackson is called to the county jail to meet with a booking officer, Hamstead, who wants to talk with her about a drunk who was booked a few hours earlier by Brown. Another prisoner has confided to Hamstead that the drunk was complaining that Brown had injured him by kicking him off a park bench and pushing him down a hill to the transport wagon. The drunk, complaining of pain in his side, was then taken to the hospital and treated for three broken ribs. When asked later about the incident, the drunk refused to cooperate and simply told Hamstead, "I fell down."

Questions for Discussion

1. How should Sgt. Jackson handle this matter?
2. What are her options? Her responsibilities?
3. What types of disciplinary policy changes should the department consider to prevent these situations from occurring?

Summary

This chapter has demonstrated the importance of police agencies' developing and implementing sound disciplinary policies and practices. Policies and training are needed for supervisors and managers to identify and respond to employee misconduct or performance problems at an early stage. Policies also ensure that discipline is administered in a consistent and equitable manner throughout the organization. Prompt, complete, and full investigations of alleged misconduct coupled with the appropriate level of discipline may minimize or even eliminate potential civil liability.

The public's trust and respect are precious commodities and can be quickly lost with the disregard or improper handling of allegations of misconduct. The public expects that police agencies will make every effort to identify and correct problems and respond to citizens' complaints in a judicious manner.

Items for Review

1. Delineate the rights that police officers possess, as well as areas in which they have limitations placed on their behavior and activity, according to court decisions and legislation.
2. Review the various forms of disciplinary actions that may be taken against police officers.
3. Explain the basic procedure to be followed by supervisors when performing an internal affairs investigation.

4. Describe the benefits of having an early warning system (EWS) to identify problem officers.

5. Provide four examples of negligent supervision of police officers that have resulted in liability.

References

Arnold, J. (1998). Internal affairs investigation: The supervisor's role. *FBI Law Enforcement Bulletin* (January):11–16.

Biehunik v. Felicetta, 441 F.2d 228 (1971).

Bonsignore v. City of New York, 521 F.Supp. 394 (1981).

Bordanaro v. McLeod, 871 F.2d 1151 (1989).

Brenckle v. Township of Shaler, 281 A.2d 920 (Pa. 1972).

Connick v. Myers, 461 U.S. 138 (1983).

Cox v. McNamara, 493 P.2d 54 (Ore. 1972).

Flood v. Kennedy, 239 N.Y.S.2d 665 (1963).

Gabrilowitz v. Newman, 582 F.2d 100 (1st Cir. 1978).

Gaffigan, S. J., and McDonald, P. P. (1997). *Police integrity: Public service with honor*. Washington, DC: U.S. Department of Justice.

Garrity v. New Jersey, 385 U.S. 483 (1967).

Gutierrez-Rodriguez v. Cargegena, 882 F.2d 553 (1st Cir., 1989).

Hester v. Milledgeville, 598 F.Supp. 1456, 1457 (M.D.Ga. 1984).

Hopwood v. City of Paducah, 424 S.W.2d 134 (Ky. 1968).

Inciardi, J. A. (1996). *Criminal justice,* 5th ed. Orlando, FL: Harcourt Brace.

Independent Commission of the Los Angeles Police Department. (1991). *Report of the independent commission*. Los Angeles: Author.

Jones v. Dodson, 727 F.2d 1329 (4th Cir. 1984).

Katz v. United States, 389 U.S. 347 (1967).

Kelley v. Johnston, 425 U.S. 238 (1976).

Krolick v. Lowery, 302 N.Y.S.2d. 109 (1969), p.115.

Lally v. Department of Police, 306 So.2d 65 (La. 1974).

Liederbach, J., Boyd, L., Taylor, R., and Kawucha, S. (2007). Is it an inside job? An examination of internal affairs complaint investigation files and the production of nonsustained findings. *Criminal Justice Policy Review*, 18:353-377.

MacNamara, J. (1995, November). Panel discussion on ethics and integrity. California Peace Officers' Association Meeting, Napa, CA.

Marusa v. District of Columbia, 484 F.2d 828 (1973).

McCarthy v. Philadelphia Civil Service Commission, 424 U.S. 645, 96 S. Ct. 1154 (1976).

McDonell v. Hunter, 611 F.Supp. 1122 (S.D. Iowa, 1985), affd. as mod., 809 F.2d 1302 (8th Cir., 1987).

McGurrin, D., and Kappeler, V. (2002). Media accounts of police sexual violence: Rotten apples or state supported violence? In K. Lersch (ed.) *Policing and misconduct*, pp. 121-142. Upper Saddle River, NJ: Prentice-Hall.

McLaughlin, V., and Bing, R. (1987). Law enforcement personnel selection. *Journal of Police Science and Administration* 15:271–276.

Morris, L. (1951). *Incredible New York*. New York: Bonanza.

Muller v. Conlisk, 429 F.2d 901 (7th Cir. 1970).

National Treasury Employees Union v. Von Raab, 489 U.S. 656 (1989).

Parish v. Luckie, 963 F.2d 201 (1992).

Pedersen, D. (2001). Rising above corruption: How to put integrity at the forefront in your department. *Law and Order* (October):136–142.

People v. Tidwell, 266 N.E.2d 787 (Ill. 1971).

Pickering v. Board of Education, 391 U.S. 563 (1968).

Police Executive Research Forum. (1981). *Police handling of officer misconduct: A model policy statement*. Washington, DC: Author.

Popow v. City of Margate, 476 F.Supp. 1237 (1979).

Ramos v. City of Chicago, 707 F.Supp. 345 (1989).

Reiter, L. (1993). *Law enforcement administrative investigations: A manual guide*. Tallahassee, FL: Lou Reiter and Associates.

Rubin, J. (2008). LAPD can't police itself, audit charges. *Los Angeles Times*. (February 12, 2008).

Sager v. City of Woodlawn Park, 543 F.Supp. 282 (D. Colo., 1982).

Sapp, A. (1994). Sexual misconduct and sexual harassment by police officers. In T. Barker & D. Carter (eds.). pp. 187–199. Cincinnati: Anderson Publishing.

Sencio, W. J. (1992). Complaint processing: Policy considerations. *The Police Chief* 7:45–48.

Soper, K. (2006). State police internal affairs unit blasted: Criminal charges could result from scathing report. *Journal Inquirer* (December 5, 2006).

Toch, H. (1995). The violence prone police officer. In W. Geller & H. Toch (eds.) *And justice for all: Understanding and controlling police abuse of force,* pp. 99-112. Washington, D.C.: PERF.

Trans World Airlines v. Hardison, 97 S.Ct. 2264 (1977).

United States v. City of Albuquerque, 12 EPD 11, 244 (10th Cir. 1976).

Wagner, A. E., and Decker, S. H. (1997). Evaluating citizen complaints against the police. In R. G. Dunham and G. P. Alpert, eds., *Critical issues in policing: Contemporary readings.* Prospect Heights, IL: Waveland.

Walker, S. (2001). *Police accountability: The role of citizen oversight*. Belmont, CA: Wadsworth.

Walker, S., Alpert, G. A., and Kenney, D. J. (2001, July). Early warning systems: Responding to the problem police officer. Washington, DC: U.S. Department of Justice, National Institute of Justice Research in Brief.

Walker, S., Alpert, G., and Kenney, D. (2000). Early warning systems for police: Concept, history, and issues. *Police Quarterly*, 3:132–152.

Williams, R. N. (1975). *Legal aspects of discipline by police administrators. Traffic Institute Publication 2705.* Evanston, IL: Northwestern University.

Worrall, J. (2002). If you build it, they will come: Consequences of improved citizen complaint review procedures. *Crime & Delinquency*, 48: 355–379.

CHAPTER 11

Police Unions and Labor Relations

Key Terms and Concepts

- Affiliation
- Appeals
- Arbitration
- Bargaining not required model
- Boston police strike
- Collective bargaining
- Contract
- Grievance
- Job action
- Labor relations
- Meet-and-confer model
- Negotiation
- Police strike
- Union
- Vote of no confidence
- Work slowdown
- Work speedup
- Work stoppage

Learning Objectives

After reading this chapter, the student will:

- understand how and why police unions came into being, and some of their past strike activities that endure in infamy
- comprehend the contemporary membership status of police unionism, including the primary organizations that support them
- know some of the salient police labor problems that unions were founded to address
- be able to relate the roles of, and the status of relations between, both police management and union leaders
- know the kinds of labor issues that can be negotiated during collective bargaining
- understand the three collective bargaining models that are in existence
- be able to explain police union contracts, including how they are developed and the kinds of benefits and elements they can contain
- know how officers may engage in grievances and appeals when employee disputes arise

Change comes from power; and power comes from organization.

—Saul Alinsky

INTRODUCTION

Labor relations has become a critical area of policing, and has a significant impact on the day to day supervision and management of police departments and individual units. Although a relatively unknown or little discussed subject of inquiry—at least when compared to homeland defense, responding to critical incidents and natural disasters, and other facets of police supervision and management—labor relations is no less serious in nature. Emotions can run very high when salaries, benefits, and general working conditions are hanging in the balance.

As a result, the police labor movement has a long and sometimes sordid and painful history, particularly when officers have elected to take drastic measures to show their displeasure with management and to attempt to effect change in their work environment. Some of their **job actions** in decades past have included **work stoppages** (strikes and "blue flu"); engaging in work **slowdowns** (reducing revenues) and **speedups** (issuing more citations, for example, and thus overwhelming the courts and jails); issuing a **vote of no confidence** (a tactic used by police unions and employee organizations to publicly voice displeasure with management.); and demonstrating their displeasure by engaging in picketing and holding sit-ins. Although there are no statistics concerning the number of police departments that are unionized, the number is considerable. (Data of the affiliations and claimed memberships of the 40 largest police agencies in the U.S. are provided below.)

Unions can have a major impact on police departments. Their activities and the contract not only affect police administrators, but also place limitations or restrictions on supervisors and managers. Thus, it is important for supervisors and managers to understand **collective bargaining**, a process whereby police employees discuss and negotiate salary, benefits, and work conditions. The result of collective bargaining is a contract. Police supervisors and managers need to understand the implications of the contract, and how they negotiate tasks and responsibilities within the confines of the contract. (Note: *Negotiation* was discussed in Chapter 5 as it primarily pertains to police managers and supervisors and their subordinates—to ensure their compliance with orders, directives, and assignments. Those same approaches and techniques also apply to *collective bargaining,* which is discussed in detail in this chapter.) Supervisors and managers also need to comprehend the relationships with employees. As a result of collective bargaining, employees have more power, and this power must be recognized and considered when dealing with employees.

This chapter explores these and other aspects of police unionization and labor relations. First, we briefly consider the history of police unions, and then explore the operation of unions and police organizations today. Next is a review of several collective bargaining models that exist, and following that is a look at police union contracts. We then consider job actions and other possible outcomes and effects of labor disagreements. Grievances and **appeals** by officers who wish to dispute the proposed labor agreement, or when they believe management is bargaining unfairly, is then covered. Two case studies are included at the chapter's end.

A BRIEF HISTORY OF POLICE UNIONS

Origins

Police employee groups started forming as early as the Civil War. These early groups were fraternal organizations, rather than unions, and even today, much of the collective bargaining that occurs in police departments is managed by these fraternal organizations (e.g., Fraternal Order of Police). The fraternal organizations primarily were concerned with employee health and welfare. For example, they were interested in death benefits and welfare insurance for their members. Police officers did not actively unionize until the passage of civil service reform, which gave them some degree of job protection.

The late 1800s and early 1900s, however, were a time of social unrest, political strife, and labor violence. After witnessing the economic gains made by trade unions, firefighters, and other public workers, the American Federation of Labor (AFL) started getting requests for charters from local police benevolent associations who were clamoring to join organized labor. The unionization of the police caused a firestorm of protest, as police executives did not want their officers forming unions and alliances with political, labor, and social activists; trade unions were viewed as a threat to the national security (DeLord, 2006a).

A number of police groups attempted to affiliate with the early American Federation of Labor. In 1897, the AFL rejected a petition by special police in Cleveland, Ohio, for a local chapter. However, by 1917, the AFL reversed its position and allowed police charters, and in September 1917 there were 37 charters with a membership of over 4,000 police officers, mostly in small and medium sized cities.

The Boston Police Strike

The Boston police strike was not the first strike by police officers in this country, but it was the most dramatic in terms of loss of life, destruction, and public attention. The Boston **police strike** was significant because it involved over 1,100 police officers; seven lives were lost and hundreds of people were injured as a result of rioting, and immense property damage was suffered before the state's national guard restored order. A number of conditions precipitated the strike:

> The morale of Boston policemen prior to the strike was low because of distressingly inadequate working conditions, among which were vermin-infested station houses, wages too low for the post-World War I inflationary period, working hours ranging between seventy-three to ninety hours per week, a requirement that officers pay for their uniforms, and the use of favoritism in assigning officers to the best positions (Burpo, 1971, pp. 3–4).

Yet, the immediate cause of the strike was Police Commissioner E.V. Curtis's refusal to recognize the **union**. He had prohibited officers from joining the union and had filed charges against several officials of the union. A citizens' committee mediated a settlement between the Commissioner and the officers that included their giving up the union charter. The Commissioner ignored the settlement and suspended a dozen officers. As a result, three-fourths of the Boston police force went on strike (Levine, 1988).

The strike lasted four days, after which, on "orders from Governor Calvin Coolidge, the Commonwealth dismissed the strikers and destroyed the union" (Levine, 1988, p. 335); 1,100 police officers lost their jobs. Entry standards were lowered to enable the Department to quickly recruit replacement officers.

President Woodrow Wilson severely condemned the police and the strike:

> A strike of policemen of a great city, leaving that city at the mercy of an army of thugs, is a crime against civilization. In my judgment the obligation of a policeman is as sacred and direct as the obligation of a soldier. He is a public servant, not a private employee, and the whole honor of the community is in his hands. He has no right to prefer any private advantage to public safety (Ziskind, 1940, p. 49).

Governor Calvin Coolidge also condemned the strike, making his now-famous declaration that "There is no right to strike against the public safety by anybody, anywhere, anytime" (Ziskind, 1940, p. 49). However, although tragic for the city, the strike did result in significant gains for Boston police. Salaries were increased by three hundred dollars, officers were no longer required to purchase their uniforms, and a pension system was created. The newly hired officers were able to reap the benefits of the strike.

The Boston police strike was also a defining moment for the fledgling police labor movement. It caused distrust and hatred of the police, caused the AFL unions to balk at calling a general strike to support the Boston police (and to revoke all its police charters), and solidified politicians' and the public's positions against police unions and organizations. Indeed, in 1969, 50 years after the Boston strike, the

AFL-CIO received a request to charter a national police union; it rejected the request. The Boston strike thus effectively halted police collectivism for many decades; it was not until 1979 that the AFL-CIO chartered the International Union of Police Associations as a national police union (DeLord, 2006).

In Boston's Aftermath

Still, since the 1960s police unionization has continued to grow—in numbers and in its militancy. As exemplified by the Boston police strike, the impetus for police unionization was poor working conditions, low salary, and oppressive management practices. Historically, police departments adhered to a military or bureaucratic management model that, more or less, treated police officers as property. Officers were seen as minions who were supposed to do as they were told. It was not until the 1970s that police management systems began to recognize that police officers were valuable assets and overall police effectiveness depended on quality police officers and their morale.

Since the 1970s, police departments have decentralized their management systems, implemented community-oriented policing that gives officers more latitude in decision making, and generally attempted to provide officers with competitive salaries and benefits.

POLICE UNIONS TODAY

As Authorized in the U.S.

As indicated above, today unions are a formidable force in policing—particularly in the Northeast, Midwest, and Western states—and they tend to play a greater role in larger departments. Unions in larger departments may even have staff working full-time to advance union causes and lobbyists who work the political system for union causes. These unions may also actively support particular political candidates and contribute to campaigns.

Once unions are recognized in a jurisdiction, the relationship between the department and the governmental entity is codified in a contract or memorandum of understanding. The **contract** specifies the rights and privileges of employees and places restrictions on the political entity and police administrators. In effect, the contract has the force of law. The contract can be changed only via re-negotiations which occur generally on a multi-year cycle as agreed upon by the union and police management.

Table 11-1 provides a breakdown of collective bargaining as it is authorized in the United States, by size of population served. As noted in the table, approximately 41 percent of all sworn police officers

TABLE 11-1 Collective Bargaining Authorized by Local Police Departments, by Size of Population Served, 2003

	Percent of Agencies Authorizing Collective Bargaining for—	
Population Served	Sworn Employees	Civilian Employees
All sizes	41%	22%
1,000,000 or more	81	63
500,000-999,999	84	67
250,000-499,999	66	54
100,000-249,999	69	60
50,000-99,999	71	59
25,000-49,999	75	59
10,000-24,999	70	48
2,500-9,999	50	21
Under 2,500	13	2

Source: Hickman, M., and Reaves, B. (2006). *Local Police Departments, 2003*. Washington, D.C.: Bureau of Justice Statistics.

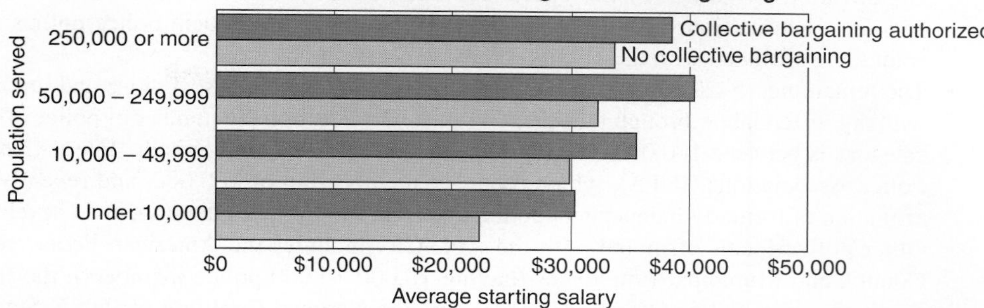

FIGURE 11-1 Starting Salaries for Entry-Level Officers in Local Police Departments Authorizing and Not Authorizing Collective Bargaining
Source: Hickman, M., and Reaves, B. (2006). *Local Police Departments, 2003.* Washington, D.C.: Bureau of Justice Statistics.

are unionized or involved in collective bargaining, as well as 22 percent of civilian employees. Also, the table shows that larger police departments tend to be more involved in collective bargaining as compared to smaller departments.

Collective bargaining also has been shown to have an impact on officers' salaries. Figure 11-1 depicts the differences in starting salaries for entry-level officers in local police agencies authorizing and not authorizing collective bargaining. In the police agencies that authorize collective bargaining, the starting salaries are about $8,900.00 higher. Of course, some of this difference is attributable to the fact that larger departments have more involvement in collective bargaining, and they generally pay higher salaries as compared to smaller agencies. Nonetheless, collective bargaining does increase police officers' wages and benefits.

Affiliations

Today a virtual maze of union affiliations constitutes the police labor movement—as contrasted with firefighters, who have been united into one worldwide union for nearly a century. Different states and jurisdictions within states have different types of unions, and many police unions have dual affiliations.

Adding to this confusion is that many people believe that a police agency is unionized only if the officers have collective bargaining rights or the officers belong to a police union affiliated with the American Federation of Labor-Congress of Industrial Organizations (AFL-CIO). In reality, when the officers form a local association, lodge, or union for the purposes of improving their wages, benefits, and conditions of employment, the officers are unionized (DeLord, 2006a).

The police labor union is divided into two camps: the independent police labor organizations and the police labor organizations affiliated with organized labor through the AFL-CIO. Approximately 80–85 percent of all police labor organizations could be classified as independent and have no **affiliation** with the AFL-CIO. Following are the major labor groups and their reported memberships:

- The independent Fraternal Order of Police (FOP) reports a membership of 310,000 and is unquestionably the nation's largest police labor organization. FOP reports that it has a lodge in all 50 states.

- The second largest independent police organization is the National Association of Police Organizations (NAPO), which reports 236,000 members. NAPO, a federation of labor unions and not a labor union per se, is composed primarily of independent police unions that did not want to be affiliated with the FOP.
- The remaining 15–20 percent of unionized officers belongs to associations and unions affiliated with organized labor through the AFL-CIO; the best guess on the number of police officers in this category is between 100,000–150,000. The largest AFL-CIO union is the International Union of Police Associations (IUPA), which reports a membership of 100,000, and recently gained the affiliation of formerly independent police unions in Los Angeles, Boston, and Cleveland.
- Other police locals affiliated with the AFL-CIO includes the American Federation of State, County, and Municipal Employees (having 10,000-15,000 police members), the International Brotherhood of Police Officers (10,000), and the National Coalition of Public Safety Officers (26,000 police and corrections officers) (DeLord, 2006a).

Table 11-2 shows the affiliations of police unions in some of the largest municipalities in the U.S.

TABLE 11-2 Affiliations of Police Unions in Some of the Largest Municipalities

The following charts represent the police union recognized as the collective bargaining agent for the rank of police officer in some of the largest municipal police departments. If no union is recognized by the city as the bargaining agent, the police union(s) with a substantial membership that includes police officers is listed.

Rank	Population	City	ST	Police Union	Affiliation	Contract
1	8,008,278	New York	NY	Patrolmen's Benevolent Association of New York City	NAPO	Yes
2	3,694,820	Los Angeles	CA	Los Angeles Police Protective League, Local 714	IUPA/NAPO	Yes
3	2,896,016	Chicago	IL	F.O.P. Lodge 7	FOP	Yes
4	1,953,631	Houston	TX	Houston Police Officers Union	NAPO	Yes
5	1,517,550	Philadelphia	PA	F.O.P. Lodge 5	FOP	Yes
6	1,321,045	Phoenix	AZ	Phoenix Law Enforcement Association	NAPO	Yes
7	1,223,400	San Diego	CA	San Diego Police Officers Association	Independent	Yes
8	1,188,580	Dallas	TX	Dallas Police Association	NAPO	No
				F.O.P Lodge 588	FOP	No
9	1,144,646	San Antonio	TX	San Antonio Police Officers Association	NCPSO/NAPO	Yes
10	951,270	Detroit	MI	Detroit Police Officers Association	NAPO	Yes
11	894,943	San Jose	CA	San Jose Peace Officers Association	Independent	Yes
12	791,926	Indianapolis	IN	F.O.P. Lodge 86	FOP	Yes
13	776,733	San Francisco	CA	San Francisco Police Officers Association, Local 911	SEIU	Yes
14	735,617	Jacksonville*	FL	F.O.P. Lodge 5/30	FOP	Yes
15	711,470	Columbus	OH	F.O.P. Lodge 9	FOP	Yes
16	656,562	Austin	TX	Austin Police Association	NCPSO/NAPO	Yes
17	651,154	Baltimore	MD	F.O.P. Lodge 3	FOP	Yes
18	650,100	Memphis	TN	Memphis Police Association	Independent	Yes
19	596,974	Milwaukee	WI	Milwaukee Police Association, Local 21	IUPA	Yes

Adapted from U.S. Dept. of Justice, Office of Community Oriented Policing Services (2006). *Police labor-management relations (Vol. I): Perspectives and practical solutions for implementing change, making reforms, and handling crises for managers and union leaders.* http://www.cops.usdoj.gov/mime/open.pdf?Item=1856, pp. 185–186.

Role of Union Leaders

To state the obvious, there is inherent conflict between management and labor. Variation in roles dictates conflict, so the challenge is whether that conflict can be kept within a healthy range. Employee associations must be an advocate for their membership; there is an expectation by the member officers that a union will be a strong, outspoken, vigorous advocate for the membership—and not become too "cozy" with management. This has profound implications for the role of union leaders. Simply put, they must maintain some level of conflict if they expect to stay in office. They must maintain some level of strain, and at least occasionally fan the fires if they are to remain in office (and police leaders who understand that are not as likely to personalize the conflict). This does not, however, preclude cooperative, productive relationships. Management and labor can work together for the better good of the organization. But there are limits to joint, cooperative effort; if everyone understands the limits there will be less rancor (Hoover et al., 2006).

Police union leaders are elected and many want to remain elected. They also have their own constituencies, and a wise union leader must attempt to balance the wants and needs of the internal ethnic, social, fraternal, and gender-based organizations and other special-interest groups against the needs of the membership as a whole. If a union leader attacks the police chief on a decision in a police misconduct case, the members may approve of the union's actions but it weakens the relationship between the police executive and union. Conversely, if the union remains silent when the members believe it needs to defend an officer, the union president risks losing his or her job. For these reasons, the average police union leader has a tenure of two to four years (DeLord and Sanders, 2006).

Union leadership also needs to exercise great caution in mixing economic demands with those pertaining to working conditions. Advocacy of an economic shift differential, for example, should be separated from advocacy of shift selection by seniority; they are not interchangeable concepts at the bargaining table, and one should not be traded for the other.

Role of Management

It is well known that the job of police executives is one of the most difficult and stressful in the nation. They have to balance the demands of the elected officials, command staff, mid-level supervisors, rank-and-file officers, government administrators, the police union, and every conceivable community organization. And, if appointed from outside their agency, they inherit their predecessor's personnel and problems. The command and mid-level supervisors in a police agency have their own agendas and the union is a major player in most agencies. The executive who maintains a cooperative relationship with the union will be able to communicate his or her message without some of the potential for conflict. The internal politics of a police agency is very complex, however. For example, if the police executive comes down hard on an officer for misconduct, the union and officers perceive the chief executive as trying to win points with the media and some community activists; if showing leniency instead, he or she is kowtowing to the union (DeLord and Sanders, 2006).

What also separates the police union from the police executive in the world of politics is that the union has the ability to endorse a candidate and work in the candidate's political campaign. Perhaps the union's greatest political advantage is its ability to contribute money to the candidate. What impact does this political involvement have? Any proposed change or reform becomes a political contest. In addition to political contributions of money, the union often seeks to influence the general pubic through press conferences, direct mail, billboards, radio, and television. Police unions have therefore become major factors in the court of public opinion, because they can deal directly with the elected officials, the media, and the public—bypassing the chief executive (DeLord, 2006b).

Union activities in the political arena—including lobbying for new laws—are discussed more below.

Status of the Relations between Management and Labor Leaders

A national survey sponsored by the federal Office of Community Oriented Policing Services (2006) determined the following:

- Monthly meetings are preferred by both police management (63 percent) and union presidents (51 percent) to discuss matters of interest. One-fourth of union representatives participate in senior command staff meetings as well.
- Management's perception is that it solicited the input of labor a majority of the time, while labor viewed itself as being included in the discussion of the issues less often, depending on the issue. Large differences of opinion existed about their respective willingness to confer on citizen complaints, scheduling, communication channels, and relations with political entities. For example, while only 6 percent of chiefs perceived they did not confer or solicit input enough from union representatives in the area of citizen complaints filed, 60 percent of union representatives felt management does not confer enough in that area.
- A minority of survey respondents, 15 percent of union leaders and 8 percent of chiefs, characterized their interactions as hostile and bitter or antagonistic. Conversely, 80 percent of chiefs and 63 percent of union leaders described their working relationship as either collaborative and fully engaged or at least cooperative and friendly (Hoover, et al., 2006).

According to this survey, today's police executives and unions are generally not that far apart in their perceptions of the roles that labor and management play in policing. They operate under a written agreement as often as not, meet formally about once a month, and acknowledge the union's status in meetings with city/county managers, with community groups, and in strategic planning meetings with various components of the agency. In their meetings they confer on a number of specific issues, many of which are perceived similarly by both sides; however, they differ in their perceptions of their respective willingness to confer on citizen complaints, scheduling, communication channels, and relations with political entities (Hoover, et al., 2006).

Police Labor Issues

The two primary issues for police management and labor collective bargaining groups are: (1) pursuit of better pay, benefits, and working conditions, and (2) broad political issues.

PAY, BENEFITS, AND WORKING CONDITIONS In terms of pay, benefits, and working conditions, police management and labor collective bargaining groups are constantly lobbying for their membership. They scrutinize their pay relative to other police departments and the pay rates of the public sector in their jurisdiction. They look for differences to point out when requesting raises. Negotiating for better pay is not a simple matter. For example, beginning salaries may be increased to attract more officers, but the salaries for veteran officers may not be raised or only moderately raised by the government. The opposite is also true. Nor is salary the only pay issue. Police departments often have specialist positions such as detective, accident investigator, K-9 handler, SWAT Officer, gang unit, field training officer, and so forth. These specialists often receive some form of pay differential or extra salary. Thus, the amount of this differential often becomes an issue when the union and government are engaged in collective bargaining.

Working conditions represent another range of bargaining issues. Unions constantly strive to have more control over working conditions, while police administrators desire to maintain a large measure of control and discretion so that they can effectively deploy personnel and manage police operations. Police employee organizations often bargain for shift assignment, criteria for transfers to

Many speciality functions like motorcycle enforcement, bike patrol, and horse mounted units are negotiated for special pay in agencies.
(Courtesy Ft. Lauderdale, Florida, P.D.)

specialized units, equipment, and promotion systems and eligibility. Unions often emphasize seniority over ability or experience. For example, if seniority were the sole or primary criterion for transferring officers to the detective unit, the unit may become staffed with personnel who are not as adept in investigations.

NEGOTIATION There is a wealth of issues that police unions attempt to influence. Bargaining does not involve one issue, but it often includes large numbers of issues. The union attempts to make gains while management attempts to hold the line. If the union cannot make gains in one area, it will use the issue to make demands in other areas. At the same time, management attempts to gain concessions from the union on issues.

Negotiating should never be one-sided. From a management perspective, negotiating should be a "quid pro quo" process whereby when management accedes to a demand, the union should make concessions in other areas. It should also be recognized that bargaining is a continuous process. What the union does not get in one contract certainly will be an issue when negotiating the next contract. Contracts generally are in effect from two to four years.

Negotiations are conducted by teams from management and labor. Each side generally is allowed the same number of personnel in the negotiation sessions; this number is often set out in the contract. The **negotiation** process usually begins cordially with casual conversation in an effort to develop a cooperative atmosphere, and once relations are established, each side presents its position. Both sides examine the complete contract to determine if there are areas that both sides can agree upon. If there are such areas, they will be excluded from the negotiations. Once this occurs, disagreed upon issues are discussed, with each side presenting data and information supporting its position. At this point, the negotiations can be rather contentious as each side vehemently argues its position. These negotiations can last for months as each side attempts to garner support for its position. In the end, issues are settled with the manner depending on the jurisdiction's bargaining model.

POLITICAL ACTIVITIES As noted above, police unions today are also extensively involved in political activities, both in terms of: (1) support of political candidates and (2) lobbying for and against legislation at the local, state, and federal levels. Unions often openly support particular candidates via endorsements, urging membership to vote for a candidate, and making contributions to campaigns. This is especially true for city and county council candidates. The union reasons that if it can influence one or a few of the council members, it can wrestle more benefits from the governing body. In terms of lobbying, police unions often lobby for local ordinances and state statues that are perceived as supportive to the police. Because state legislatures control the extent and nature of police unionization, state programs that provide grants to police departments, and personnel issues such as retirement systems, the union often takes an active role in state-wide political elections and matters.

The many other work-related areas that can be negotiated and ultimately put into the contract are delineated in Figure 11-2, next page.

MODELS OF COLLECTIVE BARGAINING

For a department to be involved in the collective bargaining process, it must be authorized by state law. Thus, police collective bargaining occurs on a state-by-state basis. The ability of the police union to negotiate over wages, hours, and conditions of employment changes the labor-management relationship. Thirty-six states have some form of collective bargaining rights for police officers (DeLord, 2006b). Most contracts also include a grievance procedure that will require management and labor to mediate or arbitrate problems and issues and at least discuss proposed changes. According to DeLord (2006b:17), police unions not having the right to collectively bargain are restricted to "collective begging" with the elected officials. When public employers can dictate the terms of employment and discipline at will, executives are more likely to be heavy-handed and avoid mediating disputes with the union. Therefore, having collective bargaining does provide for periodic interaction between both sides.

Three Models

There is a great deal of variation as to how police departments engage in collective bargaining. Collective bargaining varies from state to state depending on statutes. That is, each state places requirements on police and governmental labor negotiations. Nonetheless, three general models have emerged: (1) the binding arbitration model, (2) the meet-and-confer model, and (3) bargaining not required model.

BINDING ARBITRATION In states that allow binding arbitration, employees are given the right to select and be represented by exclusive representatives (Fraternal Order of Police, Patrolmen's Benevolent Association, American Federation of State, County, and Municipal Employees, International Brotherhood of Teamsters, etc.). Employees vote and select who will represent them in the collective bargaining process. Once this occurs, the organization or entity exclusively negotiates with the governmental entity. The union's primary obligation to its membership is "fair representation." In other words, the union must address all grievances in a fair and non-discriminatory manner (Aitchison, 2004).

The governmental entity and the union are required to bargain in good faith. When the two sides come to an impasse or are unable to agree on an issue, the two sides submit the issue and their positions to a "neutral" third party or arbitrator. The arbitrator then decides the outcome with the decision conforming to state laws and labor standards. The arbitrator's decision is made based on the supporting documentation and arguments supplied by the union and management. Aitchison (2004) has identified three models that have been adopted by the states when arbitrators engage in binding arbitration. First, there is "issue-by-issue" arbitration where the arbitrator examines and makes a decision on each

1. Union Recognition (establishes the union as the bargaining agent)
2. Management Rights (lists areas that are not negotiable in contract negotiations)
3. Check-Off (allows union dues to be collected via paycheck deductions)
4. Bulletin Boards and Ballot Boxes (describes where the union can post information)
5. Prohibitions of Strikes (prohibits strikes, usually mandated by state statute)
6. Discharge and Discipline (describes disciplinary procedures)
7. Appeal Procedure (describes how officers appeal disciplinary outcomes)
8. Grievance Procedure (describes the filing and handling of grievances)
9. Complaint Procedure (describes how a police officer can file a complaint about working conditions)
10. Seniority (describes how seniority is calculated for promotions, transfers, etc.)
11. Probationary Employees (enumerates the length of the probationary period)
12. Lay-Offs (describes the conditions that must exist for layoffs and order of people being laid off)
13. Leave Provisions (provides procedures for sick leave, annual leave or vacation, unpaid leaves, and military leaves)
14. Non-Discrimination (requires non-discrimination in decisions)
15. Hours of Work and Duty Shifts (enumerates the shift structure for officers)
16. Union Activities (describes what union activities are permissible)
17. Outside Employment and Employees Duties (describes restrictions on outside employment)
18. Citizen Complaints (describes how citizen complaints are handled by the department)

18a. Employee's Bill of Rights (incorporates officers' rights into the contract)

18b. Relief from Duty (details circumstances for an officer's being relieved from duty by a superior)

19. Attendance in Court, Conferences, Training, and Other Meetings (describes the procedures for attendance at these functions)
20. Holidays (lists the holidays that officers receive)
21. Overtime and Call-In Pay (describes the circumstances and payment for overtime and call-ins)
22. Allowance for Clothing (enumerates the amount of clothing allowance officers receive)
23. Health Care (describes officers' health insurance coverage and related contribution or costs)
24. Injuries In the Line of Duty/Temporary Disability (describes departmental procedures for assisting officers who are injured in the line of duty)
25. Limited Duty (describes light duty assignments for off-duty officers becoming ill or injured)
26. Union Business (enumerates number of union members who attend certain meetings with the department and duty assignments)
27. Safety Committee (establishes a safety committee that meets monthly and mandates that recommendations be forwarded to the mayor)
28. Longevity (specifies number of years of service for longevity pay and calculations)
29. Savings Clause (notes that if a provision of the contract is ruled illegal or unconstitutional by the courts, the remaining sections of the contract remain in force)
30. Health Care for Retirees (outlines city responsibilities for retired officers' health care coverage)
31. Residency (allows officers to reside outside the city)
32. Maintenance of Benefits (requires the city to maintain the benefits as established in the contract)
33. Examinations and Promotion Procedure (specifies procedures for promotion)
34. Pensions (describes procedures for the pension and contributions made by officers and the city)
35. Shift Differential (establishes pay differential and amount for shifts)
36. College Incentive Pay (establishes college incentive pay and enumerates its operation)
37. Wages (enumerates the annual raises for the duration of the contract)
38. Job Performance Interview (establishes that the department can counsel employees whose performance is below satisfactory)
39. Drug Testing (establishes random drug testing in the department)
40. Out-of-Classification Pay (establishes pay standards for employees who work in jobs with a different pay classification)
41. Specialty Pay (describes pay differential for officers in specialist positions)
42. Premium Pay (enumerates a higher pay supplement for officers working in certain high skilled positions)
43. Compensatory Time (describes how officers will be reimbursed for time in excess of regularly worked hours)
44. Wage Supplement for Card Employees (establishes a pay scale for certain employees)
45. Continuing Negotiations (sets procedures to ensure that the union and city negotiate on a timely basis)
46. Trade Time (establishes a procedure where officers can trade shifts)
47. Duration of Agreement (enumerates the period of time covered by the contract)

FIGURE 11-2 Uniontown City, U.S.A., Police Department Union Contract Elements

unresolved issue independently: a decision on one issue does not affect decisions on other issues. The final decision on an issue does not have to be a position that was supported by either the union or management, and in many cases, the final decision is a compromise. Second, is the "final offer issue-by-issue" outcome. Again, the arbitrator decides each issue independently, and a decision or the facts relative to one issue do not affect decisions relative to other issues. Because the arbitrator's final decision must support or be consistent with either the union or management's bargaining position, in final offer issue-by-issue, arbitrators have only two choices: either the union or management's position relative to each issue. Here there are no compromises. Finally, is "total package" arbitration. Total package arbitration is similar to final offer issue-by-issue arbitration except in total package arbitration the arbitrator must pick the total package of either management or the union. There are no compromises, and it is a winner takes all exercise.

In binding arbitration, arbitrators do not have total autonomy when making decisions. Most states establish criteria that arbitrators must use when making decisions. Generally, they must consider the prevailing wages and benefits in the area and for similar police agencies in the state. Both management and the union often provide data supporting their positions using statistics focusing on these criteria. Both sides often skew or present the data in a fashion that supports their positions. The arbitrator must ferret through the information to determine actual benchmark wages and benefits.

It is not clear if one form of binding arbitration is better than the other two forms. One attribute of total package arbitration is that it forces both sides to work toward agreements, and it forces both sides to give due diligence to each issue. Since the arbitrator must select one of the two packages, both sides understand that they can lose across the board. This often is ample motivation to move closer to an agreement.

There is some question as to whether this process is the most equitable. As established, the arbitrator is unbiased and attempts to pursue an outcome that is fair and reasonable to all parties. However, it should be noted that in most states each side must approve of the arbitrator. When approving an arbitrator both sides will examine potential arbitrators' records—how they have decided in previous negotiations. Unions will not approve an arbitrator who is perceived to have favored management too often, and management will not approve an arbitrator who is seen as deciding in favor of unions too frequently. Arbitrators, in order to remain employed, must maintain a record where about half of their decisions favor each side. This ultimately can affect individual decisions where decisions are made in order to maintain this balance as opposed to the merits of the issue. This problem may be more critical in the issue-by-issue or final issue-by-issue forms of binding arbitration. Unconsciously, the arbitrator may rule in favor of one party because he or she ruled in favor of the other party in another issue. When this occurs, the arbitration process has been circumvented, at least to some extent.

MEET-AND-CONFER The **meet-and-confer model** is similar to the binding arbitration model. Here, police officers are allowed to form and join a union or collective bargaining entity and negotiate with management. However, management is legally obligated only to meet and confer with the employee group. There is no mechanism to resolve impasses on issues. When there is an impasse, the employer can unilaterally implement its best offer to the employees. Basically, officers must accept what the government offers. Management must accomplish two tasks. First, management has to meet with the union in a timely manner. That is, when the union requests a meeting, the employer must make reasonable accommodations and meet with the union representatives. Second, management must negotiate with union representatives and attempt to agree on matters of concern to the union. Although management should negotiate in good faith, management does not have an obligation or often the motivation to accept the union's proposals. At best, this model results in officers being able to convey their concerns to management, and management providing officers with information about the department's operation. This sharing of information may allow the two sides to come to a better understanding about all the issues.

BARGAINING NOT REQUIRED There are twelve states that have the **bargaining not required model**. In these states, collective bargaining has not been authorized by the state, or such labor practices have been deemed unconstitutional. For example, Indiana passed a statute allowing police officers to bargain collectively, but the courts later ruled the statute unconstitutional. There are cases where some cities or counties in these states voluntarily have enacted some form of collective bargaining, usually in the form of meet and confer, for their employees.

The absence of any form of bargaining results in a lack of communications between police administrators and rank-and-file officers. It is important for management to become aware of officers' problems and concerns. If a police department has a negotiation process in place it would have an impact on administrative responses to problems and ultimately officer job satisfaction. If a department does not have collective bargaining, it should have some mechanism to poll officers to identify issues so that they can be addressed. At the same time, supervisors and managers should monitor the morale of their units and personnel to identify problems and take corrective actions.

POLICE UNION CONTRACTS

The result of negotiations between the union and the governmental entity is a contract or memorandum of understanding. As the title implies, it is binding on both parties, and essentially, has the force of law. That is, unless otherwise agreed upon, all parties must abide by the contract's provisions. Should either side, management or the union, propose a change, it cannot be made unless management and the union both agree to the change. When there is a dispute over the interpretation of the contract or its administration, the question is sorted out by an arbitrator or sometimes in the courts.

Union contracts must fall within the purview of any governing state statutes. For example, states that allow collective bargaining for police officers require a no-strike clause in the contract or strikes are specifically prohibited by the governing statute. Statutes may also be restrictive, by detailing items that are not negotiable and those work conditions that must be bargained. As a result, there generally are three classes of bargaining areas. First, mandatory subjects are those conditions that must be bargained by the union and political entity. Second, are illegal subjects, which cannot be negotiated. These areas, such as right to strike, generally are prohibited by statute. State legislatures often recognize that police administrators must have the flexibility to efficiently and effectively administer their departments and establish these illegal or non-negotiable subjects, which are often referred to as management prerogatives. Management prerogatives include things such as determining: (1) the number of police officers, (2) the police organization, (3) work standards, (4) the shift configuration for units in the department, (5) the number of officers assigned to various units in the department, and (6) the hiring, promoting, and transferring of officers within the department. Third, are permissible subjects, which are areas that can be negotiated by the two parties. The mandatory, illegal, and permissible negotiation areas vary from state to state and even across departments within a state depending on statutes and policies within a particular jurisdiction.

As noted above, the contract is a binding legal document. As such, it must be written with precision. There can be no misinterpretation since any misunderstandings may result in grievances or some form of arbitration. Figure 11-2 provides an example of the various elements in a hypothetical police department union contract. Notice that the contract is extensive and addresses numerous areas.

One point of contention in collective bargaining is who is covered by the contract. This is a point of negotiation. For example, are sergeants covered by the contract? Generally, this is specified in the contract itself. When unions only represent certain employees in a department, it usually results in multiple unions. For example, some large police departments have unions for (1) officers, (2) sergeants, (3) lieutenants, (4) captains, and (5) civilian personnel. Multiple unions compound management's problems when attempting to solve personnel and operational issues.

GRIEVANCES AND APPEALS

Conflicts and disagreements exist in every organization, including police departments. Such conflicts may occur between officers or between officers and their superiors. Many police departments have grievance procedures that are used to mediate such conflicts. In unionized departments, there generally is a provision in the contract that outlines how grievances are handled. All police departments should have a formalized grievance procedure to adjudicate grievances. This allows for problems to be aired and rectified with minimum negative impact on the department and its morale.

The purpose of grievance procedures is to establish a fair and expeditious process for handling employee disputes that are not disciplinary in nature. Grievance procedures often involve collective bargaining issues, conditions of employment, or employer-employee relations. **Grievances** may cover a broad range of issues, including salaries, overtime, leave, hours of work, allowances, retirement, opportunity for advancement, performance evaluations, workplace conditions, tenure, disciplinary actions, supervisory methods, and administrative practices.

The preferred method for settling officers' grievances is through informal discussion. The employee explains his or her grievance to the immediate supervisor. An important aspect of supervision involves allowing employees to vent their frustrations, because most complaints can be handled through informal discussions. Those complaints that cannot be dealt with informally are usually handled through a more formal grievance process, as described next. A formal grievance begins with the employee submitting the grievance in writing to the immediate supervisor, as illustrated in Figure 11-3.

The process for formally handling grievances will vary among agencies and may involve several levels of action. Following is an example of how a grievance may proceed:

Level I: A grievance is submitted in writing to the unit commander after informal discussions with the supervisor have failed to resolve the issue. The commander will be given five days to respond to the employee's grievance. If the employee is dissatisfied with the outcome, the grievance moves to the next level.

Level II: At this level, the grievance proceeds to the chief of police, who will be given a specified time (usually five days) to render a decision. In unionized departments, grievances often go directly to the police chief without first being examined by the unit commander.

Level III: If the employee is not satisfied with the chief's decision, the grievance may proceed to the city or county manager, as is appropriate. The manager will usually meet with the employee and/or representatives from the bargaining association, if the department is unionized, and attempt to resolve the matter. An additional 5 to 10 days is usually allowed for the manager to render a decision. In non-union police departments, the city manager generally makes a final determination. Some jurisdictions allow the grievance outcome to be appealed to the city council.

Level IV: In unionized police departments, if the grievance is still not resolved, either party may request that the matter be submitted to arbitration. **Arbitration** involves a neutral, outside person, often selected from a list of arbitrators from the Federal Mediation and Conciliation Service. An arbitrator will conduct a hearing, listen to both parties, and usually reach a decision within 20 to 30 days. The decision of the arbitrator can be final and binding. This does not prohibit the employee from appealing the decision to a state court.

Police Department
Formal Grievance Form

Grievance #____________

Employee Name: ____________ Work Phone: ____________
Department Assigned: ____________
Date of Occurrence: ____________
Location of Occurrence: ____________

Name of: 1. Department Head: ____________
2. Division Head: ____________
3. Immediate Supervisor: ____________

Statement of Grievance: ____________

Witnesses: ____________

What article(s) and or section(s) of the labor agreement of rules and regulations do you believe have been violated?____________

What remedy are you requesting? ____________

Employee Signature Signature of Labor Representative

FIGURE 11-3 Employee Grievance Form

The actions of supervisors in dealing with grievances are vital to their successful resolution. Failure to act on grievances quickly may result in serious morale problems within an agency. Snow (1990) offered some helpful advice for supervisors when dealing with employee grievances:

Give employees your attention. Grievances are important to officers and must be dealt with quickly so that officers do not think that their concerns are being ignored.

Let officers vent. Do not interrupt officers while they are expressing their grievances. Let them fully explain their concerns and never let them think that you have already made a decision.

Search for the facts. Separate facts from rumors and half-truths. Search for the underlying causes of problems—small issues often are symptoms of a larger hidden problem.

Seek the advice of peers. Talk to other supervisors or experienced officers who may have dealt with similar issues and find out what their solutions were.

Do not trivialize grievances. Grievances are often emotional and volatile issues and should be treated with dignity and respect, regardless of their veracity.

Explain your decision. Take the time to explain the logic and reasoning of your decision with the employee. Even if an officer does not agree with a decision, he or she may accept it based on your explanation and reasoning.

End on a positive note. Often, an officer only wants someone to talk to and listen to about the complaint. Supervisors should attempt to conclude interviews on a positive note and with some resolution in mind.

CASE STUDIES

Following are two case studies that allow the reader to consider some police management-labor problems and possible solutions as they concern this chapter's content.

Case Study #1

Repressing the Rumor Mill

The chief of police chairs a monthly meeting involving both union and command personnel to discuss issues that concern both sides and in an attempt to quash any departmental rumors before they adversely impact morale. The meetings have been ongoing for about six months, and they are cordial and productive in nature. Yet, no notes have ever been taken to document the discussions held. Today, however, the chief expresses a concern to the group that while the meetings appear to be going well and many issues are being resolved, the rumor mill seems to have become rampant with misinformation—including threats of grievances about perceived issues within all ranks. The chief is obviously very concerned and frustrated, and asks that both the union president and command staff discuss ways in which communication may be improved to reduce these rumors and the threats of grievances.

Questions for Discussion

1. What might be some of the underlying reasons for the obvious breakdown in communications among the officers?
2. What mechanisms could be put in place to resolve the rumor and grievance issues?
3. Whose responsibility is it to resolve these issues?

Case Study #2

Breach of Contract or Administrative Prerogative?

The new police association president is in a meeting with the chief of police to discuss a concern regarding supervisors' treatment of union representatives. The situation is as follows: officers bid on the basis of seniority every six months for their duty shifts, and one team of six officers is composed of three union representatives. The supervisors for that shift have taken it upon themselves to move some of the officers to different teams, so that no one team is adversely impacted by their absence or work relating to union representation responsibilities. (Union representatives are officers designated by the association to accompany officers during interviews relating to internal and external complaints so as to ensure the officers' rights are protected. The officer's right to have a union representative present during these interviews is provided by state law and the union's labor contract.) The association president complains to the chief that such movement of the union officers is a violation of the contract. The chief counters that this is an issue his command staff has struggled with over the years, and that there are three other teams with similar situations that are under consideration for union representative movement. The chief also says that he could invoke his management rights under the contract and be very tough on this issue, but would rather work with the president on some alternatives.

Questions for Discussion

1. What are the different issues and concerns that were created by moving the officers?
2. What options would you suggest to alleviate the problem of multiple representatives assigned to one team?
3. What process do you believe must be followed to pursue your options?

Summary

This chapter examined police collective bargaining and unions. The police labor movement has a profound impact on police services, supervision, and management. As noted, police involvement in collective bargaining has a long and fractured history. Police strikes in the early 1900s resulted in a long-term prohibition of police unions. It took several decades for the states to allow police officers to bargain collectively. There are a number of different unions representing police officers—some of which are traditional unions, and others that are fraternal organizations that have evolved into unions.

There are three collective bargaining models, ranging from no collective bargaining to binding arbitration. Some states have not allowed the police and other public employees to be engaged in collective bargaining. The binding arbitration model gives police officers more input into management and their compensation and work conditions. Collective bargaining often places a great deal of pressure on supervisors and managers as they often are caught in the middle between officers and governmental administrators and legislative bodies. Supervisors and managers are responsible for ensuring that police work is conducted effectively and efficiently. This is not always an easy task given that the collective bargaining process is an extremely emotional process since it affects officers' livelihoods.

Finally, the grievance procedure process was examined. The grievance procedure is a formal process that allows subordinate officers to air problems and concerns to management. It forces administrators to abide by laws, policies, and the contract. Moreover, it can have a positive effect on the department by forcing organizational change. Police departments are bureaucracies and it is important for them to abide by guidelines.

Items for Review

1. How did police unions evolve?
2. What was the Boston police strike; how did it affect the police labor movement?
3. To what extent is collective bargaining authorized in the U.S.?
4. What are some of the largest and most prominent police unions in the U.S.?
5. Relations between both police management and union leaders could be described in what way?
6. What are the primary issues that occur when police officers are negotiating with government bodies?
7. What are the three models of collective bargaining?
8. What types of clauses or issues are generally found in a police labor contract?
9. What is a grievance, and how should supervisors deal with employees who have grievances?

References

Aitchison, W. (2004). *The rights of law enforcement officers*. Portland: LRIS.

Burpo, W. (1971). *The police labor movement: Problems and perspectives.* Springfield, IL: Charles C. Thomas.

DeLord, R. G. (2006a). *Disorganized labor: The mutinous side of police unions.* In U.S. Department of Justice, Office of Community Oriented Policing Services, *Police labor-management relations (Vol. I): Perspectives and practical solutions for implementing change, making reforms, and handling crises for managers and union leaders,* http://www.cops.usdoj.gov/files/ric/Publications/e07063417.pdf p. 39–44 (Accessed April 25, 2008).

DeLord, R. G. (2006b). *American policing: Launched in controversy and still controversial today*. In U.S. Department of Justice, Office of Community Oriented Policing Services, *Police labor-management relations (Vol. I): Perspectives and practical solutions for implementing change, making reforms, and handling crises for managers and union leaders,* http://www.cops.usdoj.gov/mime/open.pdf?Item=1856, pp. 13–18 (Accessed April 25, 2008).

DeLord, R. G., and Sanders, J. (2006). *Understanding the crosswinds from the community as they affect law enforcement*. In U.S. Department of Justice, Office of Community Oriented Policing Services, *Police labor-management relations (Vol. I): Perspectives and practical solutions for implementing change, making reforms, and handling crises for managers and union leaders,* http://www.cops.usdoj.gov/mime/open.pdf?Item=1856, pp. 7–12 (Accessed April 25, 2008).

Drake, J. (2007). Detectives vote no confidence in DA: Union leadership reacts to Boston jurisdiction issue. http://www.boston.com/news/local/articles/2007/09/21/detectives_vote_no_confidence_in_da/ (Accessed 4/23/08).

Hoover, L., Dowling, J. L., and Blair, G. (2006). *Management and labor in community policing: Charting a course*. In U.S. Department of Justice, Office of Community Oriented Policing Services, *Police labor-management relations (Vol. I): Perspectives and practical solutions for implementing change, making reforms, and handling crises for managers and union leaders,* http://www.cops.usdoj.gov/mime/open.pdf?Item=1856, pp. xix–xxix (Accessed April 25, 2008).

Levine, M. (1988). A historical overview of police unionization in the United States. *Police Journal*, 61: 334–343.

Melady, M. (2007). Police officers choose new union representation. http://www.masscops.com/content/view/52/2/ (Accessed 4/23/08).

O'Meilia, T. (2008). Palm Beach police union vote set. *PalmBeachPost.Com.* (Accessed 4/23/08).

Snow, R. (1990). A right to complain: Grievance procedures for small departments. *Law and Order* 5:39–41.

Ziskind, D. (1940). One thousand strikes of government employees. New York: Ayer.

PART THREE

Supervising Work of Police

CHAPTER 12

Deploying and Scheduling Personnel

Key Terms and Concepts

- Call management and prioritizing
- Calls for service (CFS)
- Circadian rhythm
- Computer-aided dispatch (CAD)
- Delayed response
- Determining patrol size
- Differential police response (DPR)
- Fair Labor Standards Act (FLSA)
- Foot patrol
- Kansas City patrol studies
- Managing overtime
- Military leave
- Patrol planning
- Reducing demands for police service
- Rotating shifts
- Shift configurations
- Shift work sleep disorder (SWSD)
- Split force
- Team policing

Learning Objectives

After reading this chapter, the student will:

- understand why patrol planning and resource allocation are key considerations in providing quality police service, and some common means of determining adequate patrol force size
- know of several key studies on the patrol function
- be able to explain whether or not it is necessary for officers to respond to all calls for service
- have an understanding of what shift schedules are most prominently used in policing, and some advantages of certain shift configurations over others
- know how shift work and scheduling can deprive officers of rest, and possibly result in fatigue and poor performance
- be informed about the unique nature of officer deployment under community policing
- understand problems concerning the supervisor's management of overtime work
- have a basic understanding of the Fair Labor Standards Act as well as labor unions' impact on officers' shift scheduling
- understand the rights of police officers being activated as full-time military personnel and the challenges faced by police departments they work for

We need a sense of value of time—that is, of the best way to divide one's time into one's activities.

—ARNOLD BENNET

INTRODUCTION

The police do not have the luxury of deciding whether or not to work around-the-clock shifts; police organizations are bound by their 24-hour, 7-days-per-week responsibility to the public to deploy officers to beats in shifts. Therefore, the scheduling and deployment of patrol officers are primary concerns for police administrators, middle managers, and supervisors alike, all of whom struggle on a daily basis with balancing the needs of officers with those of the department and the community. For these practitioners, ensuring complete shift coverage is a complex task. This chapter examines the issues surrounding the scheduling and deploying of police officers to satisfy departmental service delivery objectives.

These matters are approached from primarily a *qualitative* point of view, rather than one that is highly quantitative. It is assumed that the complex, quantitative aspects of deployment and scheduling can be accomplished or are greatly aided by computer software (discussed in the section on patrol planning), in-service training sessions for those persons already employed and having scheduling responsibilities, and available literature. Furthermore, once a police agency's executives adopt and implement a particular staffing pattern, that pattern is not likely to change often; therefore, supervisors and managers do not have to spend every duty day studying staffing schedules.

But what *does* change is the *philosophical,* or qualitative aspect of personnel deployment and scheduling. As will be seen, the current adoption of the community oriented policing and problem solving (COPPS) strategy has fostered the need for greater examination, flexibility, and modification of personnel deployment. Once the COPPS philosophy is adopted, the task falls to the supervisor to see that personnel are deployed in keeping with the needs of that strategy and are given the necessary time to engage in COPPS activities.

This chapter first looks at the need for patrol planning, followed by an overview of some of the earlier studies of the patrol functions and some contemporary methods for determining the patrol force size and allocating resources. We then examine a question that is at the heart of police history: whether or not officers must respond to every call; here we also look at several alternative patrol responses that can free officers from the burden of having to go to every home and business and handle every call.

Next is a look at several aspects and configurations of shift schedules, including their characteristics and use; the advantages provided by some shift configurations over others; the effects of shift work and sleep deprivation on individual officer fatigue; a comparison of permanent and **rotating shifts**; and applicable federal labor laws as well as union considerations. We then discuss some deployment strategies, particularly given the unique requirements under the COPPS initiative. After a brief section on supervisors' management of overtime, we consider the effects of **military leave** on police agencies, and the legal rights of officers who return from active military duty. Two case studies conclude the chapter.

PATROL PLANNING

The largest, most costly, and most visible function in a police agency is patrol. Yet patrol typically receives the least amount of planning or analysis. As an example, patrol beats are all too often created by convenient streets, railroad tracks, rivers, and so forth, rather than by thoughtful planning and analysis of officer workload by geographical area. Few police agencies pay regular attention to evaluating and adjusting patrol plans to meet service demands. Instead, patrol is often the first division for which a police administration seeks to reduce personnel in order to enhance specialized units or to create new programs. This practice often leaves the patrol division in need of personnel and often results in morale problems and unnecessary delays in responding to **calls for service (CFS)**. The unfortunate consequence of this situation is that supervisors are left to manage the demands of patrol by reacting to crises rather than by thoughtful planning.

Planning is an important, powerful tool for helping police managers cope with the backlash of shrinking budgets and accompanying personnel cutbacks that have plagued police agencies since the 1970s. **Patrol planning** enables managers to properly assess service demands so that resources may be appropriately allocated across shifts and proportionate to workload. Computer software can design various combinations of shift patterns; print staffing reports for up to a year; provide quick access to all employee information, such as seniority date, shift preferences, and phone number; see an entire month's shifts at a glance; and quickly edit assignments. Several private corporations now produce and advertise such software in professional trade magazines, such as *The Police Chief,* published by the International Association of Chiefs of Police, and *Law and Order* magazine. Administrators and supervisors who want to maximize their resources would do well to consider investing in such software.

A lack of proper patrol planning may be attributed to several factors. First, if a police agency lacks a planning unit, planning (aside from that involving the budget) is usually nonexistent. The lack of data also presents a problem. Few police agencies have sufficient data for analyzing their CFS, time spent on calls by officers, time that officers are available for CFS and other work, the number of units assigned, and so on. Even when this data exists, few agencies have the trained staff to conduct in-depth analyses. The natural resistance to new ideas by some people may also create barriers to change. Many agencies are tradition bound and resist any new approaches to change patrol practices.

The primary purpose of patrol planning is to keep supervisors and managers apprised of how resources are being utilized. This enables them to make informed decisions about departmental operations and also to develop future plans. A patrol plan should be based on an analysis of data concerning the tasks that officers perform during their shifts of duty. These plans should also be flexible and constantly reviewed to meet the changing needs and goals of an organization.

EARLY STUDIES OF THE PATROL FUNCTION

To set the stage for much of what follows, we first look at some of the major research efforts and findings concerning the patrol function. Beginning in the mid-1970s, police departments began to question the efficacy and methods of patrol, and whether a patrol officer's response to every CFS in non-emergency situations was needed in order to produce effective outcomes (discussed below). Several studies concerning the patrol function were conducted and greatly affected our assumptions concerning patrol:

Kansas City Preventive Patrol Experiment. Normal, proactive (saturation), and reactive (emergencies only) patrols were conducted in 15 of 24 beats in the city's south patrol division. The normal (control) strategy involved conventional single patrol car response to CFS; the proactive beats had increased police preventive patrol and visibility by tripling the number of cars on patrol; and the reactive strategy virtually eliminated patrol cars. No significant differences in crime reduction were found in any of the experimental beat areas, regardless of the level of patrol. This experiment suggested that random police patrol was not a factor in deterring crime (Kelling, 1974).

Kansas City Response Time Study. This study evaluated whether rapid response to calls increased the likelihood of arresting offenders. It was discovered that the most important factor in arresting offenders was not the speed at which the police responded, but the delay in calling the police. Simply, the fastest response could not compensate for delays in reporting the incident (Bieck and Kessler, 1977).

Team Policing Experiment. **Team policing** was a popular reform effort that sought to improve crime prevention and reduction efforts by assigning teams of officers to a particular neighborhood and giving them responsibility for all services in that area. An evaluation of its implementation in seven cities in the United States suggested that the experiment was largely a failure. Findings revealed that poor planning and implementation by chief administrators, confusion by officers about what they were supposed to do, and resistance by middle managers who resented sharing their authority with sergeants and officers contributed to its failure (Sherman, 1973).

One- Versus Two-Officer Patrol Cars. In a study of the effectiveness of one- versus two-officer patrol cars, Hale (1981) suggested that officer productivity and operational efficiency were in fact increased by using *one-officer* patrol units. Officer safety concerns can be addressed by establishing a policy that requires the dispatching of two cars to high-risk CFS. Wrobleski and Hess (1993) added that one-officer patrol vehicles can patrol twice the area, and that solo officers are generally more cautious and more attentive to their patrol duties since they do not have a partner to engage in conversation.

Newark and Flint Foot Patrol Studies. Evidence on the effects of **foot patrol** is somewhat mixed. In Newark, New Jersey, findings suggested that citizen fear of crime was reduced while citizen satisfaction with the police increased; however, foot patrols had no significant impact on reported crime or victimization (Police Foundation, 1981). In Flint, Michigan, findings suggested that the neighborhood foot patrol program appeared to decrease crime, increase citizens' satisfaction with the police, and reduce public fear

The NYPD utilizes the COMPSTAT (computer statistics) process, meeting monthly to review crime trends, plan tactics, and allocate resources.
(Courtesy NYPD Police Unit)

(Trojanowicz, 1986). As a result, these findings should be interpreted with caution until more information is made available.

RESOURCE ALLOCATION

Another important part of police leadership lies in how to best allocate resources, especially when new resources are difficult to obtain and the police are being asked to do more with less. Next, we examine some considerations for determining how large the patrol force should be, and how patrol resources should be deployed.

Determining Patrol Force Size

The collection and analysis of data are the foundation of proper patrol deployment. Unfortunately, as mentioned earlier, many police agencies do not adhere to such rational and scientific approaches. Three crude methods are used by police departments to determine resource needs (Roberg and Kuykendall, 1995:284):

Intuitive. This is basically educated guesswork based on the experience and judgment of police managers. It is probably the most commonly used method for small agencies when the number of incidents and officers available is so low that more analytical analysis may not be necessary for determining when and where officers should be deployed.

Workload. This requires comprehensive information, including standards of expected performance, community expectations, and the prioritization of police activities. Although rarely used by an entire police agency, it is most often used for determining resource needs for patrol or specific programs, such as crime prevention.

Comparative. Often the most common method used by police agencies, the comparative method is based on a comparison of agencies by number of officers per 1,000 residents. Data is available in the *Uniform Crime Reports* (UCR), published annually (U.S. Department of Justice, Federal Bureau of Investigation, 2007). UCR data reveals a national average of 3.0 full-time, sworn police officers per 1,000 residents in the United States; the range is 2.4 officers in communities with populations of 25,000 to 99,999 residents to 3.8 officers in cities with 250,000 or more residents; surprisingly, perhaps, suburban and rural counties averaged 4.2 officers.

There are higher-level, very quantitative methods for determining patrol force size and allocation that will not be covered here. Computer models are available to assist with these endeavors, for calculating such factors as:

- Total numbers of CFS
- Officer-initiated activities
- Administrative activities
- Number of CFS by hour, shift, beat, and reporting area
- Average dispatch delay (in minutes)
- Average travel time (in minutes)
- Average on-scene time (in minutes)
- Average service time (in minutes)
- Average number of backup patrol units per call
- Probability that all units are busy
- Average number of free units

Car Planning and Computer Modeling

After patrol personnel have been assigned according to needs of time and location, the supervisor or manager must deploy them to beats or patrol car districts. Separate car plans should be established for each shift to equalize workloads for all officers. The boundaries for the beats in a six-car plan on the day shift might be different from the boundaries in a six-car plan on the night shift because of changing needs at various times of the day. For example, a congested industrial area might present quite different problems on the day shift from those on the night shift when the businesses are closed (Iannone and Iannone, 2001). And, as we have seen earlier, the number of patrol vehicles in use will also vary by time of day and day of week.

The car plan in use will normally be dictated by the number of officers on duty and available for field patrol. If two-officer units are used, adjustments will be necessary. Using one-officer units, a nine-car plan will be required to cover nine beats, unless two of the beats use two-officer patrol units, in which case 11 officers would be required.

Ideally, patrol districts should be grouped into beats so that each will contain as nearly as practicable an equal percentage of the total police work. Each beat in a 10-car plan would theoretically cover 10 percent of the work, each beat in a 5-car plan would ideally cover 20 percent of the work, and so on. By trying out different beats according to ideal percentage of workload and most desirable boundaries, the supervisor will eventually develop a variety of reasonably effective car plans from which he or she can select those that are most workable. Note that beats will not be equal in area, since area, as represented by street miles, is only one factor used in determining relative need for patrol (Iannone and Iannone, 2001).

Computer-based analysis and allocation models were developed as early as the 1960s. These models assist administrators who often struggle with shift-related issues, such as fixed versus rotating schedules, one- versus two-officer cars, and compressed schedules. Some of the first programs developed were the Patrol Car Allocation Model (PCAM), by the RAND Corporation; Hypercube Queueing Model, by Public Systems Evaluation, Inc.; and Patrol Plan/Beat Plan, by the Institute of Public Program Analysis. These automated systems were capable of performing a number of staff distribution functions and could simplify the process of determining allocation needs and designing beats (Levine and McEwen, 1985). The Statistical Package for Social Sciences (SPSS) can also be used to analyze workload and develop schedules. This comprehensive statistical package is personal–computer-based, inexpensive, and simple to run with some training. It may also be merged with mapping programs that are commonly used by police to obtain graphic representations of crime issues (e.g., location, population density, and reports of drug activity).

Clearly, a comprehensive workload analysis provides the foundation for determining allocation needs and deployment schemes. It provides the basic information for determining the number of patrol officers who are required to staff shifts each day of the week. Once an analysis is completed, managers can select the most appropriate deployment schemes to attain departmental objectives.

MUST OFFICERS RESPOND TO EVERY CALL?

Reducing Demands for Police Services

Our discussion thus far assumes that every CFS requires the response of a uniformed patrol officer. But is that necessary? Increasing workloads, shrinking budgets, and increased public demands for service are key factors in police administrators' decisions to employ alternative methods for handling non-emergency CFS (see Exhibit 12-1). Indeed, dispatching a patrol unit to the scene of every call seriously hampers COPPS efforts—and many of those calls could be handled by alternative call-taking methods, as discussed next (also see Peak and Glensor, 2008). These alternative response methods are commonly referred to as *differential police response*. They reduce patrol officers' workloads, allowing them to spend more time with directed patrol activities, initial investigations, case follow-up, and neighborhood problem-solving activities.

One of the major purposes of developing alternative response strategies is that those calls requiring rapid mobile response can receive priority, while other calls are handled by methods that both satisfy the citizen and accomplish the needs of the department. Differential response also provides a tremendous opportunity for administrators to gain some control over limited resources. The potential savings in officers' hours can have a significant impact on allocation and deployment.

One way to reduce police calls for service is to eliminate the calls from initially coming in. Exhibit 12-1 shows what the Akron, Ohio, Police Department has done to reduce high demands for service placed on its officers.

EXHIBIT 12-1 Akron's Approach to Reducing Demand for Police Service

Recently the Akron, Ohio, Police Department, working with the community, established a program to reduce the number of calls for service (CFS) for patrol officers so they could better use their time proactively patrolling and solving problems. (Although this exhibit would fit very well in Chapter 4, on community policing and problem solving (COPPS), it also shows how demands on police time can be addressed.)

Following are some of the projects that were undertaken:

- New beat lines were created—a major change, since this had not been done in more than 60 years. A committee of eight officers, led by a sergeant, analyzed CFS data and performed driving time trials to determine response times; the result is balanced workloads in the beat sectors.
- Repeat calls research showed that 37 addresses required nearly 2,000 CFS per year; officers analyzed each site and developed specific strategies to reduce CFS; this resulted in a 57 percent reduction in CFS for these problem addresses.
- Finding that people living in rental properties were committing most of the neighborhood crimes and tracing ownership records through city health department records, a list of property owners was compiled. Two hundred owners attended subsequent meetings and were informed about landlord-tenant rights: screening applicants, evicting criminals, and abating nuisances.
- False alarms were a drain on resources, so officers met with the city licensing bureau and determined that many alarm users were not licensed. Officers worked with property owners to bring those systems into compliance and began levying fines for false alarms; such calls were reduced by 10 percent.
- CFS relating to prostitution were increasing, so police formed a committee with the community. Judges and prosecutors expedited the cases, the jail created more space for offenders, and enforcement and undercover efforts were increased. Arrests increased by 26 percent and prostitution complaints decreased by 15 percent.
- Residential speeding created a high number of CFS, so the department initiated a warning letter program; police encouraged area residents to obtain license plate numbers of speeding vehicles and provide them to police, who sent the vehicle owners a letter informing them of the complaint, thus reducing speeding CFS.

By engaging the community and focusing their efforts in these areas, which composed about one-fourth of all CFS, the department has been able to significantly reduced CFS, work smarter, and give officers more time to engage in other proactive and problem solving activities.

Source: Adapted from Michael Matulavich, "A Comprehensive Approach to Reducing Demand for Services," *The Police Chief*, April 2006, pp. 66–71.

Call Management and Prioritizing CFS

Call management is a process for screening and prioritizing CFS. Today most police agencies have **computer-aided dispatch (CAD)** systems that are capable of prioritizing calls by their importance. Obviously, more dangerous and in-progress calls such as robberies and assaults would receive the highest priority and an immediate response from patrol units, while a general request for information may bring a delayed response. Police departments have clearly established dispatch protocols that determine the priority of call responses, such as the following:

Priority 1: Danger to life and/or property is imminent, or a crime of a serious nature is in progress. Examples include an armed robbery in progress, a shooting with the suspect on the scene, a major accident, and so on.

Priority 2: Threat to a person or property is possible or a breach of the peace is occurring. Examples include a loud argument or verbal disturbance, an unruly shoplifter in the custody of store security, loud music or party, and so on.

Priority 3: No threat to life or to property exists, and a delay in response would not cause undue inconvenience to the citizen. Examples include theft of property that occurred days ago, a request for a house watch, a dead animal in the road, and so on.

Oftentimes the volume of CFS will exceed the number of personnel who are available to respond. In this case, police agencies are forced to hold the calls and delay their response. Policies generally will guide the amount of time in which a call may be delayed. For example, Priority 1 calls may require an immediate response in all cases, Priority 2 calls can be held for 15 minutes, and Priority 3 can be held for 30 minutes. When a pending call cannot be assigned to an officer within the established time limit, it is usually the responsibility of the dispatcher to notify a field supervisor or watch commander. The supervisor may need to direct communications to relieve an

Computer aided dispatch (CAD) systems prioritize calls based on their seriousness, and send assigned beat officers to handle the call for service.
(*Courtesy Citrus Heights, California, P.D.*)

officer from a nonessential activity, such as lunch or another less serious call, or to hold the call for the next available officer.

Other Alternative Responses

A number of alternatives are available to reduce officer workload and increase productivity, producing more time for officers to perform other activities. They have been developed and tested by the National Institute of Justice, and they include telephone report units, delayed mobile response (stacking calls, setting appointments), walk-in reports, and use of nonsworn personnel in lieu of patrol officers (such as civilian evidence technicians, animal control officers, community service specialists). Each is discussed briefly next.

TELEPHONE REPORTING One of the most effective call alternative strategies for relieving officer workload is the Telephone Report Unit (TRU). Reports are handled over the telephone rather than by a patrol officer dispatched to the scene. TRUs provide several advantages for police agencies and the public. For example, a Priority 3 call (discussed earlier) can take 45 to 60 minutes for an officer to respond to, while a telephone report can be handled in 10 to 15 minutes and at the convenience of the caller. A telephone reporting unit may handle as much as 25 to 50 percent of an agency's non-investigative reports. This accounts for a considerable amount of the workload and frees officers in the field to engage more in community problem solving.

In order to be effective, a call classification system and prioritization scheme are needed so that call takers can properly classify incoming calls. A training program is also required for call takers, dispatchers, and officers who must be familiar with the new procedures. Evaluations of this approach have consistently shown it to be efficient and without a loss in citizen satisfaction. In addition to the volume of work that can be handled by TRUs, experience has shown that they provide major savings in the amount of time taken to complete a report and also save money on vehicle maintenance costs. They also afford sworn officers more time for self-initiated activities and arrests (Levine and McEwen, 1985).

DELAYED RESPONSE **Delayed response** means that the presence of a police officer is required at the scene, but the incident is sufficiently minor in nature that a rapid dispatch is not necessary. Such instances include "cold" larcenies and burglaries, unoccupied suspicious vehicle calls, and vandalism calls. The trend today is to develop formal delayed response strategies that specify the types of calls that can be delayed, and for how long. Factors to be considered are the seriousness of the call, presence or absence of injuries, and amount of damage. Most departments' policies state a maximum delay time, such as 30 or 45 minutes, after which the closest available unit is assigned to the call (Levine and McEwen, 1985).

Although the delayed response does not directly reduce officer workload, it does help make the existing workload more manageable. It increases the likelihood that officers will receive calls in their area of assignment, resulting in fewer cross-beat dispatches, and prevents officers from being interrupted while on another assignment (such as COPPS activities).

The call taker must inform the citizen that an officer will not arrive immediately; studies have found that once the call taker informs the citizen of the expected police arrival time, citizen satisfaction is not adversely affected by the delay (Levine and McEwen, 1985).

WALK-IN/MAIL-IN/WEB REPORTING Many police agencies also have instituted programs that encourage citizens to come to the nearest police facility at their convenience to file a report, or the police may send a report package to citizens to be completed and returned by mail. Most recently, agencies are utilizing their Web sites to allow Internet reporting of certain crimes. The recent trend by police agencies to decentralize patrol operations through various COPPS initiatives has resulted in an increase in neighborhood police mini-stations. These provide an excellent and convenient place for citizens to complete walk-in reports or to pick up or deliver reporting packages.

USE OF NONSWORN PERSONNEL The use of volunteer and nonsworn personnel to handle nonemergency CFS has gained considerable popularity over the years. Many agencies utilize volunteers who have been trained in citizen police academies, reserve police academies, and senior volunteer programs to handle a bulk of the workload traditionally handled by uniformed officers.

Another concept used by many police agencies to reduce patrol officer workload is the Community Service Officer (CSO) program, using nonsworn personnel in the field and to respond to CFS, thus eliminating the requirement for an officer's presence. A CSO may engage in traffic accident investigations, take vandalism reports, perform parking enforcement, conduct basic crime scene investigations and collect evidence, dust for fingerprints, and perform other related duties. In some agencies, CSOs also staff mini-stations to handle telephone and mail-in reporting requests, again eliminating the need for an officer at these locations.

The civilianization of police agencies is another area that should be explored. It makes little sense to assign a fully trained and qualified police officer to administrative or support duties when those responsibilities can be better handled by nonsworn personnel. Some of the areas being civilianized in police agencies include dispatching, research and planning, crime analysis, finance, parking enforcement, custody, technical/computer support, and animal control.

SHIFT SCHEDULING

As noted above, police organizations are bound by their 24-hour responsibility to public problems to deploy officers to beats in shifts. However, research on shift work strongly suggests that administrators should carefully consider the benefits and hazards of various shift schemes—and supervisors need to closely monitor the alertness of their officers. First, human beings are naturally day oriented or diurnal in their activity patterns. Shift work disrupts the body's complex biological clock, known as the **circadian rhythm**, and can result in stress-related illnesses, fatigue-induced accidents, family crises, and lower life expectancy. Furthermore, there is a higher probability of accidents and errors during shifts when officers may be fatigued, several of which are discussed below; indeed, night shift work has been associated with three times as many on-the-job accidents (Rosenberg, 2005).

Different Shift Configurations in Use

Prior to examining the nature and implications of shift scheduling on agencies and officers, it may help to first see a breakdown of the shifts that police are currently working. A recent survey of 287 police agencies by the Police Foundation resulted in the following information (Amendola et al., 2006):

- The more prevalent shift length was the traditional 8-hour shift (40.1 percent). However, for the large agencies (201 officers or more) the 10-hour shift was the most common (35 percent), but that is closely followed by the 8-hour shift (32.5 percent).
- While 12-hour shifts are increasingly attractive to many people and agencies, they are most likely to be implemented in smaller agencies (50 to 100 officers) (28.5 percent); only 19.5 percent of the mid-size (101 to 200 officers) and 15 percent of larger agencies have done so.

TABLE 12-1 Distribution of Shift Length by Agency Size

Number Sworn Officers	Total	8 HR (%)	9 HR (%)	10 HR (%)	11 HR (%)	12 HR (%)	Multiple* (%)
50 to 100	165 (58.5)	68 (41.2)	3 (2.0)	37 (22.4)	–	47 (28.5)	10 (6.1)
101 to 200	82 (28.6)	34 (41.5)	2 (2.4)	27 (32.9)	1 (1.2)	16 (19.5)	2 (2.4)
201+	40 (13.9)	13 (32.5)	–	14 (35.0)	2 (5.0)	6 (15.0)	5 (12.5)
Totals	287	115 (40.1)	5 (1.7)	78 (27.2)	3 (1.0)	69 (24.0)	17 (5.9)

*Agency has a combination of shift lengths (8, 9, 10, 11 and/or 12 hour shifts)

Source: Amendola, K. L., Hamilton, E. E., and Wyckoff, L. A. (2006). Law enforcement shift schedules: Results of a random nationwide survey of police agencies. http://www.policefoundation.org/pdf/ShiftScheduleSurveyResults.pdf (Accessed October 8, 2007).

- Rotating shifts are still employed to a significant extent (46 percent). Again, these shifts are more prevalent in small agencies (52.1 percent) and become less common as agency size increases (41.5 and 30 percent, respectively).
- While some agencies use multiple shift lengths, this is most common in larger agencies (12.5 percent), possibly due to the greater flexibility of having more staff.
- Less traditional shift configurations—such as 9- and 11-hour shifts—are very uncommon, with less than 3 percent of agencies using them.

Table 12-1 shows the distribution of shift length by agency size; Table 12-2 shows the distribution of shift length by agency size and by rotating and fixed shifts.

TABLE 12-2 Distribution of Shift Type by Agency Size

Number Sworn Officers	Total (%)	Fixed Shift (%)	Rotating Shift (%)	No Response
50 to 100	165 (58.5)	79 (47.9)	86 (52.1)	7
101 to 200	82 (28.6)	48 (58.5)	34 (41.5)	2
201+	40 (13.9)	28 (70.0)	12 (30.0)	2
Totals	287 (100)	155 (54.0)	132 (46.0)	11

Source: Amendola, K. L., Hamilton, E. E., and Wyckoff, L. A. (2006). Law enforcement shift schedules: Results of a random nationwide survey of police agencies. http://www.policefoundation.org/pdf/ShiftScheduleSurveyResults.pdf (Accessed October 8, 2007).

Characteristics of the Major Shift Schedules

As will be seen, each compressed schedule carries certain benefits and, possibly, drawbacks. Of course, the supervisor's and manager's primary task considering a compressed schedule is that the schedule meet the needs of the department and employee. Following are some of the types of compressed work schedules that have been implemented and tested by agencies across the United States:

5-day, 8-hour schedule (5–2 [8]). As shown in Table 12-1, the 5–2 (8) work schedule remains the most common format used by police agencies (used by 40 percent of all agencies). Many jurisdictions schedule these shifts to run from 6 A.M. to P.M., 2 P.M. to 10 P.M., and 10 P.M. to 6 A.M., or something similar; this avoids having a shift change at midnight, when taverns and bars are emptying, and affords having the morning shift change completed prior to the increased work and school traffic. Also, some jurisdictions add an overlapping 7 P.M. to 3 A.M. shift to assist evening and night officers, again during the busiest time of their shifts-bars and taverns closing, and when buildings and residences are more prone to being burglarized under cover of darkness.

4-day, 10-hour schedule (4–3 [10]). Under the 4–3 (10) shift plan, officers work four 10-hour days per week, with three days off. The 10-hour shift configuration (and its three days off) is attractive for many officers but, as shown in Table 12-1, only about 27.2 percent of all agencies employ it. But perhaps there needs to be a greater appreciation of the overlapping nature of the 10-hour shifts, matching the number of officers on duty with the varying activity levels. More specifically, every police jurisdiction has certain times of the day when additional officers are needed. Some simple examples will better make the point (Oliver, 2005:104).

Assume that workload increases in a city every evening between 3 P.M. and 9 P.M. Ten-hour shifts can be scheduled to increase the coverage during that time by overlapping two of the three shifts, as shown below:

Day shift:	11 A.M. to 9 P.M.
Evening shift:	3 P.M. to 1A.M.
Night shift:	1 A.M. to 11 A.M.

Note that the day shift and evening shifts overlap from 3 P.M. to 9 P.M., when there is the greatest period of activity. The number of officers on duty during this six-hour period would be doubled.

Another example concerns a mid-sized jurisdiction having two peak periods, during commute times, from 5 A.M. to 11 A.M., and from 3 P.M. to 9 P.M. This can be addressed as follows:

	Schedule One	**Schedule Two**
Day shift:	5 A.M. to 3 P.M.	11 A.M .to 9 P.M.
Evening shift	3 P.M. to 1 A.M.	3 P.M. to 1 A.M.
Night shift	1 A.M. to 11 A.M.	1 A.M. to 11 A.M.

In the first schedule, the night shift overlaps the day shift from 5 A.M. to 11 A.M. to add extra coverage during the morning peak; in the second schedule, the day shift overlaps the evening shift from 3 P.M. to 9 P.M. to add coverage for the evening peak. Note that 10-hour shifts can be operated with as little as five officers.

3-day, 12-hour schedule (3–4 [12]). The 3/12 plan, used in about a quarter of all agencies (see Table 12-1) fits neatly into a 24-hour day for scheduling. Normally, officers are assigned to work three days a week, with four days off for three weeks, and four days a week with three days off for the fourth week of a 28-day cycle. Again, proponents claim the benefits of increased productivity and employee morale as justification for 3/12 shifts (Schissler, 1996). Management voices concerns regarding increased fatigue and potential increased costs associated with the Fair Labor Standards Act, discussed later, as primary issues. Nonetheless, the 12-hour plan is enjoying increased support. It is

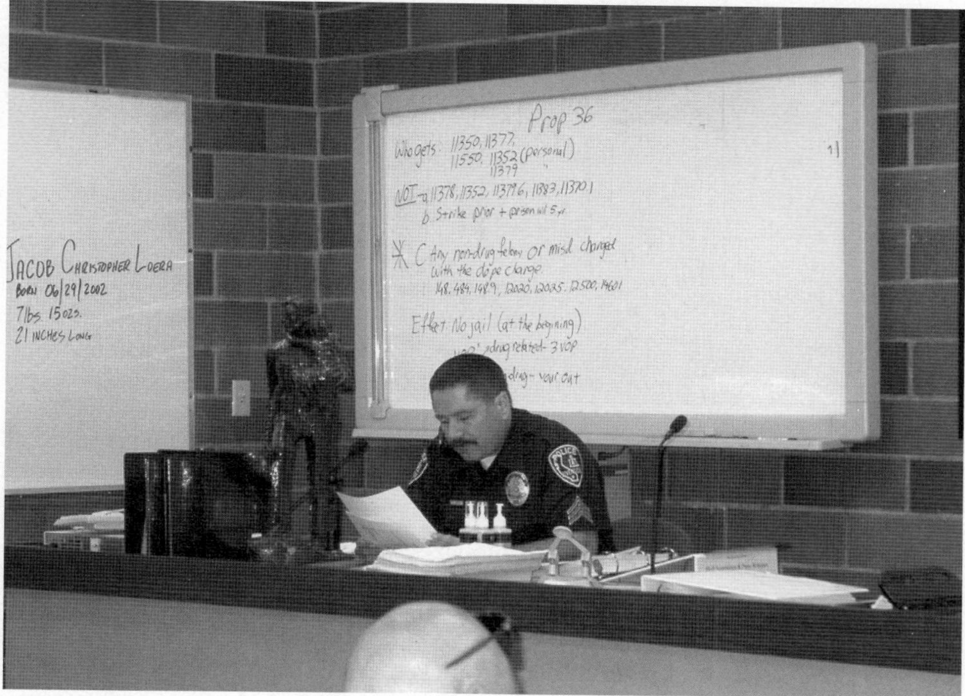

During briefing sessions at the beginning of each shift, supervisors must properly assign and deploy personnel.
(Courtesy Riverside, California, Police Department.)

touted by many agencies as resulting in higher officer morale and productivity, with reduced sick leave time taken.

5-day, 9-hour schedule (5–2 [9]). As shown in Table 12-1, 9- and 11-hour workdays are very uncommon in policing, with less than 3 percent of agencies using them. Where they are popular, it may be more so with nonuniformed assignments, such as detective units and administration.

No single shift-scheduling configuration fits all needs, nor would we recommend one shift pattern over the others. Administrators should decide on the shift that accomplishes a balance between organizational objectives and employee needs. Maintaining staffing levels, productivity, fatigue, equipment, and overtime costs should be evaluated carefully before deciding on a schedule.

Why Shift Matters: Effects of Shift Work and Sleep Deprivation on Officers

OFFICER FATIGUE: A NATIONAL REALITY Police around-the-clock responsibilities can obviously take a toll. Indeed, many people working or who have worked on the graveyard (night) shift and had trouble adjusting their sleeping and eating patterns can attest to the deleterious effects that can develop, and how cumulative fatigue can sap their mental and physical abilities; this level of fatigue is exacerbated if they were, for example, trying to attend university classes or take care of other business during the daytime. Even if sleeping well during the daytime, graveyard officers often have to attend court, training, or other such functions during normal working hours, and that can also impinge on their sleep time. For these officers, the circadian rhythm concept, discussed next, probably takes on a very personal meaning.

Tired police officers are a national reality. The majority of officers work rotating shifts or at night, which means drowsiness and fatigue are a way of life. According to one study, 90 percent of officers reported driving on duty while drowsy; one-fourth said they had actually fallen asleep while at the wheel. This is obviously a problem that cannot be ignored—particularly if an officer has **shift work sleep disorder (SWSD)**, and experiences problems falling asleep, staying asleep, or waking up (Rosenberg, 2005).

Perhaps the whole idea of shift scheduling takes on a greater level of importance when viewed in light of the physiological effects of sleep and rest deprivation on police officers. When a person is sleep deprived, the cerebral cortex—the largest structure of the brain where planning, analyzing, reasoning, and decision making occur—does not function properly. Several grave errors in judgment and performance can result. For example, a sleep-deprived officer can still fire a weapon or engage in pursuit driving, but may have decreased ability in making accurate, split-second decisions that are required. Detectives working complicated cases may have difficulty in analyzing details and developing solutions. Detectives and patrol officers may be more prone to making errors and forgetting necessary steps, such as collecting evidence at a crime scene. They may become more forgetful in general, and experience mood swings ranging from depression to anger to euphoria. They may have attention deficits, and, say, while on a surveillance operation may have difficulty in maintaining vigilance. Their response time also increases, so it may take longer for them to follow instructions (Kolasinski Morgan, 2005).

Any of the effects described above can negatively impact police personnel; furthermore, a combination of these effects can be even more dangerous. For officers who cannot get regular and sufficient sleep, there are some secondary alternatives:

- Go to the coffee pot. Caffeine, being a stimulant, can increase alertness to some degree; however, large doses of caffeine can make a person jittery and negatively affect performance.
- Take short "power" naps. Research provides evidence that naps of 15 to 20 minutes in duration are optimally effective (Kolasinski Morgan, 2005). Of course, this option is not available to officers while on duty; perhaps a short nap prior to going to work can help.

Increased caffeine and napping, however, are still second-best methods of mitigating the effects of sleep deprivation. Regular and sufficient sleep is best, and supervisors should monitor and encourage good sleep habits for optimal performance. Officers with sleep disorders should seek medical attention from specialists in that field and obtain strategies and possibly medication to help with coping with symptoms of SWSD.

WHAT SUPERVISORS CAN DO Given the above physiological effects of sleep deprivation, it becomes very important that departments develop shifts that assure the safety and longevity of officers and provide efficient and effective services to the public. O'Neill and Cushing (1991:71–73) provided the following advice for administrators when creating shifts:

1. A system of steady shifts with selection based, at least in part, on fair and equitable criteria such as seniority grade. Shift selection could provide for 75 percent of the positions to be filled by seniority and 25 percent of the positions filled at management's discretion.
2. A steady midnight shift in which the workweek is limited to four consecutive days. Officer's court dates would be scheduled for the day preceding their first night of work, and this would be considered a workday.
3. Redeployment of personnel so that only the required *minimum* number of officers and supervisors are on duty from 2 A.M. to 6 P.M. This would more accurately reflect the demand for service by assigning more officers to shifts where they are needed most.

4. In general, no changing of shifts within a time period should be permitted without making allowances for proper rest. In those rare instances when this must be done, several days of advance notice must be given. There should be no changing of shifts for purely disciplinary reasons. Officers should be permitted to bid for another shift at least twice during a year, and vacancies should be announced.

Permanent Versus Rotating Shifts

As noted above in the Police Foundation survey, rotating shifts are commonplace in policing, with nearly half of all agencies using them; so a few additional comments are in order. There are advantages and disadvantages to both fixed and rotating shifts. The primary advantages of having personnel work a permanent or fixed shift is its simplicity of scheduling and assignment of officers according to workload; fewer physiological problems for personnel; fringe benefits for senior officers (such as better choice of days off); easier court scheduling, and the fact that studies have indicated that most officers prefer to work fixed shifts (Brunner, 1976). The disadvantages of fixed shifts include the time-honored tradition of placing rookie officers on the graveyard shift, which then has the greatest number of the least-experienced personnel; the stress on younger officers who may be assigned to higher workload shifts; and the officers' lack of experience of working various shifts.

Rotating shifts also offer some advantages, including the fact that rotating officers have an opportunity to experience the different kind of work that occurs on each shift and have different times of day off for their personal or family needs. But the disadvantages are that rotation creates disruptions in officers' home lives and their pursuit of higher education, as well as fatigue. The physical adjustment to rotating shifts may be the equivalent of "jet lag."

One reason for giving strong consideration today to permanent shift assignments concerns the number of police agencies that are implementing COPPS. Under this philosophy, shift rotation can negate the officers' attempts to solve neighborhood problems on their beats. Herman Goldstein (1990:160), the founder of the problem oriented policing concept, argued that:

> The ultimate form of decentralization [occurs when] officers are assigned permanently, *for a minimum of several years,* to a specific area. Such an arrangement enables an officer to get to know the problems of a community, the strengths and weaknesses of existing systems of control, and the various resources that are useful in solving problems. Changes in the time during which a police officer works seriously detract from the potential to cement relationships between a police officer and [citizens]. (emphasis added)

Labor Considerations: FLSA and Unions

For some police administrators, the **Fair Labor Standards Act (FLSA)** (at 29 U.S.C. 203 et seq.) has become a budgetary and operational nightmare (Randels, 1992). The act provides minimum pay and overtime provisions covering both public- and private-sector employees and contains special provisions for firefighters and police officers. Although there has been some discussion in Congress concerning the repeal or modification of the act, at the present time it is still a legislative force that administrators, middle managers, and supervisors must reckon with. Indeed, one observer referred to the FLSA as the criminal justice administrator's "worst nightmare come true" (Lund, 1991:4).

The act was passed in 1938 to protect the rights and working conditions of employees in the private sector. During that time, long hours, poor wages, and substandard work conditions plagued most businesses. The FLSA placed a number of restrictions on employers to improve these conditions. Then, in 1985, the U.S. Supreme Court brought local police employees under the coverage of the FLSA. In this major (and costly) decision, *Garcia v. San Antonio Transit Authority,* the Court held, 5 to 4, that Congress legally imposed the requirements of the FLSA on state and local governments.

Criminal justice operations often require overtime and participation in off-duty activities such as court appearances and training sessions. The FLSA comes into play when overtime salaries must be paid. It provides that an employer must generally pay employees time and a half for all hours worked over 40 per week. Overtime must also be paid to personnel for all work in excess of 43 hours in a 7-day cycle or 171 hours in a 28-day period. Public safety employees may accrue a maximum of 480 hours of "comp" time, which, if not utilized as leave, must be paid off on separation from employment at the employee's final rate of pay or at the average pay over the last three years, whichever is greater (Swanson et al., 1993). Furthermore, employers usually cannot require employees to take compensatory time in lieu of cash. The primary issue with FLSA is the rigidity of application of what is compensable work. The act prohibits an agency from taking "volunteered time" from employees.

An officer who works the night shift must receive pay for attending training or testifying in court during the day. Further, officers who are ordered to remain at home in anticipation of emergency actions must be compensated. Notably, however, the FLSA's overtime provisions do not apply to persons employed in a bona fide executive, administrative, or professional capacity. In criminal justice, the act has generally been held to apply to detectives and sergeants but not to those of the rank of lieutenant and above.

Garcia prompted an onslaught of litigation by police and fire department employees of state and local governmental entities. The issues are broad but include paying overtime compensation to K-9 and equestrian officers who care for departmental animals while "off duty," overtime pay for officers who access their work computer and conduct business from home, pay for academy recruits who are given mandatory homework assignments, and standby and on-call pay for supervisors and officers who are assigned to units that require their unscheduled return to work. These are just a few of the many FLSA issues that are being litigated in courts across the nation.

The fiscal and operational repercussions of the FLSA could be staggering for some agencies, depending on past practices. For example, in one West Coast police department, the city was required to pay each of its six K-9 officers large sums in back pay for FLSA claims associated with the care, feeding, and training of the department's dogs. This example alone should be a warning to police administrators to review their department policies and practices and ensure that they conform to FLSA requirements.

Police unions consider officer deployment and scheduling to be issues that should be negotiated with management, as a condition of work. The number of persons assigned to a patrol car or section of the community, how seniority and education will be used in assignments, and hours worked and shift selection by seniority are areas that were traditionally considered to be management prerogatives but are now negotiable. Critics argue that this kind of union activity is detrimental to the effective management of the department and the provision of services to the community (Bouza, 1985). Others, however, blame poor management and unfair treatment of employees as fostering such union activity (Kleismet, 1985).

OTHER DEPLOYMENT STRATEGIES

Several methods for deploying officers to patrol duties have been explored over the years. The most common deployment schemes involve basic officer, split force, and special unit plans. Next, we briefly discuss each, as well as directed patrol. We begin the section with a consideration of the unique deployment requirements of a community policing and problem solving (COPPS) initiative.

Community Policing and Problem Solving

As was seen in Chapter 4, COPPS is less of a deployment strategy and more an overarching management philosophy that impacts how an entire organization addresses crime detection and prevention.

One of the strongest needs of the COPPS strategy involves changes in how patrol officers are deployed, including an emphasis on geography, and not just on shift time. Officers must be given the requisite time for neighborhood interaction and relationships. Decisions must be made concerning matters such as duties and job descriptions of COPPS officers, functions to be performed, staffing levels, and neighborhood boundaries.

A new set of district and post boundaries might need to be created that match the major neighborhood areas of the city, ensuring that those areas generating the greatest number of CFS were in the middle of districts and posts, thus providing for strong accountability for policing those areas. Very often, some police officers have little uncommitted time during a tour of duty, while others have large blocks of uncommitted time. As a general rule, no more than 40 percent of an officer's time should be devoted to handling CFS.

The time between calls is the key element in determining if officers have time for problem solving. It is not uncommon to find that officers have more than three hours between calls for other activities. The available time is normally spread throughout the shift, however, varying from 10 minutes to 45 minutes between calls. If we assume a problem-solving project takes 45 minutes, then the officer may have few blocks of uninterrupted time for an assignment. Time between calls varies considerably depending on the number of calls for a particular shift, the types of calls, and how much time they require. One or two fewer calls can make a big difference in the availability of uninterrupted time.

Obviously, citizen calls are important and cannot be ignored. But the aim should be to handle citizen calls in an efficient and expedient manner. In addition to telephone reporting and walk-in/mail-in reporting, discussed earlier, there are three methods for overcoming the problem of finding time for problem solving while still handling calls effectively (Peak and Glensor, 2008:155–157):

1. Allow units to perform problem-solving assignments as self-initiated activities. Under this approach, a unit would contact the dispatcher and go out of service for a problem-solving assignment. The unit would be interrupted only for an emergency call in its area of responsibility.
2. Schedule one or two units to devote a predetermined part of their shift to problem solving. As an example, a supervisor could designate one or two units each day to devote the first half of their shift or even just one hour to problem solving. Their calls would be handled by other units so that they have an uninterrupted block of time.
3. Review the department policy on "assist" units. In some departments, several units show up at the scene of a call even though they are not needed. A department should undergo a detailed study of the types of calls for which assist units are actually appearing, with the aim of reducing the number of assists.

In summary, the overall aim should be to provide officers with uninterrupted amounts of time for problem-solving assignments. There are many ways to accomplish this aim, but they require a concerted planning effort by the department.

Other Approaches

BASIC OFFICER PLAN Under this approach, officers are assigned to a geographic area that has been designed with neighborhoods in mind. This is the typical beat plan configuration described earlier. Most CAD systems adjust beat plans according to the number of officers available during any given shift. The basic officer plan assigns officers to fixed shifts.

SPLIT FORCE The **split force** plan splits patrol into two groups. One group consists of three-fourths of the patrol officers who handle CFS in a normal fashion. The second group of officers performs specialized functions in high-crime areas, often in plainclothes. The split force concept is used by many agencies to free officers to engage in COPPS activities. All officers respond to emergency calls under this plan. An evaluation conducted by the Wilmington, Delaware, Police Department found that police productivity increased by 20 percent, whereas crime decreased 18 percent during the first year of implementation (Krajick, 1978).

SPECIAL UNITS Many agencies also have developed special teams to handle certain community concerns. These teams may be dedicated solely to COPPS, gang activities, adult repeat offenders, or traffic matters and may utilize a variety of patrol tactics, including bicycle patrol, footbeats, horse patrol, or other means of transportation. The key to the effectiveness of any specialized unit is that community problems drive the tactics. Departments must be sure that the various patrol tactics benefit the agency's responses to community problems. Few agencies can afford to implement these approaches purely to improve police-community relations.

DIRECTED PATROL Directed patrol efforts were implemented in an effort to increase patrol productivity. Directed patrol is used by supervisors to direct officers to use their available time in a more planned and rational manner than traditional random patrol. Directed patrol utilizes crime analysis and shift designs as a tool to accomplish its objectives. With this data, a patrol supervisor can deploy officers to attend to specific beat problems.

A RELATED CONSIDERATION: MANAGING OVERTIME

Although costly, a certain amount of overtime is inevitable, so supervisors and managers must be realistic about what can be achieved in controlling it. Some shifts must be extended because time-consuming problems occur at any time. Sensational crimes or natural disasters are impossible to predict; police work also entails court appearances, roll calls, meetings, holidays, and standby time (when supervisors and officers must be available in the event of an emergency or are waiting at home to be called into court).

How does a police agency control overtime? The answer is by recording, analyzing, managing, and supervising. The key element that overshadows all others is management. Useful records systems cannot be constructed unless managers anticipate what they need to know. Management is also essential for analysis, and analysis needs to be done before responsive data systems can be designed. Even new computer-based information systems cannot assist if they pour out data that is not used (Bayley and Worden, 1998).

Supervision of overtime is often seen as the first line of defense against abuses. Managers often complain that one of their major responsibilities is controlling overtime; it is often critical to how they are judged as leaders. At the same time, first-line supervisors can be made the scapegoats for the failures of management, even though most of the factors that determine overtime, such as contract regulations, calls for service, crime emergencies, vacations, injuries, retirements, and special events, are beyond their control. Although first-line supervisors formally approve overtime, in some departments their ability to refuse is restricted. Furthermore, in many agencies, first-line supervisors frequently are not given the information needed to anticipate demands and to adjust work schedules.

Responsible overtime management requires leadership from the top. If the chief executive is indifferent about overtime, middle managers and supervisors will be at risk for criticism or even discipline if overtime problems occur. City councils and other outside persons should understand that overtime cannot be effectively controlled by supervisors and should not allow senior officers to pass the responsibility for **managing overtime** to junior officers.

EFFECTS OF MILITARY LEAVE

Certainly the past several years have witnessed greater challenges for many police agencies having United States Reserve and state National Guard personnel who are activated in the Middle Eastern war effort. Although call-ups are typically for 6- to 12-month deployments, some may be longer. The impact of such call-ups on agencies serving small jurisdictions can be severe (Hickman, 2006).

State and federal laws require employers to provide this leave of absence for activated personnel, and to provide medical benefits and reemployment rights. Under the law—the Uniformed Services Employment and Reemployment Rights Act of 1994, at 43 U.S. Code 38—a veteran's right to reemployment includes the right to restoration of employee benefits in which he or she, and his or her dependents, participated at the time the service leave began, as well as to benefits for which the veteran would have become eligible. When a returning veteran is reemployed, the employer is required to provide:

- Prompt reinstatement
- Accrued seniority, as if continuously employed (including all rights and benefits determined by seniority as well as status, pay, and credit for pension benefits)
- Training or retraining and other accommodations
- Special protection against discharge except for cause

Obviously a major concern for the veteran is whether or not he will be earning the same salary or wage if called up that was being earned in the civilian police job, as well as other civilian benefits that were in place. Many cities and counties are also sensitive to this issue; following are some examples of how local governments are responding to the financial concern (Brown, 2004):

- Shreveport, Louisiana, guarantees reinstatement, pays the difference between active military pay and regular city wages if city wages are greater, continues to co-pay health insurance, and permits service credit allowed under the pension plans.
- Dover, New Hampshire, passed a resolution providing all city-related benefits (health, dental and life insurance, leave accruals, access to city recreation facilities, and so on).
- San Diego, California, provides supplemental pay and continues all employer-sponsored benefits for employees called back for duty.
- Broward County, Florida, continues the employee's full pay for the first 30 calendar days, and thereafter supplements the military income up to the level of base pay they were earning at the time of the call-up.

Many, like Lubbock, Texas, supplement reservists' salary to insure that their families are not affected financially.

CASE STUDIES

Applying the materials presented in this chapter to the following case studies, the reader will get a "real-world" flavor of the issues confronting today's police supervisors and managers concerning personnel deployment and scheduling. Note that the second case study has no absolutely right or wrong answers; rather, it is intended to serve mainly as a "brainteaser," and to provide some insight as to the challenges that can arise in scheduling personnel.

Case Study #1

"Who's on First?" (Or, Who Should Work When?)

Industry City is rapidly growing, and in the past five years, the police department has doubled its number of officers. As a result, it is not uncommon to find that the officers assigned to the evening and night shifts have less than three years of experience. It is also common to find considerable disparity in beat workloads as the city has grown, with far greater numbers of calls for service now coming from the industrial and city park areas. Contributing to this workload disparity is the fact that several veteran officers have recently been called up for active duty in the Air National Guard unit. There is also a shortage of qualified field training officers for the evening shifts because the majority of veteran officers are on day shift or on a special assignment. All sworn officers work a straight 5-day, 8-hour week, with shift rotation every four months; all special assignments on day shift, such as detective work, are seniority based. It seems that toward the end of the four-month shift period, just prior to rotation, there is increased fatigue and complaints by officers about having to adjust their work and personal lives when shifts change again; they also complain that there is little or no opportunity to attend university classes in the daytime. The collective bargaining unit for the department's rank-and-file officers has indicated that it is going to be taking a much closer look at alternative shift patterns, and that it is concerned about the lack of opportunities for the younger officers to work other shifts and on special assignments. Much interest—and solid arguments—has been expressed by the patrol officers in their working 4/10 or 3/12 shift schemes. There have also been increased levels of traffic accidents, sick time usage, and citizens' complaints involving the younger graveyard shift officers. The union has sent a letter to the chief requesting a discussion of these matters. You, the training supervisor, have been directed by your chief to provide an evaluation of the prevalence, benefits, and concerns of various shift schedules and rotations.

Questions for Discussion

1. What would you report to your chief regarding what are the most popularly used—and not used—shift schedules now employed in the U.S.?
2. Compared to the current situation, what are some of the advantages and disadvantages that officers would likely realize if the department adopted the 4/10 or the 3/12 shift schedule? If it discontinued the shift rotations? What are the implications if Industry City is already engaged in, or is about to implement, the community policing and problem solving strategy?
3. What could be underlying the night-shift officers' traffic accident, fatigue, and citizen complaint problems, and what might be done to analyze and correct them?
4. What labor considerations might be posed by a shift rotation or some non-traditional shift scheduling plan?
5. What protections do federal laws apply to those police officers who are returning to Industrial City following their active duty military service upon their return?

Case Study #2

Scheduling School

You are to assume the role of Sergeant Doe in the Gotham City Police Department. This is your first shift since leaving for a two-week vacation; the date is June 10. Not counting yourself or your middle-managers, you are in charge of a 12-person patrol team and work 4:00 P.M. to midnight (swing shift), with Sundays and Mondays off. Due to the increased activities that occur during the summer months, it is the policy of your department to not allow more than two officers to take vacation or training leave at a time. You have two senior officers (Officers A and B) off on vacation for the entire month of June. Some urgent scheduling issues have come up for the week of June 16-22. Your lieutenant needs you to work up the swing-shift schedule. The following issues have arisen:

Officer H is on vacation for the week.

Officer K injured her knee over the weekend and is on sick leave.

Officers C and D have to teach at the academy on Wednesday and Thursday.

Officer D's wife is having surgery on Friday. He has requested Saturday/Sunday as days off.

The Human Resources Division is offering Workplace Violence Training on Friday, June 19th, and wants as many officers as possible to attend. No officers have Fridays off, so you schedule as many officers as possible to attend this training. Officer L is the regional gang unit liaison and Officer J is the regional drug unit liaison, but both are available for other assignments as exigencies arise. Your lieutenant wants to know if you can maintain minimum staffing of 6 officers per day without any overtime expense.

Questions for Discussion

1. See how well you do with this situation.

Summary

The patrol function is the backbone of police work and requires the greatest number of personnel and financial resources (i.e., salary, training, equipment). Therefore, this chapter has sought to focus on that aspect of patrol that is largely overlooked and taken for granted: officer deployment and scheduling.

Our discussion was premised on a simple reality: the question of whether or not to work around-the-clock shifts is not an option for the police, who must constantly be on duty. Therefore, the determination and proper utilization of patrol personnel (and, in a related vein, the use of overtime) is a major role for police supervisors and managers.

The chapter included discussions of the need for patrol planning; some means for determining the adequate patrol force size; whether or not officers must or should respond to every call for service under community policing and problem solving (and some alternative patrol responses that are available for use); various configurations of shift schedules, including their characteristics and use; the effects of shift work and sleep deprivation on individual officer fatigue; a comparison of permanent and rotating shifts; applicable federal labor law and union considerations; managing overtime; and the effects on deployment from, and legal rights of, personnel who serve on active military duty.

This chapter has demonstrated that ensuring 24-hour, 7-days-per-week shift coverage is not an easy task; many problems and pitfalls can enter into the mix. These challenges will likely never go away, so today's police supervisors and managers must therefore be very knowledgeable about personnel deployment and strategies that best fit the needs of the department.

Items for Review

1. Describe the purposes of patrol planning and some of the factors that contribute to the overall lack of proper patrol planning in police agencies.
2. Discuss the three methods most often used by police departments to determine resource needs.
3. Explain what are the most—and least—favored shift schedules in the U.S., as well as advantages and disadvantages of those three that are the most prominent.
4. Describe some of the factors to be considered when attempting to properly deploy officers by peak workloads, beat location, and time of day.
5. Discuss some alternative patrol responses for police handling of citizen calls for service that reduce officers' workload and avoid the need to respond to every call for service.
6. Compare permanent shifts versus rotating shifts, including advantages and drawbacks of both.
7. Describe the effects of the Fair Labor Standards Act and police unions on shift scheduling.
8. Examine the primary methods for deploying officers, including the basic officer, split force, special unit, and directed patrol plans.
9. Explain why the police must be deployed differently with the community policing and problem solving strategy.
10. Explain why overtime management is so important, as well as the supervisors' and managers' roles in directing and controlling overtime.
11. Delineate the means by which shift work and scheduling can deprive officers of rest, and result in fatigue and possibly even dangerous on-the-job performance.
12. Describe the protections federal law affords police officers who are called up for active duty in the military.

References

Amendola, K. L., Hamilton, E. E., and Wyckoff, L. A. (2006). Law enforcement shift schedules: Results of a random nationwide survey of police agencies. http://www.policefoundation.org/pdf/ShiftScheduleSurveyResults.pdf (Accessed October 8, 2007).

Aschoff, J. (1965). Circadian rhythms in man. *Science* 148:1427–1432.

Bayley, D. H., and Worden, R. E. (1998). *Police overtime: An examination of key issues.* Washington, DC: U.S. Department of Justice, National Institute of Justice Research in Brief.

Bieck, W., and Kessler, D. (1977). *Response time analysis.* Kansas City, MO: Board of Police Commissioners.

Bouza, A. V. (1985). Police unions: Paper tigers or roaring lions? In W. A. Geller, ed., *Police leadership in America: Crisis and opportunity.* New York: Praeger, pp. 241–280.

Brown, J. (2004). Military leave: Supporting employees. *The Police Chief* (November):30-33.

Brunner, G. D. (1976). Law enforcement officers' work schedules reactions. *The Police Chief* (January):30–31.

Garcia v. San Antonio Metropolitan Transit Authority, 469 U.S. 528 (1985).

Goldstein, H. (1990). *Problem oriented policing.* New York: McGraw-Hill.

Hale, C. D. (1981). *Police operations and management.* New York: John Wiley.

Hickman, M. L. (2006). Impact of the military reserve activation on police staffing. *The Police Chief* (October):62-72.

Iannone, N. F., and Iannone, M. P. (2001). *Supervision of police personnel,* 6th ed. Upper Saddle River, NJ: Prentice Hall.

Kelling, G. L. (1974). *The Kansas City preventive patrol experiment: A summary report.* Washington, DC: Police Foundation.

Kleismet, R. B. (1985). The chief and the union: May the force be with you. In W. A. Geller, ed., *Police leadership in America: Crisis and opportunity.* New York: Praeger, pp. 281–285.

Kolasinski Morgan, E. M. (2005). The science of sleep. *Law and Order* (July):106-113.

Krajick, K. (1978). Does patrol prevent crime? *Police Magazine* 1 (September):4–16.

Levine, M. J., and McEwen, J. T. (1985). *Patrol deployment.* Washington, DC: U.S. Department of Justice.

Lund, L. (1991). The "ten commandments" of risk management for jail administrators. *Detention Reporter* 4 (June):4.

McEwen, J. T., Conners, E., and Cohen, M. (1986). *Evaluation of the differential police response field test.* Washington, DC: National Institute of Justice.

Oliver, B. (2005). Ten-hour shifts: A good fit. *Law and Order* (July):102-105.

O'Neill, J. L., and Cushing, M. A. (1991). *The impact of shift work on police officers.* Washington, DC: Police Executive Research Forum.

Peak, K. J., and Glensor, R. W. (2008). *Community policing and problem solving: Strategies and practices,* 5th ed. Upper Saddle River, NJ: Prentice Hall.

Police Foundation. (1981). *The Newark foot patrol experiment.* Washington, DC: Author.

Randels, E. L. (1992). The Fair Labor Standards Act: An administrative nightmare. *The Police Chief* (5):28–32.

Roberg, R. R., and Kuykendall, J. (1995). *Police organization and management: Behavior, theory, and processes.* Pacific Grove, CA: Brooks/Cole.

Rosenberg, R. (2005). Working the beat when you are beat. *Law and Order* (July):115-117; see also Moore-Ede, M. C., and Richardson, G. S. (1985). Medical implications of shift work. *Annual Review of Medicine* 17:608.

Schissler, T. M. (1996). Shift work and police scheduling. *Law and Order* (May):61–64.

Sherman, L. (1973). *Team policing: Seven case studies.* Washington, DC: Police Foundation.

Swanson, C. R., Territo, L., and Taylor, R. W. (1993). *Police administration.* Upper Saddle River, NJ: Prentice Hall.

Trojanowicz, R. C. (1986). Evaluating a neighborhood foot patrol program: The Flint, Michigan project. In Dennis P. Rosenbaum, ed., *Community crime prevention: Does it work?* Beverly Hills, CA: Sage, pp. 157–78.

U.S. Department of Justice, Federal Bureau of Investigation. (2007).*Crime in the United States–2006: Uniform Crime Reports,* http://www.fbi.gov/ucr/cius2006/data/table_70.html (Accessed October 22, 2007).

Wrobleski, H. M., and Hess, K. M. (1993). *Introduction to law enforcement and criminal justice.* St. Paul, MN: West.

CHAPTER 13

Managing and Supervising Police Operations

Key Terms and Concepts

- Calls for service
- Clearance rate
- DUI enforcement
- Investigative process
- Priority call system
- Tactical units
- Ticket quota
- Traffic function
- Vehicular pursuit

Chapter Learning Objectives

After reading this chapter, the student will:

- be able to identify the operational units in a police organization
- know how calls for service represent a major driving force for the police
- understand how patrol, criminal investigation, and traffic units operate in the police department, as well as understand the managerial and supervisory roles in these operational units
- know the role and function of tactical units
- be able to explain the serious nature of vehicular pursuits as they concern human lives, property, and civil liability

Give us the tools, and we will finish the job.
—Sir Winston Churchill, 1941

INTRODUCTION

Police departments are complex organizations in that they are expected to provide a wide range of services to the public. Citizens make all sorts of demands on law enforcement agencies. These demands range from apprehending criminals such as burglars, rapists, and murderers, to providing basic services such as finding lost children, directing traffic so that motorists can travel more easily, and providing directions to people who are lost. There perhaps is no organization as complex as a police department in terms of the services that it provides. Police officers are expected to possess numerous skills so that they can perform these duties proficiently.

In terms of organizational theory, complex organizations have line and staff units. Line units are engaged in performing the organization's work, while staff units provide support or facilitate the work of the line units. Staff units in a police department include training, planning, vehicle maintenance, crime analysis, and so on. These units help ensure that line units are able to function properly and efficiently. Line units realistically cannot function without such support. Line units, on the other hand, are those units that engage in the actual police work. When people come into contact with police officers, they interact with officers in line units.

This chapter examines those line, or operational, units. Police departments have three primary operational divisions: (1) patrol, (2) criminal investigation, and (3) traffic enforcement. Patrol officers patrol the streets, answer calls for service, make arrests, and deal with public problems and crimes. As a result of patrolling, they also prevent crime. Criminal investigation or detectives are involved in the investigation of crimes. They solve cases, arrest perpetrators, and recover stolen property. Finally, traffic enforcement is responsible for ensuring that citizens abide by traffic laws, and they also investigate traffic crashes.

These three broad operational divisions are addressed in this chapter, and three case studies are provided as well.

THE ORGANIZING OF OPERATIONS

O. W. Wilson, the father of modern police administration, observed almost 60 years ago that the patrol function is the backbone of a police department (1950). That observation may arguably be true today, but certainly other major types of police operations (e.g., investigations and youth services) loom large as well. However, patrol officers provide the bulk of services to citizens, and even though most people attribute the roles of investigating crimes and arresting criminals to detectives, patrol officers make more arrests and solve more crimes than detectives do.

Patrol officers are the department's front line in crime fighting and in terms of providing services to citizens. To a large extent, detectives and traffic officers support patrol officers. When detectives investigate crime and traffic officers are engaged in enforcing traffic laws and investigating traffic crashes, it allows patrol officers to remain on the job in their beats. Thus, patrol remains the primary operational unit in any police department, and as such, it requires constant attention from managers and supervisors.

The size of a department dictates the organization of operational units and how they function. In large cities such as Chicago, New York, Kansas City, or Atlanta, it is too difficult to operate these units from one central location. The city is broken down into manageable areas that are sometimes referred to as precincts, sectors, districts, or divisions. For example, Hickman and Reaves (2006) found that in cities with a population of 1 million or more, the police departments had an average of 17 precincts, while departments serving a population of 25,000 to 499,000 had an average of 4 precincts. These areas, to a large extent, equate to self-sustained, smaller departments.

In most cases, a captain oversees the operations in an area, including the work of patrol officers, detectives, and a host of staff support. In terms of patrol, an area is staffed with lieutenant shift commanders, usually three, who command each watch or shift—a time frame usually 8 or 10 hours in duration. The lieutenants are responsible for all patrol activities during the shift. Within each shift, a sergeant or corporal reports to the lieutenant, and supervises squads, generally made up of four to eight officers. Medium-sized departments operate in essentially the same way, except that one captain manages operations for the entire area—there are not multiple areas or precincts. Small departments often have sergeants as shift commanders and possibly a lieutenant who has the responsibility for patrol.

Criminal investigation and traffic have command and supervisory structures that operate independently of patrol. In larger departments with precincts, detectives and traffic officers may be assigned to the precinct, but they have their own commanders and supervisors. Patrol, detective, and traffic commanders report to the precinct commander who coordinates their activities to ensure that the units work together and cooperatively when tackling problems. This is especially true in community policing departments. Many problems are complex, often requiring patrol officers, detectives, and traffic officers to provide a comprehensive response.

As noted, large departments have detectives assigned to the precincts. However, not all investigative activities operate out of the precinct stations. A breakdown of the investigative units in the Kansas City, Missouri Police Department is provided in Table 13-3, presented later in this chapter as it relates to organizing the investigative function. Notice that there are a number of specialized units that are not assigned to the precincts. These include units such as pawn shop section, undercover narcotics, vice, and forgery. The investigation of many crimes is conducted by a centralized unit that works cases across all precincts. Which crimes are investigated by precinct detectives, and which are investigated by a centralized investigative unit is determined by the organizational structure and enumerated in policies.

MANAGING AND SUPERVISING PATROL

Primary Responsibilities

In all but the largest departments, patrol is the only unit that assigns officers on a 24-hour basis—patrol officers are always available, and when personnel from other units are not available, patrol officers handle all activities. As noted above, the patrol function normally includes about 70 percent of all sworn officers. For the most part, patrol has specific responsibilities. Alpert and Dunham (1997) have identified eleven primary responsibilities:

1. Deterring crime through routine patrol
2. Enforcing laws
3. Investigating criminal behavior
4. Apprehending offenders
5. Writing reports
6. Coordinating efforts with prosecutors
7. Assisting people in danger or in need of assistance
8. Resolving conflicts
9. Responding to disorders and keeping the peace
10. Maintaining order
11. Expediting the flow of pedestrian and automobile traffic

The list prepared by Alpert and Dunham represents a traditional view of police patrol activities. Kappeler and Gaines (2008) note that the incorporation of COPPS in policing has changed patrol's role to some extent. Today, patrol officers are expected to take the time to work more closely with citizens in the community to identify problems and solicit citizen cooperation and assistance when attempting to solve them. Nonetheless, officers are still expected to handle those responsibilities identified by Alpert and Dunham. An important responsibility of patrol managers and supervisors is to ensure that officers do not neglect any of these responsibilities. Police officers have a tendency to favor law enforcement–related tasks and often see COPPS and service tasks as less important. Managers and supervisors must ensure that officers balance these responsibilities.

Calls for Service: The Driving Force for Patrol

Historically, it was believed that the primary purpose of patrol was to prevent crime by being omnipresent; if patrol officers patrol randomly and frequently, criminals would be dissuaded from committing crime because of the officers' presence. However, the Kansas City Patrol Study found that patrol had little impact on crime (Kelling, Pate, Dieckman, and Brown, 1974). When patrol levels were changed—decreased or increased—in Kansas City, it had little impact on crime. Today, we recognize that patrol officers are distributed across a jurisdiction so that they can respond to calls for service in a more timely fashion. **Calls for service** remain the driving force behind patrol operations, but officers also focus on the problems that cause the calls: bars that serve drunken patrons, drug selling locations, juvenile hangouts, and so on.

Police departments receive calls requesting all sorts of services and reporting numerous problems. These calls come to the police department via a 911 telephone number. The advent of 911 has resulted in a substantial increase in the number of calls to police departments. Because the overwhelming majority of 911 calls are non-emergency in nature, police call-takers are not able to receive the emergency calls in a timely fashion. A number of departments are now implementing 311 telephone numbers, which are non-emergency. The idea is that citizens should reserve 911 only when there is an emergency, allowing police call-takers to be able to handle emergencies more rapidly.

As noted, police departments receive a large number of calls. For example, the Baltimore Police Department receives over one million calls a year (Mazerolle, Rogan, Frank, Famega, and Eck, 2005). Many of these calls are emergencies, while the majority are non-emergency. Departments frequently receive more calls than there are officers to respond to them. Police departments, in an effort to manage calls, use dispatch priority systems, and a variety of such systems are operational across the country. For example, Table 13-1 provides a breakdown of the calls to which the Boston Police Department responded.

Calls are handled based on their priority. That is, priority one calls will receive officer attention before other calls. A little over one-fifth of the Boston police calls required an immediate response,

TABLE 13-1 Boston Police Department's Priority Call System

Priority	Types of Calls	Percent of Total
1	Immediate Response	20.3
2	Medium Priority Response	34.8
3	Low Priority Response	32.5
9	Administrative	8.2
	Walk-ins to Department	4.1

Source: Adapted from Nesbary, D. (2008). "Handling emergency calls for service: Organizational production of crime statistics." *Policing: An International Journal of Police Management & Strategies,* 21(4): 576-599.

which is similar to most large American police departments. These calls consist of crimes in progress, reported serious crimes, disturbances, and accidents that involve personal injury or result in traffic congestion. Medium and low priority calls, which represent the bulk of calls to a police department, are handled as officers become available. Most departments attempt to respond to all calls, but in some cases during extremely busy periods, the volume of workload does not allow officers to respond to all calls. When this occurs, administrative and low priority calls will remain unanswered.

One of the primary responsibilities of a supervisor is to back officers on calls, especially priority one calls. In doing so, the supervisor performs several functions. First, safety is enhanced, especially if a situation gets out of hand. The sergeant helps to protect the officer and control the situation. Second, the supervisor ensures that officers follow correct departmental policies and guidelines and criminal procedures. Supervisors often provide on-the-scene advice and training, especially for newer officers. Third, supervisors can ensure that officers clear calls and get back into service as soon as possible, especially during peak workload periods. In this case, the sergeant is a time manager. The supervisor plays a key role in ensuring that proper police action is taken at the scene of each call. Even when sergeants do not back officers at the scene of calls, they should monitor the radio to determine if all procedures are followed at calls.

Managing Calls for Service and Other Activities

Managers play a key role by monitoring calls and ensuring that they are responded to properly. Patrol or shift commanders may discuss calls with sergeants or officers to ensure procedures are followed. To some extent, the sergeant and the shift or watch commander share this responsibility, but ultimately, the commander must ensure that operations are within the dictates of policy.

In some cases, a shift commander may reassign officers from one area to another when necessitated by the distribution of the calls. When doing so, the shift commander is attempting to maintain beat integrity. That is, officers should be assigned geographically so that they can expediently respond to calls, and normally, patrol commanders attempt to ensure that at least one patrol unit is assigned to each beat. If calls become substantially backed up in one area, the commander likely will shift patrol personnel. Patrol shift commanders also may determine that some of the calls should be assigned to other units such as criminal investigation or traffic, and work with the dispatcher to ensure that calls are properly assigned, thus relieving patrol of some of the workload. This is important during peak workload periods.

Perhaps the most important responsibility of patrol commanders is to monitor staffing levels and ensure that all beats are staffed. Generally, a commander will have a specific number of officers. However, availability changes as the result of vacations, sick leave, holidays, training, and court appearances. In many instances, officer unavailability is not scheduled or foreseen. If too many officers are on some form of leave, the commander does not have the personnel to cover all the required patrol beats. Many departments have policies that dictate minimum patrol staffing. Thus, it is important that patrol commanders monitor staffing levels, or it may require overtime compensation to staff the beats or the assignment of sergeants to staff the beats. This negatively affects patrol's ability to manage operations.

There are periods of time when patrol officers are not assigned calls. The volume of calls fluctuates by hour of the day and day of the week (see Chapter 12). Thus, there are periods where officers are running from call to call and calls are stacked or in queue. There are other times when officers have very little to occupy them; the volume of calls subsides. For example, Famega (2005) examined a number of workload studies and found that on the average, 75 percent of a patrol officer's time is not devoted to answering calls for service. This does not mean that officers are not working. Some of this time is devoted to completing reports, serving warrants, or other administrative duties. They are also involved in self-initiated activities such as investigating suspicious persons, vehicles, and situations and writing traffic citations. Primarily, however, officers are patrolling. There is a certain amount of patrol officer time that remains flexible, which has two implications. First, patrol commanders should ensure that their patrol staffing levels result in equalized or minimum coverage to respond to calls for service. More officers should be assigned during periods that have higher numbers of calls, usually night hours and Fridays and Saturdays. Second, given the amount of non-committed time or patrol time available to officers, patrol commanders and supervisors can ensure that patrol officers are involved in COPPS activities. Slack workload periods should be identified, and officers should be given COPPS assignments to build community relationships or to tackle a crime or disorder problem in a given neighborhood. This helps maximize the department's patrol resources, and it results in an enhanced COPPS program.

Methods of Patrol

Police departments have developed a number of methods of patrol, including automobile, foot, bicycle, aircraft, horse, and watercraft patrol. The primary method remains automobile patrol since patrol officers assigned to automobile patrols can cover larger geographical areas -and obviously respond to calls more quickly with automobile patrol-than with, say, bicycle, foot, or horse patrols. Nonetheless, there are instances where other forms of patrol are useful and departments across the United States use these other methods. It is important that when alternative forms of patrol are used, they should fulfill a specific need. They should not be deployed as a novelty. Table 13-2 provides a breakdown of the departments that use various forms of patrol.

AUTOMOBILE PATROL As noted, the primary method of patrol is automobile patrol because officers can cover larger geographical areas and respond more rapidly to calls for service and crimes in progress. One automobile patrol unit can cover the same area as several foot patrol officers or bicycle officers. Moreover, motorized officers are able to carry equipment such as special weapons. Automobiles provide officers with a measure of protection when confronting unruly crowds or when

TABLE 13-2 Types of Routine Patrol Other than Automobile Used by Local Police Departments, by Size of Population Served

	Percent of agencies using each type of patrol on a routine basis				
Population served	Foot	Bicycle	Motorcycle	Marine	Horse
All sizes	59%	38%	14%	4%	2%
1,000,000 or more	75%	100%	81%	63%	63%
500,000-999,999	79	95	100	41	63
250,000-499,999	76	83	93	32	59
100,000-249,999	57	83	89	14	18
50,000-99,999	54	64	63	14	7
25,000-49,999	47	60	49	8	2
10,000-24,999	53	58	21	5	2
2,500-9,999	61	43	8	3	–
Under 2,500	61	18	3	2	–

–Less than 0.5%.

Hickman, M., and Reaves, B. (2006). *Local Police Departments, 2003.* Washington, D.C.: Bureau of Justice Statistics.

responding to disorders. They also are not impeded as a result of inclement weather. Almost all police departments use automobile patrols

FOOT PATROL During the first decades of the twentieth century and earlier, foot patrol was the primary mode of patrolling. With the advent of the automobile, foot patrols were largely abandoned by American police departments. The acceptance of COPPS resulted in a resurgence in foot patrols. Foot patrols were seen as a method by which the police could work closer with citizens and develop better ties to the community. A number of police departments began to implement them. As displayed in Table 13-2, 59 percent of all police departments use foot patrols today.

Foot patrols are seen as having a great deal of utility, especially when departments are implementing COPPS. There were two early studies in Flint, Michigan, and Newark, New Jersey, that showed that foot patrols substantially reduced citizens' fear of crime. This occurred even though actual crime did not decline in the foot patrol areas. The reduction in fear was the result of citizens being able to see police officers on a regular basis, and in some cases, develop personal relationships with them (Gaines and Kappeler, 2007).

Foot patrols should be implemented when and where they provide an advantage over other forms of patrol. Generally, they should be deployed in those areas where officers will come into contact with large numbers of citizens. Prime examples include business and entertainment districts where there are large numbers of people and in public, high-density housing. Because there is a high concentration of citizens in these areas, officers come into contact with larger numbers of citizens, enhancing police-community relations and gathering information about crime and disorder problems. Obviously, they should be deployed only when the pedestrian traffic results in a substantial number of contacts.

BICYCLE PATROL Bicycle patrols are fairly popular in American policing with about 38 percent of departments reporting using them (Hickman and Reaves, 2006). They provide more coverage than foot patrols, but less as compared to automobile patrols. They have some of the same benefits as foot patrols. Gaines and Kappeler (2007) note that they: (1) result in greater contact with the public, (2) are a stealth form of patrol, and (3) provide for more coverage. Bicycle patrols have the capacity of covering several square blocks. Clark (2003) examined bicycle patrols in Cincinnati, Ohio, and found that bicycle patrol officers were more productive as compared to automobile patrol officers, except for felony arrests. The bike officers addressed more vice incidents, made more misdemeanor arrests, served more warrants, assisted more citizens, and performed more field interrogations. Menton (2008) examined bike patrols in four cities and found similar results.

It seems that bicycle patrols have a great deal of underutilized promise, and supervisors and patrol managers can help departments realize this potential. First, they should ensure that bike officers are properly trained. They must be trained not only how to use the bicycle as a patrol vehicle, but also that bike patrol officers are able to perform a number of functions beyond providing citizens with information. As a stealth method of patrolling, bike officers are able to intervene in numerous instances of crime and disorder. Like foot patrols, bike patrols should be assigned to areas where there is a high concentration of people or problems. Patrol commanders should monitor the daily activities of bike patrol officers to ensure that they are meeting expected levels of productivity.

HORSE PATROL As noted in Table 13-2, only about two percent of police departments in the United States use horse patrols. Many departments do not use them because of the expense. Horses are expensive to acquire and maintain. Moreover, they must be transported to their patrol areas each day. Nevertheless, there are several functions that horse patrols can perform. Many large cities use them in downtown areas. Officers on horseback are able to see over crowds, allowing them to observe for problems. They can maneuver through congested pedestrian and vehicular traffic with little difficulty.

Horse patrols provide a department with a substantial amount of public relations, especially when they are used in areas where there are large numbers of families and children. They are often used in parks. They frequently can be seen in the national parks in Washington, D.C. Horses allow officers to traverse difficult terrain and enable officers to cover all areas in the park fairly rapidly. Horses are also valuable in crowd control. Essentially, a number of horses can form a line and push or move a crowd. People generally retreat in the face of horses because of their size.

MARINE PATROL Most states and many counties and cities have an agency or unit that performs marine patrol. According to Hickman and Reaves (2006) about four percent of departments have a marine patrol. They patrol lakes and rivers, especially in areas where there is a substantial amount of recreational boating. In these cases, they observe for violations of boating laws and unsafe behavior. For example, these officers make a substantial number of driving while under the influence arrests. These units are necessitated by the large number of boating accidents and deaths that occur each year. For the most part, marine patrols are used to ensure safety.

Marine patrols are also used in areas where there is narcotics smuggling and the illegal entry of foreign aliens. For example, the U.S. Coast Guard inspects numerous vessels when they enter United States waters. They often inspect them for drugs and aliens. With the need to secure our borders, the Coast Guard is now observing for terrorists, anything that can be used to make a weapon of mass destruction, and other contraband. Numerous county and city police departments have units that are performing these functions at the local level.

AIR PATROL A number of police departments now deploy fixed-wing aircraft or helicopters, which serve a number of functions, including search and rescue. Many sheriffs' departments in the west have aircraft for this purpose. Some counties have endless miles of desolate forests, mountains, deserts, and other rough terrain, and hikers and campers often get lost or become injured, necessitating a search and rescue mission. These often are best accomplished via helicopters.

Helicopters are used in a number of cities to assist patrol officers and detectives. For example, patrol officers may be chasing someone in a vehicle or on foot and officers in a helicopter will watch the suspect and report his or her whereabouts to the officers on the ground to facilitate the suspect's capture. A number of states used fixed-wing aircraft for speed enforcement. Officers in the aircraft will clock speeders while officers on the ground issue citations. This type of enforcement is especially useful in areas where there are large numbers of speeders. Finally, agencies in marijuana producing states will use aircraft to spot marijuana patches. Aircraft can search large areas with little expense. Once observed, officers on the ground are dispatched to destroy the crops.

Aircraft units are expensive operations. In addition to the cost of acquiring the aircraft, there are considerable expenditures in training pilots, maintaining the craft, and operational costs. McLean (1990) estimated that the cost to purchase and equip a police helicopter could range from $1 million to $10 million when all expenses including command and control are included. Only about one percent of departments have some type of aircraft.

In summary, there are several methods used to deploy patrol officers. The decision to acquire resources and establish these units is vested with police administrators and governmental officials. Police managers, on the other hand, should appraise the resources available to them and ensure those resources are deployed to produce maximum benefit—accomplish unit goals and objectives. Managers should recognize the benefits and liabilities of each method of patrol and deploy them where they contribute the greatest. Methods of patrol should be matched with problems.

Specialized Tactical Units

Many larger departments have specialized tactical units that are assigned to patrol. These units are not to be confused with special weapons and tactics units (SWAT). SWAT teams respond to special situations such as hostage, barricaded persons, dangerous crimes in progress, and the service of warrants for criminals with a history of violence. Specialized **tactical units** are designed to provide additional resources that can be used to attack specific crime or disorder problems or hot spots of activity. They are also designed to provide patrol commanders with a measure of flexibility.

Larger and middle sized police departments use crime analysis to identify crime problems and trends. These units can identify areas with entrenched or emerging crime problems. Patrol commanders often deploy officers across beats and consequently, often do not have the resources to concentrate on these types of problems. A specialized tactical unit provides patrol commanders with flexibility—they can assign officers in this unit or squad to address these problems. For example, if the department receives several reports of drunkenness, fights and disorders in an area or at a particular location, the commander can deploy officers from a specialized tactical unit to deal with the problem. In this case, officers would saturate the area and make a number of arrests. This could occur repeatedly until the problem is abated. Sometimes specialized tactical officers attempt to arrest repeat offenders. Departments can identify those offenders who committed greater numbers of crimes, and specialized tactical officers have the time and flexibility to attempt to find and arrest them. A specialized patrol unit or squad becomes a supplemental force that can be used for problem solving or other community policing activities. Commanders can constantly review crime statistics and identify new targets for the unit.

CRIMINAL INVESTIGATION

Goals and Types

Most citizens are familiar with criminal investigation or detectives as a result of television shows and movies. Detectives are seen as individuals who collect evidence, interrogate suspects, and make arrests once they have enough evidence to establish probable cause. Bennett and Hess (2007: 8) note that the goals of criminal investigations are as follows:

1. Determine whether a crime has been committed.
2. Legally obtain information and evidence to identify the responsible persons.
3. Arrest the suspect.
4. Recover stolen property.
5. Present the best possible case to the prosecutor.

Approximately 10 to 15 percent of a department's sworn officers are assigned to criminal investigation in large and medium sized departments. In small departments that do not have detectives, investigations are assigned to patrol officers. Medium and large departments have units or divisions that are assigned to investigate crimes. As such, managers and supervisors are responsible for ensuring that these units achieve the above goals. They assign cases to detectives and follow up to ensure that all possible leads are exhausted. They review cases to ensure that cases are properly documented and ready for prosecution.

There have been a number of studies examining criminal investigation. For the most part, the results indicated that detectives should concentrate on those cases that are solvable. Kuykendall (1986) and Sanders (1977) described cases as: (1) walk-throughs, (2) where-are-they, and (3) whodunits. Walk-throughs are those cases that are essentially solved. There is ample evidence to present to the

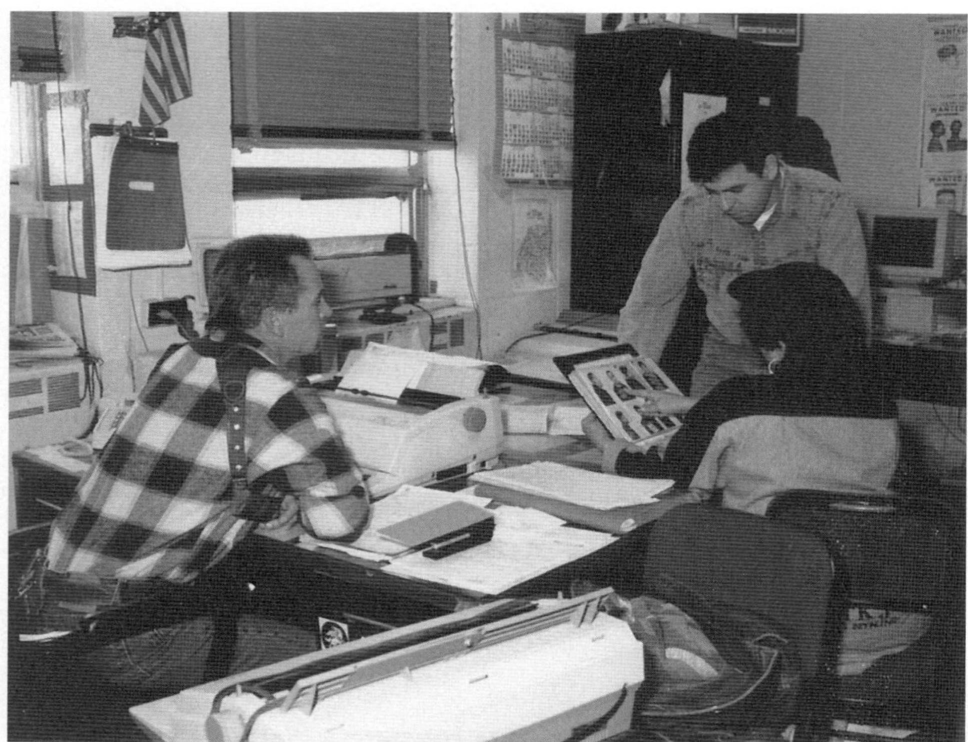

Detectives view a suspect photo lineup. Supervising a specialized unit in detectives, training, or administration requires additional skills, knowledge, and abilities.
Courtesy NYPD Photo Unit

prosecutor, and the perpetrator is in custody. In where-are-they cases, the perpetrator has been identified, and the police must locate and arrest him or her. The whodunits are cases that are unsolved; the perpetrator has not been identified. The whodunits are the most difficult cases.

The Investigative Process

Most departments divide investigations into a preliminary investigation and a follow-up investigation. Preliminary investigations are performed by patrol, while the follow-ups are assigned to detectives. It is critical that a department have a policy dictating what actions are to be taken during the preliminary investigation. Generally, patrol officers will take a crime report, identify and interview witnesses, and ensure that physical evidence is collected. Physical evidence is usually collected by detectives or crime scene specialists in larger departments, and in smaller departments, the evidence is collected by patrol officers. In some cases, patrol officers will perform a neighborhood canvas where neighbors are contacted to determine if they have any information that can assist in the investigation. Patrol supervisors must ensure that preliminary investigative tasks are completed correctly. If not, valuable evidence and information may be lost. Patrol supervisors should review officers' crime reports to ensure that they are complete, comprehensive, accurate, and well written. The crime report is the foundation for the detective's follow-up investigation, and if information is not present, it may result in the case not being solved or the detective having to retrace the steps that were supposed to be performed by the patrol officer. Supervisors should also ensure that officers adhere to proper criminal procedures so that valuable evidence is not rejected by the court.

Once the preliminary investigation is completed, the case is assigned to a detective. The detective reviews the crime report—which was completed by the patrol officer and contains a summary of the crime and evidence. Then possibly re-contacts victims and witnesses in an effort to obtain additional information. The investigation is somewhat analogous to a puzzle. The detective attempts to put the pieces of information and evidence together to identify the perpetrator and build a case for prosecution. Investigative supervisors monitor detectives' progress and ensure that they examine all possible evidence.

Eck (1983) noted that there are three categories of assigned cases facing detectives: (1) weak cases that will not be solved regardless of the investigative effort, (2) cases with moderate levels of evidence that can be solved with considerable effort, and (3) cases with strong evidence that can be solved with minimum effort. Eck notes that detectives should concentrate on the cases with moderate and strong evidence. In doing so, more cases will be cleared. They will clear a higher percentage of the cases with moderate and strong evidence, and they will clear a certain number of cases with weak evidence since some of the perpetrators they arrest committed those crimes. It must be remembered that detectives cannot manufacture evidence if none exists, and time spent on solvable cases results in better outcomes.

Organizing the Investigative Function

Smaller departments with a few or small number of detectives are not specialized. That is, cases are equally distributed across the detectives without regard to the type of case being investigated. Larger departments have specialized units within the detective bureau or unit, and the largest departments such as Chicago, Kansas City, New York, and Miami have a number of specialized units. Investigative specialization allows detectives to concentrate on specific types of crime. This allows them to develop expertise, be able to identify modus operandi, become familiar with individuals who have repeatedly committed certain types of crimes in the past, and recognize the types of physical evidence that may be present at a crime scene.

Table 13-3 provides a breakdown of the primary units in the investigation bureau for the Kansas City, Missouri, Police Department.

As displayed in Table 13-3, the Kansas City Police Department has a number of units and sections within its investigations bureau. The unit configuration is similar to other large police departments throughout the nation. Each of these units is staffed with detectives and civilian employees who are responsible for investigating a specific set of crimes. Each unit has a commander and supervisors who are responsible for ensuring that work is completed effectively. Large departments like Kansas City have a substantial workload that justifies this level of organization and specialization.

Managing Criminal Investigation Units

As noted above, some police departments have a variety of investigative units. Generally, these units are commanded by a captain or a lieutenant depending on the size of the unit. The commanders are responsible for ensuring that their units operate effectively, addressing personnel and administrative issues. In addition, they must also ensure that the units are maximizing investigative efforts. Are detectives solving cases and are they presenting good cases to prosecutors? These commanders, then, perform a number of managerial actions.

Most importantly, commanders should constantly monitor the productivity or **clearance rates** of the unit and individual detectives. In terms of the unit, the clearance rates should be tracked over time

TABLE 13-3 The Investigative Units. Housed in the Kansas City, Missouri, Police Department

Division	Units
Violent Crimes Division	• Homicide Unit. Investigates all murders and has a Cold Case Section to investigate cold cases. • Robbery Unit. Investigates robberies. • Special Victims Unit. Includes a Juvenile Section, Sex Crimes Section, and Domestic Violence Section. Detectives investigate these crimes and provide assistance to victims.
Property Crimes Division	There are six property crime sections that are assigned to precincts and investigate property crimes: • Pawn Shop Section. Checks pawn shops for stolen property. • Bomb and Arson Section. Investigates cases involving bombs, bomb threats, and arson cases. • Fraud Section. Investigates fraud and identity theft cases. • Forgery Section. Investigates cases of forgery and check fraud. • Forensic Computer Crimes Section. Investigates crimes including theft of computer related information and fraud cases involving computers.
Narcotics & Vice Division	• Metro Meth Unit. Investigates the manufacture and distribution of methamphetamine. • Career Criminal Section. Focuses on repeat offenders. • Interdiction Section. Deploys officers in an effort to intercept drugs coming into the city. • Financial Investigations Section. Investigates cases of money laundering and drug monies. • Undercover Section. Conducts undercover investigations focusing on suppliers and wholesalers. • Vice Section. Investigates prostitution, pornography, and gambling. • Street Undercover Section. Contains undercover officers who target street dealers. • Tactical Enforcement Squad. Responds to dangerous situations including hostages, barricaded persons, and arrests of armed suspects. • Gang Squad. Investigates gangs and gang-related crimes.
Investigations Support Division	• DARE Section. Provides DARE instructions in the local schools. • Police Athletic League. Provides sports programs for youths in the city. • Fugitive Apprehension/Arraignment Section. Serves warrants and apprehends wanted fugitives. • Property and Evidence Section. Stores and secures evidence and property, maintaining the chain of evidence.
Regional Criminalistics Division	• Crime Scene Investigation Section. Collects and processes evidence at crime scenes. • Fingerprint and ID Section. Ensures that suspect fingerprints and mug shots are processed and processes fingerprints collected at crime scenes. • Crime Laboratory. Analyzes physical evidence collected at crime scenes. • Forensic Photography Evidence Section. Photographs evidence for criminal cases. • Special Equipment Unit. Maintains specialized equipment that is used in investigations.

to determine if clearances are maintained at acceptable levels. There will be periods where these rates will be higher or lower, but on average there should be some consistency. Commanders can also compare their units' clearance rates with other departments that are similar in size. When there are drastic changes in clearance rates, the unit commander should attempt to determine why and take remedial action if necessary. At the same time, the productivity of individual detectives should be monitored by examining a detective's clearance rate over time and comparing it with the clearance rates of other detectives in the unit. This is especially important for detectives who have been recently appointed to the detective position and for detectives who have been transferred from other investigative units. Detectives who consistently have high clearance rates should be used to mentor new detectives, and their investigative procedures should be shared with all other detectives.

Investigative managers cannot compare clearance rates across the various units in the detective bureau. Property crimes are the most difficult to solve since they generally do not have a victim or witness that was present when the crime occurred. Homicide, on the other hand, has the highest clearance rate since these cases often have multiple leads and physical evidence. Thus, each individual investigative unit's progress and productivity should be evaluated independently of other investigative units.

Commanders should also review the final product: the case presentation in court. Commanders should review detectives' conviction rates, keeping in mind that, because convictions largely rest with juries, judges, and prosecutors, detectives do not necessarily have control over the outcomes. Nonetheless, substantial deviations should be noted and investigated. Commanders should meet with prosecutors periodically to evaluate detectives' court presentations. If problems are identified, detectives can be provided training or mentoring.

Commanders should also monitor quality control—the quality of the investigation as documented by the case jacket. Here, commanders should review completed case jackets, which contain all the reports, witness statements, and confessions and other suspect information. It is not necessary to review every case, but periodically, a random selection of cases should be reviewed at a minimum. The review should examine the accuracy, completeness, and grammar of the reports, and determine whether or not the case jacket contains all necessary reports and information, and whether or not all leads were identified and followed. When deficiencies are identified, they should be discussed with the detective and where applicable, his or her supervisor.

Another quality control issue is the preliminary reports. Patrol officers frequently consider report writing to be drudgery, and they often put little effort or time in writing them. When they have errors or are incomplete, detectives do not have the information they need to proceed with their investigations. Patrol officers' reports, in most departments, are supposed to be reviewed by the patrol supervisor, but in some cases, they may perform an inadequate review. If the criminal investigation supervisor or manager sees a consistent pattern of inadequate reports, he or she should work with patrol commanders to rectify the problem.

TRAFFIC ENFORCEMENT

Supervisory Responsibilities

Traffic enforcement has two primary responsibilities: (1) to ensure the safe and expedient flow of vehicular and pedestrian traffic and (2) to investigate traffic crashes to determine cause. Traffic enforcement is conducted via: (1) enforcement, (2) education, and (3) engineering. In terms of enforcement, traffic officers write citations in an effort to reduce traffic crashes. They should not be involved in writing tickets to generate revenue for the government. The police should also be involved in educating the public about driver and pedestrian safety. Education programming can reduce crashes in a community. Engineering refers to officers identifying dangerous road conditions such as unsafe intersections or other environmental conditions that contribute to a large number of crashes. The installation of stop signs, improving traffic stop lights, and reducing the posted speed in some areas may result in a reduction of traffic crashes.

TABLE 13-4 Traffic and Vehicle-related Functions of Local Police Departments, by Size of Population Served

	Percent of agencies responsible for—				
Population served	**Traffic law enforcement**	**Accident investigation**	**Traffic direction/control**	**Parking enforcement**	**Commercial vehicle enforcement**
All sizes	100%	97%	89%	86%	38%
1,000,000 or more	100%	100%	88%	88%	81%
500,000-999,999	100	100	97	71	57
250,000-499,999	100	100	95	73	61
100,000-249,999	100	99	94	81	56
50,000-99,999	100	99	90	88	51
25,000-49,999	100	99	91	93	52
10,000-24,999	100	99	95	92	45
2,500-9,999	100	98	90	89	39
Under 2,500	100	94	86	81	32

Source: Hickman, M., and Reaves, B. (2006). *Local Police Departments, 2003.* Washington, D.C.: Bureau of Justice Statistics, p. 18

Traffic units are responsible for a range of police activities. Table 13-4 provides a breakdown of responsibilities by population size.

All departments are involved in traffic law enforcement and the vast majority is involved in the investigation of traffic crashes, traffic control or direction, and parking enforcement. Only about 40 percent of departments are involved in commercial vehicle enforcement. Commercial vehicle enforcement involves ensuring that commercial vehicles have the proper licenses and permits. It ensures that trucks are not overloaded, which makes them unsafe. It should be noted that large trucks are over-represented in traffic crashes so laws relative to commercial vehicles should be strictly enforced. There generally is a state agency responsible for the enforcement of commercial vehicle codes in those jurisdictions where officers do not enforce these codes.

One of the primary supervisory responsibilities for traffic supervisors is to ensure that traffic officers are writing citations that contribute to safety. That is, traffic officers should write citations at locations with high numbers of accidents, and the citations should be written for the offenses that contribute the most to the traffic crashes. For example, it does little good for officers to write citations for speeding in an area where following too closely causes most of the traffic crashes. An analysis of accident reports can yield information necessary to an effective traffic enforcement program. Supervisors should inform officers of high crash locations and the driving violations that contribute to them.

Ticket Quotas?

Citizens often accuse the police of having **ticket quotas**. They believe that officers must write a minimum number of tickets each day. Few departments have official quotas; however, most departments have unofficial quotas. The two primary tasks of traffic officers are to enforce traffic laws (write citations) and investigate traffic crashes. Traffic officers, therefore, are expected to write tickets. Generally, the work group–traffic officers set quotas by establishing an average, over time, that is adhered to by the group, and is accepted by supervisors and managers, and does not result in officers having to work hard throughout the shift. Police managers cannot officially establish quotas, for if they do, the news media will likely discover the policy and publicize it. This results in a number of public relations problems.

One common problem with traffic officers is that they have a tendency to "cherry pick" citations. All officers know locations where they can write large numbers of tickets in a short period of time. Some officers will go to these locations, quickly write the required or expected number of citations, and essentially goof off for the remaining part of the shift. This is why it is important for supervisors to monitor the types of citations that are written. Supervisors can encourage officers to enforce traffic laws in locations where there is a high volume of accidents. This is an often neglected responsibility, but it is extremely important.

DUI Enforcement

Driving while under the influence (DUI) is a high enforcement priority for traffic and patrol officers. Drivers who are under the influence are over-represented in traffic crashes and fatalities. Historically, DUI laws were under-enforced; police officers did not see the importance of strictly enforcing the DUI laws, or assigned higher priority to other police activities. In the 1980s, **DUI enforcement** became a focal point for opinion and activism. Organizations such as Mothers Against Drug Drivers (MADD) and Students Against Drunk Drivers (SADD) formed and conducted public relations campaigns against drunk drivers, and to some extent, police departments for under-enforcing laws. As a result of public attention, police departments began to strictly enforce DUI laws and states made their laws stricter by lowering the blood-alcohol content levels in the statutes. The federal government gave numerous police departments grants to enhance DUI enforcement.

Today, DUI is seen as a serious offense. In some jurisdictions, repeat DUI offenses are felonies. Most police departments strictly enforce DUI laws. Such enforcement reduces traffic crashes and injuries, and it often prevents negative publicity. When multiple DUI related traffic fatalities occur, it often results in public scrutiny of the police and their enforcement priorities.

Traffic Enforcement Cameras

A relatively new innovation in traffic enforcement is stoplight cameras. Essentially, these cameras are operated by a private company, which installs and maintains the cameras and collects fines. Once fines are collected, a portion of the revenue is given to the city or jurisdiction where the camera is located. In most jurisdictions, the police have little or nothing to do with the traffic light cameras, but the public perceives that they are police operated. Traffic stoplight cameras cause some measure of friction between the police and pubic in some jurisdictions.

The stated objective for installing these cameras is to reduce the number vehicles running red lights as well as traffic crashes that are caused by these violations. However, this rationale is somewhat dubious. Many governmental officials see them as a source of revenue. For example, the City of Dallas budgeted $15 million in revenue for its 62 cameras for the 2007-2008 fiscal year (MSNBC, March 20, 2008), which is a sizable amount of income even for a city the size of Dallas. There is some evidence that the cameras are a form of policing for profit, which undermines public confidence in the police. This occurs even though the police department has nothing to do with the camera systems.

There are a number of problems associated with traffic light cameras. First, they do reduce the number of T-bone collisions (vehicles proceeding through a stop light and hitting another vehicle broadside), but they increase the number of rear-end collisions. Thus, it is unclear if they indeed reduce accidents. Second, most of the citations issued are for rolling through the light while making a right-hand turn. Officials in Los Angeles estimate that 80 percent of the citations are for right-hand turns (Connell, 2008). This no doubt is a violation, but it is questionable how unsafe the practice is. The overwhelming majority of people making such turns ensure that it is safe to do so. Third, there have been instances where the yellow or caution light at such intersections is in effect for a shorter period of time than at other stoplights, thus increasing the number of violations and citations issued. This is not only dangerous, but unethical. Fourth, the fines for these violations are quite high since the company operating the camera systems receives a substantial portion of the revenue. Police departments should consider all the facts when called upon to support the installation of these devices.

VEHICULAR PURSUITS

A High-Stakes Operation

Few patrol operational issues are of greater concern to police leadership than police pursuits. Civil litigation arising out of collisions involving police pursuits reveal it to be a high-stakes undertaking with serious and sometimes tragic results (Hill, 2002). About 350 people are killed each year during police pursuits (National Highway Traffic Safety Administration, 2006); many of the resulting deaths and injuries involved innocent third parties or stemmed from minor traffic violations. The U.S. Supreme Court, as seen later, has strengthened most progressive chase policies; but the Court has also conferred a responsibility that must be borne by the police. Pursuits place the police in a delicate balancing act. On the one hand, there is the need to show that flight from the law is no way to freedom. On the other hand, if a police agency completely bans high speed pursuits, its credibility with both law-abiding citizens and law violators may suffer; public knowledge that the agency has a no-pursuit policy may encourage people to flee, decreasing the probability of apprehension (Eisenberg, 1999). Still, according to Belotto (1999:86), because of safety and liability concerns, "a growing number of agencies have the position that if the bad guy puts the pedal to the metal, its a 'freebie.' They will not pursue him."

High-speed pursuit is indeed a threat to everyone within range of the pursuit, including suspects, their passengers, or other drivers or bystanders. One police trainer asks a simple question of officers to determine whether or not to continue a pursuit: "'Is this person a threat to the public safety other than the fact the police are chasing him?' If the officer cannot objectively answer 'yes,' the pursuit should be terminated" (Williams, 1997).

The following incidents demonstrate the dangerous nature of police pursuits:

- In Omaha, Nebraska, a 70-mile-per-hour pursuit through a residential neighborhood of a motorcyclist for an expired license plate ended when the motorcyclist ran a stop sign, crashing into another vehicle and killing the female passenger on the motorcycle.
- A sheriff's deputy in Florida intentionally rammed a vehicle during a pursuit for an outstanding misdemeanor warrant, causing a collision and killing a backseat passenger.
- A police officer pursuing a shoplifter in Mobile, Alabama, crashed into a mall security vehicle, seriously injuring the guard.

These and other tragic stories are all too common, and certainly the onus is on police chief executives to develop pursuit policies—considering input from line personnel, supervisors and managers, and attorneys versed in civil liability—and remain vigilant in seeing that they are enforced. Pursuit policies provide general guidelines for the officer and supervisor. The courts will evaluate these policy issues when considering whether or not an agency or its officers or supervisors should be held culpable for damages or injuries resulting from pursuits. At the International Association of Chiefs of Police (IACP) Annual Conference in 1996, its membership adopted a resolution and model pursuit policy to serve as a guideline for police executives. The resolution and policy, based on recommendations from the National Commission on Law Enforcement Driving Safety, was provided to the IACP's Highway

The danger of high-speed police pursuits is all too evident in the number that result in accidents, injuries, or death.
Courtesy Sparks, Nevada, Police Department

Safety Committee. The resolution and policy as shown in Figure 13-1 is purposely generic in nature so that agencies can individualize it to their specific needs.

The Supreme Court's View

In May 1990, two Sacramento County, California, deputies responded to a fight call. At the scene they observed a motorcycle with two riders approaching their vehicle at high speed; turning on their red lights, the deputies ordered the driver to stop. The motorcycle operator began to elude the officers, who initiated a pursuit reaching speeds of more than 100 miles per hour over about 1.3 miles. The pursuit ended when the motorcycle crashed; when that occurred, the deputies' vehicle could not stop in time and struck the bike's passenger, killing him; his family brought suit, claiming the pursuit violated the crash victim's due process rights under the Fourteenth Amendment. In May 1998, the U. S. Supreme Court, in *County of Sacramento v. Lewis* (118 S.Ct. 1708), ruled in this case, holding that the proper standard to be employed in these cases is whether the officer's conduct during the pursuit was conscience-shocking (conduct or character that is offensive to a reasonable person's sense of moral goodness); it further determined that high-speed chases with no intent to harm suspects do not give rise to liability under the Fourteenth Amendment (at p. 1720). The Court closed the door on the liability for officers involved in pursuits that do not "shock the conscience."

Supervisory Roles and Liability

The responsibility falls to the field supervisor to see that proper methods are employed by patrol officers during pursuits—whether the pursuit simply involves a primary pursuing officer and a backup, or more elaborate methods, such as the following two methods. The first is "boxing," where three

Following are selected portions of the Sample Vehicular Pursuit Policy that was approved at the 103rd Annual Conference of the International Association of Chiefs of Police in Phoenix, Arizona, on September 30, 1996. Note the responsibilities of the supervisor as they pertain to communications, coordination, participation, and possible termination as they relate to the pursuit:

I. *Purpose*
The purpose of this policy is to establish guidelines for making decisions with regard to pursuits.

II. *Policy*
Vehicular pursuit of fleeing suspects can present a danger to the lives of the public, officers, and suspects involved in the pursuit. It is the responsibility of the agency to assist officers in the safe performance of their duties. To fulfill these obligations, it shall be the policy of this law enforcement agency to regulate the manner in which vehicular pursuits are undertaken and performed.

III. *Procedures*
A. Initiation of Pursuit
1. The decision to initiate pursuit must be based on the pursuing officer's conclusion that the immediate danger to the officer and the public created by the pursuit is less than the immediate or potential danger to the public should the suspect remain at large.
2. Any law enforcement officer in an authorized emergency vehicle may initiate a vehicular pursuit when the suspect exhibits the intention to avoid apprehension by refusing to stop when properly directed to do so. Pursuit may also be justified if the officer reasonably believes that the suspect, if allowed to flee, would present a danger to human life or cause serious injury.
3. In deciding whether to initiate pursuit, the officer shall take into consideration:
a. Road, weather, and environmental conditions.
b. Population density and vehicular and pedestrian traffic.
c. The relative performance capabilities of the pursuit vehicle and the vehicle being pursued.
d. The seriousness of the offense.
e. The presence of other persons in the police vehicle.
Upon engaging in a pursuit, the officer shall notify communications of the location, direction, and speed of the pursuit, the description of the pursued vehicle, and the initial purpose of the stop. When engaged in pursuit, officers shall not drive with reckless disregard for the safety of other road users.

B. Supervisory Responsibilities
1. When made aware of a vehicular pursuit, the appropriate supervisor shall monitor incoming information, coordinate and direct activities as needed to ensure that proper procedures are used, and have the discretion to terminate the pursuit.
2. Where possible a supervisory officer shall respond to the location where a vehicle has been stopped following a pursuit.

FIGURE 13-1 IACP Model Pursuit Policy
Source: Reprinted from *The Police Chief,* Vol. 64, No. 1, pp. 20–21, 1997. Copyright by the International Association of Chiefs of Police, 515 North Washington Street, Alexandria, VA 22314, USA. Further reproduction without express written permission is strictly prohibited.

police vehicles are positioned at the front, rear, and side of the suspect vehicle during the chase. The three police vehicles slow in unison, causing the offender to slow and eventually stop. This technique can result in damage to any or all of the vehicles involved. The second termination tactic, "precision immobilization technique," involves a police vehicle making contact with a suspect vehicle. The officer gently pushes one of the rear quarter panels of the suspect vehicle in order to displace its forward motion, causing it to spin. This technique also involves considerable risk to the officer and suspect

(Eisenberg, 1999). Both of these methods—and other tactics employed during pursuits—are obviously potentially perilous and require extensive officer training to obtain proficiency.

Oversight of pursuits enables a third party—the supervisor—who is not emotionally involved to guard against what has been termed a pursuit fixation, wherein pursuing officers throw caution to the wind. Supervisors need to set the rules on what will be tolerated and what level of performance is expected during a pursuit. They must clearly establish that once the pursuit team is in place, other officers not directly involved should show restraint and drive parallel to the pursuit, obeying all traffic laws (Belotto, 1999).

Supervisors depend on the communications of other officers for the information needed to make the decisions demanded by the courts. The supervisor should ask by radio for the following information: the speed and direction of the fleeing suspect vehicle; the offense, suspected offense, or status (i.e., warrants) of the suspect; the number of police units involved in the pursuit; and the suspect's actions (is he close to putting others in danger with his driving?) (Williams, 1997). Supervisors are to serve as the "safety officer" of the pursuit—a role they may not wish to take because they do not want to be unpopular with their officers, but one which is far better than attending an officer's funeral or visiting one in the hospital. It is obvious that the liabilities associated with police pursuits should be a primary concern of every police chief executive officer. The courts have awarded numerous six- and seven-figure settlements to plaintiffs seeking redress for injuries, damages, or deaths resulting from police pursuits. The development of pursuit policies and officer and supervisor training can help to protect agencies against liability suits.

It is the responsibility of command personnel and supervisors to ensure that officers thoroughly understand and comply with pursuit policies. In addition to the policy issues and supervisory information identified above, other factors considered by the courts to evaluate pursuit liability involve the following:

> *The reason for the pursuit*. Does it justify the actions taken by the officer?
>
> *Driving conditions*. Any factor that could hinder an officer's ability to safely conduct a pursuit should be considered sufficient reason to terminate.
>
> *The use of police warning devices*. Typically, lights and siren are required by state statutes.
>
> *Excessive speed*. This often depends on conditions of the environment. For example, a 30-mile-per-hour pursuit in a school zone may be considered excessive and dangerous.
>
> *Demonstrations of due regard in officers' actions*. Officers who choose the course of safety will create the least danger to all parties affected and maintain the highest degree of protection from liability.
>
> *The use of deadly force*. There are few instances in which officers can justify driving tactics that result in the death of a fleeing driver; such situations include roadblocks, boxing in, and ramming.
>
> *Departmental policies and state law*. These must be obeyed; to do otherwise greatly increases the potential liability of both the officer and department.
>
> *Appropriate supervision and training*. In the absence of such measures, the department will be subject to a finding of negligence, and liability will attach. (Falcone, Charles, and Wells, 1994:60)

Police pursuits represent an ongoing, hazardous problem. Therefore, efforts must continue to develop electromagnetic-field devices that officers can place on the roadway and use to interrupt the electronic ignition systems in suspect vehicles and terminate pursuits. In the meantime, tire deflation devices, which can end chases by slowly deflating one or more tires of a suspect's vehicle, have been welcomed by the police.

CASE STUDIES

Following are three case studies that enable the reader to consider some of the substantive issues described in the chapter and to consider some options as solutions to problems.

Case Study #1

C.S.I.: Boone City

John McCauley recently was promoted to the rank of captain in charge of criminal investigations in Boone City. Previously, he was a lieutenant in patrol and earlier in his career he was a detective; therefore, he has limited experience in managing criminal investigations. The detectives in the unit view him suspiciously because of his lack of investigative experience. The unit is divided into several sections: burglary, crimes against persons (homicide, sexual assault, and robbery), narcotics, and general investigations, which includes fraud, cybercrimes, vice, and identity theft. The veteran detectives and supervisors have assured McCauley that things are working smoothly and that they will show him the ropes. On the other hand, the assistant chief in charge of the operations bureau advises him that the previous captain was not a strong leader and allowed the detectives to dictate policies and priorities for the unit. He wants McCauley to take a more assertive role in the unit, increase the detectives' clearance rates, and generally do more thorough investigations of a larger proportion of cases.

Questions for Discussion

1. How can Captain McCauley evaluate the overall effectiveness of his unit?
2. McCauley wants to provide the assistant chief with a plan of action. What should be the major elements in this plan?
3. How should McCauley go about evaluating individual detectives?

Case Study #2

I've Been Robbed!

Sergeant John Simpson recently was transferred to the second patrol watch under Captain John Waters. Simpson's precinct is an area that encompasses businesses, strip malls, and lower-middle class residential areas. The area contains a number of bars and nightclubs that historically have reputations as being wide open with a number of patrons who are rowdy and intoxicated. The bars often have fights requiring multiple patrol units to break them up. Recently the area has witnessed a substantial increase in robberies of consumers frequenting the area's mall and retail businesses. The media has published a number of stories about the problem, and the chief of police has been feeling the heat. The chief has directed Captain Waters to deal with the problem, and he tasks Simpson with the responsibility of developing and implementing a plan to deal with the problem.

Questions for Discussion

(Note: you may wish to review and incorporate some problem analysis methods discussed in Chapter 4 of this textbook.)

1. How should Simpson study the problem?
2. What alternatives should Simpson consider?
3. What additional resources might be necessary to reduce the robbery problem?

Case Study #3

Pete the Pursuer

Members of the Bentonville County Sheriff's Department have been involved in several vehicle pursuits within the last year. One such incident resulted in the death of a 14-year-old juvenile who crashed during a pursuit while he was joyriding in his parents' car. This tragedy sparked a massive public outcry and criticism of the police department for using excessive force. A lawsuit is pending against the department and individual officers involved in the pursuit. You, the sheriff, immediately changed and tightened the department's policy regarding pursuits, now requiring that a supervisor cancel any pursuit that does not involve a violent felony crime or other circumstances that would justify the danger and potential liability. All officers have been trained in the new policy. A separate policy prohibits the firing of warning shots unless "circumstances warrant." It is now about 9:00 p.m. and Deputy Pete Prusso is patrolling in an industrial park in his sector. Prusso, having graduated from the police academy and field training about 6 months ago, engages in vehicle and foot pursuits at every opportunity. He is providing extra patrol as a result of reports of vandalism and theft of building materials in one area of the county. A parked vehicle attracts his attention because private vehicles are not normally parked in the area at this time. As Prusso approaches the vehicle with his cruiser's lights off and spotlight on, he notices the brake lights on the vehicle flash on and off. Prusso exits his vehicle for a closer look, and the vehicle takes off at a high rate of speed in his direction. Seeing the vehicle coming at him from about 30 yards away, Prusso fires a warning shot into the ground. When it is about 15 yards away, the vehicle veers away from him and then leaves at a high rate of speed. As the escaping vehicle passes by, Ripley yells for the driver to halt, then fires again, striking the side of the vehicle. He then takes off in pursuit of the vehicle, and radios dispatch concerning his pursuit. The shift commander—a patrol lieutenant—hears this radio transmission.

Questions for Discussion

1. What are the central issues involved?
2. Is the deputy in compliance with the use-of-force policy? Defend your answer.
3. Should the lieutenant "shut down" Prusso's pursuit? Explain.
4. Should the deputy have fired warning shots under these circumstances? Why or why not?
5. What kinds of policies and procedures would normally cover Prusso's actions? Would your Internal Affairs Unit find that the deputy was at fault with any of them? Which of the deputy's actions do you as sheriff feel should result in disciplinary action against Prusso? Why or why not?
6. Are additional policies and training sessions needed? Explain your answers.

Summary

This chapter examines managerial and supervisory issues in police operations, patrol, criminal investigation, and traffic. Operational units comprise the bulk of personnel and activities in a police department—they are the units that provide police services to the public. Therefore, it is important that these units function effectively, and effectiveness is largely dependent on how well these units are managed and supervised.

Patrol represents the largest unit in a police department with approximately 70 percent of sworn personnel. Patrol officers are assigned to beats and are responsible for all activities within their beats. Supervisors must monitor patrol officers' activities in a number of areas. They must ensure that they are able to answer calls for service, especially during peak times. Additionally, during periods when there are fewer calls, supervisors should encourage officers to become involved in COPPS activities (discussed in Chapter 4). Supervisors and managers must constantly evaluate officers' workload and plan and make assignments.

Criminal investigation or detectives are responsible for investigating crimes. As a result of their investigations, they solve crimes, arrest perpetrators, and recover stolen property. The primary responsibility for investigative managers and supervisors is case management. They assign cases to detectives and monitor their progress. They ensure that detectives have ample time to investigate the cases in their caseload. They encourage detectives to concentrate on important cases—cases that are high profile and those that can be solved. Finally, they ensure that detectives complete their investigations, examine all evidence, document their cases, and are able to assist in the prosecution of the case.

Finally, the traffic unit is responsible for reducing traffic crashes and expediting the flow of traffic. These officers do this through enforcement, education, and engineering. Traffic officers should write tickets at locations with a high number of traffic crashes, and the citations should be for those violations that cause the crashes. If this does not occur, then traffic enforcement will not have a substantial impact on the number of traffic crashes. Traffic officers should pay particular attention to those violations that result in the largest number of accidents, especially injury and fatal accidents. This means that DUI enforcement should be a high priority. Another responsibility for police supervisors and managers of the traffic unit is the oversight of the **vehicular pursuit** function. Because of the high potential for liability and the high level of danger involved, supervisors and managers must ensure that officers involved in vehicular pursuit follow the procedures and policies that are in place to ensure the safety of officers, those they are pursuing, and innocent bystanders.

Items for Review

1. Explain how operational units are organized in large police departments.
2. How does a supervisor or manager manage patrol officers' time, and how do calls for service enter into that responsibility?
3. What are the primary responsibilities of a patrol supervisor?
4. What are the major units that can be organized in a large police department and how do those units interact with precinct commanders?
5. How do investigative supervisors and managers manage detectives' cases?
6. What are the primary responsibilities of a traffic unit?
7. How and why are vehicular pursuits both a hazard in terms of life and property as well as from the standpoint of police liability?

References

Alpert, G., and Dunham, R. (1997). *Policing urban America*. Prospect Heights, IL: Waveland Press.

Belotto, A. (1999). Supervisors govern pursuits. *Law and Order* (January):86.

Bennett, W., and Hess, K. (2007). *Criminal investigation*. Belmont, CA: Wadsworth.

Clark, W. (2003). Electric bicycles: High-tech tools for law enforcement. *Law Enforcement Technology*, 78-82.

Connell, R. (2008). Red-light cameras catch right turns and lots of revenue. *Los Angeles Times*, (May 19, 2008): A1, A13.

Eck, J. (1983). *Solving crimes: The investigation of burglary and robbery.* Washington, D.C.: PERF.

Eisenberg, C. B. (1999). Pursuit management. *Law and Order* (March):73-77.

Falcone, D. N., Charles, M. T., and Wells, E. (1994). A study of pursuits in Illinois. *The Police Chief* 61 (March):59-64.

Famega, C. (2005). Variation in officer downtime: A review of the research. *Policing: An International Journal of Police Strategies & Management*, 28: 388-414.

Gaines, L., and Kappeler, V. (2007). *Policing in America*. Newark, NJ: LexisNexis.

Hickman, M., and Reaves, B. (2006). *Local police departments, 2003.* Washington, D.C.: Bureau of Justice Statistics.

Hill, J. (2002). High-speed police pursuits: Dangers, dynamics, and risk reduction. *FBI Law Enforcement Bulletin* (July):14-18.

Kappeler, V., and Gaines, L. (2008). *Community policing: A contemporary perspective*. Newark, NJ: LexisNexis.

Kelling, G., Pate, T., Dieckman, D., and Brown, C. (1974). *The Kansas City Preventive Patrol Experiment: A summary report*. Washington, D.C.: The Police Foundation.

Kuykendall, J. (1986). The municipal police detective: An historical analysis. *Criminology*, 24: 175-201.

Mazerolle, L., Rogan, D., Frank, J., Famega, C., and Eck, J. (2005). Managing calls to the police with 911/311 systems. *NIJ Reseach for Practice*. Washington, D.C.: National Institute of Justice.

McLean, H. (1990). Getting high on crime. *Law and Order*, 38(7): 30-36.

Menton, C. (2008). Bicycle patrols: An underutilized resource. *Policing: An International Journal of Police Strategies & Management*. 31: 93-108.

MSNBC. (March 20, 2008). http://www.msnbc.msn.com/id/23710970/.

National Highway Traffic Safety Administration. (2006). National Highway Traffic SafetyAdministration statistics. Washington, D.C.: Author.

Nesbary, D. (2008). Handling emergency calls for service: Organizational production of crime statistics. *Policing: An International Journal of Police Management & Strategies*, 21(4): 576-599.

Sanders, W. (1977). *Detective work*. New York: Free Press.

Williams, G. T. (1997). When do we keep pursuing? Justifying high-speed pursuits. *The Police Chief* (March):24-27.

Wilson, O. (1950). *Police administration*. New York: McGraw-Hill Book Co.

CHAPTER 14

On Patrol: Responses to Difficult Crime Problems

KEY TERMS AND CONCEPTS

- **"A gathering storm" of crime**
- Clandestine drug labs
- Crimes in progress
- Domestic violence
- **Drug issues**
- Gangs
- Gang Resistance Education and Training (G.R.E.A.T.)
- Gun ownership
- Methamphetamine
- **Notification of managers and supervisors**
- Open-air drug markets
- **Police initiatives (for all types of crimes discussed in this chapter)**
- Raves
- School violence

LEARNING OBJECTIVES

After reading this chapter, the student will:

- be aware of why some police leaders see a "gathering storm" looming in the nation's violent crime rate, and why they feel as they do
- know how patrol officers can meet the goals of the patrol function
- understand the nature of domestic violence, and some contemporary police strategies for dealing with it
- be knowledgeable about several unique challenges posed by illegal drug use—methamphetamine use, clandestine drug labs, open-air trafficking, and rave parties—and some contemporary police strategies for dealing with them
- have a fundamental understanding of the current gang problem, and what the police have undertaken to cope with it
- comprehend the serious nature of school violence, and how the police can prepare and respond to such incidents
- know what is involved with crimes in progress, and related police initiatives
- know when supervisors and managers should be notified concerning unusual or critical incidents

Big jobs usually go to the men who prove their ability to outgrow small ones.

—RALPH WALDO EMERSON

INTRODUCTION

Many situations and problems confront patrol supervisors and middle managers as they direct their daily operations; they must also ensure that patrol officers' work activities are conducted according to agency expectations. During any tour of duty, police officers can encounter situations that are extraordinary and unique when compared with the majority of general calls for service and that require special attention.

This chapter opens with a discussion of what one person termed "a gathering storm" in view of the recent rise in crimes of violence in America, some reasons offered for the increase, and what that increase portends for all of us, including the police. Next is a general discussion of the scope of patrol operations, including the kinds of goals or objectives that patrol officers possess when responding to calls for service (CFS).

Then, six potentially deadly situations and problems that confront police officers and their leaders are addressed: domestic violence, drug abuse, gangs, school violence, crimes in progress, and gun ownership. Where appropriate, the emphasis in this chapter is on the kinds of strategies that police are undertaking for handling these problems. Then, because these and other kinds of critical incidents may be too overwhelming for street officers to handle, policy guidelines are considered for when a superior officer should be notified. The chapter concludes with two case studies.

Note that some if not all of the incidents discussed in this chapter, such as crimes in progress and domestic disputes, are often addressed in city ordinances or agency policies and procedures that spell out how officers are to deal with them; some are now also dealt with in state statutes. It is incumbent on supervisors and managers to know and understand those mandates—as well as ensure that officers adhere to them.

Finally, because they have a far greater direct role in overseeing patrol officers, and because this chapter focuses on street crimes, the primary emphasis will be on first-line supervisory personnel, and less on middle managers. Nonetheless, middle managers are assigned to the patrol function; they will find themselves confronted with managing the supervisors who are handling the problems discussed in this chapter, if not actively on the street, then administratively in their office, in a policy making capacity.

"A GATHERING STORM..."

"We have a gathering storm of crime." That is how Los Angeles Police Chief William Bratton characterized his prognosis of violent crimes in America at a recent summit meeting. Bratton—then also serving as President of the Police Executive Research Forum, as well as the creator of CompStat, discussed in Chapter 4—and the other 170 mayors, police chiefs and public officials in attendance noted that violent crime is accelerating at an alarming pace.

Indeed, the Federal Bureau of Investigation recently reported significant increases in violent crime throughout the country in three of the four violent crime categories: homicide, robberies, and aggravated assaults. More broadly, violent crime increases during 2004 and 2005 reversed a 13-year decline in violent crime rates, which occurred from 1992 through 2003 (U.S. Department of Justice, Federal Bureau of Investigation, 2007).

Concerned that these violent crime increases represent the front end of a tipping point of an epidemic of violence not seen for years, the summit's goal was to paint a picture of violent crime across the country and determine the nature and the extent of the problem (Simonetti, 2006).

Many of these officials described a culture of violence, concentrated in parts of their cities, where arguments over seemingly minor issues escalate to the retaliatory murder of additional people. Cities reported that their successful efforts to suppress drug markets had the unintended consequence of increasing street robberies for criminal enterprises; all complained about the proliferation of handguns, and that much of the violent crime is disproportionately impacting sections of the African-American and Hispanic communities. Also, more and more offenders who have spent time in a juvenile or an adult detention facility return to their communities—often poorly prepared in their previous work experience or education.

Summit attendees described a need for early intervention and many pointed to school and truancy programs that were initiated or reactivated. A number of localities are focusing their resources on hot spots and focused deterrence. Both police and elected officials alike were greatly concerned that the country has reached a critical point with violence, and, if it is not dealt with now, the country could very well witness a return to the crime heights of the early nineties (Simonetti, 2006).

In many jurisdictions, the redirection of federal resources to homeland security—what one person called "the monster that ate criminal justice"—has left cities more vulnerable to spikes in violent crime. Homeland security, in the minds of many police executives, has turned into "a zero sum game" between criminal justice funding and homeland security funding (Simonetti, 2006:12). They expressed concern that local police departments cannot be effective homeland security partners if they are

The spoils of war—gangs, guns, and drug-related violence—will continue to challenge the police in the twenty-first century.
(Courtesy NYPD Photo Unit)

overwhelmed by their core mission responsibilities; in other words, they must sacrifice hometown security for homeland security. There needs to be a more coordinated approach between homeland security and neighborhood safety. Local police departments are, they argue, the country's first line of defense.

MEETING THE GOALS OF THE PATROL FUNCTION

To understand the scope of patrol operations, we must consider the myriad possible CFS handled by the police. These range from simple requests for information or assistance to emergency situations.

One of the primary responsibilities of patrol supervisors and managers is to manage and control the scene of dangerous calls and to supervise officers' handling of such incidents. Also, supervisors and managers must address a number of calls that can be classified as tactical or critical incidents (discussed in Chapter 15), which have the potential to become life threatening. Any of these situations can take a turn for the worse and result in personal injury to citizens or officers. For this reason, the direct involvement of supervisors in such incidents is most important.

Police officers also have a number of resources at their disposal when responding to CFS, ranging from providing information or assistance to the use of deadly force. Both officers and supervisors must ensure that these responses meet the needs of the situation and that they do not go beyond the level that is necessary. If a situation calls for an arrest to be made, officers should take the suspect into custody.

It should be noted that when officers engage in various activities, they are attempting to achieve some goal or objective. Possible goals include (1) protecting an endangered citizen, (2) protecting the officer himself or herself or other officers, (3) preventing a crime, (4) defusing a potentially violent situation, (5) solving a crime, (6) serving court papers, (7) ensuring the orderly flow of traffic and pedestrians, (8) helping or serving citizens, or (9) collecting information. The goal that officers select is contingent on the situation; it is the ultimate responsibility of supervisors and managers to ensure that officers employ the proper response.

The following sections explore several types of CFS from operational and supervisory perspectives; all can require the immediate attention and involvement of a supervisor and manager.

DOMESTIC VIOLENCE SITUATIONS

The Problem

Domestic disputes are some of the most common—and potentially most dangerous—calls for police service. They may result in anything from from simple assault to homicide. **Domestic violence** tends to be underreported; therefore there are wide differences in estimates. For example, the Domestic Violence Prevention Fund (2007) reports that estimates range from 960,000 to three million incidents of violence against a current or former spouse, boyfriend, or girlfriend per year. The problem is extensive (Sampson, 2007).

Police commonly express frustration that many of the battered women they deal with do not leave their batterers. However, for a variety of reasons—fear, a bond and support for her batterer, need for affection (that often follows battering), a feel there is no place to go—they resist leaving an abuser.

Police Initiatives

Before they can attempt to deal with domestic violence, the police must first gain an understanding of their local problem. Aggregating and analyzing data is important for understanding the context and

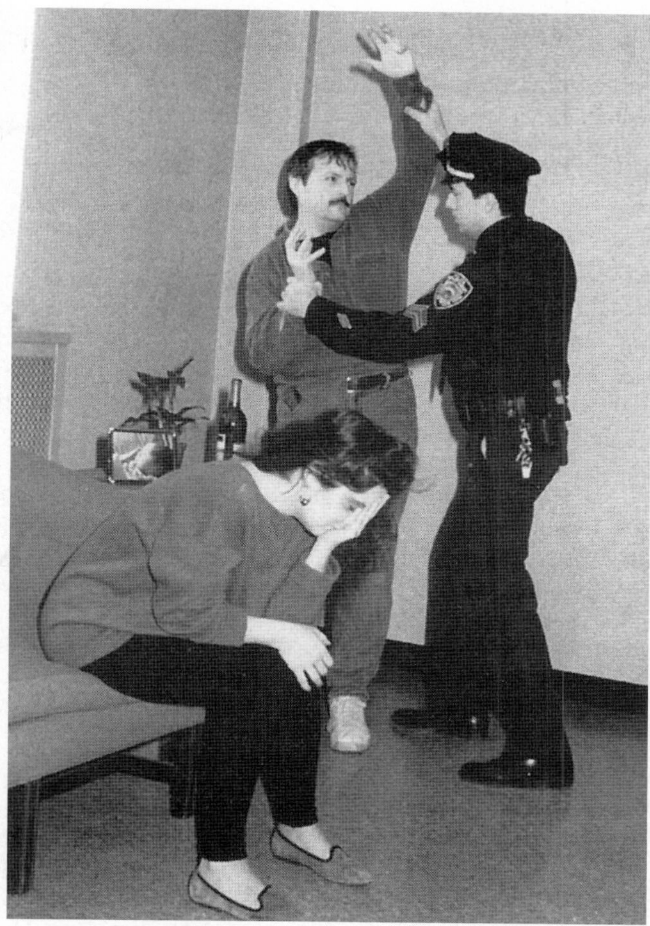

Role playing is one of the best methods for teaching officers how to handle difficult situations. Here a supervisor participates in domestic violence training.
(Courtesy NYPD Photo Unit)

history of domestic assaults, both at the community and individual levels. Calls for service, offense/incident reports, and databases from local social service agencies can assist in obtaining information about:

- ***victims*** (their number, gender, children living with them, those who were repeat victims, level of violence against them, those who are homeless, and so on);
- ***offenders*** (what percentage were arrested at the scene, had a prior arrest record, were on probation or parole, violated restraining orders against them, and so forth); and
- ***incidents*** (how many, who is the primary aggressor, time and locations of occurrences) (Sampson, 2007).

The methods to protect the victim or deter the offender can include a variety of situational crime prevention opportunity blocking mechanisms, such as the following:

- increased police surveillance of victims' homes
- greater coordination with other parts of the criminal justice system

- pendant alarms for at-risk victims
- video cameras placed in high-risk victims' homes
- cocoon watch over victims
- target hardening of victims' vulnerable properties
- police watch of offenders
- police opposition to bail
- electronic ankle bracelet monitoring of high-risk released offenders
- alarm-activated recording devices with two-way speech capability (allowing victims to speak directly to the police, and vice versa) (Sampson, 2007)

Some police agencies participate in domestic violence awareness campaigns and school programming, such as classroom instruction to teens about dating violence and ways to handle conflict. Domestic violence prevention messages may target the general population or specific populations. For example, campaigns may be designed to encourage victim reporting, deter potential offenders, or raise the consciousness of potential witnesses of abuse (neighbors, friends, relatives). However, the effect of these prevention strategies is unknown.

Police and other members of a domestic violence reduction collaborative should encourage people to call the police if they are victims of, witnesses to, or know a victim of, domestic violence. Prevention and education efforts should include this as a core message. A study of more than 2,500 domestic violence victims concluded that calling the police had a strong deterrent effect on revictimization, even when the police did not make an arrest, when the offender had a prior history of violence against the victim, and when the assault was sexual. Calling the police was beneficial even when the violence was severe (Sampson, 2007).

DRUG ISSUES

The Problem: Methamphetamine

The United States has long been in the throes of a grave drug problem. More than 1.8 million U.S. citizens are arrested for drug abuse violations per year (U.S. Department of Justice, Bureau of Justice Statistics, 2007a). The social costs of drug abuse are inestimable; drug abuse has given rise to a wide variety of related criminal acts, and resulted in innumerable gun-wielding gang members across the United States who are fighting to expand their turf.

In addition to crimes of manufacture, sale, and possession, drugs are related to criminality in additional ways; they have detrimental effects on the user's behavior and generate acts of violence (Hunt and Kuck, 2007). Now, methamphetamine has exploded onto the scene, with more than 12 million people age 12 and older reporting that they have used this relatively cheap, easy-to-make drug during their lifetime (Office of National Drug Control Policy, 2007).

Police Initiatives

Methamphetamine (meth) is a central nervous system stimulant often referred to as crank, speed, ice, or crystal. Developed in clandestine laboratories often located in remote areas, meth is cheap and addictive. Its negative effects can include physical addiction, psychotic behavioral episodes, and brain damage; chronic use can cause anxiety, confusion, insomnia, paranoia, and delusions. It is a serious health hazard to anyone who comes into reasonable contact with the precursor drugs used to produce methamphetamine, including police, medical, and fire personnel (Hunt and Kuck, 2007; Orchowsky et al., 2007).

Listed below are some successful police initiatives that have been undertaken in several communities to address their growing meth problem (U.S. Department of Justice, 2003). One study of 117 street-level drug initiatives found that the most successful were those that used a range of partnerships with community and other government agencies (Mazerolle et al., 2007). Note the use of such collaborative approaches in the examples below:

- The *Oklahoma City, Oklahoma*, Police Department focused on increased enforcement, training, and a partnership with a drug court to deal with meth problems. Officers used undercover buys, confidential informants, surveillance, and assistance from patrol officers making traffic stops to apprehend meth users and distributors. A 70 percent increase in the number of meth labs seized occurred in the first year of the initiative.
- In *Little Rock, Arkansas*, police focused on increased enforcement and training of all officers regarding meth identification and response. They established a telephone hotline for citizens to call if they suspected meth activity, launched an information campaign for retailers of precursor chemicals (including giving the police license plate numbers of purchasers of large quantities), and held interviews with jail detainees regarding meth use and manufacturing to better understand the meth market.
- *Salt Lake City* used enhanced enforcement and prosecution, child endangerment laws, civil remedies to reduce neighborhood impacts, public awareness campaigns, and the formation of a meth training team. More than 30 city, county, and federal agencies participated.
- *Minneapolis, Minnesota*, police first collected data using interviews with probationers and drug court clients. Then the department developed general training videos on lab identification and identification at traffic stops, and trained community groups; officers; and transit, housing, sanitation, and park employees who might come into contact with clandestine meth labs.

The Problem: Clandestine Drug Labs

A problem that is closely related to meth manufacturing and sales is **clandestine drug labs**. (Meth accounts for 80 to 90 percent of the labs' total drug production.) Dealing with clandestine drug labs requires extraordinarily high levels of technical expertise. Responders must understand illicit drug chemistry; how to neutralize the risks of explosions, fires, fumes, and burns; and how to handle and dispose of hazardous materials (HAZMAT). They must also know of the federal, state, and local laws governing chemical manufacturing and distribution, HAZMAT, and occupational safety (Scott, 2002).

Police Initiatives

Police responses to the problem of drug labs include:

- Using federal and state organized crime and racketeering statutes toward dismantling more sophisticated "super labs," run by syndicates
- Searching the homes and vehicles of former lab operators who are on probation and parole regularly, to determine if they have resumed operating a lab
- Seizing and filing for forfeiture of clandestine drug lab operators' assets (although this strategy is probably not effective with smaller labs)
- Enforcing environmental protection laws, because the burden of proof under these laws is typically less than that required for criminal convictions
- Filing civil actions against persons who allow their properties to be used as clandestine drug labs, as well as filing nuisance abatement actions and eviction actions
- Monitoring the sale and distribution of essential and precursor chemicals used in such labs (Scott, 2002).

The Problem: Open-Air Drug Markets

Open-air drug markets represent the lowest level of the drug distribution network. Open markets provide buyers a ready place to obtain the drugs they want, and sellers are able to maximize customer access. Dealing with open-air markets presents a considerable challenge for the police (Harocopos and Hough, 2005).

Police Initiatives

Following are some approaches to open-air drug activities that the police have undertaken—with the caveat that, whichever approach they choose, it is unlikely that they will be able to eradicate the open-air drug market completely:

- Policing the area in a highly visible fashion (including foot patrol) may disrupt the drug market and make it inconvenient for sellers and buyers to engage in drug transactions.
- Enforcing the law intensively. The effect of such a crackdown is dependent on the drug market that is targeted and the amount of resources available—such as using street surveillance and intelligence gathering, a hotline for area residents, and increases in drug treatment services.
- Undertaking intelligence-led investigative work. Information from drug hotlines and local residents can help to identify and analyse a problem. In addition any arrest may produce information if officers debrief the offender, and drug buyers may lead undercover officers to drug locations.
- Arresting drug buyers, in "reverse stings." This response serves to impact the demand side of the market and works best against new or occasional drug users. Some police have found that the process of being arrested, charged, and being forced to appear in court acted as a deterrent (Harocopos and Hough, 2005).

The Problem: Raves

A serious problem that can involve serious drug abuse are **raves**—dance parties that feature fast-paced, repetitive electronic music and light shows. Drug use is intended to enhance ravers' sensations and boost their energy so they can dance for long periods, usually starting late at night and going into the morning hours. Raves are enormously popular among young people and involve a blend of attitudes, drugs, and behaviors not found in other forms of youth culture (Scott, 2002).

Police concerns include drug overdoses, drug trafficking, noise, driving under the influence, and traffic control. Evidence suggests the drug most closely associated with rave parties—ecstasy—when used habitually, can cause permanent brain damage.

Police Initiatives

To better understand the extent of the local rave problem, police should conduct an analysis that answers a number of questions concerning rave incidents, location, and management. Some police responses that have met with success include: regulating rave venues to ensure basic health and safety measures are in use, encouraging property owners to exercise control over raves, prohibiting juveniles and adults from being admitted to the same raves, applying nuisance abatement laws where appropriate, prosecuting rave operators and property owners for drug-related offenses, and educating ravers about the risks of drug use and overexertion (Scott, 2002). Police should first perform an analytical assessment of the problem: What is the calls for service (CFS) pattern for the area? Are the arrestees youths who are truant from school? When is the activity occurring? Is lighting inadequate? Are grounds littered and vandalized? Are vacant apartments available to foster drug activity? Do abandoned vehicles provide convenient places for drug stashes?

GANGS

The Problem

Gangs have been a significant crime problem in this nation for several decades. It has long been known that the age range of gang members is broadening and becoming younger; the typical age range of gang members is about 14 to 24; youngsters generally begin hanging out with gangs at 12 or 13 years of age, join the gang at 13 or 14, and are first arrested at 14 (Huff, 1998). Furthermore, they have also spread into rural areas.

According to estimates by the National Criminal Justice Reference Service, there are more than 24,500 gangs and more than 772,000 gang members in the United States, in more than 3,300 jurisdictions. Like drug abuse, street gangs can have a significantly damaging effect on a community. Gangs play a role in firearms transactions and violence, drug sales and use, home invasions, car theft, homicide, and a number of other crime problems (U.S. Department of Justice, National Criminal Justice Reference Service, 2003).

Police Initiatives

As with raves and other problems mentioned above, the police must attempt a problem analysis of the involved street gangs, because gangs are particular to time and place (McGoin, 2005).

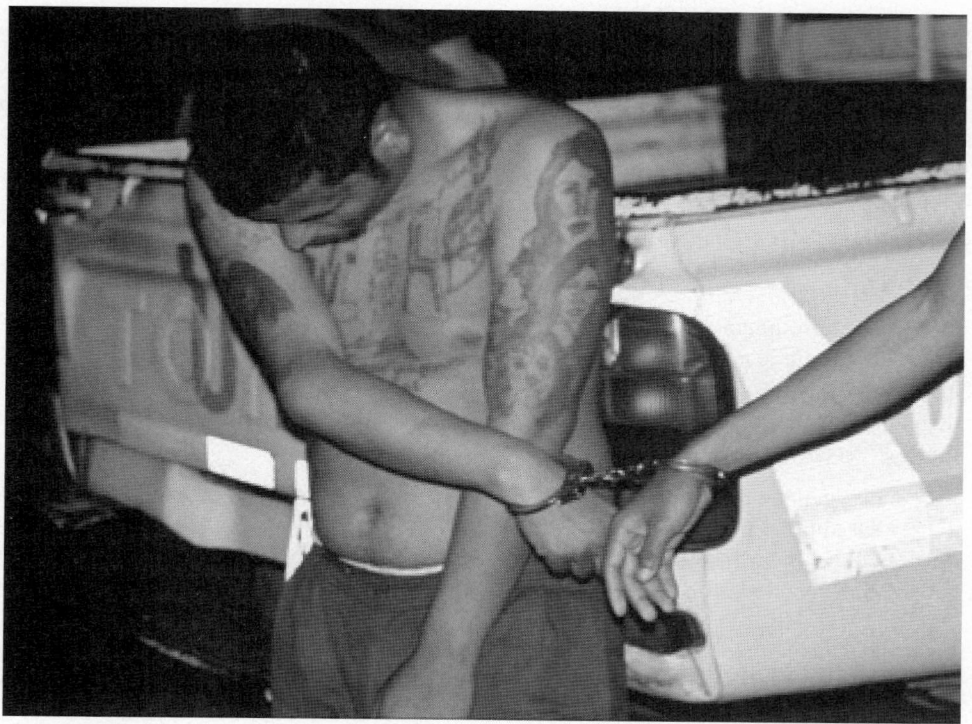

An MS-13 suspect bearing gang tattoos is handcuffed. In 2004, the FBI created the MS-13 National Gang Task Force. A year later, the FBI helped create the National Gang Intelligence Center. *(Courtesy FBI)*

Four types of programs exist for addressing gangs: prevention, intervention, suppression, and comprehensive strategies (McGoin, 2005):

- Prevention programs are typically aimed at groups that pose some risk, or more broadly, at general populations. For example, a prevention program may focus on preschool children who reside in gang neighborhoods before they show any symptoms of having joined the gang life. Perhaps the best known of these programs is **Gang Resistance Education and Training (G.R.E.A.T.)**. Although evaluation results of G.R.E.A.T. show no long-term impact on gang membership or delinquent behavior, they suggest positive short-term effects on gang-related behavior and attitudes.
- Intervention strategies typically address individuals or places that have manifested some problem. In most cases, such programs attempt to persuade gang members or gang-affiliated youth to abandon their current lifestyle or to reduce gang-related crime. At this stage, defining the type of gang of interest, the level of individual involvement in the gang, as well as the specific problem of focus becomes extremely important and integral to any success. Interventions may include a gang truce or the use of non-members to persuade gang members to leave gang life.
- Suppression programs also have the aim of reducing gang activities, but they typically rely on the law as a guide and on criminal justice agencies as the primary, and often only, partners. Deterrence principles often include law enforcement task forces or units and sentencing enhancements.
- However, suppression tactics alone are rarely successful in the long term. Even if a program appears successful in the short term, gangs tend to endure because the police can rarely eradicate them completely, nor do they have the resources to sustain such an intensive focus over time and across all gangs and gang members. In addition, crime may simply be displaced. Suppression tactics are important, but appear to provide the most benefit when part of a larger, comprehensive program.

SCHOOL VIOLENCE

The Problem

One Web site comments that "No one gives an oink about prom night or football, cos just getting home from school safe is a gamble and a blessing" (Cyberwolfman's Web Asylum, 2007). While that statement may be a gross exaggeration in the great majority of school districts across America, no one can deny that our schools have become much more potentially dangerous settings. Witness the following litany of recent school shootings:

- A suspended 14-year old student shot four people in October 2007 in his downtown Cleveland, Ohio, high school before killing himself (MSNBC, 2007).
- A heavily armed truck driver barricaded himself in a one-room Amish schoolhouse in Pennsylvania, killing five girls execution-style before killing himself (CNN.com, 2007).

Also in 2007:

- In Huntersville, North Carolina, a teenager shot and killed himself shortly after pointing a handgun at two other students in a high school parking lot (FOXNews.com, 2007).
- In Tacoma, Washington, an 18-year-old male high school student was arrested for shooting and killing a 17-year-old male student at their school. The suspect allegedly shot the victim in the face and then stood over him, firing twice more (CNN.com, 2007).

As wrenching as the above incidents were (and there were certainly many more such incidents than are listed above), the worst high school shooting since the 1999 massacre of 13 people at Columbine High School in Littleton, Colorado, occurred at the Red Lake Indian Reservation, Minnesota, in March 2005; ten people were killed (the shooter killed nine and then himself) and seven were injured in a rampage by a high school student (FOXNews.com, 2007). Nor does the above litany include the many occasions for which schools are evacuated and attacks are thwarted each year due to advance threats and warnings of shooting and violence.

And just as troubling is the fact that now such shooting sprees are occurring more frequently on postsecondary campuses as well; in 2007:

- Thirty-three people were killed on the campus of Virginia Tech in the deadliest rampage in American history (*The New York Times*, 2007).
- An 18-year old boy shot two students at Delaware State University (MSNBC, 2007).

And in an unbelievable turn, the mother of a 14-year old Pennsylvania boy—who was planning an attack at a high school—bought him a handgun and two rifles, one a semiautomatic, because he felt bullied (the boy also possessed about 30 air-powered guns, swords, knives, a bomb-making book, and videos of the aforementioned Columbine attack) (FOXNews.com, 2007).

Many who use violence in schools now fit what has become a familiar and virtually predictable profile: they had made frequent threats, were bullied, and were plagued with mental health issues. At times, however, a disagreement among students is settled with some type of weapon. About 5 percent of today's students are chronic rule breakers and are generally out of control most of the time. Students in schools where violence occurs will not focus on studies, perform at high academic levels, or even stay in school ("An overview of violence in the schools," 2001). Other common traits among the perpetrators of **school violence** include an orientation toward violent shows, videos, and music; easy access to weapons; suicidal tendencies and above-average intelligence; and the presence of ample warning signs, either in writing or talking about killing others (Egan, 1998).

Police Initiatives

Police leaders can partner with school administrators to help prepare them for acts of school violence and creating safer schools. First, they can ensure that basic crime prevention techniques are being employed: having all school visitors check in at the office; monitoring campus perimeters and hallways; making certain that area police agencies have maps or site plans of schools as well as master keys to all school classrooms and offices; having a warning signal when a school encounters a threat or emergency; and ensuring that the police and school personnel remain in constant contact during a crisis (Bridges, 1999).

It is also recommended that representatives from the police, the schools, and the community come together to sign memoranda of understanding (MOU) that clearly define what each organization or agency will do from the beginning if a school-violence crisis occurs (Band and Harpold, 1999). Some schools now hold regular meetings among faculty, administrators, and the police; problem-solving classes for the students; and regular reviews by the police and teachers to identify problem students (Kenney, 1998). Furthermore, police can (and often must) take their gang-suppression measures into the elementary and secondary schools. Studies have found that the percentage of 12- to 17-year-old students reporting the presence of gangs at school nearly doubled during the mid-1990s; indeed, about 8 percent of students surveyed reported that gangs are involved in three types of crimes at their schools: violence, drug sales, or gun possession (Howell and Lynch, 2000).

Other strategies have been suggested toward helping to prevent school violence:

- Publicizing the philosophy that a gang presence will not be tolerated, and institutionalizing a code of conduct
- Alerting students and parents about school rules and punishments for infractions
- Creating alternative schools for those students who cannot function in a regular classroom
- Training teachers, parents, and school staff to identify children who are most at risk for violent behavior
- Developing community initiatives focused on breaking family cycles of violence, and providing programs on parenting, conflict resolution, anger management, and recovery from substance abuse
- Establishing peer counseling in schools to give troubled youths the opportunity to talk to someone their own age
- Teaching children that it is not "tattling" to go to a school teacher or staff member if they know someone who is discussing "killing" (Marlin and Vogt, 1999)

CRIMES IN PROGRESS

Lethal Potential

Responding to **crimes in progress** is one of the most dangerous types of CFS. Large numbers of police officers are killed answering crimes in progress calls each year.

The danger comes from the fact that in most cases, perpetrators know the police are coming and have time to seek a defensive advantage. Also, on arrival the officers are extremely vulnerable as they exit their patrol vehicle, approach the location, attempt to obtain information, and search out any suspects.

Police officers frequently do not use their emergency equipment (lights and siren) in an effort to "run silent" and keep perpetrators from knowing of their response. This creates a dangerous situation, especially if officers are responding at a high rate of speed. Automobile accidents frequently occur, and police officers are held at fault. Therefore, police departments must ensure that when officers are not using their emergency equipment, they do not violate traffic laws and constantly have their vehicles under control. It is critical that supervisors ensure that officers follow state statutes and departmental policies in this regard.

Police Initiatives

Once a crime has been reported, it is critical that call takers or dispatchers obtain as much information as possible. It is especially important that the exact location of the incident, descriptions of suspects and vehicles and their whereabouts, possible weapons involved, and witness and victim information are obtained. If a suspect is on the scene, the dispatcher should maintain contact with the caller and provide updated information to all responding officers.

Sufficient police units should be dispatched to the scene of a crime in progress. Supervisors should ensure that responding units converge on the scene from different directions so that as many getaway routes as possible can be observed by police officers. In fact, supervisors should coordinate and direct officers' responses to ensure that the maximum number of avenues of escape are covered. Even when a description of the perpetrators or their vehicle is not available, officers should look for suspicious vehicles and conduct field interviews. These field interviews often result in the capture of the suspects or the identification of witnesses.

When responding to a crime in progress, it is critical that the dispatcher and responding officers work as a team. Field supervisors must ensure that responding officers follow police procedures and are equipped with the best possible information. Every tactical action taken by officers is guided by information obtained by the dispatcher. It is the field supervisor's responsibility to ensure that both perform according to procedures.

GUN OWNERSHIP

Certainly a problem that is related to those discussed above for the police—and all of society—is the proliferation of guns in the United States. An estimated 34 percent of the citizens own firearms in this nation, and more than 200 million firearms are estimated to be in private hands. The United States is also the leading supplier of conventional arms to the developing world; more than 300 U.S. companies produce arms and/or ammunition, and more than 4 million firearms are manufactured annually for domestic sale or export (Reuters, 2007). Furthermore, nearly a half million victims of violent crimes each year state that they faced an offender with a firearm, and about two-thirds of the murders committed each year involve the use of firearms (U.S. Department of Justice, Bureau of Justice Statistics, 2007b).

Washington, D.C.'s handgun ban, enacted in 1976, was one of the toughest laws in the nation; it was illegal to buy, sell, or own a handgun in the District, and residents could keep shotguns or rifles only if they were stored unloaded, and either disassembled or disabled with trigger locks. A resident challenged this firearm ban, and in late 2007 the U.S. Supreme Court decided to consider Americans' "right to bear arms" (Brant and Taylor, 2007).

The issue at stake-one that Americans have argued about for decades-concerned the Second Amendment's wording concerning "A well regulated militia, being necessary to the security of a free state, the right of the people to keep and bear arms, shall not be infringed." The Supreme Court had never squarely addressed the question of what the Framers intended: Did they mean to provide an individual right for private citizens to bear arms? Or, rather, was the lagnuage was intended solely to provide for state militias, which are now long defunct (Brant and Taylor, 2007)?

In June 2008 the Supreme Court rendered its decision, in District of Columbia v. Heller; it said the D.C. ban did in fact violate the Second Amendment, delivering a bold and unmistakable endorsement of the individual right to own guns. The opinion, the last of the Court's 2007–2008 term, wiped away years of lower court decisions holding that the intent of the amendment, ratified more than 200 years ago, was to tie the right of gun possession to militia service. However, the ruling left open the possibility of states barring possession of firearms by felons or the mentally ill, or forbidding carrying arms near schools or in government buildings. The Court also indicated that the use of certain types of weapons could be restricted without running afoul of the Second Amendment. These omissions, according to legal scholars, virtually ensure future legal battles (Washington Post, 2008).

WHEN ALL HELL BREAKS LOOSE: NOTIFYING MANAGERS AND SUPERVISORS

Police managers and supervisors cannot work 24 hours a day, 7 days per week. Nonetheless, critical incidents may well be occasions when ranking personnel should be notified, as the task at hand is too overwhelming for subordinates only. This is known as the "exception principle" of management: Each rank should handle only the situations that its subordinate officers lack the authority and capacity to handle or one that may have further implications. Then, a superior officer must be notified for future guidance or simply to inform him or her of what is going on (Fulton, 1998).

Although subject to change depending on local custom and guidelines (which should be put in writing), police supervisors and/or managers should be appropriately notified when incidents involve:

- Serious injuries to officers or employees
- Use of force (when serious death or injury occurs as a result of officer actions)
- Multi-jurisdictional officers (officers from other jurisdictions within the geographic boundaries assigned to a particular police manager or commander; such notification can prevent jurisdictional or "turf" problems from flaring up later)
- Off-duty officer conduct that is unusual or unlawful in nature
- Serious crimes (the term *serious* will vary in meaning from one jurisdiction to the next)
- Prominent public figures (from politicians to rock stars, the interest generated by such incidents often becomes highly publicized) (Fulton, 1998)

CASE STUDIES

The following two case studies deal with some of the issues that supervisors and managers must confront concerning patrol. Note that it might be helpful for you to consider and apply some of the methods and techniques that were discussed in Chapter 4 concerning community policing and problem solving (particularly with the case study concerning juvenile problems).

Case Study #1

Another Day, Another (Seemingly) Drab Domestic Dispute

Officers Ben Collins and Earl James respond to a domestic violence call at the Kendall household. The officers are very familiar with the Kendalls. It seems that every Friday night the husband and wife get drunk and eventually begin to assault each other. The state has enacted a mandatory arrest law for domestic violence that requires that the primary aggressor be arrested. Who exactly is the primary aggressor can never be determined in the case of the Kendalls, because they are uncooperative with the police. In fact, in the 38 previous responses to their home, only three arrests have been made—for assaults on the police officers, not domestic violence. Tonight was no different. Officers Collins and James arrived at the Kendalls' home to face an onslaught of vulgarities from both of them. Both were quite drunk and displayed the usual matching bruises. Sgt. Caplan also responds and observes his officers' vain attempts to resolve the situation. After witnessing the normal discord, drunkenness, and vulgarities, and believing his officers have other more pressing problems to deal with, Sgt. Caplan orders them to leave the home and return back to their patrol duties. Three hours later, a neighbor calls police dispatch to report the sound of gunshots from the Kendall residence; they respond and find that Mrs. Kendall has killed her husband with a shotgun.

Questions for Discussion

1. Could this situation have been prevented? How?
2. Is the supervisor liable in any manner?
3. Which, if any, laws were violated by the manner in which the police addressed the problem?

Case Study #2

Juvenile Un-justice

Hermitage Glen, your city's low-income public housing area, has experienced consistently higher crime rates than the rest of the city. Nearly half of the violent crimes reported occurred in this section of the city, which for a long time has been a depressed, low-income area, lacking in adequate services. The city housing authority was established to support the area, but its efforts have failed.

An analysis of the five public housing complexes in the Glen substantiated that high crime rates and blatant street dealing by gangs exist. Eighty-six percent of the occupants live in households headed by single females. Large groups of school-age youth in the housing complexes appear to be selling drugs during school hours. The truancy, dropout, and suspension rates in Glen schools are the highest in the city, and it also reported that bullying is commonplace in the area's middle and high schools. The highest number of pregnant teenagers in the school system reside in this area. Few of the juveniles observed in the complexes have legitimate jobs, and most of them appeared to be attracted to drug dealing by the easy money. As officers approach drug hangouts within the complexes, young lookouts (aged 12 to 16) call out "Heat!" to alert the dealers to discard their drugs and disperse. A strategy is needed to provide programs to deter youth from joining gangs and selling or using drugs; you, with expertise in community oriented policing and problem solving, are assigned to develop responses to the problem.

Questions for Discussion

1. What programs can you identify that might be implemented for dealing with the gang aspect of the problem?
2. What recommendations would you make for addressing the youths' poverty, unemployment, low self-esteem, and bullying problems?
3. What ideas might you put forth for providing positive role models for the youths?
4. What, if any, civic groups and religious organizations might be enlisted to assist with the problems?
5. What enhanced enforcement approaches would you suggest be taken?
6. How might the truancy, dropout, and pregnancy problems be alleviated?
7. How will you assess any projects or programs that are undertaken to determine whether or not the situation has improved?

Summary

This chapter focused on several situations that pose substantial danger in terms of life and safety to those who work patrol, and that pose significant challenges to their supervisors and managers. We began with a discussion of our nation's violent nature in general (characterized by one expert as "a gathering storm"), then we looked at the scope of patrol operations, and considered several unique problems—domestic violence, drug abuse, gangs, school violence, crimes in progress, and **gun ownership**—that now confront the police all too often.

Several examples were provided of the kinds of initiatives that police are undertaking for handling these problems—initiatives that should be noted by officers, supervisors, and managers alike. As Edmund Burke observed in the eighteenth century, "Example is the school of mankind," and there is certainly merit in looking at what some agencies have done toward addressing these complex problems.

As we noted at the chapter outset, the supervisor is at the heart of the police response to patrol operations. Since supervisors back up officers on potentially dangerous and complex calls, they are ultimately responsible for successful outcomes and for ensuring that commanders are notified of situations and that adequate resources are provided. Supervisors must also take charge at the scene until other support units arrive.

Items for Review

1. Explain what is meant by the term "a gathering storm" and what it means concerning recent developments in the nation's violent crime rate.
2. Delineate the supervisor's and patrol officer's goals for meeting the patrol function.
3. Describe the general nature of domestic violence, and review the kinds of activities in which the police are engaged in attempting to reduce the incidence of such situations.
4. Explain the nature of today's drug problem—including methamphetamine, drug labs, open-air markets, and rave parties, and the enforcement and non-enforcement tactics that are used by police for dealing with them.
5. Define a *gang*, and describe the major initiatives that have been attempted in police and community responses to gang problems.
6. Provide an explanation for today's problem with school violence, and what the police must do in order to be in a state of readiness for such incidents.
7. What is the extent of gun ownership in the U.S., and what are the issues involved in the U.S. Supreme Court's consideration of the Second Amendment's right to bear arms?
8. Explain the supervisor's role when police respond to crimes in progress, and the officer's role in notifying supervisors when the worst has happened.

References

An overview of violence in the schools. (2001). http://eric-web.tc.columbia.edu/monographs/uds107/preventing_introduction.html (Accessed 14 June).

Band, S. R., and Harpold, J. A. (1999). School violence: Lessons learned. *FBI Law Enforcement Bulletin* (September):10.

Brant, M., and Taylor, Jr., S. (2007). A new shot at history. *Newsweek*, December 3, p. 43.

Bridges, D. (1999). Safeguarding our schools. *FBI Law Enforcement Bulletin* (September):21–23.

CNN.com. (2007). Fifth girl dies after Amish school shooting. http://www.cnn.com/2006/US/10/02/amish.shooting/index.html (Accessed October 12).

CNN.com. (2007). Student dies in school shooting; suspect arrested. http://www.cnn.com/2007/US/01/03/school.shooting/index.html (Accessed October 12).

Cyberwolfman's Web Asylum. (2007). http://www.cyberwolfman.com/main.htm (Accessed October 12).

Domestic Violence Prevention Fund. (2007). Domestic violence is a serious, widespread social problem in America: The facts. http://www.endabuse.org/resources/facts/ (Accessed October 12).

Egan, T. (1998). Killing sprees at nation's schools share number of common traits. *The Springfield State-Journal Register* (June):9.

FOXNews.com. (2007). Major U.S. school shootings. http://www.foxnews.com/story/0,2933,300976,00.html (Accessed October 12).

FOXNews.com. (2007). N.C. teenager kills himself after threatening fellow high school students at gunpoint. http://www.foxnews.com/story/0,2933,266843,00.html (Accessed October 12).

FOXNews.com. (2007). Mother bought guns for Pennsylvania boy, charged with school plot (October 12). http://www.foxnews.com/story/0,2933,301379,00.html (accessed October 26, 2008).

Fulton, R. (1998). Supervisory notifications. *Law Enforcement Technology* (November):66.

Harocopos, A., and Hough, M. (2005). *Drug dealing in open-air markets*. Washington, D.C.: U.S. Department of Justice, Office of Community Oriented Policing Services.

Howell, J. C., and Lynch, J. P. (2000, August). *Youth gangs in schools*. Washington, DC: U.S. Department of Justice.

Huff, C. R. (1998). *Comparing the criminal behavior of youth gangs and at-risk youths*. Washington, D.C.: National Institute of Justice Research in Brief.

Hunt, D. E., and Kuck, S. (2007). *Methamphetamine abuse: Challenges for law enforcement and communities*. Washington, D.C.: National Institute of Justice Journal, Issue No. 284.

Kenney, D. (1998, August). *Crime in the schools: A problem-solving approach*. Washington, D.C.: National Institute of Justice Research Preview.

Marlin, G., and Vogt, B. (1999). Violence in the schools. *The Police Chief* (April):169–172.

Mazerolle, L., Soole, D. W., and Rombouts, S. (2007). *Disrupting street-level drug markets*. Washington, D.C.: U.S. Department of Justice, Office of Community Oriented Policing Services.

McGoin, J. M. (2005). *Street gangs and interventions: Innovative problem solving with network analysis*. Washington, D.C.: U.S. Department of Justice, Office of Community Oriented Policing Services.

MSNBC. (2007). Del. School shooting suspect charged in court (September 24). http://www.msnbc.msn.com/id/20957758/ (Accessed October 12).

MSNBC. (2007). 4 shot at Cleveland school. http://www.msnbc.msn.com/id/21224357/ (Accessed October 12).

The New York Times. (2007). Virginia Tech shooting leaves 33 dead (April 16). http://www.nytimes.com/2007/04/16/us/16cnd-shooting.html (Accessed October 12).

Office of National Drug Control Policy. (2007). Drug facts. http://www.whitehousedrugpolicy.gov/publications/factsht/methamph/#background (Accessed October 17).

Orchowsky, S., Poulin, M., and Puryear, V. (2007). Fighting the spread of methamphetamine. *Justice Research and Statistics Association Forum* 25(9) (June):1–8.

Reuters. (2007). "Guns and gun ownership in the United States." http://www.reuters.com/articlePrint?articleId=USN1743414020070417 (Accessed February 15, 2008).

Sampson, R. (2007). *Domestic violence*. Washington, D.C.: U.S. Department of Justice, Office of Community Oriented Policing Services, 2007.

Scott, M. S. (2002). *Clandestine drug labs*. Washington, D.C.: U.S. Department of Justice, Office of Community Oriented Policing Services.

Scott, M. S. (2002). *Rave parties*. Washington, D.C.: U.S. Department of Justice, Office of Community Oriented Policing Services.

Simonetti, M. R. (2006). *Police chief concerns: A gathering storm— violent crime in America*. Washington, D.C.: Police Executive Research Forum.

U.S. Department of Justice (2003). *Combating methamphetamine laboratories and abuse: strategies for success*. Washington, D.C.: Office of Community Oriented Policing Services.

U.S. Department of Justice, Bureau of Justice Statistics. (2007a). Drug and crime facts. http://www.ojp.usdoj.gov/bjs/dcf/enforce.htm#arrests (Accessed October 19).

U.S. Department of Justice, Bureau of Justice Statistics. (2007b). Firearms and crime statistics. http://www.ojp.usdoj.gov/bjs/guns.htm (Accessed January 12, 2008).

U.S. Department of Justice, Federal Bureau of Investigation. (2007). *Crime in the United States– 2006: Uniform crime reports*. http://www.fbi.gov/ucr/cius2006/data/table_01.html (Accessed October 22).

U.S. Department of Justice, National Criminal Justice Reference Service. (2003). In the spotlight: Gang resources. http://www.ncjrs.org/gangs/summary.html (Accessed May 27).

Washington Post, "Justices Reject D.C. Ban On Handgun Ownership," washingtonpost. com, http://www.washingtonpost.com/wp-dyn/content/story/2008/06/23/ST2008062300649.html (Accessed November 14, 2008).

CHAPTER 15

Disasters and Critical Incidents

Key Terms and Concepts

- Critical incident
- Hazardous material training (HAZMAT)
- Homeland Security Presidential Directive–5
- Incident command system (ICS)
- Mass demonstrations
- Mutual aid agreements
- Natural disasters
- National Incident Management System (NIMS)
- Special Operations and Response Teams (SORT) teams
- Special Weapons and Tactics (SWAT) teams
- Tactical concerns

Learning Objectives

After reading this chapter, the student will:

- be able to define and identify critical incidents and disasters
- understand the key elements of the National Incident Management System (NIMS) and its component parts, including the Incident Command System in planning for and dealing with crises
- know some of the supervisory and managerial responsibilities when addressing such disasters as major fires, hurricanes, airplane crashes, and hazardous materials
- comprehend supervisory and managerial responsibilities with respect to hostage, mass demonstration, and bomb situations
- be able to explain why tactical police units were formed, their general composition and efficacy, and some tactical responses for dealing with crises
- be knowledgeable about mutual aid agreements and memoranda of understanding, and their importance for addressing crises

You gain strength, courage, and confidence by every experience in which you really stop to look fear in the face. You are able to say to yourself, "I lived through this horror. I can take the next thing that comes along." … You must do the thing you think you cannot do.

—Eleanor Roosevelt

I am more afraid of an army of 100 sheep led by a lion that an army of 100 lions led by a sheep.

—TALLEYRAND

INTRODUCTION

A devastating earthquake. Massive flooding. Mudslides. Wildfires. These natural disasters occurred during the 1990s in the state of California alone, causing pain and suffering for hundreds of thousands of Americans, and even death for some others. Such disasters present the utmost challenges to the police in terms of saving lives and protecting property. (California, of course, also experienced a disaster of human origin in the early 1990s—widespread rioting following the trials connected with the Rodney King incident.) These kinds of catastrophic events happen nearly everywhere; no locale in this country is immune from such acts of nature. Other incidents may occur by some form of accident (such as a train or plane crash) or environmental hazard (such as chemical spills).

Critical incidents also arise. A **critical incident** may be defined as "any high-risk encounter with police-civilian contacts when officers reasonably believe they are legally justified in using deadly force, regardless of whether they use such force" (Stevens, 1999:48). Examples of such incidents involve emotionally disturbed offenders, domestic terrorism (discussed in Chapter 16), hostage takers, barricaded subjects, riots, high-risk warrant service, and sniper incidents. All such events pose serious threats to the police and citizens alike.

Command and control by police supervisors during the first few critical minutes of such incidents will often determine the incidents' ultimate outcomes and the safety of those involved (Kaiser, 1990). The incident commander or officer in charge (terms used in this chapter to include both supervisors [sergeants] and managers [lieutenants] who are often given the responsibility for command and control at such scenes) must be familiar with the agency's (and, in many cases, multiagency and regional) basic operating procedures for handling critical incidents as well as the procurement of necessary personnel and equipment to prevent the further escalation of a crisis.

This chapter explores several types of critical situations from operational and command and control perspectives. We begin with a review of the relatively new, executive mandated National Incident Management System (NIMS) that has been operationalized nationwide for addressing disasters and critical incidents; included here is an examination of one particular area of emphasis within NIMS—the Incident Command System (ICS)—that has been developed to assist public agencies to respond to major occurrences. Then, we examine selected disasters (hurricanes and floods, major fires, airplane crashes, and hazardous materials) as well as selected critical incidents (barricaded persons and hostage situations, mass demonstrations, bombing incidents, and the use of police tactical units). Two case studies are provided at chapter's end to illustrate the complexities of being in command when such incidents arise.

An underlying theme is that incident commanders must see that the preparatory foundation is laid for such catastrophic occurrences, as well as know and understand the resources that are available to them from federal, state, and local agencies; they must also be cognizant of the protocols for working within established interagency cooperative procedures, as set forth in mutual aid agreements, all of which are discussed in this chapter. Also note that in Chapter 16 we examine subjects that are today closely entwined with the topics of this chapter: homeland defense and terrorism.

PREPARING FOR THE WORST: A NATIONAL INCIDENT MANAGEMENT SYSTEM

In **Homeland Security Presidential Directive–5**, *Management of Domestic Incidents,* President George W. Bush directed the Department of Homeland Security (DHS) secretary to develop and administer a **National Incident Management System (NIMS)**. The purpose of this system is to provide a consistent nationwide approach for federal, state, and local governments to work effectively together to prepare for, prevent, respond to, and recover from disasters and domestic incidents. This directive requires all federal departments and agencies to adopt the NIMS and to use it—and to make its adoption and use by state and local agencies a condition for federal preparedness assistance beginning in fiscal year 2005 (U.S. Department of Homeland Security, 2004; also see Herron, 2004; Jamieson 2005; and Weiss and Davis, 2007).

The NIMS is a lengthy document that cannot be duplicated here in its entirety; therefore, the following discussion is limited to some of its primary components, with primary emphasis placed on the **Incident Command System (ICS)**.

Command and Management

A. ***The Incident Command System.*** The ICS was created to coordinate response personnel from more than one agency or teams from more than one jurisdiction, and has been adopted to help local police agencies respond to disasters, critical incidents, and terrorist incidents. A key strength of ICS is its unified command component, which is composed of four sections: operations, planning, logistics, and finance. Under ICS, all agencies go to the same location and establish a unified command post (Buntin, 2001). The most critical period of time for controlling a crisis is those initial moments when first responders arrive at the scene. They must quickly contain the situation, analyze the extent of the crisis, request additional resources and special teams if needed, and communicate available information and intelligence to higher headquarters. Their initial actions provide a vital link to the total police response, and will often determine its outcome.

Next we briefly review the five major functions of ICS—command, operations, planning, logistics, and finance/administration.

1. ***Command.*** The command staff is responsible for overall management of the incident. When an incident occurs within a single jurisdiction, without any overlap, a single incident commander should be designated with overall incident management responsibility, to develop the objectives on which an actual action plan will be based. The unified command (UC) concept is used in multi-jurisdictional or multi-agency incidents, to provide guidelines for agencies with different legal, geographic, and functional responsibilities to coordinate, plan, and interact effectively. The composition of the UC will depend on the location(s) and type of incident.
2. ***Operations.*** The operations section is responsible for all activities focused on reduction of immediate hazard, saving lives and property, establishing control of the situation, and restoring normal operations. Resources for this section might include specially trained, single-agency personnel and equipment, and even special task forces and strike teams.
3. ***Planning.*** The planning section collects, evaluates, and disseminates incident situation information and intelligence to the incident commander or unified command, prepares status reports, displays situation information, and maintains status of resources assigned to the incident.

4. ***Logistics.*** The logistics section is responsible for all support requirements needed to facilitate effective incident management: facilities, transportation, supplies, equipment maintenance and fuel, food services, communications and technology support, and emergency medical services.
5. ***Finance/Administration.*** This section is not required at all incidents, but will be involved where incident management activities require finance and other administrative support services—compensation/claims, determining costs, procurement, and so on. Law enforcement executives should also create budget line-item codes and emergency purchase orders before such an event, so they will be readily available and accessible.

B. ***ICS Initial Duties and Responsibilities.*** The following checklist provides some of the necessary information for quickly assessing the personnel, equipment, and other resources needed during the initial stages of any critical incident:

1. What is the exact nature and size of the incident?
2. What are the location's characteristics and its surroundings?
3. Are there dangers present to persons and property, such as armed suspects, fires, or hazardous materials?
4. Are there any unusual circumstances, such as snipers, explosives, or broken utilities present?
5. Is there a need to evacuate, and are anti-looting measures required?
6. Is traffic control needed?
7. Are additional personnel for inner and outer perimeter, evacuation, rescue, **special weapons and tactics (SWAT)**, negotiators, or other specialists needed?
8. Will a command post (CP) and staging area for additional personnel and emergency support be needed?
9. What emergency equipment and personnel are needed, and what safe routes are available for their response to the staging area?
10. What other needs are there (food and drink for long-term incidents, tactical units, rescue operations, bomb squad, K-9, tow trucks, and so on) (Iannone and Iannone, 2001)?

C. ***Multi-agency Coordination Systems.*** A multi-agency coordination system is a combination of facilities, equipment, personnel, procedures, and communications integrated into a common system to coordinate and support domestic incident management activities. Multi-agency coordination systems may contain emergency operations centers (EOCs), which represent the physical location at which the coordination of information and resources to support incident management activities normally takes place. An Incident Command Post (ICP) located at or in the immediate vicinity of an incident site, although primarily focused on the tactical on-scene response, may perform an EOC-like function in smaller-scale incidents or during the initial phase of the response to larger, more complex events. For complex incidents, EOCs may be staffed by personnel representing multiple jurisdictions and functional disciplines (e.g., a bioterrorism incident would likely include a mix of law enforcement, emergency management, public health, and medical personnel).

D. ***Public Information Systems.*** These refer to processes, procedures, and systems for communicating timely and accurate information to the public during crisis or emergency situations. The answer to the question, "How much do we tell the public?" is a simple one: you tell them everything that does not need to be safeguarded for valid reasons of security. Openness and candor are essential, and keeping the public informed will render good results. Teamwork between personnel of different agencies is also key before and after an incident—especially in those circumstances where there are many radio frequencies and institutional policies in play (the ICS, discussed above, can be of assistance here) (Keating, 2001).

E. *Preparedness*

1. ***Planning.*** Plans describe how personnel, equipment, and other resources are used to support incident management and incident response activities. They provide mechanisms and systems for setting priorities, integrating multiple entities and functions, and ensuring that communications and other systems are available.
2. ***Training.*** Training includes standard courses on multi-agency incident command and management, organizational structure, and operational procedures, as well as the use of supporting technologies.
3. ***Exercises.*** Incident management organizations and personnel must participate in realistic exercises—including those of a multi-jurisdictional nature—to improve integration and interoperability and optimize resource utilization during incident operations.
4. ***Personnel qualification and certification.*** It is important to remember that "experts are called experts for a reason," and a terrorist attack or other critical incident might involve local funeral directors, dentists, physicians, biochemists, bomb experts, crane operators, and many others.
5. ***Equipment acquisition and certification.*** Incident organizations and personnel at all levels rely on various types of equipment to perform their missions; the acquisition of equipment that will perform to certain standards—and that will operate with similar equipment used by other jurisdictions—is critical.
6. ***Mutual aid.*** Interagency **mutual aid agreements** are essential for responding to attacks and disasters. They allow for the sharing of resources among participating agencies and the establishment of clear policies concerning command and control when an attack or a disaster occurs. Few agencies have the capability of handling a major tactical incident alone, and must rely on the assistance of larger neighboring metropolitan agencies, county sheriff's departments, or state agencies and federal agencies for assistance (Buntin, 2001; also see Weiss and Davis, 2005).

Tactical Concerns

Tactical problems present many unique concerns and dangers for the incident commander's consideration. FBI training for managing confrontational situations adopts De Jong's (1994) principles into a five-phase framework for organization and deploying personnel and resources to tactical incidents:

Preconfrontation/Preparation Phase. When preparing for a situation that may be confrontational and may require a tactical response, preparation and planning are key to successful outcomes. Training should address individual officers' tactical skills, team skills (such as hostage negotiators, SWAT, and command post staff), and systems skills (agency's capabilities to manage a command post). Multiagency exercises provide one method for training and testing an agency's preparation and capabilities.

Contingency Planning. Contingency planning focuses on identifying any potential problems, logistical requirements, strategies and tactics, communications needs, and command and control requirements for any potential tactical situation. Contingency planning provides a basis for developing standard operating procedures.

Immediate Response Phase. Control of the scene and isolating the threat are paramount in any response to a tactical situation. An initial assessment of the situation may be provided by answering the questions provided earlier. Establishing an inner and outer perimeter will help isolate the suspect and keep all nonessential personnel a safe distance from danger. As a situation progresses in severity or time, attention must be given to a variety of concerns, including ongoing intelligence about suspects and hostages; establishing a command post to handle logistics, tactics, and negotiations separately; and documenting all actions taken.

Deliberate/Specific Planning Phase. During this phase, strategies for responding to the incident are developed. These may include maintaining negotiations, emergency or deliberate assault, or surrender. Tactical response plans are carefully briefed by all tactical personnel and coordinated with all other responses before initiation.

Resolution Phase. Resolution entails maintaining control, negotiations, and intelligence during an incident. The goal of this phase is to end the incident without injury to anyone involved. Surrender is preferred, but assault may be necessary, depending on the circumstances. Assault tactics should consider all available intelligence information. A direct assault is often the last resort and consideration. An after-action report should be completed following every tactical incident, identifying which tactics were successful and which were not, so that appropriate changes can be made for future operations.

These matters will guide incident commanders during the first few minutes of their arrival at scenes requiring tactical operations; the type of situation will dictate further measures that need to be taken.

A number of federal, state, and local organizations exist to help prepare for, respond to, and recover from major disasters. Of particular note at the federal level is the National Domestic Preparedness Office, which is run through the FBI and coordinates all efforts of the Department of Defense, the Federal Emergency Management Agency (FEMA), the Department of Health and Human Services, the Department of Energy, and the Environmental Protection Agency to assist state and local first responders with planning, training, and equipment necessary to deal with a conventional weapon or a weapon of mass destruction incident (U.S. Department of Justice, 2001).

DISASTERS: NATURAL AND ACCIDENTAL CALAMITIES

When Nature Rages . . .

Every year, millions of people throughout the United States are victims of natural disasters. The aftermath of an earthquake, tornado, flood, or fire presents many challenges for the police.

As noted in the chapter introduction, **natural disasters** do not discriminate by jurisdiction; the largest and smallest of communities may be victim to the catastrophic effects of a natural disaster. Within minutes of such events, large numbers of people may be endangered and police and emergency services personnel face a variety of complex problems; these events also require significant coordination and efforts to control and reduce the aftereffects of these unusual situations.

Figure 15-1 shows the life cycle of disasters and describes the process through which managers prepare for emergencies and disasters, respond to them when they occur, help people and institutions recover from them, mitigate their effects, reduce the risk of loss, and prevent disasters from occurring.

The effective management of disaster situations requires that incident commanders know what to do and how to respond quickly. Lifesaving measures, rescues, and evacuations will occupy much of the

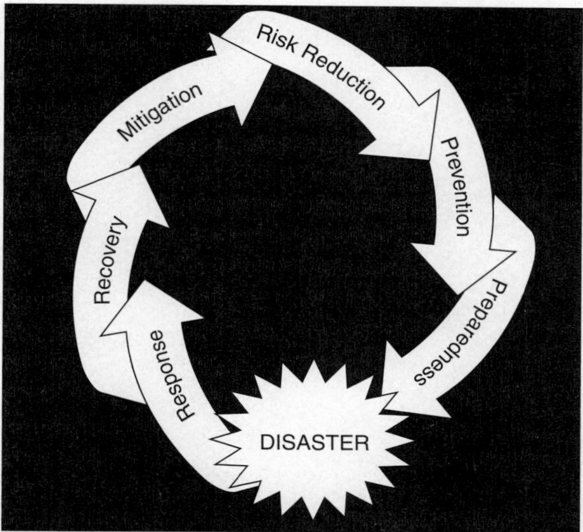

FIGURE 15-1 Life Cycle of Disasters
Source: Federal Emergency Management Agency (FEMA), *Damage Control: FEMA and the Anatomy of Emergency Management, http://www.fss.gsa.gov/pub/mtips/sep_oct02/c.pdf October 2002* (accessed October 27, 2008).

decision making during the initial stages of a disaster. Coordinating the responses of other emergency and fire personnel and support agencies will also be a concern.

Hurricanes and Floods: Lessons from Katrina

By now much has been written about Hurricane Katrina—which devastated New Orleans in August 2005—and the slow governmental response to aid evacuation from the area. Certainly many lessons were learned from this natural disaster, which laid bare the price of not being prepared. Termed "a walk through hell" (Garrett, 2005), Katrina crippled the city and reduced people to living in a manner seen only in Third World countries, without the amenities we have long taken for granted.

Much time was also spent post-Katrina in an endeavor to point the finger of culpability. What is more critical for the future of emergency planning, however, is to learn from past mistakes and remember the need to thoroughly define governments' roles and responsibilities—who should do what—when such disasters occur. Here we will merely scratch the surface with respect to the lack of planning, errors made, and lessons learned from this tragic event.

As stated by Walters and Kettl (2005:20), "only one thing disintegrated as fast as the earthen levees that were supposed to protect the city, and that was the intergovernmental relationship that is supposed to connect local, state, and federal agencies before, during, and after such a catastrophe." Certainly a broad lesson learned from Katrina is that all emergencies are, initially at least, local—or local and state—events, because those levels of government provide the initial responders and responses. The extent to which the response develops depends on a host of factors, including the size of the incident and what plans and agreements are in place prior to any event.

A primary consideration is that police and other first responders in the jurisdiction—and their families—first be taken out of harm's way. Katrina trapped at least 30 New Orleans police officers in their own homes. Furthermore, these responders will not be effective or want to enter a danger zone if

New Orleans, September 20, 2005. The city's Ninth Ward took a severe blow from Hurricane Katrina's winds and floodwaters; devastation is seen in every direction. Some sections of the city were under as much as eight feet of water.
(Courtesy FEMA)

their own families are in great peril; they must not be placed in a position where they have to choose between work and the well-being of their families.

In addition, coordination and communication problems between levels of government must be addressed before a disaster strikes (Schafer and Levin, 2007; Walters and Kettl, 2005). A lack of working police radios and cell phones created a logistical nightmare during Katrina. Without functioning communications systems, chaos was inevitable (Arey and Wilder, 2005). Communication systems need not be elaborate; simply being on the same frequency or being familiar with who will be on what frequency and discussing in advance how communication will occur if radio frequencies are jammed or cell towers are down can help tremendously (Garrett, 2005).

An agency should also create contingency plans for dealing with fewer officers than expected during such a major disaster; agencies might even consider surveying officers beforehand to determine whether or not they would be able to report to duty, and how they would ensure their families are provided for so that they could report for work (Garrett, 2005). If, for example, a 300-officer department will have only 200 officers available for duty during a crisis, the agency must lay plans accordingly.

Emergency plans should also concentrate on transportation issues for evacuation: what means of transportation will be available? Where will this transportation be located? Who will transfer the modes of transportation into the key positions? When will they be available? Preplanning should also include such matters as positioning portable restrooms; providing alternative means of transportation if roads become impassable; providing food and water to evacuees; and establishing shelters for those persons who have lost their homes (Garrett, 2005).

Certainly proactive, ongoing tabletop and full-scale exercises to assess preparation for all of the above contingencies should be provided pre-incident. This training should include local, state, and federal authorities. And the NIMS and ICS, discussed above, should be clearly understood and able to be put into play prior to the occurrence of any such disaster.

Major Fires, Airplane Crashes, Hazardous Materials

MAJOR FIRES The magnitude and scope of a major fire present immediate dangers to the public as well as police and fire personnel responding to such incidents. During any major fire, the incident commander should meet with his or her counterpart in the fire department to determine what police control measures may be required. The police commander should direct any resources necessary to support the fire department in its immediate rescue and evacuation efforts. Additionally, personnel should be assigned to the perimeter to control traffic and crowds of onlookers and protect fire apparatus and hoses. A vehicle driving over a fire hose can rupture it and risk the lives of firefighters who may be inside a structure using the hose for protection and suppression of the fire.

When a fire is extinguished, the scene should be protected for investigation. The police are also responsible for the protection of the property from looters. In some cases, police may have to establish a perimeter around an entire neighborhood affected by a fire and check the identification of persons asking to enter the property to retrieve personal belongings.

The wheels from downed TWA Flight 800—which killed 230 people in 1996 off Long Island—are carefully brought to shore.
(Courtesy NYPD Photo Unit)

The Oakland Hills, California, fire in the early 1990s provides a good example of the complexities and dangers involved in major fires. On that day, hot and dry gusts of winds swept the Monterey pine- and eucalyptus-covered upscale neighborhoods in the Oakland-Berkeley hills. Twenty-five firefighters were on-scene overhauling hot spots from a fire the previous day when embers blew into dry areas and quickly ignited a fire that was soon out of control. Immediate evacuation efforts were initiated by police and fire officials and mutual aid was requested. Twenty-five persons died, 150 were injured, and more than 3,000 residences were destroyed in a 5.25-mile area, totaling more than $1.5 billion in damages. An after-action report pointed to the need for enhanced mutual aid, increased availability of water, stricter fire codes and ordinances, improved communications, and vegetation management (Parker, 1992).

AIRPLANE CRASHES The aftermath of an airplane falling from the sky with passengers and scattering plane parts is catastrophic. Police and fire personnel are usually the first to arrive at the scene of an airplane crash; they must assume the gruesome task of fire suppression, lifesaving, containment, and protection of the scene until the responsible investigators arrive. Police leaders must also be concerned with crowd and traffic control and the looting of the personal effects of passengers.

The containment of a crash scene is often complicated by the large area or type of geography involved; sometimes planes plunge into swamps or large areas of water.

Military aircraft are particularly problematic and present many potential dangers for the on-scene commanders and officers. Depending on the type of military aircraft involved, the existence of conventional and nuclear weapons, explosives charges for ejection canopies, and the presence of classified or top secret materials make the handling of a military aircraft accident additionally difficult. As a result, many agencies located near military bases conduct joint crash response exercises and have developed mutual aid agreements for handling such occurrences.

An incident commander's primary tasks in these cases are similar to those for any aircraft accident and include coordinating immediate lifesaving and rescue operations and containing and protecting the scene until responsible authorities arrive. In most cases, and in accordance with National Transportation Safety Board (NTSB) regulations, Federal Aviation Administration (FAA) investigators will respond and assume responsibility for the investigation and coordinate their efforts with the assistance of local authorities.

HAZARDOUS MATERIALS The U.S. Department of Transportation (2008) estimates that more than four billion tons of hazardous materials are transported annually in the United States by air, highway, rail, and vessel. In fact, more than 800,000 hazardous materials shipments occur every day—365 days a year. And spills and accidents can and do occur during such transport; in 2007, for example, there were more than 19,000 HAZMAT incidents in the U.S., resulting in 10 fatalities and more than 200 people being injured—and more than $68 million in damages (U.S. Department of Transportation, 2007). Obviously the potential exists for accidents to occur in any small town or large metropolitan area.

These incidents reinforce the need for police education and training concerning hazardous materials. Police are often one of the first responders to hazardous materials accidents and can quickly become victims themselves if the proper precautions are not taken. Recently, however, the need for such training has been recognized, and **hazardous materials training (HAZMAT)** is now included in mandated Peace Officers Standards and Training curriculums.

Police are considered first responders, and their responsibility is simply to recognize and report any suspected HAZMAT condition to the proper authorities. Many local fire departments now have a special HAZMAT team trained to deal with these conditions. More extensive situations may require the response of state or federal agencies for assistance.

When on the scene of a suspected HAZMAT situation, the incident commander should quickly evaluate the threat, notify the proper authorities, and establish a perimeter large enough to protect the public and officers from the effects of the hazard or spill. The commander should determine how large a perimeter is needed, as winds, water, and other environmental conditions may aggravate a problem. Some hazardous materials are also susceptible to fire or explosion.

A HAZMAT incident of any size will require the response of several agencies, including police, fire, specialized HAZMAT response teams, and ambulance services for those injured. It is recommended that agencies develop response plans that account for the many different types of emergencies that may occur. These plans should include the following issues:

1. Pre-emergency planning and coordination with outside parties
2. Personnel roles, lines of authority, training, and communication
3. Emergency prevention
4. Determining safe distances
5. Site security and control
6. Evacuation routes and procedures
7. Decontamination procedures
8. Emergency medical treatment and first aid
9. Critiques of response and follow up
10. Proper use of personnel and equipment (Donahue, 1993:5)

A hazardous materials accident in Casa Grande, Arizona, serves as an example of how a lack of preplanning, misunderstandings about command and control, and communications problems can lead to major problems. Police and fire units responded to reports of smoke coming from a railcar that was parked near the city's downtown area. Railroad officials failed to inform responding personnel that the car contained chemical white phosphorous. Decisions to evacuate were delayed for 40 minutes, and no formal system was established for evacuation of households in imminent danger. A command post was never established, and information about the dangers involved was not transmitted to additional responding units. Subsequently, five police officers succumbed to toxic smoke as a result of the absence of self-contained breathing apparatuses. Despite the availability of six HAZMAT teams in the state, none were called for assistance. Crowd problems developed because police failed to announce the dangers through the media. Obviously, this occurrence serves as a case study in how *not* to treat a critical incident involving hazardous materials.

CRITICAL INCIDENTS: HOSTAGE, MASS DEMONSTRATION, AND BOMB SITUATIONS

Barricaded Persons and Hostages

Armed suspects who take hostages or barricade themselves represent one of the most dangerous situations confronting the police. By virtue of their motives, hostage takers are extremely dangerous to police officers and citizens. The four categories of hostage takers are (1) traditional (criminal trapped at the scene of a crime or while escaping from a crime scene), (2) terrorists, (3) prisoners who take a hostage(s) while escaping, and (4) the mentally disturbed (Peak, 2000).

The traditional or criminal type often takes hostages to gain leverage to bargain for freedom. The second type, terrorists, are probably the most dangerous of the four types. When terrorists take hostages, the operation is usually well planned and executed; furthermore, terrorists are often prepared to die for their cause and will quickly kill hostages, may be sophisticated fighters, and have probably studied antiterrorist strategies used by police.

The third type of hostage situation involves prisoners who take hostages, usually correctional personnel, to get publicity for perceived inhumane conditions and other grievances. The final type of hostage taker, the mentally disturbed person, is the most prevalent and perhaps least dangerous, if properly trained police personnel are dealing with them. They can be paranoid schizophrenic; have a bipolar disorder; be antisocial personality types; or suffer from hallucinations, feelings of persecution, or depression (Peak, 2000).

Remsberg (1986) has identified four reasons why people take hostages:

1. ***Persons seeking attention:*** This is often the motivation for gang members, criminals, or persons with mental disorders taking hostages; for example, four gunmen who took 30 hostages in a 1991 Sacramento electronics store were attempting to obtain recognition and respect for their gang.
2. ***Power:*** The hostage taker has a psychological need to control or dominate. For example, an employee may take hostages in the workplace to prevent his dismissal.
3. ***Revenge:*** The hostage taker is attempting to right some wrong. Many hostage situations involving families are the result of revenge.
4. ***Despair:*** The perpetrator is hopeless because of his or her job or financial or family situation. Hostage takers acting from despair commonly commit suicide or force the issue so that the police will kill them. Many hostage takers are experiencing multiple stressors. They frequently lack family support systems and therefore have no emotional outlets. They often feel isolated, alienated, and desperate. (Fuselier, Van Zandt, and Lanceley, 1991)

These incidents are high profile in terms of media coverage; every detail of the event is usually reported in the news. Therefore, the police must follow proper procedures in barricade and hostage situations. Police officials must proceed deliberately but cautiously, and an assault should be conducted only as a last resort or if absolute safety can be ensured.

Although no hard and fast rules apply to such cases, the incident commander at the scene must decide whether or not to accede to the hostage taker's demands. Generally, no deals will be made. But the incident commander must judge each case on its own merits and recognize that the successful negotiation of a hostage's release will take considerable time and patience.

Incident commanders should also evaluate the situation and ensure that they respond accordingly. For example, if the hostage taker's motive is attention, negotiators should respond in a firm, caring manner. Getting tough only exacerbates the situation. The power-motivated hostage taker requires a different approach. The negotiator must display power and force but also must be willing to give and take. When revenge is involved, homicide is even more likely. Negotiators should express compassion but should be prepared to move at the slightest opportunity. Finally, the despair-motivated hostage taker is the most difficult. The negotiator must realistically provide encouragement and support as opposed to false hope, which can backfire and result in violence. The negotiator must also communicate with the incident commander, in order that tactical decisions can be made.

As part of a tactical plan for neutralizing and arresting the hostage taker, the incident commander should ensure that the following tasks are being performed (adapted from Iannone and Iannone, 2001:272):

1. ***Secure the premises:*** Officers should be posted at the front and rear of the premises and in other locations to prevent an escape.
2. ***Command post:*** Locate in a safe, strategic area upwind from the scene to avoid contamination if gas is used.
3. ***Injured persons:*** Give aid, interview, and remove.

4. ***Communications:*** Notify headquarters of the situation.
5. ***Personnel support:*** Acquire necessary personnel to cordon off the area and for operations at the scene.
6. ***Special equipment:*** Request gas grenades, masks, body armor, sharpshooters and rifles, portable communications equipment, loudspeakers for communicating with the suspect, portable lights and generators, helicopter patrol, and ambulance and fire vehicles as needed.
7. ***Staging area:*** Locate staging area where officers and equipment are to report upwind from scene of incident.
8. ***Identify officers as they report:*** Assign them to positions where they can secure escape routes without exposing themselves to crossfire.
9. ***Evacuation:*** Persons in the area who may be endangered by gunfire or other police operations should be removed to a safe location.
10. ***Field intelligence:*** Collate intelligence from police and civilians regarding the suspect, victim, and location. Determine the type of crimes committed, the purpose in barricading or seizing a hostage, the suspect's physical and mental condition and attitudes concerning police and society, and a physical description. Disseminate the latter information to personnel, so they will not mistake the hostage for the suspect.

Negotiations, for the most part, are extremely effective in bringing hostage situations to a successful end; however, the police must be tactically prepared if negotiations fail and the lives of hostages are endangered. When negotiations fail, the incident commander will turn to the tactical commander to initiate a tactical plan for assaulting the barricade (negotiators and SWAT personnel often have separate command posts and plans). Entry into a barricade absolutely is the last resort.

The FBI and other entities conduct excellent training programs for professional hostage negotiators; this is a delicate and difficult subject that requires much more training and in-depth analysis than we are able to do here.

Management of Mass Demonstrations

Our country was born out of civil disorder; the Boston Tea Party, which helped to initiate the War of Independence, was an act of civil disobedience as a result of an unfair tax on imported tea. In 1863, a riot in New York City left approximately 2,000 people dead. More recently, the riots as a result of the civil rights movement and the Vietnam War affected every American citizen. Many of our major cities have experienced devastating riots, and many of our best-known universities had major riots and demonstrations that pitted students against university administrators and the police. Clearly, civil disorder is a natural part of our society and has been present ever since there were governments.

But civil disorder and **mass demonstrations** can erupt from a variety of causes, including fan displeasure following an athletic event; a police shooting; the aftermath of a court decision (such as that of Rodney King in Los Angeles); a meeting of a global international organization dealing with the rules of trade between nations (as in Seattle in 1999); or an arrest at an abortion clinic. And such mass demonstrations can quickly turn into deadly riots; as the executive director of the Police Executive Research Forum observed, "Perhaps there is no greater challenge for police officers in a democracy than that of managing mass demonstrations" (Wexler, 2006: i).

Since the events in Seattle, the police have become more mindful that large-scale events present a number of issues, including:

- How to effectively manage police resources to deal with large numbers of people
- How to work with business/community members who are not involved in the event, but who have an expectation that the police will protect them and their property

- How to effectively gather information for a planned or spontaneous mass demonstration
- How to identify the policy issues and what procedures and safeguards should be in place for mass arrests
- How to determine what level of force should be used when demonstrators become unruly
- How to integrate resources and maintain accountability (Wexler, quoted in Narr et al., 2006:i–ii)

As noted with the other disaster and critical-incident topics discussed in this chapter, the police should engage in *pre-event planning* if they know in advance of a mass demonstration in their jurisdiction, in order to lay the foundation for informed and competent decision making and to avoid major problems. Such preplanning should include, but not be limited to, the following considerations:

- Holding formal meetings with event organizers to learn details of the event
- Identify potential protest groups
- Identify partner law enforcement agencies and meet to discuss equipment needs as well as mutual aid and cross-jurisdictional issues
- Hold formal meetings with all stakeholders (such as elected officials, businesses, public transportation, public utilities, and medical facilities) who can provide support
- Establish a media strategy for maintaining community contact and disseminating information
- Determine command and control (see ICS, discussed above)
- Appoint operational and tactical commanders
- Review the rules of engagement for a hostile event
- Address intelligence issues (such as gathering and processing information)
- Arrange for logistical support, such as food and water for offices, vehicles, fuel, radios, and mass arrest supplies (Narr et al., 2006: 11–13).

Finally, it should be noted that crowds develop into unruly mobs through a series of three stages (Adams, 1994). During the first stage, the crowd consists of a conglomeration of individuals who are together because of the excitement or a feeling of some impending event. They tend to be individualistic, but they have the potential to rapidly band together, especially if some event causes them to focus their attention. The second stage occurs when leaders or agitators are able to gain individuals' attention and cause them to focus on some objective or perceived threat. The third stage occurs when the mob reaches critical mass and focuses on some objective. At this point, the crowd likely will get out of control, resulting in destruction of property and injury to citizens.

When a crowd situation occurs, the police have four primary objectives: containment, dispersal, reentry prevention, and arrest of violators (Adams, 1994). Anytime there is a disorder, the police should first attempt to contain it or prevent it from growing larger. Containment is achieved by establishing blockades and barriers to prevent others from entering into the area, and should be accomplished only when the police have adequate personnel on the scene. Then police should quickly contain the situation and begin to disperse members of the crowd, by forcing the passive participants on the edges to leave the area. Reducing the size of the crowd will effectively lessen the remaining participants' courage; then, as the crowd becomes smaller, it will be easier for the police to deal with the core or more troublesome members. Finally, the police should attempt to arrest those persons who are responsible for inciting the riot or disorder and the individuals who cause personal injury or property damage (the decision to make an on-scene arrest must be weighed against the potential that the arrest will further incite the rioters and cause more harm). The police should also conspicuously take video and still photographs of the crowd; photographs serve to discourage rioters from criminal behavior, frighten the more timid into leaving the area, and serve as evidence in court.

Bomb Incidents: What Supervisors and Managers Must Know, and Why

In an age of constant terror warnings and concerns, can anyone in policing afford to not have at least a fundamental knowledge of bombs? While the U.S. Bureau of Alcohol, Tobacco, Firearms, and Explosives maintains a Bomb Data Center, the Center does not release information concerning the number and kinds of explosive incidents that occur each year except to authorized law enforcement agencies.

Bombs are not difficult to make: half of all bombings carried out in the U.S. involve pipe bombs. These simple devices use black powder inside a container which, upon building up slowly, then explodes and releases a deadly wave of shrapnel. These bombs are a favorite of suicide terrorists. Therefore, if an officer walked into a home on a routine call and noticed that all metal in the house—utensils, doorknobs, and hardware—was rusted, would he or she know this is a strong indicator of a chemical reaction from preparing a bomb? Would the officer recognize other signs of bomb activity, such as containers, gas balloons, fuses, explosive fillers, and even contaminants such as rat poison that may be present? Would he or she realize that an unusually high number of cellular phones may also be an indication, because of their popular use as detonation devices? Or that other accessories might be present, such as alcohol, aluminum foil, petroleum jelly, protective gloves, scales, tubing, and wires (Morganstern, 2005)?

Perhaps first and foremost, field supervisors and officers need to remember that explosive devices may be easily concealed. Any suspicious unattended object—a briefcase, an abandoned bag with or without wires visible, a gas canister, a knapsack, or even a shopping bag—that has been placed in an odd location might prudently require an immediate evacuation of the area.

The bombing of the Alfred P. Murrah Federal Building in Oklahoma City required a tremendous amount of command and control.
(Courtesy Captain Jim Madeau, Washoe County, Nevada, Sheriff's Office)

When a bomb report or suspicious object call comes in, a search should be organized that is systematic and thorough so that it can be completed in the least amount of time possible. Some agencies also have trained dogs to search for explosives. A police officer might be matched with an employee of the establishment, because an employee is more likely to be familiar with the premises and be able to identify suspicious packages or out-of-place items. Police should caution any employees assisting in the search not to touch any suspected device and to summon an officer if one is found. Then, if a device is not found, the person who is responsible for the premises should be advised; police personnel should avoid telling anyone the building is safe or suggesting that employees may return to work. This is the duty of the responsible employee on the scene, and for the police to do so could incur a tremendous liability if a bomb were to explode and injure anyone.

If a suspected bomb is found, the officer in charge should ensure that trained bomb specialists are summoned to the scene. There should be no attempt by on-scene officers to remove or disarm the device while waiting for expert assistance. Officers should be directed to establish a perimeter a safe distance around the device in the event of an explosion so that no one would suffer injuries if the bomb exploded.

The dangers inherent in any bomb incident or other crisis require that a decision be made concerning the evacuation of persons from a business or their residence. Under many circumstances, the police do not have the legal authority to force people to leave their personal property or business. Exceptions occur when police encounter persons who are mentally incompetent, crippled, aged, young, or sick. In these instances, the police may assume responsibility for their safe removal from danger.

In 1978, the U.S. Bureau of Alcohol, Tobacco, Firearms, and Explosives developed a National Response team (NRT) to assist federal, state, and local investigators at the scenes of significant explosives incidents. The NRT has four regions in the U.S., and each region can respond within 24 hours to investigate such incidents, reconstructing the scene, identifying the seat of the blast, conducting interviews, and sifting through debris to obtain evidence pertaining to the explosion. Providing its services free of charge, the NRT maintains a fleet of vehicles that are fully self-contained and carry computer, recording, communications, and evidence collecting equipment (U.S. Department of Justice, Bureau of Alcohol, Tobacco, Firearms, and Explosives, 2008). In addition, the aforementioned Bomb Data Center maintains a National Explosives Tracing Center that assists police agencies in systematically tracking explosives from manufacturer to purchaser or possessor for the purpose of identifying suspects involved in criminal violations, establishing stolen status, and proving ownership. Explosives manufacturers, importers, wholesalers, and retail dealers in the U.S. and foreign countries cooperate by providing information concerning the manufacture, importation, or sale of explosive devices (U.S. Bureau of Alcohol, Tobacco, Firearms, and Explosives, 2008).

Use of Tactical Units

The Los Angeles Police Department developed the first special weapons and tactics (SWAT) units in 1967, following increased incidences of "urban violence, including snipings, political assassinations, and urban guerrilla warfare" (Los Angeles Police Department, 1974:101). Following its lead, a large number of police agencies have had SWAT teams since the 1970s, although many use a softer, more expansive title for their team, such as **Special Operations and Response Team**, or "**SORT**."

Since their inception, such teams have been trained to address critical incidents. Team members are normally highly trained, wear distinctive clothing, are well equipped with automatic weapons and gear, may be accompanied by a mobile command post with elaborate communications systems, and are often highly specialized (including, for example, a leader, scout, sharpshooter, observer, rear guard, and so on) (Center for Research on Criminal Justice, 1975).

In a critical incident today, it is recommended that most teams have 21 officers: a commander, a four-officer entry team, another four-officer secondary entry or emergency response team, a four-officer sniper complement, and eight officers to provide a containment function/perimeter team (Green, 2001). Obviously, many small agencies would be unable to maintain a well-trained unit of this size.

A national survey of 51 law enforcement agencies with SWAT units was recently completed; together, the units reported 92 critical incidents over a three-year period. In terms of outcomes, they reported surrender or arrest of the suspect in 71 (65 percent) of the incidents without gunfire or lethal force being employed. Those findings were compared with 106 agencies in the same survey that did not have a SWAT unit; they had 212 critical incidents over the same three-year period. In those incidents, suspects surrendered or were arrested without gunfire or lethal force in 93 (44 percent) of the incidents. Therefore, the study concluded that agencies with police tactical units resolve critical incidents far more safely than those agencies without such units and suggested that the reason for this finding is the greater adequacy in resources and tactics when dealing with such incidents (Stevens, 1999).

CASE STUDIES

The following two case studies afford the reader a small taste of the kinds of tactical operations that are confronted by the police all too frequently.

Case Study #1

When the Going Gets Tough ...

An estranged husband, Donald Blair, goes to his ex-wife's school, where she is a fifth-grade teacher. A residential area borders the school on the north side; on the south side is a large shopping center with a restaurant and several other small stores; a four-lane thoroughfare borders the school on the west side; and a daycare center and a retirement home are on the east. Blair enters the cafeteria, where the majority of the school's children, teachers, and the principal are having lunch. He pulls out an AR-15 automatic weapon, screams to his ex-wife that she's made his life miserable, and threatens to kill her. He also states that no one is to leave the room, or he will kill them. The school nurse, passing by in the hallway, overhears the commotion and immediately contacts the police. Sgt. Hawthorne is in charge of this district and responds to the scene. The first officers to arrive see several teachers and kids running away from the school building. One of the teachers points out Blair's pickup truck, parked in front of the school; inside the truck are several survival guides, empty ammunition boxes, and pipe bomb materials.

Questions for Discussion

1. As supervisor on the scene, use the checklist provided earlier and identify what Sgt. Hawthorne would need to do during the initial stages to gain control of this situation.
2. What additional personnel, equipment, and other resources might be needed?

Case Study #2

Dealing with Spills That Kill

Metro City is a medium-sized community located in the Midwest. Three smaller incorporated cities border its jurisdiction. Union Rails, Inc., has informed the police chief of Metro City that it plans to increase the number of trains going daily through the downtown area, and that several of those trains will be carrying hazardous industrial materials. Each rail car containing such materials will be appropriately marked, and bills of lading identifying the cargo and its hazard will be available. The railroad is requesting a meeting with local officials to discuss the area's HAZMAT response capabilities in the event of an accident. Metro City has no such plan. As a police supervisor for planning and development, Sgt. Young has been directed to provide the police chief with recommendations concerning the impact on the cities of transporting HAZMAT materials through the urban area; Young must also determine what the jurisdictions need to do to prepare for the increase in rail traffic.

Questions for Discussion

1. Which governmental agencies in the tri-city area would need to be involved in developing this plan?
2. What types of personnel training would be required, and where could the police agencies acquire this training for their officers?
3. Are there any other issues or concerns that Sgt. Young would need to identify for the chief?

Summary

This chapter has examined the supervisor's and manager's roles in both human- and nature-generated critical incident management, including disasters of all types.

A point of emphasis in this chapter is that these kinds of occurrences require preplanned responses. It simply will not do for incident commanders to await their occurrence before developing plans for coping with them; the potential cost in human lives and property is too great to be left to on-the-job training and decision making "on the fly." It behooves all police personnel, especially incident commanders as well as the first responders at such scenes, to know and understand their own agency's and existing multi-agencies', regional protocol and procedures as well as mutual aid agreements for addressing these situations. Anything less would be a disservice to the public they serve.

Items For Review

1. What is the primary purpose of the National Incident Management System, and what are its primary component parts?
2. Define what is meant by *Incident Command System* as well as its component parts.

3. Describe some of the personnel, equipment, and other resources that are needed during the initial stages of any critical incident.
4. Explain the four-phase framework for organizing and deploying personnel and resources for tactical problems.
5. List the four types of hostage takers, and some of the approaches taken by the police in dealing with them.
6. Describe the primary preplanning activities that the police should do for dealing with mass demonstrations.
7. Explain the duties of an officer in charge during a bomb search.
8. Discuss the kinds of natural disasters that can occur, and how supervisors and managers can help to ensure that their agencies are prepared to deal with them.
9. Explain how a tactical unit's officers, role, and equipment are different from those of standard police personnel.
10. Explain what the term *hazardous materials* includes, and how the police respond to incidents involving such materials.

References

Adams, T. F. (1994). *Police field operations.* Upper Saddle River, NJ: Prentice Hall.

Arey, J., and Wilder, A. (2005). New Orleans police respond to Katrina. *Law and Order* (October): 108–113.

Bolgiano, D. G. (2001). Military support of domestic law enforcement operations: Working within Posse Comitatus. *FBI Law Enforcement Bulletin* (December): 16–24.

Buntin, J. (2001). Disaster master. *Governing* (December):34–38.

Carlson, J. (1999). Critical incident management in the ultimate crisis. *FBI Law Enforcement Bulletin* (March):19.

Center for Research on Criminal Justice. (1975). *The iron fist and the velvet glove: An analysis of the U.S. police.* Berkeley, CA: Author.

De Jong, D. (1994). Civil disorder: Preparing for the worst. *FBI Law Enforcement Bulletin* (3):1–7.

Donahue, M. L. (1993). Hazardous materials training: A necessity for today's law enforcement. *FBI Law Enforcement Bulletin* 11:1–6.

Fuselier, G. D., Van Zandt, C. R., and Lanceley, F. J. (1991). Hostage/barricade incidents: High-risk factors and actions criteria. *FBI Law Enforcement Bulletin* (1):6–12.

Garrett, R. (2005). A walk through hell. *Law Enforcement Technology* (October): 32-39.

Green, D. (2001). Implementing a multi-jurisdictional SWAT team. *Law and Order* (March):68–73.

Herron, S. M. (2004). The national incident management system. *The Police Chief* (November): 20–28.

Iannone, N. F., and Iannone, M. P. (2001). *Supervision of police personnel,* 6th ed. Upper Saddle River, NJ: Prentice Hall.

Jamieson, G. (2005). NIMS and the incident command system. *The Police Chief* (February): 68-78.

Kaiser, N. (1990). The tactical incident: A total police response. *FBI Law Enforcement Bulletin* 8:14–18.

Keating, F. (2001). Catastrophic terrorism: Local response to a national threat. *Journal of Homeland Security* (August) http://www.homelandsecurity.org/journal/Articles/Keating.htm (Accessed October 27, 2008).

Los Angeles Police Department. (1974). *Special weapons and tactics.* Los Angeles: Author.

Morganstern, H. (2005). Bomb basics: What law enforcement needs to know and why. *Law enforcement technology* (August): 8-17.

Morris, J. (2001). Task forces formed to recommend means to improve aviation security. *The Dallas Morning News* (September 16):1A.

Narr, T., Toliver, J., Murphy, J., McFarland, M., and Ederheimer, J. (2006). *Police management of mass demonstrations: Identifying issues and successful approaches.* Washington, D.C.; Police Executive Research Forum.

Parker, D. R. (1992). *Report of the Oakland Berkeley hills fire*. Oakland, CA.: Oakland Office of Fire Services.

Peak, K. J. (2000). *Policing America: Methods, issues, challenges,* 3d ed. Upper Saddle River, NJ: Prentice Hall.

Ragavan, C. (2001). FBI, Inc.: How the world's premier police corporation totally hit the skids. *U.S. News and World Report* (June 18):14.

Remsberg, C. (1986). *The tactical edge: Surviving high risk patrol.* Northbrook, IL: Calibre Press.

Schafer, J.A., and Levin, B. H. (2007). Policing and mass casualty events. Washington, D.C.: U.S. Department of Justice, Federal Bureau of Investigation, Futures Working Group.

Stevens, D. J. (1999). Police tactical units and community response. *Law and Order* (March):48–52.

U.S. Bureau of Alcohol, Tobacco, Firearms, and Explosives. (2008). National explosive tracing center. http://www.atf.gov/aexis2/trac.htm (Accessed 25 April).

U.S. Department of Homeland Security. (2004). *National incident management system*. Washington, D.C.: Author, pp. viii, ix.

U.S. Department of Justice, Bureau of Alcohol, Tobacco, Firearms, and Explosives. (2008). National response team. http://www.atf.gov/pub/gen_pub/atf_p35101.pdf (Accessed 25 April).

U.S. Department of Justice, Federal Bureau of Investigation, National Domestic Preparedness Office. (2001). http://www.fas.org/irp/agency/doj/fbi/ndpo/ (Accessed 5 January).

U.S. Department of Transportation, Hazardous Materials Information System. (2007) . HAZMAT summary by indicent state. http://hazmat.dot.gov/pubs/inc/data/2007/2007state_hwy.pdf (Accessed April 16, 2008).

U.S. Department of Transportation, Pipeline and Hazardous Materials Safety Administration. (2008). Hazardous materials transportation modules. http://www.phmsa.dot.gov/staticfiles/PHMSA/DownloadableFiles/Files/MOD_intro_stu.pdf (Accessed 16 April).

Walters, J., and Kettl, D. (2005). The Katrina breakdown. *Governing* (December):20-25.

Weiss, J., and Davis, M. (2007). Continuity of operation when disaster strikes. *Law and Order* (July):25–35.

Weiss, J., and Davis, M. (2005). Mutual aid when disaster strikes. *Law and Order* (August):114-121.

Wexler, C. (2006). Foreword. In Narr, T., Toliver, J., Murphy, J., McFarland, M., and Ederheimer, J., *Police management of mass demonstrations: Identifying issues and successful approaches.* Washington, D.C.: Police Executive Research Forum.

PART FOUR

Major Challenges

CHAPTER 16

Homeland Security and Policing

Key Terms and Concepts

- Biological Weapons of Mass Destruction
- Chemical Weapons of Mass Destruction
- Community Oriented Policing and Problem Solving (COPPS)
- Earth Liberation Front
- Emergency response
- Fusion center
- Homeland security
- Infrastructure
- National Infrastructure Protection Plan (NIPP)
- Nuclear Weapons of Mass Destruction
- Officer safety
- Terrorist threat categories
- Weapons of mass destruction (WMD)

Learning Objectives

After reading this chapter, the student will:

- know the various terrorist threats, both internal and external to the United States
- know the different types of weapons of mass destruction as well as their effects
- understand how policing will likely change, particularly in the areas of community policing with the advent of the homeland security mandate
- be able to delineate how intelligence plays a key role in policing, and how fusion centers assist in this endeavor
- know the levels of protection required in homeland security and how they are applied at the various levels
- understand why officer safety is a major issue with regard to acts of terrorism
- comprehend what is meant by threat assessment and critical infrastructure identification
- know what the police must do in terms of an immediate response to acts of terrorism
- be able to explain how community oriented policing and problem solving (COPPS) can assist in homeland defense

Novus ordo seclorum. ["A new order of the ages."]

— Latin inscription, below the pyramid on the U.S. one dollar bill

INTRODUCTION

"What does the future hold?" "What is going to happen to our nation?" These are questions that probably all of us have asked ourselves, especially following the catastrophic events of September 11, 2001. One thing is undeniable: Our society is constantly changing, and, as Postman (1989:19) said, we cannot afford to [be in the new millennium] with our eyes firmly fixed on the rearview mirror. Anticipating and being prepared for what the future holds is a complex undertaking; still, our nation's police are charged with protecting citizens from minor crimes to major catastrophes, of both human and natural origin (Several of which were discussed in Chapter 15).

Therefore, in an era of terrorism and homeland security, the popular police slogan "to protect and to serve" takes on a new meaning. When a disaster or terrorist attack occurs, even though federal agencies play a major role in mediating their effects, local police and other public safety personnel are the first to respond and must care for the injured, control the situation, and minimize the damage that has occurred. Thus, local police agencies have a monumental task when there is a catastrophic event. The importance of a police presence during national emergencies was demonstrated in New Orleans in the wake of Hurricane Katrina and in New York City after the 9/11 attacks; and in both situations, the police were overwhelmed. We now recognize the importance of local police agencies not only in terms of responding to such events, but also that police agencies are on the front line in terms of preventing terrorist attacks in our communities.

This chapter broadly examines homeland security as it relates to local police agencies and roles of individual officers as threat assessors and first responders. We begin with an overview of homeland security, including a description of the terrorist threat. Next we look at the ultimate threat to our well-being: weapons of mass destruction. Next is an overview of the federal Department of Homeland Security and its initiative to protect our national infrastructure, and then we consider the responsibilities of local police agencies in terms of threat assessment, identifying primary targets in our critical infrastructure, partnering with the private sector, ensuring officer safety, and as first responders to acts of terrorism. The chapter concludes with two case studies.

THE TERRORIST THREAT

Today we live in a dangerous world in which war, famine, and politics are causing substantial discontent on every continent. Much of this anger is directed toward the United States. There is a litany of reasons ranging from our support for Israel to the perceived ill treatment of citizens of other countries by American multi-national corporations to our wars in Afghanistan and Iraq. Terrorists see the United States as a method to rally support and hatred. They regularly burn American flags and pictures of American presidents. They are able to keep the political waters boiling with their rhetoric, which in turn, results in an increasing number of people who hate America and who are potential terrorists.

There are a number of groups that desire to carry out attacks—attacks that embolden and strengthen these groups—on the United States. The most prominent groups are mentioned here. Hamas, which is housed in Palestine and at the center of the Israeli-Palestinian conflict, gets its support from Kuwait, Iran, and Saudi Arabia. It routinely attacks civilian Israeli targets. Hezbollah is located in Lebanon and receives financial and logistic support from Syria and Iran. In 2006, Hezbollah battled the Israeli army to a standstill. In the past, Hezbollah has attacked American targets oversees and it is conceivable that it will stage attacks in the United States in the future (National Intelligence Council, 2007). The Islamic Jihad is an umbrella organization with groups or cells throughout the Middle East

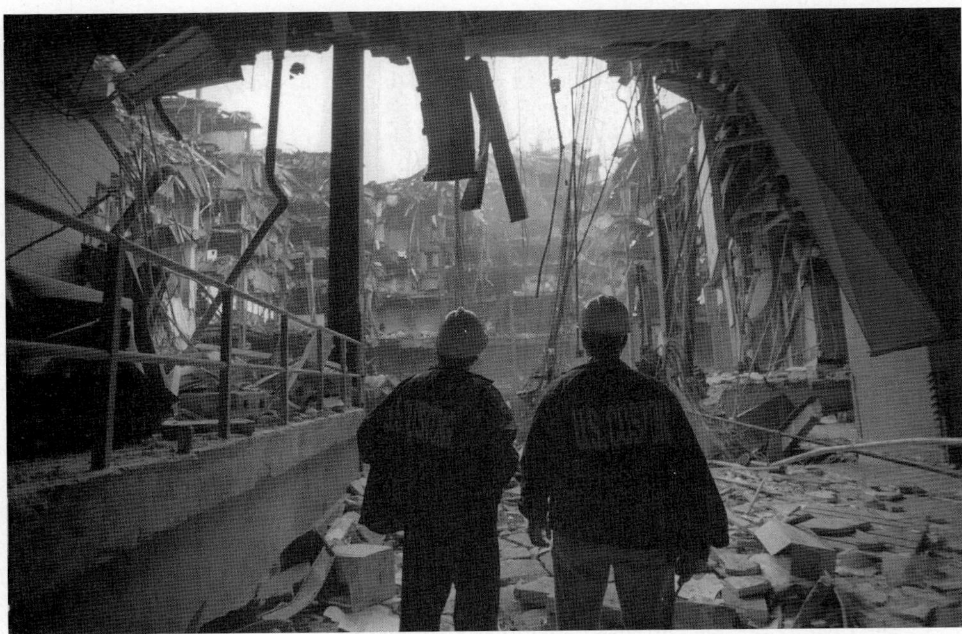

Customs agents review the damage from inside the NYC Custom House after the terrorist attack. *(Courtesy U.S. Customs and Border Protection)*

including Palestine, Egypt, Yemen, and Turkey. The Islamic Jihad has staged a number of attacks, primarily suicide bombings, on Israel. The most known and feared group is Al Qaeda. Al Qaeda is led by Osama bin Laden. It is a Sunni Muslim group thought to have terrorist cells throughout the world, including the United States. Al Qaeda was responsible for the 9/11 attacks in New York City and Washington, D.C. It was also responsible for the 1998 attacks on U.S. embassies in Africa and the 2000 attack on the USS Cole in Yemen. There are many other, smaller, groups that profess their desire to attack the United States as well.

When thinking about terrorism and attacks on the United States, we too often think only of foreign or Middle Eastern groups. However, the United States has a number of internal terrorist groups that have waged attacks on American soil. These groups can be divided into two distinct categories: (1) right-wing hate groups and (2) environmental-animal rights groups.

Right-wing extremist groups are located throughout the United States and include a number of militias, Christian based groups, and the Ku Klux Klan. The best known example of right-wing terrorism in the United States is the 1995 bombing of the Alfred P. Murrah Federal Building in Oklahoma City. The bombing was carried out by Timothy McVeigh and Terry Nichols, members of a right-wing group. They discharged 5,000 pounds of explosives that resulted in 168 deaths and the demolishing of the building. Members of the Arizona Patriots were convicted of plotting to bomb the Simon Wiesenthal Center. They raised money by committing a series of robberies. Members of the Patriot Council plotted to use ricin, a poisonous biological agent, to attack government installations and officials. Members of this group were the first to be charged under the Biological Weapons Anti-Terrorism Act. Members of the Oklahoma Constitutional Militia were arrested and convicted for planning attacks on gay and lesbian bars, abortion clinics, and the offices of the Southern Poverty Law Center. The Ku Klux Klan has a long history of terrorist acts against African-Americans, Jews, and Catholics. Best known for cross burnings, its members have been implicated in bombings and other related activities. Again, there are numerous right-wing organizations in America that profess hatred for the government, taxation, minorities, and religious groups.

There are also Jewish extremist groups. The Jewish Defense League (JDL) was founded in New York City. The JDL targeted groups that it labeled as anti-Semitic and Arab groups. In 2001, members of the JDL were arrested for planning to kill a Lebanese-American Congressman and blow up a mosque in California. JDL members have been active in demonstrations and other activist activities.

A number of extremist groups are engaged in environmental and animal rights terrorist activities. According to White (2009) the **Earth Liberation Front** (ELF) formed in 1992 in the United Kingdom and quickly migrated to the United States. Today, it is composed of a number of radicals from Earth First, the Animal Liberation Front (ALF) and other environmentalists who are opposed to the destruction of our environment. ELF does not stage attacks on people, but has been involved in a number of attacks on property. Their aim is to cause as much economic damage to those who destroy the environment. Martin (2003) notes that members have destroyed a forest station in Oregon, poisoned Mars candy bars, destroyed a livestock research laboratory at the University of California at Davis, spiked trees in logging areas, liberated minks in Wisconsin, and committed arson at a Vail, Colorado ski resort. Additionally, animal rights support groups have attacked numerous individuals, universities, and private entities involved in animal research.

The FBI divides the current international **terrorist threat** into three **categories**:

1. ***Foreign sponsors of international terrorism.*** Seven countries—Iran, Iraq, Syria, Sudan, Libya, Cuba, and North Korea—are designated as such sponsors and view terrorism as a tool of foreign policy. They fund, organize, network, and provide other support to formal terrorist groups and extremists.
2. ***Formalized terrorist groups.*** Autonomous organizations (such as bin Laden's al Qaeda, Afghanistan's Taliban, Iranian-backed Hezbollah, Egyptian Al-Gama'a Al-Islamiyya, and Palestinian HAMAS) have their own infrastructures, personnel, finances, and training facilities. Examples of this type are the al Qaeda terrorists who attacked the World Trade Center and the Pentagon in 2001.
3. ***Loosely affiliated international radical extremists.*** As noted, examples are the persons who bombed the World Trade Center in 1993. They do not represent a particular nation but may pose the most urgent threat to the United States because they remain relatively unknown to law enforcement agencies. (Lewis, 1999)

These international groups now pose another source of concern to law enforcement agencies: They are cooperating among themselves. For example, a terrorist manual is circulating among some of them, and al Qaeda is known to maintain close ties with Hezbollah (Doane, 2001). Another concern is their choice of weapons; although terrorists continue to rely on conventional weapons such as bombs and small arms, indications are that terrorists and other criminals may consider using unconventional chemical (including nerve gas, sarin, or other chemical cocktails whose ingredients are readily available) or biological weapons in an attack in the United States at some point in the future (Lewis, 1999).

In sum, a terrorist attack can come from a number of directions involving a variety of actors. This makes the jobs of police managers and supervisors more complex in that they must be aware of numerous groups' activities. It means that police officials must be prepared for a variety of contingencies.

THE ULTIMATE THREAT: WEAPONS OF MASS DESTRUCTION

Nature and Effects

In terms of homeland security, the greatest threat is **weapons of mass destruction (WMD)** (Henry and King, 2004). WMDs can be biological, chemical, or nuclear (discussed below). WMDs have the potential capacity to cause large numbers of deaths and injuries and destruction, especially in heavily populated areas. For example, exploding a small nuclear devise in a city such as Chicago, New York, or Los Angeles could inflict substantial destruction. Moreover, it would have residual effects. It would overload the police and other first responders and hospitals. It would substantially affect the economy, having an impact on thousands of persons who were not directly affected by the explosion. It would cripple a city, resulting in numerous problems that could potentially last for years or decades. To some extent, the primary purpose of using WMDs is not the initial death and injuries, but the residual effects that possibly could be more destructive to a country than the initial impact. Destroying a primary communications center might result in initial deaths and injuries and loss of property, but the loss of the communications would also have a dramatic impact on our society. WMDs include a wide range of weapons that are more dangerous than commonly used conventional weapons.

A WMD is any explosive, incendiary, poison gas, chemical, biological, or nuclear device that can have substantial wide-spread devastation. WMDs differ from conventional weapons in that conventional explosives generally target and affect a specific area. WMDs have the potential of spreading destruction across a wide area affecting hundreds if not thousands of people. Moreover, they have longer residual effects. For example, it would require considerable effort, time, and expense to clean up an area that had been attacked by a biological, chemical, or nuclear devise. These longer-term effects would result in substantial problems in terms of health problems, fear, and a weakened economy.

Nuclear Weapons of Mass Destruction

Of all the weapons of mass destruction, nuclear devices raise the most concern. Even a small nuclear weapon detonated in one of our large cities would result in catastrophic destruction and large numbers of casualties. Moreover, the presence of nuclear materials—radiation—would result in long-term problems for the country.

A nuclear device can be constructed from highly enriched uranium or plutonium. There are two ways terrorists could acquire a nuclear weapon. First, they could steal or purchase one that has been constructed by another country. Second, they can acquire the materials and construct one. The Union of Concerned Scientists notes that terrorists most likely will attempt to acquire the materials and construct a device. If terrorists are able to acquire all the necessary components, it is not difficult to construct a nuclear weapon. Only a relatively small amount of nuclear materials are required to build a bomb. There are a number of Middle Eastern countries that currently have the knowledge and capability, and some of these countries and individuals in those countries are sympathetic with extremist causes. Indeed, scientists in Pakistan have shared technical information to other countries in the Middle East. Moreover, a number of the extremist groups have the funding necessary to purchase materials, expertise, or weapons.

Nuclear weapons can be used in at least three different ways: (1) a dirty bomb, (2) attacks on nuclear power plants, and (3) diversion of nuclear material or weapons. Dirty bombs use conventional explosive materials but are wrapped or contain some type of radioactive material. The conventional explosion causes the radioactive materials to be dispersed, resulting in contamination. A dirty bomb does not necessarily have to contain highly enriched uranium or plutonium; it could contain radioactive waste products that are produced at commercial power plants or hospitals. Radioactive waste generally has fewer security precautions as compared to highly enriched uranium or plutonium.

A Predator drone such as those used to patrol the borders.
(Courtesy U.S. Customs and Border Protection)

There have been previous attempts to use a dirty bomb. In 1996, Islamic rebels from Chechnya planted such a device in a park in Moscow. Although not detonated, it contained dynamite and Cesium 137, a by-product of nuclear fission. In 2002, Abdullah Al Muhajir, also known as Jose Padilla, was arrested by federal authorities for plotting to construct and detonate a dirty bomb in the United States. There is evidence that terrorists see a dirty bomb as a plausible weapon that could inflict substantial damage. Currently, there is only one hospital with facilities to treat persons suffering from radiation exposure.

Crashing a large aircraft or by using large amounts of explosives at a nuclear power plant could have the same effects as a dirty bomb except the effects would be of a larger magnitude. Such an explosion could cause the reactor core to melt down (such as occurred at Chernobyl) or spent fuel waste to be spread across a large geographical area. The effects could be devastating, and the clean-up could take decades. As discussed above, if terrorists acquired a nuclear weapon detonated in the United States it would have devastating effects on America.

Biological Weapons of Mass Destruction

Because there are numerous contagions that pose a real health threat to large numbers of people, biological terrorism is a genuine threat to the United States. Diseases such as smallpox and anthrax could infect large numbers of people over a large geographical area. There is a great deal of speculation that terrorist groups possess or are attempting to possess biological weapons. There was substantial publicity and public fear in 2001 when someone sent anthrax via mail to several locations in the United States causing five deaths. In dealing with biological terrorism, containment and prevention are of the utmost importance.

Ackerman and Moran (n.d.) note there are three types of biological agents that are considered suitable for bioterrorism:

1. Bacterial organisms such as those that cause anthrax, plague, and tularemia.
2. Viruses including those that cause smallpox and ebola.
3. Toxins including botulinum toxin (derived from a bacterium), ricin (derived from the caster bean plant), and saxitoxin (derived from marine animals). Toxins are not alive and cannot multiply like bacteria or viruses, and therefore have the same attributes associated with chemical weapons.

Mere possession of an agent does not make it a weapon. The agent must be "weaponized"; that is, the would-be terrorist must develop or possess a mechanism that can disperse or disseminate the agent within a target area. Biological weapons may or may not be contagious; anthrax, for example, is not contagious, while smallpox is. Whether contagious or not, most biological agents have an incubation period; generally it takes one to two weeks after contamination before there is an onset of the disease within the host or victim. This allows the perpetrator to distance him- or herself from the scene before law enforcement officials become aware of the act. It also enables the disease to take hold or spread for a time before medical experts can begin responding to the problem. We know very little about the effectiveness of biological weapons in terms of casualties. Most of the information we have is from military uses and experiments. However, perhaps the greatest problem with many biological agents is the effect on the population. An outbreak of smallpox could result in a great deal of disorder.

There are several reasons why a group or country might use bioterrorism. Some groups see these weapons as meeting their ideological desires. For example, racist groups might use them to attempt to wipe out their perceived enemies. Some religious groups may see these weapons as a means to bring about the apocalypse. A number of Middle Eastern groups have a stated goal of wiping Israel off the face of the map. Biological weapons could be seen as a tool to accomplish this objective.

Chemical Weapons of Mass Destruction

As displayed in Figure 16-1, the Centers for Disease Control and Prevention (CDC) has compiled a listing of the various chemical compounds that may be used in some type of chemical attack, breaking them down into basic categories. A variety of toxic compounds are contained within each of these categories.

Used historically, chemical warfare was a primary weapon in World War I and in the Iraqi-Iranian War. The use of chemical weapons in World War I caused one million casualties. Thus, chemical weapons are not new. However, countries continue to develop new, more deadly compounds that pose a greater risk to the United States.

Chemical weapons have different levels of toxicity and lethality. Some of the chemicals that may be used are insecticides, which have a low level of toxicity, but are readily available. Insecticides have been used, but the results have been limited to nonexistent. On the other hand, weapons grade chemical weapons are potentially dangerous. Chemical weapons such as mustard gas, sarin, and VX are extremely lethal. As with biological weapons, the effectiveness of a chemical threat is to a large extent based on the delivery system. Many experts believe that chemical weapons cannot pound the same level of casualties as nuclear or biological weapons. Thousands of pound of the chemical would have to be effectively released to have a significant impact. A primary difference between chemical agents and biological agents is that the chemical agents have an immediate effect. This results in crippling any response or providing any warning to civilian populations.

* Biotoxins
* Blister Agents/Vesicants
* Blood Agents
* Caustics (Acids)
* Choking/Lung/Pulmonary Agents
* Incapacitating Agents
* Long-Acting Anticoagulants
* Metals
* Nerve Agents
* Organic Solvents
* Riot Control Agents/Tear Gas
* Toxic Alcohols
* Vomiting Agents

FIGURE 16-1 Chemical Weapons of Mass Destruction
Source: U.S. Department of Health and Human Services, Centers for Disease Control and Prevention, "Chemical Emergencies Overview," http://www.bt.cdc.gov/chemical/overview.asp#categories (Accessed June 18, 2008).

DEPARTMENT OF HOMELAND SECURITY

Organization and Responsibilities

Although **homeland security** encompasses all levels of government, the federal government is primarily responsible for security of the homeland. This responsibility lies with the Department of Homeland Security (DHS) at the Cabinet level. The DHS was organized by President George W. Bush by combining a number of agencies from other Cabinet-level departments. The largest Cabinet-level department in the federal government, the DHS currently has approximately 180,000 employees. It was formed to better coordinate the numerous agencies that can play a role in case of a terrorist attack on the United States. Additionally, it has a number of corollary responsibilities. First, through the Federal Emergency Management Agency (FEMA) and other agencies within the Department, the DHS responds to natural and man-made disasters including terrorist attacks. The DHS also coordinates with other agencies to prevent and minimize terrorist attacks. For example, because traditional and organized crimes are associated with terrorist organizations, especially in the areas of procuring financial resources and money laundering, the DHS works with the appropriate agencies to thwart and investigate these activities and crimes, especially as they relate to terrorist organizations. Figure 16-2 shows the Department of Homeland Security's organizational chart.

A major difficulty with the initial organization was that the agencies that were transferred to the DHS had previously established goals, responsibilities, and operational procedures. The move to the DHS resulted in the assignment of new responsibilities and priorities. The difficulties occurred when agencies attempted to integrate these new homeland security responsibilities into their current operations (see Perrow, 2006). Horizontal integration issues made it unclear as to what the agencies' new responsibilities were, and no organizational structure previously existed to ensure that new responsibilities were conducted effectively. Integration of new responsibilities into the agencies has been piecemeal and evolutionary.

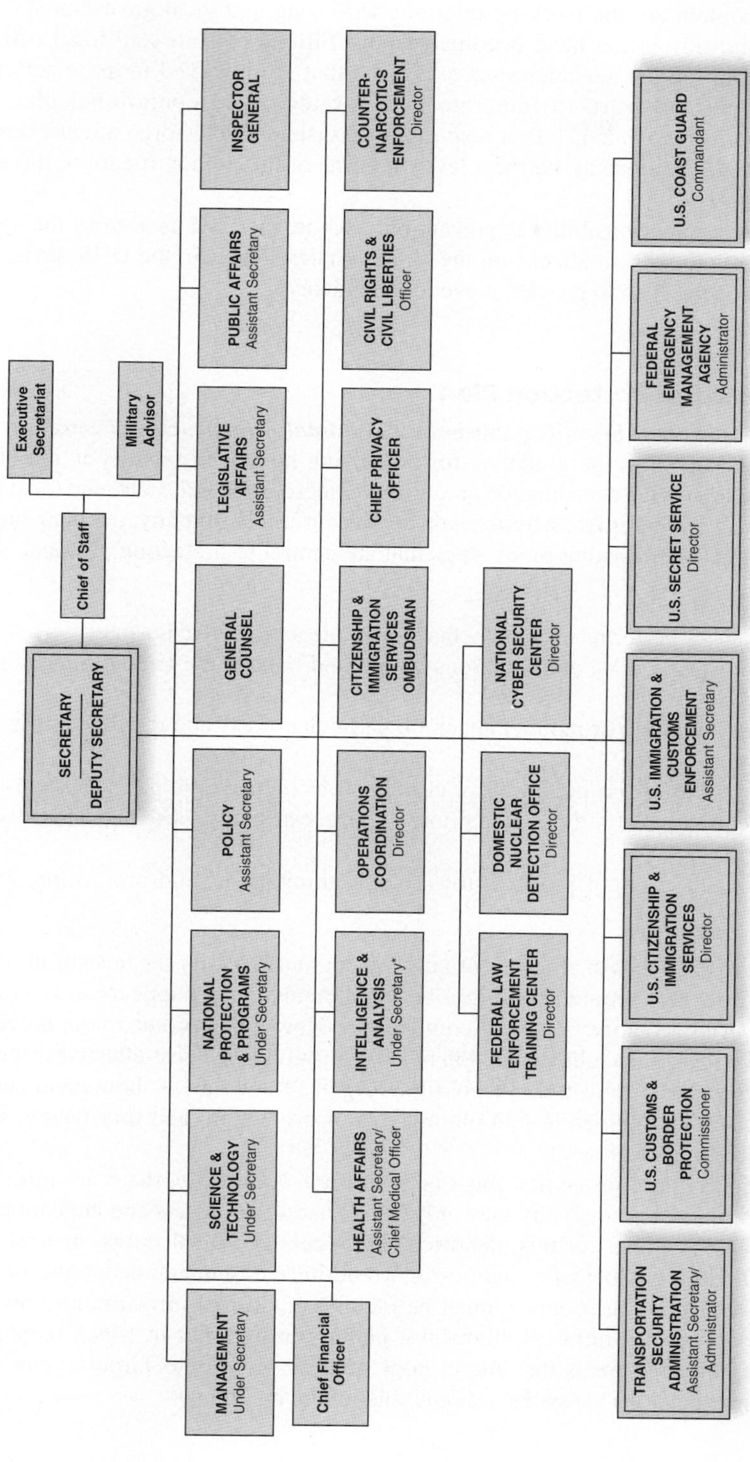

FIGURE 16-2 Department of Homeland Security organizational chart.
Source: *Department of Homeland Security.* http://www.dhs.gov/xabout/structure/editorial_0644.shtm

Compounding the problem are the working relations with state and local governments. To a large extent, prevention and mitigation have become responsibilities of state and local officials even though there are several federal agencies such as FEMA that are involved in these activities. State and federal agencies must work to integrate their strategic and operational planning. Although there have been efforts to enhance first response to disasters and terrorist attacks through grants and training, little has been done at the local level in terms of threat identification, threat assessment, and target assessment.

The Department's primary responsibility is prevention. That is, the DHS is seen as the agency that will coordinate all efforts to prevent attacks on the United States. As such, the DHS devised the National Infrastructure Protection Plan to provide prevention guidance.

The National Infrastructure Protection Plan

In 2002, the Department of Homeland Security published the ***National Infrastructure Protection Plan* (NIPP)**. This document has served as the guideline for organizing homeland security in the United States. The plan is designed to provide coordination among the numerous federal, state, and local agencies in protecting the nation's critical **infrastructure** and key resources. Essentially, the plan enumerates a homeland security process consisting of six steps that are central to protecting physical, cyber, and human assets:

1. Establish security goals or performance targets that constitute a protective posture.
2. Identify assets, systems, networks, and functions within and outside the United States that require a level of protection.
3. Assess risks in terms of a direct or indirect attack on particular assets and the probability that a target will be attacked.
4. Establish priorities in terms of risk and levels of current protection and mitigation systems.
5. Implement protective programs for those high priority assets, especially those that currently have low levels of protection.
6. Measure effectiveness in terms of progress toward hardening assets and preventing attacks. (DHS, 2006: 30)

First, homeland security officials at all levels of government must identify the level of protection necessary for assets and how that protection should be implemented. This appears to be a rather straightforward process, but in actuality, it is very complicated. How much protection is necessary? Too little protection leaves targets vulnerable, while too much protection is not cost-effective, especially in light of limited resources and a multitude of possible targets. Nonetheless, homeland security officials must develop goals that enumerate minimum levels of protection, and this system should consider all types of possible targets or assets.

Second, all assets that require protection must be identified. Nationally, there are millions of such assets, while at the local level, a small city may only have a handful of assets and large cities may have hundreds or thousands. The focus of this identification process is critical infrastructure—those targets that can result in a large number of casualties or would have a dramatic economic or social impact on a community, a state, or the country must be identified. Critical infrastructure includes: petrochemical plants and operations, railways, highways, public transit, areas in which large public gatherings occur, shopping areas or malls that attract large numbers of people, airports, gun stores, financial institutions, communications networks, schools, and public buildings.

Third, once critical infrastructure assets have been identified, local agencies must make some sort of an assessment as to the probability of attack. This is difficult, because there is little experience in this arena. Local officials really do not have any baseline data to make judgments about the probability of attacks. Therefore, they must develop some kind of protection and response model for all the assets in the community, which involves a substantial amount of work, especially in light of the fact that police departments have not received additional resources and their traditional law enforcement responsibilities tend to increase over time. Nonetheless, police agencies must develop protection and response plans for critical infrastructure.

Fourth, since it is an insurmountable task to provide protection for every asset in most jurisdictions, individual departments must prioritize assets in terms of the level of protection and effort exerted. Prioritizing in this way is a difficult chore since, again, police departments do not have experience in this arena. For example, should more attention be given to a high school or a petroleum storage facility? In the end, value judgments must be made, and any prioritized list ultimately will be subjective. Although all assets should be secured at some level, departments must ensure that high priority assets meet a minimum standard not only in terms of security but also in terms of potential response.

Fifth, as noted above, all critical infrastructure assets must be identified. Then departments must evaluate each asset's level of protection and determine whether or not they are secure. They must also establish the minimum level of security that is required for the asset. Departments must then work to provide some level of protection, which may result in the formulation of new policies that affect patrol operations or the creation of closer working relationships with asset owners or private security firms that are employed to provide security.

Finally, police agencies must continually evaluate security systems. As noted above, once security systems are in place, it must be insured that they meet some minimum level. Security systems may be neglected and deteriorate over time. The operations that occur or the amount and kinds of products within the facility may change over time. Therefore, the police must periodically make assessments to ensure that the level of security matches the critical asset. If there are deficiencies, the police must work to harden the target.

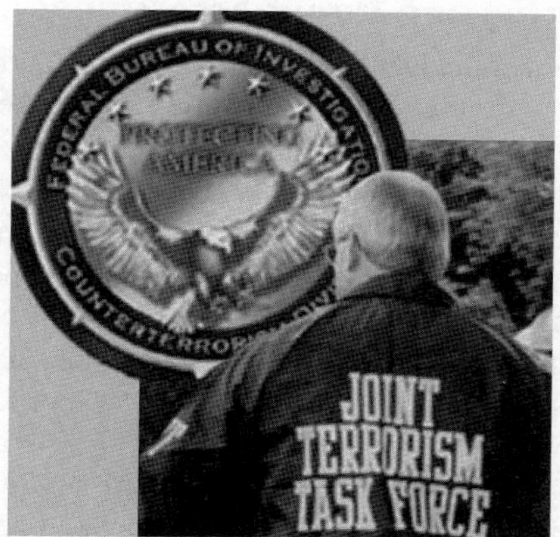

The FBI and local law enforcement team up across the United States in Joint Terrorism Task Forces (JTTF) to evaluate and respond to any local threats of terrorism.
(Courtesy of the Federal Bureau of Investigation.)

HOMELAND SECURITY AT THE LOCAL LEVEL

"Think Globally, Act Locally"

Homeland security today represents a major operational area for state and local governments. If there is a terrorist attack or major disaster, state and local officials are first to respond. During this initial response, they must control the situation and mitigate the damage as much as possible. It may take days or even weeks, as in Hurricane Katrina, for the necessary federal assets to arrive on the scene. This places a substantial burden on local and state resources, which are limited and often inadequate, especially if a major disaster occurs.

The federal government has approached homeland security from a top-down perspective, focusing, to a large extent, on identifying and apprehending terrorist suspects in the United States and abroad. The federal government has initiated improvements in airline security, and mounted efforts to improve border security, although border security has little to do with reducing the threat to potential targets.

There is substantial consternation over the role of local agencies in protecting local assets. However, we must "think globally and act locally" (Carter, n.d.). Essentially, attacks on a local asset can come from anywhere in the world, but local authorities will assume a large amount of the responsibility to prevent an attack and mitigate it if an attack does in fact occur.

Local agencies must develop strategies and policies to deal with homeland security. As noted, it is the local agencies that at least initially will be responsible for response and protection. However, states and local units of government have not received realistic, workable guidance in constructing and implementing such strategies. Currently, it appears that the states and local units of government are engaged in four homeland security activities:

1. Threat assessment via intelligence gathering (intelligence-led policing)
2. Critical infrastructure identification
3. Partnerships between law enforcement and critical infrastructure security personnel
4. Public education

Next we briefly discuss each of these activities.

Intelligence-Led Policing and Threat Assessment

To address threat assessment at the local level, local police departments must become involved in identifying potential terrorists and suspect activities, although there is some debate as to whether terror intelligence gathering should be a federal function or involve state and local agencies (Thacher, 2005). Currently, police departments are improving their intelligence capacity through intelligence-led policing (Carter, n.d.), which essentially is the enhancement of police intelligence gathering capability. Most major police departments already have some form of intelligence gathering capabilities. In the past, these efforts have been aimed at collecting information about organized crime, drug trafficking, and gangs. Intelligence-led policing dictates that departments not only begin collecting information about possible terrorists and possible targets, but also that they should enhance their intelligence gathering and usage skills. It is logical to include possible terrorists and terrorist activities, especially considering that narcotics trafficking is extensively used to finance terrorism (Kleiman, 2004; McCaffrey and Basso, 2003). Of course, one of the major difficulties for local departments in collecting terrorist intelligence is that unlike other organized crime groups, little is known about who might be a terrorist and their potential activities. For the most part, there is an absence of baseline data or information to guide intelligence and investigative activities. Rhetorically, it is too late to gather information about possible terrorists once they have been identified as terrorists. Nonetheless, departments are encouraged to begin gathering information on "persons of interest" who fit some profile of terrorists. As witnessed with the 9/11 attacks, one undiscovered attack can result in the loss of thousands of lives.

Intelligence-led policing is compatible with and complementary to community policing. Police officers across the country are now working more closely with citizens and communities. These relationships provide a vast reservoir of "eyes and ears" for the police, which not only enhances problem solving, but also provides a way to collect intelligence about suspicious persons and activities in a community. Intelligence gathered in the community can be collated and compared to other intelligence to provide a clearer picture of the activities in a jurisdiction. It is important for police managers and supervisors to reinforce this new mandate.

Fusion Centers

A new innovation in intelligence collection is fusion centers. A number of cities and counties have partnered with the Federal Bureau of Investigation to form terrorism early warning groups or fusion centers (Sullivan, 2006). The **fusion center** provides overarching coordination of all response and counter-terrorism elements within a community or metropolitan area. As information or intelligence is gathered by local and federal agencies it is fed into the fusion center where it is analyzed. The fusion center is a comprehensive approach in that it allows for the analysis of information from a variety of sources. It is the most comprehensive manner by which to collect and analyze data for a particular geographical area. Once analyzed, terrorist threat or activity information is generated and supplied to affected constituents. The fusion centers include medical personnel and fire department personnel as well as law enforcement personnel. The medical personnel can act as an early warning system for a biological attack by providing the fusion center with information about suspicious diseases or illnesses, and the firefighter personnel can provide information about suspicious fires or chemical problems. The fusion center also allows for more comprehensive planning and a better coordinated response should a terrorist event occur.

Critical Infrastructure Identification

Local police departments need to take inventory of the critical infrastructure within their jurisdictions. This requires that the police identify all potential terrorist targets. This is especially important given the numerous potential targets that may exist and that attacks on different types of targets present dissimilar challenges to the police and other first responders. Local police departments must create a catalog or database of all possible terrorist targets in the jurisdiction, especially those that would result in significant damage if attacked. This process serves two functions. First, the database allows the department to comprehensively develop response plans for the various identified targets. A police department should have a response plan in place for all of these locations. Second, it results in focusing attention on areas that are of interest to possible terrorists. Once assets are identified, the police department should focus intelligence operations near and around the locations. It is very likely that if a terrorist plans to attack an asset, he or she will conduct reconnaissance. Due vigilance may result in the terrorist being identified before the act.

As police departments develop their critical infrastructure asset database, they should remember that there are all sorts of assets that must be considered. They range from areas with a large concentration of people, such as shopping malls and sporting events, to medical facilities and petrochemical facilities. Also included are transportation corridors, such as railways and roadways, and airports. Smaller, less obvious facilities or businesses such as gun shops, government buildings, and tourist attractions should also be included in any such database. The police department should develop a contingency plan for an attack on each of the critical assets in the community.

Contingengy plans include information about command and control, tactical responses, and use of other support agencies such as disaster, medical, fire, and chemical and radiological personnel. These plans are flexible in that they can be used to deploy resources for a host of problems anywhere within a jurisdiction. Police agencies use these plans sparingly as there are only a few instances that call for their application. Donahue and Tuohy (2006) note that these plans often fail for a variety of reasons, including uncoordinated leadership among the various responding agencies; failed communications including inoperability of communications systems and a lack of desire for agencies to communicate with each other; weak planning whereby plans are developed in a vacuum without the benefit of "real life" experiences; and resource constraints since most emergencies of any magnitude quickly strip a jurisdiction's resources to maintain a maximum response. Police agencies must examine their critical incident response plans and ensure that they are comprehensive and applicable to terrorist threats or attacks. Pelfrey (2005) advises that planning is the most critical aspect of homeland defense. Many departments are well equipped, but do not have adequate plans in place.

Partnering with Private Security

Each year more is spent on private security than on public police, and the private sector employs larger numbers of personnel than do public police departments (Morabito and Greenberg, 2005). Private security is a significant force in the public safety arena. Public policing and private security are not necessarily mutually exclusive domains. For example, Green (1981:25) has defined the role of private security as, "those individuals, organizations, and services other than public law enforcement and regulatory agencies that are engaged primarily in the prevention and investigation of crime, loss, or harm to specific individuals, organizations, or facilities." There is, therefore, substantial overlap between private security and the police. Because private security secures a number of potential terrorist targets, it can be an important asset for a department in its efforts to develop a comprehensive homeland security plan.

Historically, there has been little cooperation or communication between the police and private security personnel even though they endeavor to achieve the same goals. The police often saw areas or facilities that were guarded by security personnel as "dead zones." That is, they were areas that did not require police services unless called upon. However, in an effort to better protect the community from the threat of terrorism and the need to secure critical infrastructure, the police must develop close working relationships with private security firms. Often security personnel have more information about the critical asset than the police. For example, many of these facilities have controlled access and activities, and therefore, security personnel are more likely to observe people and actions that are out of the ordinary or suspicious, and independently, or in cooperation with the police, investigate them. At a minimum, the police should be aware of those facilities that are target hardened through private security, and strengthen relationships with the private security personnel who monitor them. Such relationships would: (1) improve joint response to critical incidents, (2) coordinate infrastructure protection, (3) improve communications and the interpretation of data, (4) bolster information and intelligence sharing, (5) prevent and investigate high-tech crime, and (6) devise responses to workplace violence (Ohlhausen Research Inc., 2004).

Partnerships between the police and private security are critical. Gaines and Kappeler (2008) have identified some of the activities that must occur:

1. Cooperative training on the development and implementation of potential terrorist profiles
2. Mapping of potential targets in a jurisdiction to include security assets
3. Development and coordination of critical incident plans outlining responses to acts of terror and disasters
4. Better communication between law enforcement and the private security industry

Public Education

On May 9, 2007, the Federal Bureau of Investigation arrested six suspects who had planned to attack and kill soldiers at Fort Dix in New Jersey. The initial investigative lead was supplied by an alert photography store clerk who was asked to copy a video cassette onto a DVD. The cassette contained footage of the suspects training for their attack. The alert store clerk notified the police, which resulted in an extended FBI investigation and subsequent arrests. This incident exemplifies how law enforcement can obtain valuable intelligence information from the general public.

Community policing necessitates that the police work closely with communities. One of the programs that resulted from this partnering is public education about a variety of crime and safety issues. Jurisdictions must develop programs that produce results similar to those experienced in the New Jersey case. The police should employ programs that encourage citizens to observe for and report suspicious persons and activities. These programs are similar to some of the drug and crime citizen reporting systems that have been used for decades. Lyon (2002) advises that the police should develop programs in communities or neighborhoods that are likely to engender support for the police and the reduction of terrorist activities.

Officer Safety Issues

The threat of terrorism has changed and become more deadly. Over the past several years, a new trend has developed in terrorism within the United States: a transition from more numerous low-level incidents to less frequent but more destructive attacks, with a goal to produce mass casualties and attract intense media coverage. Although the number of terrorist attacks in the United States declined during the 1990s, the number of persons killed and injured increased (Lewis, 1999).

Police officers confronting terrorists in the United States now find themselves vulnerable in six types of situations (Garrett, 2002):

1. ***Traffic stops:*** Law enforcement lacks prior knowledge of the individual being stopped; the officer may be isolated and the potential terrorist may be in a heightened state of suspicion or anger as a result of the stop.
2. ***Residence visits:*** Officers are on the extremists' home turf, putting them at a disadvantage; the visit may be routine, but the extremist may not view it as such, and the home may be armed and fortified.
3. ***Rallies/marches:*** The risk to police usually comes not from the group holding the event, but from protestors, often anarchists who hate the police and believe that the best way to confront the demonstrators is through physical violence.
4. ***Confrontations/standoffs:*** All such incidents can arise from the three previous situations.
5. ***Revenge and retaliation:*** A terrorist may be motivated by personal benefit or revenge, such as one who attempts to blow up an Internal Revenue Service office because he was audited.
6. ***Incident responses:*** These can take many forms, ranging from activities of terrorists to acts of nature.

Police departments must ensure that these threats are incorporated into training. Officers must understand and be able to respond to these threats, especially in terms of **officer safety**. Since terrorist attacks are very infrequent and have occurred only in a few American jurisdictions, most police officers are complacent. Police managers and supervisors play a large role in constantly reinforcing the threat of terrorism, police officer safety, and the need to work with citizens and private security personnel.

Immediate Police Response to an Act of Terrorism

As noted above, there are a number of weapons that can be used in a terrorist attack, and the police must be prepared for all of them. Moreover, the police must coordinate their response with other first

If First on Scene:

- Isolate/secure the scene, establish control zone
- Establish command
- Stage incoming units

If Command Has Been Established:

- Report to Command Post
- Evaluate scene safety/security (ongoing criminal activity, secondary devices, additional threats)
- Gather witness statements and document activities and occurrences
- Institute notifications (FBI, explosive ordinance squad, private security, and so forth)
- Request additional resources
- Secure outer perimeter
- Control traffic
- Use appropriate self-protective measures
- Initiate public safety measures (evacuations as necessary)
- Assist with control/isolation of patients
- Preserve evidence
- Participate in a unified command system with fire, medical, hospital, and public works agencies

FIGURE 16-3 Law Enforcement's Emergency Response to Terrorism
Adapted from U.S. Department of Justice, Federal Emergency Management Agency, *Emergency Response to Terrorism: Self-Study. Washington*, DC: Author, June 1999.

responders such as fire, emergency medical, hospitals, and disaster agencies at the local, state, and federal levels. Obviously, the type of attack will influence the response. For example, a biological attack will necessitate a response that is different from a conventional explosives attack. Nonetheless, there are some guidelines that should be followed. Figure 16-3 provides the general guidelines that law enforcement should follow when responding to a terrorist attack.

COPPS AND HOMELAND DEFENSE

In Chapter 4 we thoroughly examined community oriented policing and problem solving (COPPS). Here we revisit that concept in terms of how it can assist police effort toward ensuring the security of our nation.

When a police officer is responding to a call for service and observes a container with 50 gallons of chlorine in a corner of a garage, but no swimming pool in the back yard, would he or she know what to do with that information? When emergency medical services personnel are on a call and observe five passports from different countries, all bearing the same photograph, on the kitchen table, would they know who to contact?

Perhaps an underlying theme of this book is that information is the lifeblood of contemporary policing. Unfortunately, however, it is still common for the police, fire, and emergency services personnel to not know what the others are finding, and to take for granted that the others are aware of threat-related information such as those mentioned above.

Homeland security begins with local police and the community. The collection of information at the neighbourhood level is critical to the mission of protecting the homeland. First responders need to know how to cultivate information: what information to look for, how to collect it, and where to send it. Training of first responders in this area reduces the information gap between police and other services, and must be embraced by each agency's management in order to be effective.

There are numerous community information sources, some of which may not have occurred to the police; following are some of them, and the kinds of information they might provide:

- Business owners (information about purchasers of dangerous materials such as torches, propane, and blasting supplies)
- Employees of transportation centers and tourist attractions (information about suspicious persons and activities)
- Those who issue handgun, firearm, and liquor licenses and information about blasting materials
- Letter carriers, couriers, and delivery services drivers (information on suspicious people, activities and packages)
- College and university personnel and students (information about possession of hazardous materials by foreign exchange students, controversial speakers and research, and events)
- Storage unit managers (information on explosive or hazardous materials possibly connected to terrorist or criminal activity)
- Hotel clerks and security officers (information on suspicious guests) (Doherty, 2006)

In addition, while traumatic events like the 9/11 attacks might possibly cause police organizations to revert back to more traditional methods—even to abandon COPPS for more seemingly pedestrian, security-oriented concerns—COPPS should play a central role in the defense of our homeland. Because COPPS helps to build trust between police and their communities, deals more effectively with community concerns, and helps the police to develop knowledge of community activity, the problem-solving model is well suited to the prevention of terrorism. Departments can also use a wide variety of data sources to proactively develop detailed risk management and crisis response plans (Chapman and Schneider, 2002; Doherty, 2006).

CASE STUDIES

Following are two case studies that will provide you with some opportunities to apply some of the concepts described in this chapter.

Case Study #1

Organizing Homeland Security at Home

The state director of homeland security recently issued a policy directing all cities to prepare a comprehensive terrorist or major event response plan. He advised that the plan should concentrate on two areas: prevention and response. Although officials in the department were acutely aware of the need to move resources into homeland security, the department had not done so. In essence, the department must build its plan from the ground up. The police chief appointed Captain John Patrick to the new position of Police Homeland Security Director.

ns for Discussion

1. What areas should Captain Patrick address?
2. How should he address the city's infrastructure?
3. What new departmental standard operating procedures should be developed?
4. How should Captain Patrick attempt to involve officers from patrol and other operational units in homeland security?

Case Study #2

Collaborating with the Private Sector

As noted in this chapter, terrorist attacks would be directed at critical infrastructure assets. There are all sorts of such potential targets in any given city. Police departments should be in the process of identifying these assets. Once identified, the department should be considering some response should a terrorist attack or other significant events occur. Sergeant James Whitley has been appointed to the department's Homeland Security Unit. Captain John Patrick, the unit commander, has directed Sergeant Whitley to identify potential targets in the city. No such efforts preceded this request, so Sergeant Whitley must begin anew.

Questions for Discussion

1. What types or categories of critical infrastructure should concern Sergeant Whitley?
2. What criteria should Sergeant Whitley use? For example, the list very likely will include a gasoline storage facility, but should gasoline service stations be included as well?
3. Is there anyone in the community that Sergeant Whitley could consult to advise him on his decision making?
4. Will local politics come into play when developing this list, especially if someone's business is not included?
5. What should the department do once this list is compiled?

Summary

The 9/11 attacks on New York City and Washington, D.C. resulted in drastic changes in the American criminal justice system. Homeland security became an important function within the American system of policing. In addition, as a result of 9/11, Americans became acutely aware that they can be the victims of terrorist attacks that are planned and launched from foreign soil. 9/11 also served as a wakeup call to the federal, state, and local governments that homeland security is now imperative. Since 9/11, the federal government has spent billions of dollars attempting to improve homeland security. States now have agencies to coordinate efforts. Local police departments are now working more closely with an array of agencies so that they are prepared to respond to a possible attack.

Police managers and supervisors essentially are on the front lines. If there is an attack, the local police are the first responders, and therefore, they must be prepared. Additionally, they must coordinate efforts to prepare the citizenry for an attack and using community policing practices, get citizens involved in providing criminal intelligence. Police departments must assume new responsibilities as well continue to provide traditional services. Not only must police managers and supervisors ensure that subordinates are prepared, but they must also ensure that their responses meet the needs of the people.

Items for Review

1. List some of the terrorist organizations operating internationally and in the United States.
2. Describe the categories of weapons of mass destruction and provide examples of each.
3. What are some of the agencies in the Department of Homeland Security?
4. What are the levels of protection described in the National Infrastructure Protection Plan?
5. List the actions that a local police department should take in order to prepare for or prevent a possible terrorist attack.
6. How would you define a fusion center?
7. What are some means by which a police agency can engage in critical infrastructure identification?
8. Describe some of the officer safety issues that are involved with homeland security.
9. List the steps that should be taken when initially responding to a terrorist or major event.
10. Explain some of the ways in which COPPS can assist in homeland defense.

References

Ackerman, G., and Moran, K. (n.d.). Bioterrorism and threat assessment. Stockholm, Sweden: Weapons of Mass Destruction Commission. http://www.wmdcommission.org/files/No22.pdf (Accessed June 18, 2008).

Carter, D. (n.d.). *Law enforcement intelligence: A guide for state, local, and tribal law enforcement agencies.* Washington, D.C.: Office of Community Oriented Policing Services.

Chapman, R., and Schneider, M. C. (2002). Community policing: Now more than ever. Washington, D.C.: U.S. Department of Justice, Office of Community Oriented Policing Services.

Department of Homeland Security. (2006). *National infrastructure protection plan*. Washington, D.C.: Author.

Doane, K. (2001). It's hardly terror, inc. *U.S. News and World Reports* (June 11): 31.

Doherty, S. (2006). Community policing and homeland security. *The Police Chief* (February):78–81.

Donahue, A., and Tuohy, R. (2006). Lessons we don't learn: A study of the lessons of disasters, why we repeat them, and how we can learn from them. *Homeland Security Affairs* 2(2): 1–28.

Gaines, L., and Kappeler, V. (2008). *Policing in America.* Newark, NJ: LexisNexis.

Garrett, K. (2002). Terrorism on the homefront. *Law Enforcement Technology* (July): 22–26.

Green, G. (1981). *Introduction to security*. Stoneham, MA: Butterworth.

Henry, V., and King, D. (2004). Improving emergency preparedness and public–safety responses to terrorism and weapons of mass destruction. *Brief Treatment and Crisis Intervention*, 4(1): 11–35.

Kleiman, M. (2004). Illicit drugs and the terrorist threat: Causal links and implications for domestic drug control policy. *CRS Report to Congress*. Washington, D.C.: Congressional Research Service.

Lewis, J. (1999). Fighting terrorism in the 21st century. *FBI Law Enforcement Bulletin*, (March): 3.

Lyon, W. (2002). Partnerships, information, and public safety. *Policing*, 25: 530–543.

Martin, G. (2003). *Understanding terrorism: Challenges, perspectives, and issues*. Thousand Oaks, CA: Sage.

McCaffrey, B., and Basso, J. (2003). Narcotics, terrorism, and international crime: The convergence phenomenon. In eds. Howard, R. and Sawyer, R., *Terrorism and counterterrorism: Understanding the new security environment*, pp. 206–221. Guilford, CN: Dushkin.

Morabito, A., and Greenberg, S. (2005). *Engaging the private sector to promote homeland security: Law enforcement-private security partnerships*. Washington, D.C.: Bureau of Justice Assistance.

National Intelligence Council. (2007). *National intelligence estimate: The terrorist threat to the U.S. Homeland*. Washington, D.C.: Office of the Director of National Intelligence.

Ohlhausen Research Inc. (2004). *Private security/public policing: Vital issues and policy recommendations*. Alexandria, VA: International Association of Chiefs of Police.

Pelfrey, W.V., Jr. (2007). Local law enforcement terrorism prevention efforts: A state level case study. *Journal of Criminal Justice* 35: 313–321.

Pelfrey, W.V., Sr. (2005). The cycle of preparedness: Establishing a framework to prepare for terrorist threats. *Journal of Homeland Security and Emergency Management* 2(1): 1–21.

Perrow, C. (2006). The disaster after 9/11: The Department of Homeland Security and the intelligence reorganization. *Homeland Security Affairs* 2(1): 1–32.

Postman, N. (1989). Quoted in Osborne, D., and Gaebler, T., *Reinventing government: How the entrepreneurial spirit is transforming the public sector*. Reading, MA: Addison-Wesley.

Sullivan, J. (2006). Terrorism early warning groups: Regional intelligence to combat terrorism. In eds. Howard, R., Forest, J., and Moore, J., *Homeland Security and Terrorism,* pp. 235–245. New York: McGraw-Hill.

Thacher, D. (2005). The local role in homeland security. *Law & Society Review* 39: 635–676.

White, J. (2009). *Terrorism and homeland security*. Belmont, CA: Wadsworth-Cengage.

ADVICE THAT HAS STOOD THE TEST OF TIME: SOME PRACTICAL COUNSEL

LAO-TZU'S VIEWS

This book has covered many facets of supervision and management in its 16 chapters. Perhaps at its simplest level, the book is saying that a successful supervisor or manager influences others by example and gains the willing obedience, confidence, respect, and loyalty of subordinates. This characteristic of leadership was recognized in the sixth century B.C. by Lao-Tzu, when he wrote:

> The superior leader gets things done
> With very little motion.
> He imparts instruction not through many words
> But through a few deeds.
> He keeps informed about everything
> But interferes hardly at all.
> He is a catalyst.
> And although things wouldn't get done as well
> If he weren't there,
> When they succeed he takes no credit.
> And because he takes no credit
> Credit never leaves him.
> (quoted in Bennett and Hess, 2001:56)

ANALECTS OF CONFUCIUS AND MACHIAVELLI

The writings of two other major figures have stood the test of time. The analects (or brief passages) of Confucius (551–479 B.C.) and the writings of Machiavelli (A.D. 1469–1527) are still popular today. Many college and university students in a variety of academic disciplines have analyzed the writings of both, especially Machiavelli's *The Prince,* written in 1513. Both of these philosophers tended to agree on many points regarding the means of governance, as the following will demonstrate. After reading some quotations from each philosopher, we consider their application to police supervision and management.

> Confucius often emphasized the moralism of leaders, saying, He who rules by moral force is like the pole-star, which remains in its place while all the lesser stars do homage to it. Govern the people by regulations, keep order among them by chastisements, and they will flee from you, and lose all self-respect. Govern them by moral force, keep order among them ..., and they will ... come to you of their own accord. If the ruler is upright, all will go well even though he does not give orders. But if he himself is not upright, even though he gives orders, they will not be obeyed. (Waley, 1938:88, 173)

Confucius also believed that those people whom the leader promotes are of no small importance: "Promote those who are worthy, train those who are incompetent; that is the best form of encouragement" (Waley, 1938:92). He also believed that leaders should learn from and emulate good administrators:

> In the presence of a good man, think all the time how you may learn to equal him. In the presence of a bad man, turn your gaze within! ... Even when I am walking in a party of no more than three I can always be certain of learning from those I am with. There will be good qualities that I can select for imitation and bad ones that will teach me what requires correction in myself. (Waley, 1938:105, 127)

Unlike Confucius, Machiavelli is often maligned for being cruel; the "ends justify the means" philosophy imputed to him even today has cast a pall over his writings. Although often as biting as the "point of a stiletto" (Machiavelli, 1992:xvii) and seemingly ruthless at times ["Men ought either to be caressed or destroyed, since they will seek revenge for minor hurts but will not be able to revenge major ones," and "If you have to make a choice, to be feared is much safer than to be loved" (Machiavelli, 1992:7, 46], he, like Confucius, often spoke of the leader's need to possess character and compassion. For all of his blunt, management-oriented notions of administration, Machiavelli was prudent and pragmatic.

Like Confucius, Machiavelli believed that administrators would do well to follow examples set by other great leaders (we would encourage the reader to take some literary license with Machiavelli's writings and substitute "supervisor" and/or "manager" for "prince"):

> Men almost always prefer to walk in paths marked out by others and pattern their actions through imitation. A prudent man should always follow the footsteps of the great and imitate those who have been supreme... A prince should read history and reflect on the actions of great men. (Machiavelli, 1992:15, 41)

On the need for developing and maintaining good relations with subordinates, he wrote:

> If ... a prince ... puts his trust in the people, knows how to command, is a man of courage and doesn't lose his head in adversity, and can rouse his people to action by his own example and orders, he will never find himself betrayed, and his foundations will prove to have been well laid. The best fortress of all consists in not being hated by your people. Every prince should prefer to be considered merciful rather than cruel.... The prince must have people well disposed toward him; otherwise in times of adversity there's no hope. (Machiavelli, 1992:29, 60)

In a related, more contemporary vein, we might briefly note other writers' views of today's supervisors and managers. For example, Peter Drucker provided a compelling opinion of the importance of a supervisor: "Supervisors are, so to speak, the ligaments, the tendons and sinews of an organization. They provide the articulation. Without them, no joint can move" (quoted in Bennett and Hess, 2001:41). Similarly, the critical importance of supervisors and managers was noted by Bock (1993:39), who drew an analogy from the military:

> The old saying, "generals win battles but sergeants win wars," is true of millions of organizations—and of police departments. What a department is, to the officer on the street and the citizens of your community, is a direct result of what sergeants are and do.

As police organizations struggle with the complexities of a rapidly changing world and ever-demanding workforce, their leaders might do well to heed the analects of Confucius and the work of Machiavelli, as well as other, more contemporary observers.

CUES FOR TODAY'S SUPERVISORS AND MANAGERS

Several implications for contemporary supervisors and managers come from these philosophers. First, supervisors must lead by example, including by appearance, and occupy several roles. Lao-Tzu tells us that the successful leader is one who keeps informed, does not rant and rave, and prefers to "condemn in private, praise in public." Confucius tells us that one who leads must, above all, be moral and upright, advance subordinates, and try to learn something from each human contact.

Machiavelli also teaches us that supervisors and managers should emulate successful leaders; recruit and train competent subordinates; be able, upon newly assuming a leadership role, to maintain an adequate amount of professional distance between themselves and their subordinates, some of whom were formerly good friends with the new supervisor or manager and may now attempt to see how much they can get away with; and be able to say "no" to underlings while being compassionate toward them.

References

Bennett, W. W., and Hess, K. (2001). *Management and supervision in law enforcement,* 3rd ed. Belmont, CA: Wadsworth.

Bock, W. (1993). Generals win battles but sergeants win wars. *Law and Order* (May):39–40.

Machiavelli, N. (1992). *The prince.* R. M. Adams, trans. New York: Norton. (Original work published in 1513.)

Waley, A., trans. (1938). *The analects of Confucius.* London: Allen and Unwin.

INDEX